# Th
# Anne
# Boleyn
# Papers

# About the Author

Elizabeth Norton gained her first degree from the University of Cambridge, and her Masters from the University of Oxford. She is the author of ten books on the tudors. She lives in London.

## Praise for Elizabeth Norton

*Catherine Parr*
'Scintillating ... Norton cuts an admirably clear path through tangled Tudor intrigues' JENNY UGLOW, *THE FINANCIAL TIMES*
'Eminently readable ... Norton's strength is in her use of original sources' SARAH GRISTWOOD, *BBC HISTORY MAGAZINE*

*Bessie Blount*
'Secret of the queen that Britain "lost"' *THE SUN*
'A lucid, readable, intelligent account of the life of a woman who might have been queen' *THE GOOD BOOK GUIDE*

# The Anne Boleyn Papers

ELIZABETH NORTON

AMBERLEY

This edition first published 2013

Amberley Publishing
The Hill, Stroud
Gloucestershire, GL5 4EP

www.amberleybooks.com

British Library Cataloguing in Publication Data.
A catalogue record for this book is available from the British Library.

ISBN 978 1 4456 1288 1

Typesetting and Origination by Amberley Publishing.
Printed in the UK.

# Contents

# Introduction

Anne Boleyn, the second of Henry VIII's six wives, was one of the most famous women of her generation. Her story is well known: she has been the subject of a number of biographies in recent years, as well as appearing as a major character in historical fiction.[1] In spite of this interest, surviving information on Anne is surprisingly scant and it is necessary for historians to piece her life story together from the information that survives. For the first time, an attempt is made to present some of the most important sources for the life of Anne Boleyn in one volume, so that she can be viewed both in her own words, through her surviving letters and recorded speech and conduct, and through the words of those who knew her, or, in some cases, had access to those that had known her. The sources presented are a mixture. Some are favourable to Anne, some hostile. Some are considerably more reliable than others. They have been selected to give as complete a picture of the Tudor queen as possible: both as to her life, and with regard to the reputation that she acquired. Other sources on Anne exist and it would be impossible to include all the surviving information in one volume. Particular attention has therefore been given to documents that were last recorded in print a considerable amount of time ago, in order to make them readily accessible again to readers once more.

The lack of information regarding Anne Boleyn is particularly apparent in relation to her birth and childhood. Anne was the daughter of Sir Thomas Boleyn and his wife, Elizabeth Howard. Traditionally, she was believed to have been born in 1507, a date that was put forward by the Elizabethan historian William Camden and reiterated by the author of the early seventeenth-century *Life of Jane Dormer*.[2] While the *Life of Jane Dormer*, which is a biography of a friend of Anne's stepdaughter, Mary I, is accurate in many respects, it is clear that the author, Henry Clifford, had read Camden's own assessment of Anne since he refers to Camden's work in his text. Dating Anne's birth to 1507 therefore rests, almost entirely, on Camden's assertion. This would mean that Anne had not yet turned thirty at the time of her death and the facts of her life do not support such a late birth. Twelve was generally recognised as the minimum age at which a girl could serve as a lady in waiting and Anne, who was sent to serve Margaret of Austria in 1513, is unlikely to have been very much younger than this. Anne's own father, Sir Thomas Boleyn, also complained that, following his marriage in the last years of the fifteenth century, his wife brought him every year a child. Sir Thomas Boleyn and Elizabeth Howard had five known children: Mary, Anne, George, Thomas and Henry. Thomas and Henry died in infancy and, while it is possible that there were other children who died at similarly young ages, it seems unlikely that Anne was born so long after her parents' marriage. There continues to be considerable debate over whether Anne or her sister, Mary, was the elder. While it was Anne who first left home for a prestigious appointment, it was Mary who married first (in 1520). Mary's own grandson, Lord Hunsdon, believed that his grandmother was the elder when he petitioned Anne's daughter for the restoration of the Boleyn family earldom in the late sixteenth century.[3] This evidence, although contradicted by the inscription on Lord Hunsdon's daughter's tomb, would seem fairly conclusive and it is likely that Mary was the eldest child. She was probably born in around 1499, with Anne following in around 1501 and George a few years later.

Anne is often portrayed as an upstart but, in reality, her family were firmly members of the English nobility, in comparison with the gentry families from which Henry VIII drew his later English wives: Jane Seymour and Catherine Parr. Anne's great-grandfather, Sir Geoffrey Boleyn, had been a merchant who rose to become Lord Mayor of London in 1457 and was rewarded with a knighthood. He started a family tradition of marrying well and was able to amass a vast fortune, leaving the extraordinary sum of £1,000 to London charities at the time of his death. He also purchased the great houses of Blickling Hall in Norfolk and Hever Castle in Kent. Geoffrey's son, Sir William Boleyn, had the luck to marry Margaret Butler, whose father unexpectedly became Earl of Ormond some years after the marriage. Margaret and her sister were the earl's heiresses and Anne's father, Sir Thomas Boleyn, was therefore the grandson of an earl, as well as being considerably wealthy. His own marriage was a grand one. He married Elizabeth Howard, the daughter of the Earl of Surrey (who later reacquired the family dukedom of Norfolk under Henry VIII). The Howards were one of the premier noble families in England and Anne's uncle, the third Duke of Norfolk, had taken Anne of York, the daughter of Edward IV and sister-in-law of Henry VII as his first wife. His second marriage to Elizabeth Stafford, the sister of the royally descended Duke of Buckingham, was also prestigious. He was a leading councillor to Henry VIII.

No details survive of Anne's childhood. Assuming that she was born in around 1501, she was probably born at Blickling Hall in Norfolk. Little now remains of Anne's first childhood home, although a number of memorials to Boleyn family members survive in the neighbouring church, including a memorial brass to an aunt of Anne's who died young and who was also called Anne Boleyn. The family later moved to Hever Castle in Kent and it is this property that is most associated with Anne today. Anne's brother, George, was well educated and it is likely that his sisters shared many of his tutors during childhood. Thomas Boleyn was an ambitious man and was determined that his daughters should make their way in the world. He had been appointed as an esquire of the body to both Henry VII and Henry VIII, and he was particularly noted at court for his fluency in French. During the early years of Henry VIII's reign, he was often called upon to serve as an ambassador for the King. He apparently enjoyed a particular friendship with Margaret of Austria, the daughter of the Emperor Maximilian I who ruled the Netherlands on behalf of her young nephew, the future Emperor Charles V. In 1513, he was able to persuade Margaret to take one of his daughters into her household. The year 1513 marked the end of Anne's childhood as she left England to finish her education in one of the most cultured courts in Europe.

There is little information for Anne's time in Brussels, although it is apparent that she impressed Margaret and that she rapidly learned French.[4] It is possible that she caught her first glimpse of Henry VIII when Margaret and her court moved to Lille in August 1513 to meet with the English king and his retinue. If Anne was there, she was nowhere recorded. Her time with Margaret was brief and, in late 1514 Henry VIII requested that Thomas Boleyn supply both his daughters to serve his sister, Mary Tudor, following her marriage to the aged Louis XII of France.[5] In order to marry Louis, it was necessary for Mary Tudor's betrothal to Charles V to be broken, something that deeply rankled with Margaret of Austria. Anne may well have found that she received a frosty farewell as she journeyed to join the new French queen in October 1514. Her time with Mary Tudor proved even briefer than that with Margaret. Louis XII died on 1 January 1515, after less than three months of marriage. His widow quickly, and scandalously, married Charles Brandon, Duke of Suffolk, returning to England in disgrace. Both Anne and Mary Boleyn remained in France, transferring to the household of the new queen, Claude. Claude was always something of a political nonentity. While she was treated respectfully by her husband, Francis I, she was allowed no input into government and suffered regular pregnancies which further weakened her already precarious health. She was renowned for her piety and kept her household apart from that of the King's. In spite of this, it is certain that Anne would have been familiar with the French court. Her sister definitely was, being sent home in disgrace after it became known that she had enjoyed a casual affair with Francis I. Anne appears to have acquired no ill reputation during her time in France. It is likely that she attended the meeting between Henry VIII and Francis I known as the Field of the Cloth of Gold, in June 1520. She was also, on occasion, able to meet with her father. Few records exist for Anne's time in France, but she became French in all but birth. It was a very different Anne who finally sailed for England in early 1522 to the girl who had left, nine years before.

Anne would probably have been content to remain in France and it may have been a shock when she received word that she was to be recalled. Some controversy exists over Anne's appearance as it has long been rumoured that she suffered from a number of physical deformities, including a sixth finger on one hand and a large mole on her neck, both of which she reportedly hid artfully beneath her fashionable clothes.[6] Much of what has been said about Anne's appearance is certainly slander as it is unlikely that she could have attracted the King with the appearance suggested by some hostile sources. In spite of this, there is evidence that she may indeed have had the beginnings of a sixth finger on one hand, something that was acknowledged by her early biographer, George Wyatt. She also had dark hair and a dark complexion entirely at odds with the contemporary ideal of beauty, which favoured blonde hair and blue eyes. She was striking in appearance and her French education gave her an exotic aura on her return to England, something that was quickly recognised by the men of the court.

Anne was recalled to England in 1522 in order to make a marriage. She would have been aware, since her early childhood, that her future lay in an advantageous marriage, and it would not have been a surprise to hear that a husband had been selected for her. Anne's great-grandfather, the elderly Earl of Ormond, had died in 1515, having expressed a wish that Thomas Boleyn, his favourite grandchild, should succeed to his earldom. Unfortunately, in Ireland, the earl's cousin, Sir Piers Butler, immediately declared himself the new earl and took possession of the Ormond estates. Where a nobleman died leaving only daughters, the position concerning the inheritance of the family title was never clear-cut. In order to avoid the dispute escalating, Anne's own uncle, the Earl of Surrey (who would later become the third Duke of Norfolk and was then serving in Ireland) proposed that Sir Thomas Boleyn's only unmarried daughter, Anne, should marry Piers Butler's eldest son, James. Negotiations were already in hand when Anne returned home, although it appears that neither she, nor her father, had any enthusiasm for the match. Instead, Anne threw herself into court life, appearing in a court masque at Greenwich in March 1522, only weeks after her arrival home.[7] Anne's sister, Mary, who was at that time the King's mistress, may well have secured the prestigious role for Anne. Both sisters were among the eight ladies who appeared representing virtues besieged in a castle. Mary Boleyn took the role of Kindness, while the King's sister, Mary Tudor, queen dowager of France, played Beauty. Anne, appropriately enough as it would transpire, played Perseverance. By May 1523, Piers Butler had come to the view that the marriage between Anne and his son was unlikely to occur. This may well have been due to the inaction of the Boleyn family. Anne, who had been appointed as one of Queen Catherine of Aragon's ladies in waiting soon after her arrival in England, had, by that time, already formed an attachment of her own to Henry Percy, the heir of the Earl of Northumberland.[8] Percy, who was a similar age to Anne and a member of Cardinal Wolsey's household was a frequent visitor to the queen's apartments and it was soon noted that he displayed a particular affection for Anne. The couple appear to have entered into a secret betrothal. For Anne, it would have been a brilliant marriage. Unfortunately, before the couple could bring their scheme to fruition, Henry VIII heard of the marriage and, perhaps still hoping that the Butler marriage would occur, ordered Wolsey, his chief minister, to break off the match. Wolsey sent for Percy's father, who indignantly rushed south before forcing his son to marry a considerably wealthier bride. Anne, who became the Cardinal's enemy following his interference, was sent home to Hever Castle in disgrace.

For Anne, the loss of her marriage to Henry Percy and her position at court must have been devastating. It appears however that, while she was at Hever, she took the opportunity to reacquaint herself with a Kentish neighbour, the poet Thomas Wyatt, who was in high favour at court. Wyatt had already been married for some years by 1523 and, while he was separated from his wife, Anne would have been well aware that he could not offer her the security of marriage. In spite of the assertion of some hostile sources, it is unlikely that Anne saw her relationship with Wyatt as anything more than a harmless flirtation. Wyatt made reference to his feelings for Anne in a number of his poems, but there is no evidence that she ever became his mistress and it is more likely that Anne hoped that, after she was finally allowed to return to court in 1525, her relationship with Wyatt would bring her to the attention of more eligible suitors. If this was her hope, it proved to be correct as Wyatt, who was a favourite of the King's, soon found a rival in his sovereign for Anne's attention. Matters came to a head when Henry took a ring from Anne, wearing it as a trophy on his finger. While he was playing bowls with Wyatt, the King deliberately used the finger on which he wore Anne's ring to point at a game which he declared he had won. Wyatt, who had also taken a jewel from Anne to wear around his neck, removed it and declared that he would use it to measure who the true winner was. When Henry recognised that the jewel was Anne's, he declared 'it may be so, but then am I deceived'. He stalked away to Anne's chambers in anger.[9]

For Anne, the bowls game may have been the first indication of just how serious the King was about his interest in her and her other suitors quickly began to fall away. Henry was attracted to Anne's exotic dark looks and foreign demeanour, and he sought her out to become his mistress. A number of Henry's love letters to Anne survive. They are a remarkable testament to his affection for her, as well as his increasing desperation as she continually spurned his advances, retreating to her family home at Hever rather than accept the role of the King's mistress. It is likely that Anne, who had seen her own sister simply be discarded by the King, had no interest in following in her footsteps but, for Henry, Anne's aloofness merely spurred him on. Matters came to a head when he offered her the position of his 'official mistress', vowing to take no other mistress but her. When she declined this position as well, Henry, desperately in love with her, took the unprecedented step of offering her marriage. This was an offer that Anne was willing to accept, and she signified her agreement with the gift of a jewel fashioned to represent a maiden in a storm-tossed ship. On 5 May 1527, Henry gave a banquet for the French ambassador and publicly led Anne out as his dancing partner for the first time. Twelve days later a secret ecclesiastical court opened in London, in an attempt to annul Henry's existing marriage to Catherine of Aragon, a woman who had previously been the wife of his deceased elder brother and to whom he had been married for nearly twenty years.

By 1527, Catherine of Aragon was over forty and recognised to be long past childbearing. She had borne Henry a number of children throughout their long marriage but only a daughter, Princess Mary, had survived infancy. Years of childbearing and disappointment had left Catherine overweight and old before her time. She was nearly six years older than Henry, an age gap which, by 1527 seemed particularly noticeable. In 1527, Henry was only in his mid-thirties and was still one of the handsomest rulers in Europe. It is likely that Anne was attracted to the King and both hoped that he would quickly secure his divorce on the grounds that, by marrying his brother's widow, Henry had broken divine law. Unfortunately for the couple, Catherine, who was the daughter of the famous Queen Isabella of Castile and King Ferdinand of Aragon, had powerful relatives. In June 1527 her nephew, the Holy Roman Emperor Charles V, sacked Rome, imprisoning the Pope. For Charles, any attempt by Henry to divorce Catherine was an attack on his family honour and he swore to uphold her rights, meaning that a divorce granted by the Pope was a virtual impossibility. Anne and Henry continued to hope that the Pope could be persuaded to grant the divorce for some time, placing their hopes in a Church court that was convened at Blackfriars in 1529 and presided over by the papal legates Cardinal Campeggio and Cardinal Wolsey.[10] Although Catherine refused to attend court after making an emotional appeal to Henry on the first day of the trial, the hearing continued. However, when the time came for the Cardinals to give judgment, Campeggio declared that he had to revoke the case to Rome. For Henry and Anne, this was a major blow and it reawakened Anne's hostility towards Cardinal Wolsey. She played a major role in persuading Henry abandon his favour towards his chief minister and, on 9 October 1529 he was charged with taking orders from a foreign power (the Pope) and forced to surrender the great seal and his position as chancellor. Wolsey fully blamed Anne for his fall, referring to her as a 'serpentine enemy' and the 'Night-Crow'. Tellingly, it was Henry Percy who was ordered to arrest the cardinal at Cawood the following year.[11] The cardinal was, by then, a broken man, and he died at Leicester on 29 November 1530 on his way south to face trial in London.

By the time of Wolsey's death, Anne had already established herself as the most powerful person at court after the King. She was a queen in all but name and, by late 1528, had her own fine lodgings at court. In spite of this, she was constantly aware that she was not, in fact, the queen, and her fiery temper often got the better of her. She is recorded to have quarrelled with her uncle, the Duke of Norfolk, in early 1530.[12] She was also disliked by her aunt, the Duchess of Norfolk, who sent secret messages of support to Catherine of Aragon.[13] In the summer of 1532 she was rumoured to have quarrelled with her father over his support for an imprisoned priest.[14] Even Henry often felt the sharp-end of her tongue and, on at least one occasion, her complaints brought the King to tears.[15] Regardless of this, the couple remained publicly devoted to each other and, when Henry finally separated from Catherine in the summer of 1531, their marriage became inevitable. Anne was, for the most part, deeply unpopular in England, with the French ambassador, for example, commenting in December 1528 that 'the people remain quite hardened, and I think they would do more if they had more power'.[16] In the summer of 1532 she and Henry were forced to turn back from a hunting trip due to the hostility they encountered from the local people.[17] For Anne, it must have been particularly galling that both Catherine and her daughter, Princess Mary, were loved and she sought a number of petty victories over Catherine, on one occasion requesting the Queen's jewels for her own use.[18]

In spite of the Pope's intransience, Henry and Anne continued to search for a means by which the King could be free of his first wife. In September 1532, Henry took the unprecedented step of making Anne a peeress in her own right when she was created Lady Marquis of Pembroke in a glittering ceremony at court. The following month she and Henry crossed the channel for a meeting with the French king, Francis I, in a bid to have Anne's position recognised internationally. The meeting was a success, although Francis was able to persuade no royal French ladies to meet with the English king's 'mistress'. Emboldened, it appears that Henry and Anne finally consummated their relationship around the time of their French visit and, by the early weeks of 1533, Anne had become pregnant. The couple married in a secret ceremony on 25 January 1533, presided over by Henry's chaplain, Rowland Lee.

Although Henry had always preferred to secure his divorce through a sentence given by the Pope, by early 1533, he had given up hope of receiving papal approval and, instead, began to look around for other means to end his first marriage. Anne was instrumental in bringing the solution to Henry's attention. She had always been interested in the religious reform movement, which had little respect for the Pope and, instead, sought to advance religion through a study of the scriptures in the vernacular. Anne is known to have owned a copy of the Bible in French and, as queen, she also kept an English version on open display in a demonstration of her reformist beliefs.[19] Although never a fully-fledged Protestant, she was, not surprisingly, anti-papal. Anne read many of the works produced by reformist scholars and was in the habit of marking out passages that would interest the King. Two particular works helped guide royal policy towards the divorce: William Tyndale's *Obedience of a Christian Man* and Simon Fish's anti-clerical *The Supplication of Beggars*, both of which were introduced to the King by Anne. Henry's first move against the Pope occurred in January 1531 when he insisted to a convocation of the clergy that they purchase a pardon from him for the offence of praemunire (prioritising papal law over that of the king). The assembled clergy reluctantly agreed to pay the King's fine but, the following month, he renewed his pressure, sending a document to the clergy containing five articles for them to agree. The first insisted that they recognise him as the sole protector and supreme head of the Church in England. After much debate, a qualified title was agreed on 11 February, with the English clergy recognising Henry as 'Supreme Head of the Church of England, as far as the law of Christ allows'.[20] In practice, this rendered Henry's new title virtually meaningless but it did at least serve to emphasise the King's anger against the Pope and his intention to move against him if his divorce was not granted. In the years that followed, Henry continued to take steps to limit papal power and privileges in England. Finally, in August 1532, the death of the aged and conservative Archbishop of Canterbury, William Warham, allowed Henry to appoint a new, reformist primate. He selected Thomas Cranmer, a priest who had previously been a member of the reform-minded Thomas Boleyn's household. As soon as the papal bulls confirming Cranmer's appointment reached England, in March 1533, the new archbishop convened a Church court at Dunstable in which he formally declared that Henry's marriage to Catherine of Aragon was invalid. Even before this sentence had been passed, Anne had been publicly proclaimed as queen, appearing as Henry's wife for the first time in the Easter celebrations at court. As soon as Cranmer had given sentence against Henry's first marriage, he hurried to London to crown Anne in a grand coronation on 1 June 1533.

Both Anne and Henry expected the coronation to be quickly followed by the birth of a son. It was therefore a shock to them both when, in the afternoon of 7 September 1533, Anne gave birth to a daughter, who was named Elizabeth. In spite of her parents' disappointment, Elizabeth was given a rich christening. She was also declared heiress of England in preference to her elder half-sister, Mary, who had been declared illegitimate with her parents' divorce. Anne proved to be a fond, if distant, mother to Elizabeth and she regularly visited her daughter after she had been removed to her own household in December 1533. In order to further emphasise Elizabeth's status as Henry VIII's 'legitimate' daughter, her elder half-sister was sent to serve in her household and placed in the custody of Anne's aunt, Lady Shelton. For Anne, Mary was always a threat to the position of her own child, even after the passing of the first Act of Succession in March 1534 which reiterated that it was Anne's children who were the legitimate heirs to the King. Both Henry and Anne treated Catherine and Mary poorly, refusing to allow the pair to meet or correspond. Mary was physically forced to give precedence to her half-sister when she attempted to assert herself.

Anne devoted much of her time as queen to the promotion of the religious reform movement and her charitable works.[21] There were also lighter moments during her queenship and, in early 1524, she received the gift of a dog named Purquoy from Lady Lisle, the wife of Henry's governor of Calais.[22] According to Anne's cousin, Sir Francis Bryan, the 'little dog' was 'so proper and so well liked by the Queen that it remained not above an hour in my hands but that her Grace took it from me'.[23] Sadly, the dog did not survive for more than a few months, with Lady Lisle receiving news, in December 1534 that 'the Queen's Grace setteth much store by a pretty dog, and her Grace delighted so much in little Purkoy that after he was dead of a fall there durst nobody tell her Grace of it, till it pleased the King's Highness to tell her Grace of it'.[24] Lady Lisle, who was hoping to place one of her daughters in the queen's household was determined to please Anne, also making her the gift of a song bird in May 1534.[25] Perhaps in recognition of Lady Lisle's extravagent gifts, Anne sent her a present of a gold rosary for New Year 1535, which the peeress was assured was 'of her Grace's own wearing'.[26]

Anne was always acutely aware that she was required to present Henry with a male heir. She fell pregnant soon after Elizabeth's birth, but it appears that this pregnancy ended either in a miscarriage or a stillbirth in the summer of

1534. There is no firm evidence that she conceived again until the autumn of 1535. For Anne, her failure to produce a male child was dangerous. Henry had pursued Anne for many years before 1533 but, following their marriage, he quickly began to lose interest in her. He took a mistress in the summer of 1533 during Anne's first pregnancy and this was followed by a more lasting affair in 1534 when Anne was expecting her second child. During the early months of Anne's third pregnancy, Henry entered into a relationship with Jane Seymour, one of Anne's ladies in waiting, and it appears that the queen came upon her husband embracing her maid on his lap one day. Catherine of Aragon had died on 7 January 1536 and Henry and Anne celebrated the death at court by wearing yellow. In spite of this, Anne was far from secure and, on the very day of Catherine's funeral, she miscarried a male foetus, variously blaming the sight of Henry with Jane Seymour and her fear at the news that the King had suffered a fall from his horse for the disaster. This did nothing to mollify the King and he was heard to say that 'he would have no more boys by her' as he left Anne's chamber. Henry had not, at that stage, fully made up his mind to abandon Anne and, as late as April, he sought a recognition of her status as queen from Eustace Chapuys, Charles V's ambassador in England. By April 1536, however, there were a number of parties working against Anne in England. Chapuys, a partisan of Princess Mary, had made contact with Thomas Cromwell, the King's chief minister, who had quarrelled with Anne. Mary gave her support to a proposed marriage between the King and Jane Seymour and her supporters joined with Cromwell and the Seymours in their promotion of Jane. By late April, Henry had also decided to rid himself of Anne and marry Jane and, on 24 April 1536, he appointed a commission to investigate certain treasons which was directed at Anne herself.[27]

On 30 April 1536 Mark Smeaton, a low-born young musician in Anne's household, was flatteringly invited to dine with Cromwell at his house in Stepney. On his arrival, Smeaton was placed under arrest and taken to the Tower of London. Amid rumours that he had been tortured on the rack, Smeaton confessed to committing adultery with Anne, providing both Cromwell and Henry with the means to bring about Anne's fall.[28]

Anne was probably entirely oblivious to Smeaton's disappearance and, on 1 May 1536, she attended the May Day jousts at Greenwich with Henry. While the tournament was still ongoing, Henry surprised everyone by suddenly rising to his feet and stalking away without saying a word. He rode at once with only six attendants to Westminster, closely questioning one of the gentlemen of his privy chamber, Henry Norris, on the journey. It appears that Henry interrogated Norris on the nature of his relationship with Anne and, the next morning, he too was sent as a prisoner to the Tower.

Anne must have spent an anxious night at Greenwich after Henry's abrupt departure and, the following morning, her uncle, the Duke of Norfolk, and several other members of the King's council arrived to interrogate her. She was also taken to the Tower and, in the days that followed, she was joined there by her brother, George Boleyn, Viscount Rochford, Sir Thomas Wyatt, and the gentlemen Sir Francis Weston, William Brereton and Sir Richard Page.

With the exception of Smeaton's confession, the case against Anne appears to have rested on the evidence given by four women: Lady Wingfield, Lady Worcester, Lady Rochford and Anne herself. The judge, Sir John Spelman, who attended Anne's trial, noted that Anne had originally been accused by Lady Wingfield, who appears to have been a friend of Anne's before her death in 1533 or 1534.[29] Although no further details of Lady Wingfield's allegations survive, it has been speculated that she left a deathbed statement accusing the Queen of being morally lax.[30] A contemporary letter by John Husee to Lady Lisle also claimed that 'the first accusers, the Lady Worcester, and Nan Cobham, with one maid more. But Lady Worcester was the first ground.'[31] It appears that the Countess of Worcester, who was a member of Anne's household, took a lover and, in early 1536, was berated for her immoral conduct by her brother, Sir Anthony Browne.[32] During the confrontation, Lady Worcester declared that her conduct was not the worst and that he should look at the conduct of the Queen herself. Anne's sister-in-law, Lady Rochford, also came forward with evidence once it became clear that the King intended to proceed against Anne and her brother and it is likely that she was the source of the charges that Anne and George had laughed at the King's clothes and suggested that he was impotent. George was also later accused of questioning the paternity of Princess Elizabeth. Anne's own words in the Tower were used against her and the reports of Sir William Kingston, the lieutenant of the Tower, suggest that she spoke unguardedly, discussing conversations that she had had with some of the accused men which could be taken to suggest adultery. It was Anne who first mentioned Sir Francis Weston's name and, after she claimed that he had told her that he was in love with her, he too found himself imprisoned in the Tower. There is no evidence that any of the claims made against Anne implicated her in actual adultery and it appears more likely that Anne, who loved dancing and music, simply enjoyed the games of courtly love common at the time. Unfortunately for her, and the men with whom she was accused, however, innocent words and actions could be interpreted much more dangerously. On 12 May 1536, Norris, Brereton, Weston and Smeaton were convicted of treason after being accused 'that they had violated and had carnal knowledge of the said queen, each by himself at separate times'. No move was made to try either Wyatt or Page and they were eventually released from the Tower.[33] On 15 May, both Anne and her brother were arraigned separately in the Tower of London and, after spirited defences, were found guilty. Anne was sentenced to be burned or beheaded at the King's pleasure.

The result of Anne's trial was a foregone conclusion and, on 17 May, Archbishop Cranmer formally annulled her marriage to Henry, either on the grounds of her earlier betrothal to Henry Percy, or due to the King's earlier relationship with Mary Boleyn which, ironically, had placed Anne and Henry, in the eyes of the Church, within the same degree of consanguinity as he had been with Catherine of Aragon, his brother's widow. That same day, Anne's five 'lovers' were executed. With the deaths of the five men,

Anne must have known that her own death was inevitable. On 18 May, she swore on the sacrament that she was innocent in front of Sir William Kingston. She then took steps to prepare herself for death. On the morning of 19 May 1536, she was led out to a scaffold erected on Tower Green in front of a crowd of carefully selected witnesses. She made a final speech and began to pray before a swordsman, sent for from either Calais or St Omer by Henry VIII, stepped up behind her and severed her head with one stroke of the sword.

The documents printed in this volume detail Anne's story in both her own words (through her letters and recorded speech) and the words of contemporaries, or near-contemporaries, who recorded details of her life. The aim has been to provide as complete a picture as possible without too much interpretation or speculation, in order to allow the sources to speak for themselves. It should be recorded that there are two notable sources not fully considered here. The first is William Latymer's *Chronickille of Anne Bulleyne*, which was presented to Anne's daughter, Elizabeth, during her reign. Latymer was Anne's chaplain and so an eyewitness to what he described. Due to size constraints for this volume, it has been impossible to include it. There is however an excellent recent edition, transcribed and edited by Maria Dowling, which is listed in the bibliography. Given the accessibility of Dowling's edition, the decision has been taken to omit Latymer's *Chronickille* from this work.

A second omission is the poem written by Lancelot de Carles, a member of the French embassy in London at the time of Anne's fall. He wrote a poem on Anne's arrest and death in June 1536 which is of considerable interest. The original poem is written in French and has, as yet, received no full edition in English. A summary translation is printed here, but the decision was taken not to print the French version in full. An edition containing the French original is listed in the bibliography.

Finally, the decision has been taken to focus on sources that are directly relevant to Anne. A great deal of material survives concerning the break with Rome and the Reformation. Since a number of excellent source books already exist containing this material, much of it has been omitted here.[34] Likewise, the executions of Thomas More, John Fisher and Elizabeth Barton, the nun of Kent, although interesting elements to Anne's story, have not been detailed fully, except where sources that relate to them can be said to also be directly relevant to Anne.

The majority of the sources printed here are available in works now published online. Many have not, however, received a recent print edition. This work is therefore for those who are interested in seeing the major sources for Anne in print together for the first time. No pretence is made that new material has been uncovered: Anne has been so well studied over the years that it is unlikely that anything new and directly relating to her will be found. With a few exceptions, the sources published here are those that have been used on countless occasions by historians to reconstruct the life of Anne Boleyn. They tell her story.

Anne Boleyn was still only in her mid-thirties, at most, at the time of her death but she left a great legacy both in the religious reform, which continued to develop after her death, and in her daughter, Elizabeth, who survived to become one of England's greatest monarchs. In her own lifetime she was a controversial figure and it is possible to read the story of her eventful life both in the words that she herself left behind, and in the accounts of those that, variously, loved or loathed her.

# 1

# George Wyatt's *Life of Queen Anne Boleigne*

*George Wyatt (c. 1554–1624) was the son of Sir Thomas Wyatt the Younger, who was executed for mounting a rebellion against the Catholic Queen, Mary I, in an attempt to stop her marriage to her second cousin, Prince Philip (later Philip II) Of Spain.[1] He was the grandson of the poet and courtier, Sir Thomas Wyatt the Elder, Anne Boleyn's suitor.[2]*

*Wyatt, a Protestant, deeply admired Anne and he devoted the last three decades of his life towards study and writing, apparently intending to write a work refuting Nicholas Sander's 'The Rise and Growth of the Anglican Schism', which contained an attack on Anne Boleyn and the Reformation and was published in 1585. In order to produce his account, Wyatt assembled a great quantity of information, including obtaining the accounts of those who had known Anne. His* Life of Queen Anne Boleigne *was never completed with, for example, the preface he drafted for the work existing as a separate manuscript. His work is, however, the earliest surviving and most complete account of Anne's life. It was last printed in 1825 as an appendix to Cavendish's* Life of Wolsey *(with a further edition of the same work in 1827).*

*George Wyatt was writing from a viewpoint that was extremely favourable to Anne, as can be seen from some of his own comments on his motivation for writing, which are contained in the draft preface. Wyatt claimed that:*

Willingly therfore now my last daise I doe consecrate to the honor of God and sacred memory and worthe of that Illustrus Lady, the rather to divert the remembrance of mine owen harmes in consideringe hers, who was second wife to the renowned King Henry the 8, and mother to our late gratious Quene Elizabethe al of them beringe a most greate part in the greate and remarkable convertion in the state of religion springing in our times throughout al Christendome originall and principaly here in England a place by Gods singular goodness as may seeme destinate for many suche honors. And so in like sort al must acknowlege this Princely Lady was elect of God a most eminent agent and actor in the most dangerous and difficult part therof, in sustaininge so greate an emotion with an invincible corage and Heroical spirit, under which Atlas himself might sinke, muche more a woman who yet diynge did seale it with her blud, which livinge she so curragiously stud to support, whence hathe growen a greate part of the

Envy which hathe moved so many to writ and speake no les falsly then foulely of her as presently shalbe evident to al thos not wilfully injurious to her honor.

*His work is, obviously, far from unbiased, and it contains errors, such as the reference to Anne's conflict with Wolsey over the banned book, which he dates as having occurred after she became queen when, in fact, Wolsey had been dead for over two and a half years by the time of her coronation. Due to his viewpoint Wyatt also, naturally, recorded all the good that he heard of Anne Boleyn and omitted any of the bad. One further problem with the source that should be mentioned is that while Wyatt, as the grandson of Anne's suitor, Sir Thomas Wyatt, may have had access to additional information not available to other biographers, he also wanted to portray his grandfather in a favourable light. The relationship between Anne and Thomas Wyatt was already well known by the time that George Wyatt was writing, but it is not impossible that he would have embellished his sources to ensure that both Anne, and Thomas Wyatt, emerged with renewed reputations, particularly after the attack contained in Sander's work.*

*In spite of this, George Wyatt's work is of great value to the study of Anne Boleyn. He was especially diligent in collecting his sources and other materials, and he records a number of incidents of which the basic facts are likely to be accurate. The surviving life is a fraction of what Wyatt wanted to achieve, but, for all its problems, can be considered to be one of the most useful and influential sources used in the study of the life of Anne Boleyn.*

The peculiar means that I have had, more than others, to come to some more particular knowledge of such things as I intend to handle, ought to draw thus much from me; yet much more the request of him that hath been by authority set on work in this important business, both for the singular gifts of God in him, of wisdom, learning, integrity, and virtue; and also the encouragement I have had of late from the right reverend my Lord of Canterbury's grace, to set down what understanding I have had of this matter, is both my warrant, and a bond the more upon my conscience, to hold me urged and constrained not to neglect such an opportunity of my service to the church, my prince, and country, Principally his desire was, and my purpose in satisfying it, to deliver what I knew, touching certain things that happened to the excellent lady, the LADY ANNE BOLEIGNE, about the time of her first coming to the court. Yet, considering I had some other knowledge of things that might be found serviceable no less than that, and also might give light and life to the faithful narration of this whole matter, I have supposed it would fall best, to deliver the same, as it were, under the description of her whole life; and this the more particularly and frankly, that, all things known, those that I understood were to visit it again might take what they should think most material for their use. And would to God I could give that grace and felicity of style unto it that the worthiness of the subject doth require, notwithstanding that in this regard I am the less carefull, for that it is to pass through their hands that can give it better vesture; and I shall the more turn my care to intend the sincere and faithful delivery of that which I have received from those that both were most likely to come to the most perfect knowledge hereof, and had least cause or, otherwise for themselves, could least give just reason of suspicion to any, either of mind, or partiality, or wit, to fayne or misreport any whit hereof. And, indeed, chiefly the relation of those things that I shall set down is come from two.[3] One a lady, that first attended on her both before and after she was queen, with whose house and mine there was then kindred and strict alliance.[4] The other also a lady of noble birth, living in those times, and well acquainted with the persons that most this concerneth, from whom I am myself descended. A little, therefore, repeating the matter more high, I will derive the discourse hereof from the very spring and fountains, whence may appear most clearly by what occasion and degrees the stream of this whole cause hath grown to such an ocean as it were of memorable effects through all our parts of Christendom, not by chance or wits of men so much as even by the apparent work of God, as I hope presently to make plain to all men.

The see of *Rome* having risen, in this our age, unto a full tide of all wickedness, had overflowed all these parts of the world with the floods of her evils, whereby was occasioned and had beginning the ebb of all her pomp, power, and glory, every particular devising, as if it had been by one consent and accord (so showing it the more apparently to come of God), to provide for the time to come against her so great inundation of mischiefs. Hereof, in *England, Germany, Italy*, and in many other places, sundry persons of singular learning and piety, one succeeding another, at divers times, opened their mouths as trumpets to call men to this work upon several occasions, all rising from the outrageous corruptions and foaming filth of that see. But chiefly and most notoriously, in the time of Henry the Eighth, of famous memory, this came to pass by the just judgment of God upon her, and his mercy upon us, where the same polity by which she had in custom, and then made herself most assured, to strengthen herself in giving to princes licence to unlawful contracts.[5] (esteeming thereby to tie them and their issue the more strongly to her); the bond of so evil counsel breaking suddenly, set at liberty the certain means of this great opposition against her after almost through all Europe. So little assurance especially have evil foundations of usurped authorities against the provoked judgments of God by sin, and general displeasure of man upon just conceived indignities.

There was, at this present, presented to the eye of the court the rare and admirable beauty of the fresh and young Lady Anne Boleigne, to be attending upon the queen. In this noble imp, the graces of nature graced by gracious education, seemed even at the first to have promised bliss unto her aftertimes. She was taken at that time to have a beauty not so whitely as clear and fresh above all we may esteem, which appeared much more excellent by her favour passing sweet and cheerful; and these, both also increased by her noble presence of shape and fashion, representing both mildness and majesty more than can be expressed. There was found, indeed, upon the side of her nail upon one of her fingers, some little show of a nail, which yet was so small, by the report of those that have seen her, as the workmaster seemed to leave it an occasion of greater grace to her hand, which, with the tip of one of her other fingers, might be and was usually by her hidden without any least blemish to it.[6] Likewise there were said to be upon some parts of her body certain small moles incident to the clearest complexions. And certainly both these were none other than might more stain their writings with note of malice that have caught at such light motes in so bright beams of beauty, than in any part shadow it, as may right well appear by many arguments, but chiefly by the choice and exquisite judgments of many brave spirits that were esteemed to honour the honourable parts in her, even honoured of envy itself.[7]

Among these, two were observed to be of principal mark. The one was *Sir Thomas Wiat*, the elder, the other was the king himself. The knight, in the beginning, coming to behold the sudden appearance of this new beauty, came to be holden and surprised somewhat with the sight thereof; after much more with her witty and graceful speech, his ear also had him chained unto her, so as finally his heart seemed to say, *I could gladly yield to be tied for ever with the knot of her love,* as somewhere in his verses hath been thought his meaning was to express.[8] She, on the other part, finding him to be then married, and in the knot to have been tied then ten years, rejected all his speech of love; but yet in such sort as whatsoever tended to regard of her honour, she showed not to scorn, for the general favour and good will she perceived all men to bare him, which might the rather occasion others to turn their looks to that which a man of his worth was brought to gaze at in her, as, indeed, after it happened. The king is held to have taken his first apprehension of this love after such time as upon the doubt in those treaties of marriage with his daughter Mary, first with the Spaniard, then with the French: by some of the learned of his own land he had vehemently in their public sermons, and in his confessions to his ghostly fathers, been prayed to forsake that his incestuous life by accompanying with his brother's wife; and especially after he was moved by the cardinal, then in his greatest trust with the king, both for the better quietness of his conscience, and for more sure settling of the succession to more prosperous issue.[9]

About this time, it is said that the knight, entertaining talk with her as she was earnest at work, in sporting wise caught from her a certain small jewel hanging by a lace out of her pocket, or otherwise loose, which he thrust into his bosom, neither with any earnest request could she obtain it of him again. He kept it, therefore, and wore it after about his neck, under his cassock, promising to himself either to have it with her favour or as an occasion to have talk with her, wherein he had singular delight, and she after seemed not to make much reckoning of it, either the thing not being much worth, or not worth much striving for. The noble prince having a watchful eye upon the knight, noted him more to hover about the lady, and she the more to keep aloof of him; was whetted the more to discover to her his affection, so as rather he liked first to try of what temper the regard of her honour was, which he finding not any way to be tainted with those things his kingly majesty and means could bring to the battery, he in the end fell to win her by treaty of marriage, and in this talk took from her a ring, and that wore upon his little finger; and yet all this with such secrecy was carried, and on her part so wisely, as none or very few esteemed this other than an ordinary course of dalliance. Within few days after, it happened that the king, sporting himself at bowls, had in his company (as it falls out) divers noblemen and other courtiers of account, amongst whom might be the Duke of Suffolk, Sir F. Brian, and Sir T. Wiat, himself being more than ordinarily pleasantly disposed, and in his game taking an occasion to affirm a cast to be his that plainly appeared to be otherwise; those on the other side said, with his grace's leave, they thought not, and yet, still he pointing with his finger whereon he wore her ring, replied often it was his, and specially to the knight he said, Wiat, I tell thee it is mine, smiling upon him withal. Sir Thomas, at the length, casting his eye upon the king's finger, perceived that the king meant the lady whose ring that was, which he well knew, and pausing a little, and finding the king bent on pleasure, after the words repeated again by the king, the knight replied, And if it may like your majesty to give me leave to measure it, I hope it will be mine; and withal took from his neck the lace whereat hung the tablet, and therewith stooped to measure the cast, which the king espying, knew, and had seen her wear, and therewithal spurned away the bowl, and said, It may be so, but then am I deceived; and so broke up the game. This thing thus carried was not perceived for all this of many, but of some few it was. Now the king, resorting to his chamber, showing some discontentment in his countenance, found means to break this matter to the lady, who, with good and evident proof how the knight came by the jewel, satisfied the king so effectually that this more confirmed the king's opinion of her truth than himself at the first could have expected. Shortly, upon the return of the cardinal, the matter of the dutchess[10] cooling every day more and more, his credit also waned till it was utterly eclipsed; and that so busied the great personages that they marked the less the king's bent, the rather for that some way it seemed helpful to their working against the cardinal. The king also took here opportunity to proceed to discover his full and whole meaning unto the lady's father, to whom we may be sure the news was not a little joyful. All this notwithstanding, her virtue was not so dased with the glory of so forcible attractives, but that she stood still upon her guard, and was not, as we would suppose, so easily taken with all these appearances of happiness; whereof two things appeared to be the causes. One the love she bare ever to the queen whom she served, that was also a personage of great virtue: the other her conceit that there was not that freedom of conjunction with one that was her lord and king as with one more agreeable to her estate. These things being well perceived of, the queen shew she knew well to frame and work her advantage of, and therefore the oftener had her at cards with her, the rather also that the king might have the less her company, and the lady the more excuse to be from him; also she esteem herself the kindlier used, and yet withal the more to give the king occasion to see the nail upon her finger. And in this entertainment of time they had a certain game that I cannot name then frequented, wherein dealing, the king and queen meeting they stopped, and the young lady's hap was much to stop at a king; which the queen noting, said to her playfellow, My Lady Anne, you have good hap to stop at a king, but you are not like others, you will have all or none. So often earnest matters are delivered under game. Yet had the king his times, and she in the end yielded to give her consent of marriage to him, whom hardly ever any before was found able to keep their hold against. This was now so far to the pleasure of the king, that forthwith he with her and her father concluded to open the matter to the council, all other things being ripe thereunto, and specially for that it was not possible to keep it any longer from the talk of men near his person, and the more, the queen being found to take such knowledge thereof. It is thought then the table was diversely carried to give opinion upon this matter; some of the nobility wishing rather to have had so good hap lighted to some of their own houses; others that it had not been at all; some inclining to either of these as depending on them; but most liked better the king's own choice, both for the hope of issue, and that the greatness of great men should not grow too great to sway with in managing of matters of state. But howsoever, it appeared manifestly that presently there were practices discovered on all sides under sundry arts, on the parts of Spain, from Rome and that faction, and from the queen herself, and specially some with the king, some with the lady herself, plotted to break or stay at the least till something might fall between the cup and the lip, that might break all this purpose with one of them, if it might have been. And verily one of these may seem for this present occasion not unmeet to be recounted; which was this: There was conveyed to her a book pretending old prophecies, wherein was represented the figure of some personages, with the letter H upon one, A upon another, and K upon the third, which an expounder thereupon took upon him to interpret by the king and his wives, and to her pronouncing certain destruction if she married the king. This book coming into her chamber, she opened, and finding the contents, called to her maid of whom we have spoken before, who also bore her name: 'Come hither, Nan,' said she, 'see here a book of prophecy; this he saith is the king, this the queen, mourning, weeping and wringing her hands, and this is myself with my head off.' The maid answered, 'If I thought it true, though he were an emperor, I would not myself marry him with that condition.' 'Yes, Nan,' replied the lady, 'I think the book a bauble; yet for the hope I have that the realm may be happy by my issue, I am resolved to have him whatsoever might become of me.'

The Romish fable-framer,[11] if he may be believed, affirmeth another practice after this sort: 'That Sir Thomas Wiat coming to the council, for his better security, confessed to have had dealings with that lady, before he had any perceiving of the king's purpose of marriage; but not being credited by the king, that Wiat, as not finding it well he was not believed, affirmed he would bring the king where he might see him enjoy her. And that again being delivered by the Duke of Suffolk to the king, he yet believed it not.' But it is certain that the whole or greatest part of this is fiction; for the persons, manner, and event of these things have been utterly mistaken and misshapen. For I have heard by the report of one of right good and honourable account, and of much understanding in such things, who also hath the truth of his word in high respect, that it was Sir Francis Brian that confessed such a like thing to the king by another lady, with other success more likely, which was that the king thereupon pardoned *him* indeed, but rejected and gave over the lady ever after to him. Whether the duke might, upon the sight of that which happened at bowls, take any occasion with the king to dissuade the marriage, supposing the knight could not or would not otherwise have cleared himself and the lady, but by confessing and craving pardon for it as done before he had knowledge of the king's intention, I cannot say; and by guess I will not affirm it in any case of any, much less of so worthy and noble a personage. Only this I say, that if he did so, I believe verily that he was greatly deceived therein of his expectation; as finding that by good proof the knight could clear himself and her of that matter, even to the full assuring and ascertaining of the king of the manner of his coming by the jewel without her dishonour, and that so the duke, if he did so, might come to find himself had gone too far, as to have purchased to himself thereby mislike both of the king and queen, whereupon he might turn his heavy displeasure to the knight ever after. I know of a certainty, that the knight had a most high opinion of that princely lady's noble virtues as by trial, and chiefly in the matter of the bowls; in that she took not or interpreted ill of his deed (as herself, being in her own conscience clear), but as he meant it to the king's disport before knowledge of the marriage. This is true also, that Sir Thomas Wiat was twice sifted and lifted at, and that nobleman both times his most heavy adversary, as I have to show under the knight's own hand in his answer to his last indictment.[12] Neither could I ever learn what might be the cause of his so perpetual grudge, save only that it appeareth to be as old as this. Some man might perhaps be led to think that the duke might have a special end to draw him to enter and venture so far to the breaking off the match. And it is true that he was then married with the king's second sister, when the king had then remaining but one only daughter, and then she also questioned whether legitimate; That then also was procured a statute to cut off foreign titles; and it is true also, that after the ambition of some to occasion hereby to thrust the duke's issue, even before the proper and lawful issue of the king, into the regal seat. All this notwithstanding, I will never be induced to give that opinion of that nobleman, but rather I would think, if he did any such thing, in any sort giving colour to this fancy of the Roman legender, he did it upon zeal that in his conceit it was true, and that he thought the knight would so far confess it as done before talk of the king's marriage, when he saw he had passed so far in the measuring of the cast. And though the whole fiction have scarcely so much as shadow of colour of any appearance, yet for that part where he deviseth that Sir Thomas should before the council apeach himself and that lady, or after not being credited, offer to make the king see him to have to do with her, this showing itself sufficiently falsified to any wise and understanding reader, especially considering it particularly with the circumstances, it is so far from all likelihood, as all presumptions are flat against it, as in a word or two shall now be showed.

For that princely lady, she living in court where were so many brave gallants at that time unmarried, she was not like to cast her eye upon one that had been then married ten years. And her parents, then in good and honourable place, resident in court, and themselves of no mean condition, they would keep, no doubt, a watchful eye over her to see she should not roam to the hinderance of her own preferment, a course so foul with one where was no colour of marriage. The King's eye also was a guard upon her, as also those that pleased the king in recounting the adventures of love happening in court made it hard, specially for the shortness of time after her placing there, and the king's own love. Also she that held out against such a king where was hope of marriage, what was like she should do to the knight, where his own lady and her friends were still to attend upon their doings, whose testimonies of the honourable carriage of that lady are therefore here most strong for her? And for the knight, if he had enjoyed her, was he so far desperately wicked and a monster in love, that he would openly, purposely, and to his own disgrace, vaunt the spoil of a maid of so good friends and likelihoods of advancements, without all regard of God or man? especially when she had stood so well upon the assurance of her own innocence for the matter of the jewel without turning him to any displeasure thereby. Those that knew him best, knew him far from that dishonest disposition chiefly in this kind, and for so gross a villainy. And if he had been of that mind, yet was he known not of so little wit or understanding, upon a point that was not very likely to be known, to discover his own and her evil; where was a great deal more likelihood that, the king believing her rather than him, he was to incur a more certain and greater mischief, that might in all presumption, fall by the heavy displeasure of them both upon himself ever after. And if we could imagine him both so wretchedly dishonest, and so very a sot (neither of which could be found of him), his father then counsellor to the king, for his wisdom, years, and experience, more grave, would not have suffered him yet to quit himself so fondly and to be so mad; especially as when the king had showed not to believe it, then to run more obstinately to offer when the king had made her privy hereunto, to bring her that the king should see her also so mad as to yield to him after she had given consent of marriage to the king. Who would not believe them also mad, that would believe so mad a carriage of such a business amongst grave and wise men, howsoever the railing Romanist be so mad to write it so as he would seem mad with reason? For the king also, besides that he had more occasion and means than any other to note and observe her doings, yet much more (as the nature of generous spirits carries them) he was watchful upon the knight, as in other things so chiefly in this, not to be outrun at this garland of love; so as by himself and by the eyes of others, there was not any trip but would have been spied, no likelihood but would have carried suspicion with it; how much more would the knight's confession have sunk into his head? Would he, being so wise a prince, have forgotten that the soberness of his choice would serve much for satisfying the world, touching his divorce? Had he not time, had he not leisure to learn, to inquire and sift out all things? His care used in gathering opinions of universities, and in informing princes of the whole matter, with all circumstances in the managing this cause, by the space of some years, show he was not so passionate a lover, but also withal a wise and considerate prince. But it is said the king believed it not! Yet what? when the knight (as this tale saith) offered to make the king see it, and that avowed to the council! Could such a prince as he swallow this? Doubtless none that hath his wits will think so, none that knew the complexion of the king could induce himself to suppose a thing so incredible. The case of Sir Francis Brian's opening of his love had another effect, and shows plainly that the king was of another metal, since he cast off that Lady loved right dearly (as hath been said) without farther matter. And doubtless in this case, he believing the matter would have thrown off this lady also, the marriage not yet consummate, and he having in his own realm and abroad beauties enough to content him, and means enough also to push on some other. But it is devised the king believed it not. Not believing it, think we the knight could have escaped punishment of a slanderer, though he might by confessing, avoid the punishment of a malefactor (as they say) after? This no outrageous madman would believe. If the king would or could have passed it over, the lady in honour could not, nor might. But suppose also that supposal beyond all suppose. Though they punished it not, would they, think ye, have put him in credit and advancement after? Would they have had him chief ewerer even the very day of her coronation? Would they have employed him ambassador in that matter of the marriage? Yea, I say more! would the king also have rewarded him with a good portion of lands soon upon this? But all these were so as we have alleged them. The Chronicles have his service on that day of coronation. His embassages were twice about this matter known right well: I have seen the patents of the grant myself. And these things, the last especially, I the rather allege, for that the knight useth them himself as testimonies of the king's good opinion of him, in his defence before mentioned, which also by the king and his council in those times was liked and allowed of as his just purgation, by which they acquitted him. Finally, that his defence then may and is to be esteemed his defence now also in this case not to be contemned, and may thus be considered. This reporteth that he was twice winnowed. The matters were the same both times, the accusations so frivolous, the inducements and proofs so idle, that they prove nothing more than that there lacked no wills in his adversary to do him hurt, than that they had any least colour of matter to work it. Nothing so impertinent, nothing so unlikely that they allege not. Yea and his most trusty and best services they had the chief matters of their accusation, nothing was so fond that they ripped not up to his discredit, at the least if it might have been. Yet in all this was no word or signification of any such matter. Though it had not been brought as the ground of his accusation, would it not have been drawn forth to aggravate or induce the matter? Undoubtedly it would, either in the queen's life in his first trouble, and it would have done well to revenge if he had done her this wrong, or after to her overthrow, or else in his second trouble against him. But no one word is or was in it touching any such matters.

After so many cross billets of cunning polities, surmounted by the guiding providence of God, after so many trials of her truth, passed through by her

wise and virtuous governance, the king having every way made so thorough
proof how deep root honour had taken in her bosom, and having found
it not to be shaken even by him, this royal and famous prince Henry the
Eighth, resolving her matchless perfections meet alone to be joined with his,
now at the length concluded forthwith to knit up this marriage, although
for certain causes the same was thought more convenient to be performed
somewhat privately and secretly. On the twenty-fifth of January, therefore,
the ceremony was consummate.[13] The king also, shortly after having himself
more ascertained, and by more inward trial more assured of her spousal
truth, would yet farther testify that his opinion of her, by giving her that
highest honour he could give her virtues, in having her solemnly and royally
crowned. And thus we see they lived and loved, tokens of increasing love
perpetually increasing between them. Her mind brought him forth the rich
treasures of love of piety, love of truth, love of learning. Her body yielded
him the fruits of marriage, inestimable pledges of her faith and loyal love.
And touching the former of these, it is here first not to be forgotten, that
of her time (that is during the three years that she was queen) it is found
by good observation, that no one suffered for religion, which is the more
worthy to be noted for that it could not so be said of any time of the queens
after married to the king. And amongst other proofs of her love to religion
to be found in others, this here of me is to be added. That shortly after her
marriage, divers learned and christianly disposed persons resorting to her,
presented her with sundry books of those controversies that then began to be
questioned touching religion, and specially of the authority of the pope and
his clergy, and of their doings against kings and states. And amongst other,
there happened one of these,[14] which, as her manner was, she having read,
she had also noted with her nail as of matter worthy the king's knowledge.
The book lying in her window, her maid (of whom hath been spoken) took
it up, and as she was reading it, came to speak with her one then suitor to
her, that after married her;[15] and as they talked he took the book of her,
and she withal, called to attend on the queen, forgot it in his hands, and
she not returning in some long space, he walked forth with it in his hand,
thinking it had been hers. There encountered him soon after a gentleman
of the cardinal's of his acquaintance, and after salutations, perceiving the
book, requested to see it, and finding what it was, partly by the title, partly
by some what he read in it, he borrowed it and showed it to the cardinal.
Hereupon the suitor was sent for to the cardinal and examined of the book,
and how he came by it, and had like to have come in trouble about it, but
that it being found to have pertained to one of the queen's chamber, the
cardinal thought better to defer the matter till he had broken it to the king
first, in which meantime the suitor delivered the lady what had fallen out,
and she also to the queen, who, for her wisdom knowing more what might
grow thereupon, without delay went and imparted the matter to the king,
and showed him of the points that she had noted with her finger. And she
was but newly come from the king, but the cardinal came in with the book
in his hands to make complaint of certain points in it that he knew the king
would not like of, and withal to take occasion with him against those that

countenance such books in general, and specially women, and as might be thought with mind to go farther against the queen more directly if he had perceived the king agreeable to his meaning. But the king that somewhat afore distasted the cardinal, as we have showed, finding the notes the queen had made, all turned the more to hasten his ruin, which was also furthered on all sides.

On the other part, of her body she bare him a daughter on the seventh of September, to the great joy then of all his people, both for that the king had now issue legitimate of his own body, and for the hope of more after. The king also he expressed his joy for that fruit sprung of himself, and his yet more confirmed love towards her, caused her child openly and publickly to be proclaimed PRINCESS ELIZABETH at the solemnity of her baptising, preferring his younger daughter legitimate before the elder in unlawful wedlock. And after this again, at the prorogation of the parliament, the thirtieth of March,[16] he had every lord, knight, and burgess sworn to an act of succession, and their names subscribed to a schedule fixed to the same statute, where it was enacted, that his daughter princess Elizabeth, he having none other heir male, should succeed him to the crown. And, after were commissioners sent to all parts of the realm to take the like oath of all men and women in the land. Neither also were her virtues only enclosed in her own breast or shut up in her own person. She had procured to her chaplains,[17] men of great learning and of no less honest conversing, whom she with hers heard much, and privately she heard them willingly and gladly to admonish her, and them herself exhorted and encouraged so to do. Also at the first, she had in court drawn about her, to be attending on her, ladies of great honour, and yet of greater choice for reputation of virtue, undoubted witnesses of her spousal integrity, whom she trained upon with all commendations of well ordered government, though yet above all by her own example she shined above them all, as a torch that all might take light of, being itself still more bright. Those that have seen at *Hampton Court* the rich and exquisite works by herself, for the greater part wrought by her own hand and needle, and also of her ladies, esteem them the most precious furniture that are to be accounted amongst the most sumptuous that any prince may be possessed of. And yet far more rich and precious were those works in the sight of God which she caused her maids and those about her daily to work in shirts and smocks for the poor. But not staying here her eye for charity, her hand of bounty passed through the whole land; each place felt that heavenly flame burning in her; all times will remember it, no place leaving for vain flames, no times for idle thoughts. Her ordinary amounted to fifteen hundred pounds at the least, yearly, to be bestowed on the poor. Her provisions of stock for the poor in sundry needy parishes were very great. Out of her privy purse went not a little to like purposes. To Scholars in exhibition very much: so as in three quarters of a year her alms was summed to fourteen or fifteen thousand pounds.[18]

She waxing great again and not so fit for dalliance, the time was taken to steal the king's affection from her, when most of all she was to have been cherished. And he once showing to bend from her, many that least ought shrank from her also, and some lent on the other side; such are the flexible natures of those in courts of princes for the most part. Unkindness grew, and she was brought abed before her time with much peril of her life, and of a male child dead born, to her greater and most extreme grief. Being thus a woman full of sorrow, it was reported that the king came to her and bewailing and complaining unto her the loss of his boy, some words were heard to break out of the inward feeling of her heart's dolours, laying the fault upon unkindness, which the king more than was cause (her case at this time considered) took more hardly than otherwise he would if he had not been somewhat too much overcome with grief, or not so much alienate. Wise men in those days judged that her virtues was here her default, and that if her too much love could, as well as the other queen, have borne with his defect of love, she might have fallen into less danger, and in the end have tied him the more ever after to her when he had seen his error, and *that* she might the rather have done respecting the general liberty and custom of falling then that way. Certainly, from henceforth the harm still more increased, and he was then heard to say to her: he would have no more boys by *her*. Having thus so many, so great factions at home and abroad set loose by the distorned favour of the king, and so few to show themselves for her, what could be? what was otherlike but that all these guests lighting on her at once should prevail to overthrow her, and with her those that stood under her fall? She and her friends therefore were suddenly sent to the Tower: and this gracious queen coming unto the entry of the gate, she falling down upon her knees made that place a reverend temple to offer up her devout prayers, and as a bale there here soul beaten down with afflictions to the earth, with her faithful prayers bounded up to heaven. 'O Lord,' said she, 'help me, as I am guiltless of this whereof I am accused.' The time approached for the hearing of her cause. The place of her trial in the Tower may somewhat discover how the matter was liked to be handled. Nor there was it appointed the better to conceal the heinousness of the accusation, though that might be the pretence. For that was published in parliament that it might from thence spread abroad over all. Her very accusations speak and even plead for her; all of them, so far as I can find, carrying in themselves open proof to all men's consciences of mere matter of quarrel, and indeed of a very preparation to some hoped alteration. The most and chief of them showing to have come from *Rome,* that popish forge of cunning and treachery, as *Petrarch* long since termed it.

> *Nido di tradimenti in cui si cuova*
> *Quanto mal per lo mondo hoggi si spandi*
> Nest of treasons in which is hatch'd and bred
> What ill this day the world doth overspread.

For that most odious of them, something is to be esteemed by the apparent wrongs of the other evil handling of matters. But for this thing itself, partly it is incredible, partly by the circumstances impossible. Incredible, that she that had it her word as it were, the spirit of her mind, as hath been said, that she was *Caesar's* all, not to be touched of others, should be held with the foul desire of her brother. Again, she having so goodly a prince to please her, who also had showed himself able to content more than one, that she should yet be carried to a thing so much abhorring even womanly years and to nature itself, much more to so christian a queen. Impossible, for the necessary and no small attendance of ladies ever about her, whereof some, as after appeared, even aspired unto her place and right in the king's love; yea, by manifest prevention before their time. And indeed, hereof, it was her very accusers found it impossible to have colour to charge her with any other than her brother, which also made it no less impossible even for him alike as other. Impossible, I say, because neither she could remove so great ladies, by office appointed to attend upon her continually, from being witnesses to her doings; neither for the danger she saw she stood in, and the occasion daily sought, would she for her own wisdom, and also by the advertisements of her kindred and followers, whereof she had many of most great understanding, experience, and faith, about her. Besides, she could not but be made more wary and wakeful, if for none other cause, yet even to take away all colour from her enemies, whose eyes were everywhere upon her to pick matter, and their malicious hearts bent to make some where they found none; as plainly enough was to be seen when they were driven to those straits to take occasion at her brother's more private being with her; the more grudged at perhaps, for that it might be supposed his conference with her might be for the breaking off the king's new love. For the evidence, as I never could hear of any, so small I believe it was. But this I say, well was it said of a noble judge of late, that 'half a proof where nature leadeth was to be esteemed a whole proof.' On the contrary, in this case he would have said, whole and very absolute proofs to have been needful in such a case against nature. And I may say, by their leaves, it seems themselves they doubted their proofs would prove their reproofs, when they durst not bring them to the proof of the light in open place. For this principal matter between the queen and her brother, there was brought forth, indeed, witness, his wicked wife accuser of her own husband, even to the seeking of his blood, which I believe is hardly to be showed of any honest woman ever done. But of her, the judgment that fell out upon her, and the just punishment by law after of her naughtiness, show that what she did was more to be rid of him than of true ground against him. And that it seemeth those noblemen that went upon the queen's life found in her trial, when it may appear plainly by that defence of the knight that oft hath been here mentioned, that the young nobleman the Lord Rochford, by the common opinion of men of best understanding in those days, was counted and then openly spoken, condemned only upon some point of a statute of words then in force. And this and sundry other reasons have made me think often that upon some clause of the same law they grounded their colour also against her, and that for other matters she had cleared herself well enough. It seemeth some great ones then had their hands in drawing in that law to entangle or bridle one another, and that some of them were taken in the same net, as good men then thought worthily. Surely my Lord Cromwell and this young lord were taken in those entanglements, and the knight himself, of whom is spoken, had hardly scaped it, as may appear by his defence, if he had not by the well delivering of the goodness of his cause broken through it. And this may well serve to admonish men to be well aware how far they admit of laws that shall touch life upon construction of words; or, at the least, admitting them, how far they leave to lawyers to interpret of them, and especially that thereby they give not excuse to juries to condemn the innocent when sway of time should thrust matters upon them. Thus was she put upon her trial by men of great honour; it had been good also if some of them had not been to be suspected of too much power and no less malice. The evidence were heard indeed, but close enough, as enclosed in strong walls. Yet, to show the truth cannot by any force be altogether kept in hold, some belike of those honourable personages there, more perhaps for countenance of others' evil than for means by their own authority to do good (which also peradventure would not have been without their own certain perils), did not yet forbear to deliver out voices that caused every where to be muttered abroad, that that spotless queen in her defence had cleared herself with a most wise and noble speech. Notwithstanding such a trial, such a judgment found her guilty, and gave sentence of death upon her at home, whom others abroad, living the feel her loss, found guiltless.

The woful sentence was given; burning or heading at the king's pleasure, leaving open some small place to pity for the kind of death; which the king's conscience (no doubt) moved him to take in appointing the more honourable death. Within those walls this execution was to be done. What needed that? The love known indeed to her by the people was not to be feared of the king, her love being such to him as to her last breath she stood to acquit and defend him by her words at her death, carrying a very true image of her former love and life. 'Christian people!' said she, 'I am come to die, and according to law, and by law I am judged to death, and therefore I will speak nothing against it. I am come hither to accuse no man, nor to speak any thing of that whereof I am accused and condemned to die. But I pray God save the king, and send him long to reign over you, for a gentler and more merciful prince was there never, and to me he was ever a good, a gentle, and sovereign lord. If any person will meddle of my cause, I require him to judge the best. And thus I take my leave of the world and of you, and I heartily desire you all to pray for me. O Lord, have mercy on me! To God I commend my soul.' And so she kneeling down said, 'To Christ I commend my soul. Jesu, receive my soul!' The bloody blow came down from his trembling hand that gave it, when those about her could not but seem to themselves to have received it upon their own necks, she not so much as shrieking at it. God provided for her corpse sacred burial, even in place as it were consecrate to innocents.

# 2

# Early Life, *c*. 1501–1526

*In common with most people of her time, little information survives relating to Anne's childhood. Her birth went unrecorded and no evidence as to her education exists. It is possible to catch glimpses of Anne as she moved into early adulthood through the sources. The period up to 1526 was crowded with incident for Anne. She spent nearly nine years away from England, before returning home. Within months of returning to England, after being recalled to make an arranged marriage, she apparently fell in love for the first time.*

## Letters Relating to Anne's Time in Brussels

*Anne Boleyn's childhood effectively ended in 1513 when she was sent to serve Margaret of Austria, the regent of the Netherlands, in Brussels. Little record survives of her time in Brussels, but the two letters below demonstrate that she rapidly found favour with Margaret. Sir Thomas Boleyn undoubtedly hoped that service with Margaret, who had been raised in France, would improve Anne's French. Anne's letter to her father, her earliest surviving correspondence, was written in schoolgirl French and refers to her studies in the language. It is demonstrative of the interest that Thomas Boleyn took in Anne's education that she felt confident enough to address him in her first French letter of her own composition.*

*Extract from a letter by Margaret of Austria to Sir Thomas Boleyn[1]*
I have received your letter by the Esquire Bouton, who presented to me your daughter, who was very welcome to me, and I hope to treat her in such a fashion that you will have reason to be content with it; at least be sure that until your return there need be no other intermediary between you and me than she; and I find her of such good address and so pleasing in her youthful age that I am more beholden to you for having sent her to me than you are to me.

*Anne Boleyn to her father, Sir Thomas Boleyn[2]*
Sir, I understand by your letter that you desire that I shall be a worthy woman when I come to the Court and you inform me that the Queen will take the trouble to converse with me, which rejoices me much to think of talking with a person so wise and worthy.[3] This will make me have greater

desire to continue to speak French well and also spell, especially because you have so enjoined it on me, and with my own hand I inform you that I will observe it the best I can. Sir, I beg you to excuse me if my letter is badly written, for I assure you that the orthography is from my own understanding alone, while the others were only written by my hand, and Semmonet tells me the letter but waits so that I may do it myself, for fear that it shall not be known unless I acquaint you, and I pray you that the light of [?] may not be allowed to drive away the will which you say you have to help me, for it seems to me that you are sure [??] you can, if you please, make me a declaration of your word, and concerning me be certain that there shall be neither [??] nor ingratitude which might check or efface me affection, which is determined to [?] as much unless it shall please you to order me, and I promise you that my love is based on such great strength that it will never grow less, and I will make an end to my [?] after having commended myself right humbly to your good grace. Written at [? Veure] by

Your very humble and very obedient daughter,

Anna de Boullan

## Documents Relating to Anne's Proposed Marriage to James Butler

*Anne left Brussels in 1514 to serve Henry VIII's sister, Mary Tudor, in France. She transferred to the household of Queen Claude following Mary Tudor's return to England. Anne was recalled home from France in order to marry James Butler, the son of her father's cousin Piers Butler, who claimed to be Earl of Ormond. Anne's father, Sir Thomas Boleyn, as the grandson of the previous Earl of Ormond, claimed the title as his heir general. The matter was far from certain, however, and Piers Butler, although considerably more distantly related to the previous earl, was his heir male. In order to bring the dispute to an end, a match was suggested between Pier Butler's eldest son and Sir Thomas Boleyn's daughter by the Earl of Surrey (later the third Duke of Norfolk, Anne's uncle).*

*In their letters, both Surrey and Henry acknowledge Piers Butler as Earl of Ormond, something that would have been a blow to Thomas Boleyn's hopes. They also relied on Butler's support in Ireland, with Surrey writing to Wolsey, on 3 November 1520:*

> Beseeching your Grace to cause thankfull letters to bee sent from the Kinges Grace to the Erle of Ormond, aswele for his deligence shewed unto me, at all tymes, as also for that he shewith hym self ever, with his good advise and strenght, to bring the Kinges entended purpose to good effect. Undoubtidly he is not oonly a wyseman, and hath a true English hert, but also he is the man of moost experience of the feautes of warre in this cuntrey, of whome I have, at all tymes, the best counsaill of any of this land.[4]

*The fact that the marriage negotiations eventually came to nothing suggests that the parties were not enthusiastic. It is possible that Thomas Boleyn was unwilling to relinquish his hopes of an earldom: he eventually received the title due to Anne's relationship with Henry, forcing Piers Butler to be content with the Earldom of Ossory.*

*The letters below demonstrate Surrey's hopes that a marriage could be agreed and Henry VIII's support for the match.*

*The Lord Lieutenant and Council of Ireland to Cardinal Wolsey*[5]

Pleas it Your Grace to understand, that the second day of this moneth we came to this towne; and yesterday came hether thErl of Desmond, and to morow we wol goo to Waterford, and thErlis of Desmond and Ormond with us. We have also sent for their kynesmen and adherentes of both parties, and we shall doo oure best to bryng theyme to peas, concord, and amytie, which if it may bee doon, and from hensfurth contynued, shall greatly further the Kingis entendid purpose. We fynde the said Erl of Desmond right confourmable by his wordes, and shewith hym to bee content in all thingis to follow the Kinges pleaser, and to bee ordred after our advyse and counsaill. And asfor thErll of Ormond, we can not desire to have hym more confourmable than he is. And by our next letters we shall certify Your Grace whate conclusyon we shall take with theyme. Beseching Your Grace to helpe that the varyaunce betwixt Waterford and Rosse may bee broght to some good ende, and that they may have good and spedy expidicion; for the which both the parties have desirid us to write unto Your Grace.

And where, at our beeing with Your Grace, divers of us moeved you to cause a maryage to bee solempnysed betwene thErll of Ormondes son, beeing with Your Grace, and Sir Thomas Boleyns doughter; we thynk, yf Your Grace causid that to bee doon, and also a fynall ende to bee made betwene theyme, for the tytle of landes depending in varyaunce, it shuld cause the said Erll to bee the better wylled to see this land brought to good order; not withstanding, undoubtidly, we see not but he is as wele mynded thereunto, and as redy to geve his good advyse and counsaill in all causes for the furtherance of the same, as we can wyssh hym to bee. Other newes we have noon to certyfy Your Grace of, at this tyme, and as they shalbe occurrant, soo Your Grace shalbe advertised. Thus the Blissed Trynytie have Your Grace in his tender tuycion. Writin at Clonemel, the 6th day of October.

T. SURREY. [and others]

*Extract from Henry VIII's Response to the Earl of Surrey*[6]

*The bulk of this long letter deals with the points raised in the previous letter, and from Surrey's earlier correspondence. It then continues:*

And like as ye desire Us to indevour our selff, that a mariage may be had and made betwixt thErle of Ormondes sonne, and the doughter of Sir Thomas Bolain, Knight, Countroller of our Householde; so we woll ye bee meane to the said Erie for his agreable consent and mynde therunto, and to advertise Us, by your next letters, of what towardenesse ye shall fynde the said Erie in that bihalf. Signifying unto you, that, in the meane tyme. We shall advaunce the said matier with our Comptroller, and certifie you, how We shall finde hym inclined therunto accourdingly.

## Extract from Hall's Chronicle on Anne's Appearance at a Court Masque[7]

*The chronicler Edward Hall, a contemporary of Anne's, was born towards the end of the fifteenth century.[8] He was a gentleman and well educated, studying at Cambridge University. Hall entered public life in 1532 as a Common Sergeant of the City of London and his career steadily progressed. He later became a member of parliament for Bridgnorth. His chronicle, which charts a history of the kings of England, was a major undertaking. Hall was a firm supporter of Henry VIII, which is reflected in his chronicle. He also viewed Henry's reformation favourably and has been described as a 'Protestant'. His chronicle was one of the books burned in the Counter-Reformation of Queen Mary. There is, of course, inevitable bias in his work. However, Hall, who died in the same year as Henry, does provide some interesting, and near-contemporary, accounts of court life and the events of Henry VIII's reign. Much of Hall's information would have been obtained from the first-hand accounts of those he knew. His work is one of the most comprehensive accounts of Henry's reign, although there is an element of 'hero-worship' in his account of Henry VIII. This does not detract greatly from its usefulness as a source in relation to Anne Boleyn.*

*The extract below describes Anne's first appearance in an English court masque. The details of the masque are well-known but it is interesting to read a contemporary account. Hall, who had a love of pageantry, may not have been present at the masque, but is likely to have mixed with those who were. Certainly, the detail given by him is precise and likely to be, largely, accurate. Anne's casting as one of the eight virtues demonstrates the attention that she had attracted only, at most, weeks after her arrival at court. The principal virtue, 'Beauty', was taken by the King's sister, Mary Tudor, Queen Dowager of France. Anne's sister and Henry's then mistress, Mary Boleyn, played 'Kindness'. Anne's future sister-in-law, Jane Parker (later Lady Rochford) was also one of the virtues. Anne was 'Perseverance'. The accounts for the masque survive and include the entry: 'For the 8 ladies' garments; 8 cauls of Venice gold for the ladies' heads, 8 s. each. These things remain with the French Queen, the Countess of Devonshire, Mistress Anne Boleyn, Mistress Karre [i.e. Carey – Mary Boleyn], Mistress Parker, Mistress Browne, Mistress Danet and Mistress [name left blank in original manuscript].'[9]*

In the moneth of Marche, as you haue hard before, came certain noble men from the Emperor to the king, which the more to solace theim enterprised a Iustes *[jousts]*, he himself was chief on the one side, his courser was barded in cloth of siluer, of Denmarke embrodered with. L. L. L. of Golde, and vnder the letters a harte of a manne wounded, and greate rolles of golde with blacke letters, in whiche was written, *mon nauera*, put together it is, *ell mon ceur a nauera, she hath wounded my harte*, and thesame suite was his base.

Then folowed sir Nicolas Carewe, his base and barde was white Damaske, on whiche was embraudered with Clothe of gold: a prison and a man lokyng out at a grate, and ouer the prison came from the prisoner a rolle, in whiche was written in Frenche, in prison I am at libertie, and at libertie I am in prison, and all his apparell was garded with shakelles of siluer.

Then folowed therle of Deuonshire, the lord Roos in one suite, their apparell was white veluet, embraudered with cloth of golde, wrought in deuice an harte, trauersed crosse wise with a chayne, the which deuided the bard in foure quarters, in twoo quarters was a hand of golde holding a spere of the worlde, on the other twoo quarters was twoo handes holding two plumes of fethers, and on the borders were written my harte in betwene ioye and pein.

Then folowed Anthony Kyngston, and Anthony Kneuet, their apparell was a hart bounde in a blewe lace, embroudered on Crimosyn sattin: and written about with letters of gold, my harte is bounde.

Nicholas Darrel had a bard and base of black sattin, embraudered full of hartes, turned or broken of gold, and written in letters of siluer, my harte is broken.

Last of that bend was Anthony Broune, whiche had a bard of siluer full of speeres of the world broken, set on hartes broken al of gold written aboute in letters of blacke *sance remedy*, without remedy.

Then entered the Duke of Suffolke and his bend, all in bardes and bases of russet veluer and cloth of siluer, embraudered with braunches of paunces of golde, at these Iustes were many speres broken, whiche the straungiers highly commended.

The third day of Marche, the Cardinall made to the kyng and the Ambassadors, a great and a costly banket, and after that, a plaie and a Maske, their garmentes were russet sattin and yelowe, all the one side was yelowe, face and legge, and all the other side was russet.

On shroue tewesdaie at night, thesaid Cardinall to the kyng and ambassadors made another supper, and after supper thei came into a great chamber hanged with Arras, and there was a clothe of estate, and many braunches, and on euery braunche. xxxii. torchettes of waxe, and in the nether ende of thesame chamber was a castle, in which was a principall Tower, in which was a Cresset burning: and two other lesse Towers stode on euery side, warded and embattailed, and on euery Tower was a banner, one banner was of iii. rent hartes, the other was a ladies hand gripyng a mans harte, the third banner was a ladies hand turnyng a mannes hart: this castle was kept with ladies of straunge names, the first *Beautie*, the second *Honor*, the third *Perseueraunce*, the fourther *Kyndnes*, the fifth *Constance*, the sixte *Bountie*, the seuenthe *Mercie*, and the eight *Pitie*: these eight ladies had Millian gounes of white sattin, euery Lady had her name embraudered with golde, on their heddes calles, and Millein bonettes of gold, with Iwelles *[jewels]*. Vnder nethe the basse fortresse of the castle were other eight ladies, whose names were, *Dangier, Disdain, Gelousie, Vnkyndenes, Scorne, Malebouche, Straungenes*, these ladies were tired like to women of Inde. Then entered eight Lordes in clothe of golde cappes and all, and great mantell clokes of blewe sattin, these lordes were named. *Amorus, Noblenes, Youth, Attendaunce, Loyaltie, Pleasure, Gentlenes*, and *Libertie*, the kyng was chief of this compaignie, this compaignie was led by one all in crimosin sattin with burnyng flames of gold, called *Ardent Desire*, whiche so moued the Ladies to geue ouer the Castle, but *Scorne* and *Disdain* saied they would holde the place, then *Desire* saied the ladies should be wonne and came and encoraged the knightes, then the lordes ranne to the castle, (at whiche tyme without was shot a greate peale of gunnes) and the ladies defended the castle with Rose water and Comfittes, and the lordes threwe in Dates and Orenges, and other fruites made for pleasure, but at the last the place was wonne, but Lady *Scorne* and her compaignie stubbernely defended them with boows and balles, till they were driuen out of the place and fled. Then the lordes toke the ladies of honor as prisoners by the handes, and brought them doune, and daunced together verie pleasauntly, which much pleased the straungers, and when thei had daunced their fill, then all these disuisered[10] themselfes and wer knowen: and then was there a costly banket, and when all was done, the straungiers tooke their leaue of the king and the Cardinall, and so departed into Flaunders, geuyng to the kyng muche commendacyon.

## Extract from Cavendish's *Life of Wolsey* on the Love Between Anne Boleyn and Henry Percy[11]

*Cavendish's* Life of Wolsey *provides the first detailed evidence for Anne's early life in its discussion of her love affair with Henry Percy.*

*Until 1814, there was some debate over who the author of the* Life of Wolsey *was, with William Cavendish, the brother of the actual author, George Cavendish, usually described as the author.[12] George Cavendish, a contemporary of Anne's, has frequently been overshadowed by his more well-known brother, who famously married Bess of Hardwick.[13] George Cavendish served Cardinal Wolsey as a gentleman usher, loyally remaining with him until his death. Cavendish was then offered a similar position in the King's household but instead choose to go into retirement in the country, eventually writing his life of his old master in his old age, twenty-five years after he left court.*

*Cavendish's account of Wolsey is useful due to his proximity to the Cardinal. He knew many of the people that he describes and was present at most of the major events in the last years of the Cardinal's life. However, as has been pointed out by the editor of the most recent edition of his work, while Cavendish was present in Wolsey's household and witnessed much of what occurred, he was not privy to the Cardinal's innermost thoughts and often misunderstood, or failed to notice, Wolsey's political manouevrings. It is considered that, factually, the* Life *is, for the most part, accurate, but that Cavendish often misunderstood what was happening, presenting what he saw at 'face-value'.*

*In his account below, of the love affair between Anne and Henry Percy, Cavendish would have been an observer to much that happened and he can be considered, to a large extent, reliable. However, it is unlikely that he is correct in saying that Henry VIII ordered Wolsey to break the marriage due to his own interest in Anne and it is more likely that both the King and*

*Cardinal hoped that the Ormond marriage would materialise. Cavendish*
*may also have been inclined to think the worst of Anne, both due to Wolsey's*
*own dislike of her (set out in the extract on the fall of Wolsey printed below)*
*and his own belief in her guilt in the crimes for which she died (see his*
Metrical Visions, *also printed below).*

Thus passed the cardinal his life and time, from day to day, and year to
year, in such great wealth, joy, and triumph, and glory, having always on
his side the king's especial favour; until Fortune, of whose favour no man
is longer assured than she is disposed, began to wax something wroth with
his prosperous estate, [and] thought she would devise a mean to abate
his high port; wherefore she procured Venus, the insatiate goddess, to be
her instrument. To work her purpose, she brought the king in love with a
gentlewoman, that, after she perceived and felt the king's goodwill towards
her, and how diligent he was both to please her, and to grant all her requests,
she wrought the cardinal much displeasure; as hereafter shall be more at
large declared. This gentlewoman, the daughter of Sir Thomas Boleyn, being
at that time but only a bachelor knight, the which after, for the love of
his daughter, was promoted to higher dignities. He bare at divers several
times for the most part all the rooms of estimation in the king's house;
as Comptroller, Treasurer, Vice Chamberlain, and Lord Chamberlain. Then
was he made Viscount Rochford; and at the last created Earl of Wiltshire,
and Knight of the noble Order of the Garter; and, for his more increase
of gain and honour, he was made Lord Privy Seal, and most chiefest of
the king's privy council. Continuing therein until his son and daughter did
incur the king's indignation and displeasure. The king fantasied so much
his daughter Anne, that almost all things began to grow out of frame and
good order.

To tell you how the king's love began to take place, and what followed
thereof, I will even as much as in me lieth, declare [unto] you. This
gentlewoman, Mistress Anne Boleyn, being very young was sent into
the realm of France, and there made one of the French queen's women,
continuing there until the French queen died.[14] And then was she sent for
home again; and being again with her father, he made such means that she
was admitted to be one of Queen Katharine's maids, among whom, for her
excellent gesture and behaviour, [she] did excel all other; in so much, as the
king began to kindle the brand of amours; which was not known to any
person, ne scantly to her own person.

In so much [as] my Lord Percy, the son and heir of the Earl of
Northumberland, then attended upon the Lord Cardinal, and was also his
servitor; and when it chanced the Lord Cardinal at any time to repair to
the court, the Lord Percy would then resort for his pastime unto the queen's
chamber, and there would fall in dalliance among the queen's maidens, being
at the last more conversant with Mistress Anne Boleyn than with any other;
so that there grew such a secret love between them that, at length, they
were insured together, intending to marry. The which thing came to the
king's knowledge, who was then much offended. Wherefore he could hide no

longer his secret affection, but revealed his secret intendment unto my Lord Cardinal in that behalf; and consulted with him to infringe the precontract between them: insomuch, that after my Lord Cardinal was departed from the court, and returned home to his place at Westminster, not forgetting the king's request and counsel, being in his gallery, called there before him the said Lord Percy unto his presence, and before us his servants of his chamber, saying thus unto him. 'I marvel not a little,' quoth he, 'of thy peevish folly, that thou wouldest tangle and ensure thyself with a foolish girl yonder in the court, I mean Anne Boleyn. Dost thou not consider the estate that God hath called thee unto in this world? For after the death of thy noble father, thou art most like to inherit and possess one of the most worthiest earldoms of this realm. Therefore it had been most meet, and convenient for thee, to have sued for the consent of thy father in that behalf, and to have also made the king's highness privy thereto; requiring therein his princely favour, submitting all thy whole proceeding in all such matters unto his highness, who would not only accept thankfully your submission, but would, I assure thee, provide so for your purpose therein, that he would advance you much more nobly, and have matched you according to your estate and honour, whereby ye might have grown so by your wisdom and honourable behaviour into the king's high estimation, that it should have been much to your increase of honour. But now behold what ye have done through your wilfulness. Ye have not only offended your natural father, but also your most gracious sovereign lord, and matched yourself with one, such as neither the king, ne yet your father will be agreeable with the matter. And hereof I put you out of doubt, that I will send for your father, and at his coming, he shall either break this unadvised contract, or else disinherit thee for ever. The king's majesty himself will complain to thy father on thee, and require no less at his hand than I have said; whose highness intended to have preferred [Anne Boleyn] unto another person, with whom the king hath travelled already, and being almost at a point with the same person, although she knoweth it not, yet hath the king, most like a politic and prudent prince, conveyed the matter in such sort, that she, upon the king's motion, will be (I doubt not) right glad and agreeable to the same.' 'Sir,' (quoth the Lord Percy, all weeping), 'I knew nothing of the king's pleasure therein, for whose displeasure I am very sorry. I considered that I was of good years, and thought myself sufficient to provide me of a convenient wife, whereas my fancy served me best, not doubting but that my lord my father would have been right well persuaded. And though she be a simple maid, and having but a knight to her father, yet is she descended of right noble parentage. As by her mother she is nigh of the Norfolk blood: and of her father's side lineally descended of the Earl of Ormond, he being one of the earl's heirs general. Why should I then, sir, be any thing scrupulous to match with her, whose estate of descent is equivalent with mine when I shall be in most dignity? Therefore I most humbly require your grace of your especial favour herein; and also to entreat the king's most royal majesty most lowly on my behalf for his princely benevolence in this matter, the which I cannot deny or forsake.' 'Lo, sirs,' quoth the cardinal, 'ye may see what conformity and wisdom is in this wilful boy's head. I thought that when thou heardest me declare the king's intended pleasure and travail herein, thou wouldest have relented and wholly submitted thyself, and all thy wilful and unadvised fact, to the king's royal will and prudent pleasure, to be fully disposed and ordered by his grace's disposition, as his highness should seem good.' 'Sir, so I would,' quoth the Lord Percy, 'but in this matter I have gone so far, before many so worthy witnesses, that I know not how to avoid my self nor to discharge my conscience.'[15] 'Why, thinkest thou,' quoth the cardinal, 'that the king and I know not what we have to do in as weighty a matter as this?' 'Yes,' (quoth he) 'I warrant thee. Howbeit I can see in thee no submission to the purpose.' 'Forsooth, my Lord,' quoth the Lord Percy, 'if it please your grace, I will submit myself wholly unto the king's majesty and [your] grace in this matter, my conscience being discharged of the weighty burthen of my precontract.' 'Well then,' quoth the cardinal, 'I will send for your father out of the north parts, and he and we shall take such order for the avoiding of this thy hasty folly as shall be by the king thought most expedient. And in the mean season I charge thee, and in the king's name command thee, that thou presume not once to resort into her company, as thou intendest to avoid the king's high indignation.' And this said he rose up and went into his chamber.

Then was the Earl of Northumberland sent for in all haste, in the king's name, who upon knowledge of the king's pleasure made quick speed to the court. And at his first coming out of the north he made his first repair unto my Lord Cardinal, at whose mouth he was advertised of the cause of his hasty sending for; being in my Lord Cardinal's gallery with him in secret communication a long while. And after their long talk my Lord Cardinal called for a cup of wine, and drinking together they brake up, and so departed the earl, upon whom we were commanded to wait to convey him to his servants. And in his going away, when he came to the gallery's end, he sat him down upon a form that stood there for the waiters some time to take their ease. And being there set called his son the Lord Percy unto him, and said in our presence thus in effect. 'Son,' quoth he, 'thou hast always been a proud, presumptuous, disdainful, and a very unthrift waster, and even so hast thou now declared thyself. Therefore what joy, what comfort, what pleasure or solace should I conceive in thee, that thus without discretion and advisement hast misused thyself, having no manner of regard to me thy natural father, ne in especial unto thy sovereign lord, to whom all honest and loyal subjects bear faithful and humble obedience; ne yet to the wealth of thine own estate, but hast so unadvisedly ensured thyself to her, for whom thou hast purchased thee the king's displeasure, intolerable for any subject to sustain! But that his grace of his mere wisdom doth consider the lightness of thy head, and wilful qualities of thy person, his displeasure and indignation were sufficient to cast me and all my posterity into utter subversion and dissolution: but he being my especial and singular good lord and favourable prince, and my Lord Cardinal my good lord hath and doth clearly excuse me in thy lewd fact, and doth rather lament thy lightness than malign the same; and hath devised an order to be taken for thee; to whom both thou and I be more bound than we be able well to consider. I pray to God that this may be to thee a sufficient monition and warning to use thyself more wittier hereafter; for thus I assure thee, if thou dost not amend thy prodigality, thou wilt be the last earl of our house. For of thy natural inclination thou art disposed to be wasteful prodigal, and to consume all that thy progenitors have with great travail gathered together and kept with honour. But having the king's majesty my singular good and gracious lord, I intend (God willing) so to dispose my succession, that ye shall consume thereof but a little. For I do not purpose, I assure thee, to make thee mine heir; for, praises be to God, I have more choice of boys who, I trust, will prove themselves much better, and use them more like unto nobility, among whom I will choose and take the best and most likeliest to succeed me. Now, masters and good gentlemen,' (quoth he unto us), 'it may be your chances hereafter, when I am dead, to see the proof of these things that I have spoken to my son prove as true as I have spoken them. Yet in the mean season I desire you all to be his friends, and to tell him his fault when he doth amiss, wherein ye shall show yourselves to be much his friends.' And with that he took his leave of us. And said to his son thus: 'Go your ways, and attend upon my lord's grace your master, and see that you do your duty.' And so departed, and went his way down through the hall into his barge.

Then after long debating and consultation upon the Lord Percy's assurance, it was devised that the same should be infringed and dissolved, and that the Lord Percy should marry with one of the Earl of Shrewsbury's daughters; (as he did after); by means whereof the former contract was clearly undone. Wherewith Mistress Anne Boleyn was greatly offended, saying, that if it lay ever in her power, she would work the cardinal as much displeasure; as she did in deed after. And yet was he nothing to blame, for he practised nothing in that matter, but it was the king's only device. And even as my Lord Percy was commanded to avoid her company, even so was she commanded to avoid the court, and sent home again to her father for a season; whereat she smoked *[i.e. fumed]*: for all this while she knew nothing of the king's intended purpose.

### The Earl of Northumberland to Cromwell, Denying Any Contract or Promise of Marriage Between Anne Boleyn and Himself[16]

*This letter was written at the time of Anne's fall when her possible pre-contract to Henry Percy was closely examined as a means of invalidating her marriage to the King. In his letter, Percy (by then Earl of Northumberland) was adamant that he and Anne had not contracted a valid precontract. This appears to be at odds with what Percy earlier told Cardinal Wolsey when his relationship with Anne was discovered. It may be that Percy was trying to ensure his own safety, perhaps aware that another early suitor of Anne's, Sir Thomas Wyatt, had been committed to the Tower. Alternatively, he may have felt that the matter had already been satisfactorily investigated. It has been suggested that the delay between the breaking of his relationship with Anne and his marriage was due to the need to disentangle Percy from any legal difficulties resulting in his 'betrothal' to Anne.[17] In 1532 Percy's estranged wife, Mary Talbot, raised the possibility of a precontract with Anne in the hope that it would secure her divorce. Percy may have felt able to swear that he and Anne had not made a valid precontract following the investigation into his relationship with Anne in 1532 which apparently concluded that both he and Anne were free to marry other parties.*

Mr Secretary, This shall be to signifie unto you that I perceive by Sir Raynold Carnaby, that there is supposed a precontract between the queen and me; wherupon I was not only heretofore examined upon my oath before the Archbishopps of Canterbury and York, but also received the blessed sacrament upon the same before the Duke of Norfolk, and other the king's highnes' council learned in the spiritual law; assuring you Mr Secretary, by the said oath, and blessed body which affore I received, and hereafter intend to receive, that the same may be to my damnation, if ever there were any contracte or promise of marriage between her and me. At Newington Green, the xiijth day of Maye, in the 28th year of the reigne of our soveraigne lord King Henry the VIIIth. Your assured, Northumberland.

## Supposed Letter from Anne Boleyn to an Acquaintance, after 1524[18]

*The following letter is among the most curious documents printed here. Its mention of Anne's cousin, Henry Howard, as the Earl of Surrey must date it to after 1524 when he became entitled to the earldom after his father inherited the title of Duke of Norfolk. It can probably be dated to shortly after Anne's return to court after her rustication following the discovery of her affair with Henry Percy. The letter was first printed in 1769 as part of an article comparing the difference between current (i.e. late eighteenth-century) English manners and those of previous centuries. In order to demonstrate his point, the author printed a letter which a friend had passed to him, apparently assuring him that it was written by Anne Boleyn before she became queen. The writer himself was uncertain about the letter, confessing that 'there is something curious in the production'. However, he printed it as he received it, albeit after 'modernizing the style for the convenience of my readers'.*

*On printing the letter, the anonymous author of the article concluded that the manners of the sixteenth century were very different to those that were known in the eighteenth!*

*As the author agreed, the letter is indeed unusual. The style appears suspiciously eighteenth century rather than sixteenth, although this could, perhaps, be accounted for by the fact that its publisher has modernised the style. If it could be considered genuine, the letter would be of great interest in the study of Anne's early life – providing valuable details of her first month in London after her return to court, as well as details of her activities at home at Hever, including her diet. It would also not be beyond the realms of possibility to suggest that the 'Mary' whom Anne addresses could be her sister, Mary Boleyn, visiting Hever while Anne was at court, although, equally, Mary was, of course, a common name and there may well have been other ladies of that name to whom Anne was close.*

*There are, however, unfortunately too many errors in the letter for it to be concluded that it is genuine. The reference to the 'Lord of Leicester', for example, is telling. Until Anne's daughter created her favourite, Robert Dudley, Earl of Leicester, the title had been held by the Crown (when its holder, Henry, Earl of Derby, succeeded to the throne as Henry IV in 1399). Elizabeth Fitzgerald, 'the Fair Geraldine' referred to in the letter was also not born until 1527 and there is no evidence that she ever became Surrey's mistress, in spite of the poem addressed to her in her childhood.[19] Perhaps the forger confused Elizabeth Fitzgerald, who later became the third wife of Edward Clinton, Earl of Lincoln, with his first wife, the famously beautiful Elizabeth (or Bessie) Blount, mistress of Henry VIII? These, among other errors, strongly suggest that the letter is a forgery. It is included here for the sake of completeness but should not be considered in any way reliable.*

Dear Mary,

I have been in town almost a month, I can't say I have found any thing in London extremely agreeable, we rise so late in the morning, seldom before six o'clock, and sit up so late at night, being scarcely in bed before ten, that I am quite sick of it, and was it not for the abundance of fine things I am every day getting, I should be impatient for returning into the country. My mother, my indulgent mother, bought me yesterday, at a Merchant's in Cheapside, three new shirts that cost fourteen-pence an ell, and I am to have a pair of stuff shoes, for my Lord of Norfolk's ball, which will actually come in three shillings. The irregular life I have led since my coming to this place, has quite destroyed my appetite; you know I could manage almost a pound of bacon and a tankard of good ale for my breakfast, in the country; but here I find it difficult to get through half the quantity; though I must own, that I am generally eager enough for the dinner-hour, which is here unconscionably delayed til twelve in your polite families. I played at Hotcockles last night at the Lord of Leicester's; the Lord of Surrey was there, a very elegant young fellow, who sung us a song of his own composition on the Lord of Kildare's daughter; it was very much approved and my brother whispered me, that the fair Geraldine, so the Lord of Surrey stiles his mistress, is the finest woman of the age. – I should be glad to see her; for I hear she is as good as she is beautiful. Pray, my dear Mary, take care of the poultry, during my absence; poor things I always fed them myself: and if Margery has knitted me the crimson worsted mittings, I should be glad they were sent up the first opportunity. – Adieu, my dear Mary, I am just going to mass, and you shall speedily have the prayers, as you now have the kindest love of your own
ANNE BOLEYN

## Wyatt's Poems Referring to his Relationship with Anne

*Sir Thomas Wyatt, whose family seat was at Allington Castle in Kent, around twenty miles from Hever Castle, may have been known to Anne in childhood. Wyatt's father, Sir Henry Wyatt and Anne's father, Sir Thomas Boleyn, are known to have been associated with each other, for example, sharing the governorship of Norwich Castle from 1511.[20] The choice of 'Thomas' as Wyatt's Christian name may also suggest that Anne's father was his godfather. Wyatt was a year or two younger than Anne. He was well-educated and studied at Cambridge. In 1520 he married Elizabeth Brooke, the daughter of Lord Cobham. Although Elizabeth produced a son, Sir Thomas Wyatt the Younger, the marriage proved to be unhappy. Both parties committed adultery and had separated by the mid-1520s. Divorce in the early sixteenth century was a virtual impossibility for all but the most powerful. When Thomas Wyatt first became interested in Anne after she returned to court following the discovery of her relationship with Henry Percy, she knew that he could not offer her marriage.*

*Thomas Wyatt was one of the most dashing figures at Henry VIII's court and it is easy to see why Anne was attracted to him. One Wyatt family manuscript claims that he was known as a lion tamer at court following an incident at Allington in which a lion that he had raised from a cub suddenly attacked him as he returned home.[21] After the animal was distracted by Wyatt's greyhound, he was able to draw his sword, killing the lion.*

*Wyatt is also remembered as a poet, who left a considerable body of work behind at his death in 1542. Allusions to his relationship with Anne have long been sought in his work. The six set out below are commonly considered to describe Anne. In the first, Wyatt gives a riddle, to which the answer is 'Anna'. The second, Wyatt's most famous poem, portrays Anne as a deer, fleeing coquettishly before numerous pursuers (suitors), of which Wyatt himself is the least successful. In the poem it is finally made clear that Anne the deer belongs only to the King and that all other suitors must fall away. This poem is particularly interesting in the fact that it alludes to potential other suitors for Anne at around the time that she first attracted the King, further evidence of her prominence at the English court.*

*The third poem portrays Anne as 'Brunet', in reference to her dark hair and eyes. That it is about Anne is likely due to line 8 of the poem, which originally read 'Her that did set our country in a rore'. Wyatt perhaps changed the line to ensure that the poem was less recognisably about his relationship with her following her fall. The third, fourth and fifth poems speak of the end of Wyatt's obsession with Anne, as though he believed that he had woken up and come to his senses. The fourth poem also describes the visit made to France by the English court at the end of 1532, in order to give Anne an international prominence. This poem testifies to the fact that Wyatt had long since abandoned his interest in Anne. The fifth poem, which uses the refrain 'The Most Happy' is also likely to refer to Anne, who used those words as her motto. Once again, the poem suggests that Wyatt felt that he had moved on from his stormy and dangerous love for Anne, in favour of the calmer love of a new mistress.*

*Finally, the sixth poem is included due to the reference to 'the knot that should not slide'. Wyatt's grandson, George Wyatt, in his* Life of Queen Anne, *declared that Wyatt, on seeing Anne, admired her, 'so as finally his heart seemed to say, I could gladly yield to be tied for ever with the knot of her love, as somewhere in his verses hath been thought his meaning was to express'. George Wyatt obtained this phrase from one of his grandfather's poems, believing it to refer to Anne. The sixth poem is therefore included here, although, as with many of the other poems allegedly about Anne, the link is debatable.*[22] *Almost certainly, given the reference to the poet's ideal of golden hair, it does not, in fact, refer to Anne.*

I[23]

What word is that, that changeth not,
Though it be turn'd and made in twain?
It is mine Anna, God it wot,
The only causer of my pain;
My love that meedeth with disdain.
Yet is it loved, what will you more?
It is my salve, and eke my sore.

II[24]

Whoso list to hunt? I know where is an hind!
But as for me, alas! I may no more,
The vain travail hath wearied me so sore;
I am of them that furthest come behind.
Yet may I by no means my wearied mind,
Draw from the deer; but as she fleeth afore
Fainting I follow; I leave off therefore,
Since in a net I seek to hold the wind.
Who list her hunt, I put him out of doubt
As well as I, may spend his time in vain!
And graven with diamonds in letters plain,
There is written her fair neck round about;
'Noli me tangere; for Caesar's I am,
And wild for to hold, though I seem tame.'

III[25]

If waker[26] care; if sudden pale colour;
If many sighs with little speech to plain:
Now joy, now woe, if there my chere[27] disdain;
For hope of small, if much to fear therefore;
To haste or slack, my pace to less, or more,
Be sign of love, then do I love again.
If thou ask whom; sure, since I did refrain
Brunet, that set my wealth in such a roar,[28]
Th' unfeigned cheer of Phyllis hath the place
That Brunet had; she hath, and ever shall.
She from myself now hath me in her grace;
She hath in hand my wit, my will, and all.
My heart alone well worthy she doth stay,
Without whose help scant do I live a day.

IV[29]

Sometime I fled the fire, that me so brent,

By sea, by land, by water, and by wind;
And now the coals I follow that be quent,[30]
From Dover to Calais, with willing mind.
Lo! how desire is both forth sprung, and spent;
And he may see, that whilom was so blind,
And all his labour laughs he now to scorn,
Meshed in the briers, that erst was only torn.


*V*[31]

After great storms the calm returns,
And pleasanter it is thereby;
Fortune likewise that often turns,
Hath made me now the most happy.


The Heaven that pitied my distress,
My just desire, and my cry;
Hath made my langour to cease,
And me also the most happy.


Whereto dispaired ye, my friends?
My trust alway in her did lie
That knoweth what my thought intends;
Whereby I live the most happy.


Lo! what can take hope from that heart,
That is assured steadfastly;
Hope therefore ye that live in smart,
Whereby I am the most happy.


And I that have felt of your pain
Shall pray to God continually,
To make your hope, your health retain,
And me also the most happy.


*VI*[32]

A face that should content me wondrous well
Should not be fair but comely to behold,
With gladsome look all grief for to expel,
With sober cheer so would I that it should
Speak, without words, such words that none can tell.
The tress also should be of crisped gold.
With wit, and these, might chance I might be tied
And knit again the knot that should not slide.


## Nicholas Sander on Anne's Early Life and Supposed Love Affairs[33]
*The account below provides a highly prejudicial version of Anne's early life.*
*It has been included due to the paucity of sources regarding Anne before she*

became the subject of the King's affection and as a comparison to George Wyatt, who was inspired to write in Anne's defence following the publication of Sander's work.

Nicholas Sander's work, 'The Rise and Growth of the Anglican Schism', was published posthumously in 1585. He was born in 1527 and studied at Oxford University. The Sander family was devoutly Catholic and his mother went into exile to ensure that she could maintain her faith. Two of his sisters also became nuns.[34] Sander himself left England in 1561, due to the Protestant religious policies of Elizabeth I, remaining in exile for the rest of his life. He went to Rome where he became a priest.

In his account of the reformation, Sander set out to attack Elizabeth I, to whom he was deeply opposed. It is therefore unsurprising that he also attacked her mother, Anne Boleyn, whose reputation and the manner of her death made her an easy target.

In spite of the prejudice in Sander's work, it does have some limited merit in a study of Anne. For example, in relation to the story of Anne's birth, in which he asserted that Henry VIII was her father, it appears that he embellished an existing rumour rather than invented it. A letter from the courtier Sir George Throckmorton to Henry VIII survives from 1537, in which he claimed:

> And seeing that the king's conscience was troubled about having married his brother's wife, said to him, 'I feared if ye did marry Queen Anne your conscience would be more troubled at length, for it is thought ye have meddled both with the mother and the sister'. To this the king replied, 'never with the mother'. At this my lord Privy Seal [Thomas Cromwell] standing nearby said 'Nor never with the sister either, and therefore put that out of your mind.'[35]

Sander can therefore not be said to have been the inventor of the rumours surrounding Henry VIII and Anne's mother, Elizabeth Howard. However, he certainly embellished them.

With regard to his comments on Anne's appearance, it seems very unlikely that Anne, who was very attractive to men, could have had the number of defects that he supplied her with. However, the sympathetic George Wyatt did agree that Anne had the slightest beginning of a sixth nail on one of her hands, something that was embellished by Sander to a sixth finger.

Finally, Sander had also heard of Anne's relationship with Thomas Wyatt. While it is very unlikely that Wyatt ever informed the King that he had consummated his relationship with Anne, or that she was stained in her reputation, it does at least provide further corroboration for the fact that Anne and Wyatt's relationship was well known. His slanderous account of their relationship is echoed in the extract from the Chronicle of Henry VIII given in the final chapter of this work, in which the chronicler alleged that Anne not only attempted to consummate her relationship with Wyatt, but also kept a second lover in a chamber above her bedroom while she and Wyatt were together.

Sander's source is of most use as a demonstration of Anne's poor reputation in the reign of her daughter among English Catholic exiles and much of

*Catholic Europe. This can be contrasted with the almost saintly reputation she attained among Protestant writers anxious to please her daughter (such as John Foxe).*

### Chapter V

Anne Boleyn was the daughter of Sir Thomas Boleyn's wife; I say of his wife, because she could not have been the daughter of Sir Thomas, for she was born during his absence of two years in France on the king's affairs. Henry VIII sent him apparently on an honourable mission in order to conceal his own criminal conduct; but when Thomas Boleyn, on his return at the end of two years, saw that a child had been born in his house, he resolved, eager to punish the sin, to prosecute his wife before the delegates of the archbishop of Canterbury, and obtain a separation from her. His wife informs the king, who sends the marquis of Dorset with an order to Thomas Boleyn to refrain from prosecuting his wife, to forgive her, and be reconciled to her.

Sir Thomas Boleyn saw that he must not provoke the king's wrath, nevertheless he did not yield obedience to his orders before he learned from his wife that it was the king who had tempted her to sin, and that the child Anne was the daughter of no other than Henry VIII. His wife then entreated him on her knees to forgive her, promising better behaviour in the future. The marquis of Dorset and other personages, in their own and in the king's name, made the same request, and then Sir Thomas Boleyn became reconciled to his wife, and had Anne brought up as his own child.

But his wife had borne Sir Thomas another daughter before this one, named Mary. Upon her the king had cast his eyes when he used to visit her mother, and now, after the return of Sir Thomas, he had her brought to the court, and ruined her. The royal household consisted of men utterly abandoned – gamblers, adulterers, panders, swindlers, false swearers, blasphemers, extortioners, and even heretics; among these was one distinguished profligate, Sir Francis Bryan, of the blood and race of the Boleyn.[36] This man was once asked by the king to tell him what sort of a sin it was to ruin the mother and then the child. Bryan replied that it was a sin like that of eating a hen first and its chicken afterwards. The king burst forth into loud laughter, and said to Bryan, 'Well, you certainly are my vicar of hell.' The man had been long ago called the vicar of hell on account of his notorious impiety, henceforth he was called also the king's vicar of hell. The king, who had sinned before with the mother and the elder daughter, turned his thoughts now to the other daughter, Anne.

Anne Boleyn was rather tall of stature, with black hair, and an oval face of a sallow complexion, as if troubled with jaundice. She had a projecting tooth under the upper lip, and on her right hand six fingers. There was a large wen under her chin, and therefore to hide its ugliness she wore a high dress covering her throat. In this she was followed by the ladies of the court, who also wore high dresses, having before been in the habit of leaving their necks and the upper portion of their persons uncovered. She was handsome to look at, with a pretty mouth, amusing in her ways, playing well on the lute, and was a good dancer. She was the model and the mirror of those who were at court, for she was always well dressed, and every day made some change in the fashion of her garments. But as to the disposition of her mind, she was full of pride, ambition, envy, and impurity.

At fifteen she sinned first with her father's butler, and then with his chaplain, and forthwith was sent to France, and placed, at the expense of the king, under the care of a certain nobleman not far from Brie. Soon afterwards she appeared at the French court, where she was called the English mare, because of her shameless behaviour; and then the royal mule, when she became acquainted with the king of France.[37] She embraced the heresy of Luther to make her life and opinions consistent, but nevertheless did not cease to hear mass with the Catholics, for that was wrung from her by the custom of the king and the necessities of her own ambition.

On her return to England she was taken into the royal household, and there easily saw that the king was tired of his wife. She also detected the aims of Wolsey, how much the king was in love with herself, and how quickly he changed in his lawless affections. Not to speak of strangers to her family, she saw how her mother first, and then her sister, had been discarded by the king. What was she, then, to hope for in the end if she did not take care of herself at first? She made up her mind what to do. The more the king sought her, the more she avoided him, sanctimoniously saying that nobody but her husband should find her alone; nevertheless she did not think there was any want of modesty in talking, playing, and even in dancing with the king. In this way she so fed the fires of the king's passion that he became more and more determined to put away Catherine his wife, and to put a woman of such admirable modesty in her place. The news was carried over into France, and there it became a common report that the king of England was going to marry the mule of the king of France.

### Chapter VI

Thomas Boleyn the reputed father of Anne, was at that time in France, detained there on the king's business with Sir Antony Brown. But when he heard that the king was in love with his daughter, and wished to make her queen, he returned to England in great haste, and without the king's knowledge, thereby departing from the custom observed by ambassadors, to let the king know, while it was yet time, that which might prove hurtful to himself hereafter, if the king ever heard it from others. He applied himself to Henry Norris, one of the king's chamberlains, begging him to make his excuses to the king for his unexpected return, and to obtain for him a secret audience.

Sir Thomas then, having obtained the audience, told the king everything; how Anne was born when he was in France, and how he for that reason would have sent his wife away if he, the king, had not interfered, and if his wife had not confessed without hesitation that Anne Boleyn was the king's child. Henry replied, 'Hold your tongue, you fool, hundreds are compromised; and be her father who he may, she shall be my wife. Go back to your embassy, and do not say a word of this.' The king went away laughing, Sir Thomas being still on his knees.

To lessen men's surprise at the sudden arrival of Sir Thomas Boleyn, a report as spread abroad that he was the bearer of the picture of the duchess of Alencon to the king. But afterwards, when Sir Thomas saw that the king as bent on marrying Anne, both he and his wife took every pains and trouble to help Anne, that they might not, by some mistake or other, miss the good fortune they expected. On the other hand, throughout England, every man of sense, modesty, and honour – every man who feared God, hated exceedingly the divorce of the queen and the marriage of Anne. Above all others, the members of the king's council thought it their duty to warn him. And as they would not meddle with questions of the divine law, for they were laymen, they resolved to speak only of Anne's licentious life, or rather of her reputation, which was of the worst; and that it might not be thought that they were influenced by idle rumours, they agreed that the whole matter should be investigated.

Among the courtiers was Thomas Wyatt, who being afraid, if the king discovered afterwards how shameless Anne's life had been, that his own life might be imperilled, went before the council, for his conscience accused him grievously, as soon as he knew it to be assembled for the purpose, and confessed that he had sinned with Anne Boleyn, not imagining that the king would ever make her his wife.

The council, furnished with this information, said that it was its duty to watch over not only the life, but also the honour and good name of the king; adding that Anne Boleyn was stained in her reputation, and that, moreover, so publicly as to make it unseemly in his majesty to take her as his wife. It also told the king all that Wyatt had confessed.

Henry was silent for awhile, and then spoke. He had no doubt, he said, that the council, in saying these things, was influenced by its respect and affection for his person, but he certainly believed that these stories were the inventions of wicked men, and that he could affirm upon oath that Anne Boleyn was a woman of the purest life. Thomas Wyatt was very angry when he heard that the king would not believe him, and so he said to some of the members of the council that he would put it in the king's power to see with his own eyes the truth of his story, if he would but consent to test it, for Anne Boleyn was passionately in love with Wyatt.

Charles Brandon, the duke of Suffolk, repeated the words of Wyatt to the king, who answered that he had no wish to see anything of the king – Wyatt was a bold villain, not to be trusted. Why should I go on? The king told everything to Anne Boleyn, who shunned Wyatt; and that avoidance of him saved his life, for he too might have suffered death with the others when Anne's incest and adultery were detected ...

# 3

# The Love Letters of Henry VIII
# & Anne Boleyn

*The love letters of Henry VIII and Anne Boleyn provide an invaluable source for the early years of their relationship. In the early stages of their relationship, Anne was often away from court, perhaps in an attempt to avoid the King's ardent suit. She had seen her own sister become Henry's mistress, only to be discarded, with little reward, once he had tired of her.*

*The first letter given below is, with the exception of the later letter written by 'the Lady in the Tower', the only example of correspondence reportedly written by Anne to Henry. There is considerable doubt over the authenticity of both letters. The letter below, which was apparently written by Anne early in her court career, is a re-translation from a letter given by the Italian historian, Gregorio Leti (1630–1701) Leti came to England to write an Italian history of Elizabeth I which included a number of letters that he claimed to have seen (translated by him into Italian). Many of the letters used by Leti, including that written by Anne to Henry, no longer exist and it is therefore necessary to rely on his Italian translations. Mary-Anne Wood, who included the letter in volume 2 of her 'Letters of Royal and Illustrious Ladies' considered that the letter was genuine due to the fact that it does not portray Anne's character, in accepting the addresses of the married king, in a positive light. She reasoned that Leti, an admirer of Anne's daughter would not have deliberately created anything prejudicial to her mother. More recently, Warnicke has stated that the letter is a forgery and that, at best, it could only be viewed as a second-hand version of a document that may never have existed.*[1]

*The letter itself is not stylistically similar to Anne's other extant letters, but this could be explained by the fact that it has been translated into Italian and then back into English. No certainty can exist over this letter, although if it is indeed genuine, it provides the only direct evidence of Anne's feelings for Henry VIII. It must however be viewed with a great deal of suspicion.*

*The next seventeen letters printed are certainly genuine and were written by Henry during his courtship of Anne. They survive, oddly, in the Vatican library, something that has led to the suggestion that they were stolen from Anne by Cardinal Campeggio: this would account for the fact that his bags were searched when he reached Calais on his return to Rome. Henry evidently kept Anne's own correspondence more securely and none of Anne's replies survive.*

Letters 1, 2, 3, 4, 5, 8, 10, 11 and 12 were written in French and are printed below translated into English. The remaining letters were originally written in English. None of the letters are dated and their exact sequence is debatable. They are assembled below in probable order. The letters are a testament to Henry's devotion to Anne: in signing letter 5, Henry drew a heart around Anne's initials, stating 'H seeks AB no other R'. Letter 8 ended with the cryptic, and indecipherable letters 'O.N.R.I de R.O.M.V.E.Z.' This was evidently some code between the couple, but its meaning is now impossible to establish. Letter 11 was again signed with Anne's initials enclosed within the drawing of a heart and the words 'H seeks AB no other R'. 12 ended more simply: 'H AB R', with 'AB' once again within a heart. The letters are full of devotion to Anne, with Henry depicting himself as the hero of a courtly romance, seeking to win the love of an unattainable woman and portraying himself as Anne's servant. Of all the surviving examples of Henry's writing, the letters are the most remarkable testaments to his character and suggest that his love for Anne Boleyn, as also shown by his determination to win her, was the most passionate of his life.

The letters are interesting to read as a sequence. There are a number of areas which are particularly notable. In letter 1, Henry sent Anne a miniature portrait of himself, contained within a bracelet. He later followed the same course with Jane Seymour, presenting her with his picture in a locket which Anne reputedly ripped from her neck in jealousy.

Letter 2 speaks of Anne's decision to distance herself from Henry and her refusal to come to court, something which suggests that she did, indeed, attempt at first to deflect his interest. This accords with her determination not to become his mistress, something that was later followed by Jane Seymour, who refused to receive a letter and a gift from the King, instead insisting that she was waiting for a virtuous marriage.

Letters 3 refers to the deadly sweating sickness, which had begun to sweep through the court. In spite of Henry's attempts to reassure Anne that few women suffered from the disease, Anne did indeed fall victim, as can be seen from Henry's anxiety in letter 12 when he received word of her illness. Anne survived, but many did not, as Henry related in letter 13. Anne's own brother-in-law, William Carey, succumbed, a fact that is referred to in letter 9 in relation to Anne's 'sister's matter'. In order to assist the Carey family, Anne requested that William's sister, Eleanor, be appointed as Abbess of Wilton. This is referred to by Henry in letter 12. The appointment of the Abbess of Wilton was used in the power struggle between Anne and Wolsey, with Wolsey, who appointed his own candidate, emerging as the victor.

Letter 16, which appears to be among the latest of the letters, demonstrates that, although they stopped short of consummating their relationship, Henry and Anne were intimate with each other, with Henry writing 'wishing myself (especially of an evening) in my sweetheart's arms, whose pretty duckies[2] I trust shortly to kiss'. There is an element of frustration and longing in many of the letters, with letter 14 ending 'written with the hand of him which desireth as much to be yours as you do to have him'.

Letters 4 and 5 are the most useful of the entire sequence. In letter 4 Henry, perturbed by Anne's refusal to become his mistress, took the unusual step of offering her the position of his official mistress. This was a concept known in France and would have given Anne status at court, and recognition permanently as the King's love. Henry promised that he would take no other mistresses and would, instead, remain faithful to Anne. Although this, to Henry, may have appeared a tempting offer, Anne remained unconvinced. With her refusal, Henry took the astounding step of offering her marriage. This was something that Anne was prepared to countenance and, according to letter 5, she signalled her submission in the present of a jewel in the form of a damsel in a storm-tossed ship. Both Anne and Henry realised that they faced difficulties in securing their marriage and the letters show that Anne took a close interest in the course of Henry's divorce, with letter 6, for example, containing information about the slow journey towards England of the papal legate, Cardinal Campeggio.

Henry's letters to Anne Boleyn provide an all too brief insight into their love affair. As the divorce progressed, Anne gradually began to spend more time at court, taking on much of the role and trappings of queenship. With her residence at court, the correspondence naturally came to an end.

## Anne Boleyn to Henry VIII[3]

Sire,

It belongs only to the august mind of a great king, to whom Nature has given a heart full of generosity towards the sex, to repay by favours so extraordinary an artless and short conversation with a girl. Inexhaustable as is the treasury of your majesty's bounties, I pray you to consider that it cannot be sufficient to your generosity; for if you recompense so slight a conversation by gifts so great, what will you be able to do for those who are ready to consecrate their entire obedience to your desires? How great soever may be the bounties I have received, the joy that I feel in being loved by a king whom I adore, and to whom I would with pleasure make a sacrifice of my heart, if fortune had rendered it worthy of being offered to him, will ever be infinitely greater.

The warrant of maid of honour to the queen induces me to think that your majesty has some regard for me, since it gives me the means of seeing you oftener, and of assuring you by your own lips (which I shall do at the first opportunity) that I am,

Your majesty's very obliged and very obedient servant, without any reserve,

ANNE BOLEYN

## Henry VIII's Love Letters to Anne Boleyn[4]

*Letter 1*

My Mistress and friend, my heart and I surrender ourselves into your hands, beseeching you to hold us commended to your favour, and that by absence your affection to us may not be lessened: for it would be a great pity to increase our pain, of which absence produces enough and more than I could ever have thought could be felt, reminding us of a point in astronomy which is this: the longer the days are, the more distant is the sun, and nevertheless the hotter; so is it with our love, for by absence we are kept a distance from one another, and yet it retains its fervour, at least on my side; I hope the like on yours, assuring you that on my part the pain of absence is already too great for me; and when I think of the increase of that which I am forced to suffer, it would be almost intolerable, but for the firm hope I have of your unchangeable affection for me: and to remind you of this sometimes, and seeing that I cannot be personally present with you, I now send you the nearest thing I can to that, namely, my picture set in bracelets, with the whole of the device, which you already know, wishing myself in their place, if it should please you. This is from the hand of your loyal servant and friend, H.R.

*Letter 2*

To my mistress.

Because the time seems very long since I heard concerning your health and you, the great affection that I have for you has induced me to send you this bearer, to be better informed of your health and pleasure, and because, since my parting from you, I have been told that the opinion in which I left you is totally changed, and that you would not come to court either with your mother, if you could, or in any other manner; which report, if true, I cannot sufficiently marvel at, because I am sure that I have since never done anything to offend you, and it seems a very poor return for the great love which I bear you to keep me at a distance both from speech and the person of the woman that I esteem most in the world; and if you love me with as much affection as I hope you do, I am sure that the distance of our two persons would be a little irksome to you, though this does not belong so much to the mistress as to the servant.

Consider well, my mistress, that absence from you grieves me sorely, hoping that it is not your will that it should be so; but if I knew for certain that you voluntarily desired it, I could do no other than mourn my ill-fortune, and by degrees abate my great folly. And so, for lack of time, I make an end of this rude letter, beseeching you to give credence to this bearer in all that he will tell you from me.

Written by the hand of your entire servant,

H.R.

*Letter 3*

The uneasiness my doubts about your health gave me, disturbed and alarmed me exceedingly, and I should not have had any quiet without hearing certain tidings. But now, since you have as yet felt nothing, I hope, and am assured that it will spare you, as I hope it is doing with us. For when we were at Walton, two ushers, two valets de chambre, and your brother, fell ill, but are now quite well; and since we have returned to your house at Hunsdon, we have been perfectly well, and have not, at present, one sick person, God be praised; and I think, if you would retire from Surrey, as we did, you would escape all danger. There is another thing that may comfort you, which is, that, in truth, in this distemper few or no women have been taken ill, and, what is more, no person of our court, and few elsewhere, have died of it. For which reason I beg you, my entirely beloved, not to frighten yourself nor be too uneasy in our absence; for, wherever I am, I am yours, and yet we must sometimes submit to our misfortunes, for whoever will struggle against fate is generally but so much the farther from gaining his end: wherefore comfort yourself, and take courage, and avoid the pestilence as much as you can, for I hope shortly to make you sing, *le renvoye*. No more at present, for lack of time, but that I wish you in my arms, that I might a little dispel your unreasonable thoughts.

Written by the hand of him who is and always will be yours,
Im-H.R.-mutable.

## Letter 4

On turning over in my mind the contents of your last letters, I have put myself into great agony, not knowing how to interpret them, whether to my disadvantage, as you show in some places, or to my advantage, as I understand them in some others, beseeching you earnestly to let me know expressly your whole mind as to the love between us to. It is absolutely necessary for me to obtain this answer, having been for the whole year stricken with the dart of love, and not yet sure whether I shall fail or find a place in your heart and affection, which last point has prevented me for some time past from calling you my mistress; because, if you only love me with an ordinary love, that name is not suitable for you, because it denotes a singular love, which is far from common. But if you please to do the office of a true loyal mistress and friend, and to give up yourself body and heart to me, who will be, and have been, your most loyal servant, (if your rigour does not forbid me) I promise you that not only the name shall be given you, but also that I will take you for my only mistress, casting off all others besides you out of my thoughts and affections, and serve you only. I beseech you to give an entire answer to this my rude letter, that I may know on what and how far I may depend. And if it does not please you to answer me in writing, appoint some place where I may have it by word of mouth, and I will go thither with all my heart.

No more, for fear of tiring you,
Written by the hand of him who would willingly remain yours,
H.R.

## Letter 5

For a present so beautiful that nothing could be more so (considering the whole of it), I thank you most cordially, not only on account of the fine diamond and the ship in which the solitary damsel is tossed about, but chiefly for the fine interpretation and the too humble submission which your goodness hath used towards me in this case; for I think it would be very difficult for me to find an occasion to deserve it, if I were not assisted by your great humanity and favour, which I have always sought to seek, and will seek to preserve by all the kindness in my power, in which my hope has placed its unchangeable intention, which says, *Aut illic, aut nullibi.*[5]

The demonstrations of your affection are such, the beautiful mottoes of the letter so cordially expressed, that they oblige me for ever to honour, love, and serve you sincerely, beseeching you to continue in the same firm and constant purpose, assuring you that, on my part, I will surpass it rather than make it reciprocal, if loyalty of heart and a desire to please you can accomplish this.

I beg also, if at any time before this I have in any way offended you, that you would give me the same absolution that you ask, assuring you, that henceforward my heart shall be dedicated to you alone. I wish my person was so too. God can do it, if He pleases, to whom I pray every day for that end, hoping that at length my prayers will be heard. I wish the time may be short, but I shall think it long till we see one another.

Written by the hand of that secretary, who in heart, body, and will, is

Your loyal and most assured servant,

H.R.

## Letter 6

The reasonable request of your last letter, with the pleasure also that I take to know them true, causeth me to send you these news. The legate[6] whom we most desire arrived at Paris on Sunday or Monday last past, so that I trust by next Monday to hear of his arrival at Calais; and then I trust within awhile after to enjoy that which I have so long longed for, to God's pleasure, and both our comforts.

No more to you at this present, mine own darling, for lack of time, but that I would you were in mine arms, or I in yours, for I think it long since I kissed you.

Written after the killing of a hart, at eleven of the clock, minding, with God's grace, to-morrow, mighty timely, to kill an other, by the hand which, I trust, shortly shall be yours.

Henry R.

## Letter 7

Darling,

Though I have scant leisure, yet, remembering my promise, I thought it convenient to certify you briefly in what case our affairs stand. As touching a lodging[7] for you, we have got one by my lord cardinal's means, the like or hire of which could not have been found hereabouts for all causes, as this bearer shall more show you. As touching our other affairs, I assure you there can be no more done, nor more diligence used, nor all manner of dangers both foreseen and provided for, so that I trust it shall be hereafter to both our comforts, the specialities whereof were both too long to be written, and hardly by messenger to be declared. Wherefore, till you repair hither, I keep something in store, trusting it shall not be long to; for I have caused my lord, your father, to make his provisions with speed; and thus,

for lack of time, darling, I make an end of my letter, written with the hand
of him which I would were yours.
H.R.

### Letter 8

Though it is not fitting for a gentleman to take his lady in the place of a
servant, yet, complying with your desire, I willingly grant it you, if thereby
you can find yourself less uncomfortable in the place chosen by yourself
than you have been in that which I gave you, thanking you cordially that
you are pleased still to have some remembrance of me.
Henry R.

### Letter 9

The cause of my writing at this time, good sweetheart, is only to understand
of your good health and prosperity; whereof to know I would be as glad
as in mine own, praying God that (if it be his pleasure) to send us shortly
together, for I promise you I long for it. How be it, I trust it shall not be long
to; and seeing my darling is absent, I can do no less than to send her some
flesh, representing my name, which is hart flesh for Henry.

As touching your sister's matter, I have caused Walter Welche to write to
my lord my mind thereon, whereby I trust that Eve shall not have power
to deceive Adam; for surely, whatsoever is said, it cannot so stand with his
honour but that he must needs take her, his natural daughter, now in her
extreme necessity.

No more to you at this time, mine own darling, but that with a wish I
would we were together an evening.
With the hand of yours,
Henry R.

### Letter 10

Although, my mistress, it has not pleased you to remember the promise you
made me when I was last with you – that is, to hear good news from you,
and to have an answer to my last letter; yet it seems to me that it belongs
to a true servant (seeing that otherwise he can know nothing) to inquire
the health of his mistress, and to acquit myself of the duty of a true servant,
I send you this letter, beseeching you to apprise me of your welfare, which
I pray to God may continue as long as I desire mine own. And to cause
you yet oftener to remember me, I send you by the bearer of this a buck,
killed late last night by my own hand, hoping that when you eat of it you
may think of the hunter; and thus, for want of room, I must end my letter,
written by the hand of your servant, who very often wishes for you instead
of your brother.
H.R.

### Letter 11

The approach of the time for which I have so long waited rejoices me
so much, that it seems almost to have come already. However, the entire

accomplishment cannot be till two persons meet, which meeting is more desired by me than any thing in this world; for what joy can be greater upon earth than to have the company of her who is dearest to me, knowing likewise that she does the same on her part, the thought of which gives me the greatest pleasure.

Judge what an effect the presence of that person must have on me, whose absence has grieved my heart more than either words or writing can express, and which nothing can cure, but that begging you, my mistress, to tell your father from me, that I desire him to hasten the time appointed by two days, that he may be at court before the old term, or, at farthest, on the day prefixed; for otherwise I shall think he will not do the lover's turn, as he said he would, nor answer my expectation.

No more at present for lack of time, hoping shortly that by word of mouth I shall tell you the rest of the sufferings endured by me from your absence.

Written by the hand of the secretary, who wishes himself at the moment privately with you, and who is, and always will be,
Your loyal and most assured servant,
H. no other (A.B.) seeks. R.

*Letter 12*

There came to me suddenly in the night the most afflicting news that could have arrived. On three accounts I lament it. The first, to hear of the illness of my mistress, whom I esteem more than all the world, and whose health I desire as I do my own, so that I would gladly bear half your illness to make you well. The second, from the fear that I have of being still longer harassed by my enemy. Absence much longer, who has hitherto given me all possible uneasiness, and as far as I can judge is determined to spite me more. The third, because I pray God to rid me of this troublesome tormenter, because my physician, in whom I have most confidence, is absent at the very time when he might do me the greatest pleasure; for I should hope, by him and his means, to obtain one of my chief joys on earth – that is the care of my mistress – yet for want of him I send you my second, and hope that he will make you well. I shall then love him more than ever. I beseech you to be guided by his advice in your illness. In so doing I hope soon to see you again, which will be to me a greater comfort than all the precious jewels in the world.
Written by that secretary, who is, and for ever will be, your loyal and most assured servant,
H. no other (A.B.) seeks. R.

*Letter 13*

Since your last letters, mine own darling, Walter Welsh, Master Brown, John Care, Brion of Brearton, and John Cork, the apothecary, have fallen of the sweat in this house, and, thanked be God, all well recovered, so that as yet the plague is not fully ceased here, but I trust shortly it shall. By the mercy of God, the rest of as yet be well, and I trust shall pass it, either not to have it, or, at the least, as easily as the rest have done.

As touching the matter of Wilton, my lord cardinal hath had the nuns before him, and examined them, Mr. Bell being present; which hath certified me that, for a truth, she[8] has confessed herself (which we would have had abbess) to have had two children by two sundry priests; and further, since hath been kept by a servant of the Lord Broke that was, and that not long ago. Wherefore I would not, for all the gold in the world, clog your conscience nor mine to make her ruler of a house which is of so ungodly demeanour; nor, I trust, you would not that neither for brother nor sister, I should so disdain mine honour or conscience. And, as touching the prioress, or Dame Eleanor's eldest sister, though there is not any evident case proved against them, and that the prioress is so old that for many years she could not be as she was named; yet notwithstanding, to do you pleasure, I have done that neither of them shall have it, but that some other good and well-disposed woman shall have it, whereby the house shall be the better reformed (whereof I ensure you that it had much need), and God much the better served.

As touching your abode at Hever, do therein as best shall like you, for you know best what air doth best with you; but I would it were come thereto (if it pleased God), that neither of us need care for that, for I ensure you I think it long. Suche is fallen sick of the sweat, and therefore I send you this bearer, because I think you long to hear tidings from us, as we do likewise from you.

Written with the hand *de votre seul,*
H.R.

### Letter 14

Darling, these shall be only to advertise you that this bearer and his fellow be despatched with as many things to compass our matter, and to bring it to pass as our wits could imagine or devise; which brought to pass, as I trust, by their diligence, it shall be shortly, you and I shall have our desired end, which should be more to my heart's ease, and more quietness to my mind, than any other thing in this world; as, with God's grace, shortly I trust shall be proved, but not so soon as I would it were; yet I will ensure you there shall be no time lost that may be won, and further can not be done; for *ultra posse non est esse.* Keep him not too long with you, but desire him, for your sake, to make the more speed; for the sooner we shall have word from him, the sooner shall our matter come to pass. And thus upon trust of your short repair to London, I make an end to my letter, mine own sweet heart.

Written with the hand of him which desireth as much to be yours as you do to have him.

H.R.

### Letter 15

Darling, I heartily recommend me to you, ascertaining you that I am not a little perplexed with such things as your brother shall on my part declare unto you, to whom I pray you give full credence, for it were too long to write. In my last letters I writ to you that I trusted shortly to see you, which is better known at London than with any that is about me, whereof I not a little marvel; but lack of discreet handling must needs be the cause thereof. No more to you at this time, but that I trust shortly our meetings shall not depend upon other men's light handlings, but upon our own.

Written with the hand of him that longeth to be yours.

H.R.

*Letter 16*

Mine own sweetheart, this shall be to advertise you of the great elengeness[9] that I find here since your departing now last, than I was wont to do a whole fortnight. I think your kindness and my fervency of love causeth it; for otherwise, I would not have thought it possible that for so little a while it should have grieved me. But now that I am coming towards you, methinketh my pains be half removed; and also I am right well comforted in so much that my book maketh substantially for my matter; in looking whereof I have spent above four hours this day, which causeth me now to write the shorter letter to you at this time, because of some pain in my head; wishing myself (especially an evening) in my sweetheart's arms, whose pretty dukkys[10] I trust shortly to cusse.[11]

Written with the hand of him that was, is, and shall be yours by his own will,

H.R.

*Letter 17*

To inform you what joy it is to me to understand of your conformableness with reason, and of the suppressing of your inutile and vain thoughts with the bridle of reason. I assure you all the greatness of this world could not counterpoise for my satisfaction the knowledge and certainty thereof. Therefore, good sweetheart, continue the same, not only in this, but in all your doings hereafter; for thereby shall come, both to you and me the greatest quietness that may be in this world.

The cause why the bearer stays so long, is the gear I have had to dress up for you;[12] which I trust, ere long, to see you occupy; and then I trust to occupy yours, which shall be recompense enough to me for all my pains and labour.

The unfeigned sickness of this well-willing legate[13] doth somewhat retard this access to your person; but I trust verily, when God shall send him health, he will with diligence recompense his demur. For I know well when he hath said (touching the saying and bruit[14] that he is thought imperial), that it shall be well known in this matter that he is but imperial; and this, for lack of time. Farewell.

# Queen in Waiting, 1527–1532

*The years between 1527 and 1532 were a time of both hope and disappointment for Anne. On 5 May 1527, Henry led Anne out publicly as his partner in a dance for the first time. Only twelve days later, a secret ecclesiastical court opened to try the validity of Henry's marriage. Henry's divorce from Catherine of Aragon proved far from smooth, however.*

## Anne's Letters to Cardinal Wolsey
*Very few of Anne's letters survive. Interestingly, however, a number addressed to Cardinal Wolsey are still extant. Whether due to his animosity towards Thomas Boleyn, or his role in the breaking off of her relationship with Henry Percy, it is clear that Anne was no friend of the Cardinal. By 1527, Cardinal Wolsey was the dominant power in England after the King and Anne was aware that he was the most likely person to be able to secure the King's divorce. Her early letters to the Cardinal are obsequious in tone. Anne's rivalry with the Cardinal was, however, apparent from an early period. Henry's love letters to Anne refer to the matter of Wilton, which, in 1528, was the first area in which Anne and the Cardinal publicly disagreed.*

*Anne's brother-in-law, William Carey, died of the sweating sickness. The Abbess of Wilton died in 1528. Anne petitioned the King for Carey's sister, Eleanor, to be appointed in her place, while Wolsey sought the election of the prioress, Isabel Jordan. As Henry's letter to Anne shows, when it became clear that Eleanor Carey had given birth to two children by different priests, her candidacy became an impossibility. To please Anne, Henry promised that Wolsey's candidate would also not receive the election. He was therefore furious when the Cardinal overruled him, appointing Isabel Jordan as Abbess. A letter of Henry's survives, berating the Cardinal for his conduct and pointing out that he had expressly told him that 'his pleasure is that in no wise the Prioress have it, nor yet Dame Elinor's eldest sister for many considerations'.[1] Wolsey was able to win the King's forgiveness but Anne did not forget the slight.*

*The last letter printed here, which is very different in tone to Anne's earlier letters to the Cardinal is doubtful. Warnicke considers it to be a forgery as, like the reputed letter of Anne to Henry VIII at the beginning of their courtship, this letter exists only as a translation into Italian by Gregorio Leti. Once again it is indeed highly suspicious. It has been pointed out that the letter does not fit the known facts of Anne's relationship with Henry and that it is highly unlikely that Anne would have risked writing such a hostile letter to a man who, while in some disgrace, was still both a Cardinal and Archbishop of York. The letter is included here for completeness, but it must be viewed with concern.*[2]

*Anne Boleyn to Cardinal Wolsey*[3]

My lord, in my most humblest wise that my heart can think, I desire you to pardon me that I am so bold to trouble you with my simple and rude writing, esteeming it to proceed from her that is much desirous to know that your grace does well, as I perceive by this bearer that you do, the which I pray God long to continue, as I am most bound to pray; for I do know the great pains and troubles that you have taken for me is never like to be recompensed on my part, but alonely[4] in loving you next unto the king's grace above all creatures living. And I do not doubt but the daily proofs of my deeds shall manifestly declare and affirm my writing to be true, and I do trust you to think the same.

My lord, I do assure you, I do long to hear from you news of the legate; for I do hope, as they come from you, they shall be very good; and I am sure you desire it as much as I, and more, an it were possible; as I know it is not: and thus remaining in a stedfast hope, I make an end of my letter.

Written with the hand of her that is most bound to be

Your humble servant,

Anne Boleyn

*Postscript by Henry VIII*

The writer of this letter would not cease, till she had caused me likewise to set my hand, desiring you, though it be short, to take it in good part. I ensure you that there is neither of us but greatly desireth to see you, and are joyous to hear that you have escaped this plague so well, trusting the fury thereof to be passed, especially with them that keepeth good diet, as I trust you do. The not hearing of the legate's arrival in France causeth us somewhat to muse; notwithstanding, we trust, by your diligence and vigilancy (with the assistance of Almighty God), shortly to be eased out of that trouble. No more to you at this time, but that I pray God send you as good health and prosperity as the writer would.

By your loving sovereign and friend,

H.R.

*Anne Boleyn to Cardinal Wolsey, c. July 1528*[5]

My Lord,

In my most humble wise, that my poor heart can think, I do thank your grace for your kind letter and for your rich and goodly present, the which I shall never be able to deserve, without your help, of which I have hitherto had so great plenty, that all the days of my life I am most bound of all creatures, next the king's grace, to love and serve your grace, of the which I beseech you never to doubt, that ever I shall vary from this thought, as long as any breath is in my body. And as touching your grace's trouble with the sweat,

I thank our Lord, that them that I desired and prayed for are escaped – and that is the king's grace and you; not doubting that God has preserved you both for great causes known alonely of his high wisdom. And as for the coming of the legate, I desire that much. And if it be God's pleasure, I pray him to send this matter shortly to a good end; and then, I trust, my lord, to recompense part of your great pains. In the which I must require you, in the mean time, to accept my good-will in the stead of the power; the which must proceed partly from you, as our Lord knoweth, whom I beseech to send you long life with continuance in honour. Written with the hand of her that is most bound to be

Your humble and obedient servant,

ANNE BOLEYN

### Anne Boleyn to Cardinal Wolsey[6]

My Lord in my most humble wise I thanke your grace for the gyft thys Benefice for Master Barlo howbeit this standithe to non Effecte for it is mayd for Tonbridge and I wold have it if your plesure war so for Sonbridge for Tonbrig is in my Lord my fathers gyft be a Vowson that he hath and it is not yet Woyd I do trost that your Grace wol graunt hym Sondrig and considering the payne that he hath takyn I do thynke that it shall be vere well bestowyd and in so doyng y Rekyn my selfe moche bownde to your grace for all this that hathe takyn payne in the Kynges Matter it shalle be my daylle study to imagyn all the Ways that I can devise to do them servys and plesur and thus I make an end sendyng you agen the letter that you sent me thankyng your Grace most humbley for the payn that you take for to Wryt to me assuryng you that next the kynges letter ther is nothyng that can rejose me so moche, with the hand of her that is most bownde to be

Your humble and obedient servant

Anne Boleyn

My lord I besyche your grace with all my hart to Remember the Parson of honelayne for my sake schortly.

### Anne Boleyn to Cardinal Wolsey, 1529[7]

My lord,

After my most humble recommendations, this shall be to give unto your grace, as I am most bound, my humble thanks for the pain and travail that your grace doth take in studying, by your wisdom and great diligence, how to bring to pass honourably the greatest wealth that is possible to come to any creature living, and in especial remembering how wretched and unworthy I am in comparing to his highness. And for you, I do know myself never to have deserved by my deserts that you should take this great pain for me; yet daily of your goodness I do perceive by all my friends, and though that I had no knowledge by them, the daily proof of your deeds doth declare your words and writing towards me to be true.

Now good my lord, your discretion may consider as yet how little it is in my power to recompense you, but all only with my goodwill, the which I assure you, that after this matter is brought to pass you shall find me, as

I am bound in the mean time, to owe you my service, and then look what thing in this world I can imagine to do you pleasure in, you shall find me the gladdest woman in the world to do it. And next unto the kings grace, of one thing I make you full promise to be assured to have it, and that is my hearty love unfeignedly during my life; and being fully determined, with God's grace, never to change this purpose, I make an end of this my rude and true-meaning letter, praying our Lord to send you much increase of honour, with long life.

Written with the hand of her that beseeches your grace to accept this letter as proceeding from one that is most bound to be

Your humble and obedient servant,

ANNE BOLEYN

*Anne Boleyn to Cardinal Wolsey, 1529*[8]

My lord,

Though you are a man of great understanding, you cannot avoid being censured by every body for having drawn on yourself the hatred of a king who had raised you to the highest degree to which the greatest ambition of a man seeking his fortune can aspire. I cannot comprehend, and the king still less, how your reverent lordship, after having allured us by so many fine promises about divorce, can have repented of your purpose, and how you could have done what you have, in order to hinder the consummation of it. What, then, is your mode of proceeding? You quarrelled with the queen to favour me at the time when I was less advanced in the king's good graces; and after having therein given me the strongest marks of your affection, your lordship abandons my interests to embrace those of the queen. I acknowledge that I have put much confidence in your professions and promises, in which I find myself deceived.

But, for the future, I shall rely on nothing but the protection of Heaven and the love of my dear king, which alone will be able to set right again those plans which you have broken and spoiled, and to place me in that happy station which God wills, the king so much wishes, and which will be entirely to the advantage of the kingdom. The wrong you have done me has caused me much sorrow; but I feel infinitely more in seeing myself betrayed by a man who pretended to enter into my interests only to discover the secrets of my heart. I acknowledge that, believing you sincere, I have been too precipitate in my confidence; it is this which has induced, and still induces me, to keep more moderation in avenging myself, not being able to forget that I have been

your servant,

ANNE BOLEYN

## Extract from Cavendish's *Life of Wolsey* Concerning the King's Great Matter and Anne's Role in the Cardinal's Fall[9]

*Cavendish's account of Henry's attempts to divorce Catherine of Aragon is of great interest as he was almost certainly an eyewitness to many of the events that he describes. His discussion of the Blackfriars trial also accords with*

*other sources and he provides a comprehensive account of the manoeuvres
undertaken by Henry in order to rid himself of his wife.*

*Wolsey's servant, George Cavendish, firmly believed that Anne was behind
the downfall of his master. The account below is obviously biased in favour
of the Cardinal (who was served loyally by Cavendish until his death). It
is however useful as a source. It is clear from Cavendish's account that the
Cardinal saw his fall as Anne's doing. Cavendish's work ends with Wolsey's
death at Leicester as he was being brought south to London to face trial and,
probably, execution. Interestingly, it was Anne's old admirer, Henry Percy
(by then Earl of Northumberland), who carried out the Cardinal's arrest
at Cawood in November 1530. Percy's role in the arrest caused much talk
about Anne, who had found 'means to employ her Antient Suitor to take
Revenge in both their names'.[10]*

Then began other matters to brew and take place that occupied all men's
heads with divers imaginations, whose stomachs were therewith full filled
without any perfect digestion. The long hid and secret love between the
king and Mistress Anne Boleyn began to break out into every man's ears.
The matter was then by the king disclosed to my Lord Cardinal; whose
persuasion to the contrary, made to the king upon his knees, could not
effect: the king was so amorously affectionate, that will bare place, and high
discretion banished for the time. My lord, provoked by the king to declare
his wise opinion in this matter for the furtherance of his desired affects, who
thought it not meet for him alone to wade too far, to give his hasty judgment
or advice in so weighty a matter, desired of the king license to ask counsel
of men of ancient study, and of famous learning, both in the laws divine and
civil. That obtained, he by his legatine authority sent out his commission
unto all the bishops of this realm, and for other that were either exactly
learned in any of the said laws, or else had in any estimation for their prudent
counsel and judgment in princely affairs of long experience.

Then assembled these prelates before my Lord Cardinal at his place
in Westminster, with many other famous and notable clerks of both the
Universities (Oxford and Cambridge), and also divers out of colleges and
cathedral churches of this realm, renowned and allowed learned and of witty
discretion in the determination of doubtful questions. Then was the matter
of the king's case debated, reasoned and argued; consulting from day to
day, and time to time; that it was to men learned a goodly hearing; but in
conclusion, it seemed me, by the departing of the ancient fathers of the laws,
that they departed with one judgment contrary to the expectation of the
principal parties. I heard the opinion of some of the most famous persons,
among that sort, report, that the king's case was so obscure and doubtful for
any learned man to discuss; the points therein were so dark to be credited
that it was very hard to have any true understanding or intelligence. And
therefore they departed without any resolution or judgment. Then in this
assembly of bishops it was thought most expedient that the king should first
send out his commissioners into all the Universities of Christendom, as well
here in England as in foreign countries and regions, to have among them

his grace's case argued substantially, and to bring with them from thence the very definition of their opinions in the same, under the seals of every several University. Thus was their determination for this time; and thereupon agreed, that commissioners were incontinent appointed and sent forth about this matter into several Universities, as some to Oxford, some to Cambridge, some to Louvain, some to Paris, some to Orleans, some to Bologna, and some to Padua, and some to other. Although these commissioners had the travail, yet was the charges the king's; the which was no small sums of money, and all went out of the king's coffers into foreign regions. For as I heard it reported of credible persons (as it seemed indeed), that besides the great charges of the commissioners, there was inestimable sums of money given to the famous clerks to choke them, and in especial to such as had the governance and custody of their Universities' seals. Insomuch as they agreed, not only in opinions, but also obtained of them the Universities' seals, (the which obtained), they returned home again furnished for their purpose. At whose return there was no small joy made of the principal parties. Insomuch as the commissioners were not only ever after in great estimation, but also most liberally advanced and rewarded, far beyond their worthy deserts. Notwithstanding, they prospered, and the matter went still forward, having then (as they thought), a sure foundation to ground them upon.

These proceedings being once declared to my Lord Cardinal, [he] sent again for all the bishops, whom he made privy of the expedition of the commissioners; and for the very proof thereof he showed them the opinions of the several Universities in writing under the Universities seals. These matters being thus brought to pass, they went again to consultation how these matters should be ordered to the purpose. It was then thought good and concluded, by the advice of them all, that the king should (to avoid all ambiguities), send unto the pope a legation with the instruments, declaring the opinions of the Universities under their seals; to the which it was thought good that all these prelates in this assembly should join with the king in this legation, making intercession and suit to the pope for advice and judgment in this great and weighty matter; and if the pope would not directly consent to the same request, that then the ambassadors should farther require of him a commission to be directed (under lead), to establish a court judicial in England, *hac vice tantum*[11] directed to my Lord Cardinal, and unto the Cardinal Campeggio, (who was then Bishop of Bath), although he was a stranger, which [bishopric] the king gave him at such time as he was the pope's ambassador here in England, to hear and determine according to the just judgment of their conscience. The which after long and great suit, they obtained of the pope his commission. This done and achieved, they made return into England, making report unto the king of their expedition, trusting that his grace's pleasure and purpose should now be presently brought to pass, considering the estate of the judges, who were the Cardinal of England and Campeggio, being both his highnesses subjects in effect.

Long was the desire, and greater was the hope on all sides, expecting the coming of the legation and commission from Rome, yet at length it came. And after the arrival of the Legate Campeggio with his solemn commission in England, he being sore vexed with the gout, was constrained by force thereof to make a long journey or[12] ever he came to London; who should have been most solemnly received at Blackheath, and so with great triumph conveyed to London; but his glory was such, that he would in nowise be entertained with any such pomp or vainglory, who suddenly came by water in a wherry to his own house without Temple Bar, called then Bath Place, which was furnished for him with all manner of stuff and implements of my lord's provision; where he continued and lodged during his abode here in England.

Then after some deliberation, his commission understood, read, and perceived it was by the council determined, that the king, and the queen his wife, should be lodged at Bridewell. And that in the Black Friars a certain place should be appointed where as the king and the queen might most conveniently repair to the court, there to be erected and kept for the disputation and determination of the king's case, where as these two legates sat in judgment as notable judges; before whom the king and the queen were duly cited and summoned to appear. Which was the strangest and newest sight and device that ever was read or heard in any history or chronicle in any region; that a king and a queen [should] be convented and constrained by process compellatory to appear in any court as common persons, within their own realm or dominion, to abide the judgment and decrees of their own subjects, having the royal diadem and prerogative thereof. Is it not a world to consider the desire of wilful princes, when they fully be bent and inclined to fulfil their voluptuous appetites, against the which no reasonable persuasions will suffice; little or nothing weighing or regarding the dangerous sequel that doth ensue as well to themselves as to their realm and subjects. And above all things, there is no one thing that causeth them to be more wilful than carnal desire and voluptuous affection of foolish love. The experience is plain, in this case both manifest and evident, for what surmised inventions have been invented, what laws have been enacted, what noble and ancient monasteries overthrown and defaced, what diversities of religious opinions have risen, what executions have been committed, how many famous and notable clerks have suffered death, what charitable foundations were perverted from the relief of the poor, unto profane uses, and what alterations of good and wholesome ancient laws and customs hath been caused by will and wilful desire of the prince, almost to the subversion and dissolution of this noble realm. All men may understand what hath chanced to this region; the proof thereof hath taught all us Englishmen a common experience, the more is the pity, and is to all good men very lamentable to be considered. If eyes be not blind men may see, if ears be not stopped they may hear, and if pity be not exiled they may lament the sequel of this pernicious and inordinate carnal love. The plague whereof is not ceased (although this love lasted but a while), which our Lord quench; and take from us his indignation! *Quia pecav mus cum patribus nostris, et injuste egimus, &c.*

Ye shall understand, as I said before, that there was a court erected in the Black Friars in London, where these two cardinals sat for judges. Now will I set you out the manner and order of the court there. First, there was a court placed with tables, benches, and bars, like a consistory, a place judicial (for the judges to sit on). There was also a cloth of estate under the which sat the king; and the queen sat some distance beneath the king: under the judges' feet sat the officers of the court. The chief scribe there was Dr Stephens,[13] (who was after Bishop of Winchester); the apparitor was one Cooke, most commonly called Cooke of Winchester. Then sat there within the said court, directly before the king and the judges, the Archbishop of Canterbury, Doctor Warham, and all the other bishops. Then at both the ends, with a bar made for them, the counsellors on both sides. The doctors for the king were Doctor Sampson, that was after Bishop of Chichester, and Doctor Bell, who after was Bishop of Worcester, with divers other. The proctors on the king' part were Doctor Peter, who was after made the king's chief secretary, and Doctor Tregonell, and divers other.

Now on the other side stood the counsel for the queen, Doctor Fisher, Bishop of Rochester, and Doctor Standish, some time a Grey Friar, and then Bishop of St Asaph in Wales, two notable clerks in divinity, and in especial the Bishop of Rochester, a very godly man and a devout person, who after suffered death at Tower Hill; the which was greatly lamented through all the foreign Universities of Christendom. There was also another ancient doctor, called, as I remember, Doctor Ridley, a very small person in stature, but surely a great and an excellent clerk in divinity.

The court being thus furnished and ordered, the judges commanded the crier to proclaim silence; then was the judges' commission, which they had of the pope, published and read openly before all the audience there assembled. That done, the crier called the king, by the name of 'King Henry of England, come into the court, &c'. With that the king answered and said, 'Here, my lords!' Then he called also the queen, by the name of 'Katherine Queen of England, come into the court, &c;' who made no answer to the same, but rose up incontinent out of her chair, where as she sat, and because she could not come directly to the king for the distance which severed them, she took pain to go about unto the king, kneeling down at his feet in the sight of all the court and assembly, to whom she said in effect, in broken English, as followeth:

'Sir,' quoth she, 'I beseech you for all the loves that hath been between us, and for the love of God, let me have justice and right, take of me some pity and compassion, for I am a poor woman and a stranger born out of your dominion, I have here no assured friend, and much less indifferent counsel; I flee to you as to the head of justice within this realm. Alas! Sir, wherein have I offended you, or what occasion of displeasure? Have I designed against your will and pleasure; intending (as I perceive) to put me from you? I take God and all the world to witness, that I have been to you a true humble and obedient wife, ever conformable to your will and pleasure, that never said or did any thing to the contrary thereof, being always well pleased and contented with all things wherein you had any delight or dalliance, whether it were in little or much, I never grudged in word or countenance, or showed a visage or spark of discontentation. I loved all those whom ye loved only for your sake, whether I had cause or no; and whether they were my friends or my enemies. This twenty years I have been your true wife or more, and by me ye have had divers children, although it hath pleased God to call them out of this world, which hath been no default in me.

'And when ye had me at the first, I take God to be my judge, I was a true maid without touch of man; and whether it be true or no, I put it to your conscience. If there be any just cause by the law that ye can allege against me, either of dishonesty or any other impediment to banish and put me from you, I am well content to depart to my great shame and dishonour; and if there be none, then here I most lowly beseech you let me remain in my former estate, and receive justice at your hands. The king your father was in the time of his reign of such estimation thorough the world for his excellent wisdom, that he was accounted and called of all men the second Solomon; and my father Ferdinand, King of Spain, who was esteemed to be one of the wittiest princes that reigned in Spain, many years before, were both wise and excellent kings in wisdom and princely behaviour. It is not therefore to be doubted, but that they elected and gathered as wise counsellors about them as to their high discretions was thought meet. Also, as me seemeth, there was in those days as wise, as well learned men, and men of as good judgment as be at this present in both realms, who thought then the marriage between you and me good and lawful. Therefore it is a wonder to hear what new inventions are now invented against me, that never intended but honesty. And cause me to stand to the order and judgment of this new court, wherein ye may do me much wrong, if ye intend any cruelty; for ye may condemn me for lack of sufficient answer, having no indifferent counsel, but such as be assigned me, with whose wisdom and learning I am not acquainted. Ye must consider that they cannot be indifferent counsellors for my part which be your subjects, and taken out of your own council before, wherein they be made privy, and dare not, for your displeasure, disobey your will and intent, being once made privy thereto. Therefore I most humbly require you, in the way of charity, and for the love of God, who is the just judge, to spare me the extremity of this new court, until I may be advertised what way and order my friends in Spain will advise me to take. And if ye will not extend to me so much indifferent favour, your pleasure then be fulfilled, and to God I commit my cause!'

And with that she rose up, making a low courtesy to the king, and so departed from thence. [Many] supposed that she would have resorted again to her former place; but she took her way straight out of the house, leaning (as she was wont always to do) upon the arm of her General Receiver, called Master Griffith. And the king being advertised of her departure, commanded the crier to call her again, who called her by the name of 'Katherine Queen of England, come into the court, &c.' With that quoth Master Griffith, 'Madam, ye he called again.' 'On, on,' quoth she, 'it maketh no matter, for it is no indifferent court for me, therefore I will not tarry. Go on your ways.' And thus she departed out of that court, without any farther answer at that time, or at any other, nor would never appear at any other court after.

The king perceiving that she was departed in such sort, calling to his grace's memory all her lament words that she had pronounced before him and all the audience, said thus in effect: 'For as much,' quoth he, 'as the queen is gone, I will, in her absence, declare unto you all my lords here presently assembled, she hath been to me as true, as obedient, and as conformable a wife as I could in my fantasy wish or desire. She hath all the virtuous qualities that ought to be in a woman of her dignity, or in any other of baser estate. Surely she is also a noble woman born, if nothing were in her, but only her conditions will well declare the same.' With that quoth my Lord Cardinal, 'Sir, I most humbly beseech your highness to declare me before all this audience, whether I have been the chief inventor or first mover of this matter unto your majesty; for I am greatly suspected of all men herein.' 'My Lord Cardinal,' quoth the king, 'I can well excuse you herein. Marry (quoth he), ye have been rather against me in attempting or setting forth thereof. And to put you all out of doubt, I will declare unto you the special cause that moved me hereunto; it was a certain Scrupulosity that pricked my conscience upon divers words that were spoken at a certain time by the Bishop of Bayonne, the French King's Ambassador, who had been here long upon the debating for the conclusion of a marriage to be concluded between the princess our daughter Mary, and the Duke of Orleans, the French king's second son.'

And upon the resolution and determination thereof, he desired respite to advertise the king his master thereof, whether our daughter Mary should be legitimate, in respect of the marriage which was sometime between the queen here, and my brother the late Prince Arthur. These words were so conceived within my scrupulous conscience, that it bred a doubt within my breast, which doubt pricked, vexed, and troubled so my mind, and so disquieted me, that I was in great doubt of God's indignation; which (as seemed me), appeared right well; much the rather for that he hath not sent me any issue male; for all such issue male as I have received of the queen died incontinent after they were born; so that I doubt the punishment of God in that behalf. Thus being troubled in waves of a scrupulous conscience, and partly in despair of any issue male by her, it drave me at last to consider the estate of this realm, and the danger it stood in for lack of issue male to succeed me in this imperial dignity. I thought it good therefore in relief of the weighty burden of scrupulous conscience, and the quiet estate of this noble realm, to attempt the law therein, and whether I might take another wife in case that my first copulation with this gentlewoman were not lawful; which I intend not for any carnal concupiscence, ne for any displeasure or mislike of the queen's person or age, with whom I could be as well content to continue during my life, if our marriage may stand with God's laws, as with any woman alive; in which point consisteth all this doubt that we go now about to try by the learned wisdom and judgment of you our prelates and pastors of this realm here assembled for that purpose; to whose conscience and judgment I have committed the charge according to the which (God willing), we will be right well contented to submit ourself, to obey the same for our part. Wherein after I once perceived my conscience wounded with the doubtful case herein, I moved first this matter in confession to you, my Lord of Lincoln, my ghostly father. And for as much as then yourself were in some doubt to give me counsel, moved me to ask farther counsel of all you my lords; wherein I moved you first my Lord of Canterbury,[14] axing your license, (for as much [as] you were our metropolitan) to put this matter in question; and so I did of all you my lords, to the which ye have all granted by writing under all your seals, the which I have here to be showed.' 'That is truth if it please your highness,' quoth the Bishop of Canterbury, 'I doubt not but all my brethren here present will affirm the same.' 'No, Sir, not I,' quoth the Bishop of Rochester, 'ye have not my consent thereto.' 'No! ha' the!' quoth the king, 'look here upon this, is not this your hand and seal?' and showed him the instrument with seals. 'No forsooth, Sire,' quoth the Bishop of Rochester, 'it is not my hand nor seal!' To that quoth the king to my Lord of Canterbury, 'Sir, how say ye, is it not his hand and seal?' 'Yes, Sir,' quoth my Lord of Canterbury. 'That is not so,' quoth the Bishop of Rochester, 'for indeed you were in hand with me to have both my hand and seal, as other of my lords had already done; but then I said to you, that I would never consent to no such act, for it were much against my conscience; nor my hand and seal should never be seen at any such instrument, God willing, with much more matter touching the same communication between us.' 'You say truth,' quoth the Bishop of Canterbury, 'such words ye said unto me; but at the last ye were fully persuaded that I should for you subscribe your name, and put to a seal myself, and ye would allow the same.' 'All which words and matter,' quoth the Bishop of Rochester, 'under your correction my lord, and supportation of this noble audience, there is no thing more untrue.' 'Well, well,' quoth the king, 'it shall make no matter; we will not stand with you in argument herein, for you are but one man.' And with that the court was adjourned until the next day of this session.

The next court day the cardinals sat there again, at which time the counsel on both sides were there present. The king's counsel alleged the marriage not good from the beginning, because of the carnal knowledge committed between Prince Arthur her first husband, the king's brother, and her. This matter being very sore touched and maintained by the king's counsel; and the contrary defended by such as took upon them to be on that other part with the good queen: and to prove the same carnal copulation they alleged many coloured reasons and similitudes of truth. It was answered again negatively on the other side, by which it seemed that all their former allegations [were] very doubtful to be tried, so that it was said that no man could know the truth. 'Yes,' quoth the Bishop of Rochester, '*Ego nosco vetitatem*, I know the truth.' 'How know you the truth?' quoth my Lord Cardinal. 'Forsooth, my lord,' quoth he, '*Ego sum professor veritatis*, I know that God is truth itself, nor he never spake but truth; who saith, *quos Deus conjunxit, homo non separet*. And forasmuch as this marriage was made and joined by God to a good intent, I say that I know the truth; the which cannot be broken or loosed by the power of man upon no feigned occasion.' 'So much doth all faithful men know,' quoth my Lord Cardinal, 'as well as you. Yet this reason is not sufficient in this case; for the king's counsel doth allege divers presumptions, to prove the marriage not good at the beginning, *ergo*, say they, it was not joined by God at the beginning, and therefore it is not lawful;

for God ordaineth nor joineth nothing without a just order. Therefore it is not to be doubted but that these presumptions must be true, as it plainly appeareth; and nothing can be more true in case these allegations cannot be avoided; therefore to say that the matrimony was joined of God, ye must prove it farther than by that text which ye have alleged for your matter: for ye must first avoid the presumptions.' 'Then,' quoth one Doctor Ridley, 'it is a shame and a great dishonour to this honourable presence, that any such presumptions should be alleged in this open court, which be to all good and honest men most detestable to be rehearsed.' 'What,' quoth my Lord Cardinal, '*Domine Doctor, magis reverenter.*' 'No, no, my lord,' quoth he, 'there belongeth no reverence to be given to these abominable presumptions; for an unreverent tale would be unreverently answered.' And there they left, and proceeded no farther at that time.

Thus this court passed from session to session, and day to day, in so much that a certain day the king sent for my lord at the breaking up one day of the Court to come to him into Bridewell. And to accomplish his commandment he went unto him, and being there with him in communication in his grace's privy chamber from eleven until twelve of the clock and past at noon, my lord came out and departed from the king and took his barge at the Black Friars, and so went to his house at Westminster. The Bishop of Carlisle being with him in his barge said unto him, (wiping the sweat from his face), 'Sir,' quoth he, 'it is a very hot day.' 'Yea,' quoth my Lord Cardinal, 'if ye had been as well chafed as I have been within this hour, ye would say it were very hot.' And as soon as he came home to his house at Westminster, he went incontinent to his naked bed, where he had not lain fully the space of two hours, but that my Lord of Wiltshire[15] came to speak with him of a message from the king. My lord, having understanding of his coming, caused him to be brought unto his bed's side; and he being there, showed him the king's pleasure was, that he should incontinent (accompanied with the other Cardinal) repair unto the queen at Bridewell, into her chamber, to persuade her by their wisdoms, advising her to surrender the whole matter unto the king's hands by her own will and consent; which should be much better to her honour than to stand to the trial of law and to be condemned, which would seem much to her slander and defamation. To fulfil the king's pleasure, my lord [said] he was ready, and would prepare him to go thither out of hand, saying farther to my Lord of Wiltshire, 'Ye and other my lords of the council, which be near unto the king, are not a little to blame and misadvised to put any such fantasies into his head, whereby ye are the causes of great trouble to all the realm; and at length get you but small thanks either of God or of the world,' with many other vehement words and sentences that were like to ensue of this matter, which words caused my Lord of Wiltshire to water his eyes, kneeling all this while by my lord's bedside, and in conclusion departed. And then my lord rose up, and made him ready, taking his barge, and went straight to Bath Place to the other cardinal; and so went together unto Bridewell, directly to the queen's lodging: and they, being in her chamber of presence, showed to the gentleman usher that they came to speak with the queen's grace. The gentleman usher advertised the

queen thereof incontinent. With that she came out of her privy chamber
with a skein of white thread about her neck, into the chamber of presence,
where the cardinals were giving of attendance upon her coming. At whose
coming quoth she, 'Alack, my lords, I am very sorry to cause you to attend
upon me; what is your pleasure with me?' 'If it please you,' quoth my Lord
Cardinal, 'to go into your privy chamber, we will show you the cause of our
coming.' 'My lord,' quoth she, 'if you have any thing to say, speak it openly
before all these folks; for I fear nothing that ye can say or allege against
me, but that I would all the world should both hear and see it; therefore I
pray you speak your minds openly.' Then began my lord to speak to her in
Latin. 'Nay, good my lord,' quoth she, 'speak to me in English I beseech you;
although I understand Latin.' 'Forsooth then,' quoth my lord, 'Madam, if it
please your grace, we come both to know your mind, how ye be disposed
to do in this matter between the king and you, and also to declare secretly
our opinions and our counsel unto you, which we have intended of very
zeal and obedience that we bear to your grace.' 'My lords, I thank you
then,' quoth she, 'of your good wills; but to make answer to your request I
cannot so suddenly, for I was set among my maidens at work, thinking full
little of any such matter, wherein there needeth a longer deliberation, and
a better head than mine, to make answer to so noble wise men as ye be; I
had need of good counsel in this case, which toucheth me so near; and for
any counsel or friendship that I can find in England, [they] are nothing to
my purpose or profit. Think you, I pray you, my lords, will any Englishmen
counsel or be friendly unto me against the king's pleasure, they being his
subjects? Nay forsooth, my lords! and for my counsel in whom I do intend
to put my trust be not here; they be in Spain, in my native country. Alas, my
lords! I am a poor woman lacking both wit and understanding sufficiently
to answer such approved wise men as ye be both, in so weighty a matter.
I pray you to extend your good and indifferent minds in your authority
unto me, for I am a simple woman, destitute and barren of friendship and
counsel here in a foreign region: and as for your counsel I will not refuse
but be glad to hear.'

And with that she took my lord by the hand and led him into her privy
chamber, with the other cardinal; where they were in long communication:
we, in the other chamber, might sometime hear the queen speak very loud,
but what it was we could not understand. The communication ended, the
cardinals departed and went directly to the king, making to him relation
of their talk with the queen; and after resorted home to their houses to
supper.

Thus went this strange case forward from court-day to court-day, until
it came to the judgment, so that every man expected the judgment to be
given upon the next court-day. At which day the king came thither, and sat
within a gallery against the door of the same that looked unto the judges
where they sat, whom he might both see and hear speak, to hear what
judgment they would give in his suit; at which time all their proceedings
were first openly read in Latin. And that done, the king's learned counsel at
the bar, called fast for judgment. With that, quoth Cardinal Campeggio, 'I

will give no judgment herein until I have made relation unto the pope of all our proceedings, whose counsel and commandment in this high case I will observe. The case is too high and notable, known throughout the world, for us to give any hasty judgment, considering the highness of the persons and the doubtful allegations; and also whose commissioners we be, under whose authority we sit here. It were therefore reason, that we should make our chief head [of] counsel in the same, before we proceed to judgment definitive. I come not so far to please any man, for fear, meed, or favour, be he king or any other potentate. I have no such respect to the persons that I will offend my conscience. I will not for favour or displeasure of any high estate or mighty prince do that thing that should be against the law of God. I am an old man, both sick and impotent, looking daily for death. What should it then avail me to put my soul in the danger of God's displeasure, to my utter damnation, for the favour of any prince or high estate in this world? My coming and being here is only to see justice ministered according to my conscience, as I thought thereby the matter either good or bad. And forasmuch as I do understand, and having perceivance by the allegations and negations in this matter laid for both the parties, that the truth in this case is very doubtful to be known, and also that the party defendant will make no answer thereunto, [but] doth rather appeal from us, supposing that we be not indifferent, considering the king's high dignity and authority within this his own realm which he hath over his own subjects; and we being his subjects, and having our livings and dignities in the same, she thinketh that we cannot minister true and indifferent justice for fear of his displeasure. Therefore, to avoid all these ambiguities and obscure doubts, I intend not to damn my soul for no prince or potentate alive. I will therefore, God willing, wade no farther in this matter, unless I have the just opinion and judgment, with the assent of the pope, and such other of his counsel as hath more experience and learning in such doubtful laws than I have. Wherefore I will adjourn this court for this time, according to the order of the court in Rome, from whence this court and jurisdiction is derived. And if we should go further than our commission doth warrant us, it were folly and vain, and much to our slander and blame; and [we] might be accounted for the same breakers of the order of the higher court from whence we have (as I said) our original authorities.' With that the court was dissolved, and no more pleas holden.

With that stepped forth the Duke of Suffolk from the king, and by his commandment spake these words, with a stout and an hault countenance, 'It was never merry in England,' (quoth he), 'whilst we had cardinals among us:' which words were set forth both with such a vehement countenance, that all men marvelled what he intended; to whom no man made answer. Then the duke spake again in great despight. To the which words my Lord Cardinal, perceiving his vehemency, soberly made answer and said, 'Sir, of all men within this realm, ye have least cause to dispraise or be offended with cardinals : for if I, simple cardinal, had not been, you should have had at this present no head upon your shoulders, wherein you should have a tongue to make any such report in despight of us, who intend you no manner of displeasure; nor have we given you any occasion with such despight to be revenged with your hault words. I would ye knew it, my lord, that I and my brother here intendeth the king and his realm as much honour, wealth, and quietness, as you or any other, of what estate or degree soever he be, within this realm; and would as gladly accomplish his lawful desire as the poorest subject he hath. But, my lord, I pray you, show me what ye would do if ye were the king's commissioner in a foreign region, having a weighty matter to treat upon: and the conclusion being doubtful thereof, would ye not advertise the king's majesty or ever ye went through with the same? Yes, yes, my lord, I doubt not. Therefore I would ye should banish your hasty malice and despight out of your heart, and consider that we be but commissioners for a time, and can, ne may not, by virtue of our commission proceed to judgment, without the knowledge and consent of the chief head of our authority, and having his consent to the same; which is the pope. Therefore we do no less ne otherwise than our warrant will bear us; and if any man will be offended with us therefore, he is an unwise man. Wherefore my lord, hold your peace, and pacify yourself, and frame your tongue like a man of honour and of wisdom, and not to speak so quickly or reproachfully by your friends; for ye know best what friendship ye have received at my hands, the which I yet never revealed to no person alive before now, neither to my glory, ne to your dishonour.' And therewith the duke gave over the matter without any words to reply, and so departed and followed after the king, who was gone into Bridewell at the beginning of the duke's first words.

This matter continued long thus, and my Lord Cardinal was in displeasure with the king, for that the matter in his suit took no better success, the fault whereof was ascribed much to my lord, notwithstanding my lord excused him always by his commission, which gave him no farther authority to proceed in judgment, without knowledge of the pope, who reserved the same to himself.

At the last they were advertised by their post that the pope would take deliberation in respect of judgment until his courts were opened, which should not be before Bartholomew tide next. The king considering the time to be very long or the matter should be determined, thought it good to send a new embassy to the pope, to persuade him to show such honourable favour unto his grace, that the matter might be sooner ended than it was likely to be, or else at the next court in Rome, to rule the matter over, according to the king's request.

To this embassy was appointed Doctor Stephens, then secretary, that after was made Bishop of Winchester. Who went thither, and there tarried until the latter end of summer, as ye shall hear after.

The king commanded the queen to be removed out of the court, and sent to another place; and his highness rode in his progress, with Mistress Anne Boleyn in his company, all the grece season.[16]

It was so that the Cardinal Campeggio made suit to be discharged, that he might return again to Rome. And it chanced that the secretary, who was the king's ambassador to the pope, was returned home from Rome; whereupon it was determined that the Cardinal Campeggio should resort to the king at Grafton in Northamptonshire, and that my Lord Cardinal should accompany him thither, where Campeggio should take his leave of the king. And so they took their journey thitherward from the Moor, and came to Grafton upon the Sunday in the morning, before whose coming there rose in the court divers opinions, that the king would not speak with my Lord Cardinal; and thereupon were laid many great wagers.

These two prelates being come to the gates of the court, where they alighted from their horses, supposing that they should have been received by the head officers of the house as they were wont to be; yet for as much as Cardinal Campeggio was but a stranger in effect, the said officers received them, and conveyed him to his lodging within the court, which was prepared for him only. And after my lord had brought him thus to his lodging, he left him there and departed, supposing to have gone directly likewise to his chamber, as he was accustomed to do. And by the way as he was going, it was told him that he had no lodging appointed for him in the court. And being therewith astonied, Sir Henry Norris, Groom of the Stole [to] the king, came unto him, (but whether it was by the king's commandment or no I know not), and most humbly offered him his chamber for the time, until another might somewhere be provided for him: 'For, Sir, I assure you,' quoth he, 'here is very little room in this house, scantly sufficient for the king; therefore I beseech your grace to accept mine for the season.' Whom my lord thanked for his gentle offer, and went straight to his chamber, where as my lord shifted his riding apparel, and being thus in his chamber, divers noble persons and gentlemen, being his loving friends, came to visit him and to welcome him to the court, by whom my lord was advertised of all things touching the king's displeasure towards him; which did him no small pleasure; and caused him to be the more readily provided of sufficient excuses for his defence.

Then was my lord advertised by Master Norris, that he should prepare himself to give attendance in the chamber of presence against the king's coming thither, who was disposed there to talk with him, and with the other cardinal, who came into my lord's chamber, and they together went into the said chamber of presence, where the lords of the council stood in a row in order along the chamber. My lord putting off his cap to every of them most gently, and so did they no less to him: at which time the chamber was so furnished with noblemen, gentlemen, and other worthy persons, that only expected the meeting, and the countenance of the king and him, and what entertainment the king made him.

Then immediately after came the king into the chamber, and standing there under the cloth of estate, my lord kneeled down before him, who took my lord by the hand, and so he did the other cardinal. Then he took my lord up by both arms and caused him to stand up, whom the king, with as amiable a cheer as ever he did, called him aside, and led him by the hand to a great window, where he talked with him, and caused him to be covered.

Then, to behold the countenance of those that had made their wagers to the contrary, it would have made you to smile; and thus were they all deceived, as well worthy for their presumption. The king was in long and earnest communication with him, in so much as I heard the king say: 'How can that be: is not this your own hand?' and plucked out from his bosom a letter or writing, and showed him the same; and as I perceived that it was answered so by my lord that the king had no more to say in that matter; but said to him: 'My lord, go to your dinner, and all my lords here will keep you company; and after dinner I will resort to you again, and then we will commune further with you in this matter;' and so departed the king, and dined that same day with Mrs Anne Boleyn, in her chamber, who kept there an estate more like a queen than a simple maid.

Then was a table set up in the chamber of presence for my lord, and other lords of the council, where they all dined together; and sitting thus at dinner communing of divers matters. Quoth my lord, 'It were well done if the king would send his chaplains and bishops to their cures and benefices.' 'Yea marry,' quoth my Lord of Norfolk, 'and so it were for you too.' 'I could be contented therewith, very well,' quoth my lord, 'if it were the king's pleasure to grant me license, with his favour, to go to my benefice of Winchester.'[17] 'Nay,' quoth my Lord of Norfolk, 'to your benefice of York, where consisteth your greatest honour and charge.' 'Even as it shall please the king,' quoth my lord, and so fell into other communications. For the lords were very loth to have him planted so near the king as to be at Winchester. Immediately after dinner they fell in secret talk until the waiters had dined.

And as I heard it reported by them that waited upon the king at dinner, that Mistress Anne Boleyn was much offended with the king, as far as she durst, that he so gently entertained my lord, saying, as she sat with the king at dinner, in communication of him, 'Sir,' quoth she, 'is it not a marvellous thing to consider what debt and danger the cardinal hath brought you in with all your subjects?' 'How so, sweetheart?' quoth the king, 'Forsooth,' quoth she, 'there is not a man within all your realm, worth five pounds, but he hath indebted you unto him;' (meaning by a loan that the king had but late of his subjects). 'Well, well,' quoth the king, 'as for that there is in him no blame; for I know that matter better than you, or any other.' 'Nay, Sir,' quoth she, 'besides all that, what things hath he wrought within this realm to your great slander and dishonour? There is never a nobleman within this realm that if he had done but half so much as he hath done, but he were well worthy to lose his head. If my Lord of Norfolk, my Lord of Suffolk, my lord my father, or any other noble person within your realm had done much less than he, but they should have lost their heads or this.' 'Why, then I perceive,' quoth the king, 'ye are not the cardinal's friend?' 'Forsooth, Sir,' then quoth she, 'I have no cause, nor any other that loveth your grace, no more have your grace, if ye consider well his doings.' At this time the waiters had taken up the table, and so they ended their communication. Now ye may perceive the old malice beginning to break out, and newly to kindle the brand that after proved to a great fire, which was as much procured by his secret enemies, [of whom] I touched something before, as of herself.

After all this communication, the dinner thus ended, the king rose up and went incontinent into the chamber of presence, where as my lord, and other of the lords were attending his coming, he called my lord into the great window, and talked with him there a while very secretly. And at the last, the king took my lord by the hand and led him into his privy chamber, sitting there in consultation with him all alone without any other of the lords of the council, until it was night; the which blanked his enemies very sore, and made them to stir the coals; being in doubt what this matter would grow unto, having now none other refuge to trust to but Mistress Anne, in whom was all their whole and firm trust and affiance, without whom they doubted all their enterprise but frustrate and void.

Now was I fain, being warned that my lord had no lodging in the court, to ride into the country to provide for my lord a lodging; so that I provided a lodging for him at a house of Master Empson's, called Euston, three miles from Grafton, whither my lord came by torch light, it was so late or the king and he departed. At whose departing the king commanded him to resort again early in the morning to the intent they might finish their talk which they had then begun and not concluded.

After their departing my lord came to the said house at Euston to his lodging, where he had to supper with him divers of his friends of the court; and sitting at supper, in came to him Doctor Stephens, the secretary, late ambassador unto Rome; but to what intent he came I know not; howbeit my lord took it, that he came to dissemble a certain obedience and love towards him, or else to espy his behaviour and to hear his communication at supper. Notwithstanding my lord bade him welcome, and commanded him to sit down at the table to supper; with whom my lord had this communication, under this manner. 'Master Secretary,' quoth my lord, 'ye be welcome home out of Italy; when came ye from Rome?' 'Forsooth,' quoth he, 'I came home almost a month ago.' 'And where,' quoth my lord, 'have you been ever since?' 'Forsooth,' quoth he, 'following the court this progress.' 'Then have ye hunted, and had good game and pastime,' quoth my lord. 'Forsooth, sir,' quoth he, 'and so I have, I thank the king's majesty.' 'What good greyhounds have ye?' quoth my lord? 'I have some, sir,' quoth he. And thus in hunting, and like disports, passed they all their communication at supper; and after supper my lord and he talked secretly together, till it was midnight or they departed.

The next morning my lord rose early and rode straight to the court; at whose coming the king was ready to ride, willing my lord to resort to the council with the lords in his absence, and said he could not tarry with him, commanding him to return with Cardinal Campeggio, who had taken his leave of the king. Whereupon my lord was constrained to take his leave also of the king, with whom the king departed amiably in the sight of all men. The king's sudden departing in the morning was by the special labour of Mistress Anne, who rode with him, only to lead him about, because he should not return until the cardinals were gone, the which departed after dinner, returning again towards the Moor.

The king rode that morning to view a ground for a new park, which is called at this day Hartwell Park, where Mistress Anne had made provision for the king's dinner, fearing his return or the cardinals were gone.

Then rode my lord and the other cardinal after dinner on their way homeward, and so came to the monastery of St Alban's (whereof he himself was commendatory), and there lay one whole day; and the next day they rode to the Moor; and from thence the Cardinal Campeggio took his journey towards Rome, with the king's reward; what it was I am uncertain. Nevertheless, after his departure, the king was informed that he carried with, him great treasures of my lord's, (conveyed in great tuns) notable sums of gold and silver to Rome, whither they surmised my lord would secretly convey himself out of this realm. In so much that a post was sent speedily after the cardinal to search him; whom they overtook at Calais, where he was stayed until search was made; there was not so much money found as he received of the king's reward, and so he was dismissed and went his way.

After Cardinal Campeggio was thus departed and gone, Michaelmas Term drew near, against the which my lord returned unto his house at Westminster; and when the Term began, he went to the hall in such like sort and gesture as he was wont most commonly to do, and sat in the Chancery, being Chancellor. After which day he never sat there more. The next day he tarried at home, expecting the coming of the Dukes of Suffolk and Norfolk, [who] came not that day; but the next day they came thither unto him; to whom they declared how the king's pleasure was that he should surrender and deliver up the great seal into their hands, and to depart simplily unto Asher,[18] a house situate nigh Hampton Court, belonging to the Bishoprick of Winchester. My lord understanding their message, demanded of them what commission they had to give him any such commandment? who answered him again, that they were sufficient commissioners in that behalf, having the king's commandment by his mouth so to do. 'Yet,' quoth he, 'that is not sufficient for me, without farther commandment of the king's pleasure; for the great seal of England was delivered me by the king's own person, to enjoy during my life, with the ministration of the office and high room of chancellorship of England: for my surety whereof, I have the king's letters patent to show.' Which matter was greatly debated between the dukes and him with many stout words between them; whose words and checks he took in patience for the time: in so much that the dukes were fain to depart again without their purpose at that present; and returned again unto Windsor to the king: and what report they made I cannot tell; howbeit, the next day they came again from the king, bringing with them the king's letters; After the receipt and reading of the same by my lord, which was done with much reverence, he delivered unto them the great seal, contented to obey the king's high commandment; and seeing that the king's pleasure was to take his house, with the contents, was well pleased simply to depart to Asher; taking nothing but only some provision for his house.

And after long talk between the dukes and him, they departed, with the great seal of England, to Windsor, unto the king. Then went my Lord Cardinal and called all officers in every office in his house before him, to take account of all such stuff as they had in charge. And in his gallery there was set divers tables, whereupon a great number of rich stuffs of silk, in whole pieces, of all colours, as velvet, satin, damask, caffa, taffeta, grograine, sarcenet, and of other not in my remembrance; also there lay a thousand pieces of fine holland cloth, whereof as I heard him say afterward, there was five hundred pieces thereof, conveyed both from the king and him.

Furthermore there was also all the walls of the gallery hanged with cloth of gold, and tissue of divers makings, and cloth of silver likewise on both the sides; and rich cloths of baudkin, of divers colours. There also hung the richest suits of copes of his own provision, (which he caused to be made for his colleges of Oxford and Ipswich), that ever I saw in England. Then had he two chambers adjoining to the gallery, the one called the *gilt chamber*, and the other called, most commonly, the *council chamber*, wherein were set in each two broad and long tables, upon tressels, whereupon was set such a number of plate of all sorts, as were almost incredible. In the *gilt chamber* was set out upon the tables nothing but all gilt plate; and a cupboard standing under a window, was garnished all wholly with plate of clean gold, whereof some was set with pearl and rich stones. And in the *council chamber* was set all white plate and parcel gilt; and under the tables, in both the chambers, were set baskets with old plate, which was not esteemed but for broken plate and old, not worthy to be occupied, and books containing the value and weight of every parcel laid by them ready to be seen; and so was also books set by all manner of stuff, containing the contents of every thing. Thus every thing being brought into good order and furnished, he gave the charge of the delivery thereof unto the king, to every officer within his office, of such stuff as they had before in charge, by indenture of every parcel; for the order of his house was such, as that every officer was charged by indenture with all such parcels as belonged to their office.

Then all things being ordered as it is before rehearsed, my lord prepared him to depart by water. And before his departing, he commanded Sir William Gascoigne, his treasurer, to see these things before remembered delivered safely to the king at his repair [thither]. That done, the said Sir William said unto my lord, 'Sir, I am sorry for your grace, for I understand ye shall go straightway to the Tower.' 'Is this the good comfort and counsel,' quoth my lord, 'that ye can give your master in adversity? It hath been always your natural inclination to be very light of credit; and much more lighter in reporting of false news, I would ye should know, Sir William, and all other such blasphemers, that it is nothing more false than that, for I never (thanks be to God), deserved by no ways to come there under any arrest, although it hath pleased the king to take my house ready furnished for his pleasure at this time. I would all the world knew, and so I confess, to have nothing, either riches, honour, or dignity, that hath not grown of him and by him; therefore it is my very duty to surrender the same to him again as his very own, with all my heart, or else I were an unkind servant. Therefore go your ways, and give good attendance unto your charge, that nothing be embezzled.' And therewithal he made him ready to depart, with all his gentlemen and yeomen, which was no small number, and took his barge at his privy stairs, and so went by water unto Putney, where all his horses waited his coming. And at the taking of his barge there was no less than a thousand boats full of men and women of the city of London, waffeting up and down in Thames, expecting my lord's departing, supposing that he should have gone directly from thence to the Tower, whereat they rejoiced, and I dare be bold to say that the most part never received damage at his hands.

O wavering and new fangled multitude! Is it not a wonder to consider the inconstant mutability of this uncertain world! The common people always desiring alterations and novelties of things for the strangeness of the case; which after turneth them to small profit and commodity. For if the sequel of this matter be well considered and digested, ye shall understand that they had small cause to triumph at his fall. What hath succeeded all wise men doth know, and the common sort of them hath felt. Therefore to grudge or wonder at it, surely were but folly; to study a redress, I see not how it can be holpen, for the inclination and natural disposition of Englishmen is, and hath always been, to desire alteration of officers, which hath been thoroughly fed with long continuance in their rooms with sufficient riches and possessions; and they being put out, then cometh another hungry and a lean officer in his place, that biteth nearer the bone than the old. So the people be ever pilled and polled with hungry dogs, through their own desire of change of new officers, nature hath so wrought in the people, that it will not be redressed. Wherefore I cannot see but always men in authority be disdained with the common sort of men; and such most of all, that justly ministereth equity to all men indifferently. For where they please some one which receiveth the benefit of the law at [their] hands according to justice, there doth they in likewise displease the contrary party, who supposeth to sustain great wrong, where they have equity and right. Thus all good justices be always in contempt with some for executing of indifferency. And yet such ministers must be, for if there should be no ministers of justice the world should run full of error and abomination, and no good order kept, ne quietness among the people. There is no good man but he will commend such justices as dealeth uprightly in their rooms, and rejoice at their continuance and not at their fall; and whether this be true or no, I put it to the judgment of all discreet persons. Now let us leave, and begin again where we left.

When he was with all his train arrived and landed at Putney, he took his mule, and every man his horse. And setting forth, not past the length of a pair of garden butts, he espied a man come riding empost down the hill, in Putney town, demanding of his footmen who they thought it should be? And they answered again and said, that they supposed it should be Sir Harry Norris. And by and bye he came to my lord and saluted him, and said 'that the king's majesty had him commended to his grace, and willed him in any wise to be of good cheer, for he was as much in his highness' favour as ever he was, and so shall be.' And in token thereof, he delivered him a ring of gold, with a rich stone, which ring he knew very well, for it was always the privy token between the king and him whensoever the king would have any special matter dispatched at his hands. And said furthermore, 'that the king commanded him to be of good cheer, and take no thought, for he should not lack. And although the king hath dealt with you unkindly as ye suppose, he saith that it is for no displeasure that he beareth you, but only to satisfy more the minds of some (which he knoweth be not your friends), than for any indignation: and also ye know right well, that he is able to recompense you with twice as much as your goods amounteth unto; and all this he bade me, that I should show you, therefore, sir, take patience. And for my part, I trust to see you in better estate than ever ye were.' But when he heard Master Norris rehearse all the good and comfortable words of the king, he quickly lighted from off his mule, all alone, as though he had been the youngest person amongst us, and incontinent kneeled down in the dirt upon both his knees, holding up his hands for joy. Master Norris perceiving him so quickly from his mule upon the ground, mused, and was astonied. And therewith he alighted also, and kneeled by him, embracing him in his arms, and asked him how he did, calling upon him to credit his message. 'Master Norris,' quoth he, 'when I consider your comfortable and joyful news, I can do no less than to rejoice, for the sudden joy surmounted my memory, having no respect neither to the place or time, but thought it my very bounden duty to render thanks to God my maker, and to the king my sovereign lord and master, who hath sent me such comfort in the very place where I received the same.'

And talking with Master Norris, upon his knees in the mire, he would have pulled off his under cap of velvet, but he could not undo the knot under his chin; wherefore with violence he rent the laces and pulled it from his head, and so kneeled bare headed. And that done, he covered again his head, and arose, and would have mounted his mule, but he could not mount again with such agility as he lighted before, where his footmen had as much ado to set him in his saddle as they could have. Then rode he forth up the hill into the town, talking with Master Norris. And when he came upon Putney Heath Master Norris took his leave and would have departed. Then quoth my lord unto him, 'Gentle Norris, if I were lord of a realm, the one half thereof were insufficient a reward to give you for your pains, and good comfortable news. But, good Master Norris, consider with me, that I have nothing left me but my clothes on my back. Therefore I desire you to take this small reward of my hands;' the which was a little chain of gold, made like a bottle chain, with a cross of gold hanging thereat, wherein was a piece of the *Holy Cross*, which he wore continually about his neck next his skin; and said furthermore, 'I assure you. Master Norris, that when I was in prosperity, although it seem but small in value, yet I would not gladly have departed with it for the value of a thousand pounds. Therefore I beseech you to take it in gree, and wear it about your neck for my sake, and as often as ye shall happen to look upon it, have me in remembrance to the king's majesty, as opportunity shall serve you, unto whose Highness and clemency, I desire you to have [me] most lowly commended; for whose charitable disposition towards me, I can do nothing but only minister my prayer unto God for the preservation of his royal estate, long to reign in honour, health, and quiet life. I am his obedient subject, vassal, and poor chaplain, and do so intend, God willing, to be during my life, accounting that of myself I am of no estimation nor of no substance, but only by him and of him, whom I love better than myself, and have justly and truly served, to the best of my gross wit.' And with that he took Master Norris by the hand and bade

him farewell. And being gone but a small distance, he returned, and called
Master Norris again, and when he was returned, he said unto him: 'I am
sorry,' quoth he, 'that I have no condign token to send to the king. But if
ye would at this my Request present the king with this poor Fool, I trust
his highness would accept him well, for surely for a nobleman's pleasure
he is worth a thousand pounds.' So Master Norris took the Fool with him;
with whom my lord was fain to send six of [his] tall yeomen, to conduct
and convey the Fool to the court; for the poor Fool took on and fired so
in such a rage when he saw that he must needs depart from my lord. Yet
notwithstanding they conveyed him with Master Norris to the court, where
the king received him most gladly.

After the departure of Master Norris with his token to the king, my lord
rode straight to Asher, a house appertaining to the Bishoprick of Winchester,
situate within the county of Surrey, not far from Hampton Court, where my
lord and his family[19] continued the space of three or four weeks, without
beds, sheets, table cloths, cups and dishes to eat our meat, or to lie in.
Howbeit, there was good provision of all kind of victuals, and of drink,
both beer and wine, whereof there was sufficient and plenty. My lord was of
necessity compelled to borrow of the Bishop of Carlisle, and of Sir Thomas
Arundell, both dishes to eat his meat in, and plate to drink in, and also linen
cloths to occupy. And thus continued he in this strange estate until the feast
of All-hallow tide was past.

It chanced me upon All-hallow day to come there into the *Great Chamber*
at Asher, in the morning, to give mine attendance, where I found Master
Cromwell leaning in the great window, with a Primer in his hand, saying of
our Lady mattins; which had been since a very strange sight.[20] He prayed
not more earnestly than the tears distilled from his eyes. Whom I bade good
morrow. And with that I perceived the tears upon his cheeks. To whom I
said, 'Why Master Cromwell, what meaneth all this your sorrow? Is my lord
in any danger, for whom ye lament thus? or is it for any loss that ye have
sustained by any misadventure?'

'Nay, nay,' quoth he, 'it is my unhappy adventure, which am like to lose all
that I have travailed for all the days of my life, for doing of my master true
and diligent service.' 'Why, sir,' quoth I, 'I trust ye be too wise, to commit
any thing by my lord's commandment, otherwise than ye might do of right,
whereof ye have any cause to doubt of loss of your goods.' 'Well, well,'
quoth he, 'I cannot tell; but all things I see before mine eyes, is as it is taken;
and this I understand right well, that I am in disdain with most men for
my master's sake; and surely without just cause. Howbeit, an ill name once
gotten will not lightly be put away. I never had any promotion by my lord
to the increase of my living. And thus much will I say to you, that I intend,
God willing, this afternoon, when my lord hath dined, to ride to London,
and so to the court, where I will either make or mar, or I come again. I will
put myself in prease, to see what any man is able to lay to my charge of
untruth or misdemeanour.' 'Marry, sir,' quoth I, 'in so doing, in my conceit,
ye shall do very well and wisely, beseeching God to be your guide, and send
you good luck, even as I would myself.' And with that I was called into the

closet, to see and prepare all things ready for my lord, who intended that day to say mass there himself; and so I did.

And then my lord came thither with his chaplain, one Doctor Marshall, saying first his mattins, and heard two masses on his knees. And then after he was confessed, he himself said mass. And when he had finished mass, and all his divine service, returned into his chamber, where he dined among divers of his doctors, where as Master Cromwell dined also; and sitting at dinner, it chanced that my lord commended the true and faithful service of his gentlemen and yeomen. Whereupon Master Cromwell took an occasion to say to my lord, that in conscience he ought to consider their truth and loyal service that they did him, in this his present necessity, which never forsaketh him in all his trouble.

'It shall be well done, therefore,' said he, 'for your grace to call before you all these your most worthy gentlemen and right honest yeomen, and let them understand, that ye right well consider their patience, truth, and faithfulness; and then give them your commendation, with good words and thanks, the which shall be to them great courage to sustain your mishap in patient misery, and to spend their life and substance in your service.'

'Alas, Thomas,' quoth my lord unto him, 'ye know I have nothing to give them, and words without deeds be not often well taken. For if I had but as I have had of late, I would depart with them so frankly as they should be well content: but nothing hath no savour; and I am ashamed, and also sorry that I am not able to requite their faithful service. And although I have cause to rejoice, considering the fidelity I perceive in the number of my servants, who will not depart from me in my miserable estate, but be as diligent, obedient, and serviceable about me as they were in my great triumphant glory, yet do I lament again the want of substance to distribute among them.' 'Why, sir,' quoth Master Cromwell, 'have ye not here a number of chaplains, to whom ye have departed very liberally with spiritual promotions, in so much as some may dispend, by your grace's preferment, a thousand marks by the year, and some five hundred marks, and some more, and some less; ye have no one chaplain within all your house, or belonging unto you, but he may dispend at the least well (by your procurement and preferment), three hundred marks yearly, who had all the profit and advantage at your hands, and other your servants none at all; and yet hath your poor servants taken much more pains for you in one day than all your idle chaplains hath done in a year. Therefore if they will not freely and frankly consider your liberality, and depart with you of the same goods gotten in your service, now in your great indigence and necessity, it is pity that they live; and all the world will have them in indignation and hatred, for their abominable ingratitude to their master and lord.'

'I think no less, Thomas,' quoth my lord, 'wherefore, [I pray you,] cause all my servants to be called and to assemble without, in my great chamber, after dinner, and see them stand in order, and I will declare unto them my mind, according to your advice.' After that the board's end was taken up, Master Cromwell came to me and said, 'Heard you not, what my lord said even now?' 'Yes, sir,' quoth I, 'that I did,' 'Well, then,' quoth he, 'assemble all my lord's servants up into the great chamber;' and so I did, and when they were all there assembled, I assigned all the gentlemen to stand on the right side of the chamber, and the yeomen on the left side. And at the last my lord came thither, appareled in a white rochet upon a violet gown of cloth like a bishop's, who went straight into the great window. Standing there a while, and his chaplains about him, beholding the number of his servants divided in two parts, he could not speak unto them for tenderness of his heart; the flood of tears that distilled from his eyes declared no less: the which perceived by his servants, caused the fountains of water to gush out of their faithful hearts down their cheeks, in such abundance as it would cause a cruel heart to lament. At the last, after he had turned his face to the wall, and wiped his eyes with his handkerchief, he spake to them after this sort in effect: 'Most faithful gentleman and true hearted yeomen, I do not only lament [to see] your persons present about me, but I do lament my negligent ingratitude towards you all on my behalf, in whom hath been a great default, that in my prosperity [I] have not done for you so much as I might have done, either in word or deed, which was then in my power to do: but then I knew not my jewels and special treasures that I had of you my faithful servants in my house; but now approved experience hath taught me, and with the eyes of my discretion, which before were hid, I do perceive well the same. There was never thing that repented me more that ever I did than doth the remembrance of my oblivious negligence and ungentleness, that I have not promoted or preferred you to condign rooms and preferments, according to your demerits. Howbeit, it is not unknown to you all, that I was not so well furnished of temporal advancements, as I was of spiritual preferments. And if I should have promoted you to any of the king's offices and rooms, then should I have incurred the indignation of the king's servants, who would not much let to report in every place behind my back, that there could no office or room in the king's gift escape the cardinal and his servants, and thus should I incur the obloquy and slander before the whole world. But now it is come to this pass, that it hath pleased the king to take all that ever I have into his possession, so that I have nothing left me but my bare clothes upon my back, the which be but simple in comparison to those that ye have seen me have or this: howbeit, if they may do you any good or pleasure, I would not stick to divide them among you, yea, and the skin of my back, if it might countervail any thing in value among you. But, good gentlemen and yeomen, my trusty and faithful servants, of whom no prince hath the like, in my opinion, I most heartily require you to take with me some patience a little while, for I doubt not but that the king, considering the offence suggested against me by my mortal enemies, to be of small effect, will shortly, I doubt not, restore me again to my living, so that I shall be more able to divide some part thereof yearly among you, whereof ye shall be well assured. For the surplusage of my revenues, whatsoever shall remain at the determination of my accompts, shall be, God willing, distributed among you. For I will never hereafter esteem the goods and riches of this uncertain world but as a vain thing, more than shall be sufficient for the maintenance of mine estate and dignity, that God hath or shall call me unto in this world during my life. And if the king do not thus shortly restore me, then will I see you bestowed according to your own requests, and write for you, either to the king, or to any other noble person within this realm, to retain you into service; for I doubt not but the king, or any noble man, or worthy gentleman of this realm, will credit my letter in your commendation. Therefore, in the mean time, mine advice is, that ye repair home to your wives, such as have any: and such among you as hath none, to take this time to visit your parents and friends in the country. There is none of you all, but once in a year would require licence to visit your wives and other of your friends: take this time, I pray you, in respect thereof, and at your return I will not refuse you, if I should beg with you. I consider that the service of my house hath been such, and of such sort, that ye be not meet or apt to serve [any] man under the degree of a king; therefore I would wish you to serve no man but the king, who I am sure will not reject you. Therefore I desire you to take your pleasures for a month, and then ye may come again unto me, and I trust by that time, the king's majesty will extend his clemency upon me.' 'Sir,' quoth Master Cromwell, 'there is divers of these your yeomen, that would be glad to see their friends, but they lack money: therefore here is divers of your chaplains who have received at your hands great benefices and high dignities; let them therefore now show themselves unto you as they are bound by all humanity to do. I think their honesty and charity is not so slender and void of grace that they would not see you lack where they may help to refresh you. And for my part, although I have not received of your grace's gift one penny towards the increase of my yearly livings yet will I depart with you this towards the dispatch of your servants,' and [therewith] delivered him five pounds in gold. 'And now let us see what your chaplains will do. I think they will depart with you much more than I have done, who be more able to give you a pound than I one penny.' 'Go to, masters,' quoth he to the chaplains: in so much as some gave to him ten pounds, some ten marks, some a hundred shillings, and so some more and some less, as at that time their powers did extend; whereby my lord received among them as much money of their liberality as he gave to each of his yeomen a quarter's wages, and board wages for a month; and they departed down into the hall, where some determined to go to their friends, and some said that they would not depart from my lord until they might see him in better estate. My lord returned into his chamber lamenting the departure from his servants, making his moan unto Master Cromwell, who comforted him the best he could, and desired my lord to give him leave to go to London, where he would either make or mar or he came again, which was always his common saying. Then after long communication with my lord in secret, he departed and took his horse, and rode to London, at whose departing I was by, whom he bade farewell; and said, 'ye shall hear shortly of me, and if I speed well, I will not fail to be here again within these two days.' And so I took my leave of him, and he rode forth on his journey. Sir Rafe Sadler, (now knight), was then his clerk, and rode with him.

After that my lord had supped that night, and all men gone to bed, (being All-hallown day), it chanced so, about midnight, that one of the porters came unto my chamber door, and there knocked, and waking me, I perceived who it was; [and] asked him, 'what he would have that time of the night ?' 'Sir,' quoth the porter, 'there is a great number of horsemen at the gate, that would come in, saying to me, that it is Sir John Russell, and so it appears to me by his voice; what is your pleasure that I should do?' 'Marry,' quoth I, 'go down again, and make a great fire in your lodge, against I come to dry them;' for it rained all that night the sorest that it did all that year before. Then I rose and put on my nightgown, and came to the gates, and asked who was there. With that Master Russell spake, whom I knew by his voice, and then I caused the porter to open the gates and let them all in, who were wet to the skin; desiring Master Russell to go into the lodge to the fire; and he showed me that he was come from the king unto my lord in message, with whom he required me to speak. 'Sir,' quoth I, 'I trust your news be good?' 'Yea, I promise you on my fidelity,' quoth he, 'and so, I pray you, show him, I have brought him such news that will please him right well.' 'Then I will go,' quoth I, 'and wake him, and cause him to rise.' I went incontinent to my lord's chamber door, and waked my lord, who asked me 'what I would have?' 'Sir,' said I, 'to show you that Sir John Russell is come from the king, who is desirous to speak with you;' and then he called up one of his grooms to let me in; and being within I told him 'what a journey Sir John Russell had that night.' 'I pray God,' quoth he, 'all be for the best.' 'Yes, sir,' quoth I, 'he showed me, and so bade me tell you, that he had brought you such news as ye would greatly rejoice thereat.' 'Well, then' quoth, he, 'God be praised, and welcome be his grace! Go ye and fetch him unto me, and by that time I will be ready to talk with him.'

Then I returned from him to the lodge, and brought Master Russell from thence to my lord, who had cast on his nightgown. And when Master Russell was come into his presence, he most humbly reverenced him, upon his knee, [to] whom my lord bowed down, and took him up, and bade him welcome. 'Sir,' quoth he, 'the king commendeth him unto you;' and delivered him a great ring of gold with a Turkis, for a token; 'and willeth you to be of good cheer; who loveth you as well as ever he did, and is not a little disquieted for your troubles, whose mind is full of your remembrance. In so much as his grace, before he sat to supper, called me unto him, and commanded me to take this journey secretly to visit you, to your comfort the best of my power. And Sir, if it please your grace, I have had this night the sorest journey, for so little a way, that ever I had to my remembrance.'

My lord thanked him for his pains and good news, and demanded of him if he had supped; and he said 'Nay.' 'Well, then,' quoth my lord to me, 'cause the cooks to provide some meat for him; and cause a chamber with a good fire to be made ready for him, that he may take his rest awhile upon a bed.' All which commandment I fulfilled; and in the meantime my lord and Master Russell were in very secret communication; and in fine, Master Russell went to his chamber, taking his leave of my lord for all night, and said, 'he would not tarry but a while, for he would, God willing, be at the court at Greenwich again before day, for he would not for any thing that it were known, his being with my lord that night.' And so being in his chamber, having a small repast, rested him a while upon a bed, whilst his servants supped and dried themselves by the fire; and then incontinent he rode away with speed to the court. And shortly after his being there, my lord was restored again unto plenty of household stuff, vessels, and plate, and of all things necessary some part, so that he was indifferently furnished much better than he was of late, and yet not so abundantly as the king's pleasure was, the default whereof was in the officers, and in such as had the oversight of the delivery thereof; and yet my lord rejoiced in that little in comparison to that he had before.

Now let us return again to Master Cromwell, to see how he hath sped, since his departure last from my lord. The case stood so, that there should begin, shortly after All-hallown tide, the Parliament, and [he], being within London, devised with himself to be one of the Burgesses of the Parliament, and chanced to meet with one Sir Thomas Rush, knight, a special friend of his, whose son was appointed to be one of the Burgesses of that Parliament, of whom he obtained his room, and by that means put his foot into the Parliament House: then within two or three days after his entry into the Parliament, he came unto my lord, to Asher, with a much pleasanter countenance than he had at his departure, and meeting with me before he came to my lord, said unto me, 'that he had once adventured to put in his foot, where he trusted shortly to be better regarded, or all were done.' And when he was come to my lord, they talked together in secret manner; and that done, he rode out of hand again that night to London, because he would not be absent from the Parliament the next morning. There could nothing be spoken against my lord in the Parliament House but he would answer it incontinent, or else take until the next day, against which time he would resort to my lord to know what answer he should make in his behalf; in so much that there was no matter alleged against my lord but that he was ever ready furnished with a sufficient answer; so that at length, for his honest behaviour in his master's cause, he grew into such estimation in every man's opinion, that he was esteemed to be the most faithfullest servant to his master of all other, wherein he was of all men greatly commended.

Then was there brought in a Bill of Articles into the Parliament House to have my lord condemned of treason; against which bill Master Cromwell inveighed so discreetly, with such witty persuasions and deep reasons, that the same bill could take there no effect. Then were his enemies compelled to indite him in a *premunire*, and all was done only to the intent to entitle the king to all his goods and possessions, the which he had gathered together, and purchased for his colleges in Oxford and Ipswich, and for the maintenance of the same which was then abuilding in most sumptuous wise. Wherein when he was demanded by the judges, which were sent [to] him purposely to examine him what answer he would make to the same, he said: 'The king's highness knoweth right well whether I have offended his majesty and his laws or no, in using of my prerogative legatine, for the which ye have me indited. Notwithstanding I have the king's license in my coffers, under his hand and broad seal, for exercising and using the authority thereof, in the largest wise, within his highness' dominions, the which remaineth now in the hands of my enemies. Therefore, because I will not stand in question or trial with the king in his own cause, I am content here of mine own frank will and mind, in your presence, to confess the offence in the inditement, and put me wholly in the mercy and grace of the king, having no doubt in his godly disposition and charitable conscience, whom I know hath an high discretion to consider the truth, and my humble submission and obedience. And although I might justly stand on the trial with him therein; yet I am content to submit myself to his clemency, and thus much ye may say to him in my behalf, that I am entirely in his obedience, and do intend, God willing, to obey and fulfil all his princely pleasure in every thing that he will command me to do; whose will and pleasure I never yet disobeyed or repugned, but was always contented and glad to accomplish his desire and commandment before God, whom I ought most rathest to [have] obeyed; the which negligence now greatly repenteth me. Notwithstanding, I most heartily require you, to have me most humbly to his royal majesty commended, for whom I do and will pray for the preservation of his royal person, long to reign in honour, prosperity, and quietness, and to have the victory over his mortal and cankered enemies.' And they took their leave of him and departed.

Shortly after the king sent the Duke of Norfolk unto him in message; but what it was I am not certain. But my Lord being advertised that the duke was coming even at hand, he caused all his gentlemen to wait upon him down through the Hall into the Base Court, to receive the duke at the entry of the gates; and commanded all his yeomen to stand still in the Hall in order. And he and his gentlemen went to the gates, where he encountered with my Lord of Norfolk, whom he received bareheaded; who embraced each other: and so led him by the arm through the Hall into his chamber. And as the duke passed through the Hall, at the upper end thereof he turned again his visage down the Hall, regarding the number of the tall yeomen that stood in order there, and said: 'Sirs,' quoth he, 'your diligent and faithful service unto my lord here your master, in this time of his calamity, hath purchased for yourselves of all noble men much honesty; in so much as the king commanded me to say to you in his grace's name, that, for your true and loving service that ye have done to your master, his highness will see you all furnished at all times with services according to your demerits.' With that my Lord Cardinal put off his cap, and said to my Lord of Norfolk; 'Sir,' quoth he, 'these men be all approved men: wherefore it were pity they should want other service or living; and being sorry that I am not able to do for them as my heart doth wish, do therefore require you, my good lord, to be good lord unto them, and extend your good word for them, when ye shall see opportunity at any time hereafter; and that ye will prefer their diligent and faithful service to the king,' 'Doubt ye not thereof,' quoth my Lord of Norfolk, 'but I will do for them the best of my power: and when I shall see cause, I will be an earnest suitor for them to the king; and some of you I will retain myself in service for your honesty's sake. And as ye have begun, so continue and remain here still with my lord until ye hear more of the king's pleasure: — God's blessing and mine be with you!' And so went up into the great chamber to dinner, whom my Lord Cardinal thanked, and said unto him, 'Yet, my lord, of all other noble men, I have most cause to thank you for your noble heart and gentle nature, which ye have showed me behind my back, as my servant, Thomas Cromwell, hath made report unto me. But even as ye are a noble man in deed, so have ye showed yourself no less to all men in calamity, and in especial to me, and even as ye have abated my glory and high estate, and brought it full low, so have ye extended your honourable favour most charitably unto me, being prostrate before you. Forsooth, Sir, ye do right well deserve to bear in your arms the noble and gentle lion, whose natural inclination is, that when he hath vanquished any beast, and seeth him yielded, lying prostrate before him at his feet, then will he show most clemency unto his vanquished, and do him no more harm, ne suffer any other devouring beast to damage him: whose nature and quality ye do ensue; therefore these verses may be applied to your lordship:

*Parcere prostratis scit nobilis ira leonis:*
*Tu quoque fac simile, quisquis regnabis in orbem.*[21]

With that the water was brought them to wash before dinner, to the which my lord called my Lord of Norfolk to wash with him: but he refused of courtesy, and desired to have him excused, and said 'that it became him not to presume to wash with him any more now, than it did before in his glory.' 'Yes, forsooth,' quoth my Lord Cardinal, 'for my authority and dignity legatine is gone, wherein consisted all my high honour.' 'A straw,' quoth my Lord of Norfolk, 'for your legacy. I never esteemed your honour the more or higher for that. But I regarded your honour, for that ye were Archbishop of York, and a cardinal, whose estate of honour surmounteth any duke now being within this realm; and so will I honour you, and acknowledge the same, and bear you reverence accordingly. Therefore, I beseech you, content yourself, for I will not presume to wash with you; and therefore I pray you, hold me excused.' Then was my Lord Cardinal constrained to wash alone; and my Lord of Norfolk all alone also. When he had done, my Lord Cardinal would fain have had him to sit down on the chair, in the inner side of the table, but surely he refused the same also with much humbleness. Then was there set another chair for my Lord of Norfolk, over against my Lord Cardinal, on the outside of the table, the which was by my Lord of Norfolk based something beneath my lord, and during the dinner all their communication was of the diligent service of the gentlemen which remained with my lord there attending upon him at dinner, and how much the king and all other noble men doth esteem them with worthy commendations for so doing; and at this time how little they be esteemed in the court that are come to the king's service, and [have] forsaken their master in his necessity; whereof some he blamed by name. And with this communication, the dinner being ended, they rose from the table, and went together into my lord's bedchamber, where they continued in consultation a certain season. And being there, it chanced Master Shelley, the judge, to come thither, sent from the king; whereof relation was made to my lord, which caused the duke and him to break up their communication; and the duke desired to go into some chamber to repose him for a season. And as he was coming out of my lord's chamber, he met with Master Shelley, to whom Master Shelley made relation of the cause of his coming, and desired the duke to tarry and to assist him in doing of his message; whom he denied and said, 'I have nothing to do with your message, wherein I will not meddle;' and so departed into a chamber, where he took his rest for an hour or two. And in the mean time my lord issued out of his chamber, and came to Master Shelley to know his message. Who declared unto him, after due salutation, that the king's pleasure was to have his house at Westminster, (then called York Place, belonging to the Bishoprick of York,) intending to make of that house a palace royal; and to possess the same according to the laws of this his grace's realm. His highness hath therefore sent for all the judges, and for all his learned counsel, to know their opinions in the assurance thereof; in whose determinations it was fully resolved, that your grace should recognise, before a judge, the right thereof to be in the king and his successors; and so his highness shall be assured thereof. Wherefore it hath pleased his majesty to appoint me by his commandment to come hither, to take of you this recognisance, who hath in you such affiance, that ye will not refuse so to do accordingly. Therefore I shall desire your grace to know your good will therein.' – 'Master Shelley,' quoth my lord, 'I know that the king of his own nature is of a royal stomach, and yet not willing more than justice shall lead him unto by the law. And therefore, I counsel you, and all other fathers of the law and learned men of his council, to put no more into his head than the law may stand with good conscience; for when ye tell him, this is the law, it were well done ye should tell him also, that, although *this* be the law, yet *this* is conscience; for law without conscience is not good to be given unto a king in counsel to use for a lawful rights but always to have a respect to conscience, before the rigour of the common law, for *laus est facere quod decet, non quod licet*.[22] The king ought of his royal dignity and prerogative to mitigate the rigour of the law, where conscience hath the most force; therefore, in his royal place of equal justice, he hath constitute a chancellor, an officer to execute justice with clemency, where conscience is opposed by the rigour of the law. And therefore the Court of Chancery hath been heretofore commonly called the Court of Conscience; because it hath jurisdiction to command the high ministers of the common law to spare execution and judgment, where conscience hath most effect. Therefore I say to you in this case, although you, and other of your profession, perceive by your learning that the king may, by an order of your laws, lawfully do that thing which ye demand of me; how say you, Master Shelley, may I do it with justice and conscience, to give that thing away from me and my successors which is none of mine? If this be law, with conscience, show me your opinion, I pray you.' 'Forsooth, my lord,' quoth he, 'there is some conscience in this case; but having regard to the king's high power, and to be employed to a better use and purpose, it may the better be suffered with conscience; who is sufficient to make recompense to the church of York with double the value.' 'That I know well' quoth my lord, 'but here is no such condition neither promised nor agreed, but only a bare and simple departure with another's right for ever. And if every bishop may do the like, then might every prelate give away the patrimony of their churches which is none of theirs; and so in process of time leave nothing for their successors to maintain their dignities, which, all things considered, should be but small to the king's honour. Sir, I do not intend to stand in terms with you in this matter, but let me see your commission.' To whom Master Shelley showed the same, and that seen, and perceived by him, said again thus: 'Master Shelley,' quoth he, 'ye shall make report to the king's highness, that I am his obedient subject, and faithful chaplain and beadman,²³ whose royal commandment and request I will in no wise disobey, but most gladly fulfil: and accomplish his princely will and pleasure in all things, and in especial in this matter, in as much as ye, the fathers of the laws, say that I may lawfully do it. Therefore I charge your conscience and discharge mine. Howbeit, I pray you, show his majesty from me, that I most humbly desire his highness to call to his most gracious remembrance, that there is both heaven and hell.' And therewith the clerk, was called, who wrote my lord's recognisance, and after some secret talk Master Shelley departed. Then rose my Lord of Norfolk from his repose, and after some communication with my lord he departed.

Thus continued my lord at Asher, who received daily messages from the court, whereof some were not so good as some were bad, but yet much more evil than good. For his enemies, perceiving the great affection that the king bare always towards him, devised a mean to disquiet and disturb his patience; thinking thereby to give him an occasion to fret and chafe, that death should rather ensue than increase of health or life, the which they most desired. They feared him more after his fall than they did before in his prosperity, doubting much his readoption into authority, by reason that the king's favour remained still towards him in such force, whereby they might rather be in danger of their estates, than in any assurance, for their cruelty ministered, by their malicious inventions, surmised and brought to pass against him.

Therefore they took this order among them in their matters, that daily they would send him something, or do something against him, wherein they thought that they might give him a cause of heaviness or lamentation. As some day they would cause the king to send for four or five of his gentlemen from him to serve the king: and some other day they would lay matters newly invented against him. Another day they would take from him some of his promotions; or of their promotions whom he [had] preferred before. Then would they fetch from him some of his yeomen; in so much as the king took into service sixteen of them at once, and at one time put them into his guard. This order of life he led continually; that there was no one day but, or ever he went to bed, he had an occasion greatly to chafe or fret the heart out of his belly, but that he was a wise man, and bare all their malice in patience.

At Christmas he fell sore sick, that he was likely to die. Whereof the king being advertised, was very sorry therefore, and sent Doctor Buttes, his grace's physician, unto him, to see in what estate he was. Doctor Buttes came unto him, and finding him very sick lying in his bed; and perceiving the danger he was in repaired again unto the king. Of whom the king demanded, saying, 'How doth yonder man, have you seen him?' 'Yea, sir,' quoth he. 'How do you like him?' quoth the king. 'Forsooth, sir,' quoth he, 'if you will have him dead, I warrant your grace he will be dead within these four days, if he receive no comfort from you shortly, and Mistress Anne.' 'Marry,' quoth the king, 'God forbid that he should die. I pray you, good Master Buttes, go again unto him, and do your cure upon him; for I would not lose him for twenty thousand pounds.' 'Then must your grace,' quoth Master Buttes, 'send him first some comfortable message, as shortly as is possible.' 'Even so will I,' quoth the king, 'by you. And therefore make speed to him again, and ye shall deliver him from me this ring for a token of our good will and favour towards him, (in the which ring was engraved the king's visage within a ruby, as lively counterfeit as was possible to be devised). This ring he knoweth very well; for he gave me the same; and tell him, that I am not offended with him in my heart nothing at all, and that shall he perceive, and God send him life, very shortly. Therefore bid him be of good cheer, and pluck up his heart, and take no despair. And I charge you come not from him, until ye have brought him out of all danger of death.' And then spake he to Mistress Anne, saying, 'Good sweetheart, I pray you at this my instance, as ye love us, to send the cardinal a token with comfortable words; and in so doing ye shall do us a loving pleasure.' She being not minded to disobey the king's earnest request, whatsoever she intended in her heart towards the cardinal; took incontinent her tablet of gold hanging at her girdle, and delivered it to Master Buttes, with very gentle and comfortable words and commendations to the cardinal. And thus Master Buttes departed, and made speedy return to Asher, to my Lord Cardinal; after whom the king sent Doctor Clement, Doctor Wotton, and Doctor Cromer the Scot, to consult and assist Master Buttes for my lord's health.

After that Master Buttes had been with my lord, and delivered the king's and Mistress Anne's tokens unto him, with the most comfortable words he could devise on their behalf, whereat he rejoiced not a little, advancing him a little in his bed, and received their tokens most joyfully, thanking Master Buttes for his comfortable news and pains. Master Buttes showed him furthermore, that the king's pleasure was, that he should minister unto him for his health: and to join with him for the better and most assured and brief ways, to be had for the same, hath sent Doctor Wotton, Doctor Clement, and Doctor Cromer, to join with him in counsel and ministration. 'Therefore, my lord,' quoth he, 'it were well done that they should be called in to visit your person and estate, wherein I would be glad to hear their opinions, trusting in Almighty God that, through his grace and assistance, we shall ease you of your pains, and rid you clean from your disease and infirmity. Wherewith my lord was well pleased and contented to hear their judgments; for indeed he trusted more to the Scottish doctor than he did to any of the other, because he was the very occasion that he inhabited here in England, and before he gave him partly his exhibition in Paris. Then when they were come into his chamber, and had talked with him, he took upon him to debate his disease learnedly among them, so that they might understand that he was seen in that art. After they had taken order for ministration, it was not long or they brought him out of all danger and fear of death; and within four days they set him on his feet, and got him a good stomach to his meat. This done, and he in a good estate of amendment, they took their leave to depart, to whom my lord offered his reward; the which they refused, saying, that the king gave them in special commandment, to take nothing of him for their pains and ministration; for at their return his highness said that he would reward them of his own costs: and thus with great thanks they departed from my lord, whom they left in good estate of recovery.

After this time my lord daily amended, and so continued still at Asher until Candlemas; against which feast, the king caused to be sent him three or four cart loads of stuff, and most part thereof was locked in great standards, (except beds and kitchen-stuff,) wherein was both plate and rich hangings, and chapel-stuff. Then my lord, being thus furnished, was therewith well contented; although they whom the king assigned did not deliver him so good, ne so rich stuff, as the king's pleasure was, yet was he joyous thereof, and rendered most humble thanks to the king, and to them that appointed the said stuff for him, saying to us his servants, at the opening of the same stuff in the standards, the which we thought, and said, might have been better appointed, if it had pleased them that appointed it: 'Nay, sirs,' quoth my lord to us, 'he that hath nothing is glad of somewhat, though it be never so little, and although it be not in comparison half so much and good as we had before, yet we rejoice more of this little than we did of the great abundance that we then had; and thank the king very much for the same, trusting after this to have much more. Therefore let us all rejoice, and be glad, that God and the king hath so graciously remembered to restore us to some things to maintain our estate like a noble person.'

Then commanded he master Cromwell, being with him, to make suit to the king's majesty, that he might remove thence to some other place, for he was weary of that house of Asher: for with continual use thereof the house waxed unsavoury; supposing that if he might remove from thence he should much sooner recover his health. And also the council had put into the king's head, that the new gallery at Asher, which my lord had late before his fall newly set up, should be very necessary for the king, to take down and set it up again at Westminster; which was done accordingly, and stands at this present day there. The taking away thereof before my lord's face was to him a corrosive, which was invented by his enemies only to torment him, the which indeed discouraged him very sore to tarry any longer there. Now Master Cromwell thought it but vain and much folly to move any of the king's council to assist and prefer his suit to the king, among whom rested the number of his mortal enemies, for they would rather hinder his removing, or else remove him farther from the king, than to have holpen him to any plaice nigh the king's common trade; wherefore he refused any suit to them, and made only suit to the king's own person; whose suit the king graciously heard, and thought it very convenient to be granted; and through the special motion of Master Cromwell, the king was well

contented that he should remove to Richmond, which place my lord had
a little before repaired to his great cost and charge; for the king had made
an exchange thereof with him for Hampton Court. All this his removing
was done without the knowledge of the king's council, for if they might
have had any intelligence thereof before, then would they have persuaded
the king to the contrary: but when they were advertised, of the king's grant
and pleasure, they dissimuled their countenances in the king's presence, for
they were greatly afraid of him, lest his nigh being, the king might at length
some one time resort to him, and so call him home again, considering the
great affection and love that the king daily showed towards him; wherefore
they doubted his rising again, if they found not a mean to remove him
shortly from, the king. In so much that they thought it convenient for
their purpose to inform the king upon certain considerations which they
invented, that it were very necessary that my lord should go down into
the North unto his benefice of York, where he should be a good stay for
the country; to the which the king, supposing that they had meant no less
than good faith, granted and condescended to their suggestions; which
were forced so with wonderful imagined considerations, that the king,
understanding nothing of their intent, was lightly persuaded to the same.
Whereupon the Duke of Norfolk commanded Master Cromwell, who had
daily access unto him, to say to my lord, that it is the king's pleasure that
he should with speed go to his benefice, where lieth his cure, and look to
that according to his duty. Master Cromwell at his next repair to my lord,
who lay then at Richmond, declared: unto him what my Lord of Norfolk
said, how it was determined that he should go to his benefice. 'Well then,
Thomas,' quoth my lord, 'seeing there is no other remedy, I do intend to
go to my benefice of Winchester, and I pray you, Thomas, so show my
Lord of Norfolk.' 'Contented, sir' quoth Master Cromwell, and according
to his commandment did so. To the which my Lord of Norfolk answered
and said, 'What will he do there?' 'Nay,' quoth he, 'let him go into his
province of York, whereof he hath received his honour, and there lieth the
spiritual burden and charge of his conscience, as he ought to do, and so
show him.' The lords, who were not all his friends, having intelligence of
his intent, thought to withdraw his appetite from Winchester, and would
in no wise permit him to plant himself so nigh the king: [they] moved
therefore the king to give my lord but a pension out of Winchester, and to
distribute all the rest among the nobility and other of his worthy servants;
and in likewise to do the same with the revenues of St Albans; and of
the revenues of his colleges in Oxford and Ipswich, the which the king
took into his own hands; whereof Master Cromwell had the receipt and
government before by my lord's assignment. In consideration thereof it was
thought most convenient that he should have so still. Notwithstanding, out
of the revenues of Winchester and St Albans the king gave to some one
nobleman three hundred marks, and to some a hundred pounds, and to
some more and to some less, according to the king's royal pleasure. Now
Master Cromwell executed his office, the which he had over the lands of
the college, so justly and exactly that he was had in great estimation for

his witty behaviour therein, and also for the true, faithful, and diligent service extended towards my lord his master.

It came at length so to pass that those to whom the king's majesty had given any annuities or fees for term of life by patent out of the forenamed revenues could not be good, but [only] during my lord's life, forasmuch as the king had no longer estate or title therein, which came to him by reason of my lord's attainder in the premunire; and to make their estates good and sufficient according to their patents, it was thought necessary to have my lord's confirmation unto their grants. And this to be brought about, there was no other mean but to make suit to Master Cromwell to obtain their confirmation at my lord's hands, whom they thought might best obtain the same.

Then began both noblemen and other who had any patents of the king, out either of Winchester or St Albans, to make earnest suit to Master Cromwell for to solicit their cases to my lord, to get of him his confirmations; and for his pains therein sustained, they promised every man, not only worthily to reward him, but also to show him such pleasures as should at all times lie in their several powers, whereof they assured him. Wherein Master Cromwell perceiving an occasion and a time given him to work for himself, and to bring the thing to pass which he long wished for; intended to work so in this matter, to serve their desires, that he might the sooner bring his own enterprise to purpose.

Then at his next resort to my lord, he moved him privily in this matter to have his counsel and his advice, and so by their witty heads it was devised that they should work together by one line, to bring by their policies Master Cromwell in place and estate, where he might do himself good and my lord much profit. Now began matters to work to bring Master Cromwell into estimation in such sort as was afterwards much to his increase of dignity; and thus every man, having an occasion to sue for my lord's confirmation, made now earnest travail to Master Cromwell for these purposes, who refused none to make promise that he would do his best in that case. And having a great occasion of access to the king for the disposition of divers lands, whereof he had the artier and governance; by means whereof, and by his witty demeanour, he grew continually into the king's favour, as ye shall hear after in this history. But first let us resort to the great business about the assurance of all these patents which the king hath given to divers noblemen and other of his servants, wherein Master Cromwell made a continuance of great suit to my lord for the same, that in process of time he served all their turns so that they had their purposes, and he their good wills. Thus rose his name and friendly acceptance with ail men. The fame of his honesty and wisdom sounded so in the king's ears that, by reason of his access to the king, he perceived to be in him no less wisdom than fame had made of him report, forasmuch as he had the government and receipts of those lands which I showed you before; and the conference that he had with the king therein enforced the king to repute him a very wise man, and a meet instrument to serve his grace, as it after came to pass.

Sir, now the lords thought long to remove my lord farther from the king, and out of his common trade; wherefore among other of the lords, my Lord of Norfolk said to Master Cromwell, 'Sir,' quoth he, 'me thinketh that the cardinal your master maketh no haste northward; show him, that if he go not away shortly, I will, rather than he should tarry still, tear him with my teeth. Therefore I would advise him to prepare him away as shortly as he can, or else he shall be sent forward.' These words Master Cromwell reported to my lord at his next repair unto him, who then had a just occasion to resort to him for the dispatch of the noblemen's and others' patents. And here I will leave of this matter, and show you of my lord's being at Richmond.

My lord, having license of the king to repair and remove to Richmond, made haste to prepare him thitherward; and so he came and lodged within the great park there, which was a very pretty house and a neat, lacking no necessary rooms that to so small a house was convenient and necessary; where was to the same a very proper garden garnished with divers pleasant walks and alleys: my lord continued in this lodge from the time that he came thither, shortly after Candlemas, until it was Lent, with a privy number of servants, because of the smallness of the house, and the rest of his family went to board wages.

I will tell you a certain tale by the way of communication. Sir, as my lord was accustomed towards night to walk in the garden there, to say his service, it was my chance then to wait upon him there; and standing still in an alley, whilst he in another walked with his chaplain, saying of his service; as I stood, I espied certain images of beasts counterfeit in timber, standing in a corner under the lodge wall, to the which I repaired to behold. Among whom I saw there a dun cow, whereon I mused most, because it seemed me to be the most lively entaylled among all the rest. My lord being, as I said, walking on the other side of the garden, perceived me, came suddenly upon me at my back, unawares, [and] said: 'What have you espied here, that you so attentively look upon?' 'Forsooth, if it please your grace,' quoth I. 'Where I do behold these entaylled images; the which I suppose were ordained for to be set up within some place about the king's palace: howbeit, sir, among them all, I have most considered the dun cow, [in] the which (as it seemeth me) the workman has most apertly showed his cunning.' 'Yea, marry, sir,' quoth my lord, 'upon this dun cow dependeth a certain prophecy, the which I will show you, for peradventure ye never heard, of it before. There is a saying,' quoth he, 'that

When this cow rideth the bull,
Then, priest, beware thy scull.

[Of] which prophecy neither my lord that declared it, ne I that heard it, understood the effect; although that even then it was a-working to be brought to pass. For this cow the king gave as one of his beasts appertaining of antiquity unto his earldom of Richmond, which was his ancient inheritance; this prophecy was after expounded in this wise. This dun cow, because it was the king's beast, betokened the king; and the bull betokened Mistress Anne Boleyn, which was after queen, because that her father, Sir Thomas Boleyn, gave the same beast in his cognisance. So that when the king had married her, the which was then unknown to my lord, or to any other at that time, then was this prophecy thought of all men to be fulfilled. For what a number of priests, both religious and secular, lost their heads for offending of such laws as were then made to bring this [marriage] to effect, is not unknown to all the world. Therefore it was judged of all men that this prophecy was then fulfilled when the king and she were joined in marriage. Now, how dark and obscure riddles and prophecies be, you may behold in this same: for before it was brought to pass there was not the wisest prophesier could perfectly discuss it, as it is now come to effect and purpose. Trust therefore, by mine advice, to no kind of dark riddles and prophecies, wherein ye may, as many have been, be deceived, and brought to destruction. And many times the imaginations and travailous business to avoid such dark and strange prophecies, hath been the very occasion to bring the same the sooner to effect and perfection. Therefore let men beware to divine or assure themselves to expound any such prophecies, for who so doeth shall first deceive themselves, and, secondly, bring many into error; the experience hath been lately experienced, the more pity. But if men will needs think themselves so wise, to be assured of such blind prophecies, and will work their wills therein, either in avoiding or in fulfilling the same, God send him well to speed, for he may as well, and much more sooner, take damage than avoid the danger thereof! Let prophecies alone, a God's name, apply your vocation, and commit the exposition of such dark riddles and obscure prophecies to God, that disposeth them as his divine pleasure shall see cause to alter and change all your enterpriser and imaginations to nothing, and deceive all your expectations, and cause you to repent your great folly, the which when ye feel the smart, will yourself confess the same to be both great folly and much more madness to trust in any such fantasies. Let God therefore dispose them, who governeth and punisheth according to man's deserts, and not to all men's judgments.

You have heard herebefore what words the Duke of Norfolk had to Master Cromwell touching my lord's going to the North to his benefice of York, at such time as Master Cromwell declared the same to my lord, to whom my lord answered in this wise: 'Marry, Thomas,' quoth he, 'then it is time to be going, if my Lord of Norfolk take it so. Therefore I pray you go to the king and move his highness in my behalf, and say that I would, with all my heart, go to my benefice at York, but for want of money; desiring his grace to assist me with some money towards my journey. For ye may say that the last money that I received of his majesty hath been too little to pay my debts, compelled by his counsel so to do; therefore to constrain me to the payment thereof, and his highness having all my goods, hath been too much extremity; wherein I trust his grace will have a charitable respect. Ye may say also to my Lord of Norfolk, and other of the council, that I would depart if I had money.' 'Sir,' quoth Master Cromwell, 'I will do my best.' And after other communication he departed again, and went to London.

My lord then in the beginning of Lent [removed] out of the Lodge into the Charterhouse of Richmond, where he lay in a lodging, which Doctor Collet, sometime Dean of Paul's had made for himself, until he removed

northward, which was in the Passion Week after; and he had to the same
house a secret gallery, which went out of his chamber into the Charterhouse
church, whither he resorted every day to their service; and at afternoons he
would sit in contemplation with one or other of the most ancient fathers of
that house in his cell, who among them by their counsel persuaded him from
the vain glory of this world, and gave him divers shirts of hair, the which he
often wore afterward, whereof I am certain. And thus he continued for the
time of his abode there in godly contemplation.

Now when Master Cromwell came to the court, he chanced to move my
Lord of Norfolk that my lord would gladly depart northward but for lack
of money, wherein he desired his assistance to the king. Then went they
both jointly to the king, to whom my Lord of Norfolk declared how my
lord would gladly depart northward, if he wanted not money to bring him
thither; the king thereupon referred the assignment thereof to the council,
whereupon they were in divers opinions. Some said he should have none,
for he had sufficient of late delivered him; some would he should have
sufficient and enough; and some contrariwise would he should have but
a small sum; and some thought it much against the council's honour; and
much more against the king's high dignity to see him want the maintenance
of his estate which the king had given him in this realm; and [who] also
hath been in such estimation with the king, and in great authority under
him; it should be rather a great slander in foreign realms to the king and his
whole council, to see him want that lately had so much, and now so little.
'Therefore, rather than he should lack,' quoth one among them, '(although
he never did me good or any pleasure), yet would I lay my plate to gage
for him for a thousand pounds, rather than he should depart so simply as
some would have him for to do. Let us do to him as we would be done
unto; considering his small offence, and his inestimable substance that he
only hath departed withal the same, for satisfying of the king's pleasure,
rather than he would stand in defence with the king in defending of his
case, as he might justly have done, as ye all know. Let not malice cloak this
matter whereby that justice and mercy may take no place; ye have all your
pleasures fulfilled which ye have long desired, and now suffer conscience to
minister unto him some liberality; the day may come that some of us may
be in the same case, ye have such alterations in persons, as well assured
as ye suppose yourselves to be, and to stand upon as sure a ground, and
what hangeth over our heads we know not; I can say no more: now do as
ye list. Then after all this they began again to consult in this matter, and
after long debating and reasoning about the same, it was concluded, that
he should have by the way of prest, a thousand marks out of Winchester
Bishoprick, beforehand of his pension, which the king had granted him out
of the same, for the king had resumed the whole revenues of the Bishoprick
of Winchester into his own hands; yet the king out of the same had granted
divers great pensions unto divers noblemen and unto other of his council; so
that I do suppose, all things accompted, his part was the least. So that, when
this determination was fully concluded, they declared the same to the king,
who straightway [commanded] the said thousand marks to be delivered

out of hand to Master Cromwell; and so it was. The king, calling Master Cromwell to him secretly, bade him to resort to him again when he had received the said sum of money. And according to the same commandment he repaired again to the king; to whom the king said: 'Show my lord your master, although our council hath not assigned any sufficient sum of money to bear his charges, yet ye shall show him in my behalf, that I will send him a thousand pound, of my benevolence; and tell him that he shall not lack, and bid him be of good cheer.' Master Cromwell upon his knees most humbly thanked the king on my lord's behalf, for his great benevolence and noble heart towards my lord: 'those comfortable words of your grace,' quoth he, 'shall rejoice him more than three times the value of your noble reward.' And therewith departed from the king and came to my lord directly to Richmond; to whom he delivered the money, and showed him all the arguments in the council, which ye have heard before, with the progress of the same; and of what money it was, and whereof it was levied, which the council sent him; and of the money which the king sent him, and of his comfortable words; whereof my lord rejoiced not a little, and [was] greatly comforted. And after the receipt of this money my lord consulted with Master Cromwell about his departure, and of his journey, with the order thereof.

Then my lord prepared all things with speed for his journey into the North, and sent to London for livery clothes for his servants that should ride with him thither. Some he refused, such as he thought were not meet to serve; and some again of their own mind desired him of his favour to tarry still here in the south, being very loath to abandon their native country, their parents, wives, and children, [whom] he most gladly licensed with good will and favour, and rendered unto them his hearty thanks for their painful service and long tarriance with him in his troublesome decay and overthrow. So that now all things being furnishied towards this journey, he took the same in the beginning of the Passion Week, before Easter; and so rode to a place, then the abbot's of Westminster, called Hendon; and the next day he removed to a place called the Rye; where my Lady Parrey lay; the next day he rode to Royston, and lodged in the monastery there; and the next he removed to Huntingdon, and there lodged in the Abbey; and from thence he removed to Peterborough, and there lodged also within the Abbey, being then Palm Sunday, where he made his abode until the Thursday in Easter week, with all his train; whereof the most part went to board wages in the town, having twelve carts to carry his stuff of his own, which came from his college in Oxford, where he had three score carts to carry such necessaries as belonged to his buildings there. Upon Palm Sunday he went in procession, with the monks, bearing his palm; setting forth God's service right honourably, with such singing men as he then had remaining with him. And upon Maundy Thursday he made his Maundy in our Lady's Chapel, having fifty-nine poor men, whose feet he washed, wiped, and kissed; each of these poor men had twelve pence in money, three ells of canvass to make them shirts, a pair of new shoes, a cast of bread, three red herrings, and three white herrings, and the odd person had two shillings. Upon Easter Day in the morning he rode to the resurrection, and that day he went in procession in his cardinal's vesture, with his hat and hood on his head, and he himself sang there the high mass very devoutly; and granted clean remission to all the hearers; and there continued [he] all the holidays.

My lord continuing at Peterborough after this manner, intending to remove from thence, sent me to Sir William Fitzwilliams, a knight, which dwelt within three or four miles of Peterborough, to provide him there a lodging until Monday next following, on his journey northward. And being with him, to whom I declared my lord's request, and he being thereof very glad, rejoiced not a little that it would please my lord to visit his house in his way; saying, that he should be most heartiest welcome of any man alive, the king's majesty excepted; and that he should not need to discharge the carriage of any of his stuff for his own use during the time of his being there; but have all things furnished ready against his coming to occupy, his own bed excepted. Thus upon my report made to my lord at my return, he rejoiced of my message, commanding me therein to give warning to all his officers and servants to prepare themselves to remove from Peterborough upon Thursday next. Then every man made all things in such readiness as was convenient, paying in the town for all things as they had taken of any person for their own use, for which cause my lord caused a proclamation to be made in the town, that if any person or persons in the town or country there were offended or grieved against any of my lord's servants, that they should resort to my lord's officers, of whom they should have redress, and truly answered as the case justly required. So that, all things being furnished, my lord took his journey from Peterborough upon the Thursday in Easter week, to Master Fitzwilliams, where he was joyously received, and had right worthy and honourable entertainment at the only charge and expense of the said Master Fitzwilliams, all [the] time of his being there.

The occasion that moved Master Fitzwilliams thus to rejoice of my lord's being in his house was, that he sometime being a merchant of London and sheriff there, fell in debate with the city of London upon a grudge between the aldermen of the bench and him, upon a new corporation that he would erect of a new mystery called Merchant Taylors, contrary to the opinion of divers of the bench of aldermen of the city, which caused him to give and surrender his cloak, and departed from London, and inhabited within the country; and against the malice of all the said aldermen and other rulers in the commonweal of the city, my lord defended him, and retained him into service, whom he made first his treasurer of his house, and then after his high chamberlain; and in conclusion, for his wisdom, gravity, port, and eloquence, being a gentleman of a comely stature, made him one of the king' counsel: and [he] so continued all his life afterward. Therefore in consideration of all these gratitudes received at my lord's hands, as well in his trouble as in his preferment, was most gladest like a faithful friend of good remembrance to requite him with the semblable gratuity, and right joyous that he had any occasion to minister some pleasure, such as lay then in his power to do.

Thus my lord continued there until the Monday next; where lacked no good cheer of costly viands, both of wine and other goodly entertainment;

so that upon the said Monday my lord departed from thence unto Stamford; where he lay all that night. And the next day he removed from thence unto Grantham, and wais lodged in a gentleman's house, called Master Hall. And the next day he rode to Newark, and lodged in the castle all that night; the next day he rode to Southwell, a place of my lord's within three or four miles of Newark, where he intended to continue all that summer, as he did after.

Here I must declare to you a notable tale of communication which was done at Master FitzWilliams before his departure from thence, between [my lord] and me, the which was this: Sir, my lord being in the garden at Master FitzWilliams, walking, saying of his evensong with his chaplain, I being there giving attendance upon him, his evensong finished, [he] commanded his chaplain that bare up the train of his gown whilst he walked, to deliver me the same, and to go aside when he had done; and after the chaplain was gone a good distance, he said unto me in this wise, 'Ye have been late at London,' quoth he; 'Forsooth, my lord,' quoth I, 'not since that I was there to buy your liveries for your servants.' 'And what news was there then,' quoth he; 'heard you no communication there of me? I pray you tell me.' Then perceiving that I had a good occasion to talk my mind plainly unto him, [I] said, 'Sir, if it please your grace, it was my chance to be at a dinner in a certain place within the city, where I, among divers other honest and worshipful gentlemen happed to sit, which were for the most part of my old familiar acquaintance, wherefore they were the more bolder to enter in communication with me, understanding that I was still your grace's servant; [they] asked me a question, which I could not well assoil them.' 'What was that?' quoth my lord, 'Forsooth, sir,' quoth I, 'first they asked me how ye did, and how ye accepted your adversity, and trouble, and the loss of your goods; to the which I answered, that you were in health (thanks be to God), and took all things in good part; and so it seemed me, that they were all your indifferent friends lamenting your decay, and loss of your room and goods, doubting much that the sequel thereof could not be good in the commonwealth. For often changing of such officers which be fat fed, into the hands of such as be lean and hungry for riches, [they] will sure travail by all means to get abundance, and so the poor commons be pillaged and extorted for greedy lucre of riches and treasure: they said that ye were full fed, and intended now much to the advancement of the king's honour and the commonwealth. Also they marvelled much that ye, being of so excellent a wit and high discretion, would so simply confess yourself guilty in the premunire, wherein ye might full well have stood in the trial of your case. For they understood, by the report of some of the king's learned counsel, that your case well considered, ye had great wrong: to the which I could make, as me thought, no sufficient answer, but said, 'That I doubt not your so doing was upon some greater consideration than my wit could understand.' 'Is this,' quoth he, 'the opinion of wise men?' 'Yea, forsooth, my lord,' quoth I, 'and almost of all other men.' 'Well, then,' quoth he, 'I see that their wisdoms perceive not the ground of the matter that moved me so to do. For I considered, that my enemies had brought the matter so to pass against me, and conveyed it so, that they made it the king's case, and caused the king to take the matter into his own hands and quarrel, and after that he had upon the occasion thereof seized all my goods and possessions into his demayns, and then the quarrel to be his, rather than yield, or take a foil in the law, and thereby restore to me all my goods again, he would sooner (by the procurement of my enemies and evil willers) imagine my utter undoing and destruction; whereof the most ease therein had been for me perpetual imprisonment. And rather than I would jeopard so far, or put my life in any such hazard, yet had I most liefest to yield and confess the matter, committing the sole sum thereof, as I did, unto the king's clemency and mercy, and live at large, like a poor vicar, than to lie in prison with all the goods and honours that I had. And therefore it was the most best way for me, all things considered, to do as I have done, than to stand in trial with the king, for he would have been loath to have been noted a wrong doer, and in my submission, the king, I doubt not, had a great remorse of conscience, wherein he would rather pity me than malign me. And also there was a continual serpentine enemy about the king that would, I am well assured, if I had been found stiff necked, [have] called continually upon the king in his ear (I mean the night-crow[24]) with such a vehemency that I should with the help of her assistance [have] obtained sooner the king's indignation than his lawful favour: and his favour once lost (which I trust at this present I have) would never have been by me recovered. Therefore I thought it better for me to keep still his loving favour, with loss of my goods and dignities, than to win my goods and substance with the loss of his love and princely favour, which is but only death: *Quia indignatio principis mors est.*[25] And this was the special ground and cause that I yielded myself guilty in the premunire; which I perceive all men knew not, wherein since I understand the king hath conceived a certain prick of conscience; who took to himself the matter more grievous in his secret stomach than all men knew, for he knew whether I did offend him therein so grievously as it was made or no, to whose conscience I do commit my cause, truth, and equity.' And thus we left the substance of all this communication; although we had much more talk: yet is this sufficient to cause you to understand as well the cause of his confession in his offence, as also the cause of the loss of all his goods and treasure.

## Anne Boleyn to Stephen Gardiner, 4 April 1529[26]

*The letter below is a rare survival written by Anne from the period of the divorce. It demonstrates the close personal interest that Anne took in Henry's attempts to persuade the Pope to annul his marriage to Catherine of Aragon. Gardiner was sent to the Pope as one of Henry's ambassadors on more than one occasion, but he, along with his colleagues, was never able to persuade Clement VII to accede to the King's request.*

*Gardiner's previous mission to Italy, with Edward Foxe, had proved to be disappointing to Anne, as she herself makes clear in her letter. The pair had visited the Pope at Orvieto and received his confirmation that he would satisfy the King as far as he was able. On hearing this, Foxe had rushed back to England, sailing from Calais in April 1528. When he arrived at the court at Greenwich Henry commanded him to go straight to Anne's chamber.*

*The couple were pleased to hear the news, which led, in June 1528, to the Pope agreeing to send Cardinal Campeggio to England to hear the divorce case.*[27]

*The letter set out below relates to a later mission to Italy and demonstrates that Anne had still not entirely given up hope of the Pope resolving matters in her favour.*

Master Stephen.

I thank you for my letter, wherein I perceive the willing and faithful mind you have to do me pleasure, not doubting but as much as it is possible for man's wit to imagine, you will do. I pray God to send you well to speed in all your matters, so that you will put me in a study how to reward your service. I do trust in God you shall not repent it, and that the end of this journey shall be more pleasant to me than your first, for that was but a rejoicing hope, which ceasing, the lack of it does put to the more pain, and they that are partakers with me, as you do know. Therefore do I trust that this hard beginning shall make the better ending.

Master Stephen, I send you here the cramp-rings for you, and Master Gregory, and Master Peter; pray you to distribute them both, as she, that (you may assure them) will be glad to do them any pleasure which shall be in my power. And thus I make an end, praying God send you good health. Written at Greenwich the 4th day of April,

By your assured friend,

Anne Boleyn

## Cardinal du Bellay's Account of the Sweating Sickness in 1528[28]

*Summer 1528 saw an outbreak of the dreaded sweating sickness in England. The illness, which may have been a type of Influenza, plagued Tudor England and was notable for the speed with which it could kill an otherwise young and healthy victim. The French ambassador, Cardinal du Bellay, provided an account of the sweating sickness which is contained in his letters below. As the Cardinal relates, Anne herself succumbed to the sickness that summer, while she was at Hever. For Henry, who always feared disease, his love for Anne was not enough to overcome his terror, and he fled from her, keeping regularly updated about her condition while he remained a safe distance away. Henry's own letters to Anne Boleyn do, however, demonstrate how anxious he was for news of her.*

*Cardinal du Bellay to ?, 18 June 1528*

One of the filles de chambre of Mademoiselle de Boulen was attacked on Tuesday by the sweating sickness. The king left in great haste, and went a dozen miles off; but it is denied that the lady Anne Boleyn was sent away, as suspected, to her brother the viscount, who is in Cainet [Kent]. This disease, which broke out here four days ago, is the easiest in the world to die of. You have a slight pain in the head and at the heart; all at once you begin to sweat. There is no need for a physician; for if you uncover yourself the least in the world, or cover yourself a little too much, you are taken off without languishing, as those dreadful fevers make you do. But it is no great thing, for during the time specified about two thousand only have been attacked by it in London. Yesterday, having gone to swear the truce, they might be seen as thick as flies hurrying out of the streets and the shops into the houses, to take the sweat the instant they were seized by the distemper. I found the ambassador of Milan leaving his quarters in great haste, because two or three had been attacked by it. If, monsieur, all the ambassadors must have their share of it, in my case, at least, you will not have gained your cause, for you will not be able to boast that you have starved me to death; and moreover, the king will have gained nine months of my service, which will not have cost him any thing. By the God of Paradise, if this sickness or fever call to see me, and I must take a sweat against the grain, I shall not feel so much regret about it as those who are better off than I am; but may God keep them so! But to return to London – I assure you that the priests there have a better time of it than the physicians, except that there is not enough of them to bury the dead. If the thing lasts, corn will soon be cheap. Twelve years ago, when the same thing happened, ten thousand persons died in ten or twelve days, it is said: but it was not so sharp as it is now beginning to be. M. the legate [Wolsey] had come for the term; but he soon had his horses saddled again, and there will be neither assignation nor term. Every body is terribly alarmed.

*Cardinal du Bellay, 30 June 1528*
The lady[29] is still at her father's. The king keeps changing his abode on account of this disorder: a good many of his servants have died of it within these two or three days. Of those whom you know, only Poowith, Careu, and Couton, are dead; but Fitzwilliam, my lord William, Brown, Bryant, who is at present of the bedchamber, Norris, Wallop, Chesney, Kingston, Paget, and generally all those of the bedchamber except one, have been attacked, or are now ill. It was said yesterday, that some more of them were at the point of death: I know not if they will escape. The king is left all alone, keeping himself close. At the legate's they are playing the same game; but when all is said, those who do not expose themselves to the air rarely die; so that out of more than forty-five thousand who have been attacked in London, not two thousand have died, whatever people may say. It is true, that if you merely put your hand out of bed during the twenty-four hours, you instantly become stiff as a peacock.

P.S. Since writing my letters, I have been informed that a brother of the Earl of Derby's, and a son-in-law of the Duke of Norfolk's, have died suddenly at M. the legate's, who slipped out at the backdoor with a few servants, and would not let any body know whither he was going, that he might not be followed. The king at last stopped about twenty miles hence, at a house which M. the legate has had built, because he sees that it is of no avail to change his residence; and I have it from good authority that he has made his will, and taken the sacraments, for fear of sudden seizure. Nothing ails him, thank God! and if he should be attacked by this sickness, which

God forbid! I do not see that there would be any danger; only he must take good care of himself.

*Cardinal du Bellay, 21 July 1528*
As to the danger which is in this country, it begins to diminish hereabouts, but increases in parts where it had not been. In Kent it is rife at this moment. Mademoiselle de Boulen and her father have had the disease, but they have got over it. The day that I had it at M. de Canterbury's eighteen died of it in four hours; scarcely any escaped that day but myself, and I am not yet stout. The king has removed further than he was, and hopes that he shall not have the complaint. Still he keeps upon his guard, confesses every day, receives the sacrament on all holydays; and likewise the queen, who is with him. M. the legate does the same. The notaries have a fine time of it here; I believe there have been made a hundred-thousand wills off-hand, because those who died all went mad the instant the disorder became severe. The astrologers say that this will turn to the plague, but I think they rave.

## John Gough's Printed Account of Henry and Anne's Journey to France in 1532[30]

*Henry VIII first met his rival monarch, Francis I of France, at the Field of the Cloth of Gold in 1520, which Anne probably attended. The meeting was remarkable for its splendour, with both Henry's first wife, Catherine of Aragon, and Francis' wife, Claude, appearing splendidly dressed and attended by vast retinues of ladies.[31] On more than one occasion, the two kings left their own camps to dine with their counterpart's queen.*

*By late 1532, Henry had entirely alienated the Emperor Charles V, due to his treatment of Catherine of Aragon. He therefore sought to establish better relations with Francis, the only potential rival to the Emperor's power in Europe. This was a policy that pleased the Francophile Anne and she fully supported Henry's decision to organise a meeting in France. On 1 September 1532, Henry created her Marquis of Pembroke in her own right, to ensure that she had sufficient status for the visit. Unfortunately, however, what was undoubtedly intended to be Anne's Field of the Cloth of Gold, failed to live up to the splendour of its predecessor. Francis, who was then married to Charles V's sister, Eleanor, could supply no lady of sufficient rank who was willing to meet with Anne and she was forced to attend in an unofficial capacity.*

*The account set out below was the official account, published by Henry's printer, Wynkyn de Worde. It was expressly printed 'under the grace and privilege of our most royal and redoubted prince, King Henry the VIIIth, for John Gough dwelling at Paul's gate in Cheap'. The account is journalistic in nature and is, in effect, a press release, giving the official account of the meeting. It is of interest in the account it gives of Anne's participation in the masque and the fact that her presence was publicly announced. It provides a useful counterbalance to the reports of Eustace Chapuys, the Imperial ambassador, on Anne's role in the preparations for the meeting (see below).*

I will certify you of our news in the parts of Calais.

First, the 11th day of October [1532], which was Friday; in the morning at five o'clock, the King's Grace took his ship called the *Swallow*: and so came to Calais by ten o'clock.

And there he was received with procession, and with the Mayor and the Lord Deputy, and all the spears [knights] and the soldiers in array; with a great peal of guns: and lay in Calais till the Sunday se'nnight after [the 20th of October].

And on the 16th day of October, my lord of Norfolk, accompanied with my lord of Derby and a great number of gentlemen besides, met with the Great Master of France six miles from Calais at the 'English Pale': the said Great Master having two great lords in his company of their order, and a hundred gentlemen attending upon them. And there my lord of Norfolk and the Great Master devised the place where the two kings should meet: which was at Sandingfield. And that so done; they went both to Calais with their companies.

And the said Great Master, with divers other strangers, dined that day with the King: and after dinner, my lord of Norfolk brought them forth of their way a mile or two; and so departed for that time.

And on the Monday, the 21st day of October, the King of England took his way to meet with the French King at the place before appointed, with seven score [gentlemen] all in velvet coats afore him, lords and knights; and forty of his guard, and others to the number, as we think, of six hundred horse, and as well horsed as ever was seen.

And the King, our Master, met with the French King at Sandingfield, within the English Pale three miles. There the French King tarried for our Master the space of an hour or two: the French King being accompanied with the King of Navarre, the Cardinal de Lorraine, the Duke de Vendome; with divers others noblemen well and richly appointed, being of like number as our King was of, that is to say, six hundred persons.

There was the lovingest meeting that ever was seen; for the one embraced the other five or six times on horseback; and so did the lords on either party each to other: and so did ride hand in hand with great love the space of a mile.

At the meeting of these two noble Kings, there were [English] sakers and sakrets cast off: and at divers flights [of shot], two kites were beaten down, which were soaring in the air, with such like pastime, which greatly pleased all the nobles of both parties. And then they did light off their horses, and drank each to other. The French King drank first to our King: and when they had drunk they embraced each other again with great love; and so rode towards Boulogne, our King on the right hand.

And when they came within a mile of Boulogne, there met with the Kings, the Dauphin, being accompanied with his two brethren the Duke d'Orleans and the Duke d'Angouleme; very goodly children; and attending on them, four Cardinals; with a thousand horse, very well beseen.

And when they came near the town, the French King caused our Master to tarry, while the gunshot was shot; which was heard twenty English miles from Boulogne: and so entered the town.

Where stood the Captain with the soldiers in good order. And above them stood a hundred Switzers of the French King's Guard, in their doublets and their hose of yellow velvet cut, goodly persons; and above them, stood two hundred more of the French King's Guard, Scots and Frenchmen, in coats of yellow, blue, and crimson velvet, bearing halberts m their hands; and above them stood two hundred gentlemen, being in their gowns well and richly beseen, every man having a battle axe in his hand, and their captains standing by them.

And so they tarried in Boulogne; Monday, Tuesday, Wednesday, and Thursday all day.

The Tuesday, being the second day of this their being there, the French King gave our King rich apparel wrought with needle work purled [fringed] with gold; in the which like apparel both the Kings went to our Lady's Church at Boulogne. At that time, our King obtained release and liberty from the French King, for all prisoners at that time prisoners in Boulogne. And in like wise, did the French King in Calais of our King and Master at his being there; and obtained grace for all banished men that would make suit for their pardon. And to esteem the rich traverses [low curtains] that were in our Lady's Church in Boulogne, and in our Lady's Church in Calais likewise, for both the Kings; and rich ordinances and provision for the same: it is too much to write!

And as for the great cheer that was there, no man can express it. For the King's Grace was there entertained all at the French King's cost and charges. And every day noblemen of France desired our nobles and gentlemen home to their lodgings: where they found their houses richly hanged [with tapestry], great cupboards of plate, sumptuous fare, with singing and playing of all kinds of music. And also there was sent unto our lodgings great fare with all manner of wines for our servants; and our horses' meat was paid for: and all at their charges.

And every day the French king had at dinner and supper with him certain noblemen of England: and the King's Grace had in like wise certain of their nobles at dinner and supper; during the time of their being at Boulogne. And this continued with as great cheer and familiarity as might be. And as concerning ladies and gentlewomen, there were none.

And on the Friday following, the Kings came towards Calais. And the Dauphin, with the Cardinals and all their gentlemen, brought the Kings unto the place where they first met them; and then departed. The French King had great carriage [baggage]; for there came more than three hundred mules laden with stuff.

And so coming towards Calais, the Duke of Richmond,[32] accompanied with Bishops, and many other noblemen that were not with the King at Boulogne; and all the King's Guard, which were with all others marvellously well horsed and trimmed; they stood in a place appointed, in array and good order in the way, two miles out of Calais where the French King should come: who saluted the French King with great honour, in like manner as the King our Master was saluted at Boulogne, with amicable and goodly salutations as ever were seen. They were saluted with great melody; what with guns, and all other instruments: and the order of the town, it was a heavenly sight for the time!

First at Newnam Bridge, 400 shot; at the Block House, 30 shot; at Risbank Tower [in Calais harbour] 300 shot; within the town of Calais 2,000 shot, great and small; besides the ships. It was all numbered at 3,000 shot. And at Boulogne, by estimation, it passed not 200 shot; but they were great pieces [cannon].

Also for the order of the town there was set all serving men on the one side, in tawny coats; and soldiers on the other side, all in coats of red and blue, with halberts in their hands.

And so the Kings came riding in the midst: and so the French King went to Staple Hall; which is a princely house.

And upon Saturday, both the Kings rode to our Lady's Church to mass; and in the afternoon both their councils sat together.

And upon Sunday, both the Kings heard mass in their lodgings. And at afternoon, the King of England rode to Staple Hall to the French King; and there was both bear-baiting and bull-baiting till night.

And at night, the French King supped with our King, and there was great banqueting.

After supper, there came in a Masque, my Lady Marquess of Pembroke [i.e., Anne Boleyn], my Lady Mary [Boleyn], my lady Derby, my lady Fitz-Walter, my lady Rochford, my lady L'Isle, and my lady Wallop, gorgeously apparelled, with visors on their faces: and so came and took the French King, and other lords of France, by the hand; and danced a dance or two.

After that, the King took off their visors; and then they danced with gentlemen of France an hour after: and then they departed to their lodgings.

As for the apparel of the French lords, my tongue cannot express it, and especially the French King's apparel passeth my pen to write ; for he had a doublet set over all with stones and rich diamonds, which was valued by discreet men at a £100,000. They far passed our lords and knights in apparel and richesse.

They had great cheer in Calais, and loving also; and all at our King's costs and charges.

Also the same day that the Kings came from Boulogne, the French King made the Duke of Norfolk, and the Duke of Suffolk, of the Order of Saint Michael. And upon Monday, which was the 29th day of October, at Calais; our King made the Great Maister of France and the Admiral of France, Knights of the Garter.

And that day, there was a great wrestling between Englishmen and Frenchmen, before both the Kings. The French King had none but priests that wrestled, which were big men and strong (they were brethren); but they had most falls.

As concerning the abundance and liberal multitude of gifts that were so lovingly and cordially given on both parties (to the great honour of both the Kings) my pen or capacity cannot express it; as well among the great lords as with the lowest yeoman that bare any office in either King's house;

and specially the King's gifts, on both parties, always rewarded the one like unto the other.

And all other gifts were nothing but rich plate, and gold coin – silver was of no estimation – besides raiments, horses, geldings, falcons, bears, dogs for the game: with many other, which were too much to write.

And upon the 29th day of October, the French King departed from Calais to Paris ward: and our King brought him as far as Morgyson, which is from Calais, seven miles; and so came to Calais again.

And he purposeth, God willing, to be at Canterbury the 8th day of November, and so home. Whom God, of His goodness, ever preserve! and send good passage, and safe again into England. Amen.

## The Despatches of Eustace Chapuys Relating to the Divorce of Catherine of Aragon[33]

*With the exception of Anne's own letters and the love letters of Henry VIII, Eustace Chapuys provides the most interesting source material for Anne.*

*Eustace Chapuys (1489–1556), a lawyer from Savoy, was appointed to serve as Imperial ambassador to England from September 1529, remaining, for the most part, at his post until 1545. By the time of his arrival, Henry's attempts to divorce Catherine of Aragon had been ongoing for over two years. Chapuys was appointed by Charles V to act, effectively, as Catherine's chief advisor, and the ambassador immediately made contact with the Queen and formed a relationship of friendship with Catherine. He also developed a personal relationship with her daughter, Princess Mary. The two women relied heavily on his advice. He was fond of them and identified strongly with their cause. For example, Chapuys rushed to Catherine when he heard that she was dying, something that was a great comfort to her. He also frequently tried to persuade the Emperor to arrange a marriage for Mary in the hope that it would rescue her from her difficult situation in England.*

*Due to his close proximity to Catherine and Mary and his relationship with them, Chapuys threw himself fully behind their cause. In a number of his despatches he went so far as to urge the Emperor to invade England on their behalf. He hated Anne, whom he never referred to as queen, always calling her 'the Concubine', 'the Lady', 'the King's Mistress' or, at best, 'La Bolaing'. He was fascinated by her actions and watched her intensely, seeking out gossip that would portray her in an unflattering light. Chapuys believed that Anne murdered Catherine of Aragon with poison and that she intended to dispose of Mary in the same way. In spite of this, his desptaches make it clear that he believed that she was innocent of the crimes for which she was condemned to death. Given Chapuys' hatred of Anne, this is important evidence as to the way Anne's innocence was perceived.*

*There is no doubt that Chapuys' accounts are hostile to Anne. He sought out the worst he could in her and recorded none of the good. Without his accounts however, much of the detail of Anne's life would be lost. Much of what Chapuys recorded is likely to be accurate. For example, Anne's seizure of Catherine's barge, which caused something of an international incident, probably occurred as described. Anne's fiery temper also sounds plausible,*

as do her actions in regard to Princess Mary, who she viewed as a rival to
her own child.

Chapuys wrote regular long despatches to Charles V throughout his tenure
as ambassador, often writing in cipher. He wrote in French and these were
translated and abridged in the nineteenth century for the publication of the
Calendar of State Papers, Spanish series. The volume of the correspondence
would make it impossible to print in full in one volume. The selection below,
and in later parts of the book, focuses on Anne, Catherine and the divorce.
References to foreign affairs, such as Charles V's wars in Italy and against
the Turks, have been removed, as have other details that are not essential to
the study of Anne Boleyn.

### Eustace Chapuys to the Emperor, 4 September 1529

As I informed Your Imperial Majesty in my despatch of the 1st inst., the
dukes of Suffolk and Norfolk, and Milord Rochefort, the father of the Lady
Anne Boleyn, are the King's most favourite courtiers, and the nearest to his
person. Now that the Cardinal is absent from Court it is they who transact
all state business. It is entirely in their power, as people generally say, to
remain in office, and if the said Lady Anne chooses, the Cardinal will be
soon dismissed, and his affair settled; for she happens to be the person in
all this kingdom who hates him most, and has spoken and acted the most
openly against him. I cannot say what will be the upshot of all this, certain
it is that from this moment the affairs of the said Cardinal are beginning
to take a very bad turn. Formerly no one dared say a word against him,
but now the tables are turned, and his name is in everybody's mouth, and
what is still worse for him, libellous writings, I am told, are being circulated
about him ...

The King's affection for La Bolaing (Boleyn) increases daily. It is so great
just now that it can hardly be greater; such is the intimacy and familiarity
in which they live at present. May God remedy it all!

### Chapuys to the Emperor, 21 September 1529[34]

... The day before the Exaltation of the Cross we started from London, and
arrived the same evening at a place three miles distant from where the King
was supposed to be. Lodgings had there been prepared for us for the night,
the King residing then at a manor so small and confined that half the servants
of his household in ordinary had to lodge elsewhere. The day afterwards,
however, orders came for the Doctor [Hennege] and me to appear before
him at 11 o'clock, We reached the place at nine in the morning, and were
received at the gate by Mr Rosselz (Sir John Russell), comptroller of the
royal household who had orders to entertain us at his rooms until the King
should come out of church. Mass over, the King came, entered the audience
hall, and sent for us. As soon as he saw me from the very end of the hall,
a very spacious and long one, where he was conversing apart with some of
his Privy Councillors, he came forward and sat in the middle of it in an arm
chair, which had been prepared for him, and under a small canopy. The King,
at my approach, rose from his seat, advanced three or four paces to meet me,

and bade me most graciously to come nearer. I did not enter at once into the matter of my commission, as I thought it better to thank him first for sending his secretary to me, and for the offers made in his name. I explained again in as few words as possible my reasons for desiring that the audience should be private instead of public, and repeated almost the same words I had said to Dr Guenich (Hennege). This I did on purpose, that he might listen with greater attention to what I had to say, as did happen. For having presented Your Majesty's letter he took it in his hand, but did not attempt to open it at the time, believing it, no doubt, to be a mere credential. I then began to expound my commission without omitting any part of my instructions, adding from time to time some little remark of my own, which I considered fit for the purpose. The King, meanwhile, listened with much attention, with open mien and smiling countenance. My address at an end, the King began by welcoming me to his kingdom, and saying: 'I could really have wished that the person I sent to visit you had been more suitable; I would have chosen a better one had I had one at hand. I am very glad and happy to see that since God has been pleased to make peace between the Emperor and myself the charge of cementing and preserving that very peace has devolved upon a man of your parts, so wise and so well inclined, for if my own information and that communicated by my ambassadors be correct, I have not the least doubt that you will do your best to preserve the friendship and alliance between your master and myself. The discretion or indiscretion of ambassadors is often the cause of the enmities and quarrels of princes as it is also the cause of their friendships and alliances. As to me, the Emperor will always find me at my post as in past times, and certainly he must own that my friendship has hitherto been of some use to him. Respecting the principal point of your commission (this he said in a low tone of voice, and as graciously as before), I must candidly tell you that I do not see what reason the Emperor has for refusing to send me the brief of dispensation for the marriage between the Queen and myself,[35] when both of us conjointly have applied for it. One might say that great injury had been done to both parties by such refusal, for the Emperor must know that a Papal brief addressed to me and to the Queen, is our joint property, belongs exclusively to us, and ought to be in our hands, not in those of people whom it does not concern. In case of the Emperor claiming to have an interest in the affair, a faithful transcript might have been sufficient instead of retaining the original itself.' The King then went on reproducing the very same arguments once made by his own ambassadors and those of the Queen in Your Majesty's presence, when they went to ask for the brief, though it must be said that he occasionally amplified and coloured them as much as he could, sometimes in Latin, at others in French, saying among other things: 'I cannot help thinking, seeing the Emperor's pertinacious refusal to send us the brief of dispensation, that it must be a forgery, made, I have no doubt, without the Emperor's knowledge, for I believe him to be incapable of such an act. I have caused all the register books at Rome to be searched, and in none of them is mention made of such a brief, whereas everyone knows that if such document really emanated from the Holy See there would still remain some record or trace of it.

'Besides (continued the King) it is a wonder to me how the Emperor, being like myself a secular prince, and the case being a purely ecclesiastical one, has mixed himself up with such matters, and gone so far as to solicit urgently the prosecution of the trial at Rome; for His Majesty knows very well that this is purely an affair of conscience, and one in which, putting aside consanguinity, friendship, or any other consideration, the truth must be investigated and made patent. Had the Emperor, your master, sent us the brief of dispensation when we applied for it the whole affair might now be cleared up and decided. If so, it would have been a great pleasure and comfort to me, for the delay in the decision of this case is extremely annoying, inasmuch as so long as the matter remains in suspense the exercise of marriage is expressly forbidden to us both.

Respecting the advocation of the case to the Papal Court, the King maintained that it was far more legal, reasonable, and convenient that the case should be tried and decided here in London than anywhere else. For it was absolutely necessary (he observed) that the judges should hear what the Queen and himself, who were not people of a condition to be summoned to appear at Rome had to say; besides which there was a number of witnesses too old and infirm to quit the kingdom and give evidence so far from home in a country so troubled and distracted by war as Italy had been for many years past, and was indeed still. In consideration of which, and in order the more to facilitate the inquiry, His Holiness, the Pope, had *motu proprio,* without solicitation of any person whomsoever, but actuated merely by a sense of justice and impartiality, committed the case to two of his cardinals (Campeggio and Wolsey) to be tried in England. 'At that time (the King continued) I wrote a letter in my own hand to the Pope, saying that not only did I consider it expedient that this matter of the marriage or divorce should be investigated in this my kingdom, but that in my opinion it was quite indispensable that it should be so, as no one in his senses could venture to think of sending the case to Rome, on account of the violence of the Imperial soldiers, who had treated His Holiness in such a disrespectful and brutal manner as to make him still tremble whenever he thought of it.' For this very reason did the Pope promise them most solemnly that he would never advoke the case to Rome. This lasted until the moment when the Emperor and the Pope made league together, when by the terms of the treaty of peace and alliance concluded at Barcelona, and perhaps also through dread of the Emperor and of his army, the Pope was compelled to do the Emperor's pleasure in this respect, and grant that which for the whole previous year he had considered unfair, for he has recently decreed the advocation against all reason, and even against his own promise, that whatever the sentence of the legates, he would confirm it. That the Holy Father (he continued) was influenced by the above-mentioned considerations, and, therefore, decreed the advocation of the case merely to please the Emperor and comply with his will cannot for a moment be doubted, for certainly the commission given in the first instance by the Apostolic See to two dignitaries of the Church of such rank and authority as Cardinals Campeggio and Wolsey, the former of whom was in possession of benefices and pensions from the Emperor, could not give rise to suspicion or scruple of any kind, especially as no intimidation or persuasion was meant, which would have been dishonest and unfair in a case of this kind, in which he (the Pope) never was either principal or party. 'Besides which (said the King) I am a conscientious prince, who prefers his own salvation to all the goods and advantages of this world, as appears sufficiently from my conduct in this affair, for had I been differently situated and not so prone to obey the voice of conscience, nobody should have hindered me from adopting other measures, which I have not taken and never will take.'

With regard to the Queen's defence, the King remarked, it could be undertaken here, in London, much better and more freely than anywhere else. He had given orders to the councillors, chosen by the Queen herself, to serve and advise her faithfully, which they had done hitherto with the same affectionate and constant regard for her interests as if the action for divorce had been brought on by the meanest peasant in his dominions, some of them going as far as writing books, and maintaining what they call the Queen's rights (such were the King's words). Besides which, had the Queen wished for a counsel of foreign lawyers he would have allowed them to come, as he did in the case of the two who came from Flanders.

The King was very glad to hear (as he himself observed) of Your Majesty's conviction that the whole of this affair had no other cause and origin than the peace and tranquillity of his own conscience. Such, and no other, were his motives, as he had informed Your Majesty by his letter. That this was the real truth, as true as the Gospel, no one could doubt who had examined his conduct in the affair. As to the remark which I made in the course of my address to him, namely, that if the matter was merely one of conscience he ought to be satisfied with the exhibition of the original brief before his ambassadors, and with the attested copy sent to him, he said: 'As some suspicion hangs over the brief, a copy is not enough to set my conscience at rest. It frequently happens that transcripts are made of false documents. As to saying that my ambassadors in Spain, who were experienced men in such matters, saw and examined the original itself, that is no proof of its authenticity, for it was not shewn to them as it ought to have been, and yet they (the ambassadors) had observed certain flaws in it, of which they had not, out of respect for Your Imperial Majesty, taken any notice at the time, thereby meaning, if I am rightly informed, that one of his ambassadors, the Auditor (Ghinucci), had written to say that the brief was decidedly a forgery, inasmuch as the Papal bull and the brief itself were dated the 26th of December of the same year, whereas they ought to bear different dates, for the bulls are generally calendered from the birth of Christ, whereas the briefs are from the Incarnation. The King, himself, did not say so, but I know from a very good source that this is one of the flaws which the said Auditor of the Apostolic Chamber pretends to have found in it.

'I suppose (he added) the steps hitherto taken in this affair have been advised or suggested to the Emperor by some person or other, for his professions and tastes are not that way; indeed, I should have no difficulty in asserting, which I have not done before, that had the Emperor heard as much of this case as I happen to know he would at once desist from the prosecution.' Then he said: 'Do you imagine that I have acted lightly in this case? Not the least, I would never believe those who spoke to me without first discussing the question and consulting books about it.' I saw that the King by these words meant to drag me into a polemic about the validity of the marriage, and therefore shunned as much as possible the discussion of this point for two reasons: the first and principal the defence of Your Imperial Majesty's acts and interference in the affair; the other, that there are already books written on the subject in which this matter of the attempted divorce has been sufficiently discussed, so much so that there is no need of further argumentation for or against it.

After this the King continued: 'All these events have passed at times when difference of opinion and enmity prevailed between the Emperor and me; now that peace has been concluded things will go on differently and better,' which last sentence he repeated in a rather emphatic tone. Indeed, I found the King's manner, whilst uttering this sentiment, so different from the mildness and composure of his former speech, that I determined as previously advised by the Queen, to follow another tack, and praise and exalt him [rather than show opposition and mistrust]. I told him that he had just given such a testimony of his great penetration and talent, as well as of his consummate skill in these matters, by the easy and clear exposition of those very points which constituted the basis of my instructions, that I did not hesitate to say no man, however learned, could have done it better. 'Nevertheless (said I), I firmly believe that Your Highness inwardly approves of the Emperor's conduct in this affair, and that the objections raised against it are more intended on the part of Your Highness as a display of wit and talent than as a serious contradiction of my master's mode of thinking and behaviour in this matter.' As to any dispute arising between His Highness and the Emperor (I added), there can really be none, for united as you both are now by almost brotherly affection, if contention and dispute should arise between your two Majesties, it can only be for the purpose of your gratifying each other. This much I can vouch for the Emperor, my master, convinced as I am that his utmost wish is to please his brother of England. Your Highness, who is so wise and reasonable, cannot fail to be satisfied with the answer once given to the English ambassadors [in Spain], and with what I myself have stated in fulfilment of my charge. It is not for me to dispute the point with Your Highness, but I cannot help observing that the refusal by the Emperor to deliver the original brief of dispensation was owing – apart from other reasons and considerations elsewhere stated – principally to the great danger of its being lost on the road, or falling into bad hands, for in these eventful times, when the accomplishment of this divorce might lead to perpetual enmity between the two Princes, there would not be wanting parties ready enough to waylay the bearer and get hold of the brief, and that might be accomplished in various ways.'

The King here interrupted me by asking several times the question: 'But now pray, what are the Emperor's reasons for thus keeping the brief in his power, and not sending it to me to whom by right it belongs?' As I perceived his obstinacy on this point I could not help answering: 'If Your Highness wishes to know what my own private opinion is about the retention of this brief by the Emperor I will at once state it in corroboration of what has already been alleged elsewhere: it is founded on right, and I would have no objection to defend this right in a court of law.' The King nodded his assent, and I continued: 'That the brief itself does not belong to Your Highness, and that there is no reason whatever to compel the Emperor to surrender it can be easily proved, for if Your Highness believes it to be a forgery, and not issued from the Roman Chancery, it is quite evident that it was not addressed to Your Highness, or the cost paid out of your Royal Treasury, which are the two conditions required to claim possession of an instrument. Besides, the brief is like a letter missive from the Pope; and it is an axiom of civil law that a letter missive does not belong to the person to whom it is addressed, unless he actually receives it. Ergo, His Highness cannot assert that the instrument belongs to him, since he owns never having seen or heard of it. Even supposing that it really belonged to Your Highness, my master's interest in the affair was such as to make it rightful, and even necessary, that the brief should remain in his (the Emperor's) hands, as prescribed by common law, which ordains that instruments concerning various parties should be preserved and kept by the highest in authority amongst them who, of course, is obliged, when required, to furnish attested copies of the same to the interested parties.' Then I added, in a milder tone, not to over irritate the King, that although Your Majesty was a secular prince, not an ecclesiastical one, yet nobody could deny him the right of interference in an affair of this sort, since notwithstanding the protest entered by his ambassadors at Saragossa, it had never crossed Your Majesty's mind to exercise jurisdiction in this case, and therefore that their remonstrances and protests fell to the ground as null and inappropriate.

Respecting the cause itself, and whether it was to be tried and sentenced at Rome, or elsewhere, I had nothing to say. He had refused to comply with Your Majesty's wishes in this matter, and, therefore, nothing was left but to obey the Pope's commands and refer to the brief lately forwarded to the Cardinal of York,[36] wherein it was expressly declared that, although right and justice were against him, he (the Pope) had, out of consideration for His Highness, and to do him pleasure, delayed as much as it was in his power, the just and legitimate advocation of the case to his court. With regard to the brief which His Holiness had written to him in his own hand, it was for His Highness to consider whether it was likely that our common Father, the Pope, who had on so many occasions shewn himself hostile to Your Imperial Majesty – of which hostility and ill-will he (the King of England) could testify better than anyone else, since out of regard for him he had joined the Italian League against the Emperor – would now, out of affection for that same prince, whom he had offended and ill-treated, condescend to issue such a brief in favour of the Queen, his aunt, and against him, his best friend and ally, had he not been stirred by a sense of justice and duty, and by the sanction of his Apostolic authority? As to me, I wondered not at the Pope issuing the brief in question; my wonder was that he had not in the first instance written to say that the marriage was null and void, and that it was neither wrong nor difficult to obtain a separation and divorce.

It was evident to me that this topic was a disagreeable one for the King, and that he feared lest by going on with my argument, it should be proved, as many people here and elsewhere pretend to say, that our Holy Father had been one of the promoters of the divorce, for he suddenly interrupted me by saying: 'Enough about that Pope, this is not the first time that he has changed his mind; I have long known his versatile and fickle nature.'

With regard to his assertion that the Pope would never dare pronounce sentence in the affair, unless it was favourable to Your Majesty and to the Queen, I observed that His Highness ought to cast away all fear on that account. Your Imperial Majesty was the Prince of Christendom, who feared God most, and had the greatest regard for justice. Had he considered the marriage illegitimate, not only would he not object to a separation of the parties, but would never have consented to two persons of their rank, and so closely allied to him, living in sin. Your Majesty should show to the World that he was not an usurper or a tyrant, and although all powerful now in Italy, would not abuse his power. These last words were not much to the King's liking, for he kept repeating: 'Not so much, not so much.'

As to the difficulty which His Highness found in himself, the Queen, and the witnesses repairing to Rome, I told him plainly that the remedy was at hand. He had only to appoint agents and proctors to represent him there, not liable to suspicion as the last were, but impartial and honest men, without any jurisdiction, commission, or mandate whatsoever, save that of examining [witnesses] and proving their allegations, and justice would have its course all the same ...

*[After discussion on foreign affairs]* The King did not say more on this occasion, and even the last words passed only between us two. I replied that neither passion nor affection had command of Your Majesty's heart. That could not be doubted even in the present case, which was equally a matter of conscience for him and for the parties concerned. Upon which he (the King) interrupted me by saying: 'Well, it is getting late, and I must needs go. I shall soon be in London, where we can discuss these matters more at leisure.' My answer was: 'As to my waiting Your Highness' pleasure in London, I must observe that, although I have been appointed Imperial ambassador at this Court in case of Doctor Lee retaining that office next the Emperor's person, yet – .' Here the King again interrupted me and said: 'It is true that Doctor Lee has been recalled owing to the Emperor having left him behind in Spain, but that is no reason for your returning so soon, for I have already appointed other ambassadors to replace the Doctor, and they will soon take their departure [for Italy].' He then told me to stop to dinner, promising that I should be well entertained, and gave Mons. de Rochefort orders to that effect. After which, and when about to retire to his private apartments, he added: 'Should news come from the Emperor, or you yourself want anything, you have only to inform me of your wishes by letter, or through one of your secretaries and they shall be attended to immediately.' I then begged his permission to call on the Queen and

present the Emperor's letters to her, which he willingly granted, and then retired to his apartments.

On my leaving the Audience Hall Mr. de Rochefort,[37] the King's treasurer, and other gentlemen of the Court came to welcome me. The King then sent for the treasurer (Rochford) and others of his Privy Council and related to them part of our conversation, as I afterwards learned from Mr. de Rochefort himself, when, after our return to the hall, he, my guide (Dr Hennege), another gentleman, and myself sat down together to dine. During dinner the conversation turned naturally on Your Imperial Majesty, and I must say that the said Mr. de Rochefort inquired most kindly after your health, your passage to Italy, the suite you took thither, and other particulars; after which he remarked that the affairs of Christendom could not but go on prosperously now that its two chief heads (meaning Your Imperial Majesty and the Pope) were agreed. His not mentioning other Christian princes made me suspect that this was said rather ironically, and that perhaps he (the treasurer) would have preferred on his daughter's account that Pope and Emperor had not been so united as they are on this occasion. After dinner, however, he took me apart and said: 'The King tells me that you are thinking of leaving us soon owing to Dr Lee's recall from Spain. You must not do that.' My answer was: 'So I was determined to do at first, but since the King proposes sending another embassy to the Emperor you may tell him that I will remain, for such are my instructions which His Highness had no time to hear in full.' I can assure you replied Mr. de Rochefort that the King, my master, whatever his differences with the Emperor may have been at other times, bears him more affection than anyone can think, imagine, or describe. I would have given anything, nay, the whole of my fortune, for the Emperor to be convinced of my master's goodwill and affectionate regard, and that such being the case the two princes should certainly understand each other on all points.' 'The King may be sure,' was my answer, 'that the Emperor, my master, fully reciprocates such sentiments, and as to your saying that you would willingly give up the whole of your fortune for such conviction and assurance, I may tell you that you can be gratified at much less expense, for I will take the very first opportunity, as my instructions prescribe, of convincing you and the King of my master's sentiments.' At this juncture a gentleman came out of the King's chamber in search of Mr. de Rochefort, upon which, after promising to renew our conversation when we first met in London, he took leave of me, and went into the King's apartments.

Soon after this Mons. de Rossel (Russell) and other gentlemen of the Royal Household came to conduct me to the apartments of the Queen, who, attended by a number of gentlemen and ladies, came out of her chamber. I presented my credentials to her, and proceeded to explain in almost the same words I had used to the King, the object of my mission. The Queen seemed very much gratified at my coming, and observed that if my words and remarks to the King had been as described, no one could have executed his commission better or spoken more to her satisfaction. Respecting the Papal brief, about which the King himself had spoken with such persistence, she observed that for those who had any regard for truth and justice, and knew the ins and outs of the affair, there was no necessity for that document. After which she said: 'There are, however, matters upon which I dare not, surrounded as I am, speak to you in detail. I will send you one of my servants to explain the remainder. There is, however, one thing I must not forget, which is that if you have not yet visited Cardinal Campeggio, it is very important that you should see him as soon as possible, and thank him in my name and in that of the Emperor also for his honest and rightful behaviour, and the trouble he has taken in this affair. As to me, I am so grateful for what he has done that I should hardly know how to repay his services.' I then told her that I was the bearer of letters both from Your Imperial Majesty and from Madame[38] for the Cardinal of York, and that I wished to know whether I ought to deliver them or not. 'There is no necessity (replied the Queen), for the Cardinal's affairs are at this moment rather embroiled.' This last sentence she said in such a low tone of voice that nobody but myself could hear her, and I doubt even whether the courtiers in the room could see her actually move her lips. After this she raised her voice to its usual pitch, and inquired where Your Majesty was, and whether your health was good, and so forth. After hearing my answer to all and every one of the above questions, she asked me for the letter which she knew Your Majesty had written to her in your own hand, and which I had not yet dared present. She told me to pass it over to her physician, which I did, after which the conference ended, and I took leave of her ...

... Coming back from the Queen's apartments I found that the King was still up and conversing with Mr. de Rochefort. Secretary Rossel went in and announced me, and then came out with the following message: 'Up to this hour the King, my master, has not yet had time to look into this affair, and prepare an answer to the Emperor; were he called upon to give one immediately he could but repeat the arguments he had made use of at the conference. But His Highness purposes going back to London soon, and there, after one or more interviews, that affair and others may and will be discussed.' Meanwhile (Russell added), I was to let the King know of any news I received [from Italy], and in a like manner he would inform me of anything that came to his knowledge. He then gave orders that a beast laden with the best venison that could be procured should be sent to my lodgings in London.

I am not at all astonished at the King's not giving me an answer after dinner, as I requested, for in the first place he had then no other member of his Privy Council with him except the said Mr de Rochefort, the father of the Lady [Anne] and then the King himself was in a great hurry to repair to the meeting place of the morning, where the Lady was ready to open the chase. So that, all things considered, the constellation under which we were was by no means a favourable one for obtaining an answer to Your Majesty's letter ...

The Queen is rather concerned and frightened at this meeting of the English Estates (Parliament) which is to take place soon. She fears that something may be brewed there against her. Her fears originate in the conduct of the King, her husband, who, she says, has played his cards so well that he is likely to get a majority of votes in his favour, and may perhaps be tempted to obtain by this means what he has not yet been able to get in any other way. But I am inclined to believe that there is no fear of that, the affection of the English for Your Majesty and for the Queen being so great.

It is reported that the real cause of this Parliament having been convoked for the 2nd of November is, independently of others specified in my despatch of the 4th of September, to investigate the conduct and examine the accounts of all those functionaries who have been connected with the finances of this country. Others add that a motion will be made to abolish the Legatine Office in England, and prevent the Pope from appointing or sending in future legates to this country. Those who think so may not be far from the truth, for I now recollect that at the last sitting of the Legates (Campeggio and Wolsey) for the purpose of proroguing the case until the 2nd of October, the Duke of Suffolk got into a great passion and began to swear, and say within hearing of the King himself, of the cardinals, and of all those who had come to that piteous ceremony in order to hear whether the sentence was in favour of the Queen or against her: 'I see now the truth of what I have heard many people say; never at any time did a Papal legate do anything to the profit of England; they have always been, and will hereafter be a calamity and a sore to this country.'

I need scarcely observe that if these sentiments of the Duke gain ground with the King and the people of this country, there will be a door wide open for the Lutheran heresy to creep into England, which is the very identical threat made by the English ambassador at Rome when the Pope was pleased to grant the advocation, as I have informed Your Majesty in a previous despatch. I firmly believe that if they had nothing to fear but the Pope's excommunication and malediction, there are innumerable people in this country who would follow the Duke's advice, and make of the King and ordinary prelates as many Popes. All this for the sole purpose of having the divorce case tried in England, notwithstanding the Holy Father's inhibition, and not so much perhaps for the ill-will they bear towards ecclesiastics in general, but principally on account of their property which they covet and wish, to seize. It is to be hoped, however, that fear of Your Majesty, if no other consideration, will defeat such wicked plans.

Yesterday the Queen sent her physician to ask me to despatch immediately a courier to Your Majesty with the account of the above conference, and everything else I have seen or heard since my landing in England; also to report about the general inhibition and its publication in this country, but having told him (the physician) that the execution had been already made, both at Bruges and at Dunkirk, he immediately returned to acquaint his mistress with the fact that she might, if interrogated by the King, know what to answer. The express, who was to be the bearer of this letter, will not leave until the physician's return, which, he tells me, will take place two days hence.

The Queen has sent me word expressly to warn Your Imperial Majesty against any attempts, past or future, made by the King or by his ambassadors to persuade Your Majesty that the divorce case had been merely instituted for the discharge of his conscience. That is not the fact; the idea of the separation originated entirely in his own iniquity and malice. Whatever the peace [between the Emperor and him] the heart was not free, and he could not but show this on many occasions. The very same day the news of this last peace of Cambray arrived in London he was the first to go and announce it to the queen, which he did in these words; 'My peace with the Emperor is made, it will last as long as you Choose.' Some time ago he said at dinner: 'I fancied at one time that this treaty of Cambray would be the means of ensuring peace and tranquillity to all Christendom. I was mistaken; ambition and lust of power must still be alive in the Emperor's heart since Alessandria is, I hear, being besieged by his troops.'

As far as I can hear and judge, this King's obstinacy and his passion for the Lady are such that there is no chance of recalling him by mildness or fair words to a sense of his duty. Things having come to such a pitch, there can be no security or repose [for the Queen] unless the case be tried and decided [at Rome], and the sooner the better, for many reasons and political considerations, whereof Your Majesty is the best judge. I am convinced that the opposite party will not leave things as they are, but intend proceeding in the case. In proof of which assertion I may tell Your Majesty that a very few days ago the King proposed to the Queen to have the whole case transferred to Cambray instead of Rome, which proposition, of course, was rejected, and will not be accepted unless Your Majesty wishes it to be so. I must further state that the King has not yet consented to the advocation being intimated to him, as, among other things, it contains a summons for him to appear personally before the Pope at Rome, which, of course, he refuses, as besides his unwillingness to quit his kingdom on such an errand, there is a law in England which forbids it under pain of confiscation of property and imprisonment. Neither has he allowed the inhibition to be served to the cardinals in virtue of the first Papal brief, but only by means of a second one addressed separately and individually to the Cardinal of York, which has since been done. According to the letter of this second brief, both cardinals have now resigned their powers, as well as their delegation and jurisdiction from the Pope in due form, as Your Majesty will see by the enclosed copy of the deed of resignation, so that they can no longer proceed or mix themselves up with the affair, as if the principal execution had been directed against them ...

*25 October 1529*
... immediately after the receipt of Your Majesty's letter of the 21st I sent one of my secretaries to Court, then at Winnesor (Windsor), to inform the King that I had received letters for him, which I was ordered to deliver into his own hands, as likewise to make certain communications whenever it might please His Highness to grant me an audience. The sooner, I intimated, the better, as the matter, in my opinion, admitted of no delay.

Meanwhile, and not to lose time, perceiving that the whole government of this country was fast falling into the hands of the Duke of Norfolk; calculating also that the matters I had to communicate would be more to his taste than the marriage question for the reasons specified in my dispatch of the 8th October, I determined to seize the opportunity for which I have been so long watching, of ascertaining the final issue of the Cardinal's affairs, who, on the festival of St Luke the Evangelist, was himself disevangelized, set aside, and deprived of the office of chancellor and of his seat in the Privy Council. All scruples being thus removed which had hitherto prevented me from calling on the Duke, I hastened to visit him at his residence in this city ...

Passing on to the subject of this late peace, and the pains which the King, his master, had taken about it, I took occasion to observe that there still remained an agreement to be made, the accomplishment of which rested wholly in the King's power, and would redound more to his tranquillity and honour before God and man than anything he had yet done, namely, the difference between the Queen and himself, on which so many exhortations, representations and requests of the most gracious and kind nature had been offered and made by Your Majesty. Presuming (I said) that he (the Duke) had knowledge of the whole affair from the King, I would make no further allusion to it than to observe that, however favourably he (the Duke) might look upon it out of family considerations, and of his relationship to the lady, whom the King wished to marry, Your Majesty considered him such a true and virtuous knight as to preclude all idea of his acting – even were it the case of his own daughter – otherwise than as honour and conscience would prescribe; incapable also of instituting, or even consenting to legal proceedings in a case of such grave and important consequences without manifest reason. Your Majesty being perfectly convinced that he (the Duke) had neither been promoter nor counsellor of such a step.

The Duke's reply was that he would willingly have lost one of his hands rather than such a question had ever arisen; not that he himself had been a party to it in any way, or been appealed to or otherwise advised the measure; for the affair was entirely one of conscience and canonic law which the King had from the very beginning submitted to the consideration of ecclesiastics, doctors in theology, and other learned persons, a great number of whom had pronounced at once against the validity of the existing marriage. This opinion, however, the King was unwilling to adopt unless he had it confirmed by the highest written authorities which he had most diligently consulted and examined. With regard to the dispensation brief in Your Majesty's hands (the Duke added), the King had openly declared that he would consider himself the most ill-used prince in Christendom if the said document was not found to be a forgery, since many had told him so, and the King himself, as he believed, had expressed his conviction to me.

The Duke further went on to say that had Your Majesty remained neutral, instead of so openly taking up the part of the Queen, the affair would have been probably much sooner settled and brought to a satisfactory issue; and that it could not appear otherwise than strange that whilst he who was most interested in an affair of this sort kept aloof, and avoided appearing as a party in the suit, Your Majesty should have formally declared himself to be one.

In answer to this I carefully summed up the reasons which had influenced Your Majesty's conduct, as well as the pressure exercised upon you; and at the same time I could not but remark that the King's dissimulation, and his unwillingness to appear in the law proceedings, was but too manifest, both from his application to the College of Cardinals as from what his ambassadors had done – and were still doing – at Rome. Upon which, perceiving that the Duke appeared thoughtful, I deemed it best to change the subject, only remarking that if I had been induced to make the foregoing observation it was rather for Your Majesty's justification, and as a proof of the confidence you were willing to repose in his (the Duke's) integrity and honour ...

The news here [in London] is that the Cardinal, who has been long tottering, has at length fallen completely. Having been dismissed from the Council and also from his office as Chancellor, as I said before, he has since been compelled to draw out in his own hand a most minute inventory of all his moveable property, that nothing may be forgotten, and that he may more easily be convicted. It is added that, having of his own free will acknowledged his errors and faults, he has presented all he had to the King, which is no trifling matter. Yesterday the King came by water from Greenwich to view the said effects [presented to him by the Cardinal], bringing with him only his lady friend, her mother, and one gentleman of his chamber; and it is added that the King was much gratified and found the present more valuable even than he expected. The Cardinal through all his misfortunes kept a brave face until the day of St Luke, when all his bravadoes turned suddenly into bitter complaints, tears, and sighs, which are unceasing night and day. The King hearing of this, either moved to pity, or perhaps thinking it inconvenient that the Cardinal should die before making a full disclosure and confession of all his acts, has lately presented him with a ring by way of consolation. He is now living at a place about ten miles from London, with a very small train indeed. A son of his, who is in Paris following his studies, and of whom I have formerly written to Your Majesty, has received orders to return. People say execrable things of the Cardinal, all of which are to come to light before next Parliament, for it may be supposed that whatever be the end of this matter, those who have raised this storm against the Cardinal will not rest until they have entirely done for him, knowing full well that were he to recover his lost ascendancy and power their own lives would be in jeopardy. The person who they say feels most for the Cardinal and regrets his disgrace is the French ambassador, because all the hopes and expectations of his master rested upon his continuance in office and favour. Fears were entertained by some people here lest the Cardinal should contrive to send his valuables out of the country, and therefore a very strict watch was kept at all the ports. It was on this account that when the custom house guards asked to examine Campeggio's trunks, notwithstanding the passport received from the King, that upon his refusing to surrender the keys of them, the locks were forced, the trunks opened, and their contents inspected to that Cardinal's great displeasure. I am told that he said on the occasion to those about him 'You do me great injustice to suppose that the Cardinal [of York] could corrupt a man like myself who has been proof against the King's innumerable presents ...

The affair of the Queen, which I have purposedly reserved for the last, is in the same state, and I have nothing new to communicate, except that the Bishop of London assures me as a matter of certainty that Dr Stock (Stokesley) is gone to France for the sole and express purpose of consulting the Parisian doctors. The Queen being also aware of the fact entreats Your Majesty to send thither for a similar purpose some learned canonists, for otherwise, in the absence of a definitive sentence, any attempts made to bring the King to reason will prove unavailing, and he will continue as pertinacious and obstinate as ever.

I have tendered to her the advice recommended by Your Majesty, but she seems to think that delay, far from being profitable, will be injurious to her cause. For which reason, and others of greater force and weight now than ever, which I have already pointed out to Your Majesty, it seems desirable not to agree to the postponement of the suit as demanded by this King. This, however, remains entirely at Your Majesty's pleasure and superior discretion. The Queen also thinks that in order to avoid raising suspicion in the mind of the King, I had better cease visiting her, and she hopes to be able to find means of communicating with me in private.

*[Post Script]*

Two days after the above was written the Cardinal was judicially and definitively condemned by the great Council of the King, and declared a rebel to his authority and guilty of high treason, inasmuch as in defiance of the royal authority and the privileges of the kingdom he had obtained from the Pope, the better to support his legatine powers, the grant of several benefices which were under the direct patronage of the King and others, of which he has disposed by anticipation. Accordingly, he has been deprived of all his offices and Church preferments, and of all dignities and prerogatives. All his property, moveable or immoveable, has been adjudicated to the King, and himself sentenced to imprisonment in one of the royal prisons here in London until the King shall decide on his ultimate fate. The sentence, it is true, was pronounced in his absence, for in this particular his enemies were quite ready to please him, but two procurators were present on his behalf, to whom it was duly communicated. All this will be of difficult digestion for him, and yet I doubt whether he will escape without further punishment.

*6 December 1529*

... The above conference *[concerning Charles V's war against the Turks]* took place on a Saturday. Next day the King dined with the Queen, and whilst at table alluded to the affair, saying: that if the Christian princes agreed to support this undertaking against the Turk, he (the King) would do wonders. But as to Your Majesty's application for assistance [in money], that was quite a different affair, as he considered it a foolish and highly improper thing for king Henry of England to remit money to Your Majesty and help him to keep no less than three armies in Italy, which, in his opinion, ought to be elsewhere ...

*[A few days later, Chapuys was invited to dine at court]* The dinner at the King's table, to which we together with the French ambassador and Papal Nuncio, were invited, was a splendid one, as Mr. de Mingoval will inform Your Majesty. The King was very familiar and jovial with all of us, and never ceased, except when the music of several instruments sounded, to address us on all manner of subjects, starting questions to draw us, especially us, the Imperial ambassadors, into conversation ...

The dinner over the King took all of us three, namely, Mr. de Rosymboz, Mr. Jehan [de le Sauch], and myself, to a window of the Hall, and there, his countenance actually beaming with joy, began to say that as regarded the Turkish campaign he did not boast of what he might and would do; he was not one of those who made great promises and spoke very high, and when called upon to fulfil their words fell back; he invariably did more than he promised ...

We thanked the King for his good counsel, and assured him that such was Your Majesty's confidence in him that in any matter, even more important than the present, you would not fail to follow his advice. Again did the King return to the subject of the Clergy, as if he wished to assert that which constitutes his chief ground of complaint against them, and is the cause of his present animadversion, for he exclaimed, addressing all of us at once: 'Now, I ask you, how can the Pope grant a dispensation for an ecclesiastic to hold two bishoprics or two curacies at once if he will not allow two women to one man? for here is the point (this he said rather between his teeth): all doctors say that a dispensation in the former case is as necessary as in the other.' Our answer was, that reformation was undoubtedly much wanted, and would be the best thing in the world, if accomplished in such a manner as proposed and required [by Your Majesty], and seconded by a prince like him, who to the good qualities with which he was endowed joined considerable learning in Church matters, and of whom it could not be suspected that in so doing he wished to derogate from the authority of that same Church in matters of its jurisdiction, whether of dispensation or of any other sort. He replied, and maintained that the only power which ecclesiastics had over laymen was the absolution from sin, and he went on in this manner speaking against the Pope in terms very similar to those above stated.

After which, Mr. de Rosymboz asked permission to pay his respects to the Queen, which the King willingly granted at once, though the duke of Norpholc (Norfolk) and the rest [of the councillors] made some difficulty. The permission being granted, we all called at the apartments of the Queen, whom we found in great sorrow, so much so that she could hardly suppress her tears in our presence. We told her that, according to Your Majesty's letters, Mr. de le Sauch, there present, had consulted on her case with several of the Parisian doctors, all of whom had given their opinion that it was quite impossible to dissolve the marriage, and that neither the king of France himself nor any other prince in the World had the power of making the university give a contrary opinion. This assurance, and the hope and trust which the Queen has in Your Majesty's exertions in her behalf, somewhat relieved her from her anguish, and her conntenance gladdened; but as there were many in the room she dared not say much, nor did we venture to speak to her on the subject. She, however, promised to write or let me know her wishes by private and verbal message.

And so she did, for on the following day she wrote me a letter through her physician [Fernando Victoria], explaining the King's behaviour towards her, which, she says, is still the same, and begging me to report upon it, and particularly to recommend her poor case to Your Majesty, earnestly entreating, now that you are with the Pope, to have her cause determined judicially or otherwise, that the state of tribulation and anguish in which she lives, and which (she says) has lasted far too long, may be put an end to at once, and begging also that for the love of God, and regard for Your Majesty's honour and reputation, no further delay be made in a matter which might give rise to serious inconvenience and danger for the future. Notwithstanding that her letter to Your Majesty – which goes also by this post – is full of the same prayers and commendations she has conjured me to write, as I do, in her favour.

On St Andrew's Day, the Queen having dined with the King, said to him that she had long been suffering the pains of Purgatory on earth, and that she was very badly treated by his refusing to dine with and visit her in her apartments. The King replied: 'That she had no cause to complain of bad treatment, for she was mistress in her own household, where she could do what she pleased. As to his not dining with her for some days past, the reason was that he was so much engaged with business of all kinds, owing to the Cardinal having left the affairs of government in a state of great confusion that he had enough to do to work day and night to put them to rights again. As to his visiting her in her apartments and partaking of her bed, she ought to know that he was not her legitimate husband, as innumerable doctors and canonists, all men of honour and probity, and even his own almoner, Doctor Lee, who had once known her in Spain, were ready to maintain. That many other theologians were of the same opinion, and, moreover, that he was only waiting for the opinion of the Parisian doctors, to obtain which he had lately sent Dr Stocler (Stokesley), the same about whom I wrote to Your Majesty in my despatch of the 25th ulto. As soon (he added) as he had obtained those opinions, and others well founded upon right and canonic law, he would not fail to have them duly forwarded to Rome, and should not the Pope, in conformity with the above opinions so expressed, declare their marriage null and void, then in that case he (the King) would denounce the Pope as a heretic, and marry whom he pleased.' The Queen replied that he himself, without the help of doctors, knew perfectly well that the principal cause alleged for the divorce did not really exist, 'cart yl l'avoit trouvé pucelle,'[39] as he himself had owned upon more than one occasion. 'As to your almoner's opinion in this matter,' she continued, 'I care not a straw; he is not my judge in the present case; it is for the Pope, not for him, to decide. Respecting those of other doctors, whether Parisian or from other universities, you know very well that the principal and best lawyers in England have written in my favour. Indeed, if you give me permission to procure counsel's opinion in this matter I do not hesitate to say that for each

doctor or lawyer who might decide in your favour and against me, I shall
find 1,000 to declare that the marriage is good and indissoluble.'

After a good deal of talking and disputing on these matters the King
left the room suddenly, and, as I am told by some of those present, was
very disconcerted and downcast, so much so that at supper the Lady Anne
noticed it, and said to him reproachfully: 'Did I not tell you that whenever
you disputed with the Queen she was sure to have the upper hand? I see
that some fine morning you will succumb to her reasoning, and that you
will cast me off. I have been waiting long, and might in the meanwhile have
contracted some advantageous marriage, out of which I might have had
issue, which is the greatest consolation in this world; but alas! farewell to
my time and youth spent to no purpose at all.'

Such, I am told, was Lady Anne's language to the King on the evening
of the day that he dined with his Queen, and disputed with her as to the
legitimacy of their marriage, but as Your Majesty will no doubt hear all these
particulars from Mr. de Mingoval, as well as the influence the Lady exercises,
and the credit she has with the King, I shall say no more on this subject, and
will leave to that ambassador the care of reporting thereupon ...

*9 December 1529*

... Respecting the Queen, matters can hardly be worse than they are at
present, as Your Majesty will more fully understand through her letters and
my own report which Mr. de Mingoval took to Court. Such is the blind
passion of the King for the Lady [Anne] that I fear one of these days some
disorderly act will take place. They will no doubt employ the means which I
pointed out in my despatch of the 6th inst., perhaps, too, they will proceed in
a shorter way, and without waiting for the answer from their ambassador in
Italy – whose province it is to look after this business at Rome – may bring
it under the discussion of this Parliament, in which I am told the majority
of the members has been bribed and gained over in favour of the King. If
so, whatever may be the issue of the trial at Rome, the King will go on; and
if he can only obtain the consent of the Chamber on the plea that has been
brought forward, he will consider himself secure and justified on all sides.
I consider it, therefore, of the utmost importance that Your Majesty think
at once of such expedients as it may be advisable to adopt under present
circumstances. In my opinion, the best step to take would be that the Pope,
now that Cardinal Campeggio – who must have perfect knowledge of the
whole affair – is at Rome, should summon the theologians and doctors
now at Bologna or Rome to his presence, and cause them freely to discuss
before a consistory of cardinals this most important matter, in which not
only the interests of the Queen, but the authority of the Holy Apostolic See
are seriously compromised, so that it should be at once determined and
concluded. There is no other way, it seems to me, of solving the difficulty,
for should the Pope, or any other judge, without having the matter fairly
discussed as above, pronounce in favour of the Queen, these people are sure
to turn round and say that the sentence is unjust, for besides the suspicion
and ill-will they have of the Pope and other ecclesiastical judges, they will

allege that it is in their (the ecclesiastical) interest to do so, and to maintain that the Pope (Julius) could rightly give dispensation for the marriage, in order to increase by these means the authority of the Pope, and procure him money by such dispensations.

If, moreover, the opinions of some universities [in Spain or Flanders] could be obtained and forwarded so as to be exhibited here it would greatly help us to success. I have written to Madame, who will no doubt procure shortly that of Louvain.

I must say that up to the present it never crossed my mind that the King's blindness could be so great. One of the reasons besides a thousand more I had for not thinking so ill of him was, that I fancied the duke of Norfolk, as I was given to understand, was aiming at the hand of the Princess[40] for his own son. Yet he has evidently avoided recommending such a course, no doubt the better to court Your Majesty's favour, and also for fear of the other [lady] having male children, which would deprive his son of the succession to the kingdom, all hopes of which, as Your Majesty knows, have been for a long time lost. Nevertheless, as far as may be conjectured from the above, such a consideration does not actually exist; perhaps too they intend treating the daughter as badly as the mother. Everyone sees the King so much bent upon that unfortunate union that no one actually dares contradict him, and so in order to countenance the intended alliance the father of the Lady was yesterday created an earl.

The Princess is still at Windsor, and, people say, not very well treated considering her rank and birth. For the last week I have had no news from the Queen. She sent me lately a message to say that she was thinking and planning how I could go to her apartments without being noticed. I am waiting for her orders, but as to going thither openly and by daylight there is no chance just now; I should greatly displease the King, and what is more it would not profit her or Your Majesty ...

*13 December 1529*
After my last despatch of the 9th inst. was sent off I received the Imperial letters of the 15th ulto, of which, as well as of Your Majesty's earnest desire to do everything to assist the Queen in her trouble, I duly and at once advised her that she might receive some of that encouragement and comfort which she now needs more than ever. Indeed, she has daily more and more ground for complaint, the King's indifference to, and neglect of, her increasing rapidly, in proportion to his passionate attachment for the Lady. At no time was his love of this latter more apparent or his intention to carry out the unrighteous and scandalous act of forsaking her, and taking the other for his wife more manifest. As I have had occasion to inform Your Majesty, it is to be feared that he may do this sooner than is anticipated unless God inspire him with repentance, or Your Majesty interfere actively to prevent it, for, as I said before, the King thinks of nothing else but accomplishing his purpose, and, as the duke of Norfolk declared once to me, there is nothing the King would not grant Your Majesty were he to obtain your consent to this divorce and new marriage, even to becoming Your Majesty's slave for ever.

It is entirely in view of this that certain relatives of the Lady were lately created earls, for it was considered essential that before her being raised to the rank of Queen her own family should be somewhat exalted. In fact all the newly created earls are nearly related to each other, or close allies of the duke [of Norfolk]. When the ceremony took place Monseigneur de Rochfort had double honour, for he was the first created, and had besides two earldoms given him, one in Ireland and the other in this kingdom, whilst the others had only one title each. Indeed, his prerogatives on the occasion were not small, for the day after, the King wishing no doubt to make it appear that the honours conferred upon the new earl were entirely owing to his daughter's favour, gave a grand fête in this city, to which several ladies of the Court were invited (among them queen Blanche[41] and the two duchesses of Norfolk, the dowager and the young one), the Lady Anne taking precedence of them all, and being made to sit by the King's side, occupying the very place allotted to a crowned queen, which by the by is a thing that was never before done [in this country]. After dinner there was dancing and carousing, so that it seemed as if nothing were wanting but the priest to give away the nuptial ring and pronounce the blessing. All the time, and whilst the carousal was going on, poor queen Katharine was seven miles away from this place holding her own fête of sorrow and weeping.

The King's demoiselle has, moreover, been the chief cause and instrument of Cardinal Wolsey's ruin, for she was heard to say a few days before that it would cost her a good 20,000 crs. before she had entirely done with him, and that if she had any influence over the Pope he (the Cardinal) would have none of it. This may be considered certain and that she will do all she can here to deprive the said Cardinal of his annats, as well of all or the greater part of his ecclesiastical authority in this kingdom.

The reform [of the Clergy], about which I wrote to Your Majesty, is partly owing to the anger of these people at His Holiness advocation of the divorce case to Rome. Although many causes are assigned for it, there can be no doubt that last is the real one, and that having begun the said reform, they will go on with it as quickly as they can, and this for many evident reasons. First of all because they will get large sums of money by the sale of Church property, and a judicious investment of the same. Secondly, because as nearly all the people here hate the priests, they may perhaps gain them over and pursuade them to consent to this marriage and declare that the Pope has no power to grant dispensations in marriages or in other matters and that no more of their substance shall go to Rome in future. Indeed, it is evident that if the English [in this affair] have no other guidance but respect for the Pope they will not care much for him, and that if this state of things should last there will be no more obedience shewn to the Pope here than in Germany. Neither the leaders nor the rest [of the party] can now refrain from slandering the Pope. The other day the duke of Norfolk said openly to me that the Pope himself had been one of the first to perceive the invalidity of this marriage, and had written to say that it could in nowise stand good, and that he would declare so himself or have it legally declared, and yet that in consequence of his alliance with Your Majesty, and of his being, as it were, under your power, that same Pope now would have the case tried and determined only as Your Majesty wished. I am, moreover, much inclined to think that one of the reasons why the King was so anxious for Your Majesty's departure for Hungary, was his thinking that he might during your absence [from Italy] do what he pleased with the Pope.

In the event, however, of the divorce case being brought forward in Parliament, as there is every reason to fear, I am persuaded that the Queen will want me to offer some sort of opposition or present a protest in Your Majesty's name. Not having received special instructions upon this point, I should very much like to know how I am to act. My own impression is that some means ought and might be adopted with the Queen's approbation to weaken the action of Parliament, or at least to defer it as long as possible. Were I to propose, as if it came from myself, that since these people are so very suspicious of the Pope and of the Queen they should consent, before any confusion arises, to refer the case to Cambray, as they themselves proposed once, or if this should not meet with the King's approbation, that he should send to Paris persons free from suspicion to represent him [at the Sorbonne] and there dispute the case with the doctors and divines appointed by the Queen, I really think that some good might be done; for the proposition, if accepted, would in my opinion answer the purpose of checking the deliberations of Parliament, and affording time for Your Majesty's late instructions on this business to be carried into effect.

I likewise deem it advisable to try, in my own name of course, what can be done with the duke of Norfolk, and see whether we could not gain him over to our cause by means of some promise of help and assistance in the marriage of his son to Princess Mary, which is so much spoken of here that I consider myself perfectly justified to urge it on by pointing out the mutual advantages to be derived from it, as well as the troubles and anxieties it would remove. I have no doubt that such motives would strongly work upon the Duke and yet there is ground for fearing that such a plan, if proposed will be rejected; for should, the Queen regain her influence and position before his son's marriage takes place she is sure to have it broken off, and besides injure the Duke in many other ways; for he knows well that the Queen has never forgiven him some angry words which he and his wife, the Duchess, said on the occasion of her not allowing the latter to take precedence of her mother-in-law, by which both were much offended, especially the Duchess, who belongs to the house of Lancaster. The other motive of anxiety for the Duke is that should the King return to his duty towards the Queen, his lawful wife, and the Lady be consequently dismissed from Court, the Cardinal would in all probability regain his influence, as there is good reason for thinking owing to his uncommon ability and the King's readiness to restore him to his former favour. Indeed, everyone here perceives that the King bears the Cardinal no real ill-will, and that in acting towards him as he did, it was merely to gratify the Lady in this particular. Should, however, the King's affection for the Lady abate in the least, the Cardinal would soon find means of settling this business [of the divorce] in a manner which would not only cost the opposite party their lives, but as they suspect, make the Queen, who has lately shewn some pity for the Cardinal's fall, help his return to power. It is, therefore, highly probable that they will all look more to their own immediate advantage or risk than to any chance for the future. Nevertheless, should the Queen approve of this plan of mine I will try my best with the Duke; no harm, in my opinion, can result therefrom, and in the meantime Your Majesty may carry out the suggestions conveyed in my despatch of the 9th inst.

I must add that when the King heard, as I failed not to assure him, that Your Majesty was fully convinced that all his steps about this divorce were merely owing to his scruples and to the wish of relieving his conscience, he shewed great satisfaction.

I am not sure that Your Majesty will believe what I am about to state; but it is a fact that in spite of all that has been said, preached, and circulated in this country [about this divorce], they have never been able to convince the people of its righteousness, for they know very well that it was the Holy League that first inspired the King's enmity towards Your Majesty, and that he has ever since become more blindly and passionately fond of the Lady. People, therefore, say that it is only the King's evil destiny that impels him, for had he as he asserts, only attended to the voice of conscience, there would have been still greater affinity to contend with in this intended marriage than in that of the Queen, his wife, a fact of which everyone here speaks quite openly.[42]

Lately one or two preachers have been suborned to preach publicly that the Pope (Julius) had no power to give dispensation for the marriage of the Queen, and that it was contrary to Divine law, over which popes have no control. There are not wanting preachers who, without any other motive than the love of justice and truth, have refuted [from the pulpit] the aforesaid proposition, but the former have not yet replied. It now remains to be seen how they will make their case good. For my own part, I imagine that they will probably keep silence, knowing that the best and most learned among the English prelates have written in favour of the Queen, and that the King himself and the noblemen of his party have declared that the prelates and divines, who hold for the Queen, are indeed good and respectable men, only too much self-opinionated ...

### 31 December 1529

... With regard to the Queen's business, she is aware that the English ambassadors at Rome have written to their king that it was impossible for them legally or in any other way to obtain what he wished, and that they saw no other way open than that of persuading Your Majesty by some good means to consent to the divorce, or at least not to take an active part in the proceedings against it. The same means were to be tried with respect to the Queen, who (they said) ought to be treated differently from what she had been hitherto. That was, in the opinion of the English ambassadors, the only way of obtaining Your Majesty's consent, as well as of bringing the Queen herself to that conclusion, for to act otherwise in the affair was like knocking one's head against the wall. The Emperor, they added, was not to be won over by rigour or by worrying the Queen, but by fair means and mild persuasions.

The King, as it would seem, would fain take the advice of his ambassadors, for at these last rejoicings and entertainments he has decidedly shewn the Queen more consideration than was his wont, and the Lady [Anne] herself did not make her appearance. Yet one might easily perceive that this apparent cordiality was rather simulated than hearty, for, as Your Majesty will hear by the Queen's own letter, the King was unable to disguise his disappointment in words if he did in manner. In fact, His Most Serene Highness the King of England may feign and dissemble as much as he likes, but he must indeed be a clever wizard if he presumes to be able by such empty compliments to change the opinion of the Queen, who has been warned beforehand of the trap that has been laid for her.

Notwithstanding all the warnings that have been addressed to her from time to time, the Queen never could think that her affairs would fall so low as they are at present. She always fancied that the King, after pursuing his course for some time, would turn away, and yielding to his conscience, would change his purpose as he had done at other times, and return to reason. Now, considering the King's great obstinacy, his long and stubborn adherence to his former plans, and the things he told her a short time ago, she has lost all hope of bringing him to a sense of right and duty. So much so, that unless Your Majesty continue, as hitherto to help and assist her, she considers her case as irretrievably lost, the justice of her cause being of no avail unless strengthened by the countenance, favour, and authority of Your Majesty, for the King has distinctly told the Queen and others that in this affair, should the Pope send a refusal, he should not heed it; it was enough for him to obtain within his own kingdom such an opinion as might set his conscience at rest; and he prized and valued the church of Canterbury in England as much as the people across the sea did the Roman ...

*12 January 1529*
Today's despatch having been forwarded through the King's people, I could not write so openly on all points as I should have wished; I therefore add this by way of supplement ...

Respecting the Queen's business, the King said to me that he had now in his favour the opinions of all the learned doctors of this kingdom, even of those who at the beginning had taken her part, and who had since acknowledged their mistake. My reply was that I knew of many among the most learned of this country who maintained their first opinion as strongly as ever, and that even if the whole of his subjects, as he said, agreed entirely with him, the matter, nevertheless, was of such importance that the opinion of his own doctors was insufficient for the decision of the case, inasmuch as from their being natives of this country they might and ought to be considered suspect. The opinion of the first universities in Christendom ought to be taken, and that before attempting a divorce between two persons of such exalted rank, whose union has lasted so long, and from whom there is issue. Indeed before entering upon a question with which the power and authority of the Holy Apostolic See are so closely connected, it seemed advisable to convoke a small council.

To this the King replied that there were in his kingdom plenty of honest men, whose persuasions and writings, besides what he himself, who is well acquainted with such matters, had read in books, had had the effect of quieting his conscience, and that he had no doubt Your Majesty would be of the same opinion when you saw the allegation (information), which was shortly to be forwarded to you. That although his own conscience was perfectly at ease on that point, he had thought it well to consult the Paris doctors, 16 of whom, the principal amongst them, had sided with him. And upon my replying that the number of his partisans was wonderfully small when compared with the innumerable host of doctors in Paris, he said that those who had voted the conclusion in his favour were the most distinguished men in that university, and that a greater number might have been found, had not two doctors, one a Spaniard the other a Fleming, at the instigation of the Imperial ambassadors in France, hindered and thwarted in every possible way the labours of the person sent by him for the management of this business; a most unfair proceeding, he observed, which he could in no wise assign to Your Majesty, as emanating from your own free will, since for whatever you had done or ordered to be done in the affair the Imperial ambassadors had lately apologized in so solemn a manner that there was nothing more to say. Besides which, Your Majesty had spoken to his ambassadors in terms so humane and generous, more perhaps than the affair deserved, that he hoped Your Majesty would, in accordance with his innate goodness, his justice and integrity, only advise and recommend a course of action strictly legal.

The duke of Norfolk, nowadays the most powerful man in England, and, if I am not mistaken, he who desires most to do you service, told me the other day, among other things, as I have already informed Your Majesty, that he very much regretted my not having been at Court during these last festivals ...

The Duke then went on to say that he thanked God for the firm purpose and mutual agreement which, to judge from the reception of the English ambassadors by Your Majesty he perceived to exist between you and the King, his master, for the maintenance of peace and perfect friendship. Then, after a few minutes' reflection, he exclaimed with a deep sigh: 'Alas! there remains still one step for the removal of all scruples and the confirmation of that very friendship and alliance which might indeed become quite indissoluble, and lay the King, my master, and his kingdom under such obligation to the Emperor that money or anything else required could be easily obtained, and this step is no other than His Imperial Majesty's consent to this marriage.' 'The King,' continued the Duke, 'is so much bent upon it that I do not think anyone but God could turn him aside, for he believes it to be imperative for the welfare and tranquillity of his kingdom that he should marry again for the sake of having male succession; besides which, from the books he has read on the subject, and the discussions he has instituted throughout his kingdom, he feels quite convinced that his union with the Queen was from the beginning illegitimate ...'

After leaving the Duke, Mr. de Rochefort (Rochford), now earl of Vulchier (Wiltshire) and Vulmot (Ormonde), came up to me proffering his services, and expressing a wish to visit me at my lodgings, saying also how much gratified the King was at Your Majesty's evident desire to maintain friendly relations with him, as appeared from the gracious reception made to his ambassadors [at Bologna]. The Earl went on to say how particularly pleased the King was to see me in England, feeling sure that I should not be one of those who by evil reports sent home would try to disturb the said friendly relations, 'although,' he added, 'there being still a few points of dispute between the Emperor and the King, my master, your letters perhaps are not without their rough edges.' My reply was that from the manner in which the English ambassadors had been received [at Bologna], it was quite evident that my account of the true state of things in England had been somewhat modified, for I had not yet lost all hope in the wisdom, goodness, and magnanimity of him whom the affair principally concerned, meaning the King, who, I thought, would sooner or later perceive the true nature of the affairs under discussion. The Earl's reply was: 'I cannot persuade myself that the Emperor wishes to hinder a plan which would be so beneficial to this kingdom. I would willingly have given all I possess for the King, my master, to have been able to converse with the Emperor for a little while on this subject.' He then asked me whether I wrote to Your Majesty often, and how my despatches were forwarded, to which I purposely made no direct answer, feigning not to have understood the nature of the inquiry ...

In consequence of a message sent me by the Queen I asked the King's permission to wait upon her. I went thither accompanied by the earl of Vulchier (Wiltshire), who tried to persuade me that she was absent from home and had gone to hear a sermon. Found her, however, sitting in her room. She asked for tidings of Your Majesty, inquired what I had to say and what I thought of her affair; if I had any hope, and thought the people [at Rome] were acting well, &c. Replied in the most encouraging terms possible, which seemed to give her much satisfaction and relief ...

*13 January 1530*

... The Queen still remains at Greenwich; the King has been here [in London] for the last five days, probably to attend without interruption to the business of the said embassy, and assist in the deliberations [of the Privy Council].

The French ambassadors were a long time at Court yesterday, especially to take leave of the Lady on the occasion of the departure of one of them, Mons. de Bayonne [for France], There was much dancing, and the Lady entertained them splendidly here; nothing could have given the King greater satisfaction than to see the French ambassadors thus take leave of the Lady, and pay their respects to her ...

*20 January 1530*

... I have been told that his [M. de Bayonne, the French ambassador] brother,

Mr. de Langey, has made several presents to the Lady in the way of rings, gold neck-laces, rosaries, and other trinkets, whether in his own name or in that of his master, the King, I cannot say; but I have been told that the ambassador's object was, first to obtain the good favour of the Lady, and then sell to the King many fine jewels he has brought with him. If so, he could not have made use of a better broker. They further say that the Frenchman has at his own house very fine jewellery and precious stones of all kinds, and that he has besides given a good many to be sold under another name. Among other things, a young Frenchman has shewn me this very day one single diamond tablet, and a large cross of the same stones, for which, as he tells me, the ambassador has here refused 10,000 crs., and for which he wants 12,000. If I am to believe what the young man says, the jewels belong to a merchant of Lyons, but, as I said before, the general opinion here is that they belong to Mr. de Langey or to his master [the king of France.]

The Queen has informed me [through a confidential messenger] that the King had lately written, or was about to do so, to the archbishop of Canterbury, as chief archbishop, primate, and legate of this kingdom, to give him warning that, unless the Pope consented to the accomplishment of this marriage, his own and other ecclesiastical authority would be at an end here in England, and that he himself (the King), the nobles, and the people, provoked and hurt at the advocation of the suit to Rome, had already shewn great animosity against ecclesiastics in general, and were getting daily more and more incensed against them, and would become Lutherans in the end. He (the King) wished to give the Archbishop notice of this, because he was the Pope's vicar in England.

This information has only come from the above-mentioned quarter, and therefore it may have been said merely to frighten the Queen, as no doubt was the case when the Spanish letter, of which I sent Your Majesty a copy, was written to me ...

### 25 January 1530

On Thursday, the 20th inst., I wrote to Your Majesty of current affairs. Next day, on receiving the letters of the 23rd ult., I went to the King, who is still detained in this city by business, or perhaps, as reported, to be at a greater distance from the Queen. Was very graciously received; indeed, the warmth of the King's welcome seems to increase each time that he gives me an audience. On this occasion he inquired eagerly after Your Majesty's health and welfare, and shewed great pleasure on hearing favourable accounts of both ...

After some further conversation on less important matters, the King said that Monseigneur (his usual designation for M. de Vulchier) had set out that very morning [on an embassy to the emperor], after having, as he believed, been to call on me. Replied that M. de Vulchier had been prevented from coming to me by press of business, just before his departure; but had written to make his excuses and take leave; and that his landlord, besides, had deceived me, for when I attempted to call on the Earl that morning, expecting to find him at home, I was told that he had already taken his departure. The King then said: 'I am very glad that the Earl has started so early; that saved you the trouble of calling upon him, which, on the present occasion, and with your position at this court, would have been an immense honour for him.' Many other flattering things did the King say on this occasion, which I answered in a similar strain ...

After a long conference on these and other various topics, I took leave of the King and went away. He begged me to come to him whether I had advices to communicate or not, without ceremony, and whenever I felt inclined, for (he said) I should always be welcome.

Before my audience from the King I was met by Monsgr. de Norfolk, who remained some little time in conversation with me ... *[After some conversation on foreign affairs]* The Duke went on to say that he was now going to speak to me rather as a friend and brother than as a foreigner and ambassador. 'You are aware (he said), that my brother-in-law, the Sr. de Vulchier (Wiltshire) is not of a warlike disposition; on the contrary, he is very timid, and if, on his arrival in Italy, he should find any danger abroad, or even suspicion of it, I believe him capable of not venturing to proceed on his journey.' The Duke, therefore, begged me to write to Your Majesty, that some precautions should be taken for his security. Answered that I considered it quite superfluous to write to Your Majesty about it. He (the Duke) knew very well how former ambassadors had been treated by you, and that even if the Sr. de Vulchier (Wiltshire) were not going as ambassador from the king of England, the fact only of his being his brother-in-law would be sufficient reason for Your Majesty to take the greatest care of his safety. The Duke, nevertheless, still urged me to write and send somebody in great haste to inquire if the last post had left for Rome, and in case the messenger was not gone that he should wait until I had written the letter. Finding, however, that he had, he made me promise to write by the next, which I could not well refuse to do, having always found the said Duke well disposed to serve Your Majesty. I consider, however, all this to have been simply done to give themselves importance, and gain, reputation, and that the fear which they seem to entertain is only an excuse.

The Duke at this interview said nothing about the marriage, as he has been in the habit of doing, yet at one time he hinted at Mr. de Vulchier (Wiltshire) in a manner that would have pleased me much more if only he had gone more into the subject, for he said that though the said nobleman would not personally work in that business for which he was sent to Your Majesty, yet it was at least a very reputable thing that such a personage should go to the Imperial Court [on such a mission]. The Duke did not actually say that nevertheless the Earl [and the rest] would be glad to see the accomplishment of the marriage, but it would have been much better if he had declared that they (the ambassadors) would abstain altogether from speaking about it. I dared not interrogate him further for fear of appearing to cast doubt on his statement.

I have been told by the landlord of the house where the French ambassador lives that he has heard him say that the King, his master, had caused several learned Parisian doctors to be written to in support of this divorce and that

35 of them had already declared in favour of it; that the subject had been much argued, and that among the said doctors were some, who, fearing lest they might lose the preferments they held under Your Majesty, did not venture to give an opinion in the matter; and that a promise had been made to them in the name of the two kings that in such case more valuable benefices should be bestowed upon them. The number of doctors they have found ready for this purpose is certainly not large; but on the other hand, the amount of crowns they have been obliged to disburse has been really enormous. Now if it only turns out true that the king of France is forwarding this matter that alone should be sufficient to dissuade this king from pursuing his enterprize, seeing that whilst the latter is seeking Your Majesty's close alliance and friendship he of France is doing all he can to keep you apart, which, after all, is the surest means for him to escape the payment both of the pension and debt. But this king is so blinded by his love for the Lady that he sees nothing else but the means of having her for his wife. I hope that Your Majesty will be able to open his (the King's) eyes this time ...

### 6 February 1530

... The Queen is treated as badly and even worse than ever. The King avoids her company as much as he can. He is always here with the Lady, whilst the Queen is at Richmond. He has never been half so long without visiting her as he is at present, giving as an excuse or pretence that some one has died of the plague near her residence. He has also resumed his attempts to persuade her to become a nun; this, however, is but a delusion and loss of time, for the Queen will never condescend to consent to it. The continued trouble and annoyance which she has to undergo compel her to be importunate both by her own letters and by mine; nor will she cease to do so until her suit is brought to a final conclusion, which she hopes will take place before Your Majesty's departure from Italy.

Jean Jocquin, the French ambassador, is here, and has brought with him money to pay the private pensions which the King, his master, gives here to various persons. The day after his arrival he and Mr. de Langey (Langeais) went to Court, conducted without ceremony by one of the King's chamberlains. They were well received by the King, and had a pretty long interview. On Saturday last they were again summoned to Court, but remained a very short time. On their return they called to visit me, and invite me to dinner for the next day. They called again on Sunday to fetch me ...

The conversation turned upon Dr Stocley's (Stockesley) commission, and his attempt at Paris to obtain for the king of England a decision of the doctors of that University in favour of his divorcing the Queen, his wife, and marrying another. At first they denied all knowledge of the affair, until at last Mr. de Langey, perceiving by the questions I put, and the conjectures I formed, that I suspected him of knowing something about it, was obliged to throw off the mask and to admit that he really had cognizance of the fact. He excused his first denial by stating that he had misunderstood me. He thought I asked him whether the question had or had not been debated in the Sorbonne by the University, of which he knew nothing. Respecting the private opinion of some of its doctors he knew for certain that Dr Stocker (Stockesley) had consulted several, among whom many whom he had supposed to be favourable to his views, and ready to write in favour of this king, had certainly given opinions exactly contrary to his wishes. The same thing had happened to a Spanish doctor residing at the Sorbonne, who was soliciting votes in favour of the Queen. Mr. de Langey spoke of this with precision, as if he had been present at the affair, and I really believe, as I lately had occasion to inform Your Majesty, that he has by his master's commands taken particular interest in this matter. In this opinion I am the more confirmed that I saw yesterday a letter from an Englishman residing in Paris, wherein the offers made to such doctors as would vote in favour of this king are expressly mentioned.

The said letter from Paris states that the chief object of Jockin's mission here was to reinstate the Cardinal in the King's favour, which, had it not been for the Lady [Anne] would have been easy enough, for as I have written to Your Majesty, it is generally believed here that the King bears no hatred to the Cardinal. If there has been ill-will it has been against the wealth he had amassed and property, and not against his person, and in this respect it would seem as if the King was not entirely in the wrong, for if the Cardinal made him spend large sums of money, and declared that all the wealth he himself accumulated was entirely for the King and for his service, to have taken possession of it a little sooner than the Cardinal expected could not be a subject of offence or injury, especially since from the moment he began to suspect his disgrace up to the time of his fall, he kept always repeating that the King could not do him a greater favour than to take away and appropriate to himself everything he possessed in this world, proceeding as it did from the Royal bounty. As a further proof that the King did not bear the Cardinal any personal ill-will I may add that from the beginning he determined that his case should not be brought before Parliament, for had it been decided against him, he could not, in face of such a decision, have pardoned him as he intended to do, and has since done, as I will relate hereafter ...

As I have lately informed Your Majesty, the Cardinal has been ill, or, as some will have it, feigned illness, in the hope that the King would go and see him, which he has not done, though by way of compensation he sent him the other day the best remedy for his illness, namely, a promise of pardon and grace, as well as absolution (abolition) from all the charges brought against him. On hearing which the Cardinal immediately began to improve and is now in full convalescence. Today he is to receive the said act of grace and pardon in the form in which he applied for it. The King, moreover, is to leave him the full enjoyment of his archbishopric of York and give him besides a yearly pension of 3,000 angels on the revenues of the bishopric of Winchester, in exchange for which he is to renounce all claims on that and every other ecclesiastical benefice. Besides the 10,000 angels which the King has sent him since his condemnation, two services of plate, and tapestry hangings enough for five rooms, have been restored to him, the rest of his money and house furniture remaining in the King's hands. With regard to his house in this city, the King has within the last few days taken legal possession of it, and incorporated it in his patrimony, and in place thereof is to give another house, which will belong in future to the archbishops of York. Master Russell told me that in consequence of a few words which he said to the King in favour of the Cardinal, the Lady [Anne] had not spoken to him for nearly a month, and that six days ago the duke of Norfolk himself had declared to him that the Lady, his niece, had taken great offence at his interference, and was also very angry with him (the Duke) for not having used his influence to the utmost against the Cardinal, of which she had often complained.

After this declaration the Duke went and asked Master Russell whether he did not think that the Cardinal still cherished the wish and the hope of again returning to power, to which question he (Russell) replied that the Duke must be aware of the Cardinal's courage and ambition, they were such that he would never draw back were there a chance of again re-entering office, and that this chance might present itself should the King require his counsel and assistance in any matter which he had formerly been in the habit of transacting. Hearing which the Duke began to swear vehemently, declaring that sooner than allow the Cardinal's return to favour under such circumstances he would eat him up alive. Such were, according to Mr Russell, the Duke's words, and I understand that it is to prevent any such possibility that the Cardinal has been forbidden to approach within six or seven miles of the Court.

I have been told by a cousin of the above-named physician that during the Cardinal's late illness the Lady had sent some one to visit him and to represent her as willing to speak to the King in his favour, a report rather difficult to believe after what I have related above, and considering the enmity and hatred which she has always borne him. One of two things, either she must have thought that the Cardinal was upon his death bed, or else she must have done it in order to shew her capabilities for dissimulation and intrigue in which arts she is generally reputed to be an accomplished mistress, or else it must be owned that Jean Jockin can work miracles and has already begun to perform this one ...

*16 March 1530*
The bishop of Lincoln and an Italian cordelier, who went recently to Oxonia (Oxford), to obtain for the King the seal of that university, were driven away by the women of the place and pelted with large stones. The King, in order to punish this act of violence and prevent any more serious outbreak, also to intimidate the doctors of that university who dispute his opinion, has sent thither the duke of Suffolk, and the treasurer of the Household, charging them that where they could not meet the argumentations of the contrary party with reason, they should pay them with ready money. The Duke has committed the said women to prison, and is eagerly following up the King's commission in order to obtain the seal by bribes or threats, as it may be.

I hear, and there is much talk about it, that recently at Cantabrigie (Cambridge), whilst the point was being discussed whether the university doctors should give in their opinion as well as the seal in the King's favour, as they had been urged to do, there was a squabble and a fight, six or seven of them being left dead on the spot. This I have on sufficiently good authority, but still, as it is only a report, and I have no letters in confirmation of it, either from the place itself or from Court, I do not vouch for its truth. If the fire, however, should be thus lit, there will be hereafter more harm done and more execrable deeds perpetrated than the parties immediately concerned in the affair foresee. There can be no doubt, as I have already informed Your Majesty, that the King, by fair means or foul, will at last wring consent from the English universities, but there still remains that of Paris, which is said to have the privilege of the Apostolic See, and to be in great difficulty as to its decision; the fear is that the king of France, in fulfilment of the promise made here by his ambassador, will by 'fas aut nephas' induce that university also to give her seal, and by threats or promises through those already on their side gain over many more, oblige their opponents to absent themselves, and then bring about a unanimous decision in favour of this king. To prevent which it would be well if the Emperor would represent to the king of France that he must refrain from giving any but strictly legal help to the king of England, for that, if this cause should be publicly disputed, any tampering with those who have written on the King's side will be brought to light. And also because the Queen has innumerable adherents, who fear to commit their opinions to writing until compelled to do so, it would be well that the Pope should issue a brief to the said university, commanding that this cause be brought forward for public disputation, and laying under sentence of excommunication any who should fail to speak the exact truth concerning it. Were this done, there is no doubt, I am told, that the case would be settled as desired.

The Cardinal has not yet gone to York, probably he does not wish to remove so far from the Court, as he would then have less facility for watching his opportunity and returning to it, the hope of which he has not yet relinquished, as I gather from his physician who came the other day to speak to me about a pension which the Cardinal still holds on the bishopric of Pallance (Palencia) in Spain. The earl of Childara (Kildare), first among the Irish nobles, who has been so long a prisoner in the Tower, is soon to be set at liberty, with permission to return to Ireland. The Queen is at Vinsor (Windsor) with the King, treated as usual ...

*10 May 1530*
I have this day waited on the King, who arrived late last evening accompanied by the Lady ...

On taking leave of the King I asked and obtained permission to visit the Queen and the princess, who are to pass five or six days together at Richmond. I hope to go there to-morrow; indeed, had the permission been refused I should have gone all the same in disguise, the Queen having sent me word that she must absolutely see me one way or other.

The audience lasted a long time, and indeed had it not been that the hour for going to mass was approaching, and that the French and Venetian ambassadors were also waiting, it would have lasted longer. The said ambassadors were in the hall when I arrived, and were still there when I left the Royal chamber. The Frenchman was transacting business with the King's first secretary and Brian Tuke, but the subject could not be very important, for they were discussing it in a corner of the hall where the greater part of what was said could be overheard.

Whilst awaiting the King's audience I went into the apartments of the duke of Norfolk, who is now lodging at the Palace, and asked him the cause of the present convocation of prelates and theologians of this country. The Duke said that had I not asked the question he would of himself have volunteered to give me the required information, as many persons wrongly supposed, and perhaps I was one of them, that the assembly was for the purpose of discussing the Queen's case, and bringing about the new marriage. He assured me on his honour that there was nothing of the sort, the sole object of the convocation being to take measures for preventing the Lutheran heresy from entering this kingdom. It was for that exclusive purpose that the King had come here [to London], and he intended to be daily present at the meeting of the said prelates and doctors as one most competent to decide on those religious matters ...

The Queen, though meeting with the accustomed treatment, is so comforted by the many proofs of Your Majesty's affection, that she is now firmer than ever in her purpose. She hopes and believes that either out of regard for his own honour and reputation, or for fear of Your Majesty, the King will not dare make the other marriage. Should it take place, which may God prevent, I suspect that the King will hastily repent, and that he will be thankful to return to his first marriage if by so doing he could be freed from his second. This was also the opinion of the Cardinal (Wolsey) and of many others, for the said cardinal would willingly have given up his archbishopric [of York] that this had been attempted two years ago, for then he could not have been better revenged of an intrigue, which has caused his ruin ...

The King shews greater favour to the Lady every day; very recently coming from Windsor, he made her ride behind him on a pillion, a most unusual proceeding, and one that has greatly called forth people's attention here, so much so that two men have been, as I am informed, taken up and sent to prison merely for having mentioned the fact [and commented upon it] ...

*15 June 1530*

Immediately after the dispatch of my last letters of the 10th inst. I received information that the King had written to certain of the prelates and high officials of this country, desiring them to be present at his court on the 12th inst., each of them bringing with him his seal of office, and that such as for some sufficient cause could not be present themselves should at least send the said seals of office. On the 12th, which was last Sunday, the greater part of those who had been summoned appeared at Court, where, as I am given to understand, they were most urgently exhorted, as the representatives of one portion of the kingdom, to write conjointly to the Pope, explaining the necessity there was for the King to divorce the Queen and make another marriage, and pointing out also all the evils that would arise if this were not done. The address ended by praying His Holiness, in conformity with the opinion of the most famous universities and most learned men in Christendom, to declare the marriage between the King and Queen illegal, and authorise the King to take another wife, intimating that should His Holiness refuse to grant so just and reasonable a petition the King and his people must seek some other means of redress even if that should involve the summoning of a General Council; this last sentence being added to the document by way of a threat, as if they thought that what the Pope most fears is the calling of a Council of the Church. To give the address greater weight and authority it was to bear the signatures and official seals of all these prelates and gentlemen, and though only those well known to be on the King's side were summoned to the meeting, still they were unable at the time to come to a resolution, and therefore the meeting was adjourned until tomorrow, Corpus Christi Day. Not one of the prelates known to be favourable to the Queen received a summons, nor the Chancellor[43] either, whom they suspect. I have been told that last Sunday, when this affair of the marriage was being discussed, it was asked why the King should not (having obtained the opinion of so many competent judges on this matter) marry at once, without awaiting any further approval of his conduct, especially as he had cause to be suspicious of the Pope. But few were found to support such an extravagant motion as this, or speak against it, until one of the King's chief favourites, fearing lest he should adhere to the proposal, and be persuaded to carry out his purpose, threw himself down on his knees and implored the King to take into consideration the slight symptoms of disaffection appearing in many parts of the kingdom, and the inclination of the people, which the slightest provocation might kindle into a flame, and that if he was determined to make this marriage without awaiting the definitive judgment of the Church, that he should at least delay it until winter, when the general excitement might have somewhat subsided. Here the question remains for the present.

On this same Sunday the Queen spoke for some time with the King, exhorting him to be again to her a good prince and husband, and to quit the evil life he was leading and the bad example he was setting, and that even if he would shew no regard for her, who was, as he well knew, his true and lawful wife, that he should at least respect God and his conscience, and no longer ignore the brief which had been executed in Flanders. The King, after many words and much commendation of those who had written in his favour, said that the brief was of very little consequence, and that even if it were he should not heed it much, because the Pope was compelled to act as the Emperor wished, and with that the King left the room abruptly without saying another word.

The Queen has since sent to ask me whether the said brief should be presented to the King. My answer has been that I think it expedient to do so, as he can then no longer allege ignorance of it, and we shall be able to obtain a last monition of excommunication against him. I believe this will be done tomorrow.

I wrote lately to Your Majesty that if the Lady [Anne] could only be kept away from Court for a little while, the Queen might still regain her influence over the King, for he does not seem to bear any ill-will towards her. Quite lately he sent her some cloth begging her to have it made into shirts for him. The Lady, hearing of this, sent for the person who had taken the cloth – one of the principal gentlemen of the bedchamber – and although the King himself confessed that the cloth had been taken to the Queen by his order, she abused the bearer in the King's very presence, threatening that she would have him punished severely. Indeed, there is a talk, as I am told, of dismissing, to please the Lady, some of the officers of the Royal Household, and if so, the said gentleman will not be the last, for some time back the wife of the young Marquis and two other ladies, most devoted to the Queen, and in whom she found more comfort and consolation than in any others, were, at her request, dismissed from Court and sent home.

I have received today letters from Paris from Dr Garay of the 8th inst., in which he says that the king of France had issued a warrant commanding the university of Paris to come to a determination on the divorce affair, but that the University after having met several times in consultation, replied on the 7th instant that as the case was already in the Pope's hands to determine, it did not become them to meddle with it. In spite of this, Dr Garay says he fears that the King will give the doctors no peace until they have declared in favour of the divorce, unless Your Majesty can obtain in the meantime from the Pope the brief about which Dr Garay wrote recently in the letter that went with my last despatch, or the king of France be otherwise induced to desist from these practices. This, however, must be done at once, for according to Garay the pressure from here is considerable. He also writes to me that, following my advice, he has acquainted the Imperial ambassador in France with all these particulars. I have no doubt that he will do his duty, as he always has done, and yet should he get a special charge from Your Majesty he might speak more boldly and openly on the subject. The affair, in short, is well worth Your Majesty's attention.

Whilst writing the above I have received a letter from the Cardinal's physician, in which he tells me in rather obscure terms that his master, not knowing exactly the state of the Queen's affairs, cannot give any special advice upon them ; that if he could get fuller information he would give counsel and directions as though Paradise were to be gained through it, for his happiness, honour, and repose depended on that, and that it seemed to him that now was the time to take stronger measures and call in the assistance of the secular arm, since so little nerve was shewn [on the other side]. The physician did not further explain the Cardinal's meaning, and, therefore, I am at a loss how to interpret his message and wishes. He also said that the Lady and her party did not at all regret the delay in the proceedings, as it gave them time to carry out their plans and push on the affair, which they do daily hoping that as time goes on both Your Majesty and the Queen will be wearied out.

All these things considered, it seems as if Your Majesty ought to have matters brought to a crisis at once the best means towards which, as I have very lately pointed out, would be the removal of the said Lady from the Court; in which opinion the Cardinal also coincides, saying that when that is accomplished, the management of the affairs may be left to those who know best how to act, by which he means himself.

It would seem as if the Pope could hardly refuse to enforce so reasonable a measure, as the removal of the Lady from Court, for right and justice require it, whereas the scandal and bad example given, and the King's disobedience to Papal authority fully recommend it. The best way would be that the Pope instead of the declaration of pains and penalties to be incurred by the King, as in the said brief, should issue an order to that effect confirming the former censures, and declaring the King to have fallen under the penalties contained in the brief.

The Queen has not heard from Rome for a long time; she is expecting daily the return of the courier I sent in April; but, nevertheless, I fancy she will dispatch another one express in three days to acquaint Messire Mai with what is going on. I hear, that the King has just received letters from Rome, which I think have been the cause of his urging the above-mentioned letter to be written.

The Queen sent me word yesterday to say that she intended writing to Your Majesty by the next courier, but in consequence of the said letters received from Paris, and seeing the urgency of affairs, I have thought better not to lose the present opportunity, and therefore send this off in all haste.

*11 July 1530*
Since my last despatch I have been to see Mr. de Norfolk, who has just returned to Court after a considerable absence ...

*[following a general discussion of affairs]* The Duke after this returned to the subject of the divorce, and said that as there seemed to be no other way of bringing this business to an end, he would willingly sacrifice the greatest part of what he owned in this world if God would be pleased to take to himself the Queen and his niece[44] also, for certainly the King would never enjoy peace of mind until he had made another marriage, both for the relief of his own conscience as for the preservation of the tranquillity of this realm, which, he said, could only be attained by the existence of male posterity to succeed to his crown. Replied that the King, not being able to ensure the possession of male heirs, ought not to have put himself in the intricate position in which he was, troubling the whole of Christendom with so scandalous an example, and sowing such pestilential views in his kingdom. That the truest, most expedient, and most laudable way of promoting the happiness of his subjects and providing male succession to his crown was to marry his daughter, the Princess, now of a suitable age for marriage, and as capable of bearing male children as any other woman, and that for my own part I should like to see his (the Duke's) son chosen for her husband, as, unless the Princess were to marry a foreign prince, I could not discover a more fitting alliance for her. Said a good deal more on this subject, and ended by stating that this suggestion was entirely my own, and did not in any way proceed from Your Majesty or from the Queen. It originated only

in my personal esteem and affection for him, and I had not mentioned it
to anyone else ...

Eight days ago the Princess sent to ask the King for permission to come
and see him here before he goes away on a hunting expedition, which will
take up his time till November. The King, however, preferred going to her,
and remained [at Richmond] all last Wednesday, shewing her all possible
affection. God grant that this may last! ...

Today the French ambassador has received intelligence that 100 Parisian
doctors have given opinion in favour of this King, and that the University is
also to give its seal to that effect. This is no doubt, bad news for the Queen,
as the King will become more arrogant than ever, and have their names and
votes proclaimed throughout his kingdom. It is, moreover, to be feared that
now that he is supported by the university of Paris he may gain to his views
a considerable portion of his subjects, and also attempt the accomplishment
of his marriage without awaiting the Pope's further decision, At this the
Lady will be nothing loth, for quite lately she has been, as I am informed,
urging on the King, and telling him that Your Majesty had it not in your
power to do him any harm, and that her family alone would provide for
one year 10,000 men for his service at their own expense; and that since
Your Majesty had not suffered any qualms of conscience in marrying your
own first cousin [Isabella of Portugal], you could not decently ask others to
be more scrupulous in this matter. I am told that a short time ago the King
said to the Lady that she was under great obligation to him, since he was
offending everyone and making enemies everywhere for her sake, and that
she replied: 'That matters not, for it is foretold in ancient prophecies that
at this time a Queen shall be burnt: but even if I were to suffer a thousand
deaths, my love for you will not abate one jot.'

The Queen is to accompany the King on the hunting expedition as
usual.

*5 September 1530*
... The Queen has been suffering from high fever constantly during the last
two or three days, according to the report of her physician, but is now, thank
God, in good health. Were her indisposition to return I should think that the
arrival of the Papal Nuncio, who landed at Dover two days ago, would soon
restore her. She is treated as usual, excepting that the Lady has forbidden the
gentlemen who were in the habit of visiting her, and from whom she could
learn something of what is going on, to wait upon her any more, and has
placed some women about her to spy and report anything she may say or
do, so that she can hear but few news and those with great difficulty.

The King is still hunting and coming nearer to London every day. This
year he has attended more to business and less to sport than for a long
time previously; indeed, ever since the closing of the ports which coincided
with Brian's (Sir Francis) arrival from France bearing news that Florence
was on the point of surrendering, he has been continually engaged in
council.

*20 September 1530*

Your Majesty's instructions respecting the bishop of Bayonne[45] have been most implicitly obeyed. I have, as related in my despatches of the 5th and 14th inst., lost no opportunity of informing him of Your Majesty's great desire for the observance of peace and continuation of the friendship between his master and yourself. The day after receiving his visit I went to return the attention; but he was not in, and the following day he had left very early. I have, therefore, been unable to speak further with him and inquire what his mission to this court was. I have, nevertheless, been assured in several quarters that the ports were only closed because after his altercation with the King he (the Bishop) had threatened to leave and report to his master that one of the chief reasons for his coming over here was to bring the consent for the Princess marriage to the son of the duke of Norfolk, and to offer the eldest daughter of France to the King himself. I have not been able to discover any sign of this, nor do I think it very probable, for since the fall of the Cardinal, the French have carried on all their intrigues through the Lady and through her father and uncle, whom, as they wish to keep on friendly terms with this king, they would not dare to affront. Besides, they well know that the love of the King for the Lady is so great that he would not give her up for the eldest daughter of France, or anyone else in the world. Nor do I think it likely either that the French would attempt any such thing, for being short of money they would rather put forward some scheme either for drawing it from this country, or deferring their own payment of the debt, than propose or countenance matrimonial alliances which would, as in this case, necessitate an advance of money on their part. They would, on the contrary, have a fair excuse for retaining a part of the said debt, whilst there was a chance of the duke of Orleans marrying the Princess, and even if they should be brought to consent to her marrying the son of the duke of Norfolk it might be for the purpose of ingratiating themselves with him; besides which it might well happen that on account of the said marriage, as well as of that which the King meditates, the latter finding himself in hot water with Your Majesty, and with his subjects, would be compelled to purchase the French king's favour and aid by releasing him from the whole, or a part of his debt. Many here share my opinion on this last point ...

*13 November 1530*

Yesterday morning, Saturday, I went to Court, and met there the lords Norfolk and Wiltshire ...

I then went to the King, who, among many other familiar topics, inquired after my servant who had died of the plague ...

Whilst speaking on the above matters the King at every possible opportunity introduced the subject of his divorce, on which he spoke with much eagerness, and this not without good cause, for at a small window in the King's chamber, commanding the gallery where the King and I were speaking, was the Lady overlooking and overhearing all that passed. Begged the King from the very first not to enter upon so delicate a subject, for I had resolved not to say anything more upon it without express command from Your Majesty. And this I said because I was convinced the King would not listen to reason; but the more I tried to avoid the subject the more did the King insist on bringing it forward. He began as usual by complaining that Your Majesty thwarted him in every possible way, expecting from him what was dishonest and unreasonable; upon which I reminded the King how many things you might have done in this cause which you had refrained from doing; and that as to the dishonest demands to which he referred there was no one in the world to whom this could apply so little as to Your Majesty, who had always acted as an honourable and virtuous prince.

The King perceiving the warmth with which I uttered these last words, and that I was ever ready with my arguments, fearing, moreover, lest the Lady might overhear something that would offend her, moved away from the window and taking me to the middle of the room, said that if he had spoken so unceremoniously about Your Majesty it was for the purpose of inducing you to reprimand your ambassadors in Rome and in France, who were inventing a thousand falsehoods about him, and ended by saying that in spite of them all he would carry his purpose through. The King added that I myself had frequently sent advices from this country to Rome which had greatly contributed to embitter his case, for the Pope himself had mentioned the fact to his ambassadors. To this new attack I answered for myself, a task easy enough to accomplish, considering that I had right on my side and that my accusers were far off. The King, however, spoke with regret of the late dealings in France ...

*27 November 1530*

The continuation of the rumour, now prevailing for some time, that in the ensuing Parliament, which is to resume its labours at the feast of the Purification of our Lady, this king intends proposing some measure respecting his divorce, and also the great annoyance the Queen experiences at her cause being so long delayed, have induced her to write to Your Majesty, and to pray that you will be pleased to intercede in her favour with the Pope, and incline His Holiness to move in her case, as he promised on the reception of Miçer Mai's memorandum, at which my own secretary was present.

The Queen further prays that her suit be proceeded with at once, without further delay, as otherwise no good can result to her, but on the contrary, as Your Majesty may judge by the duplicate of the Queen's letter to the Pope [here enclosed]. On the subject of this letter I have dwelt more fully in one of my former despatches, as have also Miçer Mai and the Nuncio, the latter of whom has now confirmed all statements in his letter to the Pope, of which a copy is also enclosed.

It is said that every exertion is being made here to prepare all matters against the meeting of this Parliament, and there was also a talk of having some book in favour of the King written and printed, that people might examine the matter for themselves ...

A few days ago the duchess of Norfolk[46] sent the Queen a present of poultry, and with it an orange, inside of which was a letter from Gregory Casale, a copy of which I deem proper to send to Your Majesty. The Queen imagines that the Duchess has sent her this present and letter of her own accord, and out of the love and affection she bears her, but I am afraid that all has been done with the Duke's knowledge; at all events this seems to open a way for the Queen to communicate more freely [with her friends] and disclose her plans to the Duchess, for which purpose it has been deemed expedient to dissemble better in future.

Eight days ago the King ordered the Cardinal to be brought here [to London], on hearing which, he abstained from food for several days, much preferring (as it is said) to die in this manner than of a more ignominious and dishonourable death, of which he has some fears. In consequence of which abstinence from food he has been taken ill on the road, and is not yet arrived. There is a report that a chamber has been already prepared for him in the Tower, the same one that the duke of Buckingham once occupied.

Many reasons are assigned for the Cardinal's arrest, but all are mere conjectures. I was told by a gentleman that a short time ago the King was complaining to his Council of something which had not been done according to his wish, and that he exclaimed in great wrath that the Cardinal was a very different man from any of them for conducting State matters, and that after repeating the same words twice over he left the Council room in disgust. Since then the Duke, the Lady [Anne], and her father, have never ceased plotting against the Cardinal, especially the Lady, who has wept and wailed, regretting her lost time and honour, and threatening the King that she would go away and leave him, so much so that the King had enough to do to quiet her, and though he begged and intreated her most affectionately, and even with tears in his eyes, not to forsake him, nothing would satisfy the Lady short of the Cardinal's arrest ...

*4 December 1530*
... The cardinal of York died on St Andrew's Day about 40 miles from here, at a place where the last king Richard was defeated and killed.[47] Both lie buried in the same church, which the people begin already to call 'the Tyrants' grave'.

Many are the reports current as to the cause of his death. Some say that for several days after his arrest he would take no nourishment whatever, and that after that he either took, or was given, something to hasten his end. On Monday the captain of the guard arrived to conduct him to London, and both supped together cheerfully enough. Soon after, however, the Cardinal was taken violently ill, so much so that it was thought he could not live through the night; yet he lingered till Wednesday, and died like a good Christian, protesting, at the time of receiving the Holy Sacrament, that he had never undertaken anything against his master, the King. There has been a great deal going on at Court since his death; but his ecclesiastical benefices have not yet been disposed of. It is believed the King will retain them for some time, and pocket the revenues ...

*29 December 1530*
Two days before Christmas the seigneur de la Pomeraye arrived here and

had an audience on Christmas Eve. On St Stephen's Day he and Jehan Jocquin returned to Court, where they remained till yesterday, greatly feted, especially by the Lady. These festivities, however, have not interfered with their business, as they have had time to arrange for the mission of the bishop of Vaynchestre (Winchester), who starts for France to-day. I am informed by de la Pomeraye that this mission is intended partly to return the bishop of Bayonne's visit here, and partly to request the King's [of France] aid and support in obtaining permission [from the Pope] for the divorce case to be tried and decided in this kingdom, and that ambassador adds that as the king of England has this affair so much at heart his master cannot, on account of the great friendship existing between them, refuse to do what is in his power. The said Bishop is starting in all haste; he will be followed to-morrow by Dr Benoit (Benet), who is returning post to Rome and is to stop at the court of France for the despatches which the Bishop [of Winchester] will have ready for him there to take to Rome. The King has charged the Bishop to beg the king of France to leave Jehan Jocquin here as ambassador with de la Pomeraye, and therefore Jocquin is in any case to remain here till the Bishop's return. They would be sorry to lose Jocquin here, he is just the man for them at the present time. The King has been pleased to offer de la Pomeraye apartments in his own palace at Briduel (Bridewell).

I have not been able to obtain further information respecting the object of the Bishop's mission, nor yet of the particular means which he is to propose for the advocation of the divorce trial here: but it may be well believed that he (the Bishop) will spare neither promises nor words to induce the king of France to lend all his influence either by entreaties or threats in this direction. Therefore seeing the coldness and cowardice which have hitherto been apparent at Rome, and which will now probably increase, owing to the intervention of the king of France in the affair, it seems absolutely necessary that Your Majesty should write sharply to all those concerned in this business at Rome ...

*1 January 1531*

... The Queen told me long ago – and the information has since been confirmed from other quarters – that what these people hate most, and what keeps them in constant fear, is to see that I make no efforts whatever to court them, and to gain their friendship. Accordingly the Queen has sent me word that unless I have some very important business to transact, I am to abstain as much as possible from visiting the King or his ministers, and that she will let me know when is the fit time to do so. I have, accordingly, followed her instructions, and avoided going to Greenwich for these Christmas festivals.

P.S. – Since writing the above, a worthy man has come in haste from Greenwich assuring me that he has there heard two or three of the principal courtiers say that the King's marriage will certainly be dissolved at this next session of Parliament, and that they hope that after that the King and his friends will find the means of appeasing Your Majesty. I cannot guess on what foundation, however slight and frail, the said hope is made to rest, for

I have always given them to understand the contrary, and will again make an express declaration to that effect before the game is up. Lady [Anne] considering herself already sure of her affair, is fiercer than a lioness. She said the other day to one of the Queen's ladies-in-waiting that she wished all the Spaniards were at the bottom of the sea. And the lady attendant having observed that she (Lady Anne) should not for the sake of the Queen's honour express such sentiments, she replied that she cared not for the Queen or any of her family, and that she would rather see her hanged than have to confess that she was her Queen and mistress.

*31 January 1531*

... The very same day on which I sent to ask for an audience the same answer and excuse were offered to the Nuncio upon his making a similar application, whereas it is well known that the King is just now in very good health. This circumstance leads me to conjecture, among other things, that the King's refusal to see the Nuncio on this occasion is entirely owing to his fear that somehow or other he will be served with some summons from Rome, of which he is terribly afraid, however he may swagger about it; so much so that I hear his intention is, as he cannot do otherwise, to give in, and of his own free will, before he is actually compelled to it, separate from the Lady [Anne]. For which purpose, as I am told, the King has ordered a house which he gave her some time ago to be fitted up and prepared for her reception. It is, however, to be presumed that his intention is not to separate from her altogether, but to recall her soon, though I think that if she is once sent away God and the Queen will take care that she does not return. I have not yet been able to ascertain whether the information received on this head is correct, but hope soon to know the truth ...

Yesterday the duchess of Norfolk sent a message to the Queen to say that those of the opposite party were trying hard to win her over to their opinion, but if the whole world were to set about it they would not make her change. She was and would continue to be one of her party. At the same time she warned the Queen to take courage, for her adversaries were at their wits' end, being as much amazed and bewildered in this affair as the first day it began.

The Jew,[48] whom this king sent for, as I informed Your Majesty in a former despatch, notwithstanding all the precautions taken by Messire Mai to prevent his passage, arrived here in London six days ago. He has already seen the King twice, and been very well received, though not so well on the first as on the second audience; most likely the graciousness of his reception will gradually decrease unless he has more agreeable news than he brought at first, for I am told that his opinion is that the Queen's marriage ought not to be disputed or dissolved, but nevertheless that the King may and can very well take another wife conjointly with his first, which opinion the King has found so extravagant and absurd that he has openly declared to the Jew himself that this will not do, and that he must devise some other means of getting him out of the difficulty, for that he would never adopt, indeed would rather die than resort to such expedient, as it would be an infamous and blameable act for him to have two wives at the same time. I hear that the pith of the Jew's argument is that although the King's marriage with the widow of his brother was a true and legitimate act, yet he does not style himself properly husband of the Queen, inasmuch as according to [Jewish] law the posterity issuing from such a union is ascribed to the first husband; and as it would be unreasonable that in order to preserve the name and race of the deceased, the survivor should be prevented from having posterity of his own and bearing his name ...

*1 March 1531*

The Jew whom the King sent for, perceiving that his opinion of the case has not been considered authentic has drawn out another as vain and ill-founded as the former, propounding that it is allowable for a man to take to wife the widow of his brother, provided he do it out of his own desire and will, and with the direct intention of procuring descent to his brother's line. Without such marked intention, he maintains, the marriage is forbidden by Divine Law. God says the Jew, said so by the mouth of Moses, and cast his malediction on all those who married without such an intention, for if they did so marry no generation could spring forth from them, and if any it could not last long. And as the male children begot by the King in the Queen, his wife, have not lived long, the Jew argues and concludes that he [Henry] must have married his brother's widow without the above express intention, and consequently that his marriage is illegitimate and invalid.

Parliament is still sitting but without passing any important Act, as I have been told by some of its members, which circumstance makes them and me suspect that the King is keeping them assembled for some mysterious purpose. All are preciously tired of it, and every day several members keep asking permission to go home, which permission is readily granted to those who are known to hold for the Queen, or supposed to be her friends, though it is generally denied to the others, which fact naturally leads to the conjecture that the King intends one of these fine days to have the divorce question discussed in Parliament, and that he is only waiting for favourable news from France to take that step. Meanwhile the King will go on treating and coaxing La Guiche, who is still residing here, until he obtains from that quarter all he wishes for. Thus, one day in Lent, at a most solemn banquet, where the King dined in public with the Lady and several of his courtiers, among whom was the said La Guiche, the King drank his health as representative of the king of France, saying that if he could be sure for ever of the friendship and alliance of France he should not be afraid of all the rest, and other things to the same purpose.

The King has not attended the sessions of this Parliament since its opening until yesterday evening. He was about one hour and a half or two hours in the House of the Lords and prelates, but did not go down to the Commons. He said a good deal to them about his love of justice, and his zeal for the good administration of the kingdom and the protection of his subjects. On this topic he spoke for some time, but proposed nothing except that they should discuss and debate certain privileges and immunities of the Church in England under which malefactors in this country had at all times taken shelter, which, as he said, had been the cause of many evils not to be tolerated, and which he was determined to put down for the future. He also requested them to look into the case of the bishop of Rochester's cook,[49] which is a very strange one and happened thus. About ten days ago, in the said Bishop's house, some sort of soup was prepared, of which all who tasted (including almost all the household servants) were on the point of death, though only two actually died, besides some poor beggars to whom the soup had been distributed for charity. All, however, were taken very ill and suffered much pain. Very luckily the worthy Bishop, whom God no doubt considers very useful and necessary in this world, did not taste of the drug and thus escaped. They say that the cook having been immediately arrested on the application of the Bishop's brother, confessed at once that he had actually put into the broth some powders, which he had been given to understand would only make his fellow servants very sick without endangering their lives or doing them any harm. I have not yet been able to ascertain who it was who gave the cook such advice, nor for what purpose. The King has certainly shewn some displeasure at this, but whatever demonstrations of sorrow he makes he will not be able to avert suspicion from falling, if not on himself, for he is too noble-minded to have resource to such means – at least on the Lady and her father. The Bishop is unwell. and has been so ever since the acknowledgment subscribed by the Clergy, about which I wrote to Your Majesty on the 31st of January, and which has caused him considerable sorrow and disappointment; but notwithstanding his indisposition he intends leaving to-morrow [for his diocese], having already obtained the King's permission to that effect. I cannot, however, conceive how, being in bad health, bishop Fisher can think of exposing himself to the fatigues of such a journey, when by remaining here [in London] he might find better medical advice and more resources than anywhere else, unless it be that he chooses to be absent from the discussion of matters appertaining to the Church, or else that he fears there may be yet some relics of the powders from which he has do miraculously escaped. Should the King resume in the meantime his proceedings against the Queen, certainly his absence at this conjuncture, and that of the bishop of Duran (Durham), formerly of London, who is also away, will be exceedingly inconvenient ...

*22 March 1531*
... *[Norfolk]* said to me that there were here in London many Lutherans and that the day before the finest and most learned preacher among them in England had been arrested, and was in danger of being publicly burnt alive; at which he (the Duke), was sadly displeased, for he said the King had no fitter or better qualified man to send abroad on an embassy to a great prince, Notwithstanding that the Duke aggravated the case of this priest, nothing serious happened to him, for he was next day released from prison, as I will relate hereafter ...

The preacher above mentioned having been arrested and taken before the archbishop of Canterbury refused to answer the questions put to him unless lay members of the Privy Council should intervene in the proceedings. Owing to which the said duke of Norfolk, the earls of Auxford (Oxford), Vulchier (Wiltshire), and Tallebot (Talbot) were deputed, before whom the said priest proceeded to make his declaration and propounded heresy enough. Two days after, as I am informed, the priest, fearing lest the archbishop of Canterbury should proceed against him, appealed to the King, as chief and sovereign of the said archbishop, and was conducted to the royal presence before several bishops, who disputed with him and asked him to retract [his erroneous doctrines]. Upon which the King taking in his hand a parchment roll, where the priest's errors were stated, his eyes fell on the very first article wherein it was expressly said that the Pope was not the sovereign chief of the Christian Church. I have been told that the King said immediately: 'This proposition cannot be counted as heretical, for it is both true and certain.' Therefore, after the King had heard what the priest had to say in his own defence, he was set free and sent back to his own dwelling on condition of preaching one of these days a sermon, and retracting some of his doctrines which the King does not consider as thoroughly orthodox.

The general opinion is that the Lady [Anne] and her father, who are more Lutherans than Luther himself, have been the principal instruments of the priest's release from prison besides the natural inclination of the King himself to all those who speak in his favour and against the Pope ...

The Princess (Mary) is still staying with the Queen, her mother, which is a great consolation for her.

*14 May 1531*

... Some days ago the King dining with the Queen, as he is in the habit of doing at almost all the great Church festivals, began to speak about the truce with the Turk, of which there has been a talk for some time. The conversation then fell on Your Majesty, and on your brother, the king of the Romans, the said King extolling beyond measure, and much more than is his wont, the power, extent of dominions and resources of Your Imperial Majesty. Suddenly he changed the subject, and coming to speak about the Princess he accused the Queen of cruelty for not having ordered that her own physician should be in attendance on her daughter during her late illness. Indeed during the whole dinner there was nothing but courtesy and kindness on the part of the King. Next day, on the strength of the said gracious words and others uttered by the King on the occasion, the Queen ventured to ask permission for the Princess to come and pay them a visit, but this the King flatly refused in very rude terms, saying that the Princess could, if she chose, come and stay where the Queen was, but that he could not consent to her coming [to Greenwich], upon which the Queen very prudently and graciously replied that neither for the sake of her own daughter, nor for any other person in the world would she consent to anything that would look like a separation from her husband. And here the conversation ended ...

The King is having a great park made in front of the house[50] which once belonged to the Cardinal (Wolsey), and in order to go to it across the street has had a very long covered gallery built, for which purpose a number of houses have been pulled down to the great damage and discomfort of the proprietors without there having yet been any question of indemnifying them for their losses. All this is done to please the Lady who prefers that palace for the King's residence to any other, owing to there being no apartments for the Queen there. It is likewise to please the said Lady that the duchess of Norfolk has been dismissed [from Court] owing to her speaking too freely, and having declared in favour of the Queen much more openly than these people like her to do ...

6 June 1531

On Monday last the Papal Nuncio received letters from Rome informing him of the repeated and importunate applications made by the duke of Albany in order to obtain a suspension of the proceedings of the suit between the king and queen of England. Indeed, among other charges entrusted to the cardinal de Grammont, one was to solicit and recommend in the name of his master, the king of France, a complete suspension in the divorce suit, which the Pope thought was a fruitless attempt and loss of time, since justice must needs have its course. The king of England ought to be told that His Holiness will act most impartially in the case, and give just sentence without injury to either party. There is, therefore, no need whatever of the French king's intervention, for what the Pope did not do for the sake of the king of England himself he would certainly not do for any other prince in the World, not even for the sake of the Most Christian king of France, in whose favour he would do many other things.

The Pope in his despatch to the Nuncio mentioned also the truce concluded between the king of the Romans and the Turk, charging him, nevertheless, to exhort the King to make preparations for next year.

Believing that his visit would be neither agreeable to the King nor profitable to our cause, the Nuncio hesitated at first about going to Court, but at my persuasion went last Tuesday. He was very well received, and after explaining the causes the Pope had had for not granting the delay asked for, as well as the excuses he had made to the cardinal de Grammont upon his return to Rome, the King said that he had been already acquainted with the fact by his ambassadors. After which, and having uttered his usual complaints and recriminations against His Holiness, he said : 'The Pope is evidently doing his utmost to retain the cognizance of this affair, but he must not be deceived and lose his time in addressing to me persuasions and remonstrances, for I shall never consent to his being the judge in that affair. Even if His Holiness should do his worst by excommunicating me, and so forth, &c., I shall not mind it, for I care not a fig for all his excommunications. Let him follow his own at Rome, I will do here what I think best.' He also said that he had sent his powers to the Englishman, who had intervened at Rome on behalf of the kingdom, and had no doubt that his interposition would be admitted. On this very subject, and the conversation growing warmer, the King went on to say that if the Pope attempted to act unjustly towards him in the case, or other-wise do him injury, he would certainly retaliate for with the help of his brother, the king of France, his true and perpetual ally, he would lead an army against Rome ...

In this way the King went on attacking the Pope until, having somewhat mastered his passion, he added: 'I take the Pope to be upon the whole a worthy man, but ever since the last wars he has been so awfully afraid of the Emperor that he dares not act against his wishes.' Then he added: 'Yet as I know him to be a thoroughly good man, and of great natural tact I will send him a newly printed book on condition that he will not shew it to any living soul for some time to come. In this manner will I try to make him lean to the side of justice.' Thus saying he (the King) handed over to the Nuncio a work of which I myself had procured a copy the day before, notwithstanding all the King's precaution and care. I have sent it to Mons. de Granvelle that he may look it over, and then forward it to Miçer Mai (sic) and to Doctor Ortiz at Rome, that both may be on their guard and prepared to answer; which in my opinion is easy enough, for there is nothing in the book which goes to the root of the matter or that cannot be refuted in two words.

After the Nuncio's departure, the King was long in consultation with his privy councillors and other great men, and finding no other means of parrying the blow announced from Rome, it was decided to send some one to the Queen for the purpose of inducing her to consent to the delay of the proceedings, and to the removal of the cause somewhere else. The Queen was secretly acquainted with the fact that very evening, and on Tuesday morning, without any further communication, as the virtuous and Christian princess that she is, took the true counsel, and caused several masses of the Holy Ghost to be said, that she might be thereby enlightened and know what to answer to the King's deputation for the salvation of her soul, and the good and repose of the King, kingdom, and the whole of Christendom.

On the said day, therefore, towards eight or nine o'clock at night, just as the Queen was going to bed, there came the dukes of Norfolk and Suffolk, the young marquis [of Dorset], the earls of Tallebot (Talbot), Northumberland, Wiltshire, and several other noblemen, more than 30 in number, accompanied by the bishops of Lincoln and London, doctors Lee, Sampson, and Steve (Stephen Gardiner), the first secretary. Being introduced to the Queen' presence, the duke of Norfolk spoke for the rest and said: 'That he and the rest had come there on the part of the King, and by his express command, on State matters of great moment to him and the whole of his kingdom ; namely, to signify to her how much displeased and hurt he (the King) was at the contempt and vituperation with which he had been treated on her account by the Pope, summoned as he had been by public proclamation to appear personally at Rome: a strange measure never before enforced by the popes against the kings of England. She (the Queen) might well consider that no reason, however strong or plausible, could be sufficient for the King to abandon his kingdom. That would certainly not help her, and those who had the management of her affairs at Rome, to come to a peaceable and satisfactory settlement of the dispute. It was far better not to press the sentence as they had done and were still doing at Rome. She ought to be contented that by mutual consent of the parties a fit place and impartial judges should be chosen, as otherwise she might be the cause of great troubles and scandals throughout the kingdom, by which all those present, their children, and the rest of their posterity might be thrown into great danger and confusion. He (the Duke) and the rest came to beg and exhort her on behalf of King and kingdom to consider how many dangers they and the whole of England would run by her refusing to comply with the King's wishes, especially as she had no legitimate cause of complaint, since from the very first she had been treated as well and as honourably as any queen of England ever was, and perhaps even more so. Secondly, she ought to recollect the help and assistance given [from England] to her father, the Catholic King [Ferdinand] by means of which he was enabled to make the conquest of Navarre. Thirdly, she ought also to bear in mind the many and multifarious services which the King had rendered to Your Majesty, even during the rising of the Commons in Spain, and at many other times which (the Duke said) would take too long to relate. She ought also to consider that the King could not, and ought not to be called upon to leave his kingdom and appear at Rome or elsewhere, except of his own free will and consent, being as he was supreme chief and sovereign in his own kingdom both temporally and spiritually, as had been declared, recognized, and attested by Parliament and the Clergy, All which considerations (added the Duke) ought to remove at once all her scruples in the matter, and induce her to consent to the delay and appointment of place and judges above alluded to.'

To the Duke's speech the Queen answered: That no living soul regretted more than she did the annoyance the King had experienced, nor the contempt and humiliation whereof he complained, especially if, as the King said, she was the principal cause of it. She could not, however, think that her proctors at Rome were capable of soliciting, or those who had taken cognizance of the affair, of granting unjust terms or other than such as common right and judicial procedure required; which terms being observed no injury or harm could be done to either of the contending parties. Respecting the choice of other judges but the Pope – the only legitimate one in such cases – she would never consent to it as long as she lived, not that she expected any favour at His Holiness' hands, 'for certainly (she said) up to the present time the Pope has shewn himself so much inclined and so partial to the King that nothing more can be asked of him. I myself, and no one else have reason to complain of His Holiness;' and she went on recapitulating the many favours granted to the King since the beginning of the suit, and the injuries she herself had received. 'Nevertheless (she added), as the King himself did in the first instance appeal to His Holiness, who keeps the place and has the power of God on earth, and consequently is the image of eternal Truth – I wish and intend that truth and justice and right be recognized and declared by the minister and vicar of the said supreme Truth, namely, by the Pope, whose authority and declaration are more necessary in this case for the repose and example not only of this kingdom, but also of Christendom at large. With regard to the scandals alluded to, I confidently hope in God that as I have hitherto been preserved from being the cause thereof, His divine grace will preserve me in future. It was to avoid such scandals – which have generally their source in injustice and iniquity – that I have followed the path of truth and justice. Those who have led the King to such extremities, against which I protest, had better take heed to what they were about, and obviate such scandals.'

As to the good treatment she has received, as the Duke said, she owned it and was thankful, as well as of the assistance given to her father [Ferdinand] for the conquest of Navarre. If he had no time fully to acknowledge and requite the service, it was entirely owing to his almost sudden death, otherwise he would never have failed to repay the favours bestowed by England in that respect, as he had both the means and the power, as well as the will and the magnanimity to do so. The services rendered to Your Majesty she could remember and acknowledge in part; yet there was no necessity for further testimony, since Your Majesty had never denied them, but on the contrary bore them in mind with the full intention of repaying them, and doing the King's pleasure whenever an opportunity should offer in all things legitimate and fair. In this (the Queen added) there would be no failure nor dissimulation, for she knew for certain that Your Majesty was the King's sincere and affectionate friend; all ought to know this and try and persuade him thereof. Touching the 'supremum caput', she acknowledged the King as her chief and sovereign, and as such was ready to serve and obey him. She considered him the lord and master of the whole kingdom in temporal matters, but in the spiritual God forbid that the King should hold such an opinion, or that she ever should consent thereto, the Pope being the only true sovereign and vicar of God, having power to judge in all spiritual matters; matrimony being of this class there could therefore be no necessity to seek another arbiter.

Immediately after the Queen's answer as above Dr Lee spoke and said: 'She ought to be convinced that having been carnally known by prince Artus (Arthur), her first husband, her second marriage with the King, his brother, was a most detestable and abominable act in the eyes of God and of the World. That was a fact acknowledged, as he found, by all good English doctors, and confirmed by the universities;' and he went on adducing similar arguments in support of his opinion. To which the Queen replied: 'You had better address your allegations to others; you shall never persuade me that what you say is the truth. In this present case you are neither my counsel nor my judge, and I can very well see that what you have just said is more for the sake of flattering the King than of adhering to truth.' She then declared that she had never been known by prince Arthur, and that with regard to the dispute pending between her husband, the King, and herself, that was certainly not the fit place to bring it forward; if he (Lee) was inclined to argue for the King he had better go to Rome and plead; he would find there others than women to contend with, and who would shew him that he was far from having seen or read all that had been written on the subject.

Dr Sampson, the dean of the Chapel, spoke next, and said to the Queen that she was indeed very blameable in thus pertinaciously refusing to have the cause tried and sentenced elsewhere than at Rome, and in not allowing the suspension of the proceedings for a time. She ought not to hasten, as she was doing, the determination and sentence of the suit, for even if the worst happened for the King at Rome, and she herself was favoured, it would only be after all a sentence pronounced by contumacy, which could be easily and by various means annulled and retracted hereafter, besides which it would be the cause of increasing rather than appeasing the contention, for the only available expedient was to proceed at once to the election of judges out of Rome, as the Duke had just proposed.

To this proposition the Queen replied as she had done to the Duke, and ended by saying: 'Dean, had you experienced one half of the hard days and nights I have passed since the commencement of this wretched business you would not consider it too hasty or precipitate on my part to wish for, and try to procure, the sentence and determination of this suit, nor would you so accuse me of tenacity and obstinacy. Respecting the 'contradictes' and other terms of Law, I know nothing of them; you may go to Rome with Dr Lee and there discuss the matter at pleasure.'

Then the bishop of Lincoln began to condemn the marriage, as Dr Lee had done, adding that she had actually lived in concubinage ever since, and that God had fully manifested his abomination of such a union by sending down the malediction of sterility with which she had been visited. She could not (he said) deny a connection with her first husband, inasmuch as there were evident proofs of the contrary. The Queen's answer was that although she esteemed and loved the King as much as woman can esteem and love man, even should he be one hundred thousand times greater in quality and perfection, she would never have remained in his company one single moment against the voice of her conscience. She knew perfectly well that she was his legitimate and true wife, and that the proofs to which they alluded, if any existed to the contrary, were forged and false. This she could affirm and maintain as one who knew the truth better than anyone in the world. If any proofs were wanting that she had never known carnally prince Arthur, she could, besides the most solemn oath once taken [before Campeggio] to this effect adduce other testimony to prove theirs to be false and mendacious.

To this last asseveration of the Queen, Dr Stock (Stokesley) objected, saying : 'Were there no other testimonies in our favour the presumption of the Law would be sufficient, for you have lived a length of time under the same roof with the Prince, and shared his bed.' The Queen replied: 'I care not for such cavilling, I only regard simple truth; as to presumptions and laws, you may go and allege them at Rome with the rest.'

The Queen at last said that she was very much astonished to see so many high personages of such great power and influence in the World thus gathered round her. What could have prevailed upon them thus to assemble and come and surprise her, a poor woman without friends or counsel, she could not guess. Upon which the Duke observed that she could not really complain on that score, for she had undoubtedly the ablest counsel in all England; that is to say, the archbishop of Canterbury, the bishops of Durham, Rochester, and others. The Queen interrupted him by saying: 'Pretty counsellors those are, for if I ask Canterbury's advice he answers me that he will have nothing to do with such affairs, and keeps repeating to me the words ira principis mors est. The bishop of Durham answers that he dares not, because he is the King's subject and vassal. Rochester tells me to have good heart and hope for the best. All the others have made similar answers, so that I have been obliged to send to Flanders for lawyers, as no one here would or dared draw an appeal in my favour. This I have since done by permission and consent of the King himself at the time that he did not object to the cause being transferred to Rome. It was in pursuance of the said Royal permission that the cause was advoked to Rome, and on it I found my right.' Hearing this the earl of Wiltshire observed that the permission to appeal, to which the Queen alluded did not go so far as to have the King summoned to appear personally at Rome. To which the Queen replied that she had never solicited or sought the said summons, and that if in the pursuit of the said appeal it was deemed necessary to take such a step, she could not be made responsible for it. The duke [of Norfolk] and the earl [of Wiltshire], by way of an excuse, tried to make it appear that they had nothing to do with the affair, and were not the promoters of it. They knew nothing, they pretended, except what they had heard lawyers say on the subject. After which all the lords left the room together without anything more being said.

The bishop of London was pressed to state his argument but when he heard the answers given by the Queen to his colleagues he had not the courage to speak. Most of the others, had they had the liberty of expressing their opinion, would undoubtedly have sided with the Queen, and at least shewed their good wishes, for they kept giving evident signs of satisfaction at the Queen's answers, and elbowing each other whenever any of her replies touched the deputies to the quick. Among those who thus took up the Queen's part, though silently, was the King's first secretary, Dr Estiene (Stephen),[51] who from the beginning had treated this affair at the Pope's court, that being most likely the reason why the Lady strongly suspects and dislikes him. Many more who were present at the conference said afterwards that they had long been trying to persuade the Queen and give her good advice, but that one woman alone had refuted their arguments and defeated their plans. One of the last was Guillesfort (Guilford), the comptroller, who was heard to say that it would be a very good thing if all the doctors who had been the inventors and abettors of the plan could be tied together in a cart and sent to Rome, there to dispute and maintain their opinions, and meet with confusion and defeat as they deserved.

And it is reported that when the two dukes and some others went to announce to the King the bad result of their commission, and the reasons the Queen had stated for not acceding to their request, he (the King), who had been impatiently waiting for their return, said: 'I feared it would be so, knowing beforehand the heart and fancy of the Queen; but it is now necessary to provide for the whole affair by other means,' saying which he remained for some time thoughtful ...

After the duke [of Norfolk] had reported according to his own views his conference with the Queen, he of Suffolk drew up a summary account of the same, telling the King in so many words that the Queen was ready to obey him in all things, but that she owed obedience to two persons first. The King, imagining that he (the Duke) meant His Holiness and Your Imperial Majesty, asked very eagerly who those two were, and the Duke replied:

'God was the first; the second her soul and conscience, which the Queen said she would not lose for anything in this world,' to which answer the King made no reply.

The said duke of Suffolk and his wife would, if they dared, oppose this second marriage of the King with all their force. Only two days ago he (the Duke) and the Treasurer had a long talk together on this very topic, both agreeing that now was the time for all to join hands in trying to dissuade the King from his folly, and that the best way to attain that object was to procure sentence with as little further delay as possible, which sentence, they maintained, would meet with the approbation of many in this country. Matters being so well disposed it is imperative to have the suit pushed as vigorously as possible.

The Lady (Anne) hearing that Guilliefort (Guildford), the comptroller, was not very partial to her, has since threatened him most furiously, saying that when she becomes queen [of England], she will have him punished and deprived of his office. The Comptroller's reply has been that in that event she will not have the trouble of having him cashiered, for he himself will be the first to resign his post. After this Guildford went to the King, and having related what passed, and the Lady's threats surrendered the seals of his office on the plea of bad health. And though the King gave them back to him twice, and would not accept his resignation, saying that he ought not to mind women's talk, the Comptroller, either disgusted at the whole affair, or because he was really indisposed, insisted on giving up his office, and went home ...

*17 July 1531*

... The Queen, thinking that the suit would be over before the meeting of Parliament, has lived for some months in comparative hope and quietness of mind. Now she is very much distressed, and in great tribulation at seeing that His Holiness takes no interest whatever in the case, but on the contrary seems purposely intent upon delaying the determination of the affair so that a way to new obstacles may he opened, and the King have time and opportunity to arrest the sentence. The King himself, the Lady and her adherents, now speak out with much greater assurance than before, and say that whatever happens, sooner or later they will have the cognizance and decision of this cause revoked from Rome and brought to England, having, as they say, in their favour the conclusion of the university of Orleans to the effect that the Pope has not the right or the power of subrogating or usurping the cognizance of this affair. This intelligence, as it would appear, was communicated to the King by Dr Sampson, and I fear that Dr Foxe, now in France, will solicit the Paris doctors to sign the same conclusion. I have written to Your Majesty's ambassador in France to be on his guard, for it is now more necessary than ever that both he and Messire Mai and the rest of the Imperial ambassadors should take their measures to defeat the intrigues of the English, more necessary even than at the time when the principal article was discussed; for should the King really obtain a conclusion from three or four more universities, shaped in the same terms as that of

Orleans, the Queen's cause must be considered as half lost, since after such a declaration no prelate in Christendom will dare refuse to proceed with the case at the King's bidding, and according to his wishes. The Lady, on the other hand, declares that her marriage to the King will take place in three or four months at the latest; little by little she is already providing for her royal estate, and has during the last few days appointed an almoner, besides several other officers about her person. She always accompanies the King at his hunting parties, without any female attendants of her own, whilst the Queen herself who used formerly to follow him on such expeditions has been ordered to remain at Vinsor (Windsor); which circumstance, as may be imagined, is exceedingly aggravating to the Queen, not only on account of the King's studied separation, but because she fancies that his object in taking the Lady with him to such hunting parties is that he may accustom the lords and governors of the counties and districts he traverses on such occasions to see her with him, and that he may the better win them over to his party when Parliament meets again ...

... The young marquis [of Dorset] has been forbidden to appear at Court for some time to come, having been charged with recruiting men in Cornwall and the adjacent counties. The Queen fancies that this has been designed by the Lady, owing to the said Marquis being a good servant of hers. She has also on that very account, and because she wants to revenge herself on the duke of Suffolk, for having once brought a charge against her honour, accused, him of criminal intercourse with his own daughter. No one knows yet what will come out of all this ...

### 31 July 1531

The Queen, in pursuance of a custom which has at all times prevailed between the King and her of sending each other messages every third day by means of some countersign agreed between them, sent somebody six days ago to the King to inquire about his health, and signify the regret she had experienced at not having been able to see him before his departure for the country. For since she had been told that she could not have the pleasure and happiness of following him in his journey she imagined that she might at least have had the consolation of bidding him adieu. Yet in this, as in other things, the Queen added, it was for him to order and for her to obey his commands and have patience. The King having heard the message and observed the countersign conversed for a while with the duke of Norfolk and with Dr Steve (Stephen), and had the messenger recalled to his presence. He then said to him in great anger, as it seemed, that he was to tell the Queen that he cared not for her adieu; he had no wish to afford her the consolation of which she spoke, nor any other; and besides that it was indifferent to him whether she sent to inquire after his health or not. She had hitherto caused him much annoyance and sorrow in a thousand ways, and particularly by her attempting to disgrace and humiliate him by a summons to appear personally at Rome, and by her having also obstinately refused the very just and reasonable request made by the members of his Privy Council and other noble personages of his kingdom. All this the Queen had done out of confidence and hope in Your Majesty; but she must know that God Almighty was more powerful than Your Majesty, and in short that she had better refrain in future from sending him messages or visitors.

The Queen answered that she was exceedingly sorry at hearing of his anger and displeasure. She had given no cause or occasion for it, for whatever she had undertaken had been done with his permission and consent, and for the honour and relief of each other's conscience, as he (the King) was perfectly aware. Her hopes were not grounded solely and exclusively on Your Majesty, or any other living prince; but only on God, the true protector [of mankind] and the father of justice and truth. What Your Majesty had done in the affair was as much out of respect and consideration for his own honour as for love of her. To these sentiments the Queen added many others equally humble and honourable, but the King having read the letter was some time before he answered it. Three days after, having first consulted the members of his Privy Council, he made a reply in writing, meagre enough, in which he made no attempt whatever to refute the Queen's arguments; he only wrote that she was indeed very pertinacious in her oath that she had never been carnally known by prince Arthur, as likewise in publicly making such an assertion. She was very much mistaken if she trusted in such a statement, for he would evidently prove the contrary by means of good and competent witnesses, and if so there could be no possible doubt that the Pope (Julius II.) had no right to dispense in their marriage, as he (the King) through his learning and doctrine which everyone recognized had sufficiently proved and shewn. It would be better and wiser for her to pass her time in looking out for witnesses to prove her pretended virginity at the time of her marriage with him than spend the same time in talking about it to whomsoever would listen to her, as she was doing; and as to sending messages or writing to him, that he strongly advised her to discontinue the practice and attend to her own business. Many other insulting sentences of this kind 'de la mesme farine' did the King write in his letter, which have not yet been reported to me.

The missive, however, bore no address, most likely because they (the councillors) could not agree as to what title was to be given to the Queen, and yet they had plenty of time for deliberation; for I am told that for three consecutive days the Privy Council did nothing else but prepare the said document, which after all, if the Lady's authority and the good reasons therein alleged be taken into consideration, must have been decreed by her. The Queen at first, seeing such rude behaviour, was very much alarmed, imagining that the King might have received from Rome some assurance that sentence would be ultimately pronounced in his favour, but I persuaded her of the contrary, and that the King's aggressive language proceeded rather from want of confidence and half despair of his ever being able to attain his purpose. This reasoning of mine has quieted her fears, and she is now comparatively calm, and yet, as she herself wrote to me yesterday, the information newly conveyed to her that the Pope has, at the intercession of the king of France, granted a new delay in the proceedings is for her a source of alarm and sorrow, fearing lest His Holiness should be induced to take other measures more injurious to her cause than the said suspension, or that during that period some novelty is to be introduced at the next Parliament. I wrote back to her that His Holiness had shewn very little favour to the king of France in this instance for that he had long resisted his prayers, and granted at last that which after all was only an act of justice, which was to observe and keep the holidays. Had he refused the application he would almost have done injury to this king, inasmuch as during these same holidays the proceedings had been suspended here in England at her own request and in her favour. She ought to be aware that the Pope having been so frequently warned by Your Majesty and by other people of the dangers and scandals likely to arise from the delay, not only in this kingdom, but in the Apostolic See and the whole of Christendom, could not grant the aforesaid delay without some sound profit or advantage to accrue from it. These and other representations of mine the Queen has accepted with very good grace, and she has just written to me saying that they have had the effect of calming her fears and soothing her sorrow. The Princess is now with her, which will in a great measure alleviate her pain and mourning at the King's absence. They will pass their time in sport and visiting the royal seats around Windsor always waiting for good news from Rome with the help and favour of Your Majesty, in which all her hopes are centred ...

### 19 August 1531

Since my last, the King, on the plea of wishing to hunt in the environs of Winsor (Windsor), sent orders for his Queen to remove to Mur (More), a manor close to the abbey of St Alban's, and for the Princess to go to Richmont; which measure has seemed so strange to most people that no doubt is entertained here that he (the King) is now resolutely intent upon obtaining his divorce. As to me, I think that all this is mere artifice to induce the Queen to consent to the cognizance of the cause being again brought here, to which she will not accede whatever stratagems may be used for the purpose ...

### 9 October 1531

... There is no one here of whom the Lady is more afraid than the bishop of Rochester (Fisher), for he is just the man who without fear of any sort has always defended and upheld in the most unanswerable manner the Queen's cause, owing to which the said Lady has lately sent him a message persuading him to remain where he is, and not come to London and attend Parliament for fear he should catch fever, as he did last year.[52] The Lady may do what she likes in that respect, the Bishop is resolved, should he meet with one hundred thousand deaths, to come and speak in the Queen's favour more openly than he has ever done ...

### 24 October 1531

... Yesterday, Sunday, the King came to the house of Brian Turc (Tuke), where the two French ambassadors (Monsieur de Bayonne and Jehan Jocquin) are staying, which is about one mile from the King's present residence, and all supped together. At the upper end of the table were the King, the Lady

(Anne), and Monseigneur de Bayonne. At the lower one Jehan Jocquin, the duke of Norfolk, the earl of Wiltshire, and his wife, the Countess; the Secretary bishop-elect of Winchester, Feuunllier (Fitzwilliam) the treasurer, and two ladies. After much eating and drinking the said bishop of Bayonne took his leave, and returned to London ...

*4 January 1532*
... The Queen having been forbidden to write letters or send messages to the King, and yet wishing to fulfil her duty towards him in every respect, caused to be presented to him on New Year's Day, by one of the gentlemen of the chamber, a gold cup of great value and singular workmanship, the gift being offered in the most humble and appropriate terms for the occasion. The King, however, not only refused to accept the present, but seemed at first very angry with the gentleman who had undertaken to bring it. Yet it appears that two or three hours afterwards the King himself desired to see the cup again, praised much its shape and workmanship, and fearing lest the gentleman of his chamber who had received it from the Queen's messenger should take it back immediately – in which case the Queen might have it presented again before the courtiers, when he (the King) could not well refuse its acceptance – he ordered the gentleman not to give the cup back until the evening, which was accordingly done, and it was then returned to the Queen. The King, moreover, has sent her no New Year's gift on this occasion, but has, I hear, forbidden the members of his Privy Council, as well as the gentlemen of his chamber, and others to comply with the said custom.

The King used also on New Year's Day to send [presents] to the ladies of the Queen's Household, and to those of the Princess, but this custom, hitherto faithfully observed, has now been discontinued, and no present has been sent, which is a sign to me that unless some prompt remedy be applied the state of the Queen and of her daughter, the Princess, will become worse and worse every day. The King has not been equally uncourteous towards the Lady from whom he has accepted certain darts, worked in the Biscayan fashion, richly ornamented, and presented her in return rich hangings for one room, and a bed covered with gold and silver cloth, crimson satin, and embroidery richer than all the rest. The Lady [Anne], moreover, is still lodging where the Queen formerly was, and during the late festivities has been attended by almost the same number of the ladies as the Queen herself had formerly in her suite, as if she were already a Queen ...

*21 June 1532*
... About 12 days ago the bishop of Rochester (Fisher) preached earnestly and strongly in favour of the Queen, in consequence of which he has been in great danger of being imprisoned or incurring some other punishment. He has, it is true, shut the mouths of those who spoke for the King, but nevertheless the Queen receives no better treatment, and therefore it is clear that the remedy lies only in the hands of the Pope. So great, however, is the desire which all in general manifest for a speedy sentence in her case, that several high personages have sent word to her, and to me also, that

should the Pope decide and pronounce sentence they will take care that it is executed. In this same declaration Master Taillop agreed two days before he started for France, whither he is now gone as ambassador, though I do not believe he will remain long, for these people begin already to perceive that he is not so ardent a partisan of the divorce as he was thought at first to be, and the duke of Norfolk has been heard to say several times, 'Master Taillop is not very suitable for the charge he has undertaken, being better trained to war than to the management of political affairs.'

I beg Your Majesty's pardon if I again urge the settlement of a matter upon which depends, in my opinion, not only the repose of this queen and kingdom, but also that of all Christendom, for the Queen's case once determined, Your Majesty may dispose of this kingdom as much or better than you ever did.

### 11 July 1532

... A very piteous thing has just happened in the case of a young priest, which I will relate to you. He had hitherto lived in such honesty and virtue that I really believe there were not two men in England more generally esteemed and loved, his profession being taken into account. It appears that he had received a sum of money in new angelots, which he out of simplicity rather than malice proceeded to sweat or file, fancying perhaps that he could well do it as he occasionally did with the consecrated wafers when he found them too large. No sooner had he accomplished his task than he went to the goldsmiths to sell the filings of the said angelots, which might be worth about half a crown, and shewed them to three or four of their number to see if he could get one farthing more upon them. He was at last arrested and sent to prison, and though his case excited general pity, and people of all classes interceded for him, the King – who had lately pardoned a Frenchman and tavern keeper for the very same offence – would not hear of any extenuation, and either through his hatred of the priesthood, or to please the Lady [Anne] who, I am told, being requested by her father [the earl of Wiltshire] to intercede in favour of the prisoner, answered that he (the Earl) ought not to speak for a priest of whom there were already too many in this country, rejected the application, and the poor man, after being tried by a civil court, was sentenced to death, and without previous degradation dragged through the streets of this capital and hanged. The above lamentable case will shew you to what extremity the Clergy of this country are reduced! ...

### 29 July 1532

The King was on his way to the Northern counties where he intended to hunt [this autumn], all those who wish him away from this place having incurred great expense in provisions and so forth, when he suddenly changed his purpose, and came back to town. The causes of his return are variously explained. Some say that for the last three or four days after he started on his journey, wherever he went accompanied by the Lady, the people on the road so earnestly requested him to recall the Queen, his wife, and the women especially so insulted the Royal mistress, hooting and hissing on her passage, that he was actually obliged to retrace his steps ...

Meanwhile, it would appear that in consequence of despatches received from Rome, or fearing perhaps that the Pope is about to issue certain letters of monition compelling him to recall the Queen to Court and cast away the Lady, the King, it is said, has lately shewn his temper in a most remarkable way, and often said in public that he could not tolerate His Holiness treating him in the manner he had done hitherto. The Pope (he said) had no power over him, and he was therefore determined to accomplish this new marriage with the greatest possible solemnity and pomp. He has, I am told, issued orders for suitable preparations to be made against such an event, and Tallebot (Talbot), who is a sort of Grand Master, and has some other pre-eminence at the coronation of queens, has been sent for. No one of those present when the King made the above declaration dared remonstrate in the least, though all were exceedingly displeased at the time, and the courtiers greatly scandalized for fear he (the King) might carry his plan into execution. Though this is not probable, I have taken care to warn the Queen that she may guard against the King's threats, and watch every opportunity to arrest the intended blow ...

*26 August 1532*

My letter of the 11th inst. must have acquainted Your Majesty with the proposed interview of these two kings *[Henry VIII and Francis I of France]* at Calais, for the accomplishment of which several ships and other smaller craft are being fitted out. They say that almost all the grand officers in the kingdom, four bishops, namely, London, Bath, Lincoln, and Winchester, and 200 or 300 gentlemen have received orders to be at Canterbury on the 25th of September next. The whole suite will consist of 3,000 or 4,000 persons. Though the ambassador of France, when he last called on me, assured me most positively that there would be no ladies at the interview, neither on this side nor on the other, yet I am rather inclined to think otherwise considering the great preparations the Lady Anne is making, and the long train of female servants she is getting ready for the expedition, as the Queen informs me for a fact. Indeed, I find there is a rumour afloat that the first meeting will take place at Boulogne, and that thence the two kings will go to Calais, where they will not make a long stay, for I am told that the provision ordered from the royal purveyors for both kings at Calais is only for four days. Respecting the matters to be discussed or treated at the said meeting, I must own that hitherto I have been unable to learn anything besides what I mentioned in my last despatch to Your Imperial Majesty; only that they are beginning to speak more openly and distinctly of a marriage between this king and the eldest daughter of France, and that there have been heavy bets offered by merchants of the latter nation that the said marriage will take place. But in my humble opinion, if the French really entertain such a hope, they must be most egregiously mistaken, or else the Lady [Anne] must be labouring under a strange delusion, for she considers herself so sure of success that not later than a week ago she wrote a letter to her principal friend and favourite here, whom she holds as sister and companion, bidding her get ready against this journey and interview, where, she says, that which she has been so long wishing for will be accomplished ...

*5 September 1532*

... On Sunday last before mass the Lady Anne was created marchioness of Penebroc (Pembroke) with a fine revenue of 4,000 ducats a year. The appointment was publicly made with much ceremonious pomp, with the account of which I will not trouble Your Majesty. A most solemn mass was then celebrated by the bishop of Winchester, after which the King and the French ambassador having approached the altar certain articles were read to them and to the Bishop, which the two former signed and swore to in common. This being done, Dr Faux (Foxe) began a peroration in praise of the peace and amity thus established between the two kings, which (he remarked) was so laudable an act, and so admirably brought about and achieved that the learned Doctor could not do less than describe it as the work of God, not of man, and added in his speech that concords of this kind were the surest means of arresting the progress of the Turk, this peace not being temporal and frail like the preceding, but an inviolable and eternal one. After this the singers began to chant the Te Deum Laudamus, to the accompaniment of trumpets and other instruments. As to me, having for some days past had the bad odour of this new treaty in my nostrils, I have since tried to learn some of its particulars, though hitherto without success.

Yesterday the Seigneur de Langez (du Bellay, sieur de Langeay), arrived here sent by the king of France. What his mission may be I have not yet been able to find out, unless it be that it was agreed between this king and that of France, that the moment the latter should quit Brittany to come here, a gentleman [of his chamber] should be dispatched with the information, and that this one should do the same to advise the day of his departure for France, which, I hear, is to take place very soon. Indeed it is a settled thing that Francis will be at Boulogne on the 1st of October at the latest, and this king at Calais on the same day. They are to meet first between Boulogne and Calais, whither this king purposes taking his brother of France, that he may rest from the fatigues of the journey. Both will then go to Boulogne, and feast for three consecutive days, at the end of which this one will quit that town and return to Calais to be ready to sally out and meet the other. There the two kings will stay three or four days, it having been agreed that for the mutual security of the Royal persons an equal number of armed men from the garrisons of Calais and Boulogne shall be provided for their escort. The Lady [Anne], who is to accompany the King, will not move from Calais. It would seem, however, as if this king were much pleased at the prospect of this interview; never at any time did he shew such joy, for certainly he does nothing but talk about it all day, and, to say the truth, he has every reason to be satisfied with his success, as far as he himself and his kingdom are concerned, for this is a sort of pleasure which he may well keep to himself; not one of his subjects envies or wishes to compete with him in that respect, except perhaps the Lady, all the rest being much displeased and grumbling in the most strange manner. All his Privy Councillors are against the interview, principally the duke of Suffolk, who has publicly spoken about it in a manner that has provoked the King's anger, and been the cause of his being reprimanded in very injurious terms. The earl of Auffort (Sir John de Vere, earl of Oxford) said a week ago to one of his friends, who repeated it to me, that he feared this proposed interview would be the cause of many evils in this kingdom for various reasons which he did not specify, though he declared that the whole thing had been exclusively got up by the King, the French ambassador, and the Lady [Anne] without the intervention of the Privy Council, and that no one save those three knew what the interview was about, or what subjects would be treated therein.

For the last month considerable repairs have been made in the Tower of London, both inside and outside, refitting the apartments which were out of order &c., which circumstance makes some people believe that it is the King's intention to send the Queen thither, whilst he himself is out of the country. This, however, is highly improbable, unless the King wants to exasperate his subjects and drive them to rebellion ...

*15 September 1532*
My despatch of the 5th inst. must have acquainted Your Majesty with the arrival of the sieur de Langey (Langeay) and other occurrences of this place. That gentleman left four days ago for the country without making any stay in town, so that I have been unable to interrogate him on the object of his mission, which, as far as I can guess, is only to inquire from the resident ambassador (De la Pommeraye) and others what day has been definitely fixed for the intended meeting of the two kings. Indeed, I hear that Mr. de Langeay, in consequence of the late prorogation demanded by this king, and of his putting off the interview until the 20th of October next, has come for the purpose of excusing his master if the length of the journey and the necessary preparations should prevent him from being at Boulogne on that day. He comes also, as I have been given to understand, to offer, in his master's name, a fleet for the passage to Calais, which this king has of course refused to accept, and besides to request that the new Marchioness [the Lady Anne] may be one of the party. If this last be not one of the objects of Langeay's mission, certain it is that the French ambassador announces it in public to be such, and the King himself tacitly owns it, since he has lately written to many lords and courtiers bidding them keep their wives in readiness to accompany [to France] his dearest and most beloved cousin, the marchioness of Penvroc (Pembroke), whom he intends to take with him at the express desire of his kind brother and perpetual ally the king of France.

It is not at all improbable that the said king [of France] may have made such an invitation, knowing how pleased this king and the Lady would be, and knowing also that had he not invited the Marchioness to the interview she would have gone just the same, for the King cannot be one hour away from her. I think, moreover, that the king of France is himself very anxious to see the Lady, and personally thank her for the many good services she has rendered, and is daily rendering him, which, in the French ambassador's words, are more than his master, the King, could ever sufficiently acknowledge or repay, and I presume that besides the proper return of thanks everything will be done and said at the meeting likely to keep the Lady devoted to his interests. In short, it can be confidently asserted that the king of France has lost nothing by the demise of the cardinal of York (Wolsey), and the recovery of this Lady's favour, for besides her being more maliciously inclined, and her enjoying much greater favour, king Francis is not obliged to expend on her an annual pension of 25,000 crs. as he did on the Cardinal, but pays her only in flattery and in promises of forwarding the divorce at Rome ...

*1 October 1532*

During the last few days, owing to the prorogation asked by the French, there has seemed to lurk some suspicion here among these courtiers that the interview of the two kings will not after all take place; which suspicion was much strengthened by the fact that [Sir Francis] Brian, who was to have followed Langeay into France immediately, had not yet moved and that neither the duke of Norfolk (who came to town only the day before yesterday to purchase silk cloth), nor several of the principal lords and officers of the Crown who were to accompany the King on his journey gave any signs whatever of preparing to cross the Channel. The interview, however, is now again in the ascendant, and instead of Brian, the grand squire (Carew) is positively to leave to-morrow for France, to stir up the French and announce the immediate departure of this king, which will take place on Friday next, St Francis' Day. It appears that avoiding Rochester and other towns on account of the plague, and because people are there dying of it, the King will go from Greenwich to Gravesend in his State barge, then to the house of a gentleman where he will stay one day, and then on board a well appointed ship of 150 tons, called 'La Mignone', and in fact more than deserving this name if her strength be taken into consideration. The 'Mignone' will then sail for a small island on the Thames, where the King intends to feast and carouse for three consecutive days at the manor of a gentleman of his bed chamber, named Chennet. Thence the King will go by land to Canterbury and Dover, at which last he will again embark on the said ship 'La Mignone', calculating upon reaching Calais on the 15th inst.

But though on this matter of the journey and interview the courtiers appear cold and indifferent, certain it is that the Lady [Anne] thinks otherwise, for knowing very well how to make hay while the sun shines, she has not been slack to provide herself with rich and most expensive dresses and ornaments, which the King has ordered to be bought for the occasion. After sending her his own jewels, the King has, I hear, lately given the duke of Norfolk commission, and he has come down here on purpose, to procure through a third person those belonging to the Queen; who, I am told, said to the bearer of the Royal message: 'I cannot present the King with my jewels as he desires, inasmuch as when, on a late occasion, I, according to the custom of this kingdom, presented him with a New Year's gift he warned me to refrain from such presents in future. Besides which (she said) it is very annoying and offensive to me, and I would consider it a sin and a load upon my conscience if I were persuaded to give up my jewels for such a wicked purpose as that of ornamenting a person who is the scandal of Christendom, and is bringing vituperation and infamy upon the King, through his taking her with him to such a meeting across the Channel. Yet,' continued the Queen, 'if the King sends expressly for my jewels I am ready to obey his commands in that as well as in all other matters.' Though highly displeased and sore at the Queen's answer the King nevertheless did send a gentleman of his chamber, who brought express orders to the Queen's Chancellor, and to her Chamberlain, to see to the delivery of the said jewels besides a letter to the Queen herself in credence of the messenger, who said to her in the King's name that he was very much astonished at her not having sent her jewels forthwith when he first asked for them, as the queen of France, her sister, and many other [ladies] would have done.' Upon which the Queen gently pleaded excuse for her former refusal, and sent him the whole of her jewels, and the King, as I am given to understand, is very much pleased and glad at it.

About eight days ago, as the French ambassador was going to court, whither he had been summoned, to attend a dinner the Lady was giving to the King, at a manor-house, with which he has lately presented her, he happened to pass by my lodgings, and came in *[their discussion is then detailed]* ...

About eight days ago this king happened to meet the Princess, his daughter, in the country though he did not say much to her save asking how she was, and assuring her that henceforward he would visit her oftener. There was no question of course of the King inviting her to the place where he is now holding his court, for the Lady is with him, and she will not see or hear of the Princess, as I have already informed Your Majesty in a former despatch. I believe, nevertheless, that had not the Lady very cautiously dispatched two of her most confidential servants towards the King that they might hear and report his conversation with the Princess, his daughter, the former would have conversed with her longer, and with greater familiarity. There was in my opinion no indication of the marriage between the Princess and the duke of Orleans, so much spoken of, being mooted during the interview, for, as far as I am aware, not a word was said about it. After the King's departure [for France] the Princess will reside in Windsor, which is a strong castle in the midst of a very pleasant park and grounds. Where the Queen is to go and reside no one knows yet. She has lately been terribly afraid of the Kings marrying the Lady at the proposed interview; but is now more tranquil, owing to the said Lady herself having assured a great personage, in whom she trusts, that even if the King wished to marry her now she would never consent to it, for she wants the ceremony to take place here, in England, at the usual place appointed for the marriage and coronation of queens ...

This very moment one of my men, whom I had sent with a message to the Grand Squire [Sir Nicholas Carew] has returned, and says to me on the part of that officer, that he is going over to France much against his will with the charge of soliciting, pressing, and recommending the interview of the two kings; and he sends me word that far from executing his commission with fidelity he will do any and everything in his power to have it put off. He further sends me word that the King is not over pleased at some rumours now current respecting certain arrangements proposed. It would appear that the king of France had promised, and this king hoped that as a sort of countenance to the Lady [Anne] he would take [to Boulogne] his own sister, Madame d'Alançon, whereas it now turns out that the latter being indisposed and unable to attend, Francis proposes to take thither Madame de Vendosme[53] instead, at which these people are by no means pleased, saying that since the said Madame de Vendom had been in former times considered doubtful company she will perhaps take in her suite some of those who shared her former bad reputation; which would be a shame and insult to the ladies on this side of the Channel ...

# Queen Anne Boleyn, 1533–1536

*Anne Boleyn and Henry VIII married secretly in early 1533. The marriage was publicised at Easter 1533 when Anne appeared openly as queen at court for the first time. Soon afterwards, Henry's marriage to Catherine of Aragon was declared invalid by Archbishop Cranmer (a former chaplain of Anne's father) and Anne was crowned. Within months of the marriage, Henry's affection for Anne appears to have cooled and there were stormy scenes when she discovered that he had taken a mistress. In spite of this, Anne was fully able to establish herself as queen. She presided over her own household and took a particular interest in the religious reform, promoting religious reformers and openly encouraging the publication of the scriptures in to vernacular. She took an active interest in her daughter, Princess Elizabeth, although she, like Henry, was openly hostile towards Catherine of Aragon and Princess Mary.*

## Nicholas Harpsfield's Account of the Marriage of Henry VIII and Anne Boleyn[1]

*Nicholas Harpsfield (1519–1575) was a Catholic priest who voluntarily went into exile during the reign of the Protestant Edward VI. He wrote a number of works on English history, including a biography of Thomas More, as well as his most famous work 'A Treatise on the Pretended Divorce Between Henry VIII and Catherine of Aragon'.*

*Harpsfield's work, like Sander's, was written from the Catholic viewpoint and, as such, it contains both an attack on Henry's attempts to divorce Catherine of Aragon and on the character of Anne Boleyn. Although, like Sander, Harpsfield wrote from a Catholic viewpoint, his work is not entirely inaccurate and is of value to historians. The extract below has been included due to the fact that accounts of the secret wedding ceremony of Henry and Anne are rare. The account may largely be false. It is particularly unlikely that the officiating priest would have believed that Henry had a papal licence to marry by early 1533, for example. Harpsfield does, at least, convey the clandestine and hurried nature of the wedding.*

*It has been suggested that Henry and Anne actually underwent two marriage ceremonies. The chronicler, Edward Hall, who wrote during Henry's reign, claimed that 'the kyng after his returne [from Calais], maried priuily the lady Anne Bulleyn, on Sainct Erkenwaldes daie [14 November 1532], whiche mariage was kept so secrete, that very fewe knewe it, til she was greate with child, at Easter after'.*[2] *The couple's daughter, Princess Elizabeth, must have been conceived in around December 1532 and so it is not impossible that, buoyed with the success of the French meeting, the couple decided to marry on their return. However, evidence for a January 1533 ceremony is more compelling and it would seem unnecessary for the couple to have two marriage ceremonies before Henry's marriage to Catherine of Aragon had been officially ruled invalid. It seems more likely that the January 1533 ceremony, set out by Harpsfield below, was the only marriage ceremony celebrated by the couple.*

The King was married to [the] Lady Anne Bulleyne long ere there was any divorce made by the said Archbishop [of Canterbury]. The which marriage was secretly made at Whitehall very early before day, none being present but Mr Norris and Mr Henage of the Privy Chamber and the Lady Barkeley, with Mr Rowland[3] the King's chaplain, that was afterward made Bishop of Coventry and Lichfield. To whom the King told that now he had gotten of the Pope a lycence to marry another wife, and yet to avoid business and tumult the thing must be done (quoth the King) very secretly; and thereupon a time and place was appointed to the said Master Rowland to solemnize the said marriage.

At which time Mr Rowland being come accordingly, and seeing all things ready for celebration of mass and to solemnize the marriage, being in a great dump and staggering, came to the King and said – 'Sir, I trust you have the Pope's lycence, both that you may marry and that I may join you together in marriage.' 'What else?' quoth the King. Upon this he turned to the altar and revested himself, but yet not so satisfied, and troubled in mind he cometh eftsoones to the King and saith – 'This matter toucheth us all very nighe, and therefore it is expedient that the lycence be read before us all, or else we run all – and I more deep than any other – into excommunication in marrying your grace without any baynes asking, and in a place unhallowed, and no divorce as yet promulged of the first matrimony.' The King, looking upon him very amiably, 'Why, Master Rowland,' quoth he, 'think you me a man of so small faith and credit, you, I say, that do well know my life passed, and even now have heard my confession? or think you me a man of so small and slender foresight and consideration of my affairs that unless all things were safe and sure I would enterprize this matter? I have truly a lycence, but it is reposed in another sure[r] place whereto no man resorteth but myself, which, if it were seen, should discharge us all. But if I should, now that it waxeth towards day, fetch it, and be seen so early abroad, there would rise a rumour and talk thereof other than were convenient. Goe forth in God's name, and do that which appertaineth to you. I will take upon me all other danger.' Whereupon he went to mass, and celebrated also all ceremonies belonging to marriage.

# Thomas Cranmer to Master Hawkins Concerning the Sentence of Divorce between Henry VIII and Catherine of Aragon[4]

*The letter below contains Thomas Cranmer's account of Henry's divorce and Anne's coronation. The new Archbishop of Canterbury went to Dunstable, which was close to where Catherine of Aragon was staying, in order to convene a Church council to rule on the validity of Henry VIII's first marriage. The result was a foregone conclusion, as everyone was aware and it would have been no surprise to Cranmer that Catherine refused to recognise the validity of his actions. Henry and Anne had, in any event, been married for some months before Henry's first marriage was finally declared invalid.*

*The second part of the letter contains an account of Anne's coronation. It is of particular interest as Cranmer, who, of course, crowned Anne himself, was the only major participant in the ceremony to leave an account.*

In my most hartie wise I commende me unto you and even so woulde be right gladd to here of your welfare &c. Thes be to advertise you that inasmoche as you nowe and than take some paynes in writyng vnto me I woulde be lothe you shuld thynke your Labour utterly lost and forgotten for lake of wrytyng agayne, therefore and bycause I reken you be somedele desirous of suche newis as hathe byn here with us of late in the Kyngis graces matters, I entend to enforme you a parte therof accordyng to the tenure and purporte vsyd in that behalf. Ande fyrste as towchyng the small determynacion and concludyng of the Matter of devorse betwene my Lady Kateren and the Kyngs grace, whiche said matter after the Convocacion in that behalf hadde determyned and aggreed accordyng to the former consent of the Vniversites, yt was thowght convenient by the Kyng and his lernyd councll that I shuld repayre unto Dunstable, which ys withing iiij. myles vnto Amptell where the said Lady Kateren kepeth her howse, and there to call her before me, to here the fynall Sentance in this said mateir. Notwithstandyng she would not att all obey therunto, for whan she was by doctour Lee cited to appe[ar] by a daye she utterly refused the same, sayinge that inasmoche as her cause was before the Pope she would have none other Judge, and therfore woulde not take me for her Judge. Nevertheless the viijth daye of Maye, accordyng to the said appoyntment, I came vnto Dunstable, my Lorde of Lyncoln beyng assistante vnto me, and my Lorde of Wyncehester, Doctour Bell, D. Claybroke, D. Trygonnel, D. Hewis, D. Olyver, D. Brytten, Mr Bedell, with diuerse other lernyd in the Lawe beyng councellors in the Lawe for the King's parte. And soo there at our commyng kepte a Courte for the apperance of the said Lady Kateren, where were examyned certeyn witnes whiche testified that she was lawfully cited and called to appere, whome for fawte of apperance was declared contumax, procedyng in the said cause agaynste her in penam contumacian as the processe of the Lawe therunto belongeth, whiche contynewed xv. dayes after our cummyng thither. And the morow after Assension daye I gave finall Sentance therin howe that it was indispensable for the Pope to lycense any suche marieges.

This donne, and after our reiornyng home agayne The Kings Highnes prepared al thyngs convenient for the coronacion of the Queene, whiche also was after suche a maner as foloweth. The Thursdaye nexte before the feaste of pentecost the Kyng and the Queene beyng at Grenewyche, all the Craftes of London thereunto well appoynted, in severall bargis deckyd after the most gorgiouse and sumptuous maner, with dyverse pagiantes thereunto belongyng, repayred and wayted all together upon the Mayre of London, and so, well furnysshed, cam all vnto Grenewiche, where they taryed and wayted for the Queenes commyng to her barge; which so done they brought her unto the tower, tromppets, shambes, and other dyverse instrumentes all the wayes playng and makyng greate melodie, which, as ys reported, was as combly donne as neuer was lyke in any tyme nyghe to our rememberaunce: and so her grace cam to the tower on Thursdaye at nyghte abowte v. of the clocke, where also was suche a pele of gonnes as hathe not byn harde lyke a great while before. And the same nyghte and Frydaye aldaye the Kyng and Queene taryed there, and on Frydaye at nyght the Kyngs grace made xviij Knyghts of the Bathe whose creacion was not alonly so strange to hereof, as also their garmentes stranger to beholde or loke on; whiche said Knightes, the nexte daye, whiche was Saturday, rydde before the Queene's grace thorowte the Citie of London towards Westminster palice, over and besyds the moste parte of the nobles of the Realme whiche lyke accompanied her grace thorowe owte the said citie, She syttyng in her heere [hair],⁵ upon a Horse Lytter, rychely appareled, and iiij knyghtes of the v. ports beryng a Canapye over her hedd. And after her cam iiij. riche charettes, one of them emptie and iij. other furnysshed with diverse auncient old lades; and after the[m] cam a great trayne of other Lades and gyntillwomen: whyche said Progresse, from the begynnyng to thendyng, extendid half a myle in leyngthe by estimacion or thereaboute. To whome also as she came alongeste the Citie was shewid many costely pagients, with diverse other encomyes spoken of chyldren to her, Wyne also runyng at certeyne Condits plentiously. And so procedyng thorowte the streats passid furthe vnto Westminster Hall, where was a certeyn Banket prepared for her, which donne, she was conveyd owte of the bake syde of the palice into a Barge and so vnto Yorke Place, where the Kyng's grace was before her comyng, for this you muste ever presuppose that his grace came allwayes before her secretlye in a Barge aswell frome Grenewyche to the tower as from the tower to Yorke place.

Nowe than on Soundaye was the Coronacion, which allso was of such a maner.

In the mornynge ther assymble[d] withe me at Westminster Churche the bysshop of Yorke, the B. of London, the B. of Wynchester, the B. of Lyncoln, the B. of Bathe, and the B. of Saint Asse, the Abbote of Westminstre with x or xij moo [more] Abbottes, whiche all revestred ourselfs in our pontificalibus, and, soo furnysshed, withe our Crosses and Crossiers, procedid oute of th'Abbey in a procession unto Westminstre Hall, where we receyved the Queene apareled in a Robe of pu[r]ple velvet, and all the ladyes and gentillwomen in robes and gownes of scarlet accordyng to the maner vsed before tyme in such besynes: and so her Grace sustayned of eche syde with ij bysshops, the Bysshope of London ande the Bysshop of Wynchester, came furthe in processyon unto the Churche of Westminster, she in her here [hair], my Lord of Suffolke berying before herr the Crowne, and ij other Lords beryng also before her a Ceptur and a white Rodde, and so entred up into the highe Alter, where diverse Ceremoneys used aboute her, I did sett the Crowne on her hedde, and than was songe Te Deum, &c. And after that was song a solempne Masse, all which while her grace satt crowned upon a scaffold whiche was made betwene the Highe Alter and the Qwyer in Westminstre Churche, which Masse and ceremonyes donne and fynysshed, all the Assemble of noble men broughte her into Westminstre Hall agayne, where was kepte a great solempne feaste all that daye, The good order therof were to longe to wrytte at this tyme to you. But nowe Sir you may nott ymagyn that that this Coronacion was before her mariege, for she was maried muche about sainte Paules daye last, as the Condicion therof dothe well appere by reason she ys nowe sumwhat bygg with chylde. Notwithstandyng yt hath byn reported thorowte a great parte of the realme that I maried her, whiche was playnly false, for I myself knewe not therof a fortenyght after yt was doune. And many other thyngs be also reported of me, whiche be mere lyes and tales.

Other newys have we none notable, but that one Fryth, whiche was in the tower in pryson, was appoynted by the Kyngs grace to be examyned befor me, my Lorde of London, my lorde of Wynchestre, my Lorde of Suffolke, my Lorde Channcelour, and my Lorde of Wylteshere, whose opynion was so notably erroniouse, that we culde not dyspache hym but was fayne to leve hym to the determynacion of his Ordinarye, whiche ys the bishop of London. His said opynyon ys of suche nature that he thoughte it nat necessary to be beleved as an Article of our faythe, that ther ys the very corporall presence of Christe within the Oste and Sacramente of the Alter, and holdethe of this poynte muste after the Opynion of Oecolampadious. And suerly I myself sent for hym iij or iiij tymes to perswade hym to leve that his Imaginacion, but for all that we could do therin he woulde not applye to any counsaile, notwithstandyng nowe he ys at a fynall ende with all examinacions, for my Lorde of London hathe gyven sentance and delyuerd hym to the secular power, where he loketh every daye to goo unto the fyer. And ther ys also condempned with hym one Andrewe a taylour of London for the said self same opynion.

If you have not harde of our Ambassadors lately gone over, you shall understande that my Lorde of Northf', my Lorde of Rochefode, Maste[r] Paulet, Sir Francis Bryan, Sir Antoney Browne, &c. Doctour Gooderyche, D. Aldryche, and D. Thrylbey, be gonne into France to the Frenche Kyng, and as I suppose they goo frome hyme to the Pope unto ...

Further you shall understande that ther ys many here whiche whyshe you to succede your uncle. Notwithstandyng I would you shulde not thynke the contrarye but that ther be a great sorte whiche woulde yt shuld not come to passe, nevertheless you be nether the nerar ne furder of thorwe suche idyll communicacion.

Fynally I here sende unto you a Bill for the banke of iiijc [400] Duckes de largo, whiche somme I woulde you shuld not take yt up before you have nede therof, and therfore I send yt for your commodite and necessite, for it ys none of the Kyngs graces money, nor his said grace knowethe nothyng therof, but alonelye of my benevolence to serve your purpose in case (as I said) you shulde lacke the same. And thus farr' ye well frome my manor of Croydon the xvij daye of June.

## The Noble Triumphant Coronation of Queen Anne, Wife unto the Most Noble King Henry the VIIIth[6]

*The following account of Anne's coronation was 'imprinted at London in Fleet Street by Wynkyn de Worde, for John Gough'. Like the earlier account of Anne's visit to France, it gives the official version of the event. This can be contrasted with Chapuys' comments on the coronation, at which he claimed that the crowd mocked Anne as she passed.*

First, the 29th day of May [1533], being Thursday; all the worshipful Crafts and Occupations in their best array, goodly beseen, took their barges which were splayed [displayed] with goodly banners fresh and new, with the cognizance and arms of their faculty; to the number of fifty great barges, comely beseen, and every barge had minstrels making great and sweet harmony.

Also there was the Bachelors' Barge comely beseen, decked with innumerable banners and all about hanged with rich cloth of gold; and foists [swift boats] waiting upon her, decked [adorned] with a great shot of ordnance: which descended the river afore all the barges; the Batchelors' Barge foremost. And so following in good order, every Craft in their degree and order, till they came to Greenwich, and there tarried; abiding the Queen's Grace: which was a wonderful and goodly sight to behold.

Then at three o'clock, the Queen's Grace came to her barge: and incontinent all the citizens with that goodly company set forth towards London in good array, as is before said. And to write what number of gun shots – what with chambers, and great pieces of ordnance – were shot off as she passed by, in divers places, and especially at Ratcliff and at Limehouse out of certain ships; it passeth my memory to write or to tell the number of them! And so the Queen's Grace, being in her rich barge among her nobles, the citizens accompanied her to London, unto the Tower wharf.

Also ere she came near the Tower, there were shot off innumerable pieces of ordnance, as ever there was there by any men's remembrances: where the King received her Grace with a noble loving countenance; and so gave thanks and praise to all the citizens for all their great kindness and loving labour and pains taken in that behalf, to the great joy and comfort of all the citizens.

Also to behold the wonderful number of people that ever was seen, that stood on the shore on both sides of the river; it was never seen, in one sight, out of the City of London. What in goodly lodgings and houses that be on the river side between Greenwich and London; it passeth all men's judgements to esteem the infinite number of them: wherein her Grace with all her ladies rejoiced much.

Knights made at Greenwich the Sunday before Whit-Sunday

And the Sunday before this Triumph, being the 25th day of May [1533]; the King made at his Manor of Greenwich all these knights.

Sir Christopher Danby.

Sir Christopher Hylard.

Sir Brian Hastings.

Sir Thomas Methem.

Sir Thomas Butteller.

Sir William Walgrave.

Sir William Fielding.

The Friday, were made Knights of the Bath, nineteen; whose names followeth

Also on Friday the 30th day of May, the king created and made in the Tower of London, nineteen noblemen, Knights of the Bath: whose names follow.

The Lord Marquis Dorset.

The Earl of Derby.

The Lord Clifford, son and heir to the Earl of Cumberland.

The Lord Fitz-Walter, son and heir to the Earl of Sussex.

The Lord Hastings, son and heir to the Earl of Huntingdon.

The Lord Berkeley.

The Lord Monteagle.

The Lord Vaux.

Sir Henry Parker, son and heir to the Lord Morley.

Sir William Windsor, son and heir to the Lord Windsor.

Sir John Mordaunt, son and heir to the Lord Mordaunt.

Sir Francis Weston.

Sir Thomas Arundell.

Sir John Hudleston.

Sir Thomas Ponings.

Sir Henry Saville.

Sir George Fitzwilliam, of Lincolnshire.

Sir John Tyndall.

Sir Thomas Jermey.

Also Saturday, the last day of May, the King made those Knights of the sword, in the Tower of London, whose names follow:

Sir William Drury.

Sir John Gerningham.

Sir Thomas Rush.

Sir Randolph Buerton.

Sir George Calverley.

Sir Edward Fytton.

Sir George Conyers.

Sir Robert Nedham.

Sir John Chaworth.

Sir George Gresley.

Sir John Constable.

Sir Thomas Umpton.

Sir John Horsley.

Sir Richard Lygon.
Sir John Saint Clere.
Sir Edward Maidison.
Sir Henry Feryngton.
Sir Marmaduke Tunstall.
Sir Thomas Halsall.
Sir Robert Kirkham.
Sir Anthony Windsor.
Sir Walter Hubbert.
Sir John Willoughby.
Sir Thomas Kitson.
Sir Thomas Mysseden.
Sir Thomas Foulehurst.
Sir Henry Delves.
Sir Peter Warburton.
Sir Richard Bulkeley.
Sir Thomas Laking.
Sir Walter Smith.
Sir Henry Everyngham.
Sir William Uvedall.
Sir Thomas Massingberd.
Sir William Sandon.
Sir James Baskervylle.
Sir Edmond Trafford.
Sir Arthur Eyre.
Sir Henry Sutton.
Sir John Nories,
Sir William Malory.
Sir John Harcourt.
Sir John Tyrell.
Sir William Browne.
Sir Nicholas Sturley.
Sir Randolph Manering.

Also the Sunday after Whit-sunday, being Trinity Sunday, and the 8th day of June; were made at Greenwich, these Knights following.
Sir Christopher Corwen.
Sir Geofrey Mydleton.
Sir Hugh Trevyneon.
Sir George West.
Sir Clement Herleston.
Sir Humphrey Feries.
Sir John Dawn.
Sir Richard Haughton.
Sir Thomas Langton.
Sir Edward Bowton.
Sir Henry Capel.

Also all the pavements of the City, from Charing Cross to the Tower, were covered over and cast with gravel.

And the same Saturday, being Whitsun Eve, the Mayor with all the Aldermen and the Crafts of the City prepared array in a good order to stand and receive her Grace; and with rails for every Craft to stand and lean, from the press of people.

The Mayor met the Queen's Grace at her coming forth of the Tower. All his brethren and aldermen standing in Cheap.

And upon the same Saturday, the Queen came forth from the Tower towards Westminster, in goodly array; as hereafter followeth.

She passed the streets first, with certain strangers, their horses trapped with blue silk; and themselves in blue velvet with white feathers, accompanied two and two. Likewise Squires, Knights, Barons, and Baronets, Knights of the Bath clothed in violet garments, edged with ermine like judges. Then following: the Judges of the law, and Abbots. All these estates were to the number of two hundred couple and more: two and two accompanied.

And then followed Bishops, two and two; and the Archbishops of York and Canterbury; the Ambassadors of France and Venice; the Lord Mayor with a mace: Master Garter the King of Heralds, and the King's coat armour upon him, with the Officers of Arms, appointing every estate in their degree.

Then followed two ancient Knights with old fashioned hats, powdered on their heads, disguised, who did represent the Dukes of Normandy and of Guienne, after an old custom: the Lord Constable of England for the time, being the Duke of Suffolk; the Lord William Howard, the Deputy for the time to the Lord Marshal, the Duke of Norfolk.

Then followed the Queen's Grace in her litter, costly and richly beseen, with a rich canopy over her: which was borne by the Lords of the Five Ports [i.e. Barons of the Cinque Ports], After her, following the Master of her Horse with a spare white palfrey richly appointed, and led in his hand.

Then followed her noble Ladies of Estate richly clothed in crimson powdered with ermines; to the number of twelve.

Then the Master of the Guard, with the guard on both sides of the streets in good array; and all the Constables well beseen in velvet and damask coats with white staves in their hand; setting every man in array and order in the streets until she came to Westminster.

Then followed four rich chariots with Ladies of Honour. After them followed thirty Ladies and gentlewomen richly garnished: and so the serving men after them.

And as she was departed from the Tower a marvellously great shot of guns was there fired, and shot off.

So this most noble company passed, till her Grace came to Fenchurch; where was a pageant fair and seemly, with certain children who saluted her Grace with great honour and praise, after a goodly fashion: and so passed forth to Gracechurch. Where was a rightly costly pageant of Apollo, with the Nine Muses among the mountains, sitting on the mount of Parnassus: and every of them having their instruments and apparel according to the description of poets, and namely [particularly] of Virgil; with many goodly verses to her great praise and honour.

And so she passed forth through Gracious [Gracechurch] Street unto Leaden Hall where was built a sumptuous and costly pageant in manner of a castle wherein was fashioned a heavenly roof and under it upon a green was a root or a stock, whereout sprang a multitude of white and red roses curiously wrought. So from the heavenly roof descended a white falcon,[7] and lighted upon the said stock and root: and incontinent descended an angel with goodly harmony, having a close crown between his hands, and set it on the falcon's head. And on the said floor sat Saint Anne in the highest place. And on that one side, her progeny with Scripture, that is to wit, the three Maries with their issue, that is to understand, Mary, the mother of Christ, Mary Salome the mother [actually wife] of Zebedee with the two children of them. Also Mary Cleophas with her husband Alpheus, with their four children on the other side. With other poetical verses said and sung; and with a ballad in English to her great praise and honour, and to all her progeny also.

And so she passed forth from thence, through Cornhill; and at the Conduit was a sumptuous pageant of the Three Graces. At the coming of the Queen's Grace a poet declared the nature of all those three Ladies; and gave high praises unto the Queen. And after this preamble finished, each Lady in particular spake great honour and high praise of the Queen's Grace

And so she passed forth with all her nobles till she came in Cheap. And at the Great Conduit was made a costly fountain, where out ran white wine, claret, and red wine, in great plenty, all that afternoon. And there was great melody, with speeches.

And so passed forth through Cheap to the Standard, which was costly and sumptuously garnished with gold and azure, with [coats of] arms and stories: where was great harmony and melody.

And so passed she forth by the Cross in Cheap, which was new garnished: and so through Cheap towards the lesser Conduit. And in the midway between, the Recorder of London received her before the Aldermen; with great reverence and honour saluting her Grace, with a loving and humble proposition, presenting her Grace with a rich and costly purse of gold, and in it a thousand marks in gold coin; given unto her as a free gift of honour. To whom she gave great thanks both with heart and mind.

And so her Grace passed a little further, and at the lesser Conduit was a costly and rich pageant; whereat was goodly harmony of music and other minstrels, with singing. And within that pageant were five costly seats, wherein were set these five personages, that is to wit, Juno, Pallas, Mercury, Venus, and Paris; who having a ball of gold presented it to her Grace with certain verses of great honour: and children singing a ballad to her Grace, and praise to all her ladies.

And so passed forth to Paul's Gate, where was a proper and sumptuous pageant, that is to wit, there sat three fair ladies, virgins, costly arrayed, with a fair round throne over their heads; where about was written, *Regina ANNA prospere! Procede! et regna!* that is in English, 'Queen ANNE prosper! Proceed! and reign!' The lady that sat in the midst having a table of gold in her hand, written with letters of azure, *Veni amica coronaberis,*

'Come my love! thou shalt be crowned!' And two angels having a close crown of gold between their hands. And the lady on the right hand had a table of silver, whereon was written, *DOMINE! dirige gressos meos!* 'LORD GOD! direct my ways!' The other on the left hand had in another table of silver written, this *Confide in DOMINO!* 'Trust in GOD!' And under their feet was a long roll wherein was written this, *Regina ANNA novum regis de sanguine natum, cum paries populis aurea secula tuis.* 'Queen Anne when thou shalt bear a new son of the King's blood; there shall be a golden world unto thy people!' And so the ladies cast over her head a multitude of wafers with rose leaves; and about the wafers were written with letters of gold, this posy.

And so her Grace passed forth into Paul's Churchyard, And at the East end of the Church against the School was a great scaffold, whereon stood the number of two hundred children, well beseen: who received her with poet's verses to her noble honour. When they had finished, she said 'Amen,' with a joyful smiling countenance.

And so passed forth through the long Churchyard; and so to Lud Gate, which was costly and sumptuously garnished with gold, colours, and azure; with sweet harmony of ballads to her great praise and honour; with divers sweet instruments.

And thus her Grace came through the City with great honour and royalty, and passed through Fleet Street till she came to the Standard and Conduit where was made a fair tower with four turrets with vanes. Therewithin was a great plenty of sweet instruments, with children singing. The Standard, which was of mason work, costly made with images and angels, costly gilt with gold and azure, with other colours. and divers sorts of [coats of] arms costly set out, shall there continue and remain: and within the Standard a vice with a chime. And there ran out of certain small pipes great plenty of wine all that afternoon.

And so her Grace passed through the city to Temple Bar; and so to Charing Cross: and so through Westminster into Westminster Hall, that was well and richly hanged with cloth of Arras, with a marvellous rich cupboard of plate; and there was a void of spice-plates and wine.

And that done, the Queen's Grace withdrew her into the White Hall for that night; and so to York Place by water.

The Sunday, in the morning, at eight o'clock, the Queen's Grace with noble ladies in their robes of estate, assembled with all the nobles apparelled in Parliament robes, as Dukes, Earls, Archbishops and Bishops, with Barons and the Barons of the Five Ports; with the Mayor of the City and the Aldermen in their robes, as mantles of scarlet.

The Barons of the Five Ports bare a rich canopy of cloth of gold, with staves of gold, and four bells of silver and gilt. The Abbot of Westminster with his rygals [? regalia] came into the Hall in *pontificalibus*, with his monks in their best copes; the [members of] the King's chapel in their best copes: with the Bishops, richly adorned *in pontificalibus.*

And the blue 'ray cloth spread from the high dosses [? dais] of the King's Bench unto the high altar of Westminster.

And so every man proceeding to the Minster in the best order, every man after his degree appointed to his order and office as appertaineth; came unto the place appointed: where her Grace received her crown, with all the ceremonies thereof, as thereunto belongeth. And so all ceremonies done, with the solemn Mass: they departed home in their best orders; every man to the Hall of Westminster: where the Queen's Grace withdrew for a time into her chamber appointed.

And so after a certain space, Her Grace came into the Hall. Then ye should have seen every nobleman doing their service to them appointed, in the best manner that hath been seen in any such ceremony.

The Queen's Grace washed. The Archbishop of Canterbury said grace. Then the nobles were set to the table. Therewith came the Queen's service with the service of the Archbishop. A certain space, three men with the Queen's Grace's service.

Before the said service, came the Duke of Suffolk (High Constable that day, and Steward of the feast) on horseback, and marvellously trapped in apparel with richesse. Then with him came the Lord William Howard, as Deputy to the Duke of Norfolk, in the room [office] of the Marshal of England, on horseback.

The Earl of Essex, Carver. The Earl of Sussex, Sewer. The Earl of Derby, Cupbearer. The Earl of Arundel, Butler. The Viscount Lisle, Panterer. The Lord Braye, Almoner.

These noble men did their service in such humble sort and fashion, as it was a wonder to see the pain and diligence of them; being such noble personages.

The service borne by Knights, which were to me too long to tell in order: the goodly service of kinds of meat; with their devices from the highest unto the lowest: there have not been seen a more goodly nor more honourably done in no man's days.

There were four tables in the great Hall, along the said hall.

The noblewomen, one table: sitting all on that one side.

The noblemen another table.

The Mayor of London another table, with his brethren.

The Barons of the [Cinque] Ports, with the Master of the Chancery, the fourth table.

And thus all things nobly and triumphantly done at her Coronation; her Grace returned to White Hall, with great .joy and solemnity.

And on the morrow, there were great justs at the tilt done by eighteen Lords and Knights, where were broken many spears valiantly; and some of their horses would not come at their pleasure, near unto the tilt; which was displeasure to some that there did run.

## Nicholas Udall's English Verses and Ditties at the Coronation Procession of Queen Anne Boleyn[8]

*This interesting document sets out the words spoken in praise of Anne in the pageants held during her coronation procession. They were composed to praise both Anne and her issue and demonstrate her fitness for the throne.*

*Pageants were commonly used to glorify the royal family in state occasions in the Tudor period.*

<u>At the Pageant representing the Progeny of Saint ANNE, exhibited at Cornhill, besides Leadenhall.</u>
Were pronounced unto the Queen's Grace, these words following.

BY A CHILD.
Most excellent Queen, and bounteous Lady!
Here now to see your gracious Goodness,
With such honour entering this City;
What joy we take, what hearty gladness,
No pen may write, nor any tongue express!
For of you, depend the sure felicity
And hope, both of us and our posterity.

For like as from this devout Saint ANNE
Issued this holy generation,
First CHRIST, to redeem the soul of man;
Then James th'apostle, and th'evangelist JOHN;
With these others, which in such fashion
By teaching and good life, our faith confirmed.
That from that time yet to, it hath not failed:

Right so, dear Lady! our Queen most excellent!
Highly endued with all gifts of grace,
As by your living is well apparent;
We, the Citizens, by you, in short space,
Hope such issue and descent to purchase;
Whereby the same faith shall be defended,
And this City from all dangers preserved.

Which time that we may right shortly see,
To our great comfort, joy and solace;
Grant the most high and blessed Trinity!
Most humbly beseeching your noble Grace,
Our rude simpleness showed in this place
To pardon; and, the brief time considering,
To esteem our good minds, and not the thing.

This spoken, opened a cloud, and let down a White Falcon, In the descending of which was pronounced, as followeth:

BY ANOTHER CHILD.
Behold and see the Falcon White!
How she beginneth her wings to spread,
And for our comfort to take her flight.

But where will she cease, as you do read?
A rare sight! and yet to be joyed.
On the Rose; chief flower that ever was,
This bird to 'light, that all birds doth pass!
Then out of the same cloud descended an Angel, and crowned the same Falcon
with a Crown Imperial: at which doing, was pronounced as followeth:

BY ANOTHER CHILD.
Honour and grace be to our Queen ANNE!
For whose cause an Angel celestial
Descendeth, the Falcon as white as swan,
To crown with a Diadem Imperial!
In her honour rejoice we all.
For it Cometh from GOD, and not of man.
Honour and grace be to our Queen ANNE!

Then, at the departing of the Queen's said Grace, was sung this ballad
following.

This White Falcon,
Rare and geason,
This bird shineth so bright;
Of all that are,
No bird compare
May with this Falcon White.

The virtues all,
No man mortal,
Of this bird can write.
No man earthly
Enough truly
Can praise this Falcon White.

Who will express
Great gentleness
To be in any wight;
He will not miss,
But call him this
The gentle Falcon White.

This gentle bird
As white as curd
Shineth both day and night;
Nor far ne near
Is any peer
Unto this Falcon White.

Of body small,
Of power regal,
She is, and sharp of sight;
Of courage hault
No manner fault
Is in this Falcon White.

In chastity,
Excelleth she,
Most like a virgin bright:
And worthy is
To live in bliss
Always this Falcon White.

But now to take
And use her make
Is time, as troth is plight;
That she may bring
Fruit according
For such a Falcon White.

And where by wrong,
She hath fleen long,
Uncertain where to light;
Herself repose
Upon the Rose,
Now may this Falcon White.

Whereon to rest,
And build her nest;
GOD grant her, most of might!
That England may
Rejoice alway
In this same Falcon White.

<u>At the Conduit in Cornhill was exhibited a Pageant of the Three Graces</u>
In which a Child, apparelled like a Poet, pronounced unto the Queen's
Grace these verses:

QUEEN ANNE, behold your servants, the Three Graces!
Giving unto your Grace faithful assistance.
With their most goodly amiable faces,
They attend with their continual presence,
Where your Grace goeth, Absent in your absence.
While your Grace is here, they also here dwell
About the pleasant brinks of this live well.

Now here to be, they thought it their duty,
And presently to salu[t]e you, gracious Queen!
Entering this day into this noble City,
In such triumphant wise as hath not been seen:
Which thing, to your honour and joy may it been!
These Three Sisters thought it their rebuke and shame,
This day to be slack in honouring their Dame.

Then immediately followed the speeches of the Three Graces, in this wise:

AGLAIA. HEARTY GLADNESS.
QUEEN ANNE! whom to see, this City doth rejoice;
We three Graces, ladies of all pleasance,
Clasped hand in hand, as of one mind and voice,
With our three gifts in all good assurance,
Shall never fail your Grace, to t'endue and enhance!
For I, HEARTY GLADNESS by my name called,
Shall your heart replenish with joy unfeigned.
THALEIA. STABLE HONOUR.
And I, STABLE HONOUR, gracious Queen Anne!
Joying in your joy, with this noble City,
In honour and dignity, all that I can,
Shall you advance! as your Grace is most worthy.
You to assist, I am bound by my duty.
For your virtues being incomparable,
You cannot but live, aye, most honourable.

EUPHROSYNE. CONTINUAL SUCCESS.
And for the great virtues, which I perceive
To be in your Grace, so high and excellent!
By me, CONTINUAL SUCCESS, ye receive
Long fruition, with daily increasement
Of joy and honour, without diminishment.
Never to decay, but always to arise!
All men, women, and children pray the same wise.

*At the Little Conduit in Cheapside was exhibited the judgement of PARIS*
In manner and form following:

MERCURY.
JUPITER, this apple unto thee hath sent,
Commanding, in this cause, to give
true judgement!

PARIS.
JUPITER, a strange office hath given me,
To judge which is fairest of these ladies three.

JUNO.
All riches and kingdoms be at my behest,
Give me the apple! and thou shalt have the best!

PALLAS.
Adjudge it to me! and for a kingdom,
I shall give thee incomparable wisdom!

VENUS.
Prefer me! and I shall reward thee, PARIS!
With the fairest lady that on the earth is.

PARIS.
I should break JUPITER'S high commandment,
If I should for mede or reward give judgement.

Therefore, lady VENUS! before both these twain,
Your beauty much exceeding; by my sentence,
Shall win, and have this apple. Yet, to be plain!
Here is the fourth Lady, now in presence,
Most worthy to have it of due congruence,
As peerless in riches, wit, and beauty;
Which are but sundry qualities in you three.
But for her worthiness, this apple of gold
Is too simple a reward a thousand fold!

The conclusion of this Pageant pronounced by A CHILD.

No! No! Another reward there is
Ordained for the worthiness of Her Grace;
And not to be disposed by you, PARIS!
Nor to be given here in this place.
Queen ANNE! most excellent that ever was,
For you is ready a Crown Imperial!
To your joy, honour, and glory immortal.

GOD, that of His goodness all things doth us send,
Hath sent us your Grace, our hearts to make glad.
Wherefore with as much humbleness we intend
Your noble Grace to serve, as ever Queen had.
For nothing there is, that may now make us sad,
Having your noble Grace, our refuge and rest,
Provided by Him, that knoweth what is best.

All joy, wealth, and honour, with long space of life,
Be to your Grace; with succession royal!
And He, that hath power of all prerogative,

The most blessed Trinity, GOD eternal,
Save our King HENRY in his estate royal!
Thus pray all the citizens, wife, child, and man,
GOD save King HENRY, and his Spouse Queen ANNE!

At the departing of the Queen's said Grace was sung this ballad following:

QUEEN ANNE so gent,
Of high descent.
Anne excellent
In nobleness!
Of ladies all,
You principal
Should win this ball
Of worthiness!

Passing beauty
And chastity,
With high degree,
And great riches;
So coupled be
In unity.
That chief are ye
In worthiness.

When JUPITER
His messenger
Sent down hither,
He knew certes
That you, victrice
Of all ladies,
Should have the prize
Of worthiness.

And wise PARIS
Made judge in this;
Anon, I wis,
Most high Princess!
Well understood
Your virtues good,
Your noble blood
And worthiness.

Your dignity
When he 'gan see,
The Ladies Three,
Queen ANNE peerless!

He bade give place
Unto your Grace;
As meet it was
In worthiness.

The golden ball,
Of price but small,
Have Venus shall,
The fair goddess!
Because it was
Too low and base
For your good Grace
And worthiness!

## Extract from Wriothesley's Chronicle on Anne's Coronation and the Birth of Princess Elizabeth[9]

*Wriothesley's Chronicle, which details the years between 1485 and 1559, provides much of the background detail that is known of the reign of Henry VIII and can be compared to Hall's Chronicle in scope. The author, Charles Wriothesley, a Windsor Herald from 1534, was particularly well-connected. Wriothesley was a kinsman of Henry VIII's conservative Lord Chancellor, Thomas Wriothesley, who was later created Earl of Southampton. Thomas Wriothesley was trusted enough by Henry VIII for him to be named as an executor to his Will. He served, for a time, on the council that ruled for the child king, Edward VI.*

*Events up to the eleventh year of Henry VIII's reign appear to have been heavily based on an earlier work of Richard Arnold (to whom Charles Wriothesley was related by marriage). However, the remainder of the Chronicle has been asserted to be a contemporary record, with the author recording events as they occurred.[10] For the most part, Wriothesley's Chronicle provides an accurate representation.*

Memorandum: the 12th day of Aprill, Anno Domini 1533, beinge Easter eaven, Anne Bulleine, Marques of Pembroke, was proclaymed Queene at Greenewych, and offred that daie in the Kinges Chappell as Queene of Englande.

And the Wednesdaie before the good Queene Katherin was deposed at Hanthill by the Duke of Norfolke, the Duke of Suffolke, my Lord Marques of Exceter, my Lorde of Oxforde, Lord Chamberlaine of the Kinges howse, Mr Treasorer and Mr Controwler of the Kinges howse. And from that daie after to be called Ladie Katherin, wife of Prince Arthur, dowarie of Englande, she to have by yearelie pencion for her dowarie eight thousand poundes sterlinge.

Memorandum, Thursdaie, the 29th daie of Maie, 1533, Ladie Anne, Marques of Pembroke, was receaved as Queene of Englande by all the Lordes of Englande. And the Major /sic/ and Aldermen, with all the craftes of the Cittie of London, went to Greenewych in their barges after the best fashion, with a barge also of Batchlers of the Majors crafte rytchlie behanged with cloath of golde and a foyst to wayte on her. And so all the Lordes, the Major, with all the craftes of London, brought her by water from Greenewych to the Tower of London, and ther the Kinges grace receaved her at her landinge; and then were shott at the Towre above a thousand gunnes, besides other shotts that were shott at Lymehowse, and in other shipps lying in the Thammes. And the morrowe after being Fridaie their were made divers Knightes of the Bath.

And on Saturdaie, the last daie of Maie, shee rode from the Towre of London throwe the Cittie, with a goodlie companye of Lordes, Knightes, and Gentlemen, with all the Peares of the Realme, rytchlie apparailed, and also eightene Knightes of the Bath newlie made, ridinge in blewe gownes with hoodes on their sholders purfeled with white, and white laces of silke knitt on the left sholders of their gownes. And she herself riding in a rytch chariott covered with cloath of silver, and a rich canapie of cloath of silver borne over her heade by the fower Lordes of the Portes, in gownes of Scarlett, and fower chariotts, with ladies followinge after her rytchlie behanged; and also divers other ladies and gentlewomen riding on horsebacke all in gownes made of crymson velvett; and their was divers pageants made on skaffoldes in the Cittie; and all the craftes standing in their liveries everie one in order, the Major and Aldermen standinge in Cheepeside; and when she came before them the Recorder of London made a goodlie preposition to her, and then the Major gave her a purse of cloath of golde, with a thousand markes of angell nobles in it, for a presente for the whole bodie of the Cittie; and so the Lordes brought her to the Palace at Westminster, and their left her that night.

Memorandum, the first daie of June, Quecne Anne was brought from Westminster Hall to the Abbey of Sainct Peeter's with procession, all the monkes of Westminster going in rytch copes of golde with 13 abbotts mitred; and after them all the Kinges Chappell in rych copes with fower bushopps and tow archbishopps mittred, and all the Lordes going in their Perliament roabes, and the crowne borne afore her by the Duke of Suffolke, and her tow scepters by tow Earles, and she herself going under a rytch canapie of cloath of golde, apparailed in a kirtell of crymson velvett powdred with ermyns, and a robe of purple velvett furred with powdred ermines over that, and a rich cronett with a call of pearles and stones on her hedde, and the olde Dutches of Norfolke[11] bearing upp her traine in a robe of Scarlett with a cronett of golde on her bonett, and the Lorde Boroughe, the Queenes Chamberlaine, staying the traine in the middes; and after her tenne ladies following in robes of scarlett furred with ermins and rounde cronettes of golde on their heades; and next after theim all the Queenes maides in gownes of Scarlett edged with white lettushe furre; and so was shee brought to Sainct Peeters Church at Westminster, and their sett in her seate riall, which was made on a high scaffolde before the highe aulter; and their shee was anoynted and crowned Queene of Englande by the Archbishopp of Canterberie and the Archbishoppe of Yorke, and so sate crowned in her seate riall all the masse, and offred also at the said masse; and the masse donne, they departed everie man in their degrees to Westminster Hall, she going still under the cannapie crowned with towe septers in hir handes, my Lorde of Wilshire, her father, and the Lorde Talbott leadinge her, and so theire dynned; wheras was made the most honorable feast that hath beene seene.

The great hall at Westminster was rytchlie hanged with rych cloath of Arras, and a table sett at the upper ende of the hall, going upp twelve greeses, where the Queene dyned; and a rytch cloath of estate hanged over her heade; and also fower other tables alongest the hall; and it was rayled on everie side, from the highe deasse[12] in Westminster Hall to the scaffold in the church in the Abbay.

And when she went to church to her coronation their was a raye cloath, blew, spreed from the highe desses of the Kinges Benche unto the high alter of Westminster, wheron she wente.

And when the Queenes grace had washed her handes, then came the Duke of Suffolke, High Constable that daie and stewarde of the feast, ryding on horsebacke rytchlie apparailed and trapped, and with him, also ridinge on horsebacke, the Lorde William Howarde as deputie for the Duke of Norfolke in the romth of the Marshall of Englande, and the Queenes service following them with the Archbishopps, a certaine space betwene which was borne all by knightes, the Archbishopp sitting at the Queenes borde, at the ende, on her left hande. The Earle of Sussex was sewer, the Earle of Essex carver, the Earle of Darbie cuppbearer, the Earle of Arrondell butler, the Viscount Lisle pantler, the Lord Gray almoner.

Att one of the fower tables sate all the noble ladies all on one side of the hall, at the second table the noble men, at the thirde table the Major of London with the Aldermen, att the fowerth table the Barons of the Portes with the Masters of the Chauncerie. The goodlie dishes with the delicate meates and the settles which were all gilt, with the noble service that daie done by great men of the realme, the goodlie sweete armonie of minstrells with other thinges were to long to expresse, which was a goodlie sight to see and beholde.

And when shee had dined and washed her handes she stoode a while under the canopie of estate, and behelde throwghe the hall, and then were spices brought with other delicates, which were borne all in great high plates of gold, wherof shee tooke a litle refection, and the residue geavinge among the lordes and ladies; and that donne she departed up to the White Hall, and their changed her apparell, and so departed secreetlie by water to Yorke Place, which is called White Hall, and their laie all night.

On the morrowe after was great justes at the tilte donne by eightene lordes and knightes, where was broken many speares valiantlie, but some of their horses would not come at their pleasure nere the tilt, which was great displeasure to somme of them that ranne; and, the justes donne, their was a goodlie banquett made to all the lordes, ladies, and gentlemen in the Queenes Chamber.

This yeare, on Midsommer eaven, died the French Queene, sister to the Kinge, and wife to the Duke of Suffolke, and was buried at Sainct Edmondesburie[13] in Suffolke.

This yeare, in Julie, on a Fridaie, one Frith, a servingman, a great clearke in the Greeke and Latten tonge, was brent[14] in Smithfielde, and a tailor of London with him, for heresie.

Memorandum, the viith daie of September, 1533, being Sonndaie, Queene Anne was brought to bedd of a faire daughter at three of the clocke in the after noune; and the morrowe after, being the daie of the Nativitie of Our Ladie, Te Deum was songe solempnlie at Powles, the Major and Aldermen being present, with the head craftes of the Cittie of London.

And the Wednesdaie next followinge, the most honorable yonge ladie was christened at Greenewych in the Friers Church, all the noble lordes and ladies doing service about the christening in their offices after their degrees, which was a goodlie sight to see, and their shee had geaven her to name Elizabeth; my Lord Thomas Cranmer, Archbishopp of Canterberie, godfather; the old Dutchesse of Northfolke, wydowe, my Ladie Marques of Dorcett, widowe, godmothers at the fonte, and my Ladie Marques of Exceter, godmother at the bishoppinge; and the morrowe after their was fiers made in London, and at everie fire a vessell of wyne for people to drinke for the said solempnitie.

## Anne's Letters as Queen

*Few of Anne's letters survive. The selection below demonstrates that she quickly adopted a royal style in her correspondence. The first two letters are almost identical, but are both included for the sake of completeness. They announce the birth of Elizabeth in September 1533. It was usual for the queen to personally announce the birth of a royal child and letters would often be prepared in advance to be sent out. They were not, of course, written in her own hand, but would have been approved by the Queen.*

*Interestingly, most of the other letters relate to Anne's attempts to advance followers of the religious reform movement. Anne's letter to Dr Crome is of further interest due to the fact that she was determined to promote and advance him, regardless of whether he wanted her assistance or not! The letter to the Abbot of St Mary's, York similarly hints at the fact that Anne expected to be obeyed and was not a woman to be crossed. Her promotion of the religious reform is also attested in a number of other sources concerning her life, including the early biography written of her by her chaplain, William Latymer. Latymer claimed that Anne was determined to lead by example, often reading the Bible in English at the common desk in her apartments, in order to encourage others to do so. Latymer related that Anne sent commissioners to Hailes Abbey to enquire into their famous relic of the blood of Christ. When it was discovered to be either the blood of a duck or red wax, she reported it to Henry and insisted that it be removed. Latymer further related that Anne assisted Continental reformers who had been exiled to England.[15]*

*Queen Anne Boleyn's Letter to Squire Josselin on the Birth of Princess Elizabeth[16]*
By the Queen.

Trusty & wellbeloued, wee greet you well. And whereas it hath pleased the goodness of Almighty God of his infinite mercy and grace, to send unto vs at this tyme good speed in the deliverance and bringing forth of a Princess, to the great joye and inward comfort of my Lord, vs, and of all his good and louinge Subjects of this his Realme, For the which his inestimable benevolence soe shewed unto us, we haue noe little cause to giue high thankes, laude, & praysing unto our said Maker, like as we doe most lowly, humbly, & with all the inward desire of our heart. And inasmuch as wee undoubtedly trust that this our good speed is to your great pleasure, comfort, & consolacion, Wee therfore, by these our Letters, aduertise you thereof, desiring & hartily praying you to giue with us unto Almighty God, high thankes, glory, laude, & praising; & to pray for the good health, prosperity, & continuall preseruacion of the said Princess accordingly.

Yeouen under our Signett, at my Lords Manner of Greenwich, the 7th day of September, in the 25th yeare of my said Lords Raigne. Anno Domini 1533.

*Queen Anne Boleyn to Lord Cobham, 7 September 1533*[17]
Right trusty and well beloved, we greet you well. And whereas it hath pleased the goodness of Almighty God, of his infinite mercy and grace, to send, to us, at this time, good speed in the deliverance and bringing forth of a princes, to the great joy, rejoice, and infinite comfort of my lord, us, and all his good subjects of this his realm, for the which his inestimable benevolence, so shewed unto us, we have no little cause to give high thanks, laud, and praising our said Maker, like as we do most lowly, humbly, and with all the inward desire of our heart. And inasmuch as we undoubtedly trust, that this our good speed is to your great pleasure, comfort, and consolation, we, therefore, by these our letters advertise you thereof, desiring and heartily praying you to give with us, unto Almighty God, high thanks, glory, laud, and praising; and to pray for the good health, prosperity, and continual preservation, of the said princes accordingly. Given under our signet, at my lord's manor of Greenwich, the 7th day of September, in the 20th [*sic*] year of my said lord's reign.

*Queen Anne Boleyn to the Magistrates of the City of Bristol, 1535*[18]
Trusty and well-beloved,
We greet you well, letting you to wit that for the great zeal and tender favour which we do bear towards the great advancement of it your town of Bristol, we be right desirous to have a friend of ours, who, as we know right well, is a man of right good learning, and of no less virtue and good demeanour, to be preferred into the room of master of the college of St John the Baptist, standing in Ratcliff Pit in the town aforesaid: being of your patronage, after the decease of the now incumbent of the same.

Wherefore we desire and heartily pray you that for this purpose you, at your contemplation of these our letters, will make your sufficient grant under your seal of the next advowson of the said college or hospital, unto our trusty and right-well-beloved councillors, Sir Edward Bainton, knight, our chamberlain, and Mr Nicholas Shaxton, D.D., our almoner, and to our trusty and well-beloved David Hutton. To the intent that they, immediately upon the next vacation of the same, may present thereunto our said friend; by whose good life and spiritual conversation we verily trust that such charitable order, concord, and unity shall be augmented and increased among you, as may not only be to the pleasure of Almighty God, but also to the no little rest, quietness, weal, and benefit of your said town in time to come, whereof we be right desirous. And of your good minds herein we pray you to send to us your answer in writing, by this bearer, accordingly.

Give under our signet, at my lord's manor of Westminster, the 20th of January.

### *Queen Anne Boleyn to Dr Crome, 1535*[19]

Trusty and well-beloved,

We greet you well, marvelling not a little that, albeit heretofore we have signified unto you at sundry times our pleasure concerning your promotion unto the parsonage of Aldermary, within the city of London, which we have obtained for you, yet you hitherto have deferred the taking on you of the same; by which your refusal, we think that you right little regard or esteem your own weal or advancement. We, minding nothing more than the furtherance of virtue, truth, and godly doctrine, which we trust shall be not a little increased, and right much the better advanced and established, by your better relief and residence there, signify therefore unto you, that our express mind and pleasure is that you shall use no farther delays in this matter, but take on you the cure and charge of the said benefice of Aldermary, as you tender our pleasure in any behalf.

Give under our signet, at my lord's manor of Richmond, the 20th of May.

### *Queen Anne Boleyn to Thomas Cromwell, 1535*[20]

Master secretary,

Whereas heretofore, at our instance and for our sake, you have been good master unto Robert Power, whom we put to you in service, insomuch, beside others, you granted him afore this time, as we be informed, the nomination and preferment of an abbacy or house of religion for his friend, through the which he might be the more able to maintain himself in your service; and now, as we be informed, the abbot of Wallryale in Lincolnshire[21] is lately deceased and departed this world, wherefore the said monastery is now void and without a head: wherefore we desire and heartily pray you, at the contemplation of these our letters and at our request, in preservation of your said grants to be fulfilled, to help his said friend to the preferment of the said house or monastery. And in so doing we shall hereafter have you in our remembrance, with condign thanks, &c. to be shewed unto you.

Give under our signet, at my lord's manor of Langley, the 18th day of July, in the twenty-seventh year of my said lord's reign.

ANNE THE QUEEN.

*Queen Anne Boleyn to the Abbot of St Mary's, York, 1535*[22]
ANNE QUEEN.
Trusty and well-beloved in God, we greet you well. And albeit at the time of your preferment to be head and governor of that my lord's monastery of Saint Mary beside his city of York, we then made request unto you for one dompne John Eldmer, bachelor of divinity, a man, as we [be] credibly informed, of good learning, sad demeanour, and virtuous governance, who then for the same his elect qualities stood in election (as you did) to be abbot, like as we doubt not but you remember right well, that the same dompne John Eldmer should apply and continue his study and learning at my lord's university of Cambridge for the increase of virtue and learning: wherewith at that time you were well content. Yet notwithstanding the same, you, contrary to our said request (as we be credibly informed), have not only called him from his learning at the said university, but also have intricate and charged him with sundry rooms and offices in your said monastery, to the no little disturbance and inquietation of his mind, and to alienate him as much as may be from his said study and learning: to our no little marvel. We, considering the good affection and desire the said dompne John Eldmer hath to the increase of virtue and learning, desire and heartily pray you, that you will permit and suffer him to repair again to the university for the intent aforesaid, giving unto him sufficient exhibition to the maintenance of his study there, or else to signify unto us in writing, by this bearer, a cause reasonable why you defer to accomplish our said request made unto you in that behalf.
Given under our signet, at my lord's manor of Westminster, the 13th day of May.


*Anne Boleyn to Thomas Cromwell, c. 1535*[23]
Master Secretary,
I pray you despatch with speed this matter, for mine honour lies much on it, and what should the king's attorney do with Pointz's obligation, since I have the child by the king's grace's gift, but only to trouble him hereafter, which by no means I will suffer, and thus fare you well as I would ye did.
Your loving mistress, Anne the Queen


*Queen Anne Boleyn to Thomas Cromwell (undated)*[24]
ANNE THE QUENE.
By the Quene.
Trustie and right welbiloued we grete you well. And where as we be crediblie enformed that the berer hereof Richard Herman marchaunte and citizen of Antwerpe in Brabant was in the tyme of the late lorde Cardynall[25] put and expelled frome his fredome and felowshipe of and in the Englishe house there, for nothing ells (as he affermethe) but oonly for that that he dyd bothe with his goddis and pollicie, to his greate hurte and hynderans in this Worlde, helpe to the settyng forthe of the Newe Testamente in Englisshe. We therefore desire and instantly praye you that with all spede and favoure convenient ye woll cause this good and honeste marchaunte, being my Lordis true faithfull and loving subjecte, restored to his pristine fredome, libertie, and felowshipe

aforesaid, and the soner at this oure requeste, and at your good leyser to here hym in suche thinges as he hathe to make further relacion unto you in this behalf. Yeven undir our Signete at my Lordis manoure of Grenewiche the xiiijth daye of May.

## Lady Skeffyngton to Anne Boleyn, 26 January 1536[26]

*The letter below contains a direct appeal to Anne for aid. It has been suggested that Anne was seen as 'particularly receptive to female petitioners'.[27] She is known to have assisted her aunt, Katherine Howard, in her attempts to obtain a separation from her husband. Another lady, Elizabeth Staynings, sought access to her in order to plead for the release of her husband from prison.*

*Lady Skeffyngton was the wife of Sir William Skeffyngton, Henry VIII's Lord Deputy of Ireland. She wrote her appeal to Anne on the same day that she sent a similar letter to Thomas Cromwell, enclosing a petition in which she requested sums due to her husband, as well as payment for her expenses in her return to England.*

*Anne has also often been supposed to have intervened in a petition from the Prioress of Catesby, a nunnery in Northamptonshire which was to be dissolved by Henry VIII. In a letter addressed to Thomas Cromwell, the prioress asserted that 'the queen's grace hath moved the king's majesty for me, and hath offered his highness two thousand marks in recompence of that house of Catesby'. However, given that Cromwell's commissioners did not actually reach the nunnery until the summer of 1536, the queen in question was, almost certainly, Anne's successor, Jane Seymour.[28]*

To the Quinis Most excellent Highnes.

Ytt may please Your most excellent Highnes to be advertized, that the last day of December yt pleased Almyghti God to call to his infinite merci Sir William Skeffyngton, my late husband, the Kinges Grace Deputie of this his land of Ireland; whose soule Jhesu pardon. Where fore, onles that Your Grace, of your most haboundaunt goodnes and pety, in this my greate necessite, left here comfortles, be my good and gracius Lady, to move for me unto the Kinges Highnes, that in recompence of some parte of my said late husbandes good service to His Highnes, doo shoo aswell his marcifull favours unto me, as also of his most noble liberalite be my favorable Lorde, in all suche my power requestes and peticion, as on my behalfe shalbe uttered and showed unto his Grace Counsaillour and Chefe Secretory, Maister Thomas Crumwell, surely I none other wyse accompte my selfe, and all my power childern, but cleerly undone by my said husbandes servyce; which I humble beseche your most royall estate to move unto the Kinges Highnes to have in his gracius rememeraunce the longe contynuaunce of the same my sayd husbandes faythfull, trewe, and diligent harte and service all weyse unto His Grace, to the uttermest of his lytyll power. And I, and all myne, shall daily pray to the Blessed Trenyte for the preservacion of your most high excellent estate, long to endure. Wretton at the Kynges Grace Cetty of Dublyn, the 26th day of Jenuarij.

Your humble and most obediaunt daylly Oratryx and Bedwoman,[29]
ANNE SKEFFYNGTON.

## Extract from the *Life of Jane Dormer* by Henry Clifford[30]

*The* Life of Jane Dormer *presents a highly prejudicial view of Anne Boleyn, contrasting both her, and her daughter, unfavourably to Catherine of Aragon and Princess Mary. The* Life *was written by Henry Clifford, an English Catholic. It was started shortly after Jane Dormer's death in 1613 and was apparently substantially complete by 1615.[31] It was not, however, finished until 1643, when the author presented a copy of his work to Lord Dormer, a relative of its subject.*

*Jane Dormer was born in 1538, the daughter of a former suitor to Jane Seymour, Henry VIII's third wife.[32] She served Mary I when she became queen and was close to her, marrying one of Mary's closest advisors, the Spanish Count de Feria, soon after the Queen's death. Jane, a devout Catholic, left England after Elizabeth I's accession and never returned to her homeland. She did, however, retain an interest in its affairs, as a letter that she wrote to James VI of Scotland demonstrates. In her letter, Jane, who had been acquainted with his mother, Mary, Queen of Scots, assured the King that the surest path to the English throne was for him to convert to Catholicism – advice that he was to prudently ignore. Jane Dormer employed Henry Clifford, her biographer, in her household, and became close to him, providing him with much of the information that he would use to write her biography. Jane was not, however, born until after Anne's fall, and would have had to rely on information from others. Clifford's account certainly has some value. For example, Jane may have received the account of Anne's attempts to befriend her stepdaughter directly from Princess Mary. However, it is also clear that Jane's view of Anne was prejudiced both by the people that she obtained her information from, and her own view of Anne's daughter and the changes to religion that Anne's marriage ushered in. The source should therefore be viewed with some caution: it cannot be considered a first, or even, second hand account of Anne's life and actions.*

... Queen Catharine was some five years older than the king, and very different in manners. She rose at mid-night to be present at the matins of the Religious. At five o'clock she made herself ready with what haste she might, saying that the time was lost which was spent in apparelling herself. Under her royal attire she did wear the habit of St Francis, having taken the profession of his Third Order. She fasted all Fridays and Saturdays and all the Eves of our Blessed Lady with bread and water. On Sundays she received the Blessed Sacrament, read daily the Office of the Blessed Virgin, she was the most part of the morning in the Church at holy service and after dinner read the life of that day's Saint to her maids standing by. Then she returned to the Church. She was sparing in her supper. She prayed kneeling on her knees without cushions. She was affable in conversation, courteous to all, and of an excellent and pious disposition. This lady, a mirror of goodness, was afterwards brought into infinite troubles, so to be tried as that the sweet savour of her virtues might be diffused over the whole christian world.

Henry the Eighth, weary (as it seems) of this good queen Catharine, after fifteen years' co-habitation, by the suggestion of Cardinal Wolsey begins to make scruple whether this marriage with the Lady Catharine was lawful, for that she had been before his brother's wife. Pope Julian the second gave lawful dispensation to make good the marriage. That learned and glorious martyr doctor John Fisher, the light not only of the kingdom of England but of the whole Christian world, when this divorce was in pleading, delivered to the legates a paper most learnedly written in defence of the marriage, advising them not to seek a knot in a rush nor to suffer the manifest truth of Holy Scripture and Ecclesiastical laws, sufficiently seen and examined in this cause, to be perverted; but rather to consider again and again how great mischiefs would follow by this divorce, to wit, hatred between King Henry and Charles the Emperor, and the factions of the princes who would join them. And the most grievous of all, – dissensions in matters of faith, schisms, heretics and infinite sects. 'I (said he) have in this matter laboured much and employed my utmost industry; and I dare affirm what I have not only proved in this writing, and clearly taught by the testimony of the Sacred Scriptures and of Holy Fathers, but also am ready to testify it with the shedding of my blood, that there is no power on earth that can dissolve or disjoin this marriage, which has been joined by God Himself.'

This with other learned and pious writings that the other advocates did present to the legates, although Cardinal Wolsey was one, did move them not to give sentence as the king desired and required; nor would Clement VII., then Pope, give way to it, who then being at war with the emperor was offered by King Henry to maintain four thousand [men] in his wars against Cesar. So much did he desire this divorce to marry the Lady Anne Bullen. He sought all means by gifts and corruptions to most Universities to have their favourable opinions for this his desire. Cardinal Wolsey had it intimated, in regard to his note to the emperor, that the king might marry with the Lady Margaret, a very fair woman, the widow of the Duke of Alencon, and sister to Francis, the French king.

Thomas Cranmer, chaplain to Sir Thomas Bullen, the supposed father of the Lady Anne,[33] was a man to the king's own heart. He turned as the king pleased, flattered and followed him in all his demands. He pronounced the sentence of divorce by which Queen Catharine was to be called the princess dowager of Prince Arthur and Anne was to be held lawful queen.

Mr Camden conceals the time of the marriage of Anne Bullen, for that the Lady Elizabeth's birth was in four months after. I marvel that he tells not the time of the king's espousals with her, nor of her marriage and her coronation, she being the mother of her whose life and reign he published. He says only that she was born 7th September, 1533, at Greenwich. Queen Catharine was banished from the Court to Kimbolton, where living retired with her maids until 6th January, 1536, she left this mortal life. It is said that her days were shortened by the intemperature of the unwholesome air, but chiefly by the continual increase of griefs and calamities; and some were of opinion, not without suspicion of poison, for the Lady Anne hated her extremely. When the king understood her death he shed tears and commanded all his household to wear mourning; but his new wife did clothe herself in yellow, glad of her death that she died so quietly. Her body was buried at Peterborough. She never could be persuaded after her banishment from the Court to enter into a monastery, although most desirous of that life, nor to do anything that might be in prejudice of her marriage, although exposed to many injuries and manifest dangers. Nor could she be drawn to go into Spain, or into Flanders, whither she was invited by the emperor, her nephew, where she might have had most honourable entertainment. She applied these miseries and disasters to have specially happened for the death of Prince Edward Plantagenet, son of the Duke of Clarence, brother to King Edward the Fourth; whom (most innocent) Henry VII. put to death to make the kingdom more secure to his posterity, and to induce King Ferdinand to give his daughter, this Catharine, in marriage to Prince Arthur. Before her death she wrote two pious letters, one to the king, the other to Friar Foster, her ghostly father, then in prison, after with cruel tortures a glorious martyr. Thus ended this great queen and holy princess, renowned in all nations and magnified by most writers of those times.

Within five months after, Queen Anne was brought to her reckoning for another world, but after a different life to her predecessor. It was passed most in masks, dancing, plays and such corporal delights, in which she had a special grace, – temptations to carnal pleasures and inventions to disgrace such and ruin them who were renowned for virtue. From the time that Queen Catharine was defended so stoutly and learnedly by the Bishop of Rochester she did seek by all means his destruction. One Richard Rice, a cook, was suborned to poison him, and he knew no other way to do it than to poison the common pot, which was for the whole household of the bishop. It chanced that that day according to his custom the bishop came not to dine in the parlour, but most of his family that dined there were poisoned and died thereof. Rice the cook being discovered did confess it and was publicly put to death for it. And when a gentleman brought word to the king that Sir Thomas More was then beheaded, the king being at table, and the Lady Anne standing by, the king throwing away the dice showed anger and sorrow that he was troubled and said to her, 'This is long of you; the honestest man of my kingdom is dead,' and suddenly retired chafing.

But to come to her death. The king seeming to affect Jane Seymour, and having her on his knee, as Queen Anne espied, who then was thought to be with child, she for anger and disdain miscarried, as she said, betwitting the king with it, who willed her to pardon him, and he would not displease her in that kind thereafter. But the queen, much wanting to have a manchild to succeed, and finding the king not to content her, to have her purpose did accompany with her own brother, Lord George Bullen, Viscount Rochford, Francis Weston, Henry Norris, William Brereton and Mark Sweton, a musician, all of the Privy Chamber, for which they all suffered death. Three days after that Anne Bullen herself was beheaded on 14th May, 1536, the Duke of Norfolk sitting High Steward. She was convicted and condemned by twenty-six peers, whereof her father was one, who shortly after died of grief. She was not twenty-nine years of age. We see how different were the mothers of these two queens, and of the latter the father might be doubted, for Queen Mary would never call her sister, nor be persuaded she was her father's daughter. She would say she had the face and countenance of Mark Sweton, who was a very handsome man. But we will pass to their education.

To speak briefly of the education and some passages of the life of Queen Mary, I should relate that she was bred under her virtuous mother, as well in princely splendour, as in true piety, to know and serve Almighty God and to have His holy fear before her eyes; and afterwards was commended for her further education to the Countess of Salisbury, the mother of Cardinal Pole, and cousin german to the queen her grandmother, a most pious and saint-like woman. She was declared Princess of Wales and heir of the kingdom; so bred as she hated evil; knew no foul or unclean speeches, which when her lord father understood, he would not believe it but would try it once by Sir Francis Brian, being at a mask in the court; and finding it to be true, notwithstanding, perceiving her to be prudent and of a princely spirit, did ever after more honour her. It chanced once that she and the Lady Anne Boleyn at Eltham, heard Mass together in one room. At the end of Mass, the Lady Mary made a low courtesy and went to her lodging; so did the Lady Anne, then called queen. When she came to her quarter, one of her maids told her that the Lady Mary at parting made reverence to her, she answered that she did not observe it; and said, 'If we had seen it, we would have done as much to her;' and presently sent a lady of honour to her, to excuse it; adding, that the love of none should be dearer nor more respected than hers, and she would embrace it with the kindness of a true friend. The lady that carried the message came when the Lady Mary was sat down at dinner. When admitted, she said; 'The queen salutes your grace with much affection and craves pardon, understanding that at your parting from the oratory, you made a courtesy to her, which if she had seen, she would have answered you with the like; and she desires that this may be an entrance of friendly correspondence, which your grace shall find completely to be embraced on her part.' 'It is not possible,' answered the Lady Mary, 'that the queen can send me such a message; nor is it fit she should, nor can it be so sudden, her majesty being so far from this place. You would have said, the Lady Anne Boleyn, for I can acknowledge no other queen but my mother, nor esteem them my friends who are not hers. And for the reverence that I made, it was to the altar, to her Maker and mine; and so they are deceived, and deceive her who tell her otherwise.' The Lady Anne was maddened with this answer, replying, that one day, she would pull down this high spirit.

## Queen Anne Boleyn to Lady Shelton, January 1536[34]

*The following letter was quoted by Chapuys in one of his despatches to the Emperor Charles V. Chapuys made it his business to know all that was happening in Princess Elizabeth's household in relation to her half-sister, Princess Mary. It seems unlikely that Chapuys would have deliberately sent his master a forged letter. This letter is therefore very likely to have been written by Anne. It was written after she had made another attempt to befriend Mary, offering to become a mother to her after her own mother's death. When this was refused, Anne wrote to her aunt, Lady Shelton, who had been appointed as Mary's governess, effectively washing her hands of the girl. The letter shows Anne exasperation at Mary's continuing conduct, and also the bravado with which she often responded to slights from the Imperial party.*

Mrs Shelton, my pleasure is that you do not further move the Lady Mary to be towards the King's Grace otherwise than it pleases herself. What I have done has been more for charity than for anything the king or I care what road she takes, or whether she will change her purpose, for if I have a son, as I hope shortly, I know what will happen to her; and therefore, considering the word of God, to do good to one's enemy, I wished to warn her beforehand, because I have daily experience that the king's wisdom is such as not to esteem her repentance of her rudeness and unnatural obstinacy when she has no choice. By the law of God and of the king, she ought clearly to acknowledge her error and evil conscience if her blind affection had not so blinded her eyes that she will see nothing but what pleases herself. Mrs Shelton, I beg you not to think to do me any pleasure by turning her from any of her wilful courses, because she could not do me [good] or evil; and do your duty according to the king's command, as I am assured you do.

## Mary Boleyn to Thomas Cromwell, 1534[35]

*The summer of 1534 proved to be a difficult time for Anne as it was during that period that her second pregnancy ended in either a miscarriage or a stillbirth. Henry also began a relationship with a new mistress, the so-called 'Imperial Lady', who was hostile to her, openly supporting Catherine of Aragon and Princess Mary. Anne's sister, the widowed Mary Boleyn, caused a scandal by appearing at court visibly pregnant, to her sister's fury. When Anne learned that Mary had secretly married the lowly William Stafford, she was banished from court in disgrace. The letter below, which was written by Mary, demonstrates the force of Anne's anger, and her continuing ability to influence the King, in spite of her failure to bear him a son. The letter, in its reference to 'the greatest queen in Christendom', contains a subtle dig at Anne, and suggests that the relationship between the sisters may have included some elements of rivalry. Anne did eventually forgive her sister, bringing her back to court to attend her during her final pregnancy.*

Master Secretary,
After my poor recommendations, which is smally to be regarded of me, that am a poor banished creature, this shall be to desire you to be good to my poor husband and to me. I am sure it is not unknown to you the high displeasure that both he and I have, both of the king's highness and the queen's grace, by reason of our marriage without their knowledge, wherein we both do yield ourselves faulty, and do acknowledge that we did not well

to be so hasty nor so bold, without their knowledge. But one thing, good master secretary, consider, that he was young, and love overcame reason; and for my part I saw so much honesty in him, that I loved him as well as he did me, and was in bondage, and glad I was to be at liberty: so that, for my part, I saw that all the world did set so little by me, and he so much, that I thought I could take no better way but to take him and to forsake all other ways, and live a poor, honest life with him. And so I do put no doubts but we should, if we might once be so happy to recover the king's gracious favour and the queen's. For well I might have had a greater man of birth and a higher, but I assure you I could never have had one that should have loved me so well, nor a more honest man; and besides that, he is both come of an ancient stock, and again as meet (if it was his grace's pleasure) to do the king service, as any young gentleman in his court.

Therefore, good master secretary, this shall be my suit to you, that, for the love that well I know you do bear to all my blood, though, for my part, I have not deserved it but smally, by reason of my vile conditions, as to put my husband to the king's grace that he may do his duty as all other gentlemen do. And good master secretary, sue for us to the king's highness, and beseech his highness, which ever was wont to take pity, to have pity on us; and, that it will please his grace of his goodness to speak to the queen's grace for us; for, so far as I can perceive, her grace is so highly displeased with us both that, without the king be so good lord to us as to withdraw his rigour and sue for us, we are never like to recover her grace's favour: which is too heavy to bear. And seeing there is no remedy, for God's sake help us; for we have been now a quarter of a year married, I thank God, and too late now to call that again; wherefore it is the more *almones* [alms] to help. But if I were at my liberty and might choose, I ensure you, master secretary, for my little time, I have tried so much honesty to be in him, that I had rather beg my bread with him than be the greatest queen in Christendom. And I believe verily he is in the same case with me; for I believe verily he would not forsake me to be a king.

Therefore, good master secretary, seeing we are so well together and does intend to live so honest a life, though it be but poor, show part of your goodness to us as well as you do to all the world besides; for I promise you, you have the name to help all them that hath need, and amongst all your suitors I dare be bold to say that you have no matter more to be pitied than ours; and therefore, for God's sake, be good to us, for in you is all our trust.

And I beseech you, good master secretary, pray my lord my father and my lady be so good to us, and to let me have their blessings and my husband their good will; and I will never desire more of them. Also, I pray you, desire my lord of Norfolk and my lord my brother to be good to us. I dare not write to them, they are so cruel against us; but if, with any pain that I could take with my life, I might win their good wills, I promise you there is no child living would venture more than I. And so I pray you to report by me, and you shall find my writing true, and in all points which I may please them in I shall be ready to obey them nearest my husband, whom I am most bound to; to whom I most heartily beseech you to be good unto, which, for my sake, is a poor banished man for an honest and a godly cause. And seeing that I have read in old books that some, for as just causes, have by kings and queens been pardoned by the suit of good folks, I trust is shall be our chance, through your good help, to come to the same; as knoweth the [lord] God, who send you health and heart's ease. Scribbled with her ill hand, who is your poor, humble suitor, always to command, MARY STAFFORD.

## The Despatches of Eustace Chapuys Relating to Anne's Time as Queen[36]

*Chapuys continued to observe Anne closely during her time as queen. Once again, his portrayal of Anne is, naturally, significantly biased. However, without his accounts, a great deal of Anne's life would now be lost, such as her pregnancy in 1534, which was never publicly announced.*

### 3 January 1533

... The Queen[37] has lately received intelligence that the King shews repentance at the separation, in consequence of which she fancies that God has perhaps touched his heart, and that he is about to acknowledge his error; but in my opinion she is very much mistaken, for the repentance, if there be any signs of it, proceeds less from knowledge of his sinful conduct than from fear of the infamy and evil rumours current among the people in consequence of this new marriage, and principally from a wish to save the expense of keeping so many establishments, which expense he is continually complaining of, and has ever since his return [from Calais] tried to curtail in every possible way, having already begun to reduce his household. It might also happen that the said repentance had its origin in another quarter, lest the Pope, during Your Majesty's next stay at Bologna, should be induced to pronounce sentence against him, or at least issue some brief commanding him to return to his queen. Indeed, I hear from one of his Privy Councillors that the King is very much afraid that one of these days a sentence will come from Rome, and he is already thinking, as I am told, of parrying the blow by means of another contradictory decision emanating from his Parliament, or at least of having the effects of the sentence suspended, and appealing to a General Council, which may never take place. That he (the King) considers his case at Rome as irretrievably lost, appears sufficiently from the fact of his having persistently refused of late to grant the Papal Nuncio an audience, as I duly informed Your Majesty in my despatch of the 30th of January though he promised to send soon for him.

The Queen's chaplain, who, as I wrote in a former despatch, had been long confined to prison for having preached and written in her favour, has been released during these last festivals [of the Epiphany], on condition, however, of his not writing or preaching again until a fortnight after Easter. Thus the priest has actually been set free, but the rings and jewels which the Queen lent the King for his journey to Calais still remain in bond, and God knows when they will be given back.

*27–29 January 1533*

… Doctor Cremmer (Cranmer) had not been a week here on his return from the embassy to Your Majesty when to the great astonishment of everyone he was appointed by the King to the archbishopric of Canterbury, the first and most substantial benefice in all England, since its holder becomes Primate and [Papal] Legate over all the kingdom. One of the causes why the said appointment has taken the people so much by surprise is that formerly it was not the custom for the King to fill up the vacancies before the expiration of the year within which the vacancy actually occurred, whereas the archiepiscopal see of Canterbury has not been vacant four months. There is still another reason which makes people wonder. That the expedition of the bulls may not be delayed the King has advanced out of his own pocket the sums required for that, which circumstance makes people suspect that such haste in the filling up of the see, and expedition of the bulls is chiefly owing to the King's wish that the Doctor may one of these days, as archbishop and legate of this kingdom, sanction the divorce, and authorize in this Parliament the new marriage. Indeed there is a rumour afloat that Dr Crammer, who is considered to be a Lutheran, has renounced the whole of his temporalities in favour of this king, which would be a fair way of compelling the rest of the English Clergy to do the same.

*9 February 1533*

… Besides her vehement suspicions that this sudden filling up of the archbishopric of Canterbury by the King is due to no other cause than his wish to attempt something against her, the Queen has lately had a further proof of the same; for within the last few days the King has twice boasted before his courtiers that should the Pope refuse to grant him what he is about to ask through Dr Bonnart (Bonner), who is only to take his departure to-morrow, he would immediately upon the expedition of the bulls [of Canterbury], let people know what he was about, and what he himself intended doing. She has also been told that four days ago one of the principal members of the Privy Council had assembled a number of doctors, churchmen as well as lawyers, and had proposed to them in the King's name that the opinion of all divines and canonists was that if the Queen had been 'cognue' by prince Arthur, her second marriage was null and void, and, therefore, that in order to prove the above connexion the King had, besides the presumption of right, searched for and found a document, which he shewed them, wherein it was asserted by the Catholic king [Ferdinand], and by the King's father [Henry VII] that queen Katharine had been 'cognue' by Arthur. And that the paper having been read, and minutely examined by the whole of the Assembly, they all agreed that the King, by the authority of the archbishop of Canterbury, legate of England, ought to carry out his undertaking at once. Which, being heard by the Queen, who also knows the King's great joy at the Nuncio's first overtures, she has been ever since in the greatest perplexity and doubt, so much so that she sent me yesterday three messengers, one after the other, and two more to day, begging me to dispatch this present courier in haste, and requesting in the most earnest manner that since she herself in her state of alarm and anxious care could not write to Your Majesty on the subject I should myself do it in her name, this being, as I said before, the reason of my venturing to write in greater detail.

In conclusion my advice is that His Holiness ought to delay the expedition of the bulls [of Canterbury] until the sentence is actually pronounced, or nearly so. An excuse might easily be found for such a step, or else a clause introduced in the bulls themselves, or in the form of the oath to be exacted from the Archbishop, forbidding him to mix himself up with the divorce case. I have already spoken about this to the Nuncio, who says he has already written, and will write again to His Holiness. Indeed were the Pope to know the reputation the said archbishop (Crammer) has here of belonging heart and soul to the Lutheran sect, he would not be so hasty in confirming him and expediting his bulls. I hear from a very authentic source that he has taken into his service two priests who have preached sermons against the Queen, though only out of gratitude to the father of the Lady, without whose interference they would have been sent to the stake a year ago, as I had the honour to inform Your Majesty in one of my despatches ...

The King, moreover, never talked so much or so openly as he does now of carrying his marriage into execution; so does the Lady [Anne], for she said the other day to a priest who wished to enter her service as chaplain that he must have patience for a short time until she had actually married the King. She still keeps in her possession the Queen's rings and jewels, and there is no talk for the present of her restoring them to their legitimate owner ...

*15 February 1533*
... The Lady said eight days ago, whilst dining in her own apartments, that she was as sure as she was of her own death that she should be very soon married to the King; and her father [the earl of Wiltshire] said the day before yesterday to the earl of Rotalant (Rutland) that the King was determined no longer to be so considerate as he had been but to marry his daughter at once, and that, the marriage having once taken place by the authority and sanction of Parliament it would be much easier to conciliate the opponents than at present. And upon the earl of Wiltshire asking him, Rutland, whether when the motion was brought forward in Parliament he, who was one of the King's blood, would vote for him or oppose the measure, he answered that the matter was wholly of a spiritual nature and could not be decided by Parliament. Upon which the Lady's father got into a passion as though Rutland had uttered a blasphemy, and began to taunt him in very gross language, so much so that he at last promised to vote whatever the King wanted, and sent me a message to say how matters stood, and that I was not to expect that any member of Parliament would dare offer any opposition.

I must add that the said earl of Wiltshire has never declared himself up to this moment; on the contrary, he has hitherto, as the duke of Norfolk has frequently told me, tried to dissuade the King rather than otherwise from the marriage. Which circumstance, coupled with others still more significative, such as the appointment of the new Chancellor, which the King has just

made, and the permission to three bishops who hold for the Queen to retire
to their dioceses, and appoint procurators approved by the King to represent
them in Parliament, &c., has thrown the Queen in the greatest state of
tribulation and anxiety, and she has particularly asked me to acquaint Your
Majesty with her fears ...

### 23 February 1533

The Queen perceiving the King's obstinacy to increase every day, and the
disorderly symptoms of a second marriage to grow in equal proportion, is
again compelled to apply for help, assistance and favour to Your Majesty,
on whom her last hopes are fixed.

Ever since my despatch of the 15th ulto the King has been continually
urging the archbishops of Canterbury and York, the bishops of London,
Winchester, and Lincoln, and several other doctors, Italian as well as English,
to sign their names to a letter which he has had written at his fancy, and which
as Your Majesty has no doubt been informed by Monsieur de Grandvelle, to
whom I have forwarded a copy, is a very strange document. They say that
the archbishop of York and the bishop of Winchester have not yet consented
to append their signatures, but that the elect of Canterbury has made no
difficulty or scruple whatever and has on the contrary urged it upon his
colleagues as if the affair concerned him principally. Indeed, if what a worthy
man has told me this very morning be true, a great danger is imminent. My
informer, who was going straight to the Queen to acquaint her with the fact,
assures me that the archbishop [of Canterbury] has actually pledged his most
solemn word to adhere entirely to the King's opinion in this matter of the
divorce, so much so that he has actually married the King to the Lady [Anne]
in the presence only of her father, mother, brother, and two intimate female
friends of the Lady herself, besides a priest of the diocese of Canterbury.
If so, the King could not do better to secure the archbishop's co-operation
and prevent his changing opinion hereafter, when once constituted into the
archiepiscopal dignity, as that of York and another bishop [Campeggio] did
a few years ago. Indeed, there is every reason to presume that either the said
archbishop elect of Canterbury has actually married the parties or promised
to marry them for certain considerations which I have already represented
to Your Majesty, and especially because ever since his (Cranmer's) election
he does not hesitate to say openly that he is ready to maintain with his life
that the King can take the Lady for his wife.

The rumour is afloat, and increases every day, that in order to achieve
his marriage the King is only waiting for the bulls of the said elect to come
[from Rome], and that the more to authorize the case he has commanded
those who have charge of convoking provincial synods, whilst the see is
vacant, to assemble them for the 17th of next month ...

### 8 March 1533

My despatch of the 23rd ulto contained all the news up to that date. Since
then, on the 24th, Your Majesty's letter of the 28th January came to hand.
On the same day the sieur de Langez (Langeais) arrived from France in

haste, besides a French gentleman, named Beauvoir, coming from Scotland. Both were well received and entertained as usual by the King, who invited them to dine next day at his table, together with the French ambassador in ordinary. This happened to be in Carnival time. The Lady [Anne] was present, occupying the same place and seat as the Queen in former times; the duke of Norfolk and other great lords also attended, with the single exception of the duke of Suffolk, who was not present, though expressly invited to come with the badge of the Saint Esprit ...

... On the same day of St Mathias the Lady treated the King to a banquet in her apartments, beautifully ornamented with splendid tapestry hangings, and the finest of buffets covered with gold plate. The Lady herself sat on the King's right hand, whilst the Dowager Duchess [of Norfolk] was lower down on the left, at the end of a cross table joining that of the King, where the Chancellor, the duke of Suffolk, and several other lords and ladies sat. During the dinner the King was so much engaged in play and conversation with the ladies that he scarcely talked to the rest of the company, or if he did no one could hear what he said, save once that he addressed the duchess of Norfolk, and asked her if she did not think that Madame, the marchioness, had a fine dowry and a rich marriage portion, which incident and others that I could relate will shew Your Majesty how obstinate this king is in his purpose, for since the execution of the Papal brief he has behaved much worse than before, not only in this respect, but also in his treatment of the Queen, whom he has lately caused to be hastily removed 40 miles from this city, without granting her the eight days she asked for to set her affairs in order; nor can it be expected that he will act otherwise towards her until he hears of a sentence having been pronounced in his favour, as I have already informed Your Majesty ...

*15 March 1533*

Since my last despatch, dated the 8th inst., the King has had a chaplain, and the Lady also one of hers, to preach before them that all the time he had lived with his Queen he had been in adultery and sin, and that all his good subjects ought to pray God to forgive him such an offence, and enlighten him so as to take soon another wife. 'This measure,' the preacher added, 'the members of the Privy Council ought to urge and strongly recommend, and if allowable compel the King to adopt, without taking heed of the censures and other measures decreed by the Pope, who in matters like this, in which he was evidently acting against the commands of God and against all reason, ought not to be obeyed. No wonder then (the preacher went on to say) if the King being so situated, were to take a wife of low rank, provided the virtues and secret merits of the person thus chosen should counterbalance her position, as happened in the cases of kings Saul and David.' Which words the preacher uttered with such passion and vehemence that the Queen's servants were greatly shocked, and that she herself, when she came to hear of them, wrote the letter herein enclosed, again imploring Your Majesty's help and favour lest this and other alarming appearances should indeed be a sign of her case being irretrievably lost ...

*31 March 1533*

As I had the honour of writing to Your Majesty on the 9th ult. this king was only waiting for the bulls of the archbishop of Canterbury to celebrate his new marriage. The said bulls having arrived in this city five days ago, to the great regret of everyone here, the King has marvellously pressed the synod, here assembled [in convocation] for that particular purpose, to decide at once the case, so much so that the prelates in attendance have hardly had time even to take food, and are threatened in such a manner that not one has yet dared open his mouth in opposition, with the solitary exception of the good bishop of Rochester (Fisher), whose opinion, though very just and reasonable can have no weight at all, he being positively alone by himself, against all the majority. So that in fact, the Queen herself, Fisher, and others who are in her favour, look upon the case as irretrievably lost if the very great docility of the said synod and the King's unruly passion be taken into consideration. Indeed the general belief is that before next Easter, or very shortly after, the new marriage will take place with due solemnity, for already the necessary preparations to that effect are being made and the Lady's royal household has been appointed so that nothing remains to be done but to have it publicly celebrated. All people here cry 'murder' against the Pope for his procrastination in this affair, and likewise for his not having delayed the expedition of the Canterbury bulls until after the final sentence, since he was duly warned of the imminent danger pending therefrom. Indeed there is hardly one among the courtiers, whether on the King's side or on the Queen's, who does not declare in public that His Holiness will in the end betray Your Majesty; especially the two dukes of Norfolk and Suffolk, who say that they are sure of it, and could if they chose give proofs of their assertion. Although I believe that these and other like reports proceed more from the hatred these people bear the Pope than from any real conviction of their own, yet I have deemed it my duty to inform Your Majesty thereof. However this may be, His Holiness will be one of the first to repent his doings, for he will undoubtedly lose his authority in this kingdom – a highly scandalous result for the whole of Christendom as well as a most injurious proceeding against the Queen – for among other statements made in the writ exhibited in Parliament against Papal authority it is expressly forbidden in future to apply or appeal to Rome in any case whatsoever, whether temporal or spiritual, matrimonial or other, under pain of confiscation of property, and imprisonment of the parties concerned as guilty of rebellion, enjoining that the writ is to have retroactive power, and be enforced in future suits, as well as in pleas already instituted, which clause, as may easily be understood, applies exclusively to the Queen's case. Indeed I am told by some one, though I can hardly believe it, that should the Queen still persist in her appeal to Rome, and refuse to comply with the said writ the King intends to deprive her of her dower ...

*10 April 1533*

... Last Easter Sunday the King sent the bishop of Rochester (Fisher) to prison under the custody of him of Winchester, a very strange act, that prelate being the most holy and learned in all Christendom. Which imprisonment has been made, as the King had it stated the other day in this Parliament, under colour of the bishop's (Fisher) having said that Mr. de Rochefort's[38] late mission to France was for the purpose of presenting a very large sum of money to the high chancellor of France, and to the cardinal of Lorraine, to induce the Pope by money or other means to ratify this king's new marriage, or at least to dissemble and not proceed further against the parties. That the King thought the Pope would make no difficulty, inasmuch as the marriage was already a 'fait accompli'. This much the good Bishop is accused of having said, and I do really believe that it must have been also one of the objects of Mr. de Rocheffort's mission to France; and, moreover, that in order not to hinder their negotiations with the Pope through the motions which they intend making in this Parliament, the King, a week ago, sent a message to the Papal Nuncio through the duke of Norfolk, requesting him not to write to His Holiness about the said affair. But the real cause and occasion of the good Bishop's detention is his having so manfully taken up the defence of the Pope and of the Queen, by which Your Majesty will be able to understand the state of confusion and disorder in which things are here, and the obstinacy of this king, who is wilfully working his own ruin and perdition. Indeed, I hear that whenever anyone represents to him the many inconveniences arising therefrom, and the dangers of a foreign invasion, he (the King) resolutely answers that if united and in harmony together, the English shall never be conquered by a foreign prince; and yet it seems to me as if he were doing all he can to forfeit the affection of his subjects.

Meanwhile all Englishmen, high and low, are in great alarm, and consider themselves as good as lost, believing that even if there should be no foreign invasion, civil war will break out and ruin them all. Great as their fears are, and not without reason, the general indignation is still greater, for excepting 10 or 12 persons who surround the Lady, all the rest of the nation are terribly afraid of disturbances in this country; so much so that whatever losses they might sustain through it, still they would wish Your Majesty to send here an army with which to destroy the poisonous influence of the Lady [Anne] and her adherents, and make a new reformation of all this kingdom.

I beg Your Majesty to pardon me if I venture too far on matters which are not my incumbence; but the great interest I take in Your Majesty's concerns compels me to say that, considering the very great injury done to Madame, your aunt, you can hardly avoid making war upon this king and kingdom, for it is to be feared that the moment this accursed Anne sets her foot firmly in the stirrup she will try to do the Queen all the harm she possibly can, and the Princess also, which is the thing your aunt dreads most. Indeed, I hear she has lately boasted that she will make of the Princess a maid of honour in her Royal household, that she may perhaps give her too much dinner on some occasion,[39] or marry her to some varlet, which would be an irreparable evil.[40] Besides the said dangers, which are urgent enough, and ought to be prevented, there are two weighty points to be taken into consideration: one is the bad example and great scandal of this divorce; the other the fear of this kingdom being alienated from our Holy Faith and going over to the

Lutherans, which will happen soon enough, and will be an irreparable evil, inasmuch as the King himself is shewing them the way and helping them on, and the archbishop of Canterbury is doing still worse.

An undertaking against this country would be in the opinion of many people here the easiest thing in the world just now, for this king has neither cavalry nor well trained infantry, besides which the affection of his subjects is entirely on Your Majesty's side, not only that of the common people but of the nobility in general, with the single exception of the duke of Norphorg (Norfolk) and two or three more. It is true that the better to ground the said enterprise, and remove all scruples and difficulties respecting existing treaties, it would be advisable that the Pope should invoke the aid of the secular power, and that in virtue of the censures already executed, Your Majesty should forbid all intercourse of trade between your dominions of Flanders and Spain and this kingdom to make the people rise against the promoters of this accursed marriage; and that in order to encourage and countenance them in their rising it would be advisable to fit out some ships of war, and secretly aid the Scotch with money, or give them hopes of aid, so that they may not conclude peace, which is the thing these people desire most at present ...

It is perfectly true that if it were not for the Princess's imminent danger, to which I have above alluded, and also because, should the English see Your Majesty at all lukewarm in this affair, they might lose the affection they profess you, the most prudent course to follow would be to temporize a little, and try to stop their trade with your subjects. And yet it seems to me as if this expedient was also fraught with danger; for if that be done this king will immediately try to get the king of France to make some stir, and, perhaps, also contribute his share of the expenses; though on the other hand, if he sees his kingdom suddenly invaded, he is not likely to lose his time in soliciting the aid of other princes, but will spend in his own defence the money he would otherwise have given. At any rate, it seems to me that Your Majesty would do well not to allow the English merchants who reside in your dominions of Flanders and Spain to be ill-treated, for they will be instrumental in maintaining and fostering the good-will and affection of the people to Your Majesty.

I hear that the King is about to forbid everyone, under pain of death, to speak in public or private in favour of the Queen. After that he will most likely proceed to greater extremities unless God and Your Majesty prevent it.

Again I beseech Your Majesty to forgive me if I dare give advice in such matters, for besides the above causes the great pity I have for the Queen and Princess, Your Majesty's aunt and niece, absolutely compel me to take this course ...

*15 April 1533*
... On Wednesday the said Duke [of Norfolk], and the others of whom I wrote to Your Majesty in my last despatch, called upon the Queen and delivered their message, which was in substance as follows: 'She was to renounce her

title of queen, and allow her case to be decided here, in England. If she did, she would confer a great boon on the kingdom and prevent much effusion of blood, and besides the King would treat her in future much better than she could possibly expect.' Perceiving that there was no chance of the Queen's agreeing to such terms, the deputies further told her that they came in the King's name to inform her that resistance was useless, since his marriage with the other Lady had been effected more than two months ago in the presence of several persons, without any one of them having been summoned for that purpose. Upon which, with much bowing and ceremony, and many excuses for having in obedience to the King's commands fulfilled so disagreeable a duty, the deputies withdrew. After whose departure the lord Mountjoy, the Queen's chamberlain, came to notify to her the King's intention that in future she should not be called queen, and that from one month after Easter the King would no longer provide for her personal expenses or the wages of her servants. He intended her to retire to some private house of her own, and there live on the small allowance assigned to her, and which, I am told, will scarcely be sufficient to cover the expenses of her household for the first quarter of next year. The Queen resolutely said that as long as she lived she would entitle herself queen; as to keeping house herself, she cared not to begin that duty so late in life. If the King thought that her expenses were too great, he might, if he chose, take her own personal property and place her wherever he chose, with a confessor, a physician, an apothecary, and two maids for the service of her chamber; if that even seemed too much to ask, and there was nothing left for her and her servants to live upon, she would willingly go about the world begging alms for the love of God.

Though the King is by nature kind and generously inclined, this Anne has so perverted him that he does not seem the same man. It is, therefore, to be feared that unless Your Majesty applies a prompt remedy to this evil, the Lady will not relent in her persecution until she actually finishes with queen Katharine, as she did once with cardinal Wolsey, whom she did not hate half as much. The Queen, however, is not afraid for herself; what she cares most for is the Princess.

On Saturday, the eve of Easter, Lady Anne went to mass in truly Royal state, loaded with diamonds and other precious stones, and dressed in a gorgeous suit of tissue, the train of which was carried by the daughter of the duke of Norfolk, betrothed to the duke of Richmond. She was followed by numerous damsels, and conducted to and from the church with the same or perhaps greater ceremonies and solemnities than those used with former queens on such occasions. She has now changed her title of marchioness for that of queen, and preachers specially name her so in their church prayers. At which all people here are perfectly astonished, for the whole thing seems a dream, and even those who support her party do not know whether to laugh or cry at it. The King is watching what sort of mien the people put on at this, and solicits his nobles to visit and pay their court to his new queen, whom he purposes to have crowned after Easter in the most solemn manner, and it is said that there will be banqueting and tournaments on the occasion. Indeed some think that Clarence, the king-at-arms who left for

France four days ago, is gone for the purpose of inviting knights for the tournament in imitation of the Most Christian King when he celebrated his own nuptials. I cannot say whether the coronation will take place before or after these festivities, but I am told that this king has secretly arranged with the archbishop of Canterbury, that in virtue of his office, and without application from anyone he is to summon him before his court as having two wives, upon which, without sending for the Queen, he (the Archbishop) will declare that the King can lawfully marry again, as he has done, without waiting for a dispensation, for a sentence from the Pope, or any other declaration whatever ...

About a week ago the sieur de Rochefort (George Boleyn) returned from France with the sieur de Beauvoes (Beauvoir), who started yesterday for Scotland for the purpose of inducing king James to place his differences with this king into his master's hand, and making him judge and arbiter of their differences. I have been told by a very worthy man that the duke of Albany's secretary returning from a visit to the said Beaulvoys (sic) had assured him that the said ambassador would be unable to accomplish his mission in Scotland, and that war would go on fiercer than ever. Indeed it would seem as if the Scots at this moment more prosperous than ever, for instead of being as before on the defensive, they are continually making raids on the borders. For this purpose did Mr. de Rochefort go to France as it is now ascertained. These people, as I am told, wish immensely for peace with Scotland, but God, as I said above, has taken away their senses, and they cannot see how to bring it about. The said Mr. de Rochefort, as his own servants assert, has been presented in France with 2,000 crs., no doubt for the good tidings of his sister's marriage, to whom the Most Christian King has now written a letter addressing her as queen. I fancy, moreover, that the French consider this good news, firstly: because it is likely to be the means of breaking off the friendship between Your Majesty and this king, and also, because it might ultimately be the cause of freeing the French from their debt and payment of pensions, either through sheer necessity, or for fear these people may have of their ultimately joining you, should the Pope proceed to sentence the case and have the censures executed – a thing which, in my opinion, Your Majesty ought to urge in every possible way – the French would be released from all their bonds and pecuniary obligations to this king.

The name and title which the King wishes the Queen to take, and by which he orders the people to call her, is the old dowager princess. As to princess Mary no title has yet been given to her, and I fancy they will wait to settle that until the Lady has been confined ...

## 27 April 1533

The last Easter festivals the prior of the Austin friars preached a sermon in which he expressly recommended his audience to offer up prayers for the health and welfare of queen Anne, at which recommendation the assistants were so astonished, so sorry, and so shocked that almost all left the church in high displeasure and with sad countenances without waiting for the rest of the sermon, which was only half over. At which the King was so much disgusted that he sent word to the Lord Mayor of this city that unless he wished to displease him immensely he must take care that the thing did not happen again; and he gave orders that in future no one should dare speak against his marriage. In virtue of which orders the Lord Mayor caused all the crafts and guilds to assemble in their various halls, and commanded them under pain of incurring the Royal indignation not only to abstain from murmuring about the King's marriage, but to command their own journeymen and servants, and a still more difficult task their own wives, to refrain from speaking disparagingly about the new Queen. But whatever prohibitions he may issue, the King cannot, and will not, prevent people from speaking their minds in secret, and his injunctions will have no other effect than that of completely alienating the hearts of his subjects. The King also four days ago sent another message to queen Katharine forbidding her to retain her title of Queen, or the servants of her household to give it to her. Not satisfied, moreover, with such rude treatment, he has commanded the Princess, his daughter, not to communicate with her mother in writing or otherwise; and although the Princess has since begged and entreated him to appoint some one next her person to give evidence that her messages to her mother are only in reference to her health, and proposing that her own letters and the Queen's may previously pass through the King's hands, her prayers have been completely disregarded. This prohibition (I hear) was read to the Princess the very same day that the King caused his new marriage to be announced to her. Hearing which, she was at first thoughtful, and then, as the very wise person that she is, dissembled as much as she could, and seemed even to rejoice at it. Without alluding in the least to the said marriage, and without communicating with any living soul, immediately after her dinner the Princess set about writing a letter to her father, and upon the bearer of the message asking for a verbal answer, as he had been instructed, she said she had none to give, and referred him to the letter she had just written to her father, of which she would say nothing; on its being shewn to the King I hear he was marvellously content and pleased, praising above all things the wisdom and prudence of the Princess, his daughter.

Having succeeded in the execution of his plans the King wishes now for an investigation and trial of the case, and to this end the Queen has been summoned to appear personally before the archbishop of Canterbury, on the 1st of next month, at an abbey distant 30 miles from this city, in a lonely spot, which has not been chosen without certain mysterious reasons, the King being afraid that should the proceedings be instituted here in this city, people might talk, and perhaps too make a disturbance, about it. At first the Queen was thrown into great perplexity by this summons, not knowing precisely how to take the thing, but upon my sending her my legal opinion in writing she decided not to take any notice whatever of the summons. For there is, in my opinion, no danger at all for the Queen, whatever the proceedings instituted against her may be, provided she does not renounce or modify expressly or tacitly, or in any other way relinquish the appeal she once made [to Rome], which is what the King and his ministers are cunningly aiming at in various ways; but in order to defeat this scheme of theirs I have purposely drawn out a sort of protest for her to sign, and I sincerely hope that she will not fall into the nets of calumny and wickedness that are being prepared for her ...

Preparations are being made here for the Lady's coronation, and it is said that the ceremony will be conducted more sumptuously than on any other like occasion. It is rumoured that on Ascension Day, the day fixed for it, the Lady is to appear magnificently arrayed, no difficult matter for her to accomplish since she is in possession of all the Queen's jewels, and wears them on all occasions: a most strange and unwarrantable proceeding on the part of the King, as people here think that he has actually despoiled his own legitimate Queen of her property to give it to another woman. Certainly if no prompt remedy is applied to such transgressions there is no knowing where the said Lady will stop, as I have lately written to Your Majesty.

### 27 April 1533

... For a long time back, seeing the bad disposition of affairs in this country, I have endeavoured to ascertain what the Queen's intention really is, and what else she proposes doing to escape from this evil, since it is quite evident that neither by mildness, nor by the ways of justice can the object be attained; but I have always found her so over scrupulous in her affection and respect for the King that she would consider herself irretrievably doomed to everlasting perdition were she to follow any other path that might provoke a war between Your Majesty and this king. However, some days before my writing to Your Majesty the Queen sent me word that she would willingly look out for another remedy to the evil, and that she placed herself entirely in my hands as to what that remedy was to be;[41] but since then I have been unable to hear further from her or know what she really intends doing ...

### 10 May 1533

... The King's marriage, as it is said, was celebrated with due solemnity on the day of St Paul's conversion, and as about that time Dr Bonart (Benet) came back from Rome, and the Papal Nuncio went to Court very frequently, some people here suspect that the Pope has given some sort of tacit consent to the marriage, which, however, I cannot believe, though I must observe that ever since that time the said Nuncio has not, that I know of, gone to business as often or steadily as before. And although long before the promulgation of the aforesaid statute, I had earnestly requested him that in compliance with the orders received from His Holiness, and his own promise at the time when I presented to him Your Majesty's letters, he should execute the brief against the archbishop of Canterbury, or otherwise assist me in this undertaking, he has done nothing at all, and I really suspect that he may secretly have done or said something against our cause ...

The King has issued orders for all the gentlemen to present themselves in due state at these festivals of Pentecost (Whitsuntide) to do honour to the coronation of his Lady, for which solemnity new and costly preparations are daily being made. The King, however, is sure to reimburse himself amply for all his expenses on the occasion, for it is the custom of this country at such festivals and solemnities for the King to create knights [of the Order] those who have sufficient income to support that rank. In case of anyone refusing the said knighthood so as not to be obliged to fulfil certain duties – as many do – the King used formerly to accept from them a goodish sum of money. Nowadays it is intended to take another and more certain course; whoever has a revenue of 40 pounds sterling shall be compelled to accept the said Order [of the Garter] or give up all the income of his estates, however large it may be, during three years, which amounts to a very considerable fine. Besides the displeasure caused by the ill-treatment of the Queen, which makes people murmur and inveigh against this coronation, most have no other hope than the reformation which by Your Majesty's hand is soon likely to reach this country, nor any other fear than that of being compelled by Your Majesty to declare openly for the Queen; for they say that this accursed woman [Anne] is sure to ill-treat and persecute all those known as having upheld the Queen's rights, or spoken in her favour. I mean the people of substance and rank, for whoever should undertake to punish or ill-treat all the rest would have enough to do. Indeed, I do not hesitate to say that things have now come to such a pitch that were captains of Your Majesty to land in this country they could immediately enlist as many men as they chose under their banners.

This woman in the meantime is doing all she can to win the affections of the Londoners, but she is very much mistaken, for if there was an invasion I take it that the people would keep the enlistment money and cry 'Long live the Conqueror' as they are in the habit of doing ...

*26 May 1533*
... As to Your Majesty's commands for me to exhort and persuade the Queen to remain in England notwithstanding any bad treatment she may be subjected to, that has already been done and achieved as effectually as possible, and unless the King has her forcibly sent out of this kingdom – which he would hardly dare to do – there is no danger of her voluntarily quitting this country; for besides the many wise reasons against such a measure, specified in Your Majesty's letters to me, the Queen herself thinks that were she to leave this country, she would sin against Law and against the King, whom she considers, and will as long as she lives consider, as her lawful lord and husband. Indeed, however ill-treated, she has always shewn him the same affection, and even now she has never made use of angry or irritating words, much less since she knows Your Majesty's wishes in this respect ...

*29 May 1533*
... After this the Duke [Norfolk] went on to say that the King, his master, had taken in very good part the advice I had given to Cremuel (Cromwell), to avoid all occasions of offence against Your Majesty. He had been grieved to hear that the Queen's arms had been removed from her barge, and rather ignominiously torn off and cut to pieces. He had severely reprimanded that Lady's chamberlain, not only for having caused the said arms to be removed,

but for having appropriated the said barge, lately belonging to the Queen, when there were in the river many others equally fit for the Lady's service.

I failed not to praise the King's behaviour in this particular instance, saying to the Duke that there was no need of an excuse, for what belonged to the Queen was by right the King's own. The King's resolution in this case made me hope that every regard would be had to the Queen and to the Princess, her daughter, and that both would be honourably treated, for, as I had said to Cromwell, the shade of scruple which the King felt in his conscience, and which, as he said, was the sole cause of separation from his legitimate queen, could not possibly be made to extend to the treatment of her and her daughter. Should this prove unworthy in future, the King, besides bringing on himself the wrath of God, would incur the blame of all the World, besides inflicting a great offence on Your Majesty. Hearing which, the Duke praised the Queen and the Princess, extolling their virtues and good qualities, so much so that it would have been impossible for me to speak of them in higher terms, adding that he was sure Your Majesty loved already the Princess, without having seen her, and would in future love her still more. Among other virtues of the Queen, the Duke pointed out to me as a most prominent one her great modesty, prudence, and forbearance, not only during these last disagreeable differences, but likewise on former occasions, the King having been at all times very much given to amorous intrigues. With regard to the treatment she would experience, the Duke said he was sure the King would never diminish the dowry which had been assigned to her in prince Arthur's time, amounting, as he said, to 24,000 ducats every year, more than sufficient, added the Duke, for the estate of a dowager princess if she will only reduce her expenses within proper limits. To this I replied that knowing as I did the King's benignity and generosity, I did not consider him capable of curtailing the Queen's former allowance, were it for no other reason than her virtues arid the services she had rendered him in former times, and I most earnestly entreated him to ensure that no reduction of her income should be effected. Upon which the Duke took his most solemn oath to me that he would willingly have lost 10,000 crs. Rather than not hear me speak about the treatment of the Queen and Princess in the manner I had done, for had I not by my overtures on the subject afforded him an opportunity to declare his sentiments, all the gold in the world would not have been sufficient to induce him to speak first. Now that the subject had been broached, and my wishes explained, the matter might be fairly discussed and amicably settled to the end, and he would take care that Your Majesty should have no new ground of complaint, as I had hinted to the said Cromwell ...

*[After a longer conversation]* Shortly after the Duke began to excuse himself and say that he had not been either the originator or promoter of this second marriage, but, on the contrary, had always been opposed to it, and tried to dissuade the King therefrom. Had it not been for him and for the father of the Lady, who feigned to be attacked by frenzy to have the better means of opposing it, the marriage would have been secretly contracted a year ago; and for this opposition (the Duke observed) the Lady

had been exceedingly indignant with the one and the other. In confirmation of which statement made by the Duke I can say that I have heard from a very good source, and from the lips of a person who was present [at the marriage], that eight days ago as the Lady [Anne] happened to take a piece [of cloth] to add to her dress – as ladies in a family-way are wont to do in this country, when they find their robes get too tight – her father said to her that she ought to take away the piece and thank God for the state in which she found herself, and that she (the Lady), instead of thanksgiving, replied in the presence of the dukes of Norfolk and Suffolk, and of the Treasurer of the Household (Fitzwilliam), that she was in better plight than he would have wished her to be ...

Two hours after my leaving him the Duke started on his journey, so that neither he nor his suite, in whose number is the Lady's brother, would wait to witness the pageant of the coronation, for they left the day before. This morning the Lady came from Greenwich to the Tower of London accompanied by several prelates and lords, and innumerable other people, as is customary with the queens of this country, and it must be observed that whatever sorrow and annoyance the King may have experienced, as the duke of Norfolk gave me to understand, at the seizure of the Queen's own barge, the Lady has unscrupulously made use of it at this coronation of hers, and appropriated it for her own use. May God permit that she may henceforwards be contented with possessing the barge, the jewels, and the husband of the Queen, without attempting also, as I have remarked in my preceding despatches, the life of the Queen and Princess!

The coronation pageant was all that could be desired, and went off very well, as to the number of the spectators, which was very considerable, but all looked so sad and dismal that the ceremony seemed to be a funeral rather than a pageant for I am told that the indignation of the English against their king is daily increasing, as well as the hope that Your Majesty will one of these days apply a remedy to this state of things.

Next Saturday the Lady [Anne] will traverse the whole of London, and go to the King's palace [at Bridewell], and hence, on Sunday, to Uuesmaytre (Westminster), where the solemnity of the coronation is to take place.

*16 June 1533*
Neither the haste in which the bearer of my despatch of the 7th departed, nor his quality and rank permitted my being as explicit as I might have desired, or giving a description of the entry of the Lady into this city, and the ceremony of her coronation, which has been altogether a cold, poor, and most unpleasing sight to the great regret, annoyance, and disappointment not only of the common people but likewise of all the rest, so much so that public indignation has apparently increased by one half since the said coronation. And inasmuch as I considered that it would not be very pleasing for Your Majesty to read in detail the form and order of the said ceremony, I have purposely abstained from further reference in my despatches to the said entry and coronation, though if Your Majesty has leisure and does not

object to lose time over so insignificant a narrative, I can easily send all the particulars, as I had occasion to write to Mr de Grandvelle the other day ...

### 28 June 1533

... With regard to king Francis' favour and help in this affair I fancy that no great reliance can be placed on his words, for not withstanding the promises he has made at various times he has always shewn partiality for this king, and tried to keep on good terms with the Lady, to whom within the last week he has sent by esquire St Julien a handsome and richly decorated Sedan chair and three mules with harness and accoutrements in very good order.

He (the king of France) will probably give as an excuse not to act that sentence has not yet been pronounced, but he might very easily allow the Queen, his wife,[42] to write secretly in favour of her Royal relative.

The instructions for Your Majesty's ambassadors at Rome being, as I said above, so beautifully drawn up, I might be excused adding any suggestions of my own, and thus making parade of my ignorance; yet in order the better to obey Your Majesty's commands, which is the thing in this world I most desire, I have written to the count of Cyfuentes (Don Fernando de Sylva), Your Majesty's ambassador at Rome, a letter of which the enclosed is a copy recommending the whole affair and adding a few observations. I will, therefore, forbear from saying anything more about it save to remind Your Majesty that it would be advisable that the sentence should be pronounced some time before the Lady Anne is delivered of a child, for if this happened to be a son the King would, as I have written to the Count, immediately have him sworn heir to his crown by this Parliament, which is to meet again in October, and if so, the incoveniences arising from the divorce would be much greater even than at present.

*[After meeting with the King's Privy Council]* On my way back I met both the French ambassador and Esquire St Jullien coming back from Greenwich, whither they had gone to present the Sedan chair to the Lady Anne, of which she immediately made use to go to a place 3 miles off. I talked a good while with them, but was unable to hear any news of importance.

The Princess has been unwell of late, but thank God she has now recovered, and went yesterday from a house of the archbishop of Canterbury, where she had been staying nearly a year, to another belonging to the King about 40 miles from this city. During her late illness she applied to the King, her father, for permission to have the Queen's physician and apothecary in attendance upon her, which permission the King gladly granted, and the Queen herself has been allowed to send her messages whenever she liked, and might, I dare say, have visited her if she had chosen ...

### 11 July 1533

... The King sent orders and instructions to the Chamberlain, Chancellor, Almoner, and Grand Squire of the Queen's household, as well as to her Secretary and Purveyor, to address to her several and various representations, among the rest that it could only be arrogance, selfishness, or inordinate vain glory that could induce her now to assume or usurp the title of queen, she could not allege ignorance, inasmuch as she must have known before this, that according to the decision of the principal universities in Christendom, and by the authority of the Church, he (the King) was legitimately divorced from her, and married to another who has since been crowned with due solemnity. And, moreover, that she was singularly mistaken if she thought that he could, as long as he lived, ever go back to her. That he never would do on any consideration; but if she would, as was but wise and reasonable, acquiesce in his will, and consent to what had been done and could not be undone, he would ensure her honourable treatment; otherwise he would have published throughout his Kingdom all that he had done towards ensuring her such treatment, and her own unreasonable and obstinate refusal, after which he would have her punished as his subject, which she was. And that by persevering in her obstinate refusal she would cause dissension and civil war in the kingdom and disputes as to the succession, the consequence of which would be that much blood would be spilt, the kingdom totally destroyed, and his own conscience greatly troubled. Should she (the Queen) persist in her obstinate refusal the King would be compelled to manifest his displeasure towards her and the Princess, and also towards all those who dared speak about him and the divorce, whereby all her servants and friends would fall under his Royal indignation.

To all these adjurations, which, as Your Majesty may judge, are urgent and weighty enough, especially when addressed to a person whose mind is naturally somewhat perplexed, the Queen has answered boldly and openly that knowing for certain that she is the true and legitimate wife of the King, she will never as long as she lives, on any consideration, take any other title but that of Queen, and if addressed by any other will not answer to it. Which determination of hers was not to be imputed to arrogance or desire of vain glory, for she would certainly take greater glory in being called the daughter of Ferdinand and Isabella [of Spain] than the greatest queen in the world against her own conscience, if she knew that she really had no claim to that title. With regard to the iniquitous sentence pronounced by the archbishop of Canterbury, to the corrupt practices employed in order to obtain the opinions of the Universities, and the form of this clandestine and accursed marriage, she spoke fully enough touching upon the mysterious event and other circumstances connected with it. As to the King never coming back to her, as the speakers supposed, she said that she hoped and confidently trusted that He, who in one moment worked the conversion of St Paul, and from a persecutor of Christianity turned him into an apostle, would enlighten and inspire the King's conscience, and not allow such a virtuous prince to remain so long in error to the great scandal of Christendom and contempt of Papal authority.

Touching divisions in the kingdom and the disputes as to the succession, the Queen said that was a thing for which she could not be made responsible, but rather the counsellors and advisers of this second marriage, the King having already legitimate succession acknowledged by all the kingdom; besides which no issue could come from such an abominable marriage but some lignee perverse, who would throw the kingdom into confusion if allowed to reign.

Of the publication alluded to by the said speakers the Queen said that she wished extremely that not only the kingdom of England, but also the whole of the world at large should become aware of the fact that she would never, as long as she lived, consent to such an unjust and iniquitous act, or willingly accept other treatment but that befitting a Queen; such she was and would remain.

As to the punishment with which she was threatened, if she had in any way offended the King (she said) he could punish her as his own wife, not otherwise, except by sheer force; if she were not his wife, all the world might know what amount of authority he could claim over her. With regard to the Princess, her daughter, the King who was her father could dispose of her at pleasure, though she could not help saying that any bad treatment of her, or of the servants of her household, would affect her very much. Yet neither for that not for a thousand deaths would she consent to damn her soul, or that of the King, her lord and husband. Many other things did the Queen say on this occasion which would take too much time to relate.

As soon as the King heard that the Queen would not comply with his demands, without waiting for a full report from the speakers, he caused the enclosed edict which I have had translated into French, to be printed and proclaimed throughout the City, to the sound of trumpets. After that he summoned to his presence the individuals named in the said edict, to the give them, as it is thought, new commands respecting the Queen's service, or to suborn them entirely, or for some other unknown purpose. Until now nothing has been said to them, except that Cromwell in the King's name has gratefully thanked them all for their services to the Queen, and told them that they must wait a little time until it shall be decided what order is to be established in her household. And I am told that the said Cromwell could not help saying that it was impossible for a human creature, to have given utterance to a more wise or courageous answer than that which the Queen made to the deputies, and that God and Nature had done great injury to the said queen in not making her a man, for she might have surpassed in glory and fame almost all the princes whose heroic deeds are recorded in history. Many other things did this Cromwell say in praise of the Queen. God grant that the treatment in store for her may be in accordance with that minister's words! For my part I will do my best in every possible way that she is honourably treated, and as befits her rank ...

I hear that even now the Lady [Anne] complains to the king of the Easterlings, who (she says) on the coronation day, put the Imperial eagle over the arms of England and her own, a thing which she (the Lady) considers a great insult to her, and which she would willingly punish if she could. She has likewise complained to the King that in the villages through which the Princess had the other day to pass as much rejoicing went on as if God

Almighty had come down from Heaven; at which the Lady has been very much offended, and intends giving the inhabitants of these districts a proof of her resentment ...

*30 July 1533*

... Some days ago, as the Queen was about to remove by the King's commands to a house of the bishop of Lincoln, distant 20 miles from her own residence, all the people of the neighbourhood collected to witness her departure, and shew her all possible honour and respect. Incredible are the marks of affection she received on the road; though it has been expressly forbidden to call her queen, yet the people on her passage failed not to give her that title, filling the air with their acclamations, wishing her joy, comfort, and all manner of prosperity, as well as mishap to her enemies, begging her with tears in their eyes to accept their services and make use of them, since they were ready to die for her sake. Which demonstration on the part of the people has naturally roused the jealousy of the courtiers, and no wonder, for the people's feeling shews itself daily in things of less importance. Indeed, I am told that the Lady herself was singularly displeased of late at the Easterlings and others of the German nation not having come to see the English fleet – the largest and best appointed they have had here for some time – and not having had any State ceremony on that occasion, whilst the ships were making wonderful salvoes of artillery. And the more offended was the Lady at this apparent negligence of the Easterlings that the pageant was held in this river not far from Grenuyche (Greenwich), which brought fresh to her memory the slight received at her entry into this city when the said Easterlings triumphantly raised the Austrian eagle.

However this may be, it is probable that for fear of such popular demonstrations the King in future will not allow the Queen or the Princess to travel about the kingdom.

The last news received from Rome has not been very agreeable to the King. No one knows yet what its substance may be, for they keep the matter a profound secret that the Lady may be spared any sorrow and disappointment likely to endanger the life of the child she bears in her womb. The better to conceal from her the disagreeable intelligence from Rome, the King, under plea of going to the chase, left Windsor the other day and went to Guillefort (Guildford), whither he has summoned his Privy Councillors and several doctors and canonists, who are by this time hard at work, so much so that having applied for an audience for Master Jehan de la Sauch and myself to ask for the re-opening of the staple of Calais, we have been, owing to the above occurrence, put off as usual until three days after the date of this despatch ...

The Lady [Anne], not satisfied with what has already been done, has lately importuned the King to ask the Queen for a very rich and gorgeous piece of cloth, which she herself brought from Spain, as an ornamental robe for a christening, and of which the Lady is very desirous, and as it appears, may be very soon in want. But the Queen's answer has been: 'God forbid that I should ever be so badly advised as to give help, assistance, or favour, directly or indirectly, in a case so horrible and abominable as this.' Such has been her answer to the King's own request, but whether the thing will stop there or not remains to be seen ...

### 23 *August 1533*

... There was last week some appearance, as I informed Your Majesty, that owing to the news received from Rome, and the late decision of the Rota in the divorce case, the King's great affection and passionate love for the Lady had greatly diminished, and that he was beginning somewhat to acknowledge his error; but now, after holding a conference with his doctors and canonists, he is again more persistent than ever, the latter having given him to understand that the Pope has done him great injury; that the sentence declaring his second marriage illegal nowise binds him to the first; and, moreover, that the appeal he has addressed to the future Council will have the effect of protecting him against all censures and acts emanating from the Apostolic See of whatever kind they may be. In consequence of this advice the King has now turned coat and resumed his former course, inasmuch as I hear that he has lately been encouraged by a letter received from the duke of Norfolk telling him that he ought not to care a straw whether the Pope issues sentence or not in this affair of his, since there would not be wanting people willing to defend his right at the point of the sword. That the best and surest means of obviating his present difficulty was to allow all the English emigrants to return home and restore them their property and lands. Which piece of advice, on the part of the Duke, has been so much to the King's taste that he keeps repeating it at all hours of the day to the gentlemen of his chamber.

The Duke's letter has also had another effect on the King. Ever since its receipt he has commenced re-arranging the Queen's household, changing the officers who had taken the oath to her as Princess Dowager, and allowing her about 30,000 crs. a year for her maintenance, out of which 12,000 will be pocket money for her wherewith to pay the ladies of her chamber. The rest to be administered by a royal deputy who will attend to the table and pay the servants, wages, &c.

The Queen, as may be presumed, is very discontented at this arrangement, and has written to me that she would rather die or go out begging for a charity than consent to it, even if they offered her seven millions of ducats every year. This she says under the impression that if she ever consents to any innovation or reform of her usual household it will be a burden upon her conscience; which she would rather suffer 1,000 deaths than do. I have written to her that considering the many protests already entered in good and sufficient force, and considering that she is bound to have patience, the repetition of the said protests can in no manner prejudice her right, and that I was of opinion that if she could not attain her object, rather than proceed to the extremities of which she spoke, she had better tacitly accept the terms offered to her. I will do my best to persuade the Queen to this course as more convenient and at the same time more comfortable with

Your Majesty's wishes and instructions, and if anything should happen in the meantime shall not fail to write.

### 3 September 1533

... The King, believing in the report of his physicians and astrologers, that his Lady will certainly give him a male heir, has made up his mind to solemnize the event with a pageant and tournament were it for no other purpose than to repair the fault of the last which were shamefully bad. Already some of the Lady's favourites have sent to Flanders for horses. The King has likewise caused to be taken out of his treasure room one of the most magnificent and gorgeous beds that could be thought of, which was once part of the ransom paid for the delivery of a duke of Alençon. Very fortunately for the Lady the said bed has been in her possession for the last two months; otherwise she would not have it now, for it appears that she being sometime ago very jealous of the King, and not without legitimate cause, made use of certain words which he (the King) very much disliked, telling her that she must shut her eyes and endure as those who were better than herself had done, and that she ought to know that he could at any time lower her as much as he had raised her. Owing to which angry remark on the part of the King there has since been much coldness and grumbling between them, so much so that the King has been two or three days without speaking to her. True these are love quarrels, of which no great notice should be taken, and yet those who know the King's nature and temper consider the above events as of good omen and a sign that the King will soon begin to think of recalling the Queen ...

### 10 September 1533

... On Sunday last, on the eve of Lady Day, about 3 o'clock in the afternoon, the King's mistress was delivered of a girl, to the great disappointment and sorrow of the King, of the Lady herself, and of others of her party, and to the great shame and confusion of physicians, astrologers, wizards, and witches, all of whom affirmed that it would be a boy. The people in general have rejoiced at the discomfiture of those who attach faith to such divinations, and who, whatever face they may put on the present occasion, are nevertheless exceedingly affected and ashamed.

The Lord Mayor and aldermen of this city, the heads of guilds, and other citizens of note have been invited to the christening, as well as the two French ambassadors. The new-born is to be christened at Greynuich (Greenwich). The godmothers will be the mother-in-law[43] to the duke of Norfolk and the marchioness of Exeter; the archbishop of Canterbury to hold the child at the font, and the bishop of London to christen her. She is to be called Mary as the Princess: which title, as I have been informed from various quarters, will be taken away from its true and legitimate owner, and given to this spurious daughter of the King. If so we shall soon hear.

It must, therefore, be concluded that God has entirely abandoned this king, and left him a prey to his own misfortune, and to his obstinate blindness, that he may be punished and completely ruined. Indeed there is already every appearance of this, for if we consider the almost general indignation which this, the King's second marriage, and consequent acts have produced among the people, both high and low, which is likely to be increased should he, as I am assured he will, defraud the Princess of her title, for the Princess is adored, as she well deserves it, by the whole nation. I am aware that this indignation against the King and his mistress, like all other sentiments and affections of the popular masses will subside and cool down unless taken up in time and fostered at the proper moment; but still deeply rooted is it in people's minds, and so just the cause of it that it will take a long time before the nation, or at least the great majority, forgets it ...

*7–15 September 1533*
... The duke of Norfolk having, as it appears, been accused by the Lady [Anne] of too much familiarity and freedom of speech, fearing also lest I should renew the conversation on certain topics, such as the legitimacy of the princess [Mary] and her undoubted right to the succession – even in case of there being 1,000 daughters born of this new marriage – has ever since visibly avoided as much as possible my company under the plea that his time is taken up with most important business. He, has, therefore, shunned meeting me in private, and if I call and find him at home he is either surrounded by clerks and officials, or else is sure to promote some topic of general conversation which prevents my addressing him in private ...

... The Lady's daughter has been christened Elizabeth, not Mary, as I wrote in my last despatch. The christening ceremony was as dull and disagreeable as the mother's coronation. Neither at Court, nor at this city of London, nor elsewhere has there been the bonfires, illuminations, and rejoicings customary on such occasions. Immediately after the christening of this daughter of the King, a herald standing at the gate of the church proclaimed her princess of England, and previously to that, that is to say, immediately after the child's birth, the same herald announced that the good, true, and legitimate princess [of Wales] was no longer to be called so; the badges usually born by her lacquais on their coats-of-arms were instantly removed, and replaced by the King's skutcheon. In fact a rumour is afloat, and not without foundation, that her household and allowance are to be shortly reduced. May God in His infinite mercy prevent a still worse treatment!

Meanwhile the Princess, prudent and virtuous as she naturally is, has taken all these things with patience, trusting entirely in God's mercy and goodness. She has addressed to her mother, the Queen, a most wonderful letter, full of consolation and comfort. I shall not fail, however, after hearing the Queen's wishes, and receiving her orders, to remonstrate and protest against so enormous injury and injustice as the one just inflicted upon her and her daughter, the Princess, though I very much fear – and indeed am almost sure – that all my remonstrances will lead to nothing, for certainly the King's obdurate sin, and his own misfortune, have so shut his ears that no arguments of any sort or prayers shall be listened to. Indeed, something

more than mere words will be required to make him return to the right path.
– London, 7th September 1533.

Before leaving Court I begged the duke of Norfolk to grant me a private
audience, which for the reasons above alluded to he seemed not to desire
at all. The Duke then bade the brother of the Lady (George Boleyn),
as I have since learned from one who was present and overheard the
message, to go into the King's chamber, which he (George) did, returning
almost immediately after so as to cut short any conversation in which
we might be engaged. And so it was, for having requested Cromwell to
be present at the conference, I had scarcely broached the subject when
Boleyn made his appearance and our conversation was suddenly put an
end to. I had previously told them (the Duke and Chancellor) that I had
been informed that the King's newly born daughter had been proclaimed
princess of Wales. 'By so doing (said I) it is not to be presumed that the
King intends declaring his other daughter a bastard, nor depriving her of
the lawful succession to the throne.' That they might colour and repair
their error, and at the same time excuse, without prejudice or injury to
the rightful and legitimate Princess, what had already been done, I told
them that I saw no harm in the proclamation of the King's newly-born
daughter, for, after all, every Royal son or daughter ought to be so called,
but that I was only afraid that by doing so the rights of the first born
(princess Mary) might be impaired. Such, however, I presumed could not
be their intention. Hearing this the Duke and the Chancellor looked at
each other for a time without knowing what to say, and I went on with
my argument, reminding the former of what he himself told me once on
this topic, and wishing to know his opinion on the matter. Both told me
that the question was too important to be thus answered at a moment's
notice, and that besides that they had first to learn what the King's wishes
were on so delicate a point. With regard to my writing to Court and
informing Your Majesty of the result of my application, I was told by the
councillors that I might use my discretion, as they could not then give
me a more categorical one.

Just at this moment the Lady's brother came in with the message that the
King wished to see the councillors and, therefore, I had to quit the place
without speaking to him on the subject, though fully intending to renew my
visit as soon as I had learned the Queen's wishes; for I really believed then,
and I do still, that had I applied for an audience to speak about the said
matter it would have been refused.

Since my return from Court the marchioness of Exeter, who is the only
true comforter and friend the Queen and the Princess have, has informed
me that letters patent had been sent to all parts of this kingdom in which
the King bids his subjects to rejoice, and return thanks to the Almighty for
having given him an heiress. The Marchioness has likewise sent me word that
the bishop of Winchester has gone to France for the purpose of expressing
the King's regret at his brother on the other side of the Channel not having
prevented the sentence, as he fully promised to the duke of Norfolk and
might have done. The Bishop has, moreover, charge to say to the king of

France that since he had been unable to stay the Papal sentence in the affair of this divorce he is now earnestly requested to try by dint of promises, threats, or otherwise that the said sentence be revoked or at least not put into execution. She (the Marchioness) has also given me to understand that the frequent and almost daily meetings of the Privy Council are for no other purpose at present than to decide how much and in what manner the household of the Queen and Princess, and their rank and estate are to be reduced, and yet the same lady writes that the King's Privy Councillors had not yet found a solution to the affair. – London, the 15th of the month.

*10 October 1533*

Since my last despatch this king has sent word to the Princess by some of his Privy Councillors that she is to abstain in future from bearing that title, as it now belongs to his newly-born daughter, not to her; and he has also caused her household and yearly allowance to be considerably reduced. Upon which the Princess of her own accord, without consulting anyone on her own case (indeed had she asked for permission to communicate with any of her advisers she would never have obtained it) made a suitable answer to the Royal commissioners who called on her, and wrote a letter to the King, her father, saying that she would as long as she lived obey his commands, but that she really could not renounce the titles, rights, and privileges which God, Nature, and her own parents had given her. Being the daughter of a king and of a queen, putting aside other circumstances, she was rightly called Princess. The King, her father, might do his pleasure and give her any title he liked, but it should not be said of her that she had expressly or tacitly prejudiced her legitimacy, or the rights of the Queen, her mother, whose example she was determined to follow, by placing herself entirely in the hands of God, and bearing with patience all her misfortunes ...

The Queen has, moreover, charged me to beg and entreat that Your Majesty make every effort to persuade His Holiness to have the sentence carried into execution immediately, through the most rigorous and binding terms of justice, without, however, forgetting to solicit the settlement of the main case; for she really thinks that if Your Majesty and the Pope continue holding the bridle firmly, and not shewing weakness or indifference in this business, these people will come to the point and listen to reason. Indeed, whatever confidence and courage these people may shew, there can be no doubt, as the Queen herself believes and asserts, that they are full of fear and awe, which will greatly increase when they see that the Pope, in whom they still have some hope, keeps firm.

The Queen, for the sake of the King, her husband, whom she still loves and respects, dares not point out other remedies in her present case, except those of right and strict justice; but that good and holy bishop of Rochester (Fisher) advises prompt action on the part of Your Majesty, such as I recommended in one of my last despatches. Indeed, not many days ago he sent me word to say that strong measures must now be taken. In this opinion of the good and pious Bishop the majority of the English nation, as I am told, concur;

no one doubts but that Your Majesty will take the affair in hand; otherwise they fear the mere suspension of the intercourse of trade will be the cause of revolt and much trouble and confusion in this country. To obviate this the smallest sea force will suffice; innumerable people from all ranks of society, who wish for the prosperity and welfare of their country keep telling me so, and deafening my ears with their appeals.

As to my communicating with the Queen's councillors, and asking their opinion on her affairs, there has been yet no opportunity, as I have informed Your Majesty in my preceding despatches, for not one of them dares give counsel or mix himself up with the affair. What my advice is in the present emergency I need not specify, having already stated it on more than one occasion. I will not trouble Your Majesty further, but leave it to your superior wisdom and prudence in worldly affairs to decide on the best course to be followed.

I cannot guess why the King is making such haste in the reform of the Princess's household unless it be to please his mistress, whose importunate and malignant cravings are well known, or else to have occasion and excuse to ask from Parliament the help and grant in money which they are in the habit of voting on the birth of a prince or princess of England. At least such is the general belief, for Parliament has again chosen a number of its members on whom the King is to confer knighthoods, for which honour a sum of money will be got out of them, those who refuse paying also a certain sum to be exempted from the above honourable distinction. I also fancy, that in order to compel the Queen to accede to his wishes, the King is treating the Princess, his daughter, in this way; but he is very much mistaken if he thinks that he can thus convert her to his views. Perhaps, too, he imagines that by re-establishing the Princess in her rights, and causing her to be declared his heir for want of lineal male descent, he may get Your Majesty to consent to this new marriage. After all his bad star may be the cause of his being precipitated into a line of conduct which cannot fail to bring on him the animadversion and blame of all the world; and it is to feared unless a prompt and efficacious remedy be applied he will be urged on to treat the Princess with still greater indignity, and compel her by sheer force to renounce all her rights, shut her up in a nunnery, or marry her against her inclination and will. I have accordingly warned the Queen of my misgivings, and told the Princess to write down and sign a protest, which she is to keep ready at hand ...

*16 October 1533*
... Nothing new has occurred since the date of my last despatch, except that the King has made the Princess, his daughter, move from the fine house in which she was dwelling to a very wretched one, most unfit for this present season. He has done still more; the Princess's residence he has given or let – I cannot say which – to lord Rochefort, the brother of the Lady, who is already furnishing it and sending thither his household servants.

I omitted in my last despatch to specify all the names of those who had gone by the King's commands to speak to the Princess. These were the earls of Auffort (Oxford), Excez (Essex), and Succez (Sussex), and Dr Sampson, all of whom tried by prayers, threats, and persuasions innumerable to make her give up the name and title of Princess, and submit entirely to her father's will in this respect as God commands. But the Princess, I am told, replied so wisely and discreetly that the said lords knew not what to say, and all shed tears in consequence. And I hear also that following her mother's example, she would never consent to hear them in private; but insisted upon their delivering the King's message in public and before all her household assembled for the purpose. She was no doubt afraid, as she has since declared that in the absence of witnesses the King's deputies might make some statement to her prejudice or disadvantage. It is impossible for me to describe the love and affection which the English bear to their Princess, but they are already so much accustomed to see and tolerate such disorderly things that they tacitly commit the redress of the same to God and to Your Majesty.

*3 November 1533*
... Not satisfied with having taken away from his own legitimate daughter the name and title of princess, as intimated in a former despatch, the King has lately been talking of removing – and has actually begun to do so – all the officers and servants of her princely household on the plea that they have encouraged her in her disobedience. This the King has done, as he says, to daunt and intimidate her; he has even gone so far as to demand that she (the Princess) should go and live as 'demoiselle d'honneur'[44] to his bastard daughter,[45] at which, as Your Majesty may guess, both the Queen and the Princess are marvellously disturbed and in great trouble. They sent to me about a week ago for advice in this emergency, and begged I would speak to Cromwell, and see what could be done to arrest the blow. I immediately sent to the Princess a protest drawn in due form for her to sign, and keep secret, declaring that neither by word nor deed, expressly nor tacitly, has she ever consented to anything that may prejudice her or her right. I have besides put down in writing several candid and temperate statements, to be addressed to those who might come with such a proposition in her father's name. In case, however, of there being no help at all she was (I said) to have patience, for she would not have to suffer long. Should the King send some one to her on such an errand, she was to say from the very first that if the King, her father, wished it to be so, she submitted, but that she protested in due form against whatever might be done to her prejudice. These words I wrote down for her, she was to learn them by heart, and repeat them daily surrounded by her most confidential servants ...

*9 December 1533*
... The King has already appointed a household for his newly-born daughter, who will within three or four days be sent to the county of Norfolk, there

to be nursed. She will leave this city in full state, accompanied by two dukes and several great lords and gentlemen. The earl of Autfort (Oxford) will meet her 12 miles from hence, and the two dukes [of Norfolk and Suffolk] will then return to town. The Earl, after escorting the King's bastard daughter to the place where she is to be nursed, will go to the Princess, do away with her princely state, and conduct her by force to pay her court to her bastard sister. Eight days after the duke of Suffolk, the earl of Essex, the King's Comptroller, and Dr Sampson will go to the Queen, and deprive her of her chancellor, almoner, receptor and other officers of her house-hold, and remove her to a house belonging to the bishop of this place (London); and it is much to be feared that, unless God or Your Majesty remedy it, this accursed Lady will go on persecuting both the Queen and the Princess, and that no prayers or remonstrances will avail with her ...

*16 December 1533*
In consequence of the King's resolution and order as to the respective treatment of the Princess and of his bastard daughter, about which I wrote last to Your Majesty, the latter was three days since taken to a house distant 17 miles from this city; and although there was a better and a shorter route thither, yet, for the sake of pompous solemnity, and the better to impress upon the people the idea of her being the true princess of Wales, the King's bastard daughter and her suite, composed of the noblemen specified in my last, were made to traverse this city. On the ensuing morning the duke of Norfolk went himself to the Princess, and signified her father's pleasure that she should attend Court, and enter the service of his other bastard daughter, whom the Duke deliberately, and in her presence, called princess of Wales. Upon which princess Mary replied: 'That is a title which belongs to me by right, and to no one else;' after which she addressed to him many gracious, honest, and very wise remonstrances, all tending to shew that the proposals the Duke had brought from the King were both strange and unfitting. Which argument on the part of the Princess the Duke was unable to combat, so much so that he said to her that he had not gone thither to dispute, but to see the King's wishes accomplished, and his commands executed, namely, that she should be removed to the house taken for the bastard. Upon which the Princess, seeing that all her arguments and excuses would be of no avail, asked for half an hour's time to retire to her private chamber; where she remained, as I am given to understand, all the while, or nearly so, occupied in drawing out the protest whereof I once gave her the words. Thus, should she in any way be compelled by force or persuaded by deceit to renounce her rights, marry against her will, or enter a cloister, no prejudice should result to her hereafter.

When she came out of her room the Princess said to the Duke: 'Since such is my father's wish, it is not for me to disobey his injunctions; but I beg you to intercede with him that the services of many well deserving and trusty officers of my household may be rewarded, and one year's wages at least given to them.' After this she asked the Duke how many of her own servants she would be allowed to retain and take with her. The answer was that as she would find plenty of servants to attend on her where she was going, no great train of followers was needed. Accordingly the Princess set out on her journey, accompanied only by very few of her household. Her governess, daughter of the late duke of Clarence, and the King's near relative – a very honourable and virtuous lady, if there be one in England – offered, I hear, to serve the Princess at her own cost, with a good and honourable train of servants, but her offers were not accepted; nor will they ever be, for were the said lady to remain by the Princess they would no longer be able to execute their bad designs, which are evidently either to cause her to die of grief or in some other way, or else to compel her to renounce her rights, marry some low fellow, or let her fall a prey to lust, so that they may have a pretext and excuse for disinheriting her, and submitting her to all manner of bad treatment ...

Meanwhile no words can describe the sorrow and regret which such abominable conduct on the part of this king and his ministers has caused among the English people, all of whom are sensibly affected by what is now passing, and are truly indignant at his treatment of the Queen and Princess. Indeed, without taking into account the innumerable considerations, which Your Majesty's incredible wisdom will sufficiently appreciate, they are complaining to me loudly of want of action on Your Majesty's part. For many respectable and well-to-do individuals keep telling me, or sending me daily messages to the effect that they have no other wish than, and in fact only await the arrival of one of Your Majesty's ships on this coast, to rise 'en masse;' and that if they only had here in England a chief, able and willing to command them, and who dared take the initiative, they would do enough by themselves without any foreign aid ...

However this may be, and should Your Majesty decline the undertaking, the desire of the English people in general – I mean of almost all good Englishmen – is that Your Majesty at once put a stop to the intercourse of trade; for, as several of the principal English merchants, who carry on business with Flanders and Spain, sent me word only three days ago, these people would lose comparatively more by the closing of the ports than the merchants of Your Majesty's dominions. Indeed I am assured, that ever since the above measure was spoken of, the common opinion in this city, nay, in the rest of the kingdom, for they make no mystery of it, has been that, should Your Majesty order the closing of the trade for a few months only, this country would be irretrievably ruined. Your Majesty, therefore, would do well in ordering the said suspension, and thus putting a check on the doings of this king and his ministers; for I can assure you that there is nothing they are more afraid of than the above prohibition or suspension of trade, knowing very well that in that event they would have no means in their power of obviating the rebellion of the people, unless the King paid the cloth-weavers, who constitute more than half the population of England, out of his own treasury. This would require twice as much money as he (the King) can devote to that purpose, besides which, he could only do so in the expectation that the merchants of the Low Countries, being also great sufferers through it, would of themselves apply to Your Majesty for a revocation of the measure. Certainly, were the King to decide upon such a course, it would be, no doubt, the best for him to pursue, for whilst he felt the inconvenience [of having to support weavers without employment] he would by so doing gain much credit and reputation among his subjects. It is, however, the misfortune, entailed by his sinful course, that it will prevent his taking this or any other resolution profitable to himself.

There is no longer any hope of this king ever being brought to the point through persuasion, for his sin enthrals him more and more, besides which this accursed Lady has so enchanted and bewitched him that he will not dare say or do anything against her will and commands. There is still another danger to run by waiting, which is that the more forbearance Your Majesty shows in this affair, the more this king will be encouraged to persevere, or even do worse. Indeed, in my opinion, it is only his present inability which prevents his causing Your Majesty still greater annoyance; for he holds you, as he says, as his sworn enemy, and will treat you accordingly. May God inspire him with more Christian and charitable sentiments! ...

*23 December 1533*
... The duke of Suffolk and his colleague in the deputation, of whom I wrote in my last despatch, have not yet returned from the Queen. As far as I can gather, their mission has been unsuccessful. After using very strong and disrespectful language to her they proceeded to suppress all the offices of her household, such as chamberlain, chancellor, almoner, groom of her stables, and others. Next day the remainder of the Queen's male and female servants, including her own ladies in waiting, were dismissed, and replaced by men from the Northern counties, who, being more trained to war than to the usages of a Court, are supposed to have been engaged for other purposes rather than for the Queen's service. The deputies have charge of conducting the Queen, whether she will or not, to a house surrounded by water and marshes, the most insalubrious and pestilential residence in all England, as the Queen herself has been informed; owing to which, and considering the evident danger of living at such a place, she has decided not to go thither unless taken by their force.

Perceiving the Queen's stout resolution, and fearing lest some commotion or disturbance should arise [on the spot], the Royal Commissioners provided themselves with a numerous suite of retainers (those coming from the North having done the same). Besides which, the more to intimidate the Queen, her friends and servants, they summoned to the spot the magistrates of the neighbourhood, that they might help in the execution of the King's orders. The duke of Suffolk himself, before he left this city on such an errand, confessed and partook of the Communion, as his own mother-in-law[46] sent to inform me, declaring at the time of his departure that he wished some accident might happen to him on the road that should exempt him at once from accomplishing such a journey and mission.

Thus, at the request and solicitation of the Lady [Anne] whom the King dares not contradict, the Queen has by force been removed to the said house, either that they may the sooner get rid of her or else for greater security; for the place is strong, and besides is seven miles from any other, built in the centre of a lake and of certain marshes, and not to be approached, except on one side at the distance of six miles. In fact, it has been settled between the King and the said Lady that they are to look out for all occasions and ways of keeping the Queen locked up in the said island, which, as I said above, is one of the strongest places that could be imagined, for the purpose, as I hear from good quarters, all other ways and means failing, to make out that the Queen is out of her senses. The King, moreover, wishes and intends that at the next meeting of Parliament a law, statute, and ordinance be made to declare the Princess illegitimate and incapacitated from succeeding to his Crown, and that all signs of royalty in her mother, the Queen, be at once revoked and obliterated; after which, as the Lady very properly and honestly remarks, the King may take possession of all her property in land, jewels, house, furniture, and so forth, that she may be unable to dispose of, or bequeath one single farthing. In a like manner, as I am informed, the King wishes Parliament to declare that in future the Pope will have no control over the ecclesiastical affairs of this kingdom, and that all the authority will rest in future with the archbishop of Canterbury.

Your Majesty may well consider that if such cruel and abominable insults as these are tolerated, these people will not only be encouraged to accomplish their wicked and detestable purposes against the persons of the Queen and Princess, but will likewise concoct all sorts of intrigues to the prejudice of Your Majesty, whom this king has so much offended, and whom he has consequently reason to fear.

Since my last despatch I have received no answer from the King on the subject of my conversation with the Duke [of Norfolk]; and I can assign no other reason for it than the opposition of the Lady, without which, as I am given to understand, he would have sent for me, and made an answer to my application. This, of course, I have since ceased to solicit, for the considerations laid, before Your Majesty in my despatch of the 16th inst. and likewise in order to wait for the document containing the whole business.

As I informed Your Majesty, the Princess, attended only by two maids in waiting, was conducted by the duke of Suffolk to the residence of the King's bastard daughter. Arrived there the Duke asked her if she did not like to see and pay her court to the Princess [of Wales]. Upon which she answered that she knew of no other princess in England but herself; that the daughter of Madame de Penebrok (Pembroke) was no princess at all. True, if the King, her father, acknowledged her as his daughter, just as he called the duke of Richmont his son, she could treat the latter as brother, and her as sister, but in nowise as princess of Wales. Before taking leave the Duke asked her whether she had any message for the King. To which she replied: 'None, except that the princess of Wales, his daughter, asked for his blessing;' and upon the Duke observing that he would not dare take such a message to the King, she interrupted him by saying; 'Then go away, and leave me alone.' After which having repeated over and over again her former protest, and declared that what she had done and might hereafter do by the King's commands ought in nowise to prejudice her right, she retired to her chamber to shed tears, as she is now continually doing.

And I have been told that although the Duke treated the Princess rudely enough, yet upon his return to Court the King reproached him for not having faithfully accomplished his mission, but treated her too mildly, adding that he would soon find the means of humiliating her, and subduing her temper ...

*27 December 1533*

Since my last I have heard that, among other things which the duke of Suffolk and his colleagues told the Queen in the King's name, one was that they begged particularly to remind her of the many singular favours and great assistance which this king and his father [Henry VII] had at all times done to the Catholic King Ferdinand, to Your Majesty, and to the kings your ancestors on the paternal as well as maternal side, which had not been effected but at the cost of incalculable sums of money. This she could not ignore nor forget, but she ought (they said) to use discretion, and consider that all of it had been done for her sake, and that yet in return for those favours, and for the good treatment she herself had experienced at the King's hands, she had behaved most unkindly, for she had molested and worried him for many successive years, causing him to send continually messages and ambassadors to Rome and elsewhere, for the preservation of his rights and privileges, making him spend large sums of money in that service. By this time, said the Duke, she ought to be tired of tormenting and goading the King, especially now that the archbishop of Canterbury has, with the common consent (as is said) of the Anglican Church, and to the great satisfaction and repose of the kingdom, pronounced a sentence in the divorce case. Should she consent to obey that sentence, and at the same time recall her proctors from Rome, and renounce whatever had been done there in her favour and against the King, their master, she would be most greatly esteemed and beloved by the whole kingdom, besides which the King would treat her to her heart's content. If, on the contrary, she persisted in her obstinate refusal, the King would be obliged to shew his displeasure with her, would clip her wings, reduce her estate, and diminish the number of her servants, as much as he might consider necessary for her punishment. As a beginning, the King (he said) had already given orders that she should be removed, as she has actually been to the house mentioned in my last. All this, moreover, was signified by the Duke and the rest of his colleagues to the Queen, in words exceedingly bitter, rude, and uncourteous, and with many protests that, should she not comply with the King's wishes in this respect, she might be the cause of incalculable evils, effusion of blood, and great trouble in Christendom, which every good Christian ought to avoid by all means in his power. She was to take no heed (added the Duke) of the sentence given at Rome in her favour, inasmuch as, not having been pronounced according to law, and being besides unjust, it could not avail her in the least, as it contained no declaration respecting the legitimacy of her second marriage.

To these and other like charges the Queen replied in the most prudent, discreet, and masterly manner, without omitting to refute any of the arguments brought forward by the Duke and his colleagues. With regard to the recall of her agents and proctors at Rome, which she was desired to order, and the annulling of any sentences which the Pope might have given in her favour, she said that it was not in her power to do so, but in that of the King, who was nevertheless bound to obey the Papal precepts. Were she to consent to the relaxation of the ecclesiastical censures, which she would never do, His Holiness would never consent to their revocation. It was to him (the Pope), not to the archbishop of Canterbury, that the decision of the case appertained 'ex officio'. It was for him to prevent the King from living in mortal sin, not only on account of his ecclesiastical authority, which was much greater than that of the said Archbishop, but because the King himself had in the first instance applied to him for a decision.

After answering in this way each and every point touched upon in the Duke's address, the Queen ended by saying that she would suffer one thousand deaths rather than consent to or allow a thing which was so decidedly against God's law, and against the King's and her own honour and conscience. She would certainly grieve at the ill-treatment of her followers, but not even that or any other consideration would make her swerve or deviate from what she considered to be her duty. The King might treat her as he pleased, but she would never enter the mansion, of which they (the Commissioners) had spoken, unless she were dragged to it by sheer force, as otherwise she would incur the guilt of voluntary suicide, inasmuch as that which they destined for her residence was so insalubrious and pestilential.

After this the Duke and the rest of the Commissioners left the room, and summoned to their presence all the Queen's servants: some they dismissed; others they then and there arrested, and among them two very good priests, who have since been brought to this city and lodged in the Tower. Nor were the dismissed officers better treated, for they were ordered to quit the place within four-and-twenty hours under pain of death. There was also an attempt made to remove her confessor, a Spaniard and a bishop; but on the Queen alleging that she had never confessed in any other language than Spanish, they allowed him, as well as the physician and apothecary, also Spaniards, to remain in her service. They had likewise dismissed every female servant, not leaving even one of her chamber-maids; but hearing the Queen say and affirm that she would take no others into her service, that she would not undress to go to bed, and would lock the door of her chamber herself, they allowed two of them to remain; not those, however, whom the Queen would gladly have chosen. All the Queen's present servants, with the exception of her confessor, physician, and apothecary, who, as above stated, cannot speak a word of English, have been sworn upon oath not to call her by the title of Queen; against which she duly protested before the Commissioners at the time and afterwards, telling them that she should never repute them as her servants, but merely as guards, since she considered herself a prisoner from that moment.

The Commissioners remained six days at the place, that they might lock the house door and take away the keys, also that they might hear whether the Queen, through the dismissal of her servants, the threats and the manifold bad treatment she was undergoing would not change her mind; but seeing her constant and unmovable, they caused all the baggage to be packed, got litters and hackneys ready, and made other preparations for the journey. The Queen, however, on the morning of that day, locked herself up in her room; and when the Commissioners came to fetch her, she spoke to them through a hole in the wall, and said, 'If you wish to take me with you, you must break down the door.' But they dared not; for, as one of the Commissioners has since owned, such a number of people had collected there, all crying and lamenting at such unheard of cruelties, that they were actually afraid of coming by the worst.

I have been told that the place where the Queen is at present is bad and unhealthy enough, and that there will be no need of a worse one. But such are the iniquity and detestable wickedness of the Lady (Anne) that she will not be satisfied until she sees the end of both the mother and the daughter. The latter has since been deprived of the only two maids of honour, who accompanied her when the duke of Norfolk took her down to [Hatfield]. She has only one common chamber-maid, who was lately engaged for her service; and I hear that the usual practice of making her taste first the Princess's food as a precaution has been done away with, which is equivalent to opening the gates to the perils and insidious dangers from which may God Almighty preserve her!

Many Englishmen, both high and low who desire the reformation of these affairs, moved to pity, and out of affection for the Queen and for her daughter, the Princess, without taking into consideration the present state of affairs [throughout Europe], and the reasons Your Majesty and your Privy Council may have for not resenting immediately such insults, are very much scandalized at the Flemish Government having suddenly granted the intercourse of trade, as in former times, without difficulty or fear of any sort for these merchants. They had thought this a favourable opportunity at least for the Governess of the Low Countries to delay giving an answer until Your Majesty should be apprized of the state of things. True, those who think so are somewhat comforted by the idea that, perhaps, previous to the arrival or the English ships in those parts, or at least before the goods have been disposed of, the term fixed for the ecclesiastical censures and interdict will have expired; and that the Queen Regent in Flanders will then be better able, without further trouble or discussion, to forbid the inhabitants from entering into mercantile transactions with the English, – which would be a much harder blow to them, – whilst they would still be obliged to Your Majesty for allowing them to bring back their merchandize. This would be, in my humble opinion, the best, the quickest, and the most lawful remedy to be applied under the circumstances. During this time the King would, no doubt, cause all manner of measures to be taken against the Queen and the Princess, and will more and more oblige his people to maintain and support any such measures he has taken, or intends taking in future, and he himself will be encouraged to attempt or allow any bad turn against the said Queen and Princess, of which I am constantly hearing, coupled with all manner of suspicions and conjectures. Indeed ever since the Commissioners' return a rumour is being circulated at Court that the Queen is in bad health, and cannot possibly live long; which happens to be exactly the same trick of which they made use some time before the Cardinal (Wolsey) died, or even before he was ill, – thus covering beforehand any secret designs they may have formed respecting her. A worthy Englishman sent me word the other day that I ought as soon as possible to warn the Queen to take care that at night the door of her bed-chamber should be well closed, and the room itself carefully inspected for fear of anyone being there concealed, for he had heard from a good quarter that she was in danger of some trick being practised one fine night upon her. He could not positively say which, – whether to inflict bodily harm, or accuse her of adultery, or pretend that she was planning a flight to Scotland or to Wales, in order to raise there a rebellion against the King; but he assured me that the Queen is really in danger of some sort, and that he knows it from a very good source ...

*17 January 1534*
This King went a few days ago to see his bastard daughter, who is at a house 20 miles from hence, the Princess (Mary) being also with her, as I have already written to Your Majesty; and although one of the principal causes for the King's visit was evidently to persuade or force the said Princess to renounce her title, yet the Lady (dame Anne), considering the King's weakness or instability (who would dare say this?), and that the great beauty, virtue, and wisdom of the Princess might lead her father to forget his anger, and out of pity be induced to treat her better than heretofore, and allow her to bear her title, sent hastily to the King, first of all, Cremuel (Cromwell), and after him other messengers, to prevent him from speaking to or seeing the Princess. For which reason the King, before arriving at the house occupied by the Princess and by his bastard daughter, sent orders that the former should not be allowed to come to the room where he was, or appear before him. While at the house, and in the apartments of his bastard daughter, the King sent to the Princess, Cremuel, the treasurer and the captain of his body guard, the three chief people he then had with him, again to press and solicit her to renounce her title of Princess. Her answer was that she had already on a previous occasion declared her resolution as to that, and that it was mere waste of time to come again and press her to do that in which she would never acquiesce. They were very much mistaken (she said), if they thought that ill-treatment, rudeness, or even death, could change her determination; and she went on telling them many things to the same purpose, all equally wise and discreet.

Whilst the King was in the apartments of his bastard daughter, the Princess sent to beg and entreat to be allowed to kiss her father's hand; but the permission was refused, upon which, just as the King was about to mount his horse, and go away, she went up to a terrace at the top of the house to see him off. The King having been told so, or perhaps by a mere chance, turned his head towards the terrace, and saw her on her knees, with her hands clasped together by way of supplication. The King, however, took no notice, except that he nodded his head, and put his hand to his hat; upon which all those who stood by, and who before that time would hardly have dared lift their heads to look at her, glad and rejoiced, as well as encouraged, by what the King had done, bowed to her reverently, expressing as well as they could their good will and sympathy for her ...

I have just been told that the day before yesterday the Lady, after hearing of the Princess's wise and discreet answer [to the King's deputies], complained most bitterly to the King of his not holding the Princess tight enough to prevent her from getting counsel and advice from outside, as she had hitherto done; for (said she) it could not be believed that such answers as she had given really originated with her: they were, no doubt, suggested by other people. The King promised Anne to see to this, and that in future no one should see the Princess, or speak to her, without his knowing who he was. Indeed, about xx. days ago the King said to the Marquis [of Dorset?] that it was only the trust the Princess placed in Your Majesty that made her obstinate and, difficult to manage, but that he would soon bring her to book; he was not at all afraid of Your Majesty, nor of any other prince in the world. He (the Marquis) and other high vassals of his Crown had better take care what they were about, and be loyal, as he had no doubt they would be; for if they hesitated or wavered in the least, they would all lose their heads. He would keep such a guard on the Princess and her servants that no letters should be written to her or received from beyond the sea without his being previously informed of it.

Besides the hope the King has of his subjects remaining faithful to him, he has undoubtedly that of the Queen's death in the meantime; for he said, the other day, to the French ambassador, that she could not possibly live long, as she had dropsy. Now, as the Queen, to the best of my knowledge, never complained of such a disease, I have my doubts, as I have already written to Your Majesty, whether such rumours are not spread for the purpose of producing in her, one of these days, some artificial dropsy, of which she may die (God preserve her!) ...

Ever since the duke of Suffolk called on her, the Queen has not left her bedroom, except for the purpose of hearing mass in a gallery close to her apartments. She has refused to eat or drink anything that her new servants bring her. The little food she takes in this time of tribulation is prepared by her maids-in-waiting within her own bedroom; so that, in point of fact, her sitting-room, bed-chamber, and kitchen are all in one; – so poorly lodged is she. Lest Your Majesty should be inclined to think that the above account is somewhat exaggerated, and that she is not so ill-treated as she imagines, the Queen proposes, as she informs me, to write to Your Majesty concerning her present position and the treatment she receives.

*4 February 1534*

These people cease not in their intrigues against the Pope. Every day new tracts and books are published against the authority of the Apostolic See, as Your Majesty has, no doubt already learned by the copy of the one I sent by the last post, and the one herein enclosed; the substance and aim of the said tracts being to sap and destroy the authority of the Holy See, and raise discussion on several inconvenient points, such as the marriage of priests, and the bestowing of ecclesiastical benefices on laymen, which this King is aiming at, that he may by that means attach to himself a portion of the nobility, and prevent their finding fault with him for his obstinacy in pursuing his design, which is nothing short of doing away altogether with part of the ecclesiastical benefices, usurping their entire revenues in some cases, and in others taking possession of the temporal fruits.

Were it only a question, by such books and writings, of defying the Pope and the authority of the Holy See, the measure after all would not be so important; for the English people, knowing, as they do know, that all this proceeds from passion, malice, and revenge, do not attach much faith to it, but are, on the contrary, very angry with the King for doing so. The worst is that some preachers from the pulpits – wherefrom nothing should be said that is not absolutely holy and edifying – are, under cover of religious charity and devotion, inculcating on the minds of simple persons the theories propounded in such writings; whence it is to be feared that, unless the venomous root be promptly pulled up, everything here will go to ruin and perdition. And inasmuch as the doctrines propounded in the book which this King has caused to be published are in open contradiction with those of the other one which appeared once under his name, he has now printed in English a letter from Luther to him, in which he informs us that the book in question was not composed of his own free will, but that he had written it at the instigation of the cardinal of York (Wolsey) and other prelates. Your Majesty may judge from these facts how obstinate and pertinacious this King is ...

*11 February 1534*

... I had likewise thought of another course to adopt in the Princess's case, namely, that after again making the most solemn and strong protests against the violence used towards her, and the apparent danger to her life in the place where she is now made to reside, she should write to the King, and offer to relinquish the title of Princess, provided she were allowed to live with the Queen, her mother. But I have since thought that by doing so Anne might be further encouraged to execute her wicked design, for fear of the daughter being ultimately reconciled to the father; or that she might think that it would be easier for her to accomplish her end, under cover of friendship, much better than at present, when there is mutual hatred and enmity between them; besides which it might happen that the feelings of those who now favour the Princess, ignoring her reason for yielding, and the protests she has made beforehand, might cool down, and cease to have the same interest for her safety.

A worthy gentleman of this place has told me that Anne had sent a message to her father's sister,[47] in whose keeping the Princess now is, that she ought not to tolerate her using that title; should she continue to do so she was to slap her face as the cursed bastard that she was. And because the said Princess has hitherto been in the habit of breakfasting in her own room, and, when obliged to go down into the hall, has refused to eat and drink any thing, the said Anne is in despair, and has for this reason given orders that no food or drink should be served to her in her chamber.

The first Thursday in Lent the said Anne purposes to go and see her daughter, and stay with her two days. Please God that it may not be to the cost of the good Princess! We must place the whole in the hands of God, who will by His divine clemency know how to order and provide for the whole as will best fit His service, giving Your Majesty time and opportunity as well as the means of repairing the mischief done ...

### 21 February 1534

... The Princess, finding herself almost without articles of clothing, has just been obliged to send a gentleman to the King, her father, begging him to provide her with the necessary articles. The gentleman had orders from her to take any money or clothes that might be given to him, but accept no cheque or order in which her name should appear without the title of Princess. She has at the same time applied for permission to hear mass in the church quite close to the house, but this she has been unable to obtain. On the contrary, as the peasants in the neighbourhood when they saw her walk from the top of a gallery, saluted her loudly and called her Princess, she is now kept much closer than before; and nothing is done without the previous consent of the sister of Anne de Boullan's father, the lady to whom the keeping of her has lately been entrusted. I am told that the duke of Norfolk and the brother of Anne (George Boleyn) had the other day high words with the said governess because, as they thought, she treated the Princess with too great kindness and regard, when she ought to deal with her as a regular bastard that she was. The lady answered that even if it were so, and that she was the bastard daughter of a poor gentleman, her kindness, her modesty, and her virtues called forth all respect and honour. The Princess, thank God, is now in very good health; and though she cannot have fallen lower than she has from her high station yet she is so armed with patience that she bears her troubles with wonderful constancy and resignation, placing all her confidence in God, the true protector of good, right, and justice, and likewise in Your Majesty, so much so that I doubt whether she would put on a better face in prosperity than she is putting on now in the midst of her troubles. May God grant that such magnanimity on her part do not over-irritate this accursed lady [Anne], and prompt her to make haste and carry her detestable thoughts into execution.

### 7 March 1534

The King's mistress, having gone to visit her daughter (Elizabeth), sent a message to the Princess, requesting her to visit and honour her as Queen which she was. Should she do so (the message bore), she would be as well received as she could wish, and it would be the means of her regaining the good pleasure and favour of the King, her father, and of her being treated as well or perhaps better than she had ever been. The Princess's answer was, that she knew not of any other queen in England than Madame, her mother; and that should the King's mistress, as she called Anne de Bolans (Boleyn), do her the favour she spoke of, and intercede with the King, her father, she would certainly be most grateful to her. After which answer the King's mistress renewed her remonstrances, made her profuse offers, and ended by threatening; but neither her promises nor her threats could make the Princess change her mind, and she returned home highly disappointed and indignant, fully determined to put down that proud Spanish blood, as she called it, and do her worst ...

### 25 March 1534

... When the duke of Norfolk went last to the Princess for the sequestration of her property, he not only seized her best jewels and robes, as I wrote to Your Majesty, but likewise all others that she had. This was done, not only on account of her refusal to pay her respects to the Queen's mistress, but because she will not accompany the bastard, and will not walk by the side of her when they are taken anywhere. She is always in front of her or behind, and will not pay court to her unless compelled by sheer force ...

### 30 March 1534

Since the arrival of this new Scottish ambassador, the King has caused the Bill for the inheritance of, and succession to, the Crown in case of his death to be discussed in Parliament; and it has ultimately been declared and established, after entirely excluding the Princess therefrom, that the posterity left by Anne de Bolans (Boleyn) shall inherit the Crown; should there be none on that side, the succession to pass to the nearest of kin; – the declaration thereof being for the present suspended in order to stimulate the Scottish ambassadors to conclude the peace now being negotiated between the two countries, and allure them with the hope that their master will be named and specified in the Bill, if the King's words on the subject are to be believed. Parliament has also decided that in the event of the King dying before his mistress, the latter is to be regent and absolute governess of her children and kingdom. An ordinance has likewise been promulgated, prescribing that in future whoever shall give the titles of Queen and Princess to any persons except Anne herself and her daughter respectively, shall be considered guilty of the crime of lese Majesty, and condemned to confiscation of person and property. Which pain shall be incurred by all those who may hear, know of, or consent to such an infraction without immediately reporting or revealing the case, as well as by all those who might murmur or complain of the statutes passed by the said Parliament respecting the King's second marriage, and against the authority of the Pope and Apostolic See; – all of which are strange, cruel, and tyrannical acts. The King, moreover, not quite satisfied with this, and considering that though Parliament and the estates of the kingdom have done what he wanted in this particular, there might still be opposition in other quarters, intends for greater security to depute certain, commissaries to exact the oath from all his subjects.

Last Thursday, upon the Princess, Your Majesty's cousin, refusing to accompany this King's bastard daughter, who was being conducted to another house fixed for her residence, she was, by certain gentlemen deputed for the purpose, against her will and by sheer force, placed in a chaise with Anne's aunt, being in this manner obliged and compelled to pay her court to the said bastard; – not, however, without her having previously and publicly protested against the violence used with her, and declaring all the time that the act being an involuntary one could in nowise prejudice her right and title for the future.

I should never have advised the Princess to go to such an extremity for fear of her over-irritating the King, her father, and giving him occasion and excuse for treating her worse than he is doing at present, and playing her some bad trick, in order to please his mistress Anne, who never ceases day and night plotting against her. Indeed I myself had written to her, in the event of threats or violence being used, that the protest she was prepared to make, at my recommendation, her filial reverence for the King, her father, as well as the violence used on the occasion were sufficient safeguards for the future, and that her right and interests would not be prejudiced in the least; but the Queen, her mother, and some of her friends, have for some time been thinking that it was better for the Princess to act thus, and show her teeth to the King. I am of a contrary opinion; I fear the Princess will further damage her cause, and I have again written to the Queen about it, saying that if she approves of it I am ready to soften down, for her honour and advantage, the rather rigorous terms I have lately used respecting the Princess's treatment.

On Wednesday, Our Lady's Day, the new ambassador from Scotland went to pay his respects to the King and to the lady [Anne] also ...

*12 April 1534*
... On Easter Monday the ambassadors of France, namely, Morette, Catillion (Chastillon), and La Pommeraye, went to Court, where they were most welcome, at least in appearance; for it must be said that it was only towards them the King seemed to be in good humour; he himself dining privately in his own apartments without his lady, contrary to his custom at other receptions of French ambassadors. The following Tuesday La Pommeraye and Catillion (Chastillon) went to visit the King's bastard daughter, who was brought out to them splendidly accoutred and dressed, and in princely state, with all the ceremonial her governess could think of, after which they saw her quite undressed. There was, of course, no question of seeing the good princess [Mary], though I had my doubts, as they went thither, whether they might not possibly ask to see her, and announce that sentence was about to be pronounced against her mother at Rome. To prevent this I found means to make the Princess acquainted with the real state of affairs at Rome, as I had it from count Cifuentes, in a letter received the day before; and I told her

that this was the time, now more them ever, to be constant and firm in her resolution. She answered me that she would do so, and that she had received more pleasure at the news than if I had presented her with a million of gold. But, as I say, there was no need of my warning, for the French ambassadors did not even ask after the Princess ...

Your Majesty may judge how rigorously the Queen is treated in other matters, when I say that on Holy Thursday she was not allowed to serve the poor a supper, as is customary for princes to do. An order, indeed, has been issued for the poor not to approach the house where she is now, because (says the lady) the alms she once distributed among the poor are the real cause of the love and affection which the English bear her.

### 22 April 1534

... This King has lately spent two days at the house where his bastard daughter is, during which orders have been given for the Princess not to leave her room, a guard having been placed at the door by the command of the lady [Anne], who is also there with the King. Meanwhile, one of the Princess's chamber-maids, having refused to swear to the Statute or Act of Succession to this kingdom, was shut up in a room of the house, and actually compelled to swear; otherwise she would have been sent to prison, as was indeed threatened; at which the Princess was very much grieved. But this is nothing in comparison with what happened to the Princess at the same time; for the aunt of the said Anne de Boulans (Anne Boleyn), who now has charge of her, came and said that the King, her father, no longer cared whether she renounced her title willingly or not, since by the last statute (act) she had been declared illegitimate and incapable of inheriting, and that if she were in his (the King's) place she would kick her (the Princess) out of the King's house for her disobedience. And, what is still worse and more execrable, the King is known to have said that he would have her beheaded for having contravened the laws of the kingdom. Having no means of informing any living person on this last point the Princess asked to see a physician then in the house, who had once been her preceptor and physician in ordinary, but this she was refused. Upon which she found means of communicating with him without raising suspicion, for she began before all present to tell him that she had been so long without speaking Latin that she could hardly say two words rightly; and upon the physician addressing her in that language, she said to him, knowing that no one in the room could understand Latin, that the King had been heard to say the day before that he would have her beheaded. Hearing which, the physician was much taken aback, and knew not what to answer, except that the Princess's Latin was not good, and that he could not understand it; but he nevertheless contrived to send me a message immediately.

Certainly nobody in this kingdom doubts for a moment that one of these days some treachery will be executed on the Princess, unless, indeed, Your Majesty takes some preventive measure very soon. No time, therefore, should be lost, this present season being, in my opinion, the most favourable for an undertaking, – as the English in general bear much good-will towards Your

Majesty, the Queen, and the Princess, and are more irritated than ever at what is passing. Besides which, the inconveniences likely to arise from delay, as well as from this new [Lutheran] sect, which is daily increasing, might, perhaps, render the circumstances not quite so favourable later on. Many think that, were the intercourse of trade with Flanders and Spain to be closed or suspended for three or four months only, the English would let their King know where the truth lies, and teach him to reform his conduct ...

*14 May 1534*
... Although I have many a time solicited the Queen (Katharine), your Majesty's aunt, for her opinion and advice respecting the execution of the sentence, it is only two days ago that I received from her the letter herein enclosed; which, besides the adjoined declaration of the Queen's sentiments in the matter, will perhaps be a sufficient excuse for her not writing this time to Your Majesty. She hitherto imagined that the Papal sentence once delivered and intimated to the parties, this King would return to the right path; but she now perceives that it is absolutely necessary to apply stronger remedies to the evil. What these are to be, she durst not point out – firstly, because she is afraid of her letters being intercepted; and secondly, lest she should contradict in the least what she has said and written on former occasions. She is also aware that Your Majesty knows best what sort of remedy matters in this country require. Whatever that remedy may be, it must be applied shortly, otherwise the evil will be irremediable; for, owing to the means this King and many others are employing or may eventually employ according to circumstances, all will be lost; and, what is still worse, every day this new Lutheran sect increases and is reinforced, and, when once it takes root in this country, those even who have taken the Queen's part will turn round, under the impression that whatever efforts Your Majesty might make to redress the Queen's affairs here would not be so much for her sake as for the purpose of upholding the authority of the Pope, which they describe here as tyrannical ...

The Queen, Your Majesty's aunt, has lately removed to a house belonging to the heirs of Monsieur Richard Vuinfil (Wingfield), who died at Toledo whilst this King's ambassador to Your Majesty. She is personally better lodged than she was, though the house is smaller. Some time before her removal the King sent two doctors-at-law for the purpose of making her swear to the two statutes newly made in Parliament, the copies of which I enclosed to Your Majesty, on the 22nd ult.; but, instead of swearing, the Queen, as a counterpart for the intimation, read to the doctor the sentence which the Pope had given at Rome in her favour; upon which the King's deputies retired after making the household servants swear to the statutes.

A few days ago, the King asked the lady in waiting of his mistress, who had charge of the Princess, whether there were signs of her rebellious spirit and stubborn obstinacy being in any way subdued. The lady answered that she continued the same; upon which the King remarked, 'Then there must be some one near her who maintains her in her fanciful ideas by conveying news of her mother to her.' The governess replied, that, all things considered, the only person she could suspect was that very maid who, as I informed Your Majesty, was compelled to take the oath. Without further inquiry, the governess sent away the maid, who has been some days without resources, and without any one daring to receive her. At which the Princess has been much affected, and not without cause, for she was the only maid whom the Princess could trust, and by whose intermediate action she received my letters, and those of other people. The Queen herself is much grieved at this, and, above all, at the King's having lately replaced the Princess's confessor, a worthy and pious ecclesiastic, by one, who is a Lutheran, and the King's right-hand man.

The King, perceiving that he cannot subdue the Princess's temper by rude treatment or threats, and influenced perhaps by considerations of another sort, has since then treated her more honourably than usual, and addressed her in more gracious words, intimating that, were she only to give up her wilful obstinacy, and entirely obey his commands, he would propose to her, before St Michael next, such a marriage as would ensure to her the title and dignity of Queen. To which message she replied, among other good and wise words, 'God forbid that I should be so blinded by error or ambition as to confess that the King my father, and the Queen my mother, have lived so long in adultery, or that I willingly contravene the ordinances and precepts of my holy Mother the Church, by acknowledging myself illegitimate.' The Princess firmly believes that such affectation of better treatment on the part of the King covers some design on his part. It may, perhaps, be intended to disguise the poison they intend giving her; for which, as she says, she cares not in the least, firmly believing and trusting in God that she will go straight to Heaven, and be freed from this world's tribulations and troubles ...

### 19 May 1534

... It is, indeed, to be feared that upon the obstinate refusal of the Queen and Princess to comply with his wishes, the King, at the instigation of this accursed concubine of his, will play them both a bad trick The general belief here is that, when about to cross over to France, he will at least confine them both to the Tower, for fear of what may happen during his absence. And I believe him quite capable of impressing many people here with the foolish notion of applying to Parliament for a sentence against the Queen and the Princess, and making all people, without distinction, subscribe the same, – a thing in which he would meet with little or no resistance on the part of his subjects, intimidated as they are. In such an event I do not hesitate to say that prompt and efficacious measures will be needed, as I have pointed out in several of my despatches ...

### 29 May 1534

... Nobody doubts here that one of these days some treacherous act will befall the Queen, considering the rude and strange treatment to which she is daily subjected, both in words and in deeds, and which is on the increase; especially as the King's mistress has been heard to say that she will never rest until he has had her put out of the way; and that since a prophecy exists that a queen of England is to be burnt alive, she is quite justified in trying to avert that fate from herself, and make the Queen play the part of the person doomed to the faggot. Indeed, many people here suspect that the forebodings of some of the courtiers, who continually keep saying that ere long great things will be seen [in London], are in allusion to the Queen, and to the hurt they intend doing her. A few days ago the Chancellor, whilst speaking in a passion to three or four of the principal foreign merchants, said to them that in his opinion, and in that of his colleagues, all foreigners residing in England ought to be treated as they deserved, and the wings of very great people clipped; which threatening words the said merchants interpreted as alluding to the Queen. These are, indeed, monstrous things, and not easily to be believed, and yet such is the King's obstinacy, and the wickedness of this accursed woman (Anne), that everything may be apprehended ...

### 23 *June 1534*

... Upwards of ten months ago I had sent to the Queen a protest for her daughter, the Princess, to sign. This I had reason to believe had been complied with, otherwise I should have taken measures to that effect. Finding, however, that it was out of her power to obtain her daughter's signature, the Queen sent it back to me some time ago, and I have at last succeeded in making her sign the document, as Your Majesty will see. No words of mine can express the industrious and clever means which that angelical and peerless Princess has employed to get the said protest into my hands, and distract the attention of the guards by whom she is surrounded.

A gentleman worthy of credit has this day sent me word that the King's mistress has said more than once, and with great assurance, that the very moment the King crosses over [to France] to hold his interview with king Francis, and she remains governess of the kingdom, she will certainly cause the death of the said Princess by the sword or otherwise. And upon Rochefort, her brother, saying that by doing so she might offend the King, she answered him that she cared not if she did, even if she were to be burnt or flayed alive in consequence. The Princess knows very well the good intentions of that lady; but thinking that such a death is the best way of gaining Paradise, is nowise concerned at such threats, placing her trust in God, whom she has served so well at all times, and now serves better than ever. After speaking to her on the subject, whenever the permission be granted, I shall not fail to follow her advice, and address my remonstrances to the King Whether these will be of use or not is more than I can say at present ...

### 16 *July 1534*

... The day before yesterday the earl of Wiltshire and the Comptroller went again to the Princess to persuade her to renounce her title. If she did, they told her, the King would treat her much better than she could expect or even wish. In case of refusal she would meet with an opposite treatment. The Princess's answer was so prudent and wise that the commissioners went away in confusion. I had the day before informed her of the visit which she was about to receive, and wrote what I thought necessary to strengthen her in her good purpose, and keep her in good spirits and hope, as I am doing almost every day. I cannot say whether I shall in future have such opportunities, for they are threatening to have her shut up in her rooms ...

### 29 August 1534

... Having lately heard that there was a talk of change of residence for the Princess, and of making her follow and accompany the King's bastard daughter wherever she went, I received from the former no less than three different messages in twenty-four hours, asking me what she had better do. I answered her messages each time, and tried to dissipate her scruples as well as I could, writing to her that even if she were to obey implicitly the King's commands in that respect, no damage would ensue for her interests, inasmuch as the protest which I had formerly placed in her hands safeguarded her most completely. For fear, however, of the King and his Lady thinking that ill-treatment was already producing its effect on her, and that she was gradually losing courage, I strongly advised her, while maintaining her usual modesty, to speak boldly and show good heart, and yet not to carry things to such extremity as to oblige her guards to use violence as in past times. I have written at full length what she is to say in the event of her being interrogated or obliged to act against her will; not that I thought this necessary, considering the great wisdom with which she is gifted, but because she insisted upon my doing so. However this may be, I hear that the Princess has played her part so remarkably well that the Comptroller himself has actually promised her that she shall not, unless she likes, go and live with the bastard. Nevertheless, having arrived at the first gate of the house (park?) the Princess found there the bastard's chaise, and therefore she had to go first. After which, the Comptroller having given her faculty, as soon as she was in her own chaise, to go before or after, as she pleased, she suddenly went forward, and made such haste that she arrived at Greenwich one hour before the bastard, and when she came to the barge she managed so well that she occupied the most honourable seat in it. Having, moreover, sent her word that I would willingly go to Greenwich to see her pass, she replied that she should be most happy. I went thither in disguise, and had the pleasure of witnessing such grace and beauty, coupled with a true royal aspect and garb, that I felt double pity and commiseration at seeing her so ill-treated ...

### 23 September 1534

... The Princess has lately been very ill, owing to her having been obliged, whilst in delicate health, to move from where she was, and follow the bastard. In consequence of the fatigues of the journey, and of the many annoyances to which she is daily subjected, her illness increased considerably, though, thanks be to God, she has since recovered, and is now well. The King sent his own physician to visit her, and permitted that her mother's, and the apothecary who has been her medical adviser for the last three years, should also be in attendance; which permission has considerably helped to her recovery. True it is that the King had previously given orders that both his own physician and that of the Queen, as well as her apothecary, should be expressly requested and induced to go and make their reverence to the bastard before calling on the Princess, but, luckily for all parties, the messenger arrived too late. Most strict orders were then issued forbidding the said physicians and apothecary to address the Princess in any other language than English, and that in the presence of the household servants, and other inmates of the manor.

Ever since the King began to entertain doubts as to his mistress's reported pregnancy, he has renewed and increased the love which he formerly bore to another very handsome young lady of this court; and whereas the royal mistress, hearing of it, attempted to dismiss the damsel from her service, the King has been very sad, and has sent her a message to this effect: that she ought to be satisfied with what he had done for her; for, were he to commence again, he would certainly not do as much; she ought to consider where she came from, and many other things of the same kind. Yet no great stress is to be laid on such words, considering the King's versatility, and the wiliness of the said lady, who knows perfectly well how to deal with him ...

*13 October 1534*
... The wife of Mr. de Rochefort has lately been exiled from Court, owing to her having joined in a conspiracy to devise the means of sending away, through quarrelling or otherwise, the young lady to whom the King is now attached. As the credit of this latter is on the increase, and that of the King's mistress on the wane, she is visibly losing part of her pride and vainglory. The lady in question has lately sent a message to the Princess, telling her to take good heart; that her tribulations will come to an end much sooner than she expected; and to be assured that, should the opportunity occur, she will show herself her true friend and devoted servant ...

*24 October 1534*
Having lately received a message from the Princess to the effect that the King's mistress was in secret treaty with some of the household to cause her all manner of annoyances or bodily hurt, I made a pretence to go to Cromwell, and, coming to the subject of the Princess, took the opportunity of remonstrating against the ill-treatment to which she was subjected, requesting him, in the name of that affection which he once said to me he entertained towards her, and for the preservation and increase of the peace and amity between Your Majesty and his master, to prevent any injury or offence in that quarter, and not oblige the Princess to follow the King's bastard daughter wherever she went, as well as renounce her own legitimacy, and the title, which was her own. Such treatment, I said, could in nowise promote the King's views, whatever they might be; it might, on the contrary, engender some dangerous disease, at which, I was sure, the King, naturally kind and virtuous, would be highly displeased, since the loss of such a pearl as his daughter, as well as of his own reputation before the world, could not but affect him considerably.

Cromwell's answer was that certainly, as far as he himself was concerned, he had fulfilled the promise he once made me of attending with all the care in his power to the Princess's comforts, most particularly since he had spoken to her (he has only seen her once that I know of), owing to the great gifts of grace and nature which he had found in her. He had, he said, express orders from the King, his master, to look to the Princess's comforts, and see that she was well treated, and if it were found that any of the people in the household had been rude, or not done his duty towards her, he should be punished forthwith. He added that in future he should have no difficulty in having her respectfully treated, considering the paternal affection which the King bore her, and of which, notwithstanding all appearances, he (Cromwell) was as persuaded as of that which the King bore him, which was notorious and manifest enough. Well might Cromwell boast of that; for certainly the credit and authority which he enjoys with this King just now is really incredible, as great indeed as the Cardinal (Wolsey) ever enjoyed, besides which he is daily receiving fresh bounties from him.

True it is (continued Cromwell) that the King has occasionally shown displeasure at the Princess having obstinately resisted his will in what concerns the legitimacy of this, his second marriage; but, nevertheless, his paternal affection is still the same that it was, so much so that for some time past he has openly declared to some of his Privy Councillors – who, imagining they were doing pleasure to the Lady [Anne], put forward certain measures and plans to the Princess's great disadvantage – that he (the King) would never give his consent to them. Indeed it seemed as if, the better to prove his assertion, Cromwell wished to imply that he was one of those councillors who had advised on the occasion, alleging as an excuse that servants very often proposed measures which they considered agreeable or beneficial to their masters with a view to show their devotion, and also to ascertain their will and inclinations. In this instance, however, the King had so discountenanced the talebearers that there was no one at Court, neither the Lady nor any other person, who dared now speak unfavourably of the Princess.

After discoursing on other topics Cromwell went on to say that in order to raise a corner of the veil, and let me, as it were, into the secret of the King's conduct, he would tell me a fact which very few, if any, were cognisant of; namely, that not only did the King cherish the Princess, his daughter, immensely, but he loved her 100 times more than his last born, and that he would ere long give to the world an evident proof of the great affection he bore her; as he (Cromwell) would shortly have occasion to declare to me after reporting to the King my official communication on the subject; – which words in Cromwell's mouth seemed to imply, if I am not mistaken, that the King is actually thinking of having her married in some princely quarter, and that, in order to maintain the King's good-will, and increase the friendship and amity between Your Majesty and the King, his master, he and I ought to do everything in our power to soften and mend all matters relating to her, if it were only for some little time to come. He had no doubt (Cromwell said) that in time everything would be set to rights, – wishing thereby to hint that there was some appearance of the King changing his love. This last surmise Cromwell was well capable of making, though he might think otherwise, just in order to amuse people ...

The conversation ended by Master Cromwell telling me that he had positive orders from the King himself to attend to all and each of the Queen's wants, and that he had on that very day furnished 4,000 ducats for the expenses of her household. I must, however, observe that on the previous day Cromwell had held this very language to one of my secretaries, whom he questioned as to whether he was one of those who had gone to the Queen's residence, when I myself attempted to visit her. Cromwell, however, had reason to repent his having put such a question; for my man disguised so well the place where the Queen was, and the treatment made to her, that Cromwell was evidently thrown off the track. I gave him to understand that I had no wish whatever to enter into such a conversation or discuss the Queen's treatment, presuming that the King, his master, out of his magnanimity, virtue, and natural kindness, would effectually provide for all her wants, as justice and the peculiarity of her case required, more especially as his ambassador at Your Majesty's court had lately given some such assurances in his name. 'For this reason (said I to Cromwell) have I avoided, as much as possible, to touch on the subject; but since you have been the first to allude to it, and I know by experience how desirous you are that people should speak to you openly and in a straightforward manner, I am ready to tell you part of my mind on the subject.' I then told him that my information was that, far from having all her wants supplied, the Queen was poorly treated, for she had not a farthing to dispose of; which was contrary to the statement made before Parliament, that a larger income was spent upon her now than she had in former times. I granted that large sums had been paid to those about her person; but, as the Queen herself remarked, the money was not spent on her household servants, but on her guardians and keepers, as it were. Except four or five of the former, she had no one about her person. As to her old servants, some of whom had come from Spain with her, and to whom she was bound to pay pensions for their maintenance, they had all been dismissed from her service, and she had no money to give them, not even in charity. In the last two years she had had only two new dresses, &c. Cromwell's answer was that it was in the Queen's power to have as much money and as many dresses as she chose: she had only to apply for them, and send him word, and every provision would be made. Cromwell, however, can safely make such offers, knowing, as he well knows, that she will never ask for anything, nor will she either receive what is sent to her under the address of 'Old Princess Dowager', which is the title they now give her. Though it must be said that whenever Cromwell happens to name her in my presence, he does it with a certain courtly civility, – making his excuses if, by the King's command, and the order of Parliament, he is obliged to designate the mother by the title of 'Princess Dowager', and the daughter by the name of 'Madame Marie', which excuse he never fails to make whenever he mentions the Queen and Princess to me. My reply was that I would not for the world that the King, his master, the Queen, or even Your Majesty, should know that I had mixed myself up with such affairs; for, in the first place, Your Majesty would be displeased at my interference if I did not let you know first; Cromwell himself might make the necessary provision without importuning any one else; besides that, the King, his master, might, perhaps, take my interference as a sort of reproach; the Queen might also think that, speaking as I did, without her consent, and mentioning the indigence in which she lived, it might be supposed that I spoke at her instigation, and in a tone of reproach to those upon whom she depended. I then added under the same protest that it seemed to me very strange, as it seemed to every one else, that the Queen's jewels should have been taken from her to decorate the King's other wife. Indeed, the King could very well guess what reverence and veneration his Queen had for him, since she bore the insult so patiently without saying a word, and not minding what the world might say of her; in fact, that I really believed she would rather die than have to open her mouth to utter a complaint. These arguments of mine Cromwell knew not how to answer except by owning that reason was entirely on my side. After some small talk on other unimportant matters, I left the room, promising to hold another conference with him on his next return from Court.

Though Cromwell has assured me of the good-will which the King bears his daughter, the Princess, yet, putting aside other conjectures and warnings, I should scarcely have attached faith to his protestations, had there not been some evidence of their truth; for, in reality, the King gave, some time before, orders that she should be well treated; and on the Wednesday before her departure from Mur (More), she had been visited by almost all the gentlemen and ladies of the Court, however annoyed the Lady (Anne) might feel at it. The day before yesterday, being at Richmond with the King's little daughter, there came the Lady, Anne herself, accompanied by the dukes of Norfolk and Suffolk and others, and by a party of ladies, on pretence of visiting her own daughter, but in reality to see and salute the Princess, – a great novelty no doubt. The Princess, however, would not leave her room until the Lady had actually taken her departure from the house, so that she might not see her. Instead of the sedan chair covered with leather, in which the Princess travelled when, in the first instance, she was taken to the residence of the King's bastard daughter, this time, on her journey back from the More to Richmond, she had one exactly the same as the first, but covered with velvet. Arrived at Richmond, not to follow the bastard's own chair and that she might have a peep at me on her passage, the Princess allowed the little one to go by land, whilst she herself came by water. On the very evening of her departure, she settled with the bargemen as to what bank of the river she wanted them to follow. That being done, she quickly sent me word to be at a certain place on the riverside, between Greenwich and this city, in front of a detached house destined as a refuge in case of the plague; for she said she wanted to see me, and take her revenge for my having gone to Greenwich to see her off. She, therefore, managed her affairs so well with the help of the bargemen, that, instead of following the right side of the river, they followed that on which I myself stood, near enough for the Princess to see me. She then caused the barge to be uncovered, and, mounting the forecastle, did not come down until she had actually lost sight of me. She is now in pretty good health, thank God, – handsome and plump, – and, as far as I can judge, gay, and in good spirits. I had, some time before she left More to return to Richmond, advised her that since the King, her father, seemed to relent of his rigour, it behoved her not to do anything likely to irritate him; and that as the protest once written and prepared by me for her, and of which a copy was forwarded to Your Majesty, was calculated to preserve her from any danger, she was to make no faces or refuse to follow her father's bastard daughter wherever she went; not to make protests as in former times, but, on the contrary, publish and declare to the world that she was very much pleased to act according to her father's wishes. This she has done ever since, and her conduct has evidently been the cause of her father's visit to Richmond, about which I once wrote to Your Majesty, as well as the permission to come to London by water without being obliged to follow or accompany the other one.

Were it not that this King is of amiable temper and cordial nature, and that the young lady, his new mistress, is fond of the Princess, and has already worked in her favour, one might suspect that the kindness which her father has suddenly shown for her had its origin in dissimulation, and was intended to colour the sin in case the Princess came to harm; which may God forbid ...

*28 November 1534*
... Since his arrival in this city, nine days ago, the Admiral of France has been to Court no less than six different times, besides which, on Sunday last, he dined at the King's table. There has been a good deal of dancing and playing at tennis, the King taking part in the one as well as in the other sport. The Admiral, though, has only gone twice to see the ladies, and then apparently more for the sake of making himself agreeable to them than for his own pleasure; the tennis court he has not once honoured with his presence. Nor has he, as I am told, made much of the Lady [Anne], for when the King at his first audience inquired if he did not wish to call on her, the Admiral answered very coolly 'As you please', which answer was remarked by many of those present. As the said ambassador was coming out of the King's apartments at his first audience, he ceremoniously refused to precede the Duke of Norfolk, alleging that he had already explained his commission, and that he was no longer an ambassador, which was as much as saying that he had come to London merely to hear what the King had to say to him, and that he himself had brought no message whatever from his master. Tomorrow the Duke of Norfolk will entertain the Admiral, and the day after, which will be St Andrew's festival, the duke of Richmond will do the same. There was also a talk of his going to Richmond to see the chapel of the Order [of the Garter]; but it appears that he would more willingly take the road to France, if it were for no other motive than getting an answer to a despatch which he sent home on Tuesday last by express, the only one he has drawn up since his arrival ...

*19 December 1534*

On the receipt of Your Majesty's letter of the 9th ult., I immediately
proceeded, in compliance with the orders therein contained, to inform both
the Queen and the Princess of what concerned each of them in particular. It
has been of such consolation and comfort to them that no words of mine
could convey an idea of the joy both have experienced at it. Indeed, I may
say that they were greatly in need of such consolation, considering the rude
treatment they have been, and are still, subjected to, which, far from being
amended, is apparently waxing worse and worse every day. Nor is there
the least hope of an alleviation of their mutual sorrows taking place in the
future, nor of their household officers and servants being restored to them,
as they seem to write to Your Majesty from Rome. On the contrary, every
day the household of the Queen and Princess is more and more reduced.
Only the other day, as I had the honour to inform Your Majesty, one of the
Princess's maids, the same who was sent to prison, though released shortly
after, was forbidden to return to her service. I really believe, however, that
all this ill-treatment of the Princess has principally originated in the hatred
of the Lady Anne, and is carried on without the King's knowledge, who
occasionally shows love and affection to his daughter. Of this he has lately
given manifest testimony, for the Princess, having fallen ill, he immediately
sent his own chief physician to attend on her, intimating that nothing would
grieve him so much as the loss of his daughter. Having, moreover, heard
from the physician's lips that her illness was partly the result of the worry
and extreme annoyance to which she had been subjected, the King began
to sigh deeply and exclaim: 'Is it not a great misfortune that my daughter
should be so obstinate, and persevere in a line of conduct that prevents my
treating her as I should wish, and she deserves?' And upon the physician
himself insinuating that, if sent to the residence of the Queen, her mother,
the Princess might live there at less expense, be more honourably treated,
and recover more surely, and besides, that in case of mishap (which may
God forbid), all suspicion of foul play might be removed by the presence
of so many witnesses, the King owned to him that he was right in what he
said, but that there was one great drawback in such a plan, which was that
were the Princess sent to reside with her mother, it would be impossible for
him to bring her to his wishes, and make her renounce her legitimacy and
her right to the succession.

Since the date of Your Majesty's letters, several of mine must have been
received, containing a full and satisfactory answer to most points touched
on in them, owing to which, I shall be as brief as possible. With regard to
the Lady (Anne) it is quite true that occasionally this king seems to be angry
with her; but, as I have already observed in some of my previous dispatches,
such outbreaks are merely lovers' quarrels, of which no great notice need
be taken, unless, indeed, the King's passion for the young lady, about whom
I once wrote to Your Majesty, should continue and was stronger than it is
at present, of which, however, there is no certainty considering this king's
fickle and capricious humour. I hear from the Grand Squire (Guildford),
that upon the Lady [Anne] addressing certain remonstrances to the King,

and complaining that the young lady in question did not treat her with due respect in words or deeds, the King went away in a great passion, complaining loudly of her importunity and vexatiousness. Neither is there any further sign of the King's ill-humour towards the Lady's relatives, except that which is naturally connected with their occasional quarrels; though it must be said, that Rocheford's wife was dismissed from Court owing to the above mentioned cause, and that he himself has been unfavourably treated by the King in a question or dispute he had with Master Bryan. The Lady's sister also was banished from Court three months ago; but her exile was necessary, in consequence of gross misconduct, and it would not have been either honourable or decent for her to appear at Court enceinte [pregnant].

Though I was at first given to understand that the Admiral of France, had actually made overtures concerning the marriage of the Princess to the Dauphin, yet I hear from a good quarter, that previously to the receipt of Your Majesty's letter, an application for her hand had been made for the duke of Angoulême, and that this king had twice refused to entertain the subject, taking it as a hoax or mere joke on the part of the Admiral; and that upon the latter, at a second audience, insisting that he had mandate from his master, to apply for such a marriage, this king maintained that Francis could not have spoken seriously of that affair, but merely by way of a joke, so that when the Admiral mentioned the subject a third time, he was actually obliged, as I have been told, to exhibit his written instructions under the great seal of France, which, according to the testimony of a worthy citizen, who knows the person who held them in his hand and read them throughout, contained among other commissions that of applying for the aforesaid marriage, exhorting this king to return to the obedience of the Roman Church, and acknowledge the legitimacy of his daughter. According to information received the King's answer was, that he had no objection to the marriage, provided the Princess and her intended husband made firm and solemn renunciation of all rights and titles they might have, or pretend to have, to the crown of England. It is highly probable that when the Admiral spoke to me of the great service he expected to render shortly to the Princess, he alluded to this very marriage, which he imagined might be effected. However this may be, I very much doubt of the marriage ever taking place; when both Kings come to consider the probable consequences of such an alliance, they will cool upon it most likely and drop it altogether ...

*1 January 1535*
... I have no doubt he [Mr Darcy, an English exile] will be delighted to hear that the earl of Northumberland[48] is no longer such a friend of this king and of his ministers as he used to be, for the Earl's physician tells me that his master had lately complained to him of certain wrongs and injuries received at the hands of members of this government, and had declared that those who had so behaved towards him would soon have to repent of their ill-doings. The English people (he added) were so indignant at the oppressions and excessive tyranny they suffered, that the least effort on the

part of Your Majesty would be the means of working the King's perdition and ruin. The King, said the Earl, had no other hope at present but the Turk's great military power, in which his friends trusted and glorified, but which after all was a most abominable trust. The Earl went on charging the King's mistress with arrogance and wickedness, saying, among other things, that a few days ago she had heaped more injuries on the duke of Norfolk than on a dog, so much so, that the Duke was obliged to quit the Royal chamber, and that, though finding only in the hall a gentleman to whom he no longer bore affection, such was his anger that he forgot entirely whom he was addressing, and began to complain in the bitterest terms of the said Royal mistress, bestowing on her the most opprobrious epithets, and calling her among other things 'grande putain'. [i.e. a great whore] ...

The Princess has been warned that the King, her father, in virtue of the rigorous statute lately made against all those refusing to take the oath on the occasion of his new marriage, is about to summon her, immediately after these festivals, to renounce her title, and swear to the said statute, bidding her on pain of death no longer to take, or allow any one to give her, the title of 'Princess', or call Madame, her mother, 'Queen'. But I take it that even if she should be sent to the Tower, or put to death, with which she is frequently threatened, the Princess will never change her purpose. The same may be said respecting the Queen mother ...

### 14 January 1535

... I hear also from an authentic source that this king and his Privy Councillors are much concerned and astonished at their not receiving news from the court of France respecting the negotiations between this king and the Admiral, and that they begin to think and fear that there may be some intelligence between that government and Your Majesty. This king, however, hopes that if he can only hold an interview with King Francis, as they have already almost agreed to do, he will be able to defeat any other plans of Your Majesty in that quarter. The better to persuade king Francis to the meeting, and that the latter may not excuse himself, as he did last year, I am told that this king has come to no resolution at all on the matters proposed by the Admiral, delaying his final and conclusive answer till the time when he and king Francis shall meet. Such was this king's answer when asked for a decision on the several points brought forward by the Admiral, and especially concerning the Princess's marriage to the duke of Angouleme, at which the Admiral, as stated, was anything but pleased, and still less so at what the King himself told him on the occasion of the banquet given to him the day before his departure, for being seated near the Lady whilst the dance was going on, the latter began to laugh most immoderately, at which the Admiral was much annoyed, and knitting his eyebrows said, 'How is that, madam; are you mocking me?' Upon which, the lady, after somewhat restraining her laughter, made her excuses, saying, 'I could not help laughing at the King's proposition of introducing your secretary to me, for whilst he was looking out for him he happened to meet a lady, who was the cause of his forgetting everything.' I cannot say whether the excuse was accepted or not, or whether the Admiral found it a sufficient one, but I can vouch for the truth of the anecdote. On the other hand, the King, the Lady, and her friends have not taken in good part, as I hear, the circumstance of the Admiral not having given any signs of satisfaction or pleasure at anything that has been shown to him, not even at the Tower of London, and the war ammunition there stored, at which those deputed to conduct him through the building were anything but pleased. I say nothing about the remainder, because I calculate that Your Majesty knows enough of this by my several despatches ...

*25 April 1535*
... The Princess, thank God, is already well. The King, her father, at my prayer, sent his physician to her, and gave him his own horses to ride; for the want of which, among other causes and reasons, he (the physician) had at first excused himself from going. However, upon the King telling him that it was for himself an affair of honour, and that he had promised me that, notwithstanding the Queen's physician being in attendance, his own should also be present, his excuses were waived, and he actually went. I hear that the excuses of the former did not proceed from backwardness in doing service to the Princess, but because he wished to remove the suspicion the King and his lady have of his being attached to her, and of having been the cause of the Princess being lodged closer to the Queen, her mother, and being actually under the care of her physician. I must, moreover, observe that the King's physician having, as he has, the entrance to the Royal chamber, among the grandees and Privy Councillors, frequently hears many things said, and has positively told his colleague, the Queen's physician, that there are only two means of remedying the affairs of the Queen and Princess as well as those of this kingdom; the first is for God to visit the King with some slight illness or other, during which he may of himself acknowledge his error and repent, and therefore listen patiently and with good-will to the remonstrances which his people may address to him. The other is to attempt force, of which the King himself (said he) and those who have the reins of the government in their hands are marvellously afraid. Indeed the Royal physician maintains that, should war be declared, this King would take the greatest care of the Queen and Princess, in the hope that at all events they might act as mediators for a peace. Should one or other of the two above remedies be delayed (said he) both the Queen and the Princess would be in great danger of their lives. It was (he added) a very lucky thing for the King, his master, that Your Majesty was not aware of the facility of an invasion, which, if undertaken at this present season, would, in his opinion, meet with complete success ...

*June 1535*
After the two first conferences held by the King's deputies, the sieur de Rochefort left Calais, and arrived here the 15th ult. Before going to the King, he called on his sister (Anne), and had a long talk with her; yet the news he brought from Calais could not be very agreeable, for the Grand Esquire tells me that then and there, and ever since, the lady has not ceased

inveighing against the king of France, and the French in general. On the 15th, and on the 17th, which was the day of Corpus Christi, the King and his Council were closely engaged in consultation, as is generally believed, respecting the news brought by Rochefort; both King and Council being so disappointed at it that they could not conceal their discontent. Nor has the French ambassador here escaped his share of the annoyance caused by Rochefort's sudden return from Calais, for the latter brought no news for him, and he himself was not summoned to Court; to which may be added that on Corpus Day, he remained at Cromwell's lodging from the afternoon till 10 o'clock at night, waiting for that Secretary's return from Court, who, as he himself told me, dispatched him with two words, the ambassador leaving the house sad and dejected ...

*16 June 1535*

... As soon as this King heard that the bishop of Rochester (Fisher) had been created cardinal, he was so angry and indignant at it that he said to many who were present at the time, that he would soon give him another and better hat, for he would send the Bishop's head to Rome for that purpose; immediately after which he sent to the Tower for the members of his Privy Council to summon again the Bishop to their presence, as well as Master Mur (More), and make them acknowledge him as head of the Church, threatening, unless they did so, to have them executed as traitors before St John's Day. But no threats or promises have as yet had any effect on them, and it is generally believed that both will be shortly executed. As, however, they happen to be men of great reputation and credit throughout this kingdom, the King has already ordered that sermons should be preached against them in almost all the churches of this city. That work commenced on Sunday last, and is to continue through the next in order to silence the murmurs of the people. Yet as there seems to be no sufficient cause to sentence them to death, the King is looking out for some misprision of treason to convict them thereof, and an investigation is now being carried, on to ascertain whether the Bishop really applied to Rome for the cardinal's hat, to which end several relatives of his, and even gaolers and guards, have been arrested. It is impossible to describe the sorrow and affliction of the Queen and Princess at hearing of such doings, they themselves being afraid that after the execution of those personages, the King may proceed to further violence, as I have already informed Your Majesty.

Out of spite for the said nomination, and to vent more openly his hatred of the Roman Church, the King has sent orders and letters patent to all the bishops, curates, and other preachers in his dominions to propound certain articles against the Apostolic Church. He has likewise commanded every schoolmaster to teach his scholars to speak ill of Papal authority, and likewise that in all missals, breviaries, and books of hours, whether it be in the almanacks or elsewhere, the Pope's name should be erased. It is also reported that an order exists that the reading of the Gospels should in all churches be in French; – the whole of this being, no doubt, done for the purpose of infecting his people with Lutheran doctrines, and rendering them more obstinate and prone to repulse foreign invasion, from whichever side it may come, as I have already had occasion to inform Your Majesty ...

### 30 June 1535

... On the 17th inst. the good and holy bishop of Rochester was sentenced to death for having refused to swear to the statutes lately made against the Pope, and the Queen's rights, and on the 22nd he was publicly beheaded at the same place where the duke of Buckingham was executed. There is no describing the immeasurable regret and pity felt by all people. They tell me that on the scaffold he was often and often solicited to comply with the King's wishes, grace and pardon being offered to him in the King's name, but that he kept firm to the last and died most exemplarily. They gave him as a confessor a sworn enemy of his, and the staunchest Lutheran in the world, as well as the originator of all the devilish acts practised here; who, however, was so much edified by the Bishop's countenance and noble behaviour on the scaffold that he ceases not to say that one of the best and holiest men in the world has been executed. Cromwell tells me that the Pope (Paul) was the real cause of the Bishop's death, for having foolishly made a cardinal of the King's bitterest enemy; and that the reason he alleged was still more foolish, for when he heard of the Bishop's execution he said to Sir Gregory da Casale, 'I did it in contemplation of the approaching Council, for as I intended to summon cardinals from all provinces and kingdoms in the world, I thought of him, and gave him a hat that he might represent England therein.' ...

### ? July 1535

... He [Henry VIII] the other day nearly murdered his own fool, a simple and innocent man, because he happened to speak well in his presence of the Queen and Princess, and called the concubine 'ribaude' and her daughter 'bastard'. He has now been banished from Court, and has gone to the Grand Esquire [Nicholas Carew], who has sheltered and hidden him.

### 23 September 1535

The English have greatly rejoiced at the news of the Emperor's victory over Barbarossa, all except the King, the concubine, Cromwell, and a few of their adherents, who, as my secretary reports, were as astonished and displeased as dogs falling out of a window. Cromwell himself could scarcely breathe when he first heard of it ...

### 13 October 1535

The bailiff of Troyes left four days ago to return home leisurely and without haste; neither is the bishop of Vuynchestre (Winchester), whom this King is sending to France, in any great hurry; so that, in point of fact, there does not seem to be much warmth or intimacy in their mutual relations and dealings just now. Of what these are, or may have been, I know nothing positively, except what I lately wrote to Your Majesty, though I have frequently held long conversations both with the bailiff himself and with the resident ambassador. The only pertinent question I have heard them make individually, is, whether

Your Majesty was thinking, or not, before all things, of having a General Council assembled, which (said they) was by far a more praiseworthy act than the conquest of Tunis, and more wanted than the recovery of the countries which the Turk holds in Christendom; and whether it was not far preferable to try and attempt that the pure Faith, uncontaminated by heresy, should reign over Christian princes without danger to their conscience and souls, even if they should experience some little harm in their persons and fortunes. What Your Majesty had already achieved or might achieve hereafter (continued the French ambassador) in that line would be of very little use without the meeting of a General Council. Which argument, and others of a similar nature and tendency, both Frenchmen repeated several times to me. In addition to which, I must say that baron Grammont, the ambassador's brother, has many a time asked one of my men, by way of a joke, whether it was true that the Council had already assembled, and was about to begin its deliberations; which insidious question, makes me think that king Francis is after no good, plotting to prevent the assembling of the Council, and that the English will do their utmost to help in the same direction, that being the thing they fear most.

Both the ambassador and the bailiff have lately visited the little bastard (Elizabeth), yielding, as they tell me, to the frequent importunities of her mother, the royal mistress. The former, as both have since assured me, had, under some pretence or other, delayed his visit until the bailiff's arrival; whose opinion, after all, was that both ought to go to the bastard's residence, were it for no other object than the chance of meeting there the Princess, whom they wanted very much to see. Without that hope (they say) they would never have accepted the mother's invitation. Unluckily for them, they did not see the Princess; for not only was she shut up in her room, as they themselves told me, but all the windows through which she might be seen were closed. This part of their statement I do not believe; I rather think that the Princess, following my instructions, and the advice I gave her in writing at her request, in order also to disguise the annoyance likely to be caused by the Frenchman's visit, show her filial obedience, and avoid, at the same time, all occasion of provoking her father's anger, kept aloof and remained indoors, playing on the spinet. Even if she had been inclined to act otherwise, I presume that her modesty would have prevented her from placing herself behind a glass window, where she could be seen ...

*13 December 1535*
... As to listening to any proposals of fresh understanding put forward by this King's ministers, I have taken all possible care to avoid it. It strikes me that Master Cromwell considers Your Majesty's important occupations at this moment a sufficient excuse for your delaying an answer; yet both the King and himself, seeing no appearance of Your Majesty granting their demands, as men without resolution, obstinately blind, and despairing now of any help on the side of France, are evidently trying to gain time, placing all their hope, as all bad payers do, in the demise of their creditors. Cromwell himself no longer complains to me, as he once did, of the delay of that answer, though

he never ceases sending me messages through a confidential friend of his, who has called on me several times for the last fortnight, to beg and entreat for my good offices in obtaining an answer to his propositions in the King's name. Whenever I have occasion to send one of my men to him, he never fails to admonish him to urge the matter on me; yet, with all that, as I say, there is no sign of any fresh proposal; and about a week ago he again, though incidentally as it were, brought forward the marriage of the prince of Spain [Philip] to this King's last-born daughter [Elizabeth].

Having called upon him about ten days ago to solicit the payment of certain arrears due to the Queen, and at the same time hear news from the King's court, Cromwell told me that he had just despatched a man to inform the King of the indisposition of the Queen, who, he said, was very poorly. As I was not aware of that, I naturally was somewhat alarmed at the news, and asked for permission to go and visit her, or send one of my men thither. This he readily granted, authorising me at once to send someone to inquire, and signing letters to that effect; but as to his allowing me to visit her, that he could not do; he would, however, speak to the King about it, and on his return from Court would let me know the answer. He has not spoken to me since, nor have I again mentioned the subject to him; for, thank God, the Queen has recovered, and is now well. As I was coming out of Cromwell's rooms, I received a letter from the Queen's physician, stating that, with God's help, there was no fear for the present; and that, should I not hear of her being worse, I was not to trouble myself with asking for leave to see her; I therefore have since desisted from the application ...

The present despatch being closed, I received a letter from the Queen, Your Majesty's aunt, which goes along with this. In addition to its contents, which are sad enough; she commands me to call your attention to her sufferings, and relates to you several particulars, which would move a stone to pity and commiseration; but having frequently written to Your Majesty about this, and knowing that in your prudence and wisdom you know better than anyone in this world what remedy can and is to be applied under the present circumstances, and, moreover, that you have those affairs more at heart than the Queen herself, I will abstain from troubling you further on that score.

*30 December 1535*

... Yesterday, Wednesday, having received a letter from the Queen's physician to the effect that she had had a relapse, and was much worse than a month ago, and that it would be a source of content and satisfaction for the said Queen, as well as of consolation for all the members of her household, if I would ask leave to go and visit her, I immediately dispatched one of my secretaries to Court to ask for the said leave. Cromwell sent me word that there would be no difficulty at all in obtaining it, but that I ought to go first to the King, who wished to speak to me on very important matters, and, therefore that I was to be in Greenwich without fail to-day at 1 o'clock p.m., as the King would go thither from Eltham, where he is at present residing. Yet, though Cromwell repeated several times the same injunction, and begged my man over and over again not to forget his message, he has this very morning sent me his own secretary to ask what my decision was, that he might let the King know, and prepare him for my visit at Greenwich; thus showing the great desire the King himself and Cromwell had that I should go to Court on that particular day.

Accordingly at the appointed hour I found on Greenwich pier Mr. de Chenay, who was waiting by the King's command to conduct me to the 'place des lices', where I met the King. After a most courteous and kind reception, the King embraced me, and put his hands round my neck, walked for some time with me in the presence of all the courtiers, telling me many things which would take me too much time to recount or write down. Among the things he told me, one was that, hearing from his secretary, Cromwell, that I wished to visit the sick lady, he had advanced the day appointed for our meeting, inasmuch as, the matter being important and requiring haste, all other business audiences might well be abandoned, or at least postponed ...

After much talking on various matters I asked the King what he wished Your Majesty to do. He said to me that he wished Your Majesty would refrain from favouring the two ladies (meaning queen Katharine and the Princess), and have the sentence in favour of the Queen revoked. I represented to him that I saw no cause or reason for your doing so, and that even if Your Majesty felt inclined, it was not in your power to accede to his wishes, besides which I had no express mandate to debate on such matters. The only thing I could do to please him (said I) was to inform Your Majesty of his wish. I assured him that you would do anything to please him as far as your honour and conscience would permit. The King then said, among other things, that he was pretty sure that the Pope had urged Your Majesty to do your worst against him. He also owned that the report of Your Majesty having offered to the king of France to conquer this kingdom of England, and give it over to him, seemed to be a regular hoax.

At last the King said that he imagined Queen Katherine, whom he did not name otherwise than by the appellation of 'Madame' would not live long, and that once dead, he thought Your Majesty would no longer have a pretence for mixing yourself up with the affairs of England, and would refrain from further pursuits in the matter of the marriages. My reply was that the demise of the Queen could not profit any one, and that at all events the sentence was a necessity.

I had already left the King's chamber, and was quitting the Royal palace altogether, when the duke of Suffolk overtook me with a message from the King to say that just at that moment news had come that the Queen was 'in extremis', and that if I went to her lodgings I should hardly find her alive; adding, on his own account, that with her death all impediments and scruples between Your Majesty and him would finally be removed. I really believe that the danger is not so great as they represent, for otherwise her physician would have written to me that her condition was grave. However this may be, I am now going to mount my horse and go to Kimbolton.[49] I have also asked the King's permission for the Princess to go and visit her mother; he at first refused, but on my representing the case duly, he said that he would consider about it, and let me know the result. I must add that it was at the request of the Princess herself that I made the application.

*9 January 1536*

I stated in my despatch of the 30th of December ulto., almost immediately after closing it I mounted my horse in order to repair in all possible haste to the Queen's residence, followed by a numerous suite of my own servants and friends. Arrived at Kimbolton, the Queen sent immediately for me; and lest people should imagine that her illness was a feint, and also for fear of a friend of Cromwell's whom that secretary had sent to accompany me, or rather to act as a spy on my movements and report what I might say or do during my visit, she (the Queen) was of opinion – as I also was – that the said guide, as well as the principal officers of her household, such as her own chamberlain, who had not seen her for more than a year, and many others, should witness the interview. After making my reverence, and kissing the Queen's hand, she was pleased, out of sheer kindness and benevolence, and without any occasion or merit it on my part, to thank me for the many services which, she said, I had rendered her on former occasions, as well as the trouble I had taken in coming down to visit her, at a time too when, if it should please God to take her to Himself, it would at least be a consolation to die as it were in my arms, and not all alone like a beast.

I failed not to give her on this occasion all possible hope of a speedy recovery, as well as of the prospect there was of her being shortly removed to other quarters, since the King, of his own accord, had recently offered to let her choose among various royal manors of his own that he named to me, and likewise to pay certain arrears of pension due to her, adding for her greater consolation that the King had been very sorry to hear of her illness.

After this I entreated her to take courage, and do her best to get well. If not entirely for her own sake, I said she ought at least to consider that on her recovery and life depended in a great measure the union, peace, and welfare of Christendom. To enforce which, I made use of several arguments, as previously preconcerted between her and myself, through the intermediary of a third person, all this being said aloud that the guide I have alluded to, and several others present at the interview, might, if necessary, report our conversation, and my words be the cause of greater care being taken to preserve her life.

After some more conversation on the above topics the Queen bade me retire and rest after the fatigues of my journey. She herself longed for some, as she had not slept two hours for the last six days. Not long after this she again sent for me, and we talked together for two long hours; and I must say that although, for fear of overtiring her, I made several attempts to get up and leave the room, she would not hear of it, saying that I afforded her great pleasure and consolation by remaining where I was. Out of the four days I staid at Kimbolton not one passed without my paying her an equally long visit, the whole of her commendations and charges being reduced to this: her personal concerns and will; the state of Your Majesty's affairs abroad; complaints of her own misfortunes and those of the Princess, her daughter, as well as of the delay in the proposed remedy, which delay, she said, was the cause of infinite evil among all honest and worthy people of this country, of great damage to their persons and property, and of great danger to their souls. But on my representing that Your Majesty, considering the circumstances of the case and the momentous affairs you had in hand, as well as the impediments thrown by others in your way, could not possibly do more now than you have hitherto done, – after explaining to her that the unavoidable delay, to which she alluded, had by no means been unfavourable, since not only was there a chance now of the French, who had hitherto solicited the friendship and alliance of England, turning henceforward their backs upon it, but another still greater boon had sprung therefrom, which was that the Pope and the Apostolic See, in view of the execution of the holy bishop of Rochester, and other disorderly acts committed in England, now were earnestly trying to procure the remedy to so many evils, and that such a remedy would now come very apropos, since, springing directly from His Holiness and the Apostolic See, whatever happened afterwards could in nowise be imputed to her, – the Queen seemed satisfied with my reasoning, and approved entirely of the delay. With regard to the heresies and scandals of this country, I said that she knew well that God occasionally allowed such evils to spring up in the world for the greater exaltation of the good and confusion of the bad, and that heresy had not yet taken such deep hold in this country as not to be soon up-rooted when those who had momentarily swerved from the Faith would, no doubt, become after a time its most strenuous defenders, as did Saint Paul after his fall. This speech of mine made the Queen happy and contented, whereas formerly she had certain conscientious fears as to whether the evils and heresies of this country might not have been principally caused by the divorce affair.

After four days spent in the above manner, perceiving that the Queen began little by little to recover her sleep and to get rest, – that her stomach retained food, and that she was evidently getting much better, – she herself was of opinion, as well as her physician, who now considered her out of danger, that I ought at once to return home, not only in order not to abuse the permission granted to me by the King, but also to ask for a better residence for her, as promised at my departure from London. I took, therefore, leave of the Queen on Tuesday evening; she being then, to all appearance, happy and contented, so much so that on the very evening of my departure I saw her smile two or three times, and half an hour after I had left she would still joke with one of my suite, rather inclined to a jest, who had casually remained behind.

On the following Wednesday, in the morning, according to the testimony of one of the grooms of her chamber, the Queen slept well, and her physician gave full hope of her recovery; so much so that he advised me to return to London immediately, adding that should there be a relapse or danger of life he would not fail to let me know. I then started and rode as leisurely as possible to wait for news, though I must say none came to me on the road.

This morning, however, on my sending to Master Cromwell to inquire when and at what hour I could have audience from the King, to thank him for the good, cheer made to me during the journey, and also to speak to him about the new house for the Queen, he communicated to my secretary the very grievous, painful, and lamentable news of the death of the, very virtuous and holy Queen, which occurred on Friday, the day after the Epiphany, towards two o'clock in the afternoon. Which intelligence, I must confess to Your Majesty, has been one of the most cruel and painful that could reach me under any circumstances; for I am afraid the good Princess her daughter will die of grief, or else that the King's concubine will carry out her threat of putting her to death, which she will certainly do unless a prompt remedy be applied to counteract her wicked designs. Meanwhile I shall do my best to comfort and console her, and if Your Majesty would only write her a letter I have no doubt that will powerfully contribute towards it. I cannot at present furnish Your Majesty with any details of the Queen's death, nor say how she has disposed of her property and affairs, for hitherto not one of her household servants has come to town, nor can I say whether they are at liberty or under arrest

This very evening, having sent a message to Cromwell to enquire what they intend doing in this emergency, as I, on my side, am fully prepared to pay my last duties to the deceased Queen, he told my man that just as he was passing the threshold of his door, he (Cromwell) had dispatched one of his own clerks to inform me by the King's command of the Queen's demise, and that the Privy Council had decided that a very solemn and honourable funeral service should be performed for the deceased, not only on account of her many virtues, and of her having once been the wife of prince Arthur of Wales, but also for her high descent and her affinity to the Royal house of England; and that if I chose to attend the funeral the King would send black cloth for my mourning, and that of my clerks and servants. Time and place, however, for the ceremony had not yet been fixed, but I should be informed in due time.

My answer to the above message was that, supposing the whole affair would be properly conducted, and as befitted a person of the Queen's rank, I willingly accepted the invitation, and would be present at the funeral; and with regard to mourning that the King need not take any trouble about it, for I was already provided with the black cloth necessary, &c. The Queen's illness began about five weeks ago, as I had the honour to inform Your Majesty. The day after the Nativity she had a relapse. The symptoms were pains in the stomach, so violent and acute that she could not retain the smallest particle of food or drink. I have many a time asked the physician who attended her, whether he had any suspicions of poison having been administered. His answer has always been that he had some doubts about it, for that since she had drunk of beer brought from Wales, she had never felt well. The poison, if there was any, must have been very subtle and refined, for he had been unable to discover externally any traces of it in her body, such as pure and simple poison would inevitably leave. Should she be embalmed, he added, we shall know for certain.

I am exceedingly sorry to have to convey such painful news to Your Majesty, knowing, as I do, how much grieved you will be. Please God that I may be able hereafter to communicate more pleasant ones.

21 *January* 1536

... Your Majesty's letter of the 29th has likewise come to hand, as well as the singularly wise and prudent considerations therein contained on the perplexing condition of the late good Queen and Princess's affairs, which considerations and remarks I myself did not fail to represent to the two ladies themselves, mother and daughter, whenever there was an opportunity, though, I must own, by no means so distinctly and cleverly expressed as in Your Majesty's letter to me.

Among other representations I made to them both, one was that I doubted much whether they would not have to consent in the end, and, take any oaths this King might wish to impose on them; since, besides the many inconveniences pointed out in Your Majesty's letter as likely to result from their holding out, innumerable people in this country might lose courage for resistance, and join at once in the new heresies against the Apostolic See. The danger lay not so much in the King's proceeding legally to punish what he considered their pertinacious disobedience to his commands, as in his obtaining his object under colour of perfect reconciliation and by good treatment. I feared not (I said) the King himself; I feared the concubine, who had often sworn to take away their lives, and who will never rest until she has accomplished her object, believing, as she did, and does still, that, owing to this King's capricious humour and temper, her position will not be secure as long as the two ladies, mother and daughter, live. She would then have better opportunities than before of executing her damnable purpose, by having poison of some sort administered to them, as, owing to the King's apparent reconciliation, there would be less suspicion, and consequently less vigilance. Indeed had the two ladies yielded to the King's wishes by renouncing their respective rights, and therefore experienced more favourable treatment at his hands, there would no longer exist any cause for fearing them, and consequently there could be no suspicion of foul play on the part of their sworn enemy.

The King, therefore, and the concubine, impatient at the delay, and perceiving that legal proceedings were being taken at Rome, knowing also that should Your Majesty go thither the cause would certainly be hastened on, and a more rigorous sentence pronounced, had already decided, as it appears from what I shall say hereafter, to put an end at once to the good Queen's pleading. It was more convenient, the King and his concubine thought, that the mother should die before the daughter for many reasons, one being that, among others, she was the principal party in the suit at Rome; there was also less hope of making her yield to them, since, owing to her age and other circumstances, they must have felt that the mother would hold more firmly to her determination than the Princess, her daughter; to which may he added that the Queen, not being naturally subject to English law, they could not legally compel her as they might the daughter. There was, besides, another very potent reason for this King and his concubine wishing that the mother should die before the daughter, namely, their cupidity and insatiable lust of money, as in the event of the Queen dying before the daughter they would not be obliged to return her dowry.

Now that the good Queen is dead, they are trying in various ways to catch the Princess in their net, and make her subscribe to their damnable statutes and detestable opinions; so much so that the other day Cromwell, in conversation with one of my men, was not ashamed to say that there was no reason to mourn so much at the death of the Queen, which after all must be considered as most advantageous for the preservation of the friendship between Your Majesty and the King, his master, since in future he and I might communicate and talk more frankly on the subject; that it only remained for us now to induce the Princess to accede to the King's will and wishes; which end he (Cromwell) was sure that I could, if I chose, promote move efficiently than any other living man; and that it was necessary that I should do my best for the accomplishment of that object, as, besides the pleasure I might give the King by doing so, the Princess herself would be greatly benefited through it, since by submitting to the King's will she would be much better treated than ever she had been.

A bait of this sort has already been thrown out, for, according to a message received from the Princess, the concubine has lately sent her word through her own aunt, under whose keeping she still is, as I have informed Your Majesty, that should she consent to wave her obstinacy, and be obedient, like a dutiful daughter, to her father's commands, she (the concubine) would at once become her warmest friend, and a second mother to her, and that, if she wished to go to Court, she should be exempted from being her train-bearer, and might walk by her side. And I am also told that the governess is continually begging and entreating her in the warmest possible terms to reconsider these offers. Nevertheless, the Princess's answer has always been that no daughter in the world would be move obedient to her father's wishes and commands than she herself is prepared to be, provided her honour and conscience are safeguarded.

According to another message received from the Princess, the King says that he will shortly send to her certain of his Privy Councillors for the purpose of summoning her to swear to the statutes; and she asks me how she is to answer the summons in case of its being made, which is most likely. My answer in writing has been that, in my opinion, she ought to show greater firmness and determination now than ever, more courage and persistence, coupled with the requisite modesty; for if these people once believe her to be the least shaken in her purpose, they are sure to go on persecuting her to the end without leaving her a moment's peace. I fancied (said I to her) that they would not now insist upon her renouncing openly her rights, nor directly disowning the Pope's authority in Church matters; they, most likely, would press her to swear to the concubine as Queen, alleging that her own mother being dead, there could be no excuse now for opposition on that head. I have, therefore, written to her to avoid as much as possible entering into conversation or dispute with the King's deputies, if they should go to her, to request them to leave her in peace, praying God for the soul of her deceased mother, as well as imploring His help in her present situation, she being a poor orphan without experience, aid, or counsel. She was to tell the deputies that she herself knew nothing of civil or canon law, and was unable to answer and meet their arguments, and therefore begged and entreated them to intercede with the King, her father, to have pity on her ignorance or incapacity. If, moreover, she chose to go on with, her excuses, she might add that, considering it was not the custom here, in England, to impose oaths upon queens – that ceremony not having taken place when her mother was married to the King, her father – she could not help thinking that the whole of this had been planned to do her injury. That were she to become in future a queen, her present renunciation of her rights would he invalid; she would inherit the Crown all the same. One thing she recollected, which was that in the consistorial sentence respecting her father's marriage, it was fully stated that whilst his first marriage was declared good, valid, and legitimate, his second was pronounced null and void, it being expressly stated, that lady Anne could never assume the title of queen. Lastly, it seemed to her as if she could not conscientiously contravene the Pope's commands, for were she to do so, and derogate from other articles in the sentence, she would evidently impair her own rights.

I have likewise written to the Princess that, if she thought it advisable, she might say to her governess that it was time lost to press such affairs on her at the present juncture, for she would rather lose ten lives, if she had them, than submit and consent to what they wanted of her, without being better informed, thereupon. She might add, that in order to enlighten and instruct her on the subject, people abroad could be found – for those in England she thoroughly mistrusted – to impart the requisite information and doctrine on such delicate points; and that should the King, her father, grant her a respite until she was of age, which was not now far off, perhaps God would inspire her with the wish of entering into a religious house and devoting herself entirely to Him, in which case she thought her conscience would be completely safe-guarded. Should the King grant this respite, she might perhaps acquire more solid information on the subject than she now possesses. The delay asked for could in nowise prejudice the King's interests, but would, on the contrary, be beneficial to him, for were she now to accede and consent to what is wanted of her, the act, when she was of age, would still be more valid and efficient. This much I wrote to the Princess, not in a resolute manner and by way of advice, but merely for the sake of argument, to be used if convenient. I shall consider the matter over and over again, and look out for other means of parrying the impending blow, or at least averting it for some time. If, however, the King and his concubine have decided to make her swallow poison, neither the tender of the oath itself, nor any other thing we might think of, would be of any use ...

Since my despatch of the 9th instant no courier has left this capital by whom to write to Your Majesty. Immediately after the death of the good Queen I despatched one of my own men [to Kimbolton], in order to ascertain what had occurred after my departure from that place, to console the poor servants of the Queen's household in their affliction, and see what could be done for them, as well as with regard to the funeral, in case the Queen had made any dispositions in that respect. My man came back three days ago, and informed me that two days after my departure [from Kimbolton] the Queen seemed to improve considerably in health, and that in the afternoon of the Epiphany she herself without the help of any of her maids, combed and tied her hair. That next day, about midnight, she inquired what time it was, and whether it was already near dawn. This enquiry the Queen made several times, for no other purpose, as she herself afterwards declared, than to be able to hear mass and receive the Holy Sacrament: and although the bishop of Llandaff, her confessor, offered to say mass for her before four o'clock in the morning, she would not consent to it, alleging and citing several authoritative passages in Latin to prove that it could not be done. At dawn she heard mass, and took the Holy Sacrament with the greatest fervour and devotion that could be imagined; after which she went on repeating various prayers, begging those who were present to pray for the salvation of her soul, and that God would pardon and forgive the King, her husband, for the wrong he had done her, inspire him to follow the right path, and give him good counsel. After which the Queen received extreme unction, she herself replying distinctly to all the questions of the ritual in a clear audible voice.

Knowing that in England no woman surviving her husband can make a will, the Queen, for fear of infringing the law of the land, would not dispose of her property otherwise than by way of supplication and, request to the King. She accordingly begged her physician to draw out a paper with certain testamentary clause, which she ordered to be brought to me immediately after signing it with her own hand. In that paper, in which she gave directions for certain small sums of money to be distributed among the servants living with her at the time, the good Queen declared that she wished to be buried at a convent of Observant Friars of the Order of St Francis, to which she bequeathed her robes and dresses to be used as Church ornaments. The furs she had, she reserved for the Princess, her daughter, to whom she likewise bequeathed a necklace with a cross, which she herself had brought from Spain. Such were the good Queen's testamentary dispositions. With regard, to her burial and donation to the Observants, Cromwell said, to one of my men whom I sent to him for the purpose, that it was quite impossible, inasmuch as there was no convent of that order then existing in all England; but that any other bequest to the Princess, or to her own family servants would, be complied, with as completely and honourably as I could wish.

The day after I sent my man [to Greenwich] to inquire from Master Cromwell what the Kings wishes were on the whole, and beg that the late Queen's physician and apothecary should be sent to the Princess's abode. And, although Cromwell promised to introduce my man to the King's presence, that he himself might convey my message and speak in my name, nothing was done about it, save that Cromwell sent for him and took him to a room of the Royal palace, where the ambassadors from Scotland, now returning to France, happened to be at the time, and there kept him long talking to him, all the time inquiring after my health, asking whether I took exercise in the mornings, and so forth; all this being done, as I imagine, to make the ambassadors there present, believe that mighty matters were then being discussed between us two, and that I had sent my man thither for the purpose. Cromwell at last answered, in a colder manner than the preceding day, as if he were answering in his master's name, that before granting my application with regard to the Queen's bequests the King wished to see those robes and furs of which I spoke, and that if the Princess wished to possess what her mother had bequeathed to her, she was first to show due obedience to her father, the King, adding that it was for me to persuade her to that course. With regard to the late Queen's physician there was no difficulty at all. If my man called at his (Cromwell's) own residence, he would furnish him with proper letters of introduction for the governess. When my man went next day to ask for .the letters, he was put off till the day after, and then Cromwell told him that a gentleman, the same who had accompanied me to Kimbolton on my visit to the Queen, would call and explain his views on the subject. He also begged my man to try and induce me not to refuse or avoid giving audience to the gentleman in question ...

The good Queen breathed her last at 2 o'clock in the afternoon. Eight hours afterwards, by the King's express commands, the inspection of her body was made, without her confessor or physician or any other officer of her household being present, save the fire-lighter in the house, a servant of his, and a companion of the latter, who proceeded at once to open the body. Neither of them had practised surgery, and yet they had often performed the same operation, especially the principal or head of them, who, after making the examination, went to the bishop of Llandaff, the Queen's confessor, and declared to him in great secrecy, and as if his life depended on it, that he had found the Queen's body and the intestines perfectly sound and healthy, as if nothing had happened, with the single exception of the heart, which was completely black, and of a most hideous aspect; after washing it in three different waters, and finding that it did not change colour, he cut it in two, and found that it was the same inside, so much so that after being washed several times it never changed colour. The man also said that he found inside the heart something black and round, which adhered strongly to the concavities. And moreover, after this spontaneous declaration on the part of the man, my secretary having asked the Queen's physician whether he thought the Queen had died of poison, the latter answered that in his opinion there was no doubt about it, for the bishop [of Llandaff] had been told so under confession, and besides that, had not the secret been revealed, the symptoms, the course, and the fatal end of her illness were a proof of that.

No words can describe the joy and delight which this King and the promoters of his concubinate have felt at the demise of the good Queen, especially the earl of Vulcher (Wiltshire), and his son, who must have said to themselves, What a pity it was that the Princess had not kept her mother company. The King himself on Saturday, when he received the news, was heard to exclaim, 'Thank God, we are now free from any fear of war, and the time has come for dealing with the French much more to our advantage than heretofore, for if they once suspect my becoming the Emperor's friend and ally now that the real cause of our enmity no longer exists I shall be able to do anything I like with them.' On the following day, which was Sunday, the King dressed entirely in yellow from head to foot, with the single exception of a white feather in his cap. His bastard daughter (Elizabeth) was triumphantly taken to church to the sound of trumpets and with great display. Then, after dinner, the King went to the hall, where the ladies were dancing, and there made great demonstration of joy, and at last went into his own apartments, took the little bastard, carried her in his arms, and began to show her first to one, then to another, and did the same on the following days. Since then his joy has somewhat subsided; he has no longer made such demonstrations, but to make up for it, as it were, has been tilting and running lances at Grinduys (Greenwich). On the other hand, if I am to believe the reports that come to me from every quarter, I must say that the displeasure and grief generally felt at the Queen's demise is really incredible, as well as the indignation of the people against the King. All charge him with being the cause of the Queen's death, which I imagine has been produced partly by poison and partly by despondency and grief; besides which, the joy which the King himself, as abovesaid, manifested upon hearing the news, has considerably confirmed people in that belief ...

There has been some rumour here that this King intended going personally to his daughter, the Princess, or sending some high personage to condole with her, and that on that ground the news of her mother's death would be kept from her as long as possible. I hear, however, that nothing of the sort is the case. Four days after the Queen's demise the governess herself went straight to the Princess, and most unceremoniously, without the least preparation, announced to her the sad event. I myself had previously written to the Princess a letter of condolence, and sent it to one of her maids in waiting with instructions to put it into her hands the moment her mother's death should be notified to her. This was done; and I must say that the Princess received such consolation and comfort through it that soon after she herself wrote to me a very good and well penned answer, in which, after thanking me immensely for the invaluable good I have done her, she begged me to let the King know that, unless she were immediately removed from the house and company in which she was, she should consider herself as good as lost; and that, following my advice, she would in the midst of her tribulations do her best to show that courage and constancy of which I had spoken to her, and at all events prepare for death.

In the evening of the day on which the Queen's death was notified to her, the Princess begged her governess to write a letter to the King, asking for the physician and apothecary who had attended on her, rather, as I imagine, to make inquiries and hear the particulars of her last illness, than because she herself wanted their services. To which request of the Princess the King answered, that her complaint, if any, was not the result of illness, but merely of natural affliction, and therefore that she needed no physician nor apothecary at all. The Princess then wrote to me, praying, among other things, that I should solicit and procure the personal attendance of those two officials on the plea that she was really unwell, and could not do without them; which I did forthwith, as Your Majesty must have heard.

The day before yesterday I forwarded to her the letter which Your Majesty had written to the Queen, her mother, as well as another from the Queen Regent of Flanders,[50] both of which arrived too late. The letters, however, have been of great consolation to the Princess, as she herself wrote to me half an hour ago; for since her mother's death she writes oftener than before, for no other purpose, as I imagine, than to give a proof of that courage and firmness which I am continually recommending to her. I must add that her good sense, incomparable virtues, and unheard-of patience under the circumstances, enable her to bear with fortitude the loss of a mother whom she loved and cherished as much, perhaps more than any daughter ever did; – the Queen, her mother, having always been her principal refuge in all her tribulations.

Great preparations are being made for the burial of the good Queen, and according to a message received from Master Cromwell the funeral is to be conducted with such a pomp and magnificence that those present will scarcely believe their eyes. It is to take place on the 1st of February; the chief mourner to be the King's own niece, that is to say, the daughter of the duke of Suffolk; next to her will go the Duchess, her mother;[51] then the wife of the duke of Norfolk, and several other ladies in great numbers. And from what I hear, it is intended to distribute mourning apparel to no less than 600 women of a lower class. As to the lords and gentlemen, nothing has yet transpired as to who they are to be, nor how many. Master Cromwell himself, as I have written to Your Majesty, pressed me on two different occasions to accept the mourning cloth, which this King offered for the purpose no doubt of securing my attendance at the funeral, which is what he greatly desires; but by the advice of the Queen Regent of Flanders (Mary), of the Princess herself, and of many other worthy personages, I have declined, and, refused the cloth proffered ; alleging as an excuse that I was already prepared, and had some of it at home, but in reality because I was unwilling to attend a funeral, which, however costly and magnificent, is not that befitting a queen of England ...

# 6

# A Memorial from
# George Constantyne to
# Thomas Lord Cromwell

*The memorial of George Constantyne (or Constantine), an eye witness to many of the events surrounding Anne's fall is, if genuine, of major importance.[1] Although only parts of the following document are relevant to Anne, it has not been printed since 1831 and is a difficult text to obtain. It is therefore printed in full. The source is also useful in relation to Henry's attempts to find a fourth wife after the death of Jane Seymour in 1537.*

*Some caution must be taken over Constantyne's memorial. The original document has never been produced and the publication was made using a transcript prepared by John Payne Collier. During his lifetime, Collier was rumoured to have created sources for use in his own historical works and it is therefore possible that Constantyne's memorial may also be a forgery.[2] It was, however, considered to be genuine by Thomas Amyot, the Treasurer of the Society of Antiquaries and it is regularly used by historians. In recent years Collier's reputation has also been somewhat rehabilitated, with it being claimed that he was actually one of the leading scholars of his period.[3] If genuine, it is a particularly useful source in relation to information on the men who were accused of adultery with Anne. It is generally accepted by historians as an original source.*

*George Constantyne was a servant of Henry Norris at the time of his arrest for adultery with Anne. In 1539, he was arrested following a controversial conversation with John Barlow, Dean of Westbury, who reported him to Thomas Cromwell. His memorial was a record of that conversation addressed to Cromwell. Constantyne is interesting in relation to Norris's arrest, William Brereton (with whom he had attended school in childhood) and the deaths of the five men accused with Anne. He was a follower of the religious reform. After persecution under Mary I, he was made an archdeacon by Anne's daughter, Elizabeth I.*

<u>Instructions for my Lorde Privey Seale as towchinge the whole communication betwixt John Barlow Deane of Westbury, Thomas Barlow Prebendary there, clerkys, and George Constantyne of Lawhaden, in their journey from Westbury vnto Slebech in Southwales.</u>

Fyrst on twisdaye being the xix[th] daye of August in the xxxj[th] yere of the reyne of our Soverayne Lorde Kynge Henry the viij[th], I George Constantyne came to Westbury from Bristow on fote, and there supped with the Deane, who asked me what tydinges, And I said none but good; that God be thanked the Kynges majestie was myrrye upon Sonday; And forther I sayed that I hearde saye that the late Bisshops of Salisbury and of Worcestre had an hundred merkes pension vnder the Kynges broad seale. What, sayed the Deane, owt of their Bishopryckes, or owt of the Kynges cofers? I can not tell that sayed I, but yf they can be contented they never lyved so myrryly in their lyves, yf they have that and the Kynges favour withall. I am glad sayed the Deane, for now I have hope that I shall have my money that the Bisshop of Worcestre oweth me, namynge xxvj^li or xxx^li, but I am sure that he shall never receave penny of his pension, for he shalbe hanged I warrante hym or⁴ christmasse. Na, sayed I, God forbidde, for I thinke he will nother write nor preach contrary to th'act of Parleament, he ys too wise. But he shalbe examined sayed the Dean, and I warrante he will never subscribe. As for the Bisshop of Salisbury, I heare saye he begynneth to relente. I can not tell, sayed I, but they saye at Bristowe that the Bisshop of Bath his servants geve hym good promise. And thacte of Parleamente ys not that men shuld other be examined or subscribe to the same, for it requireth no soch thinge, for it ys of authorytie it self withowt any mans subscription. Well, sayed the Deane, ye shall se that a waye wilbe founde for hym. Is Doctor Barnes come home yet? Yee mary, sayed I, he came to the cowrte apon Sondaye. Jesu mercy, sayed the Deane, And it was sayed in Bristow that he preached in London against th'acte apon oure Lady daye. And then, sayed I, he was not within Englonde. What newes hath he brought? sayed the Deane. In good fayeth I can not tell, sayed I, but he ys very sad. Did he spayeke with the kyng? sayed the Deane. No mary, sayed I, but as he showed me had lycence because of his werynes to departe vnto the Kynges nearer comyng to London, vnto the tyme he were sende for. Sende for? sayed the Deane, Na, I warrante you the kynge will not speake with him. I know not that, sayed I, but Doctor Barnes tolde me that my Lorde Privey Seale⁵ wolde have had hym taryed to have spoken with the kynge, but that he prayed lycence because of his werynesse. Forther I tolde the Deane that I cowld heare of no Commission that was owt for this last acte. Neverthelesse, sayed I, I will aduyse all my frendes to kepe them owt of daunger. And so I desyred the Deane at after supper that he wold lycence me to goo to Bristow, for I had dyvers thinges to bye for my selfe and I wold be ready to wayete upon hym in the mornyng, at which time he appoynted to take his journey towards St Dauids. And thus I wente to Bristow, where I was busye all the xx^te daye, and the xxj daye tyll it was x of the clock. For the trewth ys I was at that tyme veraye loth to ryde in the Deanes company, and therfore taryed a daye longer at Bristow, which notwithstandinge upon thursdaye being the xxj day of August, I founde the Deane at the ferry at Auste wayetinge for passage. And so as it was my fortune I joyned with hym in company, and at Chepstow we laie all that night, where as he made me hearty chere as me thought and that all malice was forgoten; So that I toke the man for whoale changed, and that all was remitted, & was veraye glad it was my chaunce to over take hym. But that daye nor night we had no communycation but myrrly. Now on the morrow, the xxij daye of August, we rodde towarde Abergevenye, which waye we had this communication, The Deane, Syr Thomas, and I; which communication, because I will bringe in faythfully and sensiblie, I haue brought it in a colloqui, because I will not trowble your Lordship with 'he sayeth, & I sayed, & Syr Thomas sayde'.

DEANE. THOMAS. GEORGE

DEANE. By Gods mercy, it ys good tydinges that ye told vs the last night that there ys no Commission owt as yet for the last acte. THOMAS. By Saynt Mary, I am glad of it, if it be true. GEORGE. I promise you I cowlde heare of none, and yet I enquired for it, Wherefore I trust there wilbe a moderation in it. DEANE. By Gods mercy it had neade so, for it ys too vnreasonable. THOMAS. I did ever thinke that mariage of Priestes shulde haue gone forwarde at this Parleament. DEANE. My Lorde of Cantorbury was ferre to blame in the matter. GEORGE. Why my Lorde of Cantorbury moare then my Lorde of St Dauids & other? DEANE. Ye speake wisely indeed; For if my Lorde of Cantorbury had sticked, there was never a man there that wold have subscribed, I dare saye. GEORGE. Well, we know not the worke of God. If it be his pleasure it ys as easy for hym to overcome with few as with many; but I thinke veryly that my Lorde Privey Seale persuaded my Lorde of Cantorbury, and that for other considerations than we do know; or els I am sure avoyding the Kynges indignation he wold not haue subscribed, which in deade he shuld in conscience rather haue aventured, if he were not in conscience therto persuaded. I praye you what hath it avayled the Bishop of Rochester to subscribe: he had as good a charter of his life as the best of them? As I can heare, my Lorde Privey Seale ys vtterly persuaded as the acte ys. DEANE. It ys marveil if it so be. GEORGE. Wonderfull are the wayes of the Lorde, Kynges heartys are in the hande of God. He turneth them as he lusteth. How mercyfully, how plentifully and purely hath God sende his worde vnto vs here in England! Agayne, how vnthankefully, how rebelliously, how carnally and vnwillingly do we receave it! Who ys ther almost that will haue a bible but he must be compelled therto? How loth be our Priestes to teach the commaundementes, th'articles of the faith, and the Pater noster in English! Agayne how vnwillinge be the people to lerne it! Yee they gest at it, callinge it the new Pater noster and new lernynge; So that as, helpe me God, if we amende not, I feare we shalbe in moare bondage and blindnes then ever we ware. I pray you was not one of the best preachers in christendome Bisshop of Worcester? And now there ys one made that never preached that I hearde, excepte it were the Popes law. But alas, beside our noughtines, cowardenes and covetousnes ys th'occasion of moch of this. The cowardnes of our Bisshops to tell trowth and stande bye it, while they might be hearde, and the covetousnes of our visitors. For in all our visitations we have had no thinge reformed but our purses. DEANE. By Gods mercy thow saiest trowth; those be two pratty sinnes, how saye ye? GEORGE. Mary cowardnesse and covetousnes; And so we came to fowle waye that the Deane and I were rydinge together, & then we fell in communication alone after this manner worde for worde, as I can call to remembrance.

DEANE. GEORGE.

DEANE. Hearest of no maryage towarde? GEORGE. I can not tell what I shuld saye; but me thinke it great pittie that the Kynge ys so longe withowt a Quene; his Grace might yet haue many fayre childern to Gods pleasure and the comforte of the realme; my father might be graundefather to an elder man than the Kynges maiestie, and yet ys lustie, I thanke God. DEANE. How old ys he? GEORGE. Mary IIJ$^{xx}$ yere olde and twelve, & yet the last sommer he roode xxxij myles apon one daye afore two a clocke, & sayed he was not wery when he had done. DEANE. But hearest any thinge of any Maryage? GEORGE. I can not tell what I shuld saye. There be two spoken of. DEANE. Yee, mary, the duches of Myllaen and one of Cleif.[6] GEORGE. That ys trew. How call ye the little Doctor that ys gone to Cleif? DEANE. Doctor Woten. GEORGE. Mary as I heare saye, he sende hym home lately, that ys with hym of the Privey Chamber, I haue forgoten his name. DEANE. Mary his name ys Berde. GEORGE. It ys Berde in deade. Now Syr this Berde ys come home and sende thider warde agayne with the kynges payntour;[7] I pray you kepe this gere secret. DEANE. Mary I warrant you. GEORGE. I maye tell you there ys good hope, yet, that all shalbe well inough if that maryage go forwarde. For the duke of Cleif doeth favour Gods worde, and ys a mighty Prince now; for he hath Gelder lande in his hande to, and that against the Emperor's will; for the olde Duke of Gelder, that ys now deed, solde to the Emperor the reversion of it, & he was ever a skowrge for the Pope when there was any thinge betwixt the Pope and the french kynge. DEANE. Mary I lyke that well that Berde ys gone agayne so shortly. GEORGE. Na surely the matter ys broken of Myllaen, for she ys in no possession of Millaen, nor hath any profit therof. DEANE. I dare saye Myllaen hath cost more good men of Warre their lyves, then are at this houre in all cristendome. GEORGE. And agayn she demaundeth two thinges, of which I trust shull never be granted the tone. DEANE. What be those? GEORGE. Mary she wold haue the kynge accepte the Bisshop of Rome's dispensation. DEANE. That ys sure they will not meddle withowt his dispensation. GEORGE. And also they wold haue pledges. DEANE. Why pledges? GEORGE. Mary she sayeth that the kynges maiestie was in so litle space rydde of the Quenes, that she dare not trust his cownceill, though she durst trust his maiestie. For her cownceill suspecteth that her great Aunte was poysoned;[8] that the second was innocentlye put to deeth;[9] And the thred lost for lacke of kepinge in her child bed.[10] In good fayth to saye the trouth, I can not tell whether this was her awnsware of Myllaen or of Cleif. I hearde a mutteringe of soch a thinge afore Whitsontyde, but because I haue no grownde of it, I am loth to speake it, but I pray you let it go no forther. Now Syr if it were th'answare of her of Cleif, surely it was a great occasion of the last acte. DEANE. By Gods mercy ye saye trowth: but heare ye no thinge of Myllaen more? GEORGE. Not a whit, but as I haue tolde you. DEANE. Ys Doctour Petre gone, can ye tell? GEORGE. He toke me by th'ande at the cowrte apon Sondaye, and asked how my Lorde fared. DEANE. Then ys that of Myllaen dashed. GEORGE. Why dashed? DEANE. For he was appoynted to be sende to her of Myllaen. GEORGE. I praye God it be dashed. For of this am I sure that it ys not possible that there can be faythfull amytie betwixt the Kynge, the Emperor, and the French kynge, so longe as the kynge receaveth not the Pope, who ys their God in erth. And alas for this last acte, how can the Germaynes be our frendes, when we conclude them heretiques in our actes of Parleamente. DEANE. Ye saye trueth, but then it ys likly that it was she of Cleif that gave this awnsware of pledges and that was th'occasion of the acte. GEORGE. I beleve the same. It ys lyke so. DEANE. Yee, by Sainte Mary, and now maye fortune they of Cleif be better advised. GEORGE. I trust so. And that maye fortune ys the stoppinge of the commissions.

Then rodde we with the company, and I showed the Deane that Erasmus Sarcerius had written against my Lorde of Winchester's boke de vera obedientia. And I showed the Deane that he wrote veraye gently. And that he named hym not, but only a 'certen Bisshop'. And the end of his boke was declaringe, quod deficere ab externa tyrannide Romani Pontificis, non erat vera defectio, sed ab ipsa doctrina Romani Pontificis, erat vere deficere. And therwith in his boke he doeth boeth recite the common places which he taketh pro ipsa doctrina, & confuteth them. And thus communyng, and other trifles, we came to Abergaveny, where we dyned, And the same night rode to Brecknock to bed, And by the waye we had this communicacyon, Syr Thomas hearing for the most parte, but he spake veraye litle or no thinge.

GEORGE. DEANE.
If there shuld be any pledges sende into Cleif, in good faith I wolde the Erle of Surraye shulde be one of them. DEANE. It ys the most folish prowde boye that ys in Englande. GEORGE. What, man, he hath a wife & a childe, & ye call hym boye? DEANE. By Gods mercy me thinke he exceadeth. GEORGE. What then? he ys wise for all that, as I heare. And as for pride, experience will correcte well inough. No merveil though a yonge man, so noble a mans sonne & heyre apparante be prowde; For we be to prowde ourselves withowt those qualities. But I wold wish that he shuld be one to be sente thider for that he shulde there be fully instructed in Gods worde and of experience. For if the Duke of Northfolke were as fully persuaded in it as he ys in the contrary, he shuld do moch good, for he ys a ernest man, a bold man and a witty, in all his matters. DEANE. It ys trew & ye saye well in that.

And then we comuned agayne of Sarcerius's boke in this manner:

DEANE. GEORGE.
I wold I might se the boke written agaynst the bisshop of Winchester. GEORGE. Mary I have it, And wold gladlyer se his awnsware, for he ys lerned, & as I thinke, the wittiest, the boldest, and the best lerned in his facultie that ys in Englonde, and a greate rethorition, but of veraye corrupte Judgement. Truly I can not beleve he will awnsware, for Erasmus ys to stronge for hym in his matter. DEANE. He hath done moch hurte I promise you. GEORGE. Na ther ys no man hath done so moch hurte in this matter as the bisshop of Durrham, for he by hys stilnes sobernes and subteltie worketh more then ten soch as Winchester, & he ys a lerned man too. And

a wonderfull thinge my Lorde Privey Seale brought hym in. DEANE. Ye saye the trowth. GEORGE. But these two Bisshops if they were as well lerned in Gods worde as they be in the Popes law, and as ernest to set the worde forth as they be traditions, they were bisshops in deade; but alas by them, and soch, we have no thinge, in a manner but translatio Imperii, so that they make of the kynge as it were a Pope. And dispensations be sold now dearer by the half then they were in the popish tyme. DEANE. By Gods mercye ye saye trewth. GEORGE. I wold not cownceill my Lorde Privey Seale to trust them to moch for all that. For I dare saye this, that they will do the best they can to have hym owte, yf they can se hym at an advantage. I wold trust them, if I cowld se one of them ones promote or set forwarde but one that ys suspected to favour Gods worde.

And thus we came to Brecknock, where we laye all night, we thre in one chamber. And there the Deane & I rehersed our comunycacyon of the maryage vnto Syr Thomas as we were in our beddes. And the Deane asked me where I had it. And I sayed of George Elyot, but the trueth ys I had it of Thomas Parnell.

Apon Setterdaye, beinge the xxiij daye of August, we rode toward Kermarddyn, And in our journey in the mornynge we communed as foloweth:

DEANE. GEORGE.
A my fayth the gere ye showed vs of the maryage ys lyckly. But I never hearde of the Quenes that they shuld be thus handled. GEORGE. In good fayth nor I; nother yet I never suspected, but I promise you there was moch mutteringe of Quene Annes deeth. DEANE. There was in deade. GEORGE. And it ys the thinge that I marked as well, as ever I marked any thinge. DEANE. Did ye so? And I can tell nothinge of it for I was at that tyme at St Dauids. GEORGE. Na, ye were in the diocese of St Assaph. For my Lorde was that tyme in Scotlonde. And I was the same tyme Mr. Norice's servante.[11] I wrote a Letter of comforth vnto hym, and that after he was condemned. I haue the copie of the same Letter in my howse. DEANE. He had not your Letter. GEORGE. Yes I delyvered it vnsealed vnto Mr Lieftenant,[12] And he delyvered it Mr Noryce. DEANE. I pray the what canst thow tell of the matter? Let vs heare. GEORGE. The first that was taken was Markys,[13] And he was at Stepneth in examinacyon on Maye even. I can not tell how he was examined, but apon Maye daye in the mornynge he was in the towre, the trewth ys he confessed it, but yet the sayeing was that he was fyrst grevously racked, which I cowlde never know of a trewth. Apon May daye Mr Noryce justed.[14] And after justinge the Kynge rode sodenly to Westminster, and all the waye as I heard saye, had Mr Noryce in examinacyon and promised hym his pardon in case he wolde utter the trewth. But what so ever cowld be sayed or done, Mr Norice wold confess no thinge to the Kynge, where vpon he was committed to the towre in the mornynge. And by the waye as his chapleyn tolde me he confessed,[15] but he sayed at his arrayning, when his owne confession was layed afore hym, that he was deceaved to do the same by the Erle of Hampton that now ys.[16] But what so ever he sayed, he

was cast. DEANE. But what can ye tell of Brerton? GEORGE. By my troeth, yf any of them was innocent, it was he. For other he was innocente or els he dyed worst of them all.[17] DEANE. How so? GEORGE. Apon thursdaye afore Maye daye in the mornynge I spake with hym abowt nyne of the clocke, And he tolde me that there was no waye but one with any matter. For I did aske hym & was bold apon hym because we were borne within foure myles together, And also we wente to grammar scole together. And the same daye afore ij of the clock was he in the towre as ferre as the best. What was layed against hym I know not nor never hearde. But at his deeth these were his wordes: I haue deserved to dye if it were a thousande deethes, But the cause wherfore I dye judge not: But yf ye judge, judge the best. This he spake iij or foure tymes. If he were gyltie, I saye therfore that he dyed worst of them all. DEANE. Why, how dyed the others? GEORGE. Mary in a manner confessed all but Mr Norice, who sayed allmost nothinge at all. DEANE. How do ye know it? GEORGE. Mary I hearde them, and wrote every worde that they spake. DEANE. What sayed the others? GEORGE. The lorde of Ratchforde, after many wordes, to the effecte sayed this. I desyre you that no man wilbe discoraged from the Gospell for my fall. For if I had lyved accordinge to the gospel as I loved it, and spake of it, I had never come to this. Wherfore sayed he Syrs for Gods love, leave not the gospel, but speake lesse and lyve better. For I had rather have one good lyver accordinge to the gospel then ten bablers. And Weston sayed; I had thought to haue lyved in abhominacion yet this twenty or thrittie yeres & then to haue made amendes. I thought little it wold haue come to this: willinge all other to take example at hym. And Markes sayed: Masters I pray you all praye for me, for I haue deserved the deeth. And the Quene sayed: I do not entende to reason my cause, but I committe me to Christ wholy, in whome ys my whole trust, desirynge you all to praye for the Kynges maiestie that he maye longe regne over you, for he ys a veraye noble prince and full gently hath handled me. DEANE. Know ye any thinge of the examinacyon of her? GEORGE. Her brother and she were examined at the towre. I hearde saye he had escaped had it not byn for a Letter. Almost all the lordes that were in the realme were there. And the duke of Northfolke, vncle to them both, he was, as it was told me, in the Kynges place and Judge. It were pittie he shuld be alyve if he shuld judge then against right. DEANE. A marvelouse case, and a great fall. GEORGE. So it was. Now Syr, because that she was a favorer of Gods worde, at the leest wise so taken, I tell you few men wolde beleve that she was so abhominable. As I be saved afore God I cowld not beleve it, afore I hearde them speake at their deeth. For there were that sayed that moch money wold haue byn layed that daye, & that great oddes, that the Lorde Ratchforde shulde haue byn quytte.[18] DEANE. I never hearde so moch before, as that the Duke of Northfolke was judge. GEORGE. So I hearde saye, And that the water ronne in his eyes.[19] I blame hym not though it greved hym.

We had also comunicacyon of the boke made agenst Luther in the Kynges name.

DEANE. GEORGE.

The Kyngs grace ys marvelously well lerned. GEORGE. He ys surely well lerned, and of a great witte, or els he cowld not haue brought matters to passe as he hath done. And besyde he hath a great grace of gentlenesse which ys moch to be commended in a prince. DEANE. He ys exceadinge well lerned, for he wrote a boke agenst Luther, a great while agoo. GEORGE. By my trowth, I thinke it was no more his graces makynge then yours. DEANE. I ever thought It had been his. GEORGE. It ys not possible. For it ys abowte xviij yeres agoo sence that boke was written. And that tyme the kynge was more geven to yowth and lesse to his boke then his grace ys now. DEAN. Is not the Kynge lerned? GEORGE. I thinke he ys best lerned of any prince in Christendome, but I take hym not to be so well lerned. For that boke ys made of men of great studye & sayeth as moch in matters it entreateth as maye be sayed. DEANE. Who made it then? GEORGE. Mary they that be lerned thinke it was the doinge of the Bisshop of Yorke that now ys, & Mr More. And that the Cardinals policie was to have it put forth in the Kynges name, therby thinkynge to make the kynge and the bisshop of Rome joyned for ever. DEANE. And I beleved ever that he had byn exceadingly well lerned. GEORGE. So he ys I saye for a prince. But ever take hede to this. The worlde ever flatters them that be in authoritie. And what so ever they saye or do ys clerkly, wisely, and exceadingly well done, and sayed. Solomon hath soch a sayenge as I remember: Loquutus est dives et stulte, et omnes applaudent illi: loquutus est pauper et sapienter, et derident illum. DEANE. That ys a pratty sayenge. How do you know that the Kynge ys not so well lerned? GEORGE. Mary his maiestie reasoned with me hymselfe almost nyne yeres agoo. And beside that it ys not possible he shuld be so well lerned, a Kynge hauynge soch busynesse & so great entysementes to pleasures. Lernynge requireth almost, yea all together, an whole man. DEANE. What ys the Kynge now lustie? GEORGE. His grace was lustie, but it greved me at the hearte to se his grace halte so moch apon his sore legge. By my trowth, if I myght speake with his grace so that I had hope he wolde heare me I wolde move hym to kepe the diate of Gwaiacum, I durst aventure my lyfe It wolde heale hym. DEANE. But ye durst not. GEORGE. By God but I durst. What made it any matter for my lyfe or twentye thousande soch for the preservacion of his lyfe? DEANE. Ye shuld have tolde Doctour Buttes so. GEORGE. I did not remember it when I spake with hym, And I know well inough that it ys a thinge the phisicions will not medle with. For none of the olde autours write of it. And it ys in a maner agenst the common rules of phisick. But it were a small thinge for the preservacyon of his Grace if one were loked owt of the Kynges complexion and that had a sore legge & so to prove it. Now then if it wolde heale hym, why shuld it not heale the Kynge as well? It healeth the pockes, the gowte, the spue, the colyck, yee any ulceracyon that ys curable. And the lepre if it be but new begonne. And it healeth the rote so that it shall not lightly breake owt agayne. It healeth some in fourtene dayes, some in a month. I never knew any that was curable but it cured hym in vj wekes. If he kept it well. And it were not moch for the Kynge for his owne health & to preserve hym longe healthy to the realme for to take payne for so longe. DEANE. Ye saye trowth. But where lerned ye it? It ys a gaye thinge. GEORGE. Mary I was a surgyon in Brabant a whoale yere and haue occupied it. And besyde that I haue knowen dyvers in Englande healed with it. And in good fayth, seinge that conjugium sacerdotum ys concluded agenst Gods worde, I entende to study the same facultie agayne. I will loke over myne olde bokes. I am glad that I haue them yet.

Thus comunynge we came to Llangadoc to dyner, where we dyned ffrendly together. Where ys also one Mr Thomas Jones, a servante of the Kynges, and a great Ruler in that contrey. At after dyner withowt comunicacyon of any matters but husbandre and howsholdinge, we rodde to Kermarddyn.[20] And there we supped and laye all night, And in the morninge apon Sondaye, beinge the xxiiij[th] daye of August, we rode to Slebech together, two myles by yonde my howse, And dyned there at Roger Barlowes with great kyndnesse as I toke it. And thence I toke my leave of the Deane to my wife, apon condicyon that I wold come that waye in the mornynge towarde Saynte Dauids. And so I did. And the Deane layed no thinge to my charge all this tyme, nor his brother Syr Thomas nor any other man. No nor when he came to Sainte Dauids hym selfe apon twesdaye he layed no thinge agenst me. But apon Wensdaye the xxvij[th] daye of August then he began to accuse me. Now of what mynde the Deane doeth accuse me I trust your lordship doeth perceaue, in that ye haue knowen his malyce towarde me longe. And forther your lordship maye perceave in case it please the same to aske Master Syr Richarde Crumwell, who moved hym to write two letters vnto my Lorde my Master agenst me. Also the Duke of Northfolke his grace can shew who moved hym to speake to my lorde my Master agenst me. The Deane forther hath sklandered me for a Sacramentary, which ys, yf any thinge can be worse, more heynous then treason. It greved me, I take God to recorde, more then my person to heare your Lordship so greatly note me of heresye. The Deane and his brethren Syr Thomas Barlow & Roger Barlow haue contynually geven me good reporte, And I am sure haue holpen well to that note. I am in prison if they can fynde that ever I medled in any matters but these: Justificacyon and by lyvinge faith: Pilgremage: Invocacyon of Saintes: Worshippinge of Images: cownterfayted religions: trustinge to ceremonies & abuse of them: Ignorante and superstitious prayeinge: superstitious fastes & conjugium sacerdotum, Of the which I never reasoned sence the acte. And I refuse all favour. But Mr Dean ys a man, that can make of a pece a whole tale, and if he haue a man downe he can invente as hym lusteth. I haue faythfully written our comunicacyon wherin my conscience accuseth me of no treason. If the Dean and his brother other wise leven it, I pray God forgeve them: for in good faith I thanke God I haue forgeven them in my hearte or[21] I came owt of your lordships chamber. But I praye God kepe all symple honest heartes owt of their company. They maye agree at their pleasure, for comynge from Wales they laye every night together, And spende most parte of their journey in repeting their lessons with addicyons & detractions at their pleasure. Which if it will so be taken, or without justice maye so be taken, I can not saye but with Susan: Angustiae sunt mihi vndique. For with the note of a traytor I desyre not to lyve, no not though

I myght, I thank God. Nor my hearte, God knoweth, never wisshed the kynges majestie nor any of his honorable cownceill but prosperous honour and myndes to know God, to love God, and to feare God. I trust what so ever come of me, I shall beare this testimonie afore his eyes from whom ys no thinge hydde, not the secretes of the hearte. To whom be all honour & glorie for ever Amen.

# 7

# The Fall of Anne Boleyn, May 1536

*On the very day of Catherine's funeral, Anne suffered another miscarriage, losing a son. This was damaging for the Queen, but there was no indication that Henry intended to end his marriage, in spite of his anger. Anne was in a vulnerable position in the early months of 1536 as the death of Catherine of Aragon was, in fact, damaging for her. While Catherine lived, Henry knew that he would be expected to return to her if he abandoned Anne. With her death, he was free to choose a third wife if he wished, providing that he could rid himself effectively of Anne. As late as April 1536, Henry insisted on the Imperial ambassador, Eustace Chapuys, recognising Anne as queen for the first time. However, Anne's enemies were already moving against her. Events came to a head on 1 May 1536 when Henry rose abruptly from watching the May Day jousts and rode with only a small company to Westminster, leaving a perplexed Anne at Greenwich.*

## The Despatches of Eustace Chapuys Relating to the Fall of Anne Boleyn[1]

*Far from being an impartial observer, Chapuys played a decisive role in the fall of Anne Boleyn. As his despatches set out, when he learned that Anne had quarrelled with Thomas Cromwell, he set out to attempt to bring the minister into the plot against Anne. It was Chapuys who also secured Princess Mary's support for Jane Seymour in her attempts to supplant Anne Boleyn.*

*In working to bring about Anne's fall, Chapuys exceeded the orders that he had received from Charles V. With Catherine of Aragon's death in January 1536, Charles was prepared to make peace with Henry, even if the price of this was the recognition of Anne Boleyn. In his despatches, Chapuys makes little of his meeting with Anne at Easter, but it was significant. By giving reverence to her, Chapuys effectively confirmed that Charles recognised her as queen. This was Anne's final triumph. Within a few short weeks she was dead.*

*29 January 1536*
... The Princess's governess having lately informed her niece, the Royal mistress,[2] that the former disregarded entirely the offers made to her in her name, and would rather suffer a hundred deaths than change her opinion,

or do anything against her honor and conscience, the concubine addressed a letter, or rather defamatory libel, to the governess, at which the Princess has been laughing ever since ...[3]

I heard some days ago from various quarters, though I must say none sufficiently reliable, that the King's concubine, though she showed great joy at the news of the good Queen's death, and gave a good present to the messenger who brought her the intelligence, had, nevertheless, cried and lamented, herself on the occasion, fearing lest she herself might be brought to the same end as her. And this very morning, some one coming from the lady mentioned in my letter of the 21st of November ultimo, and also from her husband, has stated that both had heard from the lips of one of the principal courtiers that this King had said to one of them in great secrecy, and as if in confession, that he had been seduced and forced into this second marriage by means of sortileges and charms, and that, owing to that, he held it as null. God (he said) had well shown his displeasure at it by denying him male children. He, therefore, considered that he could take a third wife, which he said he wished much to do.

I must say that this intelligence, though coming from sufficiently authentic quarters, seems to me almost incredible. I will consider what appearance or sign of truth there may be in the report, and look out for the means of letting the governess – who, as I said before, is the concubine's aunt – have a hint of it through a third person, that she may take in future better care of the Princess, and treat her well. My intermediary agent on this occasion has been instructed by me to treat the said governess in the most friendly terms possible, and assure her that, should the Princess recover her state, she will experience no displeasure at her hands, but, on the contrary, shall be favoured and rewarded. This much have I thought of promising her in the Princess's name in order to guard against possible events.

Both the physician and apothecary of the late Queen (as I lately informed Your Majesty) have been to visit the Princess who, thanks to God, is now in good health. They have spent two days at the house, not that she herself required their attendance and advice, but because she wanted, as I informed Your Majesty, to hear from them the particulars of the illness and death of the Queen, her mother. It is, however, a wonder to me that the King, after giving the said physician and apothecary permission, at my request, to go to — and visit the Princess, should have scarcely allowed them to speak to her in private, no more than my own servants, who went thither at the same time. Not one of them has had permission to see the Princess in her apartments, and yet she seems to be taking good revenge on her guardians just now, for she hardly ceases writing to me, having now greater opportunity than ever she had, inasmuch as on account of her mourning she remains mostly in her rooms alone ...

*17 February 1536*
... On that very day the good queen of England's burial took place, which was attended by four bishops and as many abbots, besides the ladies mentioned in my preceding despatches. No other person of rank or name was present

except the comptroller of the Royal household. The place where she lies in the cathedral church [of Peterborough] is a good way from the high altar, and in a less honourable position than that of several bishops buried in the same church. Had she not been a dowager Princess, as they have held her both in life and death, but simply a baroness, they could not have chosen a less distinguished place of rest for her, as the people who understand this sort of thing tell me. Such have been the wonderful display and incredible magnificence which these people gave me to understand would be lavished in honour and memory of one whose great virtues and royal relationship certainly entitled her to uncommon honours!! Perhaps one of these days they will repair their fault, and erect a suitable monument or institute some pious foundation to her memory in some suitable spot or other.

On the same day that the Queen was buried this King's concubine miscarried of a child, who had the appearance of a male about three months and a half old, at which miscarriage the King has certainly shown great disappointment and sorrow. The concubine herself has since attempted to throw all the blame on the duke of Norfolk, whom she hates, pretending that her mishap was entirely owing to the shock she received when, six days before, he (the Duke) came to announce to her the King's fall from his horse. But the King knows very well that it was not that, for his accident was announced to her in a manner not to create alarm; besides which, when she heard of it, she seemed quite indifferent to it. Upon the whole, the general opinion is that the concubine's miscarriage was entirely owing to defective constitution, and her utter inability to bear male children; whilst others imagine that the fear of the King treating her as he treated his late Queen, – which is not unlikely, considering his behaviour towards a damsel of the Court, named Miss Seymour, to whom he has latterly made very valuable presents – is the real cause of it all. The Princess's governess, her daughters, and a niece of hers, have greatly mourned over the concubines miscarriage, never ceasing to interrogate one of the Princess's most familiar maids in waiting on the subject, and asking whether their mistress had been informed of Anne's miscarriage, for if she had, as was most likely, they still would not for the world that she knew the rest of the affair and its causes, thereby intending to say that there was fear of the King's taking another wife.

The Princess, thanks to God, is doing well. She changed her lodgings last Saturday, and on her journey to her new residence was better attended and provided with money and every necessary than she has been for a long time past. That came very apropos, for she was thus enabled to distribute alms on the road, the King, her father, having sent her one hundred crs. or thereabouts to expend as she pleased. There is a rumour, as Master Cromwell sent me word immediately after the Queen's demise, that the King intends increasing the Princess's household and estate. May it be so, and may God, forbid that there should be a snake in the grass, or any other danger to her. It seems to me as if the King had only been waiting for his mistress' confinement. Had she been delivered of a son, as both were almost sure would be the case, he would, certainly have summoned, the Princess to swear to the statutes. I do not know what he may do now. I have warned the Princess to consider whether, in case of her being much pressed to take the oath and thereby reduced to extremities, it would not be expedient for her to offer, the very moment the King, her father, had a son, to accede to his wishes, and in the meanwhile begin from this day to flatter and, make herself agreeable to the governess. As soon as I get an answer to my message I shall not fail to apprize Your Majesty ...

### 24 *February* 1536

... Some courtiers tell me that for the three last months this King has not spoken ten times to his concubine, and that when the news of her miscarriage was brought to him, he only observed, 'I see that God will not give me male children;' and that, having gone to visit her, on leaving her room he added by way of farewell, with much ill grace, 'When you are up I will come and speak to you.' It seems that the concubine has assigned two causes for her miscarriage; one is the King's fall from his horse some time before; the other the love she bears him, which she says is greater and more vehement than that of the late Queen, so much so that whenever she hears of his loving another woman but her, she is broken-hearted. The King, however, has been much disappointed as well as hurt at Anne's excuses at least he has all the appearance of being much discontented with her, for during these last days of festival and rejoicing he has remained in London, leaving Anne at Greenwich, whereas in former times he could hardly be one hour without her ...

Just at this moment I am in receipt of a message from the Princess to say that after leaving me Cromwell had, by the King's command and in his name, sent for a cross which the Queen, her mother, had bequeathed to her. I fancy that the cross is not set with precious stones, and that the gold of it is not worth 10 crs., but that there is inside a piece of the true cross, – an object of great devotion and consolation to the Princess. By which act Your Majesty may well calculate what faith and reliance can be placed in these people's words. I apprehend that God will never grant them His grace that they may acknowledge their error, and avoid the punishment of their execrable crimes and misdeeds.

### 1 *April* 1536

... The other day, as the young marquis [of Dorset], the dowager countess of Childra (Kildare), Monsieur de Montague, and several others, were dining with me at this embassy, the last-named Lord, after complaining of the bad state of affairs in this country, went on to say that this King's mistress and Secretary Cromwell were on bad terms just now, and that there had been a talk of a new marriage for this King. Which rumour agrees well with my own news from the court of France, where, according to letters I have received, courtiers maintain that this king has actually applied, for the hand of Francis' daughter. Hearing this, and for the purpose of procuring information, and, if possible, learning what truth there was in the report, I called on Cromwell, and told him that I had purposely avoided visiting him many a time for fear of arousing his Royal mistress' suspicions, owing to the reasons he himself had explained to me. I recollected very well his telling me that she (Anne Boleyn) would like to see his head off his shoulders. Such a threat, I said, was constantly before my eyes, causing me great care and anxiety, and I sincerely wished him a more gracious mistress than she was, one more grateful for the immense services he (Cromwell) had rendered the King. He ought to take care not to offend or over-irritate her, or else he must renounce all hope of that perfect reconciliation we both were trying to bring about. I therefore begged and entreated him, in such an event, to guard against her attacks more effectually than the cardinal (Wolsey) had done, which I hoped his dexterity and prudence would be able to accomplish. If it were true, as I had been told, that the King, his master, was now thinking of a fresh marriage, that would, no doubt, be the way of preserving him (Cromwell) from many inconveniences, and likewise the best thing for the King to do, disappointed, as he had hitherto been, of male issue. Whatever might be said or preached on that score from the pulpit, the King knew very well that his marriage to Anne could never be held as valid, for many reasons, which I left to his consideration; and although from another marriage, more legitimate than his last, the King might possibly have male issue, which would eventually turn out to the Princess's prejudice, yet the love and affection I bore the King, and him in particular, as well as my earnest desire for the peace, honour, and prosperity of England, made me wish that he (Cromwell) should have another royal mistress, not out of hatred of Anne Boleyn, for she had never done me any harm, but for his own sake.

Cromwell seemed to take my words in good part, and thanked me for the affection I professed to him, &c., saying that he was well aware of the precarious nature of human affairs, to say nothing of those appertaining to royal courts; he had for a long time back known this, having had continually before his eyes several examples of it of a domestic nature. He had, however, admitted to himself that the day might come when fate would strike him as it had struck his predecessors in office: then he would arm himself with patience and place himself for the rest in the hands of God. True, it was, as I had hinted to him, that he would have to implore God's help if he wished to escape from dangers and inconveniences of that sort; and that he did, and he would, besides, do his utmost to avoid danger. After that Cromwell began to excuse himself for having promoted the King's marriage [to Anne]. True, it was (he said), that seeing the King so much bent upon it, and so determined, he (Cromwell) had paved the way towards it. Although the King, his master, was still inclined to pay his court to ladies, yet it was generally believed that in future he would lead a more moral life than hitherto – a chaste and marital one with his present Queen. This Cromwell said to me in such a cold indifferent manner that I had a strong suspicion that he meant just the contrary. Indeed, I observed whilst he said so, that not knowing what mien to put on, he leant against the window close to which we were both standing, and put his hand to his mouth to prevent the smile on his lips, or to conceal it altogether from me should it come on; adding, shortly after: 'of one thing, however, you may be sure, namely, that should the King, my master, want another wife, it is certainly not among the French that he will look for one'.

After which he said that upon the arrival of Your Majesty's answer to the overtures that had been made to me, we would treat of all those matters, and come to an understanding upon the whole. At last, when I was about to depart, he said that although I had once refused to accept a horse, which he wanted to present to me, now I could not, without suspicion of anger or ill-will on my part, decline the gift of one which the earl of Sussex had presented to him the day before; and I must add that, whatever my excuses, I was literally obliged to accept the present ...

[*following his interview with Cromwell*] I receive a message from the marchioness [of Dorset], confirming the information I once had from Master Geliot, namely, that some days ago, the King being here in London, and, the young Miss Seymour, to whom he is paying court at Greenwich, he sent her a purse full of sovereigns, together with a letter, and that the young damsel, to whom he is paying court, after respectfully kissing the letter, returned it to the messenger without opening it, and then falling on her knees, begged the royal messenger to entreat the King in her name to consider that she was a well-born damsel, the daughter of good and honourable parents without blame or reproach of any kind; there was no treasure in this world that she valued as much as her honour, and on no account would she lose it, even if she were to die a thousand deaths. That if the King wished to make her a present of money, she requested him to reserve it for such a time as God would be pleased to send her some advantageous marriage.

The marchioness also sent me word that in consequence of this refusal the King's love for the said damsel had marvellously increased, and that he had said to her that not only did he praise and commend her virtuous behaviour on the occasion, but that in order to prove the sincerity of his love, and the honesty of his views towards her, he had resolved not to converse with her in future, except in the presence of one of her relatives, and that for this reason the King had taken away from Master Cromwell's apartments in the palace a room, to which he can, when he likes, have access through certain galleries without being seen, of which room the young lady's elder brother and his wife have already taken possession for the express purpose of her repairing thither. But I hear that the young lady has been well tutored and warned by those among this King's courtiers who hate the concubine, telling her not in any wise to give in to the King's fancy unless he makes her his Queen, upon which the damsel is quite resolved. She has likewise been advised to tell the King frankly, and without reserve, how much his subjects abominate the marriage contracted with the concubine, and that not one considers it legitimate, and that this declaration ought to be made in the presence of witnesses of the titled nobility of this kingdom, who are to attest the truth of her statements should the King request them on their oath and fealty to do so. The marchioness wishes that I or some one else, on Your Majesty's part, would take this affair in hand, and certainly, if my opinion on such a point is needed, I do not hesitate to say that whoever could help in its execution would do a meritorious work, as it would prove a further security for the person of the Princess, a remedy for the heretical doctrines and practices of the concubine – the principal cause of the spread of Lutheranism in this country – as well as be the means of clearing the King from the taint of a most abominable and adulterous marriage. The Princess herself would be glad of this, even if she were eventually deprived of her rights to the English crown by the birth of male children. I shall again inform her to-day of what is going on, and, with her advice, will act in such a manner that if we cannot gain, at least we shall lose nothing by the event.

*21 April 1536*
*Written after Chapuys received instructions from the Emperor ordering him to come to terms with Henry VIII, even if it meant acknowledging his marriage to Anne Boleyn.*

The night of the day on which Your Majesty's letter of the 28th came to hand, was entirely spent in deciphering its contents, which being done, on Easter Day, after dinner, I went to call on Master Cromwell at a very fine house, which the King has presented him with, completely furnished, three leagues from this city. Before communicating the news received from Your Majesty, or showing the letters I had for him, I reminded him of our frequent conversations with respect to mutual friendship and amity, and especially of our conference on the eve of St Mathias. Finding him as firm and constant as ever in his purpose, and as determined to bring the negotiation to an issue; hearing from his own lips, and without any allusion on my part, that his indignation at French behaviour had lately increased, I did not hesitate to hand over to him Your Majesty's letter, which he kissed and received most reverently, assuring me over and over again that he really knew not how to acknowledge the immense favour and honour you did him by deigning to write to such an insignificant person as he was ...

[Following *a longer interview with Cromwell*] I was hardly in the saddle to return home than Cromwell sent one of his clerks to inform the King in all haste that I was the bearer of wonderfully pleasing news. Next day, which was Easter Monday, Cromwell himself went to Court, before the King's levee, and in the afternoon of that day sent me word that he had shown Your Majesty's letter to the King, and literally recited all our conversation. The King had heard the account with pleasure, and desired that I should appear at Court on the following Tuesday, at about 10 o'clock in the morning, where I should be welcome, and get such an answer as would greatly please me ...

At Court I had from the Privy Councillors and other lords such a cordial and honourable reception that nothing better could be wished for, all and every one of them coming up to congratulate one upon the prosperous news just received, praising, above all things, the good offices which they presumed I had rendered, for the accomplishment of so desirable a work. The concubine's brother, lord Rochefort, among the rest, signalised himself most particularly by his hearty congratulations. I could not help hinting to him that I had no doubt he was as much pleased as any other of the King's courtiers at the favorable prospect of affairs, and believed he would co-operate as well as the rest to ensure the success of one which could not fail to be beneficial to the community at large, and especially to himself and family. Rochefort seemed particularly pleased at this hint of mine, and I myself dissembled as much as I could, avoiding all occasion of entering into conversation with him or discussing his Lutheran principles, of which he is so proud that he cannot abstain from boasting of them in public.

Before the King left his apartments to go to Chapel and hear mass, Cromwell came to me, and asked in the King's name whether I did not wish to visit the concubine in her rooms, and kiss her hand; the King would be particularly pleased by my doing so, yet if I had the least objection, he referred entirely to my will. My answer was that for a long time back I had professed to be the King's slave, and had no other wish than to execute his commands; but that it seemed to me that for many reasons, which I would tell the King himself the very first time I had an audience from him, my visit to the lady under present circumstances would be highly inconvenient. I begged Cromwell to make my excuses, as though from himself and try to dissuade the King therefrom, as, in my opinion, it could only be detrimental to the negociation in hand. Cromwell went away, and soon after returned, saying that the King had taken my excuses in good part, and hoped that very shortly all matters would be speedily settled to the satisfaction of the parties. He then said to me that after dinner I could speak with the King at leisure, and that on leaving him, I should, according to custom, go into the Council room, and explain my charge. I replied that it seemed to me as if the matters under discussion were so honest and reasonable, and had been so long ago anticipated, that the King might take at once a resolution upon them; or else he (Cromwell), to whom Your Majesty's credentials had been addressed, could report to the Council much better than I myself could. I added that until I had heard what the King's intentions and will were respecting the whole or part of the proposed negociation I strongly objected to appear before the Privy Council, though I purposed addressing each of them in particular, and doing anything else they might advise.

Soon after this I saw the King pass; he made me a most gracious bow, holding his cap in his hand, and not allowing me to remain longer uncovered. He asked me how I was, and how I had passed my time since the last time he had seen me. He added that I was welcome, asked for news of Your Majesty, and seemed delighted to hear you were in good health. After that he asked where Your Majesty was, and on my answering that the courier stated that at his departure from Rome he had left you close to that city, he replied that to judge from the date of Your Majesty's letter to his secretary it would appear that on the departure of the courier from Rome you were at Gaeta. He then asked me whether Your Majesty intended making a long stay at Rome, and on my answering that I did not think so, unless thereby you could be of use to him and do his pleasure – sure as I was that for such a purpose and end Your Majesty would have no difficulty in making a longer stay, or doing other things for his honour and for love of him – he smiled and made another bow. He then said that he imagined it would have been far better for Your Majesty's plans and interests not to have gone so soon to Rome, but to have remained longer in the kingdom of Naples, in order to throw the bait to those who wanted it, and catch them more securely within your nets. My answer was that there was still plenty of time left for dissimulation, thereby meaning that I was sure Your Majesty in this, as well as in other matters, would act conformably with his advice, as that of his oldest friend, brother, and almost father, as he would gather by what I should have the honour to tell him more at leisure. 'Certainly' replied the King, 'We will talk of that and other matters.' I was conducted to the Chapel by lord Rochefort, the concubine's brother, and when the offering came a great many people flocked round the King, out of curiosity, and wishing no doubt to know what sort of a mien the concubine and I should put on; yet I must say that she was affable and, courteous enough on the occasion, for on my being placed behind the door by which she entered the chapel, she turned round to return the reverence which I made her when she passed.[4]

After mass the King went to dine with the concubine in her apartments, all the courtiers accompanying him except myself who was conducted by lord Rochefort to the Royal presence chamber, where I dined with the principal courtiers. As I afterwards learned from a distinguished officer of the Royal household, who was there present, the concubine asked the King during dinner why I had not come as the other ambassadors had done, and that the King had answered that there were good reasons for it. Nevertheless, another courtier affirms that he heard the concubine say to the King after dinner, that it was a great shame for the king of France to treat his own uncle, the duke of Savoy, as he was doing, and make preparations for the invasion of Milan for no other purpose, as she said, than to prevent and mar the enterprise against the Turk, and that it seemed as if the Most Christian, weary of life owing to his sufferings and bad health, wished to put an end to his days as soon as possible ...

*29 April 1536*
... The Grand Esquire, Master Caro (Sir Nicholas Carew), was on St George's Day invested with the Order of the Garter, in the room of Mr. De Bourgain, who died some time ago. This has been a source of great disappointment and sorrow for lord Rochefort, who wanted it for himself, and still more for the concubine, who has not had sufficient credit to get her own brother knighted. In fact, it will not be Carew's fault if the aforesaid concubine, though a cousin of his, is not overthrown one of these days, for I hear that he is daily conspiring against her, and trying to persuade Miss Seymour and her friends to accomplish her ruin. Indeed, only four days ago the said Carew and certain gentlemen of the King's chamber sent word to the Princess to take courage, for very shortly her rival would be dismissed, the King being so tired of the said concubine that he could not bear her any longer. Besides which, Montagu's brother said to me yesterday, at dinner, that the day before the bishop of London had been questioned [by some courtier] as to whether the King could or could not abandon the said concubine, and that the bishop had refused to give an opinion on the subject unless the King himself asked him for it. Even then he would, before he answered, try and ascertain what the King's intentions were, thereby implying, no doubt, that the King in his opinion could certainly desert his concubine; but that

knowing well the King's fickleness, he would not run the risk of offending her by proffering such advice. The bishop was once, it must be observed, the principal cause and instrument of this King's first divorce; he now repents of it, and would willingly be the abettor of a second one, were it for no other reason than the well-known fact of the said concubine and all her race being most abominable and rank Lutherans.

### 2 May 1536

Your Majesty recollects no doubt what I wrote at the beginning of last month, in reference to my conversation with Master Cromwell on this king's divorce from his concubine. Having since heard the Princess's opinion and pleasure on this particular matter, which is that I should watch the proceedings, and if possible help to accomplish the said divorce, were it for no other purpose than for the King's honour and the relief of his conscience, as she (the Princess) did not care a straw (said the message) whether the King, her father, had or had not from a new and legitimate marriage male children who might take away from her the succession to the Crown. Nor did she wish for the King's divorce out of revenge for the many injuries inflicted on her mother, the late Queen, and on herself. Those she had willingly forgiven and forgotten for the honour of God, and she now bore no ill-will to any one whomsoever.

In consequence of this message from the Princess, I have since employed various means for the accomplishment of the said affair, sometimes talking about it to Master Cromwell, and to such others as seemed to me most fit for the purpose. I have not written sooner to Your Majesty on this particular subject, because I was naturally waiting for the issue of the affair one way or other; but it has since come to a head much sooner and more satisfactorily than one could have thought, to the greater ignominy and shame of the lady herself, who has actually been brought from Greenwich to this city under the escort of the duke of Norfolk, and of the two chamberlains – that of the Kingdom, and that of the Royal Chamber – and allowed only four maid-servants in attendance. The reason for all this, as the rumour goes, is, that she has for a length of time lived in adultery with a spinet-player of her chamber, who has this very morning been confined to the Tower, as well as Mr Norris, this king's principal and most favoured groom-in-waiting, for not having revealed what he knew of the said adulterous connexion. Rochefort, the brother, was likewise sent to the Tower six hours before. I hear, moreover, from certain authentic quarters, that before the discovery of the lady's criminal connexion, the King had already resolved to abandon her, for there were many witnesses ready to testify and to prove that more than nine years ago a marriage had been contracted and consummated between the said Anne Boleyn and the earl of Nortambellan (Northumberland), and that the King would have declared himself much sooner, had not one of his Privy Councillors hinted that he could not divorce himself from Anne without tacitly acknowledging the validity of his first marriage, and thus falling under the authority of the Pope, whom he fears.

The above is certainly a most astounding piece of intelligence, and yet if we consider the sudden change from yesterday to this day, and the King's sudden departure from Greenwich to come here, there must still be a great cause for wonder. Not to delay, however, the departure of the express bearer of this my despatch – from whose lips Your Majesty may learn the details of the affair – I will abstain from further particulars. Such are its greatness and importance under present circumstances that I considered it my duty to despatch the express messenger at once without waiting for the catastrophe. Should this be such as to warrant my despatching another messenger, I shall not fail to do so ...

*18 May 1536 [addressed to de Granvelle]*
I could not, if I wished, write to you more news of this country than those contained in my despatch to the Emperor. I hope, however, to be able to make up for the shortness of this letter by sending you in my next the faithful account and true chronicle of the mien and language which the English Messalina, or Agrippina,[5] held during her imprisonment, in which account you will, no doubt, find very remarkable things, as the lady under whose custody and keeping she was has not concealed a single thing from me.

From the very beginning of her incarceration the lady I allude to sent to communicate to me certain facts concerning the Messalina, apart, among others, that she heard her say that she could not imagine who could have made her lose the King's favour and love save me, for she pretends that from the very moment of my arrival at this court, the King no longer looked upon her with the same eyes as before. I confess that I was rather flattered by the compliment, and consider myself very lucky at having escaped her vengeance; for kind-hearted and merciful as she is, she would without remorse have cast me to the dogs. Two other English gentlemen have been imprisoned along with her, and it is suspected that a good many more will share the same fate; for the King has been heard to say that he believes that upwards of 100 gentlemen have had criminal connexion with her. You never saw a prince or husband show or wear his horns more patiently and lightly than this one does.[6] I leave you to guess the cause of it.

Owing to my last illness, and also because I am waiting for the *extremum actum fabulæ*, and presume that George, the courier, must have told you my prognostications with regard to the Messalina's fate, I will not write more for the present. — London, 18 May 1536.

I have just heard that yesterday, the 18th, the archbishop of Canterbury (Cranmer) declared and pronounced by way of sentence the lady's daughter (Elizabeth) to be a bastard, and begotten by master Norris, not by the King, which is equivalent to remove a cog from the Princess's eyes. I hope, therefore, that whatever difficulties the King may have hitherto made to have her declared true heir to the kingdom will now be removed, and that he will now have her declared and sworn to as such, and as his legitimate daughter born of a marriage legitimated *propter bonam fidem parentum*.[7] I have also been informed that the said archbishop of Canterbury had pronounced the marriage of the King and of his mistress to have been unlawful and null in consequence of the King himself having had connexion with Anne's sister, and that both he and she being aware and well acquainted with such an impediment, the good faith of the parents could not possibly legitimize the daughter.

Though what I am about to say on this subject may have no sufficient foundation, yet I feel bound to inform you that many people here imagine that most of the newly-created bishops will soon have their desert; for there is a report that, by persuading the King's mistress that there was no necessity for the confession [of her sins], they have encouraged her and made her more audacious and licentious in the prosecution of her detestable and abominable vices; and what is still more blameable on the part of the said bishops, they have taught her that, according to their sect, it was allowable for a woman to ask for aid and help in other quarters, even among her own relatives, whenever the husband was not considered idoneous[8] or sufficiently able to satisfy her wishes.

Before her marriage to the King, and in order to enhance the love she bore him, the Royal concubine used to say that there existed a prophecy that about this time a queen of England was to be burnt alive; but that, to please the King, she cared not if she was that queen. After the marriage she often said in jest that part of the prophecies had already been fulfilled, and yet she had not been condemned to death by fire. One could very well repeat to her what was once said to Caesar: *Venere idus, sed nondum prœterire*, the days have commenced, but have not yet ended.

I have not the least doubt that if His Majesty intends to treat and come to some sort of arrangement with these people, some personage of authority and rank ought now to be sent, and if he could but come before the closing of this Parliament, the affairs of the Princess and other matters might be satisfactorily adjusted. Should the said personage come before St John's Day, he might assist, as I believe, at the King's approaching marriage and the coronation of the new queen, which is to be celebrated with great solemnity and pomp, the King intending, as I am told, to perform wonders, for he has already ordered a large ship to be built, like the Bucentaur of Venice, to bring the lady from Greenwich to this city, and commanded other things for the occasion.

### 19 May 1536

... I cannot well describe the great joy the inhabitants of this city have lately experienced and manifested, not only at the fall and ruin of the concubine, but at the hope that the Princess will be soon reinstated in her rights. I must say, however, that as yet the King has shown no intention of bringing about the said reinstatement, but has on the contrary obstinately refused to contemplate it, on the two different occasions that his Privy Council has spoken about it. I hear, nevertheless, from many authentic quarters, that even before the arrest of the concubine, and when speaking to mistress Jane Seymour about their future marriage, the lady proposed to him to replace the Princess in her former position; and on the King telling her that she must be out of her senses to think of such a thing, and that she ought to study the welfare and exaltation of her own children, if she had any by him, instead of looking out for the good of others, the said Jane Seymour replied that in soliciting the Princess's reinstatement she thought she was asking for the good, the repose, and tranquillity of himself, of the children they themselves might have, and of the kingdom in general, inasmuch as should the reinstatement not take place, neither Your Majesty nor the English people would be satisfied, and the ruin and desolation of the country would inevitably ensue.

Such a wish on the part of the said lady is very commendable indeed, and I purpose using all means in my power in keeping her to her good intentions. I also mean to go to the King about it, two or three days hence, and visit one by one the members of his Privy Council, and if I can personally, or by means of my friends, influence some of the lords and gentlemen who have been summoned for the next Parliament – which is to meet on the 8th of next month – I shall not fail to do so, for I really believe there will be a question of excluding the little bastard from the succession to the Crown, and praying this King to marry again. It should be observed that in the meantime, and in order to conceal from the public his love for Jane Seymour, the King has made her reside seven miles from this city, at the house of the Grand Squire [Sir Nicholas Carew], a rumour having been previously spread among the public that the King has not the least wish of marrying again unless he be actually urged to it by his subjects. Many messages, moreover, have I already received from various members to the effect that at the meeting of Parliament they will uphold, at the peril of their lives, the Princess's rights.

On the afternoon of the very day on which the concubine was lodged in the Tower, as the duke of Richmond went to his father, the King, to ask for his blessing, according to the English custom, the latter said with tears, that both he and his sister, meaning the Princess, ought to thank God for having escaped from the hands of that woman, who had planned their death by poison, from which I conclude that the King knew something of her wicked intentions.

On the 12th inst. Master Norris, first chamberlain to this king, Master Obouston (Weston) who used to sleep in the King's chamber, Master Bruton (Brereton), the gentleman in waiting, about whom I wrote to Your Majesty by my secretary, were condemned as traitors, and sentenced to death. Of these, only the last-named confessed having slept with the concubine on three different occasions; all the others were sentenced on mere presumption or on very slight grounds, without legal proof or valid confession. On the 15th the concubine herself and her brother (George), were tried by a tribunal composed of the principal lords of the kingdom, and convicted of treason, the duke of Norfolk presiding over it and reading the sentence to the culprits. I am told that the earl of Wiltshire wished also to be present at the trial [of his daughter and son], as he had been at that of the other four. Neither the concubine nor her brother were taken to Westminster as the other criminals had been; they were tried within the Tower, and yet the trial was far from being kept secret, for upwards of 2,000 people were present.

The chief charge against the concubine was her having had connexion with her own brother (George) and other accomplices; having actually promised, to marry Norris after the King's demise, her having received from, and given to, the said Norris certain medals indicative that both were bound together and aimed at the King's death; that she had poisoned the late Queen, and meditated doing the same with the Princess. These charges she obstinately denied; others she answered satisfactorily enough, though she confessed having given money to Ubaiston (Weston) and to several other gentlemen. She was likewise charged, as was her brother, with having ridiculed the King, and laughed at his manner of dressing, showing in many ways that she did not love him, and was tired of married life with him.

The brother, as I say, was charged with having had connexion with her; no proof of his guilt was produced except that of his having once passed many hours in her company, and other little follies. He answered so well that many who were present at the trial, and heard what he said, had no difficulty in waging two to one that he would be acquitted, the more so that no witnesses were called to give evidence against him or against her, as is customary in such cases, when the accused denies the charge brought against him. I cannot omit another charge in the indictment, namely, that the concubine, his sister, had said to his wife that the King was impotent. This, however, was not read in public; it was given to him in writing, under protest that he was only to say yes or no, without reading aloud the accusation; but to the great annoyance of Cromwell and others, he (George Boleyn) read it aloud and said that he was unwilling to engender or create suspicion in a matter likely to prejudice the issue the King might have from another marriage. He was likewise charged with having spread the rumour or expressed a doubt as to Anne's daughter (Elizabeth) being the King's, to which charge, however, he made no answer.

Both were tried separately without seeing each other. The concubine was sentenced first to be burnt alive, or beheaded at the King's pleasure. When the sentence was read to her, she received it quite calmly, and said that she was prepared to die, but was extremely sorry to hear that others, who were innocent and the King's loyal subjects, should share her fate and die through her. She ended by begging that some time should be allowed for her to prepare her soul for death.

After reading the sentence to him, the brother said to his judges that since die he must he would no longer plead 'not guilty', but would own that he deserved death. His last prayer to the King was that certain debts, which he named, should be paid out of his personal estate.

Although the generality of people here are glad of the execution of the said concubine, still a few find fault and grumble at the manner in which the proceedings against her have been conducted, and the condemnation of her and the rest, which is generally thought strange enough. People speak variously about the King, and certainly the slander will not cease when they hear of what passed and is passing between him and his new mistress, Jane Seymour. Already it sounds badly in the ears of the public that the King, after such ignominy and discredit as the concubine has brought on his head, should manifest more joy and pleasure now, since her arrest and trial, than he has ever done on other occasions, for he has daily gone out to dine here and there with ladies, and sometimes has remained with them till after midnight. I hear that on one occasion, returning by the river to Greenwich, the royal barge was actually filled with minstrels and musicians of his chamber, playing on all sorts of instruments or singing; which state of things was by many a one compared to the joy and pleasure a man feels in getting rid of a thin, old, and vicious hack in the hope of getting soon a fine horse to ride – a very peculiarly agreeable task for this king. The other night, whilst supping with several ladies at the house of the bishop of Carlion (Carlisle), he (the King) manifested incredible joy at the arrest of Anne, as the Bishop himself came and told me the day after. Indeed, he related to me that, among other topics of conversation, the King touched on that of the concubine; telling him: 'For a long time back had I predicted what would be the end of this affair, so much so that I have written a tragedy, which I have here by me.' Saying which, he took out of his breast pocket a small book all written in his own handy and handed it over to the Bishop, who, however, did not examine its contents. Perhaps these were certain ballads, which the King himself is known to have composed once, and of which the concubine and her brother had made fun, as of productions entirely worthless, which circumstance was one of the principal charges brought against them at the trial.

Three days after the concubine's arrest the Princess was removed to other quarters, most honorably attended and escorted on the way, not only by all the officers of the little bastard's household, but by several gentlemen and ladies, who had formerly been in her mother's service and in her own, and who, on hearing the news, went thither to congratulate her. Though the governess herself had no objection to their remaining in the house, the Princess, following my advice, has declined their services, and will retain no one near her person that is not previously accepted and appointed by her father, the King. Indeed, my great fear is, among others, that when the moment comes for the Estates to ask for the reinstatement of the Princess in her rights and titles, the King is likely to answer that it cannot be done unless she previously swears to, and conforms with, the irritating statutes concerning the King's second marriage as well as against Papal authority; which act of acquiescence, in my opinion, it will be extremely difficult to obtain from the Princess, though my advice is that she ought to agree to the whole of it so long as her conscience is not aggrieved, nor her rights and titles impaired through it. Please Your Majesty to instruct me what your wishes and intentions on this point are, that I may act accordingly.

Today lord Rocheford, and the other four gentlemen above-named, were all beheaded in front of the Tower. Notwithstanding the great efforts made by the resident French ambassador, the bishop of Tarbes, and by another one, called the sieur de Vintemille (Vintimiglia), who arrived the day before yesterday, to save the life of Vaston (Weston), he suffered death like the rest. To make matters worse for the concubine it was arranged that she should witness their execution from the windows of her prison. Rochefort before dying declared himself to be innocent of all the charges brought against him, though he owned that he deserved death for having been contaminated with the new heresies, and having caused many others to be infected with them. He had no doubt, said he on the scaffold, that God had punished him for that, and, therefore, he recommended all to forsake heretical doctrines and practices, and return to true faith and religion. Which words on the mouth of such a man as lord Rochefort will be the cause of innumerable people here making amends for their sins, and being converted.

The concubine herself is to be beheaded without fail tomorrow, or on Friday, at the latest, and I have my reasons for saying that the King is very impatient, and would have liked the execution to have already taken place; for the day before Anne's condemnation he sent the Grand Squire and many others in quest of Mistress Seymour, and made her come to within one mile of his own residence, where she is being splendidly entertained and served by cooks and officers of the royal household. And I have been told by one of her female relatives, who dined with her on the morning of the very day of Anne's condemnation, that the King sent her a message to say, that at three, in the afternoon of that day, she would receive news of the sentence, and so it was, for he despatched Master Briant [Sir Francis Bryan] in all haste to give her the intelligence. So that to all appearances there cannot be the least doubt that the King will soon take the said Seymour to wife, some people believing, and even asserting, that the marriage settlements have already been drawn up ...

After writing to Your Majesty as above, I thought I might delay the departure of this courier for 24 hours, in order to report the execution of the concubine, who was beheaded this very morning at 9 o'clock within the Tower, in the presence of the King's Chancellor, of Master Cromwell, and of many other members of the King's Privy Council, besides a considerable number of other people, though no foreigners were allowed to witness the execution. I hear that, although the heads and bodies of those executed the day before yesterday have been buried, the head of the concubine will be exposed on the bridge, at least for some time. She confessed, and took the Sacrament yesterday. No one ever shewed more courage or greater readiness to meet death than she did, having, as the report goes, begged and solicited those under whose keeping she was to hasten the execution. When orders came from the King to have it delayed until today, she seemed sorry, and begged and entreated the governor of the Tower (Sir William Kingston), for God's sake, to go to the King, and beg of him that, since she was well disposed and prepared for death, she should be dispatched immediately. The lady in whose keeping she has been sends me word, in great secrecy, that before and after her receiving the Holy Sacrament, she affirmed, on peril of her soul's damnation, that she had not misconducted herself so far as her husband the King was concerned ...

## The Chronicle of Henry VIII from the Death of Catherine of Aragon to the Execution of Anne Boleyn[9]
*The so-called 'Spanish Chronicle' was written before 1552 by a Spanish*

*merchant residing in London.*[10] *The author is unknown, although he was perhaps Antonio de Guaras, who came to England with Eustace Chapuys in 1529. Given the author's Imperial background, it is unsurprising that it presents a deeply hostile picture of Anne. Much of what is contained in the Chronicle is also inaccurate, for example, the Chronicler switches Henry's marriages with Anne of Cleves and Catherine Howard round, making Catherine his fourth wife and Anne his fifth. To compound this error, he also ascribed a prominent role in the fall of Catherine Howard to Thomas Cromwell, who had, in fact, been dead for over a year when her alleged crimes came to light. In spite of this, the chronicler was almost certainly an eye witness to some of the events that he described, he was, for example, one of the crowd appointed to welcome Anne of Cleves at her official reception to England.*[11] *Other details were provided by contemporary gossip and it appears that the chronicler lacked court connections.*

*Anne's early biographer, P. Friedmann, considered that, while there were a number of factual inaccuracies in the Chronicle's account (such as making no mention of Weston and describing George Boleyn as a duke), there may be some truth in the account.*[12] *He pointed out that there was a Sir Thomas Percy at court at the time of Anne's fall (the brother of her former suitor, Henry Percy) and it is possible that he did indeed quarrel with Mark Smeaton. Friedmann considered the account of the 'Spanish Chronicle' to be a report of 'the story which seems to have been accepted by the Spanish merchants who resided in London towards the close of Henry's reign'. It is, perhaps, fair to say, that the Chronicle presents a significantly embellished account, based on rumours, that may have some aspects of truth buried within it. It is necessary to use caution when using the Chronicle in relation to the fall of Anne Boleyn. The account of Anne's relationship with Smeaton seems scarcely credible. No Margery is known to have served Anne, although she was close to a lady named Margaret Horsman (mentioned in Edward Baynton's letter below).*

*Chapter XXVI: How Anne Boleyn committed adultery, and how it was found out*

Soon after the death of the sainted Queen Katharine, Anne Boleyn, who ostentatiously tried to attract to her service the best-looking men and best dancers to be found, heard that in the city of London there was a young fellow who was one of the prettiest monochord players and deftest dancers in the land. They told her he was the son of a poor carpenter, and she sent for him to play before her, asking him what his name was, to which he replied, 'My lady, my name is Mark.' Then the Queen sent for her minions, amongst whom was one called Master Norris, and another Master Brereton, to whom the Queen showed great favour. She ordered Mark to play, Master Norris leading her out to dance, and Mark played some virginals so prettily, that while she was dancing she said to Norris, 'What do you think of it, does not the lad play well?' and whilst they were passing near Mark, Norris answered gently, 'Lady, I should well like him to play sometimes, if it were possible, when we are together.' The Queen laughed, and Mark took notice

of everything that passed. When that dance was finished, the Queen wanted
to dance with Mark, and made one of her ladies play. So Mark danced
with her; and he tripped it so well, and so gracefully, that she at once fell
in love with him, and told him she wished him to live there. Mark fell on
his knees and kissed her hand, and she ordered one hundred nobles to be
given to him to buy clothes, and the next day Mark came all tricked out,
looking like the son of a gentleman. He never left the palace, and the Queen
persuaded the King to give him a salary of one hundred pounds, and from
that time forward Anne always had Mark to play to her. One morning, when
the Queen was in bed, she sent for Mark to play whilst she lay in bed, and
ordered her ladies to dance. They began dancing; and after a while, when
Anne saw that they were becoming very merry, she ordered one of the ladies
to play whilst the others danced. When she saw they were intoxicated with
their dancing, she called Mark to her, and he fell on his knee by her bedside,
and she had time to tell him that she was in love with him, whereupon he
was much surprised; but being of a base sort, he gave ear to all the Queen
said to him, forgetting, the sinner, that only two months before he was a
poor fellow, and that the King had given him a good income, and might
give him much more; so he answered, 'Madam, I am your servant; you may
command me.' And the lady bade him keep it secret, and she would find
means to compass her desires. Very few days after that the King went to
Windsor, which is twenty-five miles from there, and stayed a fortnight before
he came back; so Anne, seeing she had time, confided in an old woman of
her chamber, who, as it afterwards turned out, knew the Queen's secrets;
and this bad old woman, instead of putting obstacles in the way, said 'Leave
it to me, Madam, I will find means to bring him to you whenever you want
him.' Anne was so enamoured that every hour seemed a year.

One night, whilst all the ladies were dancing, the old woman called Mark
and said to him gently, so that none should overhear, 'You must come with
me;' and he, as he knew it was to the Queen's chamber he had to go, was
nothing loth. So she took him to an ante-chamber, where she and another
lady slept, next to the Queen's room, and in this ante-chamber there was
a closet like a store-room, where she kept sweetmeats, candied fruits, and
other preserves which the Queen sometimes asked for. To conceal him more
perfectly the old woman put him into this closet, and told him to stay there
till she came for him, and to take great care he was not heard. Then she
shut him up and returned to the great hall where they were dancing, and
made sign to the Queen, who understood her, and, although it was not
late, she pretended to be ill, and the dancing ceased. She then retired to her
chamber with her ladies, whilst the old woman said to her, 'Madam, when
you are in bed and all the ladies are asleep, you can call me and ask for
some preserves, which I will bring, and Mark shall come with me, for he is
in the closet now.'

The Queen went to bed and ordered all her ladies to retire to their
respective beds, which were in an adjoining gallery like a refectory, and
when they were all gone but the old lady and the lady who slept with her, she
sent them off too. When she thought they would all be asleep, she called the

old woman, and said, 'Margaret, bring me a little marmalade.' She called it out very loudly, so that the ladies in the gallery might hear as well as Mark, who was in the closet. The old woman went to the closet and made Mark undress, and took the marmalade to the Queen, leading Mark by the hand. The lady who was in the old woman's bed did not see them when they went out of the closet, and the old woman left Mark behind the Queen's bed, and said out loud, 'Here is the marmalade, my lady.' Then Anne said to the old woman, 'Go along; go to bed.'

As soon as the old woman had gone Anne went round to the back of the bed and grasped the youth's arm, who was all trembling, and made him get into bed. He soon lost his bashfulness, and remained that night and many others, so that in a short time this Mark flaunted out to such an extent that there was not a gentleman at court who was so fine, and Anne never dined without having Mark to serve her.

Here the devil was even with her, for as she formerly showed great favour to Mr Norris and the other gentleman, Brereton, and forgot them as soon as Mark came into the field, these gentlemen were both grieved, each one for himself. Anne saw this, and called Master Norris to her, and spoke to him quietly, it is believed to tell him to go to her that night, for as Mark was expecting his usual summons from the old woman, she told him he could not go. As Mark saw Anne speaking to Master Norris, and had heard what they had said on the former occasion, he suspected what was going on.

The next day Mark was called by the Queen and told to play whilst she summoned Brereton to dance with her, and it is suspected that on that night Brereton was invited to visit her, as Mark waited in vain to be called.

The next night the old woman called Mark, and he could not refrain from telling the Queen what was in his heart. Anne laughed at him, and as he saw she was deceiving him, he said no more; and that night the Queen gave him a purse full of gold pieces, and told him to get ready for the ridings on May-day, to which the King was coming.

The next day Mark bought three of the best horses that could be found, and tricked himself out so bravely, that there was no gentleman at Court who spent so much money either in arms, liveries for his servants, or trappings for his horses.

There was much jealousy of him, and many murmured to see him so smart and lavish. One of the Queen's household had some words with him, and Mark threatened him, which offended the gentleman very much; and Mark, being always suspicious of him, conveyed his suspicions to the Queen, who sent for the gentleman and said to him, 'Thomas Percy,' for that was his name, 'I desire that there shall be no quarrelling with Mark, and if any annoyance is caused him I shall be very angry.' Percy answered, 'Madam, you are aware that I have served you for many years, and I will not be ill-used by one who only came yesterday.' But the Queen ordered them to be good friends, and Percy could easily see that she bore great love for Mark; so he must needs go to Secretary Cromwell, and said to him, 'I wish to speak to you.' 'Say what thou wishest, Percy,' answered the Secretary, and then Percy said, 'Your worship will know that it is hardly three months since Mark came to Court, and that he only has one hundred pounds salary from the King, of which he has only received a third, and he has just bought three horses that have cost him over five hundred ducats, as well as very rich arms and fine liveries for his servants for the day of the ridings, such as no gentleman at Court has been able to do, and many are wondering where he has got the money. I can tell you more, for I know that on many occasions he has been in the Queen's chamber, and your worship should look to it.' Cromwell answered him, 'Hold thy tongue, Percy, and keep this secret; when the King comes back I shall learn the truth; meanwhile keep your eyes open and see if you note any signs, and who speaks to Mark.'

Percy did not forget it; and one night before the King returned the old woman called Mark whilst the ladies were dancing, and Percy was on the look-out, but Mark, seeing him watching, was clever enough to return to the dance instead of going with the old woman, so Percy discovered nothing that night. The next morning the Queen sent for Mark, and as soon as Percy knew that he was in the chamber he went to Secretary Cromwell and told him what he had seen the night before, and how he was now playing in the Queen's chamber. Cromwell said, 'Hold thy tongue for the present, Percy; the King is coming tomorrow and the next day is May-day, when the jousts will be held, and I will find out a way to discover the truth.'

*Chapter XXVII How Cromwell took Mark to London and learnt from him what had happened*

The night before they held the jousts the King came to Greenwich, and all the gentlemen were very gay, particularly Master Norris and Master Brereton. On the day of the jousts, which was the 1st of May, Cromwell was going to London and sent for Mark, and said, 'Mark, come and dine with me, and after dinner we will return together.' Mark, suspecting nothing, accepted the invitation; and when they arrived at Cromwell's house in London, before dinner, he took Mark by the hand and led him into his chamber, where there were six gentlemen of his, and as soon as he had got him in the chamber he said, 'Mark, I have wanted to speak to you for some days, and I have had no opportunity till now. Not only I, but many other gentlemen, have noticed that you are ruffling it very bravely of late. We know that four months ago you had nothing, for your father has hardly bread to eat, and now you are buying horses and arms, and have made showy devices and liveries such as no lord of rank can excel. Suspicion has arisen either that you have stolen the money or that someone had given it to you, although it is a great deal for anyone to give unless it were the King or Queen, and the King has been away for a fortnight. I give you notice now that you will have to tell me the truth before you leave here, either by force or good-will.'

Mark, understanding as soon as Cromwell began to speak that the affair was no joke, did not know what to say, and became confused. 'You had better tell the truth willingly,' said Cromwell; and then Mark said that the money had been lent to him; to which Cromwell answered, 'How can that be, that the merchants lend so much money, unless on plate, gold, or revenue, and at heavy interest, whilst you have nothing to pledge except that chain you wear. I am sorry you will not tell what you know with a good grace.'

Then he called two stout young fellows of his, and asked for a rope and a cudgel, and ordered them to put the rope, which was full of knots, round Mark's head, and twisted it with the cudgel until Mark cried out, 'Sir Secretary, no more, I will tell the truth,' and then he said, 'The Queen gave me the money.' 'Ah, Mark,' said Cromwell, 'I know the Queen gave you a hundred nobles, but what you have bought has cost over a thousand, and that is a great gift even for a Queen to a servant of low degree such as you. If you do not tell me all the truth I swear by the life of the King I will torture you till you do.' Mark replied, 'Sir, I tell you truly that she gave it to me.' Then Cromwell ordered him a few more twists of the cord, and poor Mark, overcome by the torment, cried out, 'No more, Sir, I will tell you everything that has happened.' And then he confessed all, and told everything as we have related it, and how it came to pass.

When the Secretary heard it he was terror-stricken, and asked Mark if he knew of anyone else besides himself who had relations with the Queen. Mark, to escape further torture, told all he had seen of Master Norris and Brereton, and swore that he knew no more. Then Cromwell wrote a letter to the King, and sent Mark to the Tower.

*Chapter XXVIII: How Cromwell wrote to the King, and how the Queen and her gentlemen-in-waiting were arrested*

The Secretary at once wrote to the King, and sent Mark's confession to him by a nephew of his called Richard Cromwell, the letter being conceived as follows: 'Your Majesty will understand that, jealous of your honour, and seeing certain things passing in your palace, I determined to investigate and discover the truth. Your Majesty will recollect that Mark has hardly been in your service four months and only has £100 salary, and yet all the Court notices his splendour, and that he had spent a large sum for these jousts, all of which has aroused suspicions in the minds of certain gentlemen, and I have examined Mark, who has made the confession which I enclose to your Majesty in this letter.'

When the King read this confession his meal did not at all agree with him; but, like a valiant prince, he dissembled, and presently ordered his boat to be got ready, and went to Westminster. He ordered that the jousts should not be stopped, but when the festivities were over that Master Norris and Brereton, and Master Wyatt, should be secretly arrested and taken to the Tower. The Queen did not know the King had gone, and went to the balconies where the jousts were to be held, and asked where he was, and was told that he was busy.

Presently came all the gentlemen who were to ride, and Master Norris and Brereton came, looking very smart, and their servants in gay liveries; but the Queen looked, and not seeing Mark, asked why he had not come out. She was told that he was not there, but had gone to London, and had not come back. So the jousts began, and Master Wyatt did better than anybody.

This Master Wyatt was a very gallant gentleman, and there was no prettier man at Court than he was. When the jousts were finished and they were disarming, the captain of the guard came and called Master Norris and Master Brereton, and said to them, 'The King calls for you.' So they went with him, and a boat being in waiting, they were carried off to the Tower without anyone hearing anything about it. Then Cromwell's nephew said to Master Wyatt, 'Sir, the Secretary, my master, sends to beg you to favour him by going to speak with him, as he is rather unwell, and is in London.' So Wyatt went with him.

It seems that the King sent to Cromwell to tell him to have Wyatt fetched in order to examine him. When they arrived in London Cromwell took Master Wyatt apart, and said to him, 'Master Wyatt, you well know the great love I have always borne you, and I must tell you that it would cut me to the heart if you were guilty in the matter of which I wish to speak.' Then he told him all that had passed; and Master Wyatt was astounded, and replied with great spirit, 'Sir Secretary, by the faith I owe to God and my King and lord, I have no reason to distrust, for I have not wronged him even in thought. The King well knows what I told him before he was married.' Then Cromwell told him he would have to go to the Tower, but that he would promise to stand his friend, to which Wyatt answered, 'I will go willingly, for as I am stainless I have nothing to fear.' He went out with Richard Cromwell, and nobody suspected that he was a prisoner; and when he arrived at the Tower Richard said to the captain of the Tower, 'Sir Captain, Secretary Cromwell sends to beg you to do all honour to Master Wyatt.' So the captain put him into a chamber over the door, where we will leave him, to say how the Queen and the Duke her brother were arrested.

*Chapter XXIX: How the Queen and her brother the Duke were arrested*
On the 2nd of May the captain of the guard with a hundred halberdiers came to Greenwich in the King's great barge, and went to the Queen, and said to her, 'My lady, the King has sent me for you;' and she, very much astonished, asked the captain where the King was. She was told he was at Westminster; and she at once got ready, and embarked with all her ladies, thinking she was to be taken to Westminster, but when she saw they stopped at the Tower, she asked whether the King was there. The captain of the Tower appeared, and the captain of the guard addressed him, saying, 'I bring you here the Queen, whom the King orders you to keep prisoner, and very carefully guarded.' Thereupon the captain took Anne by the arm, and she, as soon as she heard that she was a prisoner, exclaimed loudly in the hearing of many, 'I entered with more ceremony the last time I came.' They ordered two of her ladies to remain with her, and the rest to be taken to Westminster, and amongst them one very attractive, of whom we shall have to speak further on.

As soon as the King learnt that she was in the Tower, he ordered the Duke her brother to be arrested, and taken thither, the old woman having already been taken. The King then wished the Queen to be examined, and he sent Secretary Cromwell, the Archbishop of Canterbury, the Duke of Norfolk, and the Chancellor, who were expressly ordered by the King to treat her with no respect or consideration. They desired the Archbishop to be spokesman, and he said these words to her, 'Madam, there is no one in the realm, after my lord the King, who is so distressed at your bad conduct as I am, for all these gentlemen well know I owe my dignity to your good-will;' and Anne, before he could say any more, interrupted him with, 'My lord Bishop, I know what is your errand; waste no more time; I have never wronged the King, but I know well that he is tired of me, as he was before of the good lady Katharine.' Then the Bishop continued, 'Say no such thing, Madam, for your evil courses have been clearly seen; and if you desire to read the confession which Mark has made, it will be shown to you.' Anne, in a great rage, replied, 'Go to! It has all been done as I say, because the King has fallen in love, as I know, with Jane Seymour, and does not know how to get rid of me. Well, let him do as he likes, he will get nothing more out of me; and any confession that has been made is false.'

With that, as they saw they should extract nothing from her, they determined to leave; but before doing so the Duke of Norfolk said to her, 'Madam, if it be true that the Duke your brother has shared your guilt, a great punishment indeed should be yours and his as well.' To which she answered, 'Duke, say no such thing; my brother is blameless; and if he has been in my chamber to speak with me, surely he might do so without suspicion, being my brother, and they cannot accuse him for that. I know that the King has had him arrested, so that there should be none left to take my part. You need not trouble to stop talking with me, for you will find out no more.' So they went away; and when they told the King how she had answered, he said, 'She has a stout heart, but she shall pay for it;' and he sent them to the Duke to see how he would answer. To explain why the Duke had been arrested, it should be told that the King was informed that he had been seen on several occasions going in and out of the Queen's room dressed only in his night-clothes. When the gentlemen went to him, he said, 'I do not know why the King has had me arrested, for I never wronged him in word or deed. If my sister has done so, let her bear the penalty.' Then the Chancellor replied, 'Duke, it was ground for suspicion that you should go so often to her chamber at night, and tell the ladies to leave you. It was a very bold thing to do, and you deserve great punishment.' 'But look you, Chancellor,' answered the Duke, 'even if I did go to speak with her somtimes when she was unwell, surely that is no proof that I was so wicked as to do so great a crime and treason to the King.' Then the Duke of Norfolk said, 'Hold thy peace, Duke, the King's will must be done after all.' So they left him, and presently put old Margaret to the torture, who told the whole story of how she had arranged that Mark and Master Norris and Brereton should all have access to the Queen unknown to each other. She was asked about Master Wyatt, but she said she had never even seen him speak to the Queen privately, but always openly, whereupon Secretary Cromwell was glad, for he was very fond of Master Wyatt.

So the gentlemen ordered the old woman to be burnt that night within the Tower, and they took her confession to the King; and the King ordered all the prisoners to be beheaded, and the Duke as well, so the next day the Duke, Master Norris, Brereton, and Mark were executed.

*Chapter XXX: How the duke, and Norris, and Brereton, and Mark were beheaded the next day*

We have told how the old woman was ordered to be burned in the great courtyard of the Tower, and they made the Queen see it from an iron-barred window. She said, 'Why do you grieve me so? I wish they would burn me with her.' To which the keeper answered, 'Madam, another death is reserved for you.' 'I do not care for all the harm they can do me now,' she said, 'for they can never deny I was a crowned Queen, although I was a poor woman.'

The next day they brought out the Duke and the others, and it was a surprising sight to see the great crowd there was. There came with the culprits over five hundred halberdiers, and when the Duke ascended, a gentleman said to him, 'My lord Duke if you have anything to say, you can say it.' Then the Duke turned to the people and said in the hearing of many, 'I beg you pray to God for me; for by the trial I have to pass through I am blameless, and never even knew that my sister was bad. Guiltless as I am, I pray God to have mercy upon my soul.' Then he lay upon the ground with his head on the block, the headsman gave three strokes, and so died this poor Duke.

Then Master Norris mounted, and made a great long prayer; and then, turning to the people, he said, 'I do not think any gentleman at Court owes more to the King than I do, and none have been more ungrateful and regardless of it than I have. I deserve the death they condemn me to, and worse still, and so I pray to God for mercy on my soul, and acknowledge the justice of my sentence.' Then he cast himself on the ground, and was beheaded.

The next was Brereton, who said nothing but 'I have offended God and the King; pray for me,' and he was executed.

The last was Mark, and he cried out in a loud voice that all could hear, 'Oh, woe is me! Only four months ago I was a poor man, and my good fortune raised me to better things, and would have lifted me higher still, but for the devil's tempting, and my inability to resist the pride which has been my undoing. I thought treason would never come to light, but I confess now I erred, and do not deserve so honourable a death as that which the King has ordered me. I ask pardon of God and the King, for I have wronged him more than any other, and I beg you, gentlemen, to pray to God for me;' and then he threw himself down and was beheaded; but before he died he said, 'Gentlemen, I ask pardon of Master Percy, for he would have been killed if I had not been arrested, as I had set men on to murder him;' and fortunately Master Percy was there and answered, 'God pardon thee, Mark, as I pardon thee.'

The good Wyatt was witnessing all this from a window of the Tower, and all the people thought that he also was to be brought out and executed; but Wyatt that night wrote a letter to the King, and sent it to him by a cousin of his, which letter was as follows.

*Chapter XXXI: How Master Wyatt wrote a letter to the King and how he was pardoned*

The night before the Duke and the others were led out to execution, the good Wyatt was assured that he would be spared; so he got some paper and ink and wrote the following to the King: "Your Majesty knows that before marrying Queen Anne you said to me, Wyatt, I am going to marry Anne Boleyn, what do you think of it? I told your Majesty then that you had better not do so, and you asked me why; to which I replied that she was a bad woman, and your Majesty angrily ordered me to quit your presence for two years. Your Majesty did not deign on that occasion to ask my reasons for saying what I did, and since I could not then give them by word of mouth, I will do so now in writing. One day, whilst Mistress Anne's father and mother were at the Court eight miles from Greenwich, where, as all the world knows, they were stationed, I took horse and went thither, arriving when Anne was already in bed. I mounted to her chamber, and as soon as she saw me she said, 'Good God! Master Wyatt, what are you doing here at this hour?' I answered her, 'Lady, a heart tormented as mine has been by yours for long past has urged me hither to ask for some consolation from one who has caused it so much pain.' I approached her and kissed her, and she remained quiet and silent, and even to still greater familiarities she made no objection, when suddenly I heard a great stamping over the bed in which she slept, and the lady at once rose, slipped on a skirt, and went out by a staircase which led up behind the bed; I waited for her more than an hour, but when she came down she would not allow me to approach her.

I cannot but believe that I was treated in the same way as a gentleman once was in Italy, who was as madly in love with a lady as I was, and was, by his good luck, brought to the same point, when he heard a stamping overhead, and the lady rose and went out; but the gentleman in question was wiser than I, for he very soon followed the lady upstairs, and found her in the arms of a groom, and I have no doubt I should have seen the same thing if I had been wise enough to follow her.[13] A week after she was quite at my service, and if your Majesty had deigned to hear me when you banished me, I would have told you then what I write you now."

As soon as the King read this letter, he sent to the Tower to fetch Wyatt. He came into the King's presence and kissed his hand for his pardon, and the King said to him, 'Wyatt, I am sorry I did not listen to thee when I was angry, but I was blinded by that bad woman.' And thenceforth Master Wyatt was more beloved by the King than ever he had been. A few days afterwards he sent him as ambassador to the Emperor Charles V., where he served the King well, so there is no more to say about him.

*Chapter XXXII: How Anne was beheaded, and what took place five days after the execution of the Duke and the others*

The King ordered the Queen to be beheaded. He had sent a week before to St Omer[14] for a headsman who could cut off the head with a sword instead of an axe, and nine days after they sent he arrived. The Queen was then told to confess, as she must die the next day, and she begged that she might be executed within the Tower, and that no foreigner should see her. So they erected the scaffold in the great courtyard of the Tower, and the next morning they brought her out. She would not confess, but showed a devilish spirit, and was as gay as if she was not going to die. When she arrived at the scaffold she was dressed in a night-robe of damask, with a red damask skirt, and a netted coif over her hair. This lady was very graceful, and had a long neck; and when she mounted the scaffold she saw on it many gentlemen, amongst them being the headsman, who was dressed like the rest, and not as executioner; and she looked around her on all sides to see the great number of people present, for although she was executed inside, there was a great crowd. They would not admit any foreigner, except one who had got in the night before, and who took good note of all that passed. And as the lady looked all round, she began to say these words, 'Do not think, good people, that I am sorry to die, or that I have done anything to deserve this death. My fault has been my great pride, and the great crime I committed in getting the King to leave my mistress Queen Katherine for my sake, and I pray God to pardon me for it. I say to you all that everything they have accused me of is false, and the principal reason I am to die is Jane Seymour, as I was the cause of the ill that befell my mistress.'[15]

The gentlemen would not let her say any more, and she asked which was the headsman. She was told that he would come presently, but that in the meanwhile it would be better for her to confess the truth and not be so obstinate, for she could not hope for pardon. She answered them, 'I know I shall have no pardon, but they shall know no more from me.' So seeing that she would not confess, the headsman came and knelt before her, saying, 'Madam, I crave your Majesty's pardon, for I am ordered to do this duty, and I beg you to kneel and say your prayers.' So Anne knelt, but the poor lady only kept looking about her. The headsman, being still in front of her, said in French, 'Madam, do not fear, I will wait till you tell me.' Then she said, 'You will have to take this coif off,' and she pointed to it with her left hand. The sword was hidden under a heap of straw, and the man who was to give it to the headsman was told beforehand what to do; so, in order that she should not suspect, the headsman turned to the steps by which they had mounted, and called out, 'Bring me the sword.' The lady looked towards the steps to watch for the coming of the sword, still with her hand on her coif; and the headsman made a sign with his right hand for them to give him the sword, and then, without being noticed by the lady, he struck her head off on to the ground. And so ended this lady, who would never admit or confess the truth.

Her body was presently carried to the church within the Tower and buried, and a few days afterwards her father died of grief for the loss of her and the Duke.[16] God pardon them!

## Extract from the Metrical Visions by George Cavendish Concerning the Fortunes and Fall of the Most Eminent Persons of his Time[17]

*George Cavendish, as set out above, was a contemporary of Anne Boleyn. His Dante-esque Metrical Visions, a long poem setting out a fictional author's conversations with certain deceased members of Henry VIII's court has been described as having 'little or no merit as verses'.[18] While this may, or may* not be an accurate assessment of the quality of the poetry, he did provide an interesting character summary of Anne and her supposed lovers. Cavendish was certainly acquainted with Anne and it is likely that he knew at least some of the men involved in her fall personally. His interpretation of Anne, Rochford, Weston, Norris, Brereton and Smeaton is coloured by his belief in their guilt, but it is possible to pick out details of their characters which are otherwise unrecorded in the words that he gave to them.

Cavendish, for example, portrays Anne's brother, Lord Rochford, as a man guilty of sexual sins. He does, however, also provide another side to his character, speaking of his education and the poetry that he wrote, verses which, unfortunately, no longer survive. Francis Weston is also portrayed as a sinner, something that may be echoed in his actions before his execution. Weston spent some of his last hours writing out a list of his debts, which he sent to his mother and wife. He also sent a final message, demonstrating his preparedness for death.[19] 'Father and mother and wife, I shall humbly desire you, for the salvation of my soul, to discharge me of this bill, and for to forgive me of all the offences that I have done to you, and in especial to my wife, which I desire for the love of God to forgive me, and to pray for me: for I believe prayer will do me good. God's blessing have my children and mine.' It was signed, 'By me, a great offender to God.'

Cavendish undoubtedly believed that the people that he wrote about had received their just deserts and much of what he has his subjects say must be considered fiction. However, as a fiction written by a man who knew or, at least, knew people who knew them, his work is of some value in assessing the characters of the five men who died with Anne Boleyn.

*Th'Auctor G.C.*
When I had wepte, and lamentyd my fyll,
With reason persuaded, to hold me content,
I espied certyn persons comyng me tyll[20]
Strangely disgwysed, that greatly did lament,
And as me seemed, this was ther intent,
On fortune to complayn, their cause was not slender,
And me to requier their fall to remember.

*Viscount Rocheford*
Alas! quod the first, with a full hevy chere,
And countenance sad, piteous, and lamentable,
George Bulleyn I ame, that now dothe appere;
Some tyme of Rocheford Viscount honorable,
And now a vile wretch, most myserable,
That ame constrayned with dole in my visage,
Even to resemble a very deadly image.

God gave me grace, dame Nature did hir part,
Endewed me with gyfts of natural qualities:
Dame Eloquence also taughte me the arte

In meter and verse to make pleasaunt dities,
And fortune preferred me to high dignyties
In such abondance, that combred was my witt,
To render God thanks that gave me eche whitt.

It hath not been knowen nor seldome seen,
That any of my yeres byfore this day
Into the privy councell preferred hath been:
My soverayn lord in his chamber did me assay,
Or yeres thryes nine my life had past away;
A rare thing suer seldom or never hard,
So yong a man so highly to be preferrd.

In this my welthe I had God clean forgot,
And my sensuall apetyte I did always ensewe,
Esteming in my self the thyng that I had not,
Sufficient grace this chaunce for to eschewe,
The contrary, I perceyve, causithe me now to rewe;
My folly was such that vertue I set asyde,
And forsoke God that should have been my gwyde.

My lyfe not chaste, my lyvyng bestyall;
I forced wydowes, maydens I did deflower.
All was oon to me, I spared none at all,
My appetite was all women to devoure,
My study was both day and hower,
My onleafull lechery how I might it fulfill,
Sparyng no woman to have on hyr my wyll.

Allthoughe I before hathe both seene and rede
The word of God and scriptures of auctoritie,
Yet could not I resist this onlefull deede,
Nor dreade the domes of God in my prosperitie;
Let myn estatte, therefore, a myrror to you be,
And in your mynd my dolors comprehend
For myne offences how God hath made dissend.

So how fortune can alter and change hir tyde,
That to me but late could be so good and favorable,
And at this present to frowne and set me thus aside,
Which thoughte hyr whele to stand both firme and stable,
Now have I found hyr very froward and mutable;
Where she was frendly now she is at discord,
As by experience of me Viscount Rocheford.

For where God list to punysh a man of right,
By mortal sword, farewell all resistence;

When grace faylyth, honor hath no force or myght,
Of nobilitie also it defacyth the high preeminence,
And changythe their power to feeble impotence;
Than tornyth fortune hyr whele most spedely
Example take of me for my lewde avoultrie,

All noblemen, therefore, with stedfast hart entyer,
Lyft up your corages, and think this is no fable;
Thoughe ye sit high, conceive yt in your chere,
That no worldly prynce in yerthe is perdurable;
And since that ye be of nature reasonable,
Remember in your welthe, as thyng most necessary,
That all standythe on fortune when she listeth to vary.

Alas! to declare my life in every effect,
Shame restraynyth me the playnes to confess,
Lest the abhomynation wold all the world enfect:
Yt is so vile, so detestable in words to expresse,
For which by the lawe condempned I am doughtlesse,
And for my desert, justly juged to be deade;
Behold here my body, but I have lost my hed.

*Th'Auctor G.C.*
Another was there redy to complayne
Of his evyll chaunce, crying owt, alas!
And said of all grace, no man more barayn
Than he was, that in his time so happie was,
And now onhappie fortune hath brought to passe;
That where most happiest he was but of late,
Now most onhappiest fortune hath torned hir date.

*Norres*
With welthe, worshipe, and houge aboundaunce,
My soverayn lord extendyd his benygnytie:
To be grome of his stoole he did me avaunce,
Of all his privie chamber I had the soverayntie;
Offices and romes he gave me great plentie:
Horsys, hawks, and hounds, I had of eche sort,
I wanted nothing that was for my disport.

Of welthy life I dought it never a wytt,
Thou knewest well I had, and thereof no man more,
All things of pleasure unto my fantzie fitt,
Till ambyssion blyndyd me that I forthinke sore,
From the midst of the streme dryvyn to the shore;
From welthe I say, alas! to wretchedness and waylyng,
For my mysdemenor to God and to the kyng.

My chaunce was such I had all thyng at wyll,
And in my welthe I was to hym onkynd,
That thus to me did all my mynd fulfyll,
All his benyvolence was clean owt of mynd:
Oh, alas! alas! in my hart how cowld I fynd
Ayenst my soverayn so secretly to conspier,
That so gently gave me all that I desier.

His most noble hart lamented so my chaunce,
That of his clemency he granted me my lyfe,
In case I wold, without dissimulaunce,
The trouthe declare of his onchaste wyfe,
The spotted queen, causer of all his stryfe;
But I most obstynate, with hart as hard as stone,
Denyed his grace, good cause therefore to mone.

To sighe, to sobbe, it ware but wast;
To weep, to waylle, or to lament,
Yt will not prevayle; the tyme is past:
Alas! in tyme why did I not prevent
The rage and fury of fortunes male intent?
But then I did as now all other do,
In tyme of welthe let all these thoughts goo.

Who is more willfull than he that is in welthe?
Who is more folishe than he that shold be wyse?
Who syknes soner doth forget than he that hath his helthe?
Or who is more blynd than he that hath two eyes?
Who hath most welthe doth fortune most dispise;
Even so dyd I for whant of Goddis grace:
What now remayneth but sorrow in thys case?

Sometyme in trust, and now a traytor found;
Sometyme full nighe, but now I stand afarre;
Sometyme at libertie, and now in prison bound;
Sometyme in office, and now led to the barre:
The rigor of the lawe justice will not deferre,
But for myn offences syth needs that I must die;
Farewell my frendes, loo helplesse here I lye.

*Th'Auctor G.C.*
Next hyme followed an other that was of that band,
With teares bespraynt,[21] and color pale as lead,
Yt was Weston the wanton, ye shall understand,
That wantonly lyved without feare or dreade;
For wyll without wytt did ay his brydell leade,
Followyng his fantzy and his wanton lust,

Having of mysfortune no maner mystrust.

*Weston*
Fortune (quod he) not so, but not fearyng God above,
Which knowyth the depthe of every man's mynd,
Whom I forgot to serve in dread and in love
By wanton wyll, for that I was so blynd,
Which caused my welthe full soon to outwynd;
And cheafe of all, and most to be abhord,
For my unkyndnes ayenst my soverayn lord.

Beyng but young, and skant out of the shell,
I was dayntely noryshed under the king's wyng,
Who highly favored me and loved me so well
That I had all my will and lust in every thyng,
Myndyng nothing lesse than chaunce of my endyng;
And for my dethe that present is nowe here,
I looked not for, this fyvetie or threscore yere.

My lust and my wyll were knytt in alyaunce,
And my wyll folowed lust in all his desier;
When lust was lusty, wyll did hyme advaunce
To tangle me with lust where my lust did requier:
Thus wyll and hot lust kyndeled me the fier
Of filthy concupicence, my youth yet but grean
Spared not, my lust presumed to the queene.

And for my lewd lust my will is now shent,[22]
By whom I was ruled in every motion,
Now wyll and lust makyth me sore to repent;
That wyll was my gwyd, and not sad[23] discression,
Therefore agenst wyll I ame brought to correction;
Who folowyth lust his will to obeye
May chaunce to repent, as I do this day.

Lust then gave cause why will did consent
Willfully to rage, where wytt shold restrayn
So highly to presume; to furnyshe his intent
Will was to sawcy, and wold not refrayn,
Havyng no regard to pryncely disdayn;
Wherefore by Justice now hither am I led
To satisfie the cryme with the losse of my hed.

*Th'Auctor G.C.*
Then appeared an other his chaunce to declare,
And sayd, that fortune hathe gevyn hyme a fall,
Which sowced hyme in sorrowe, and combred hyme with kare;

Yt avayllyth hyme nothyng to crye and to call,
For frends hathe he none, their helpe is but small
To socoure hyme nowe: loo, what it is to trust
To fykkyll fortune when she dothe chaynge her lust.

*Breerton*
But late I was in welthe,[24] the world can it record,
Floryshyng in favor, freshly beseen,
Gentilman of the chamber with my soverayn lord,
Tyll fortune onwares hath disceyved me clean,
Which pynchethe my hart, and rubbyth me on the splene
To thynk on my fall; remembryng myn estate
Renewyth my sorowe, my repentance comyth to late.

Furnished with romes[25] I was by the kyng,
The best I ame sewer he had in my contrie;
Steward of the Holt, a rome of great wynnyng
In the marches of Wales, the which he gave to me,
Where of tall men I had sewer great plentie
The kyng for to serve, both in town and feld,
Redely furnyshed with horse, spere, and sheld.

God of his justice, forseyng my malice,
For my busy rigor wold punyshe me of right
Mynestred unto Eton, by color of justice:
A shame to speke, more shame it is to wright;
A gentilman born, that thorowghe my myght
So shamefully was hanged upon a gallowe-tree,
Oonly of old rankor that roted was in me.

Now the lawe hath taught me justice to know,
By dyvyn dome, Goddis wordes to be trewe,
Who strykythe with the sword the sword will over-throwe;
No man shall be able the danger to eschewe;
Thexperience in me shall give you a vewe,
That rigor by rigor hath quit me my mede,
For the rigor of justice dothe cause me to blede.

Loo, here is th'end of murder and tyranny!
Loo, here is th'end of envious affeccion!
Loo, here is th'end of false conspiracy!
Loo, here is th'end of false detection
Don to the innocent by cruel correccion!
Althoughe in office I thought myself strong,
Yet here is myn end for mynestryng wrong.

*Th'Auctor G.C.*

Than came another, which had lyttil joye,
Sayeng, that some tyme I did hyme knowe
In the cardinal's chapleyn a syngyng boy,
Who humbly requered me, and lowted[26] full lowe
To wright his dekay, as last of this rowe;
And that his desier I wold not refuse,
For, by his confession, he dyd them all accuse.

*Marke Als. Smeton*

My father a carpenter, and labored with his hand,
With the swett of his face he purchast his lyvyng,
For small was his rent, much lesse was his land;
My mother in cottage used dayly spynnyng;
Loo, in what mysery was my begynnyng,
Till that gentill prynce, kyng of this realme,
Toke me de strecore et origens pauperem.

And beyng but a boy, clame uppe the hygh stage,
That bred was of naught, and brought to felicite,
Knew not myself, waxt proud in my corage,
Dysdayned my father, and wold not hyme se;
Wherfore nowe Fortune by hir mutabilitie
Hathe made so cruelly hir power for to stretch,
For my presumption, to dye lyke a wretch.

Loo, what it is, frayle youth to advance
And to set hyme uppe in welthy estate,
Or[27] sad discression had hym in governance
To brydell his lust, which now comes to late;
And thoughe by great favor I lease but my pate,
Yet deserved have I cruelly to be martred,
As I ame juged to be hanged, drawn, and quartred.

*Th'Auctor G.C.*

In the myddys of my labor intendyng to take rest,
Beyng fortossed[28] in this my long travayl,
Disposed to pawse, I made me therto prest;[29]
But as I sat musyng on Fortune so frayl,
A lady I saw sobbyng, that happe made to wayl,
Wryngyng of her hands, hir voyce she owt brayd,
Complaynyng on Fortune, thes words to me she sayd.

*Queene Anne*

Alas, wretched woman, what shall I do or say?
And why, alas, was I borne this woo to susteyn?
Oh how infortunat I ame at this day,

That raygned in joy, and now in endles payn,
The world universal hathe me in disdayn;
The slander of my name woll aye be grean,
And called of eche man the most vicious quene.

What nedythe me my name for to reherce,
For my fall, I thynk, is yet freshe in the mynd;
I dread my faults shall thy paper perce,
That thus have lyved and byn to God onkynd;
Vices preferryng, settyng vertue behynd,
Hatfull to God, to most men contrarye,
Spotted with pride, viciousnes, and cruelty.

Oh sorrowfull woman, my body and my soule
Shall ever be burdened with slander detestable!
Fame in her register my defame woll enroll,
And to race owt the same no man shall be able,
My lyfe of late hathe byn so abhomynable;
Therfor my frayltie I may both curse and ban,
Whissyng to God I had never known man.

Who was more happier, if I had byn gracious,
Than I of late, and had moore my wyll,
For my soverayn lord of me was so amorous
That all my desiers he gladly did fulfyll;
My hosbond and soverayn thought in me no ill,
He loved me so well, havyng in me great trust:
I turned trust to treason, and he chayngd all his lust.

The noblest prynce that raygned on the ground
I had to my hosbond, he toke me to hys wyfe;
At home with my father a maiden he me found,
And for my sake of pryncely prerogatyfe:
To an erle he advanced my father in his lyfe,
And preferred all them that ware of my bloode;
The most willyngest prynce to do them all good.

Whan Fortune had displayed abrode my freshe sayle,
Also had arryved me in the most joyfull port,
I thoughte that Fortune wold me never fayle,
She was so redy to avance all to my comfort;
But nowe, alas, she is as redy my vice to transport,
Changyng my joy to great indignacion,
Leavyng me in the stormes of depe desperacion.

I may be compared in every circumstance
To Athalia that destroyed Davythes lynne,

Spared not the blood by cruel vengeance
Of Goddis prophets, but brought them to rewyn:
Murder askyth murder, by murder she did fynd,
So in lyke wyse resystyng my quarell
How many have dyed and ended parell.

I was the auctor why lawes ware made
For speking ayenst me, to daynger the innocent;
And with great othes I found owt the trade
To burden mens concyence: thus I did invent
My sede to advance; it was my full intent
Lynnyally to succeed in this Emperial crown:
But howe sone hath God brought my purpose down!

Who that woll presume a purpose to achyve
Without Goddis helpe their matters for to frame,
At thend they shall but skarsly thryve,
And for ther enterprice receyve great blame
At Goddis hands, presumyng to the same
Thexperyence in me, wantyng Goddis ayd,
Wold mount aloft: how sone ame I dekayd!

Yt had byn better for myn assuraunce
To have led my lyfe in meke simplyssitie,
Owt of all daynger of Fortune's dissemblaunce,
Usyng my lyfe in wyfely chastitie
As other women, regardyng myn honestie;
Oh how myche prayse is gevyn to thos
That wold in no case ther chastitie loos.

But well away, evermore the spott
Of my default shall, aye, spryng and be grean;
For who, alas, can bear a greater blott
Than of such lyfe to bear the name onclean?
My epitaphe shall be, – 'The vicious quene
Lyethe here, of late that justly lost hir hed,
Bycause that she did spott the kyngis bed.'

But God that dyd abhorre this lothesome deade,
For that I was a quene and lyved not chast
Hathe spotted me, alas, and all my sede;
Oon for a pledge, here left behynd for bast:[30]
Thus after swete sawce folowd an egere[31] tast,
A payment fyt, full well as it apperes
Dewe unto me for myn onjust desiers.

How happy art thou, quene Jane (the kyng's next wyfe),

Whos fame from ferre dayly doth rebound
For usyng of thy chast and sober lyfe;
Allthoughe thou art deade and layed in the ground,
Yet deathe wantithe power thy fame to confound;
For of thy chast sides perpetually to record
Sprong Kyng Edward, that swete and loyal lord.

O lady most excellent, by vertue stellefied,
Assendyng the hevyns, where thou raynest aye,
Among the goddes eternal, there to be deified,
Perpetually to endure unto the last day;
And I, most wretched, what shall I do or saye?
But humbly beseche the, O Lord, for thy passion,
That my worthy deathe may be my crymes purgacion.

Now must I depart, there is non other boote;[32]
Farewell, fayer ladies, farewell, all noble dames,
That sometyme ware obedyent and kneled at my foote,
Eschewe detraction, preserve your honest names,
Geve non occasion a sparke to kyndell flames;
Remember this sentence, that is both old and trewe,
'Who will have no smoke the fier must nedes eschewe.'

Farewell, most gentill kyng; farewell my lovyng make;[33]
Farewell the pleasaunt prynce, flower of all regally,
Farewell most pityfull, and pitie on me take;
Regard my dolorous woo marcyfully with your eye,
Howe for myn offences most mekely here I dye:
Marcy, noble prynce, I crave for myn offence;
The sharped sword hathe made my recompence.

## Wyatt's Poems on Anne's Fall

*Wyatt was arrested soon after Anne's own arrest and taken to the Tower, where he was held in the Bell Tower. Of the seven men imprisoned in the Tower at the time of Anne's fall, only Wyatt and Sir Richard Page escaped with their lives, something which appears to have weighed heavily on Wyatt's mind.*

Wyatt's past connection with Anne was enough to send him to the Tower, although it was early decided that he would not be tried. Certainly, his own father, Sir Henry Wyatt, was so unconcerned on hearing the news, late at night, of his son's imprisonment, that he promptly went back to bed, only attending to the business of attempting to secure his release the following morning.[34] At least two, and possibly three, poems refer to Wyatt's imprisonment and the fall of Anne Boleyn.

Poem 1 may, or may not, refer to Wyatt's imprisonment in May 1536. The poem was written while Wyatt was a prisoner and was addressed to Anne's kinsman, Sir Francis Bryan. Wyatt's arrest in May 1536 was not his only period of incarceration and the poem may refer to a later spell of *imprisonment. However, if it does refer to his time in the Tower in May 1536 it is of interest in that Wyatt clearly sets out his innocence of the crimes of which he was accused. It also speaks of the discomforts of imprisonment and the fears with which he was beset.*

*Poem 2 more certainly refers to Anne's fall. It is a lament to the five men that died for their alleged relationships with Anne and makes it clear that Wyatt witnessed their executions from his window in the Bell Tower. This would have been a sobering sight for the poet and increased his own fears that he would follow them to the block. In the poem Wyatt pities the men and laments their fate, although, like Anne herself, he criticised Mark Smeaton for his role in accusing the Queen by his confession.*

*Poem 3 demonstrates the change in Wyatt that was occasioned by his imprisonment. The Latin refrain, which can be translated as 'It thunders through the realms' characterises the shock felt by Wyatt at the savagery of Anne's fall. The words 'These bloody days have broken my heart. My lust, my youth did them depart' also refer to Wyatt's own sense of shock and the loss of his youth that it occasioned.*

*I. Wyatt, Being in Prison, To Bryan*[35]
Sighs are my food, my drink are my tears;
Clinking of fetters would such music crave;
Stink, and close air away my life it wears;
Poor innocence is all the hope I have:
Rain, wind, or weather judge I by my ears:
Malice assaults, that righteousness should have.
Sure am I, Bryan, this wound shall heal again,
But yet, alas! the scar shall still remain.

*II. In Mourning Wise Since Daily I Increase*[36]
In mourning wise since daily I increase,
Thus should I cloak the cause of all my grief:
So pensive mind with tongue to hold his peace.
My reason sayeth there can be no relief;
Wherefore, give ear, I humbly you require,
The affects to know that thus doth make me moan.
The cause is great of all my doleful cheer
For those that were and now be dead and gone.

What though to death desert be now their call
As by their faults it doth appear right plain.
Of force I must lament that such a fall
Should light on those so wealthily did reign,
Though some perchance will say, of cruel heart,
'A traitor's death why should we thus bemoan?'
But I, alas, set this offence apart,
Must needs bewail the death of some be gone.

As for them all I do not thus lament
But as of right my reason doth me bind.
But as the most doth all their deaths repent,
Even so do I by force of mourning mind.
Some say, 'Rochford, hadst thou been not so proud,
For thy great wit each man would thee bemoan.'
Since as it is so, many cry aloud,
'It is great loss that thou art dead and gone.'

Ah, Norris, Norris, my tears begin to run
To think what hap did thee so lead or guide,
Whereby thou hast both thee and thine undone,
That so bewailed in court of every side.
In place also where thou hast never been
Both man and child doth piteously thee moan.
They say, 'Alas, thou art far overseen
By thine offences to be thus dead and gone.'

Ah, Weston, Weston, that pleasant was and young,
In active things who might with thee compare?
All words accept that thou didst speak with tongue,
So well esteemed with each where thou didst fare.
And we that now in court doth lead our life,
Most part in mind doth thee lament and moan.
But that thy faults we daily hear so rife,
All we should weep that thou art dead and gone.

Brereton, farewell, as one that least I knew.
Great was thy love with diverse, as I hear,
But common voice doth not so sore thee rue
As other twain that doth before appear.
But yet no doubt but thy friends thee lament
And other hear their piteous cry and moan.
So doth each heart for thee likewise relent
That thou giv'st cause thus to be dead and gone.

Ah, Mark, what moan should I for thee make more
Since that thy death thou hast deserved best,
Save only that mine eye is forced sore
With piteous plaint to moan thee with the rest?
A time thou hadst above thy poor degree,
The fall whereof thy friends may well bemoan.
A rotten twig upon so high a tree
Hath slipped thy hold and thou art dead and gone.

And thus, farewell, each one in hearty wise.
The axe is home, your heads be in the street.

The trickling tears doth fall so from my eyes,
I scarce may write, my paper is so wet.
But what can help when death hath played his part
Though nature's course will thus lament and moan?
Leave sobs therefore, and every Christian heart
Pray for the souls of those be dead and gone.

*III. Circa Regna Tonat*[37]
*V. Innocentia*
*Veritas Viat Fides*
*Circumdederunt me inimici mei*

Who list his wealth and ease retain,
Himself let him unknown contain.
Press not too fast in at that gate
Where the return stands by disdain,
For sure, *circa Regna tonat.*

The high mountains are blasted oft
When the low valley is mild and soft.
Fortune with Health stands at debate.
The fall is grievous from aloft.
And sure, *circa Regna tonat.*

These bloody days have broken my heart.
My lust, my youth did them depart,
And blind desire of estate.
Who hastes to climb seeks to revert.
Of truth, *circa Regna tonat.*

The bell tower showed me such sight[38]
That in my head sticks day and night.
There did I learn out of a grate,
For all favour, glory, or might,
That yet *circa Regna tonat.*

By proof, I say, there did I learn:
Wit helpeth not defence too yerne,
Of innocency to plead or prate.
Bear low, therefore, give God the stern,
For sire, *circa Regna tonat.*

## Cranmer's Letter to Henry VIII on Anne's Fall[39]

*Cranmer's letter to Henry following Anne's fall demonstrates the Archbishop's
caution and his determination to preserve the religious reform at all costs.
Alexander Ales implies that Cranmer believed Anne to be innocent (see
below), and this is also suggested by his cautious attempt in his letter to set*

*out his belief in Anne's virtue, while also agreeing with the official line in*
*condemning her. Cranmer wrote a similar letter on the fall of another friend,*
*Thomas Cromwell, when he was arrested in 1540. Cranmer was a great*
*survivor of Henry VIII's reign and he was, perhaps, aware that there was*
*little he could actually do to aid the Queen. Within days of writing, Cranmer*
*pronounced that Anne's marriage was invalid at Henry's request.*

Pleaseth it your most noble grace to be advertised, that at your grace's
commandment, by Mr Secretary's letters, written in your grace's name, I
came to Lambeth yesterday, and do there remain to know your grace's
further pleasure. And forsomuch as without your grace's commandment I
dare not, contrary to the contents of the said letters, presume to come unto
your grace's presence; nevertheless, of my most bounden duty, I can do no
less than most humbly desire your grace, by your great wisdom, and by the
assistance of God's help, somewhat to suppress the deep sorrows of your
grace's heart, and to take all adversities of God's hands both patiently and
thankfully. I cannot deny but your grace hath great causes, many ways,
of lamentable heaviness: and also, that, in the wrongful estimation of the
world, your grace's honour of every part is so highly touched, (whether
the things that commonly be spoke of be true, or not,) that I remember
not that ever Almighty God sent unto your grace any like occasion to try
your grace's constancy throughout, whether your highness can be content to
take of God's hand, as well things displeasant, as pleasant. And if he finds
in your most noble heart such an obedience unto his will, that your grace,
without murmuration and overmuch heaviness, do accept all adversities, not
less thanking him than when all things succeed after your grace's will and
pleasure, nor less procuring his glory and honour; then I suppose your grace
did never thing more acceptable unto him, since your first governance of
this your realm. And moreover, your grace shall give unto him occasion to
multiply and increase his graces and benefits unto your highness, as he did
unto his most faithful servant Job; unto whom, after his great calamities and
heaviness, for his obedient heart, and willing acceptation of God's scourge
and rod, *addidit ei Dominus cuncta duplicia*. And if it be true, that is openly
reported of the queen's grace, if men had a right estimation of things, they
should not esteem any part of your grace's honour to be touched thereby,
but her honour only to be clearly disparaged. And I am in such a perplexity,
that my mind is clean amazed: for I never had better opinion in woman, than
I had in her; which maketh me to think, that she should not be culpable.
And again, I think your highness would not have gone so far, except she
had surely been culpable. Now I think that your grace best knoweth, that,
next unto your grace, I was most bound unto her of all creatures living.
Wherefore I most humbly beseech your grace to suffer me in that, which
both God's law, nature, and also her kindness bindeth me unto; that is, that
I may with your grace's favour wish and pray for her, that she may declare
herself inculpable and innocent. And if she be found culpable, considering
your grace's goodness towards her, and from what condition your grace
of your only mere goodness took her, and set the crown upon her head; I

repute him not your grace's faithful servant and subject, nor true unto the realm, that would not desire the offence without mercy to be punished, to the example of all other. And as I loved her not a little, for the love which I judged her to bear towards God and his gospel; so, if she be proved culpable, there is not one that loveth God and his gospel that ever will favour her, but must hate her above all other; and the more they favour the gospel, the more they will hate her: for then there was never creature in our time that so much slandered the gospel. And God hath sent her this punishment, for that she feignedly hath professed his gospel in her mouth, and not in heart and deed. And though she have offended so, that she hath deserved never to be reconciled unto your grace's favour; yet Almighty God hath manifoldly declared his goodness towards your grace, and never offended you. But your grace, I am sure, knowledgeth, that you have offended him. Wherefore I trust that your grace will bear no less entire favour unto the truth of the gospel, than you did before: forsomuch as your grace's favour to the gospel was not led by affection unto her, but by zeal unto the truth. And thus I beseech Almighty God, whose gospel he hath ordained your grace to be defender of, ever to preserve your grace from evil, and give you at the end the promise of his gospel. From Lambeth, the third day of May.

After I had written this letter unto your grace, my lord chancellor, my lord of Oxford, my lord of Sussex, and my lord chamberlain of your grace's house, sent for me to come unto the star-chamber; and there declared unto me such things as your grace's pleasure was they should make me privy unto. For the which I am most bounden unto your grace. And what communication we had together, I doubt not but they will make the true report thereof unto your grace. I am exceedingly sorry that such faults can be proved by the queen, as I heard of their relation. But I am, and ever shall be, your faithful subject.

Your grace's most humble subject, and chaplain,

T. Cantuariensis

## Alexander Ales to Queen Elizabeth I, 1558[40]

*Alexander Ales (1500–1565) was a Scottish follower of the religious reform. He was present in London at the time of Anne's death and was closely acquainted with both Thomas Cromwell and Thomas Cranmer, from whom he drew much of his information on Anne.*

*Ales wrote to Anne's daughter, Elizabeth I, soon after her accession, setting out his memories of her mother and including his own interpretation of the cause of her fall. Ales' account is of particular importance in relation to his claim that, in the days before her arrest, Anne made an appeal to Henry carrying her daughter in her arms, something that is related by no other source. He is also interesting in relation to Cranmer's reaction to Anne's death, demonstrating that in spite of his letter to Henry disassociating himself from the Queen, the Archbishop felt her loss deeply.*

*Ales wrote some years after the events that he described. It is also clear that he was eager to please Elizabeth. His inclusion of a forwarding address at the end of his letter is telling: he hoped to receive some preferment from*

*the Queen. Regardless of this, Ales' account is a useful source and he
provides a favourable eye-witness account to some of the events that made
up Anne's last days.*

*Ales' letter begins with a fairly standard form of praise, comparing
Elizabeth I to a number of Biblical heroines. The first part of the letter has
been summarised as:*

Congratulates her upon her accession to the throne by the 'senatus
consultum' of the realm, and the consent of all orders, she being the true
posterity of the families of the White and Red Roses, the sole daughter of
Henry VIII., and his lawful and undoubted heir. Although the joy which
the intelligence of her accession occasioned to all the English, Scotch,
French, and Belgian exiles (driven from their home for the confession of
the pure doctrine of the Gospel), has already been made know to her by the
churches of Frankfort on the Maine and Strasburg upon their return into
Britain, yet he considers that the duty of conveying this intelligence belongs
more especially to himself, England having afforded him an asylum at the
time when he was summoned to teach in the University of Cambridge
during the lifetime of her most pious mother. He is persuaded that all
ranks will rejoice at her accession. After referring to various characters
and incidents in the Old Testament history as illustrative of his warning,
he assures her that he believes that she prayed with Esther when she
saw her father's kingdom transferred to strangers, and the Archbishop of
Canterbury killed like Abimelech the High Priest, by Doeg. She had been
exposed like a second Esther to the dangers of a violent death in her sister's
Court, because, like Mardocheus and the Jewish nation, she professed
the same religion as the martyrs did, following herein the example of her
mother.

*He then continues, in Latin:*

... I am persuaded that the true and chief cause of the hatred, the treachery, and
the false accusations laid to the charge of that most holy Queen, your most
pious mother, was this, that she persuaded the King to send an embassy into
Germany to the Princes who had embraced the Gospel. If other arguments
of the truth of this were wanting, a single one would be sufficient, namely
that before the embassy had returned, the Queen had been executed.

On account of this embassy, the Emperor Charles, (who formerly had
been so hostile to your most serene father, with whom he had a suit before
the Pope and the Papal Legate in England, Campegio, on account of his
aunt, Queen Catherine, whom the King had divorced, and because he
had married your mother, and honoured her with the regal crown,) most
grievously threatened the Princes of Germany who were associated in the
defence of the Gospel.

It was chiefly on account of this embassy that he prepared for hostilities,
and invoked the aid of the Pope, King Ferdinand,[41] the nobles of Italy, Spain,
Hungary, Bohemia, Lower Germany, and other nations.

On account of this embassy all the Bishops who were opposed to the purer doctrine of the Gospel and adhered to the Roman Pontiff, entered into a conspiracy against your mother.

And I myself in some sort was the occasion of this embassy, having been the bearer of the 'Loci Theologici' of Philip Melancthon, which that very learned man sent to the most serene King your father, and had, moreover, induced him to dedicate that book to the King's Majesty.

I was also asked by the King whether I thought Philip would come into England if His Majesty invited him, and I answered that I had very little doubt as to his inclination so to do, could he obtain the permission of John Frederic, Duke of Saxony.

From these reasons it has often occurred to me that it was a duty which I owed the Church, to write the history, or tragedy, of the death of your most holy mother, in order to illustrate the glory of God and to afford consolation to the godly. No one, as far as I know, has as yet published such a work; I have been admonished from heaven by a vision or dream, which I shall presently narrate, to make it known to the world. I will therefore recount, with brevity and simplicity, the events as they occurred, introducing no ornaments of doctrine, as is done by some historical writers thereby to recommend themselves to their readers and to obtain credence for their narrative.

Shortly after the Bishop of Hereford had been sent into Germany by the most serene King along with Dr Nicolas Heath, now Archbishop of York, it happened that Dr Stephen Gardener, Bishop of Winchester, then Ambassador with the King of France, (a most violent persecutor of all the godly, on account of the true doctrine of the Gospel, who afterwards caused Dr Ridley, Bishop of London, Hopper, of Norwich, Latimer, of Worcester, and three others to be put to death,) wrote to those friends whom he had in the Court of the King of England, conspirators like himself, to the effect that certain reports were being circulated in the Court of the King of France, and certain letters had been discovered, according to which the Queen was accused of adultery.

These letters were delivered by the steward of the Bishop of Winchester, the King's Secretary, Thomas Wrothisley, who afterwards was created Earl of Southampton, whom Dr Stephen had placed in the Court to watch over his interests. They were next shown to the Lord Crumwell, the King's ear and mind, to whom he had entrusted the entire government of the kingdom.

As Crumwell attended at the Court daily, along with Wrotisley, the affair thus became known to the King himself. He was furious, but, dissembling his wrath, he summoned Crumwell, Wrotisley, and certain others, who, as report says, hated the Queen, because she had sharply rebuked them and threatened to inform the King that under the guise of the Gospel and religion they were advancing their own interests, that they had put everything up for sale and had received bribes to confer ecclesiastical benefices upon unworthy persons, the enemies of the true doctrine, permitting the godly to be oppressed and deprived of their just rewards. To them he intrusted the investigation of the whole business.

These spies, (because they greatly feared the Queen) watch her private apartments night and day. They tempt her porter and serving man with bribes; there is nothing which they do not promise the ladies of her bedchamber. They affirm also that the King hates the Queen, because she has not presented him with an heir to the realm, nor was there any prospect of her so doing.

Not long after this the persons returned who had been charged with the investigation of the rumours which had been circulated, everything having been arranged according to their entire satisfaction. They assure the King that the affair is beyond doubt; that they had seen the Queen dancing with the gentlemen of the King's chamber, that they can produce witnesses who will vouch to the Queen having kissed her own brother, and that they have in their possession letters in which she informs him that she is pregnant.[42]

Thereupon it was decided and concluded that the Queen was an adulteress, and deserved to be burnt alive. The Councillors were summoned to meet at the King's palace at Greenwich, opposite London, on the other side of the river Thames, on April 30.

At this time I was in attendance upon Crumwell at the Court, soliciting the payment of a stipend awarded to me by the most serene King. I was known to the Evangelical Bishops, whom your most holy mother had appointed from among those schoolmasters who favoured the purer doctrine of the Gospel, and to whom she had intrusted the care of it. I was also upon intimate terms with the Archbishop of Canterbury and Latimer, to whom your most holy mother was in the habit of confessing when she went to the Lord's Table. He it was for whom she sent when she was in prison and knew that she should shortly die. Although this most holy Queen, your very pious mother, had never spoken with me, nor had I ever received ought from anyone in her name, nor do I ever expect any such thing, (for all royal Courts have hitherto been opposed to me,) yet in consequence of what I had shortly before heard respecting as well her modesty, prudence, and gravity, as her desire to promote the pure doctrine of the Gospel and her kindness to the poor, from the Archbishop of Canterbury, Bishop Latimer, and even from Crumwell himself, I was deeply grieved in my heart at that tragedy about to be enacted by the Emperor, the Pope, and the other enemies of the Gospel, whose intention it was, along with her, to bury true religion in England and thus to restore impiety and idolatry.

Never shall I forget the sorrow which I felt when I saw the most serene Queen, your most religious mother, carrying you, still a little baby, in her arms and entreating the most serene King, your father, in Greenwich Palace, from the open window of which he was looking into the courtyard, when she brought you to him.

I did not perfectly understand what had been going on, but the faces and gestures of the speakers plainly showed that the King was angry, although he could conceal his anger wonderfully well. Yet from the protracted conference of the Council, (for whom the crowd was waiting until it was quite dark, expecting that they would return to London,) it was most obvious to everyone that some deep and difficult question was being discussed.

Nor was this opinion incorrect. Scarcely had we crossed the river Thames and reached London, when the cannon thundered out, by which we understood that some persons of high rank had been committed to prison within the Tower of London. For such is the custom when any of the nobility of the realm are conveyed to that fortress, which is commonly called the Tower of London, there to be imprisoned.

Those who were present (of whom, by God's mercy, many are still alive, and have now returned into England from banishment) well know how deep was the grief of all the godly, how loud the joy of the hypocrites, the enemies of the Gospel, when the report spread in the morning that the Queen had been thrown in the Tower. They will remember the tears and lamentations of the faithful who were lamenting over the snare laid for the Queen, and the boastful triumphing of the foes of the true doctrine. I remained a sorrowful man at home, waiting for the result; for it was easy to perceive that in the event of the Queen's death, a change of religion was inevitable.

I take to witness Christ, Who shall judge the quick and the dead, that I am about to speak the truth. On the day upon which the Queen was beheaded, at sunrise, between two and three o'clock, there was revealed to me (whether I was asleep or awake I know not) the Queen's neck, after her head had been cut off, and this so plainly that I could count the nerves, the veins, and the arteries.

Terrified by this dream, or vision, I immediately arose, and crossing the river Thames I came to Lambeth, (this is the name of the Archbishop of Canterbury's palace,) and I entered the garden in which he was walking.

When the Archbishop saw me he inquired why I had come so early, for the clock had not yet struck four. I answered that I had been horrified in my sleep, and I told him the whole occurrence. He continued in silent wonder for awhile, and at length broke out into these words, 'Do not you know what is to happen to-day?' and when I answered that I had remained at home since the date of the Queen's imprisonment and knew nothing of what was going on, the Archbishop then raised his eyes to heaven and said, 'She who has been the Queen of England upon earth will to-day become a Queen in heaven.' So great was his grief that he could say nothing more, and then he burst into tears.

Terrified at this announcement I return to London sorrowing. Although my lodging was not far distant from the place of execution, yet I could not become an eye witness of the butchery of such an illustrious lady, and of the exalted personages who were beheaded along with her.

Those persons, however, who were present, (one of whom was my landlord,) and others, told me at noon, that the Earl of Wiltshire (the Queen's father) had been commanded to be an assessor along with the judges, in order that his daughter might be the more confounded, and that her grief might be the deeper. Yet she stood undismayed; nor did she ever exhibit any token of impatience, or grief, or cowardice.

The Queen was accused of having danced in the bedroom with the gentlemen of the King's chamber and of having kissed her brother, Lord Rochfort. When she made no answer to these accusations, the King's syndic or proctor, Master Polwarck, produced certain letters and bawled out that she could not deny she had written to her brother, informing him that she was pregnant. Still she continued silent.

When the sentence of death was pronounced, the Queen raised her eyes to heaven, nor did she condescend to look at her judges, but went to the place of execution. Kneeling down, she asked that time for prayer should be granted her. When she had ceased praying, she herself arranged her hair, covered her eyes, and commanded the executioner to strike.

The Queen exhibited such constancy, patience, and faith towards God that all the spectators, even her enemies, and those persons who previously had rejoiced at her misfortune out of their hatred to the doctrine of the religion which she had introduced into England, testified and proclaimed her innocence and chastity.

Without being questioned they themselves answered the accusations brought against the Queen. It is no new thing, said they, that the King's Chamberlains should dance with the ladies in the bedchamber. Nor can any proof of adultery be collected from the fact that the Queen's brother took her by the hand and led her into the dance among the other ladies, or handed her to another, especially if that person was one of the royal chamberlains. For it is a usual custom thoughout the whole of Britain that ladies married and unmarried, even the most coy, kiss not only a brother, but any honourable person, even in public. It is the custom also with young women to write to their near relatives when they have become pregnant, in order to receive their congratulations. The King also was most anxious for an heir, and longed for nothing more than to know that the Queen was pregnant.

From such arguments as those which were advanced against the Queen they affirmed that no probable suspicion of adultery could be collected; and that therefore there must have been some other reason which moved the King. Possibly it might be the same as that which induced him to seek for a cause of divorce from his former Queen, namely, the desire of having an heir.

He was still further strengthened in his desire for a new marriage by perceiving that all the male children to which the Queen gave birth came into the world dead, and that for some years past she had not conceived. For the King was apprehensive that after his own decease civil wars would break out, and that the crown would again be transferred to the family of the White Rose if he left no heir behind him.

And further, the King was angry with the Queen because of the want of success which attended the embassy which, at her instigation, he had despatched into Germany, the Princes of which would not enter into a league with him against the Emperor, unless for the defence of the purer doctrine. They demanded more money than he was willing to give, nor would they permit Philip [Melancthon] to come into England. And the King was exceedingly indignant because the Princes of Germany doubted his faith.

Moreover, they said that the Emperor, the Pope, Ferdinand, and the other Princes were banded against the King, and that he was in danger from them on account of the change of religion; nor was there anyone among the Kings and Princes who would render him assistance in the event of the Emperor declaring war against him in consequence of the divorce of his aunt, Queen Catherine, and the substitution of a second wife.

How the matter actually stood would, however, they said, speedily be made known; whether he had executed the Queen for having broken her marriage vows, or for fear of the war which was about to break out in consequence of the changes in religion, and the divorce of the Emperor's aunt. For if he executed the Queen only on account of the suspicion of adultery, no change in religion would follow; but if out of fear of the war about religion and the divorce, then Lutheranism would be driven out of England and sent back into Germany, to those Princes who would not make a treaty with the King in the matter of the divorce. If, however, he was already in love with some other woman out of his anxiety for an heir, neither could this long be kept a secret. For so ardent was he when he had begun to form an attachment, that he could give himself no rest; so much so that when he was raving about Queen Anne and some of his friends were dissuading him from the divorce, he said that he preferred the love of the Queen to half his realm. It was in vain that his Councillors, and among the number Thomas More, the Chancellor, opposed this measure; for he sent agents to all the more renowned cities in France, Italy, and Germany, to collect the suffrages of the doctors in the matter of the divorce, not without the expenditure of an immense sum of money, concerning which he also consulted Luther and Philip.

While the guests were thus talking at table in my hearing it so happened that a servant of Crumwell's came from the Court and sitting down at the table, asked the landlord to let him have something to eat, for he was exceedingly hungry.

In the meantime, while the food was being got ready, the other guests asked him what were his news? Where was the King? What was he doing? Was he sorry for the Queen? He answered by asking why should he be sorry for her? As she had already betrayed him in secrecy, so now was he openly insulting her. For just as she, while the King was oppressed with the heavy cares of state, was enjoying herself with others, so he, when the Queen was being beheaded, was enjoying himself with another woman.

While all were astonished and ordered him to hold his tongue, for he was saying what no one would believe, and that he would bring himself into peril if others heard him talking thus, he answered, 'You yourselves will speedily learn from other persons the truth of what I have been saying.'

The landlord, who was a servant of Crumwell's, hearing this, said, 'It is not fitting for us to dispute about such affairs. If they are true they will be no secret. And when I go to Court I will inquire carefully into these matters.'

The person, however, who had first spoken, answered that he had the King's orders that none but the Councillors and secretaries should be admitted, and that the gate of the country house should be kept shut in which the King had secluded himself.

Some days afterwards, when the landlord returned from the Court, before anyone asked him a question he called out with a loud voice, 'I have news to tell you.' The guests anxiously waited to know what he had to say, whereupon he added, that within a few days the King would be betrothed and shortly afterwards would be married, but without any state, in the presence of the Councillors only; for he wished to delay the coronation of his new spouse until he should see whether she would give birth to a boy.

The issue of events proved that this was the truth, for the Lady Jane was crowned Queen when she was upon the eve of the confinement in which she died.[43]

The birth of a son gave immense satisfaction to the King. But as he was afraid that he himself would not live so long as to see the child grown up, he removed out of the way all those persons of whom he was apprehensive, lest, upon his death, they should seize the crown.

Shortly before his own death, conscious of the weakness of his son, he made a will by which he declared legitimate the daughter who had been born to him by the Emperor's aunt, and ordered that she should succeed to the throne in the event of his son dying without heirs.[44] And if she also should have no heirs, that then Your Royal Highness should be acknowledged to be Queen by the kingdom.

Although Cardinal Reginald Pole, one of the family of the White Rose, (from his hatred not only to the family of the Red Rose but also to the true doctrine of the Gospel,) accomplished thus much, when he returned into England from banishment, after the death of King Edward, that the realm should be transferred to strangers, still the counsel of God, which had determined to remove other persons out of the way and to give the crown of this realm to Your Majesty, could not be thwarted either by him, by the Pope, nor by the Emperor Charles.

She also, who succeeded your mother, and who gave an heir male to the King, died, (as I have before mentioned) in childbirth. As she was near her last breath she was crowned, and with this intention, lest it should be objected to the child, when he grew up and applied for the crown, that his mother had not been a crowned Queen of England.

The brother also of this Queen Jane, although he was created Duke of Somerset by the King,[45] and made the tutor of his nephew, the son of his sister, and the Governor of the whole realm, yet shortly after the death of your illustrious father he was beheaded by means of his enemy, John Dudley, Duke of Northumberland, who in his turn was put to death by your sister, Queen Mary; he having attempted to transfer the succession to his own family upon the death of your illustrious brother, the godly King Edward.

Although your brother, King Edward, on account of his piety, was worthy of a longer life, (which I am sure Your Royal Highness would not have grudged him, but which you would have wished for him,) nevertheless the fixed decree of God remained unaltered by which you were placed in the room of your most holy mother, whose innocence God has declared by the most indisputable miracles, and proved by the testimonies of all godly men. Of this, her innocence, there can be no more evident proof than this, that whereas she left you, her only child, your father always acknowledged you as legitimate; nor could those letters which were written by your mother to her brother, which were produced as the concluding and conclusive proof that your mother deserved capital punishment, persuade the illustrious King that you were not his daughter.

Thus much have I introduced about the tragedy of your most pious mother, in order that this illustrious instance might manifest the glory of God, and that the craft and power of man in vain oppose themselves to Him.

For this and many of God's mercies the writer hopes that she will be induced to serve Him faithfully, that she will guard herself from the snares of the devil, who was the cause of her mother's death in consequence of her love for the doctrine of the Gospel while it was in its infancy, and afterwards persecuted those persons whom she appointed to watch over the Church, the Archbishop of Canterbury, Latimer, and those other most holy Bishops and martyrs, of whom the writer would be glad to see a catalogue published by Doctor Bale. For those persons whom the King appointed as 'Inspectors of Churches', under the pretext of religion, consulted their own profit. God avenged this profanation of His Name by suppressing the doctrine and punishing the individuals. True religion in England had its commencement and its end with your mother. And as soon as the King began to hate her, laws hostile to the purer doctrine of the Gospel appeared.

When I could not bear these with a good conscience, nor could my profession allow me to dissemble them (for I was filling the office of the ordinary reader in the celebrated University of Cambridge by the King's orders,) I came to the Court, and asked for my dismissal by means of Crumwell. But he retained me for about three years, with empty hopes, until it was decreed and confirmed by law that married priests should be separated from their wives and punished at the King's pleasure. But before this law was published, the Bishop of Canterbury sent Lord Pachet [Paget] from Lambeth to me at London. (I understand that he afterwards attained a high position in the Court of your sister, Queen Mary.) He directed me to call upon the Archbishop early in the morning. When I called upon him, 'Happy man that you are,' said he, 'you can escape! I wish that I might do the same; truly my see would be no hindrance to me. You must make haste to escape before the island is blocked up, unless you are willing to sign the decree, as I have, compelled by fear. I repent of what I have done. And if I had known that my only punishment would have been deposition from the archbishopric, (as I hear that my Lord Latimer is deposed,) of a truth I would not have subscribed. I am grieved, however, that you have been deprived of your salary for three years by Crumwell; that you have no funds for your travelling expenses, and that I have no ready money. Nor dare I mention this to my friends, lest the King should become aware that warning had been given by me for you to escape, and that I have provided you with the means of travelling. I give you, however, this ring as a token of my friendship. It once belonged to Thomas Wolsey, and it was presented to me by the King when he gave me the archbishopric.'

When I heard what the Bishop had to say, I immediately caused my property to be sold, and I concealed myself in the house of a German sailor until the ship was ready, in which I embarked, dressed as a soldier, along with other German troops, that I might not be detected. When I had escaped a company of searchers, I wrote to Crumwell (although he had not behaved well towards me) and warned him of the danger in which he stood at that time, and about certain other matters. For this I can vouch the testimony of John Ales, Gregory, and the Secretary, and Pachet himself. But Christopher Mount said that Crumwell did not dare to speak to me when I was going away and soliciting my dismissal, nor could he venture to give me anything, lest he should be accused to the King, but that he would send the sum that he owed me into Germany.

The next intelligence, however, which I heard of him was that he had undergone capital punishment by order of the King; to whom he had written, when in prison, saying that he was punished by the just judgment of God, because he had loved the King more than God; and that out of deference to his Sovereign he had caused many innocent persons to be put to death, not sparing your most holy mother, nor had he obeyed her directions in promoting the doctrine of the Gospel.

May Christ preserve Your Highness from the snares of the devil, and warm your heart to love the true religion, by which His Name may be sanctified and the kingdom of His Son may again reach the English nation under your sway. — Leipsic [*Leipzig*], 1 Sept. Signed: Alexander Alesius, D.

P. S. — D. Johannes Outehoffius, who presents these letters to Your Majesty, is a very learned man and the constant associate of John a Lasco in the ministry of the Gospel. He is now returning out of Poland into England, on account of the reasons which he will explain to Your Majesty. I respectfully recommend him to you.

Should you wish to send me anything, this may be done by Bishop William Barlow, or by D. Bale.

## Letters Concerning the Fall of Anne Boleyn[46]

*Following her arrest on 2 May 1536, Anne was taken to the Tower of London. Throughout her time there, she was actively spied upon by the ladies that had been appointed to wait upon her and by Sir William Kingston, the lieutenant of the Tower. Kingston's letters concerning Anne's conduct are likely to be an accurate account. The letters were written at the time of her imprisonment and addressed to Thomas Cromwell, the King's chief minister. Of particular interest are the words spoken by Anne regarding her conduct and dealings with the men with whom she was accused. Her words concerning Francis Weston were enough to send him to the Tower and it is clear that she spoke unguardedly on first arriving at the formidable fortress. She later composed herself and Kingston was surprised at how cheerfully she faced death. He records that she swore that she was innocent of the crimes of which she was charged on the sacrament, compelling evidence as to her guiltlessness. Unfortunately, Kingston's letters were badly damaged by fire some years after they were written. Where possible, missing segments have been inserted in square brackets. These have been taken from earlier partial transcripts of the letters. Parts of the letters that are no longer extant are indicated by an ellipsis (i.e. ...).*

*The approximate length of the missing portions is demonstrated by the length of the ellipsis shown.*

*1. Sir William Kingston to Secretary Cromwell, upon Queen Anne's committal to the Tower*

Thys ys to advertyse you apon my Lord of Norfolk and the kyngs counsell depart[*inge*] from the Towre I went before the quene in to hyr lodgyng, & [*then she*] sayd unto me, M. Kyngston, shall I go in to a dungyn? Now,[47] madam, y[*ou*] shall go into your logyng that you lay in at your coronacion. It ys to gu[*de*] for me, she sayd, Jesu, have mercy on me; and kneled downe wepyng a [*great*] pace, and in the same sorow fell in to agret lawyng,[48] and she hathe done [*so*] mony tymes syns. And then she desyred me to move the kyngs hynes that she [*myght*] have the sacrament in the closet by hyr chambr, that she my[*ght pray*] for mercy, for I am as clere from the company of man, as for s[*yn, sayd she as I*] am clere from you, and am the kyngs trew wedded wyf; and then sh[*e sayd*] M. Kyngston, do you know wher for I am here, and I sayd Nay, and then [*she sayd*] when saw you the kyng? and I sayd, I saw hym not syns I saw [*him in*] the Tylte yerde,[49] and then M. K. I pray you to tell me wher my [*Lord Roch*]ford ys? and I told hyr I saw hym afore dyner in the cort. O [*where ys*] my sweet brod'er? I sayd I left hym at York place, and so I dyd. I [*hear say, say*]d she, that I shuld be accused with iij men; and I can say [*no more but*] nay, withyowt I shuld oppen my body; and ther with opynd [*her gown sayeng, O Nor*]res, hast thow accused me, thow ar in the Towre with me, & [*thou and I shal*]l dy to gether: and, Marke, thou art here to. O my mother, [*thou wilt dy*] for sorow, and meche lamented my lady of Worcet[r],[50] for by ca[*wse her child*] dyd not store[51] in hyr body, and my wyf sayd what shuld [*be the cawse, she*] sayd for the sorow she toke for me: and then she sayd M. K[*ingston, shall I dy*] with yowt just[s];[52] & I sayd, the porest sugett[53] the kyng [*hath had justis, and*] ther with she lawed.[54] All thys sayings was yester ny[*ght*] . . . . . . . . . . . . . . . . . . . & thys moryng dyd talke with mestrys Cosy,[55] [*and said that Nor*]res dyd say on Sunday last unto the quene amn[*er,*[56] *that he wold sw*]ere for the quene that she was a gud woman. [*And then sayd Mrs*] Cosyn, Madam, why shuld ther be hony seche maters [*spoken of? Mary,*] sayd she, I bad hym do so, for I asked hym why he [*went nat thorough with*] hys maryage? and he made ansur he wold tary [*a time. Then said she, you*] loke for ded mens showys;[57] for yf owth cam[*e to the king but good,*] you wold loke to have me; and he sayd, yf he [*should have ony soche thought,*] he wold hys hed war of;[58] and then she sayd, [*she could undo him if she wold,*] and ther with thay fell yowt. Bot [*she said, she more feared Weston; for*] on Wysson Monday last [*Weston told he*]r that Nores cam more u[*nto her chawmbre for her then for M*]age,[59] and further . . . . . . . . . . . . . . . . . . . . . . . . . . . . . . . . Wher I was commaunded to charge the gentlewemen that y gyf thaye atende apon the quene, that ys to say, thay shuld have now commynycaseon with hyr, in lese[60] my wyf ware present, and so I dyd hit, notwithstaundyng it canot be; for my lady Bolen[61] and mestrys Cosyn lyes on the quenes palet,[62] and I and my wyf at the dore with yowt,[63] so at[64] thay most nedes talke at[65] be without; bot I have every thyng told me by mestrys Cosyn that she thynks met for mee to knowe, and tother ij gentlewemen lyes with yowt me, and as I may knowe [*the*] kings plesur in the premysses I shall folow. From the Towre this mo . . . . . . . . . .

S$^r$. syns the makyng of thys letter the quene spake of West[*on that she*] had spoke to hym by cause he dyd love hyr kynswoma[*n Mrs Skelton*[66] *and that s*]he sayd he loved not hys wyf; and he made anser to hyr [*again that he*] loved won in hyr howse better then them bothe[*; she asked him who is that? to which he answered*] that it ys your self; and then she defyed hym. WILLM KYNG[STON.]

### 2. Sir William Kyngston to Secretary Cromwell, on Queen Anne's behaviour in Prison

After your departyng yesterday, Greneway gentilman ysshar cam to me, & . . . . . . . . . M. Caro and Mast$^r$ Bryan[67] commanded hym in the kyngs name to my [*Lord of*] Rotchfort from my lady hys wyf, and the message was now more . . . . . . . . . . se how he dyd; and also she wold humly sut unto the kyngs hy[*nes*] . . . . . . . . . . for hyr husband; and so he gaf hyr thanks, and desyred me to know [*at what*] tyme he shuld cum affore the kyngs counsell, for I thynk I s[*hall not*] cum forthe tyll I cum to my jogement, wepyng very . . . . . . . . . . . . . . . . . . . . I departed from hym, and when I cam to the chambr the [*quene heard*] of me and sent for me, and sayde I here say my lord my [*brother is*] here; it ys trowth, sayd I; I am very glad, said sh[*e that we*] bothe be so ny[68] together; and I showed hyr here wase . . . . . . . . . . Weston and Brerton, and she made very gud countenans . . . . . . . . . . I also sayd, M. Page and Wyet wase mo, then she sayd he ha . . . . . . . . . . on hys fyst tother day and ye here now bot ma . . . . . . . . . . . . . . . . . . . . I shall desyre you to bayre a letter from me [*to Master*] Secretory;[69] and then I sayd, madam, tell it me by [*word of mouth & I*] will do it, and so gaf me thanks saying, I ha[*ve moche marvell*] that the kyng's counsell come not to me; and thys [*same day she*] sayd we shuld have now rayne tyll she ware [*delivered owt*] of the Towre. I pray you it may be shortly by [*cawse of the*] fayre wether. You know what I mayne. The quen[*e sayd this*] nyght that the kyng wyst[70] what he dyd wh[*an he put soche*] ij abowt hyr as my lady Boleyn and Mestres [*Cosyns, for*] thay cowd tell hyr now thyng of my [*lord her father nor*] nothyng ellys, bot she defyed them all. B[*ot upon this my lady Bolen*] sayd to hyr, seche desyre as you heve ha[*d to soche tales*] hase browthe you to thys. And then sayd [*Mrs. Stoner, Marke*[71] ys the worst cheryssht of heny m[*an in the howse, for he*] wayres yernes, she sayd that was [*becaws he was no*] gentleman. Bot he wase never in m[*y chambr but at Winchestr, and*] ther she sent for hym to ple[*y on the virginals, for there my*] logyng was [*above the kings*] . . . . . . . . . . . . . . . . . . . . . . . . . . . . . . . . . . . . . . . . . . . . . . . . . . . . . . . . . . . . . . . . . . . . . . . . . . . . . . . . . . for I never spake with hym syns, bot apon Saterday before May day, and then I fond hym standyng in the ronde wyndo in my chambr of presens, and I asked why he wase so sad, and he ansured and sayd it was now mater, and then she sayd, you may not loke to have me speke to you as I shuld do to anobull[72]

man, by cause you be aninferer[73] persson. No, no, madam, aloke[74] sufficed
me; and thus far you well . . . . . . . . . . [s]he hathe asked my wyf whether
heny body maks thayr bed . . . . . . . . . . . . . . . . . . . [m]y wyf ansured and
sayd, nay, I warant you, then she say . . . . . . . . . . . . . . . . . . y myght make
baletts Well now bot ther ys non bet . . . . . . . . . . . . . . . . . . . d that can do
it, yese sayd my wyf master Wyett by . . . . . . . . . sayed trew.
. . . . . . . . . . my lord my brod' will dy.
. . . . . . . . . . ne I am sur thys was as
. . . . . . . . . tt downe to den[r] thys day.
WILLM KYNGSTON.
. . . . . . . . . . . . . . . . . . .thys day at diner I sent M. Nores hys diner & sent
hym . . . . . . . . . . . . . . . . . . a knave to hys prest that wayted apon hym
withe . . . . . . . . . . . . . . . . . . t unto hym, and he ansured hym agayn . .
. . . . . . . . . . . . . . . . . . . . . . . . . . . . . . . . . . ny thyng of my confession
he ys worthye to have . . . . . . . . . . . . . . . . . . hyt I defy hym; and also
he desyreth to hav . . . . . . . . . . . . . . . . . . [ha]lf anowre yf it may be the
kyngs plesur.
WILLM KYNG[STON.]


*3. Sir William Kyngston to Secretary Cromwell, with further details of the
Queen's Conduct*
S[r].

The quene hathe meche desyred to have here in the closet the sacarments,
& also hyr amner[75] who she supposeth to be Devet; for won owre she ys
determyned to dy, and the next owre meche contrary to that. Yesterday
after your departyng I sent for my wyf, & also for mestrys Cossyn to know
how the[76] had done that day, they sayd she had bene very mery and made
agret dyner, and yet sone after she called for hyr supper, havyng marvell
wher I was all day; and after supper she sent for me, and at my commyng
she sayd, 'Wher have you bene all day,' and I mad ansure I had bene with
prysoners, 'so,' she sayd, 'I thowth I hard M. Treasur[er,'] I ansured he was
not here; then she be gan talke and sayd I was creuely handeled . . . . . . .
. . . a Greweche with the kyngs counsell with my lord of Norfolke that he
sayd, [*Tut, tut, tut,*] and shakyng hys hed iij or iiij tymes, and as for Master
Tresurer he was in the [*Forest of Windsor.*] You know what she meynes by
that, and named M[r]. Controler to be avery [*gentleman*] . . . . . . . . . . . . . . .
. . . . she to be a quene and crevely handeled as was never sene; bot I [*think
the king*] dose it to prove me, and dyd lawth[77] with all and was very mery,
and th[*en she said I shall have just*]ists;[78] and then I sayde have now dowt
ther[*in*]; then she sayd yf hony man [*accuse me I can say bot n*]ay, & thay
can bring now wytnes, and she had talked with the gentell[*wemen*] . . . . . . .
. . . . . . . . . . . . sayd I knew at Marks commyng to the Towre that nyght I
reysayved . . . . . . . . . . . . . . . . . . . at it was x. of the cloke or he ware well
loged, and then she sayd . . . . . . . . . knew of Nores goyng to the Towre,
and then she sayd I had . . . . . . . . . . . . . . . . . . . . next yf it had bene leyd
she had wone, and then she sayd I w[*old God I had m*]y bysshoppys for
thay wold all go to the kyng for me, for I thy[*nke the most part of*] Yngland

prays for me, and yf I dy you shall se the grette[*st punishment for m*]e withyn
thys vij yere that ever cam to Yngland, & then sh[*e sayd I shal be in heaven,
for*] I have done mony gud dedys[79] in my days,[80] bot zit I thynke [*moche
onkindnes yn the*] kyng to put seche abowt me as I never loved: I showed
[*her that the king toke theym*] to be honest and gud wemen, bot I wold have
had [*of myn owne prevy chambre,*] weche I favor most &c.[81]
WILLM KYNGST[ON.]

*4. Edward Baynton to the Treasurer: declaring that only one person, named
Mark, will confess any thing against Queen Anne*
M[r] Theasurer,
This shalbe to advertyse yow that here is myche communycacion that noman
will confesse any thyng agaynst her, but allonly Marke of any actuell thynge.
Wherfore (in my folishe conceyte) it shulde myche toche the kings hono[r]
if it shulde no farther appeere. And I cannot beleve but that the other two
bee as f[*ully*] culpapull as ever was hee. And I thynke assur[*edly*] the on
kepith the others councell. As many . . . . . . . . . . conjectures in my mynde
causeth me to thynk . . . . . . . . . . specially of the communycacion that was
last bet[*wene*] the quene and Master Norres. M[r]. Aumener[82] [*tolde*] me as I
wolde I myght speke with M[r]. S[*ecretorie*] and yow together more playnely
expresse my . . . . . . . . . . . yf case be that they have confessyd like wret . . .
. . . . . . . all thyngs as they shulde do than my n . . . . . . . . . . . . . . . . . . . at
apoynte. I have mewsed myche at . . . . . . . . . . of mastres Margery whiche
hath used her . . . . . . . . . . strangely toward me of late, being her fry[*nde*]
as I have ben. But no dowte it cann[*ot be*] but that she must be of councell
therewith, [*there*] hath ben great fryndeship betwene the q[*ene and*] her of
late. I here farther that the que[*ne*] standith styfly in her opynyon that she
wo . . . . . . . . . . whiche I thynke is in the trust that she . . . . . . . . . . ther two.
But if yo[r] busynes be suche . . . . . . . . . . . . . . not com, I wolde gladly com
and wayte . . . . . . . . . . . . . . . . . . . . ke it requysyte. From Grenewy[*che*] . .
. . . . . . . . . . . . . mornyng.
EDWARD . . . . . .

*5. Sir William Kyngston to Secretary Cromwell, 16 May 1536, upon the
preparations for the execution of my Lord Rochford and Queen Anne*
Sir,
Thys day I was with the kyng's grace and declared the petysyons of my
Lord of Rochford, wherin I was answerd. Sir, the sayd lord meche desyreth
to speke with you, weche towchet hys consyens meche as he sayth, wherin
I pray you I may know your plesur, for by cause of my promysse made
unto my sayd lord to do the same, and also I shall desyre you further to
know the kyngs plesur towchyng the quene, as well for her comfyt as for
the preparacion of skefolds and hother necessarys consernyng. The kyng's
grace showed me that my lord of Cantorbury shuld be hyr confessar, and
was here thys day with the quene; & not[83] in that mater, sir, the tyme ys
short, for the kyng supposeth the gentelmen to dy to morow, and my lord of
Rocheford with the reysydew of gentelmen, & as zit with yowt [*confession*]

weche I loke for, bot I have told my lord of Rocheford that he be in aredynes to morow to suffur execusyon, and so he accepse[84] it very well, and will do his best to be redy, Notwithstandyng he wold have reysayved hys ryghts, weche hathe not bene used and in especiall here. Sir, I shall desyre you at[85] we here may know the kyngs plesur here as shortly as may be, at[86] we here may prepayre for the same weche[87] ys necessary, for the same we here have now may for to do execusyon. Sir, I pray you have gud rymembrance in all thys for hus[88] to do, for we shalbe redy al ways to our knowlage. Zit thys day at dyner the quene sayd at[89] she shuld go to Anvures[90] & ys in hope of lyf, and thus far you well.

WILLM KYNGSTON

*6. Sir William Kingston to Lord Cromwell, 18 May 1536*

Syr,

Thys shalbe to advertyse you I have resayved your lett[r] wherin yo[*u wolde*] have strangerys[91] conveyed yowt of the Towre and so thay be by the [*meanis*] of Richard Gressum, & Will-m Loke, & Wythepoll, bot the nmbr[92] of stra[*ngers past*] not xxx. and not mony; Hothe and the imbassit[r] of the emperor had a [*servaunt*] ther and honestly put yowt. S[r] yf we have not an owre[93] serten [*as it may*] be knowen in London, I thynke he[*re*] wilbe bot few and I thynk [*a resonable*] humbur[94] ware bes: for I suppose she wyll declare hyr self to b[*e a good*] woman for all men bot for the kyng at the o[r] of hyr de[*th.[95] For thys*] mornyng she sent for me that I myght be with hyr at [*soche tyme*] asshe reysayved the gud lord to the in tent I shuld here hy[*r speke as*] towchyng her innosensy alway to be clere.[96] & in the writy[*ng of this*] she sent for me, and at my commyng she sayd, M. Kyngston, I he[*ar saye I shall*] not dy affore none, & I am very sory ther fore; for I thowth [*than to*] be dede [*an*]d past my payne. I told hyr it shuld be now[97] payne it w[*as so sottell.[98] And then she said I*] hard say the execut[r]. was very gud, and I have a ly[*ttle necke, and put he*]r hand abowt it lawyng[99] hartely.

I have sen[*e mony men &*] also wemen executed and at they have bene in gre[*te sorrowe, and to my knowle*]ge thys lady hathe meche joye and plesur in dethe. [*Sir, hyr Amner[100] is conti*]newally with hyr, and hasse byne syns ij of the clo[*cke after midnight. This is*] the effect of hony thyng that ys here at [*thys tyme, and thus fare yow*] well.

Your . . . . . . .

WILLM KYNG[STON]

## Manuscript Account of Anne's Trial[101]

*Little evidence survives regarding Anne's trial or the evidence produced against her. The account of her trial below is therefore of interest. It is taken from an anonymous manuscript which contains the names of the Lord High Stewards of England from the reign of William I until the time of Charles I, as well as accounts of notable trials held before them. The account was, at its earliest, written over a century after Anne's death. However, it does largely accord with other surviving information on her trial and may have been taken from an earlier account. What is interesting about this account*

*is that it demonstrates that Anne defended herself as ably as her brother.
It also makes it clear that the result of the trial was a foregone conclusion;
she spoke so well in her defence that observers thought that she ought to
be acquitted although, of course, she was not.*

Thomas, Duke of Norfolke, Lord High Steward of England, att the Tryall
of Queene Anne Bulloigne, who, on the 15th Day of May in the 28th yeare
of the Raigne of King Henry the Eight, was arraigned in the Tower of
London, on a scaffold for that purpose made in the Kings Hall; the Duke
of Norfolke sittinge vnder the cloath of state, the Lord Chauncellour on his
right hand, and the Duke of Suffolke on his lefte, the Earle of Surrey, sonne
of the Duke of Norfolke, sittinge directly before his Father, a degree lower,
as Earl Marshall of England; to whome were adioyned 26 other Peeres,
and among them the Queenes Father, by whome shee was to be tryed. The
Kings Commission beinge read, the accusers gaue in theire evidence, and
the wittnesses were produced. The Queene sittinge in her Chaire made for
her, (whether in regard of any infirmity, or out of honour permitted to
the wife of the Soveraigne,) haueinge an excellent quick witt, and being a
ready speaker, did so answeare to all obiections, that, had the Peeres given
in theire verdict accordinge to the expectacion of the assembly, shee had
been acquitted. But they (among whome the Duke of Suffolke, the Kings
brother-in-lawe, was Cheife, and wholy applyinge himselfe to the Kings
humour,) pronounced her guilty; Whereupon the Duke of Norfolke, bound
to proceed accordinge to the verdict of the Peeres, condemned her to Death,
either by beinge burned in the Tower Greene, or beheaded, as his Maiestie
in his pleasue shoulde thinke fitt.

The Sentence beinge denounced, the Court arose, and she was conveyed
back againe to her Chamber, the Lady Bolen her Aunt, and the Lady Kinsman
*[sic]*, wife to the Constable of the Tower, only attendinge her.

## The Trials of Anne Boleyn and Lord Rochford, 15 May 1536[102]

*This is a summary translation from the original Latin. The original is
printed in full as an appendix to Wriothesley's Chronicle (volume 1). Few
details survive of Anne's trial. The summary below is therefore of interest,
in particular in relation to the charges laid against Anne. Although the
charges against Anne appear to be specific, in reality few can possibly have
been accurate, with Anne often resident at a different location on the dates
specified. The lurid details set out were calculated to shock and appall Anne's
contemporaries.*

Record of pleas held at the Tower of London before Thos. duke of Norfolk,
treasurer and earl marshal, lord high steward, citing:

(1) Patent appointing the said Duke steward of England *hac vice* for the trial
of queen Anne and lord Rocheford. Westm., 12 May 28 Hen. VIII.

(2) Mandate to Sir John Baldewin, Sir Ric. Lister, Sir John Porte, Sir John
Spelman, Sir Walter Luke, Sir Anth. Fitzherbert, Sir Thos. Englefeld, and Sir

Will. Shelley, special commissioners of Oyer and Terminer for Middlesex, to return all indictments found against queen Anne and lord Rocheford. Westm., 13 May 28 Hen. VIII.

(3) Similar mandate to Sir John Baldewyn, Sir Walter Luke, Sir Anth. Fitzherbert, and Sir Will. Shelley, special commissioners for Kent. Westm., 13 May 28 Hen. VIII.

(4) Mandate to Sir Will. Kyngestone, constable of the Tower, to bring queen Anne and lord Rocheford before the Lord High Steward when required. Westm., 13 May 28 Hen. VIII.

(5) The Lord High Steward issued his precept, 13 May, to Sir John Baldewyn and his fellows in Middlesex, to return the indictments at the Tower before him on Monday, 15 May, and a similar precept to Sir J. Baldewyn, Luke, and his fellows in Kent ; a third precept to the constable of the Tower to bring queen Anne and lord Rocheford that day before him ; and a fourth to Ralph Felmyngham, serjeant-at-arms, to summon such and so many lords of the kingdom, peers of the said queen Anne and lord Rocheford, by whom the truth may appear.

(6) Pleas held before the duke of Norfolk, steward of England, at the Tower, on Monday, 15 May 28 Hen. VIII.

The justices bring in the indictments for Middlesex and Kent, Sir Will. Kingston produces the prisoners, and Ralph Felmyngham declares that he has summoned the peers. Proclamation being then made, the peers answer to their names ; viz., Charles duke of Suffolk, Hen. marquis of Exeter, Will, earl of Arundel, John earl of Oxford, Hen. earl of Northumberland, Ralph earl of Westmoreland, Edw. earl of Derby, Hen. earl of Worcester, Thos. earl of Rutland, Rob. earl of Sussex, Geo. earl of Huntingdon, John lord Audeley, Thos. lord La Ware, Hen. lord Mountague, Hen. lord Morley, Thos. lord Dacre, Geo. lord Cobham, Hen. lord Maltravers, Edw. lord Powes, Thos. lord Mount Egle, Edw. lord Clynton, Will, lord Sandes, Andrew lord Wyndesore, Thos. lord Wentworth, Thos. lord Burgh, and John lord Mordaunt.

(7) Indictment found at Westminster on Wednesday next after three weeks of Easter, 28 Hen. VIII. before Sir John Baldwin, &c., by the oaths of Giles Heron, Roger More, Ric. Awnsham, Thos. Byllyngton, Gregory Lovell, Jo. Worsop, Will. Goddard, Will. Blakwall, Jo. Wylford, Will. Berd, Hen. Hubbylthorn, Will. Hunyng, Rob. Walys, John England, Hen. Lodysman, and John Averey; who present that whereas queen Anne has been the wife of Henry VIII. for three-years and more, she, despising her marriage, and entertaining malice against the King, and following daily her frail and carnal lust, did falsely and traitorously procure by base conversations and kisses, touchings, gifts, and other infamous incitations, divers of the King's daily and familiar servants to be her adulterers and concubines, so that several of the King's servants yielded to her vile provocations ; viz., on 6th Oct. 25 Hen. VIII., at Westminster, and divers days before and after, she procured, by sweet words, kisses, touches, and otherwise, Hen. Noreys, of Westminster, gentleman of the privy chamber, to violate her, by reason whereof he did so at Westminster on the 12th Oct. 25 Hen. VIII.; and they had illicit intercourse at various other times, both before and after, sometimes by his procurement,

and sometimes by that of the Queen. Also the Queen, 2 Nov. 27 Hen. VIII. and several times before and after, at Westminster, procured and incited her own natural brother, Geo. Boleyn, lord Rocheford, gentleman of the privy chamber, to violate her, alluring him with her tongue in the said George's mouth, and the said George's tongue in hers, and also with kisses, presents, and jewels; whereby he, despising the commands of God, and all human laws, 5 Nov. 27 Hen. VIII., violated and carnally knew the said Queen, his own sister, at Westminster; which he also did on divers other days before and after at the same place, sometimes by his own procurement and sometimes by the Queen's. Also the Queen, 3 Dec. 25 Hen. VIII., and divers days before and after, at Westminster, procured one Will. Bryerton, late of Westminster, gentleman of the privy chamber, to violate her, whereby he did so on 8 Dec. 25 Hen. VIII., at Hampton Court, in the parish of Lytel Hampton, and on several other days before and after, sometimes by his own procurement and sometimes by the Queen's. Also the Queen, 8 May 26 Hen. VIII., and at other times before and since, procured Sir Fras. Weston, of Westminster, gentleman of the privy chamber, &c., whereby he did so on the 20 May, &c. Also the Queen, 12 April 26 Hen. VIII., and divers days before and since, at Westminster, procured Mark Smeton, groom of the privy chamber, to violate her, whereby he did so at Westminster, 26 April 27 Hen. VIII.

Moreover, the said lord Rocheford, Norreys, Bryerton, Weston, and Smeton, being thus inflamed with carnal love of the Queen, and having become very jealous of each other, gave her secret, gifts and pledges while carrying on this illicit intercourse; and the Queen, on her part, could not endure any of them to converse with any other woman, without showing great displeasure; and on the 27 Nov. 27 Hen. VIII. and other days before and after, at Westminster, she gave them great gifts to encourage them in their crimes. And further the said Queen and these other traitors, 31 Oct. 27 Hen. VIII., at Westminster, conspired the death and destruction of the King, the Queen often saying she would marry one of them as soon as the King died, and affirming that she would never love the King in her heart. And the King having a short time since become aware of the said abominable crimes and treasons against himself, took such inward displeasure and heaviness, especially from his said Queen's malice and adultery, that certain harms and perils have befallen his royal body.

And thus the said Queen and the other traitors aforesaid have committed their treasons in contempt of the Crown, and of the issue and heirs of the said King and Queen.

(8) Record of indictment and process before Baldewyn, Luke, and others, in co. Kent.

The indictment found at Deptford, on Thursday, 11 May 28 Hen. VIII., is precisely similar in character to the Middlesex indictment, except as regards times and places; viz., that the Queen at Estgrenewyche, 12 Nov. 25 Hen. VIII., and divers days before and since, allured one Hen. Noreys, late of Est Grenewyche, to violate her, whereby he did so on the 19 Nov., &c.; that on 22 Dec. 27 Hen. VIII., and divers other days, at Eltham, she allured Geo. Boleyn, lord Rocheford, &c., whereby he did so, 29 Dec., &c.; that on the

16 Nov. 25 Hen. VIII., and divers, &c., at Est Grenewyche, she allured one Will. Bryerton, late of Est Grenewyche, &c., whereby he did so, 27 Nov., &c.; that on the 6 June 26 Hen. VIII., &c., at Est Grenewyche, she allured Sir Fras. Weston, &c., whereby he did so, 20 June, &c.; that on the 13 May 26 Hen. VIII. &c., at Est Grenewyche, she allured Mark Smeton, &c., whereby he did so, 19 May 26 Hen. VIII.

And further that the said Boleyn, &c. grew jealous of each other; and the Queen, to encourage them, at Eltham, 31 Dec. 27 Hen. VIII., and divers times before and since, made them presents, &c.; that the Queen and the others, 8 Jan. 27 Hen. VIII., conspired the King's death, &c., and that she promised to marry one of the traitors whenever the King was dead, affirming she would never love him, &c.

And afterwards, Monday, 15 May, queen Anne comes to the bar before the Lord High Steward in the Tower, in the custody of Sir Will. Kingston, pleads not guilty, and puts herself on her peers; whereupon the said duke of Suffolk, marquis of Exeter, and other peers, are charged by the High Steward to say the truth; and being examined from the lowest peer to the highest, each of them severally saith that she is guilty.

Judgment: To be taken to prison in the Tower, and then, at the King's command, to the Green within the Tower, and there to be burned or beheaded as shall please the King.

The same day, lord Rocheford is brought before the High Steward in the custody of Sir Will. Kingston, and pleads not guilty. The peers are charged, with the exception of the earl of Northumberland,[103] who was suddenly taken ill, and each of them severally saith that he is guilty.

Judgment: To be taken to prison in the Tower, and then drawn through the city of London, to the gallows at Tyburn, &c., as usual in high treason.

# Anne Boleyn to Lady Wingfield, *c.* 1532[104]

*Few documents relating to the evidence produced at Anne's trial survive. Sir John Spelman, a judge who sat on the bench at Anne's trial, noted that she had originally been accused by Lady Wingfield. Lady Wingfield died in either 1533 or 1534, apparently leaving a deathbed statement accusing Anne of being morally lax. This statement no longer survives but the letter below is interesting. It was written shortly before Anne's marriage and demonstrates that she was particularly close to Lady Wingfield, declaring that she loved her almost as much as her own mother.This suggests that Anne and Lady Wingfield were close and that they may have shared some secret. It is not impossible that Anne may have consummated her relationship with Henry Percy, believing that she was legally contracted to him, and perhaps Lady Wingfield's statement related to this. Without her deathbed statement, or a full record of the trial, it is impossible now to be certain.*

Madam,

I pray you, as you love me, to give credence to my servant this bearer, touching your removing and any thing else that he shall tell you of my behalf; for I will desire you to do nothing but that shall be for your wealth.

And, madam, though at all times I have not shewed the love that I bear you as much as it was indeed, yet now I trust that you shall well prove that I loved you a great deal more than I made feign for; and assuredly, next mine own mother, I know no woman alive that I love better: and at length, with God's grace, you shall prove that it is unfeigned. And I trust you do know me for such a one that I will write nothing to comfort you in your trouble but I will abide by it as long as I live; and therefore I pray you leave your indiscreet trouble, both for displeasing of God and also for displeasing of me, that doth love you so entirely. And trusting in God that you will thus do, I make an end. With the ill hand of

Your own assured friend during my life,

ANNE ROCHEFORD

## Elizabeth, Countess of Worcester to Thomas Cromwell, 1537[105]

*It has also been suggested that the Countess of Worcester was Anne's first accuser. Lady Worcester was a member of Anne's household and, apparently when accused of immoral conduct by her brother, Sir Anthony Browne, declared that she was not the worst and that he should look at the conduct of the Queen herself. The letter below, written by the Countess nearly a year after Anne's death, demonstrates that she and the Queen were close and that Anne lent her the large sum of £100 for a purpose that she desired to keep secret from her husband. This suggests that Anne and the Countess were close and it is possible that Lady Worcester reported on the open atmosphere of Anne's household, in which she encouraged music and dancing and openly involved herself in the rituals of courtly love, as indicated by her comments in relation to Henry Norris, Mark Smeaton and Francis Weston set out in Sir William Kingston's letters (printed above).*

Mine own good lord,

I heartily commend me to you. And whereas I do perceive, by a letter sent to me from my brother, that you are special good lord unto me as touching the sum of one hundred pounds which I did borrow of queen Anne, deceased; in which thing I doubt it not but she would have been good to me: for your goodness to me in that matter I most heartily thank you, desiring you of continuance, and I, with all my friends, to the uttermost of our poor powers, shall be glad to deserve it. For I am very loath it should come to my lord my husband's knowledge, which is and hath been utterly ignorant both of the borrowing and using of the said hundred pounds. And if he should now have knowledge thereof, I am in doubt how he will take it. Wherefore I beseech you continue your good mind, and be good lord to me in this matter. Thus Almighty God preserve you.

At Tintern, the 8th day of March.

Yours to her power,

ELIZABETH WORCESTER

## Lady Rochford to Thomas Cromwell[106]

*Anne's sister-in-law, Jane Parker, Lady Rochford, appeared with her in the*

*famous masque at Greenwich in 1522.*[107] *She is a somewhat shadowy figure. She is known to have been associated with Anne Boleyn in 1534, when Chapuys reported that she had been banned from court for working with Anne in an attempt to secure the banishment of Henry's mistress, the so-called 'Imperial Lady'. Lady Rochford was the daughter of Henry Parker, Lord Morley, who had, in his youth, served Henry's grandmother, Lady Margaret Beaufort, and who was known for his conservative beliefs, later writing 'A Book of Miracles and Examples of Virtue for the Guidance of a Ruler' for the Catholic Mary I.*[108] *It has recently been suggested that Lady Rochford may have had some sympathy, and links, with Catherine of Aragon and her daughter, Princess Mary.*

*Few details survive of Lady Rochford's involvement in the arrests of her husband and sister-in-law, although it does appear that she provided information against them. It may, perhaps, have been Lady Rochford who claimed that George Boleyn questioned the legitimacy of Princess Elizabeth, that Anne and George's mocked Henry's clothes and poetry, and that Anne and George had discussed the King's impotency. The letter below is interesting due to the paucity of sources concerning Lady Rochford. It demonstrates that she was in a far from comfortable position following her husband's execution and, perhaps, accounts for her early return to court as a servant of Jane Seymour.*

Mayster Secretory, as a power[109] desolat wydow wythoute comffort, as to my specyall trust under God and my Pryns, I have me most humbly recommendyd unto youe; prayng youe, after your accustemyd gentyll maner to all them that be in suche lamentabull case as I ame in, to be meane to the Kyngs gracyous Hyghnes for me for suche power stuffe and plate as my husbonde had, whome God pardon; that of hys gracyous and mere lyberalyte I may have hyt to helpe me to my power[110] lyvyng, whiche to his Hyghnes ys nothynge to be regardyd, and to me schuld be a most hygh helpe and souccor. And farther more, where that the Kyngs Hyghnes and my Lord my father payed great soms of money for my Joynter to the Errell of Wyltchere to the some off too thowsand Marks, and I not assuryd of no more duryng the sayd Errells naturall lyff then one hundreth Marke; whyche ys veary hard for me to schyffte the worldd wythall. That youe wyll so specyally tender me in thys behalff as to enforme the Kyngs Hyghnes of these premysses, wherby I may the more tenderly be regardyd of hys gracyous persone, youre Worde in thys schall be to me a sure helpe: and God schall be to youe therfore a sure reward, whyche dothe promes good to them that dothe helpe powere[111] forsaken Wydos. And bothe my prayer and servys schall helpe to thys duryng my naturall lyff, as most bounden so to doo, God my wyttnes; whoo ever more preserve you.
JANE ROCHEFORD

## Extract from Cavendish's *Metrical Visions* on Jane, Viscountess Rochford[112]

*Lady Rochford returned to court as a widow. She became one of the leading attendants of Henry VIII's fifth wife, Catherine Howard, the cousin of Anne Boleyn. She followed her husband to the block in 1542 for her role in assisting Catherine Howard in her clandestine meetings with her lover, Thomas Culpeper.*

*As a prominent executed traitor, Lady Rochford received an entry into Cavendish's* Metrical Visions. *She is a somewhat shadowy figure and the verses provide useful information into her character. As with the previous extract from the* Metrical Visions *however, caution should be taken when using this fictionalised portrayal of Lady Rochford as fact.*

*Th'auctor G.C.*
As I drewe towards thend of my boke,
Purposyng to fynyshe that I had begon,
By chaunce, asyde, as I cast my loke,
I aspied a wydowe in blake full woo begon
*[Line blank in manuscript]*
That I wold hir a place here afford,
Whom I oons knew, Jane, Viscountess Rocheford.

*Viscountess Rocheford.*
My grave father (quod she) of the Morlas[113] lynne,
My mother of the St John's;[114] this was my parentage:
And I, alas! that dyd myself inclyne
To spot them all by this my owltrage,[115]
Brought uppe in the court all my yong age,
Withouten bridell of honest measure,
Folowing my lust and filthy pleasure.

Without respect of any wyfely truthe,
Dredles of God, from grace also exempte,
Vicously consumyng the tyme of thys my youth;
And when my beautie began to be shent;[116]
Not with myn owne harm suffced or content,
Contrary to God, I must it nedes confesse,
Other I entised by ensample of my wredchedness.

Of right me thynkith I ought to be a glass
To all the rest of great estates; and dames
Seyng me nowe, considering what I was,
Without any blott, to kepe their honest names:
Seyng that vice ne endyth without flames;
And thoughe that shame may be wayled all day,
Thereof the blott will not be washt away.

Howe bright among us yet dothe shyne the starre
Of them that ride within the chayer of Fame,
Above all things, which only did preferre

The brewte to kepe of their onbroken name;
As auctors right well dothe testifie the same
Ayenst such vices that wan the victory,
And beare the palme to their eternall glory.

As vertuous Sara, Rebecca, and Racell,
Judyth, Hester, and chast Pennelopie,
And Cornelia, that onbroken kept the shell,
And bare the lampe of onquenched chastitie,
Fleeyng excesse or superfluitie,
Where carnall lust for all his violence
Ne made them breke chastitie or obedyence.

Where sturdy Silla, to nature contrarious,
Enforced by lust hir father's heare to pull;
With Cleopatra, concubyn to Anthonyous,
With vicious Pasiphae that deled with the Bull;
And Messalyne, insacyatt, that never was full:
But ever thes wretches, vicious and discommendable
To God and nature, they lived abhominable.

Wold to God that I, in my flowryng age,
Whan I did trade the courtly life,
Had fostered byn in a symple village,
Beryng the name of and honest and chast wyfe;
Where now my slaunder for ever shall be ryfe
In every matter, both early and late,
Called the woman of vice insaciatt.

The tyme is past, and I have now receyved
The dewe dett of my onjust desiers,
Prayeng to God my fall may be conceyved
Within their harts that burn in vicious fiers;
The just God, as right allwayes requires,
That hath me punyshed for my misgovernaunce,
Ne take of me a greater vengeaunce.

## Cromwell to Gardiner and Wallop, Ambassadors in France, 14 May 1536[117]

*Cromwell's letter below, to the English ambassadors in France, provides the official account of Anne's fall. As Chapuys' despatches show, it does not, by any means, show the full extent of Henry's chief minister's involvement in Anne's arrest.*

Aftre my right harty commendacions, Albeit ye shall at this tyme receyve non answer to your letteres sent by Salisbury being the same differred[118] tyl tharryval of the baylie of Troys, Yet the kinges highnes thought convenient that I shuld aduertise you of a chaunce, as most detestably and abhomynably deuised[119] contryved ymagined doon[120] and contynued, soo most happely and graciously by thordenaunce of god reueled[121] manifested and notoriously knowen to all men. Wherof though ye haue harde[122] I doubt not the rumour, yet I shal expresse vnto youe some parte of the cummyng out, and of the kinges proceding in the same. The quenes abhomynacion both in incontynent lyving, and other offences towardes the kinges highnes was so rank and commen, that her ladyes of her privy chambre, and her chamberers could not conteyne it within their brestes, But detesting the same had soo often communications and conferences of it that at the last it cam soo plainly to the eares of some of his graces counsail that with their dieutye[123] to his Maiestie they could not concele it from him, but with greate feare, as the cace enforced declared what they harde vnto his highnes Wherupon in most secret sorte certain personnes of the privye chambre and others of her side were examyned, in whiche examynacions the matier appered soo evident, that besides that cryme, with the accidentes, there brake out a certain conspiracye of the kinges deathe, whiche extended soo farre that all we that had thexamynacion of it quaked at the daunger his grace was in, and on our knees gave him laude and prayse that he had preserued him soo long from it, and nowe manifested the most wretched and detestable determynacion of the same. Thus were certain men commytted to the towre for this cause, that is Markes[124] & Norres, and her brother thenne was she apprehended, and conveyed to the same place, aftre her was sent thither for the crymes specefied, Sir Fraunces Weston and William Brereton. And Norres Weston Brereton and Markes be already condempned to deathe, vppon arraynement in Westminster hal on Friday last. She and her brother shalbe arayned tomorowe, and wil vndoubtedlie goo the same waye. I write noo particularities, the thinges be soo abhomynable, that I thinke the like was neuer harde, and therfor I doubt not but this shalbe sufficient for your Instruction to declare the truth if ye haue occasion soo to doo. Your lordship shall get in CC li[125] of the III c[126] that were out amonges thise men, notwithstanding greate sute hath been made for the hole, whiche though the kinges highnes might give in this cace yet his maiestie doth not forget your seruice. And the third C li[127] is bestowed of the vicar of hell,[128] vppon [whom] though it be some charge vnto youe his highnes trusteth ye wil think it wel bestowed. And thus Fare you most hartely well From the Roulles in hast this xiiiith of Maye

Youre louyng assuryd freen[d]

Thomas Crumwell

## Anne's Letter to Henry VIII from the Tower[129]

*The following letter, which is not in Anne's handwriting, was found among Thomas Cromwell's papers and endorsed with the words 'To the King from the Lady in the Tower'. The letter was reputedly written on 6 May 1536, while Anne was in the Tower and it has been suggested that it is a copy of an original written or, perhaps, dictated by Anne. Stylistically, the letter does not accord with Anne's other surviving letters and it is debatable whether she would have dared to have written to Henry in such terms. On 6 May Anne still entertained some hopes that she would be allowed to retire to a nunnery and she would not have wished to jeopardise this. She would also have been concerned about Henry's reaction to the letter, which, even in the event of her own death, could be visited on her daughter or her surviving relatives. The letter must be considered extremely doubtful. However, it is not impossible that Anne found the means and time to write in the Tower. Kingston, in one of his letters to Cromwell, did indeed mention that she had asked him to forward a letter to the chief minister. She was also often outspoken with Henry during their courtship and marriage and, if anyone had dared to write to the King on such terms, it would have been Anne Boleyn.*

*The early historian John Strype mentioned a possible second letter written by Anne to Henry from the Tower, written in response to a message from the King urging her to confess. He claimed to have seen this document, although did not transcribe it in full, merely relating that it ended:*

> She could confess no more than she had already spoken. And she said, she must conceal nothing from the king, to whom she did acknowledge her self so much bound for many favours: for raising her first from a mean woman to be a marquess; next to be his queen; and now, seeing he could bestow no further honour upon her on earth, for purposing to make her, by martyrdom, a saint in heaven.[130]

*This appears to be a second letter due to the fact that it differs materially from the letter quoted below, which Strype references as published by Burnet in his* History of the Reformation.[131] *Strype was therefore aware that the paragraph quoted above does not occur in the letter below.*

Your grace's displeasure and my imprisonment are things so strange unto me, that what to write, or what to excuse, I am altogether ignorant. Whereas you send to me (willing me to confess a truth and so obtain your favour), by such a one, whom you know to be mine ancient professed enemy; I no sooner received this message by him, than I rightly conceived your meaning; and if, as you say, confessing a truth indeed may procure my safety, I shall, with all willingness and duty, perform your command. But let not your grace ever imagine that your poor wife will ever be brought to acknowledge a fault, where not so much as a thought ever proceeded. And to speak a truth, never a prince had wife more loyal in all duty, and in all true affection, than you have ever found in Anne Bolen, – with which name and place I could willingly have contented myself if God and your grace's pleasure had so been pleased. Neither did I at any time so far forget myself in my exaltation, or received queenship, but that I always looked for such alteration as I now find; for the ground of my preferment being on no surer foundation than your grace's fancy, the least alteration was fit and sufficient (I knew) to draw that fancy to some other subject.

You have chosen me from a low estate to be your queen and companion, far beyond my desert or desire; if then you found me worthy of such honour, good your grace, let not any light fancy or bad counsel of my enemies withdraw your princely favour from me, neither let that stain – that unworthy stain – of a disloyal heart towards your good grace, ever cast so foul a blot on me and on the infant princess your daughter.

Try me, good king, but let me have a lawful trial, and let not my sworn enemies sit as my accusers and as my judges: yea, let me receive an open trial, for my truth shall fear no open shames; then shall you see either mine innocency cleared, your suspicions and conscience satisfied, and ignominy and slander of the world stopped, or my guilt openly declared. So that whatever God and you may determine of, your grace may be freed from an open censure, and mine offence being so lawfully proved, your grace may be at liberty, both before God and man, not only to execute worthy punishment on me, as an unfaithful wife, but to follow your affection already settled on that party, for whose sake I am now as I am; whose name I could some good while since, have pointed unto; – your grace being not ignorant of my suspicion therein.

But if you have already determined of me, and that not only my death, but an infamous slander, must bring you the joying of your desired happiness, then I desire of God that he will pardon your great sin herein, and, likewise, my enemies, the instruments thereof, and that he will not call you to a strait account for your unprincely and cruel usage of me at his general judgment-seat, where both you and myself must shortly appear; and in whose just judgment, I doubt not (whatsoever the world may think of me) mine innocency shall be openly known and sufficiently cleared.

My last and only request shall be, that myself may only bear the burden of your grace's displeasure, and that it may not touch the innocent souls of those poor gentlemen, whom, as I understand, are likewise in strait imprisonment for my sake.

If ever I have found favour in your sight – if ever the name of Anne Bulen have been pleasing in your ears – then let me obtain this request; and so I will leave to trouble your grace any further: with mine earnest prayer to the Trinity to have your grace in his good keeping, and to direct you in all your actions.

From my doleful prison in the Tower, the 6th of May.
ANN BULEN

## Poems Supposedly Written by Anne in the Tower

*Traditionally, the two poems below have been ascribed to Anne while she was in the Tower. If she was, as suggested above, permitted the means to write two letters to her husband during her imprisonment, it is not impossible that she also found the time to write two verses. She moved in literary circles and her brother, Lord Rochford, her cousin, the Earl of Surrey, and her admirer, Sir Thomas Wyatt, were all noted poets.*

*If the two poems below can be considered to be Anne's they are notable as the only surviving examples of her writing, excepting letters. Much doubt must surround them, however. It has recently been suggested that the first was probably written by the composer Robert Johnson (c. 1583–1633).[132] The second is more*

*easily ascribed to Anne and was originally set to music by her former chaplain,*
*Robert Jordan. Both should be treated with caution however.*

*Doleful Complaints of Anne Boleyn*[133]

*I*

Defiled is my name, full sore
Through cruel spite and false report,
That I may say for evermore,
Farewell to joy, adieu comfort.
For wrongfully ye judge of me;
Unto my fame a mortal wound:
Say what ye list, it may not be,
Ye seek for that cannot be found.

*II*

O death, rock me on sleep,
Bring me on quiet rest,
Let pass my very guiltless ghost,
Out of my careful breast;
Toll on the passing bell,
Ring out the doleful knell,
Let the sound my death tell,
    For I must die,
    There is no remedy,
    For now I die.

My paines who can express?
Alas! they are so strong,
My dolour will not suffer strength,
My life for to prolong;
Toll on the passing bell,
Ring out the doleful knell,
Let the sound my death tell,
    For I must die,
    There is no remedy,
    For now I die.

Alone in prison strong,
I wail my destiny;
Wo worth this cruel hap that I
Should taste this misery.
Toll on the passing bell,
Ring out the doleful knell,
Let the sound my death tell,
    For I must die,
    There is no remedy,
    For now I die.

Farewell my pleasures past,
Welcome my present pain,
I feel my torments so increase,
That life cannot remain.
Cease now the passing bell,
Rung is my doleful knell,
For the sound my death doth tell,
   Death doth draw nigh,
   Sound my end dolefully,
   For now I die.

## Extract from the Chronicle of Calais[134]

*The Chronicle of Calais, which mainly details events from the last English possession in France, provides one of the most complete accounts of the death of Anne's brother, George Boleyn, Lord Rochford. Rochford had visited Calais on more than one occasion, which may account for the contemporary chronicler's interest in him.*

*The penitential tone of Rochford's speech should not be taken as an admission of guilt in the crimes of which he was accused. In order for a condemned prisoner to be considered to have a good death, it was necessary for them to show remorse and go to their death demonstrating a pious faith in God. Rochford's penitence at his sinful way of life is in accordance with this tradition.*

1536. The words of ser Gorge Boleyne, brothar to qwene Anne, warden of the v. portes, on the xvij. of May, when he toke his deathe at the Towre Hill at London, he sayde thre tymes, 'Christen men, I am borne undar the lawe, and judged undar the lawe, and dye undar the lawe, and the lawe hathe condemned me. Mastars all, I am not come hether for to preche, but for to dye, for I have deserved for to dye yf I had xx. lyves, more shamefully than can be devysed, for I am a wreched synnar, and I have synned shamefully, I have knowne no man so evell, and to reherse my synnes openly it were no pleaswre to you to here them, nor yet for me to reherse them, for God knowethe all; therefore, mastars all, I pray yow take hede by me, and especially my lords and gentlemen of the cowrte, the whiche I have bene amonge, take hede by me, and beware of suche a fall, and I pray to God the Fathar, God the Sonne, and the Holy Ghoste, thre persons and one God, that my deathe may be an example unto yow all, and beware, trust not in the vanitie of the worlde, and especially in the flateringe of the cowrte. And I cry God mercy, and aske all the worlde forgevenes, as willingly as I wowld have forgevenes of God; and yf I have offendyd any man that is not here now, eythar in thowght, worde, or dede, and yf ye here any suche, I pray yow hertely in my behalfe, pray them to forgyve me for God's sake. And yet, my masters all, I have one thinge for to say to yow, men do comon and saye that I have been a settar forthe of the worde of God, and one that have favored the Ghospell of Christ; and bycawse I would not that God's word shuld be slaundered by me, I say unto yow all, that yf I had followed God's worde in dede as I dyd rede it and set it forthe to my power, I had not come to this. I dyd red the Ghospell of Christe, but I dyd not follow it; yf I had, I had bene a lyves man[135] amonge yow: therefore I pray yow, mastars all, for God's sake sticke to the trwthe and folowe it, for one good followere is worthe thre redars, as God knowethe.'

The xix. of May qwene Ann Boleyn was behedyd in the Towre of London, by the hands of the hangman of Caleis, withe the swerde of Caleis.

## Extract from Wriothesley's Chronicle on Anne's Trial and Death[136]

*Wriothesley's Chronicle (which is discussed above in relation to the extract detailing Anne's coronation and the birth of Princess Elizabeth) is of particular interest in relation to Anne's trial, of which few sources survive. It is highly probable that Wriothesley would have heard what occurred at the trial from an eyewitness and his comments on Anne's strong defence against the charges is interesting. It accords with the anonymous manuscript account of the trial printed above.*

This yeare, on Maye daie, 1536, beinge Moundaie, was a great justing at Greenewych, where was chalengers my Lorde of Rochforde and others, and defenders Mr Noris and others.

And the seconde daie of Maie, Mr Noris and my Lorde of Rochforde were brought to the Towre of London as prisonners; and the same daie, about five of the clocke at night, the Queene Anne Bolleine was brought to the Towre of London by my Lord Chauncelor, the Duke of Norfolke, Mr Secretarie, and Sir William Kingston, Constable of the Tower; and when she came to the court gate, entring in, she fell downe on her knees before the said lordes, beseeching God to helpe her as she was not giltie of her accusement, and also desired the said lordes to beseech the Kinges grace to be good unto her, and so they left her their prisoner.

Item, the 12th daie of Maie, 1536, being Fridaie, their were arraygned at Westminster Sir Frances Weston, knight, Henrie Norris, esquier, Brerton, and Markes, being all fower of the Kinges Privie Chamber, and their condempned of high treason against the Kinge for using fornication with Queene Anne, wife to the Kinge, and also for conspiracie of the Kinges death, and their judged to be hanged, drawen, and quartered, their members cutt of and brent before theim, their heades cutt of and quartered; my Lord Chauncelor being the highest Commissioner he geving their judgment, with other lordes of the Kinges Counsell being presente at the same tyme.

And the morrowe after, being Satterdaie, and the thirtenth daie of Maie, Maister Fittes-Williams, Treasorer of the Kinges howse, and Mr Controoler, deposed and brooke upp the Queenes householde at Greenewich, and so discharged all her servantes of their offices clearlye.

Item, on Munday, the 15th of May, 1536, there was arreigned within the Tower of London Queene Anne, for treason againste the Kinges owne person, and there was a great scaffold made in the Kinges Hall within the

Tower of London, and there were made benches and seates for the lordes, my Lord of Northfolke sittinge under the clothe of estate, representinge there the Kinges person as Highe Steward of Englande and uncle to the Queene, he holdinge a longe white staffe in his hande, and the Earle of Surrey, his sonne and heire, sittinge at his feete before him holdinge the golden staffe for the Earle Marshall of Englande, which sayde office the saide duke had in his handes; the Lord Awdley, Chauncellour of England, sittinge on his right hande, and the Duke of Suffolke on his left hande, with other marqueses, earles, and lordes, everie one after their degrees.

And first the Kinges commission was redd, and then the Constable of the Tower and the Lieutenant brought forthe the Queene to the barre, where was made a chaire for her to sitt downe in, and then her indictment was redd afore her, whereunto she made so wise and discreet aunsweres to all thinges layde against her, excusinge herselfe with her wordes so clearlie, as thoughe she had never bene faultie to the same, and at length putt her to the triall of the Peeres of the Realme, and then were 26 of the greatest peeres there present chosen to passe on her, the Duke of Suffolke beinge highest, and, after thei had communed together, the yongest lorde of the saide inquest was called first to give verdict, who sayde guiltie, and so everie lorde and earle after their degrees sayde guiltie to the last and so condemned her. And then the Duke of Northfolke gave this sentence on her, sayinge: Because thou haste offended our Sovereigne the Kinges grace, in committinge treason against his person, and here attaynted of the same, the lawe of the realme is this, that thou haste deserved death, and thy judgment is this: That thow shalt be brent[137] here within the Tower of London on the Greene, els to have thy head smitten of as the Kinges pleasure shal be further knowne of the same; and so she was brought to warde agayne, and two ladies wayted on her, which came in with her at the first, and wayted still on her, whose names were the Ladie Kingstone and the Ladie Boleyn, her aunte.

After this, immediatlie, the Lord of Rocheforde, her brother, was arreigned for treason, which was for knowinge the Queene, his sister, carnallie, moste detestable against the lawe of God and nature allso, and treason to his Prince, and allso for conspiracie of the Kinges death: Whereunto he made aunswere so prudentlie and wiselie to all articles layde against him, that marveil it was to heare, and never would confesse anye thinge, but made himselfe as cleare as though he had never offended. Howbeit he was there condemned by 26 lordes and barons of treason, and then my Lord of Northfolke gave him this judgment: That he should goo agayne to prison in the Tower from whence he came, and to be drawne from the saide Towre of London thorowe the Cittie of London to the place of execution called Tyburne, and there to be hanged, beinge alyve cutt downe, and then his members cutt of and his bowells taken owt of his bodie and brent before him, and then his head cutt of and his bodie to be divided in 4 peeces, and his head and bodie to be sett at suche places as the King should assigne; and after this the court brake up for that tyme. The Major *[sic]* of London with certeyne Aldermen were present at this arreignment of the Queene and her brother, with the wardeins and 4 persons more of 12 of the principall craftes of London.

Allso the 17th day of May, beinge Weddensday, the Lord of Rochforde, Mr Norys, Mr Bruton, Sir Francis Weston, and Markys, were all beheaded at the Tower-hill; and the Lord of Rocheforde, brother to Queene Anne, sayde these wordes followinge on the scaffolde to the people with a lowde voyce: Maisters all, I am come hither not to preach and make a sermon, but to dye, as the lawe hath fownde me, and to the lawe I submitt me, desiringe you all, and speciallie you my maisters of the Courte, that you will trust on God speciallie, and not on the vanities of the worlde, for if I had so done, I thincke I had bene alyve as yee be now; allso I desire you to helpe to the settinge forthe of the true worde of God; and whereas I am sclaundered by it, I have bene diligent to reade it and set it furth trulye; but if I had bene as diligent to observe it, and done and Iyved thereafter, as I was to read it and sett it forthe, I had not come hereto, wherefore I beseche you all to be workers and Iyve thereafter, and not to reade it and lyve not there after. As for myne offences, it can not prevayle you to heare them that I dye here for, but I beseche God that I may be an example to you all, and that all you may be wayre by me, and hartelye I require you all to pray for me, and to forgive me if I have offended you, and I forgive you all, and God save the Kinge. Their bodies with their heades were buried within the Tower of London; the Lord of Rochfordes bodie and head within the chappell of the Tower, Mr Weston and Norys in the church yeard of the same in one grave, Mr Bruton and Markes in another grave in the same churche yerde within the Tower of London.

And the same day, in the after-noone, at a solemne court kept at Lambeth by the Lord Archbishoppe of Canterburie and the doctors of the lawe, the King was divorsed from his wife Queene Anne, and there at the same cowrte was a privie contract approved that she had made to the Earle of Northumberlande afore the Kings tyme; and so she was discharged, and was never lawfull Queene of England, and there it was approved the same.

The Fridaye followinge, beinge the 19th day of May, 1536, and the 28th yeare of King Henry the VIIIth, at eight of the clocke in the morninge, Anne Bulleyn, Queene, was brought to execution on the greene within the Tower of London, by the great White Tower; the Lord Chauncelloure of England, the Duke of Richmond, Duke of Suffolke, with the moste of the Kings Councell, as erles, lordes, and nobles of this realme, beinge present at the same; allso the Major of London, with the Alldermen and Sheriffs, and certayne of the best craftes of London, beinge there present allso. On a scaffolde made there for the sayde execution the sayde Queen Ann sayde thus: Maisters, I here humblye submitt me to the lawe as the lawe hath judged me, and as for myne offences, I here accuse no man, God knoweth them; I remitt them to God, beseechinge him to have mercye on my sowle, and I beseche Jesu save my sovereigne and maister the Kinge, the moste godlye, noble, and gentle Prince that is, and longe to reigne over yow; which wordes were spoken with a goodlye smilinge countenance; and this done, she kneeled downe on her knees and sayde: To Jesu Christe I commend my sowle; and suddenlye the hangman smote of her heade at a stroke with a sworde; her bodye with the head was buried in the Chappell within the Tower of London, in the queere there, the same daye at afternoone, when she had reygned as Queene three yeares, lackinge 14 dayes, from her coronation to her death.

## English Summary of the Poem on Anne Composed by Lancelot de Carles, a Member of the French Embassy in London on 2 June 1536[138]

*Lancelot de Carles, a member of the French embassy to London at the time of Anne's fall, produced a long poem in French less than a month after Anne's death. As the earliest 'biography' of Anne, the poem is of great interest. Its usefulness continues to be debated today. De Carles may well have had information on Anne's early life in France and the way that she was perceived. He was also present in England at the time of her death. However, as a member of the French embassy he would not have been privy to much of what was happening. His account is therefore, to a large extent, likely to have been based on rumour and information deliberately passed to the French ambassadors. It is also clear that de Carles was a sympathiser with Princess Mary, something that colours his view of Anne. Anne's biographer, Eric Ives, in particular, argues that caution should be taken in using de Carles, pointing out that he later sent a presentation copy of his poem to Henry VIII and that he relied on official information provided to the French embassy. His poem agrees with Cromwell's own account of what happened, sent to the English ambassadors in France (printed above).[139]*

*No full English translation has been produced. However, a good English summary was prepared in the nineteenth century, which is printed below. Details of the French original can be found in the bibliography.*

Speaks of her having first left this country when Mary[140] went to France 'to accomplish the alliance of the two Kings'. She learned the language from ladies of honour. After Mary's return to England she was retained by Claude and became so accomplished that you would never have thought her an English, but a French woman. She learned to sing and dance, to play the lute and other instruments, and to order her discourse wisely. She was beautiful and of an elegant figure, and still more attractive in her eyes, which invited to conversation, &c. On her return her eyes fascinated Henry, who made her, first a marchioness, and afterwards Queen, 1 June 1533. Describes the birth and baptism of Elizabeth, the establishment of the royal supremacy, and the death of More and the Carthusians, of which Anne was accused of being the cause. Hence a severe ordinance was issued against any that spoke ill of her; which shut people's mouths when they knew what ought not to be concealed. Meanwhile queen Katharine suffered patiently her degradation and even being separated from her daughter. Anne, on the other hand, had her way in all things; she could go where she pleased, and if perhaps taken with the love of some favoured person, she could treat her friends according to her pleasure, owing to the ordinance. But that law could not secure to her lasting friendships, and the King daily cooled in his affection. Anne met with divers ominous occurrences that presaged evil; – st a fire in her chamber, then the King had a fall from horseback which it was thought would prove fatal, and caused her to give premature birth to a dead son. Nevertheless she did not leave off her evil conversation, which at length brought her to shame.

A lord of the Privy Council[141] seeing clear evidence that his sister[142] loved certain persons with a dishonourable love, admonished her fraternally. She acknowledged her offence, but said it was little in her case in comparison with that of the Queen, as he might ascertain from Mark [Smeaton], declaring that she was guilty of incest with her own brother. The brother did not know what to do on this intelligence, and took counsel with two friends of the King, with whom he went to the King himself and one reported it in the name of all three. The King was astonished, and his colour changed at the revelation, but he thanked the gentlemen. The Queen, meanwhile, took her pleasure unconscious of the discovery, seeing dogs and animals that day fight in a park. In the evening there was a ball, and the King treated her as if he knew no cause of displeasure. But Mark was then in prison and was forced to answer the accusation against him. Without being tortured he deliberately said that the Queen had three times yielded to his passion. The King was thus convinced, but made no show of it, and gave himself up to enjoyment. Especially on the 1 May, he got up a tournay with several combatants; among others, my lord of Rocheford, the Queen's brother, showed his skill in breaking lances and vaulting on horseback. Norris, also, best loved of the King, presented himself well armed, but his horse refused the lists and turned away as if conscious of the impending calamity to his master. The King seeing this, presented Norris with his own horse; who, however, knew that he could not keep it long. He, Waston (Weston), and Barton (Brereton) did great feats of arms, and the King showed them great kindness 'dissimulant leur ruyne prochaine'. The Queen looked on from a high place, 'et souvent envoioit les doulz regards', to encourage the combatants, who knew nothing of their danger. Immediately after the tournay archers were ordered to arrest Norris, and were much astonished and grieved, considering his virtue and intimacy with the King, that he should have committed disloyalty. Before he went to prison the King desired to speak to him, offering to spare his life and goods, although he was guilty, if he would tell him the truth. But being told the accusation, Norris offered to maintain the contrary with his body in any place. He was accordingly sent to the Tower. The Queen was conducted thither next day by the duke of Norfolk, and her brother also, who said he had well merited his fate. Weston and Barton followed, and pages also. The city rejoiced on hearing the report, hoping that the Princess would be restored. The whole town awaited her coming with delight.

> Et n'eussiez veu jusque aux petis enfans
> Que tous chantans et d'aise triumphans.
> Il n'y a cueur si triste qui ne rye
> En attendant la princesse Marie.

But she did not remove from her lodging, and did not avenge herself by blaming the Queen when she heard that she was a prisoner; but only wished she had behaved better to the King, and hoped God would help her, adding:

Et si sa fille est au Roy, je promectz
Qu'a mon pouvoir ne luy fauldray jamais.

Here follows a eulogy of the Princess, describing her education in astronomy, mathematics, logic, morals, politics, Latin, Greek, &c. The expectation that she would be restored made the King apprehensive of some commotion; to appease which he caused his thanks to be conveyed to the people for their good will to him and his daughter, but told them they need not be anxious about her return, for they would shortly be satisfied. The joy of the people on this was converted into sorrow and they dispersed.

The Queen, meanwhile, having no further hope in this world, would confess nothing.

Riens ne confesse, et ne resiste fort
Comme voulant presque estre delivre
De vivre icy, pour aulz cieulz aller vivre;
Et l'espoir tant en icelle surmonte,
Que de la mort ne tient plus aucun compte.

But she did not give up her greatness, but spoke to the lords as a mistress. Those who came to interrogate were astonished. They afterwards went to Rochford, who said he knew that death awaited him and would say the truth, but raising his eyes to Heaven denied the accusations against him. They next went to Norris, Waston, and Barton, who all likewise refused to confess, except Mark, who had done so already. The King ordered the trial at Westminster, which was held after the manner of the country.

Description of the process of indictment and how the archers of the guard turn the back [of the axe] to the prisoners in going, but after sentence of guilty the edge is turned towards their faces; the trial at Westminster; the verdict; whereupon suddenly the axe was turned towards them; and the sentence. Everyone was moved at their misfortune, especially at the case of Waston, who was young and of old lineage and high accomplishments; but no one dared plead for him, except his mother, who, oppressed with grief, petitioned the King, and his wife, who offered rents and goods for his deliverance. But the King was determined the sentence should be carried out. If money could have availed, the fine would have been 100,000 crowns.

Rochford was not tried at Westminster, but at the Tower, with the Queen. His calm behaviour, and good defence. More himself did not reply better. The judges at first were of different opinions, but at last one view overturned the other and they were unanimous. The duke of Norfolk as president, though maternal uncle of the accused, asked them if he was guilty or not, and one replied guilty. Rochford then merely requested the judges that they would ask the King to pay his debts. The Queen then was summoned by an usher. She seemed unmoved as a stock, and came away with her young ladies, not as one who had to defend her cause but with the bearing of one coming to great honour. She returned the salutations of the lords with her accustomed politeness, and took her seat. She defended herself soberly against the charges, her face saying more for her than her words; for she said little, but no one to look at her would have thought her guilty. In the end the judges said she must resign her crown to their hands; which she did at once without resistance, but protested she had never misconducted herself towards the King. She was then degraded from all her titles, countess, marchioness, and princess, which she said she gave up willingly to the King who had conferred them. Sentence of death, either by sword or fire, at the pleasure of the King, was pronounced by Norfolk. Her face did not change, but she appealed to God whether the sentence was deserved; then turning to the judges, said she would not dispute with them, but believed there was some other reason for which she was condemned than the cause alleged, of which her conscience acquitted her, as she had always been faithful to the King. But she did not say this to preserve her life, for she was quite prepared to die. Her speech made even her bitterest enemies pity her.

Meanwhile the prisoners prepared to die and took the Sacrament. Description of the execution of Rochford, with his dying speech.[143] The other four said nothing, as if they had commissioned Rochford to speak for them, except Mark, who persisted in what he said that he was justly punished for his misdeeds.

The Queen, in expectation of her last day, took the Sacrament. Then the day of her death was announced to her, at which she was more joyful than before. She asked about the patience shown by her brother and the others; but when told that Mark confessed that he had merited his death, her face changed somewhat. 'Did he not exonerate me,' she said, 'before he died, of the public infamy he laid on me? Alas! I fear his soul will suffer for it.'

Next day, expecting her end, she desired that no one would trouble her devotions that morning. But when the appointed hour passed she was disappointed, – not that she desired death, but thought herself prepared to die and feared that delay would weaken her. She, however, consoled her ladies several times, telling them that was not a thing to be regretted by Christians, and she hoped to be quit of all unhappiness, with various other good counsels. When the captain came to tell her the hour approached and that she should make ready, she bade him for his part see to acquit himself of his charge, for she had been long prepared. So she went to the place of execution with an untroubled countenance. Her face and complexion never were so beautiful. She gracefully addressed the people from the scaffold with a voice somewhat overcome by weakness, but which gathered strength as she went on. She begged her hearers to forgive her if she had not used them all with becoming gentleness, and asked for their prayers. It was needless, she said, to relate why she was there, but she prayed the Judge of all the world to have compassion on those who had condemned her, and she begged them to pray for the King, in whom she had always found great kindness, fear of God, and love of his subjects. The spectators could not refrain from tears. She herself having put off her white collar and hood that the blow might not be impeded, knelt, and said several times 'O Christ, receive my spirit!'

One of her ladies in tears came forward to do the last office and cover her face with a linen cloth. The executioner then, himself distressed, divided her neck at a blow. The head and body were taken up by the ladies, whom you would have thought bereft of their souls, such was their weakness; but fearing to let their mistress be touched by unworthy hands, forced themselves to do so. Half dead themselves, they carried the body, wrapped in a white covering, to the place of burial within the Tower. Her brother was buried beside her, Weston and Norris after them. Barton and Mark also were buried together.

The ladies were then as sheep without a shepherd, but it will not be long before they meet with their former treatment, because already the King has taken a fancy to a choice lady. And hereby, Monseigneur, is accomplished a great part of a certain prophecy which is believed to be true, because nothing notable has happened which it has not foretold. Other great things yet are predicted of which the people are assured. If I see them take place I will let you know, for never were such news. People say it is the year of marvels.

## Translation of a Letter from a Portuguese Gentleman to a Friend in Lisbon, Describing the Execution of Anne Boleyn, Lord Rochford, Brereton, Norris, Smeaton and Weston[144]

*The source set out below has been described as probably being written by an eye witness, and as the most authentic source for Anne's fall and death.[145] It is possible that the author, a foreigner, may have been able to witness Anne's death as, while Sir William Kingston was instructed to remove all foreigners from the Tower, the author of the Spanish Chronicle also claimed to have been able to gain access to witness Anne's final moments.*

*Like de Carles, the account is near-contemporary to Anne's fall and a useful source. There are, however, some errors in the events it details and it is clear that the writer was not privy to much of what was happening at court, instead relying on rumour and official channels of information.*

Having within these few days discoursed largely to your good Lordship, touching the manner in which the Queen of England had been found guilty, and the sort of punishment which the King's Council did doom her to suffer, as also how his said Majesty had willed that the brother of the Queen should be put to death; And having likewise fully discoursed to you concerning that person, who more out of envy and jealousy than out of love towards the King, did betray this accursed secret, and together with it, the names of those who had joined in the evil doings of the unchaste Queen, it now seemeth proper, and, in truth, mine especial duty, to write to you all the circumstances which belonged to that act of cruel justice.

When that sorrowful day came, which was to bring their last hour to those unhappy wretches who had bought a brief pleasure with a dreadful peril, even the peril of their life and honour, a scaffold was build up before the Tower of London, on a Wednesday, which was the 17th day of May. And then they led out of the Tower wherein they had been imprisoned, the Queen's brother and the four accused gentlemen, all closely guarded as they are wont to guard those guilty of such things. And my Lord of Reujafort, [Rochford] for that was the name of the Queen's brother, said, three several times, with a loud voice, to the whole city there gathered together – 'O ye gentlemen and Christians, I was born under the law, and I die under the law, forasmuch as it is the law which hath condemned me.' And then he proceeded to speak in this wise. 'Ye gentlemen here present, I come not hither to preach unto you, but to die. Nor do I now seek for any thing, in the sorrowful plight in which I here stand, save that I may soon bathe my dry and parched lips in the living fountain of God's everlasting and infinite mercy. And I beseech you all, in his holy name, to pray unto him for me, confessing truly that I deserve death, even though I had a thousand lives – yea even to die with far more and worse shame and dishonour than hath ever been heard of before. For I am a miserable sinner, who have grievously and often times offended; nay and in very truth, I know not of any more perverse or wicked sinner than I have been up until now. Nevertheless, I mean not openly now to relate what my many sins may have been, since in sooth it can yield you no profit, nor me any pleasure here to reckon them up; enough be it that God knoweth them all. And ye, Gentlemen of the Court, mine especial and ancient familiars, I beseech you, of all love, that ye take heed not to fall into the error of my ways, and that ye be warned by my example; and I pray to the Father, Son, and Holy Ghost, Three Persons in One God, that ye may wisely profit by the same, and that from my mishap ye may learn not to set your thoughts upon the vanities of this world, and least of all, upon the flatteries of the Court, and the favours and treacheries of Fortune, which only raiseth men aloft that with so much the greater force she may dash them again upon the ground. She in truth it is who is the cause that, as ye all witness, my miserable head is now to be dissevered from my neck; or rather, in greater truth, the fault is mine, and it is I who ought to be blamed for having adventured to lean on Fortune, who hath prove herself fickle and false unto me, and who now maketh me a sad example to you all and to the whole world. And do ye all, Sirs, take notice, that in this my sorrowful condition, I pray for the mercy of God Almighty, and that I do moreover forgive all men, with all my heart and mind, even as truly as I hope that the Lord God will forgive me. And if so be that I should in aught have offended any man not now here present, do ye entreat him, when ye chance to meet him, that he also may of his charity forgive me; for, having lived the life of a sinner, I would fain die the death of a Christian man.

'Nor must I fail (while it be yet time) to tell you all, gentle and simple, now hearkening to me, that I was a great reader and a mighty debater of the Word of God, and one of those who most favoured the Gospel of Jesu Christ. Wherefore, lest the Word of God should be brought into reproach on my account, I now tell you all, Sirs, that if I had, in very deed, kept his holy Word, even as I read and reasoned about it with all the strength of my wit, certain am I that I should not be in the piteous condition wherein I now stand. Truly and diligently did I read the Gospel of Christ Jesu, but I turned not to profit that which I did read; the which had I done, of a surety I had not fallen into so great errors. Wherefore I do beseech you all, for the love of our Lord God, that ye do at all seasons, hold by the truth, and speak it, and embrace it; for beyond all peradventure, better profiteth he who readeth not and yet doeth well, than he who readeth much and yet liveth in sin.'

Having made an end of speaking, he knelt down upon his knees, and his head was stricken off. And so befell it likewise to the other four gentlemen; one was called Monsire Nestorn, [Weston]; another Breton, [Brereton]; another Norris, Chamberlain to the Kings Majesty; and the fourth of this sorrowful company was Mark [Smeton]; the which said no more than that they besought the bystanders to pray for them, and that they yielded themselves to death with joy and exceeding gladness of heart.

After this, on the next Friday, which was the 19th of the same month, the Queen was beheaded according to the manner and custom of Paris, that is to say, with a sword, which thing had not before been seen in this land of England. And a scaffold, having four or five steps, was then and there set up. And the unhappy Queen, assisted by the Captain of the Tower, came forth, together with the four ladies who accompanied her; and she was wholly habited in a robe of black damask, made in such guise that the cape, which was white, did fall on the outer side thereof. And she then besought the Captain of the Tower that he would in no wise hasten the minute of her death, until she should have spoken that which she had in mind to say: which he consenting to, she said as followeth:–

'Good friends, I am not come here to excuse or to justify myself, forasmuch as I know full well that aught that I could say in my defence doth not appertain unto you, and that I could draw no hope of life from the same. But I come here only to die, and thus to yield myself humbly to the will of the King my Lord. And if in my life I did ever offend the King's Grace, surely with my death I do now atone for the same. And I blame not judges, nor any other manner of person, nor any thing save the cruel law of the land by which I die. But be this, and be my faults as they may, I beseech you all, good friends, to pray for the life of the King my Sovereign Lord and your's, who is one of the best princes on the face of the earth, and who hath always treated me so well that better could not be: wherefore I submit to death with a good will, humbly asking pardon of all the world.'

Then, with her own hands, she took her coifs from her head, and delivered them to one of her ladies, and then putting on a little cap of linen to cover her hair withal, she said, 'Alas, poor head! in a very brief space thou wilt roll in the dust on this scaffold; and as in life thou didst not merit to wear the crown of a queen, so in death, thou deservest not a better doom than this. And ye, my damsels, who, whilst I lived, ever shewed yourselves so diligent in my service, and who are now to be present at my last hour and mortal agony, as in good fortune ye were faithful to me, so even at this my miserable death ye do not forsake me. And as I cannot reward you for your true service to me, I pray you take comfort for my loss; howbeit, forget me not; and be always faithful to the King's Grace, and to her whom with happier fortune ye may have as your Queen and Mistress. And esteem your honour far beyond your life; and in your prayers to the Lord Jesu, forget not to pray for my soul.'[146]

And being minded to say no more, she knelt down upon both knees, and one of her ladies covered her eyes with a bandage, and then they withdrew themselves some little space, and knelt down over against the scaffold, bewailing bitterly and shedding many tears. And thus, and without more to say or do, was her head stricken off; she making no confession of her fault, and only saying, 'O Lord God, have pity on my soul;' and one of her ladies then took up the head, and the others the body, and covering them with a sheet, did put them into a chest which there stood ready, and carried them to the church which is within the Tower, where, they say, she lieth buried with the others.

The Council then declared, that the Queen's daughter was the child of her brother; and that as the child of a private person, the child be forthwith removed from that place; and that the King should again receive that Princess who was the daughter of the former and the true Queen, as his own and real daughter, and as being his successor in the kingdom; and the King did so receive her with the utmost graciousness.[147] Other matter have I not to write to you, saving that I kiss your hands, and do recommend myself humbly to your favour. From London, the 10th day of June, 1536.

## Anonymous Imperialist Account of Anne's Death from the Archives at Brussels[148]

*This is another near-contemporary account of Anne's death by a foreigner. It is of particular interest in relation to the deaths of the five men accused with Anne. The account of Rochford's speech accords well with other sources, such as the Chronicle of Calais. The deaths of the other four men can be contrasted with Constantyne who set out what they said at their deaths. It has recently been suggested that the writer was not present at the deaths of the five men, but was able to witness Anne's death two days later.[149]*

Lord Rochfort, brother of the wicked Queen Anne Boleyn, has been beheaded with an axe on a scaffold in front of the Tower.

The said lord made a good Catholic address to the people. He said that he had not come there to preach to them, but rather to serve as a mirror and an example. He acknowledged the crimes which he had committed against God, and against the King his sovereign; there was no occasion for him, he said, to repeat the cause for which he was condemned; they would have little pleasure in hearing him tell it. He prayed God, and he prayed the King, to pardon his offences; and all others whom he might have injured he also prayed to forgive him as heartily as he forgave every one. He bade his hearers avoid the vanities of the world, and the flatteries of the Court which had brought him to the shameful end which had overtaken him. Had he obeyed the lessons of that Gospel which he had so often read, he said he should not have fallen so far; it was worth more to be a good doer than a good reader. Finally, he forgave those who had adjudged him to die, and he desired them to pray God for his soul.

After Lord Rochfort came Mr Norris, first gentleman of the bedchamber to the King; next to him Weston and Brereton, gentlemen of the bedchamber also; and then Mark the musician. These four said nothing except to pray for

God's and the King's forgiveness, and to bid us pray for their souls. Brereton and Mark were afterwards quartered.

The wicked Queen herself suffered last on a scaffold within the Tower, the gates being open. She was led up by the lieutenant, feeble and half-stupified, and she looked back from time to time at four of her ladies by whom she was attended. On reaching the platform she prayed to be allowed to say something to the people. She would not speak a word, she said, which was not good. The lieutenant gave permission, and, raising her eyes to heaven, she begged God and the King to forgive her offences, and she bade the people pray God to protect the King, for he was a good, kind, gracious, and loving Prince.

This done, they removed an ermine cloak which she had on, and she herself took off her head-dress, which was in the English fashion.[150] One of her attendants gave her a cap into which she gathered her hair. She then knelt; a lady bound her eyes, and incontinently the executioner did his office. When the head fell, a white handkerchief was thrown over it, and one of the four ladies took it up and carried it away. The other three lifted the body, and bore it with the head into the adjoining chapel in the Tower.

It is said that she was condemned to be burnt alive, but the King commuted the sentence into decapitation.

## Extract from Foxe's *Actes and Monuments* on the Deaths of Catherine of Aragon and Anne Boleyn[151]

*The martyrologist, John Foxe (1517–1587) wrote his famous* Actes and Monuments, *which is commonly known as the* Book of Martyrs *during the reign of Anne's daughter, Elizabeth. Foxe was staunchly Protestant and his depiction of Anne as a saintly figure, working towards the promulgation of reform in England is very similar to that provided by Anne's chaplain, William Latymer, in his account of her. Foxe was a contemporary of Anne and, while it is very unlikely that he ever saw her, he was able to interview those who had known her. His account therefore has much merit and provides a useful counterpoint to the many hostile accounts of her life. It must, however, always be remembered that his primary aim was to glorify the Protestant religion and the reformation in England. His depiction of Anne as a Protestant saint is considerably exaggerated. Anne is certainly known to have had an interest in reform, but she died in the Catholic faith, as can be seen by her comments to Sir William Kingston (set out in his letters above) about believing that she would go to Heaven due to her good deeds. Her decision to swear her innocence on the sacrament on the day before her death was also a testament to her traditional beliefs. It seems likely that, had she lived longer, Anne would have developed a more Protestant outlook, as did many of her contemporaries, such as one of her successors as Henry's wife, Catherine Parr. She cannot be considered to be England's first Protestant queen however.*

The same year in which William Tyndale was burned, which was A.D. 1536, in the beginning of the year, first died lady Katharine, princess dowager, in the month of January.

After whom, the same year also, in the month of May next following, followeth the death also of queen Anne, who had now been married to the king the space of three years. In certain records thus we find, that the king, being in his jousts at Greenwich, suddenly with a few persons departed to Westminster, and, the next day after, queen Anne, his wife, was had to the Tower, with the lord Rochford her brother, and certain others, and, the nineteenth day after, was beheaded. The words of this worthy and christian lady at her death were these:

### The Words of Queen Anne at her Death

Good christian people! I am come hither to die, for according to the law, and by the law, I am judged to death; and therefore I will speak nothing against it. I come hither to accuse no man, nor to speak any thing of that whereof I am accused and condemned to die; but I pray God save the king, and send him long to reign over you, for a gentler, or a more merciful prince was there never; and to me he was ever a good, a gentle, and a sovereign lord. And if any person will meddle of my cause, I require them to judge the best. And thus I take my leave of the world, and of you all, and I heartily desire you all to pray for me. O Lord have mercy on me! To God I commend my soul.

And so she kneeled down, saying, 'To Christ I commend my Queen soul:' 'Jesu, receive my soul.' Repeating the same divers times, till at length the stroke was given, and her head was stricken off.

And this was the end of that godly lady and queen. Godly I call her, for sundry respects, whatsoever the cause was, or quarrel objected against her. First, her last words spoken at her death declared no less her sincere faith and trust in Christ, than did her quiet modesty utter forth the goodness of the cause and matter, whatsoever it was. Besides that to such as wisely can judge upon cases occurrent, this also may seem to give a great clearing unto her, that the king, the third day after, was married in his whites unto another. Certain this was, that for the rare and singular gifts of her mind, so well instructed, and given toward God, with such a fervent desire unto the truth and setting forth of sincere religion, joined with like gentleness, modesty, and pity toward all men, there have not many such queens before her borne the crown of England. Principally this one commendation she left behind her, that during her life, the religion of Christ most happily flourished, and had a right prosperous course.

Many things might be written more of the manifold virtues, and the quiet moderation of her mild nature, how lowly she would bear, not only to be admonished, but also of her own accord would require her chaplains plainly and freely to tell whatsoever they saw in her amiss. Also, how bountiful she was to the poor, passing not only the common example of other queens, but also the revenues almost of her estate; insomuch that the alms which she gave in three quarters of a year, in distribution, is summed to the number of fourteen or fifteen thousand pounds;[152] besides the great piece of money which her grace intended to impart into four sundry quarters of the realm, as for a stock there to be employed to the behoof of poor artificers and occupiers. Again, what a zealous defender she was of Christ's gospel all the world doth know, and her acts do and will declare to the world's end. Amongst which other her acts this is one, that she placed Master Hugh Latimer in the bishopric of Worcester, and also preferred Dr Shaxton to his bishopric, being then accounted a good man. Furthermore, what a true faith she bare unto the Lord, this one example may stand for many: for that when king Henry was with her at Woodstock, and there, being afraid of an old blind prophecy, for which neither he nor other kings before him durst hunt in the said park of Woodstock, nor enter into the town of Oxford, at last, through the christian and faithful counsel of that queen, he was so armed against all infidelity, that both he hunted in the aforesaid park, and also entered into the town of Oxford, and had no harm. But because, touching the memorable virtues of this worthy queen, partly we have said something before, partly because more also is promised to be declared of her virtuous life (the Lord so permitting) by others who then were about her, I will cease in this matter further to proceed.

## Extract from Hall's Chronicle on the Death of Anne Boleyn[153]

*The Chronicler, Edward Hall, provides a basic narrative of Anne's arrest and death which, given his admiration for Henry VIII, is likely to be very close to the official account. Hall's work is notable for its inclusion of Anne's final speech, which appears to be an accurate version.*

On May day were a solempne Iustes kept at Grenewyche, and sodainly from the Iustes the kyng departed hauyng not aboue vi. persons with him, and came in the evening from Grenewyche in his place at Westminster. Of this sodain departyng many men mused, but most chiefely the quene, who the next day was apprehended and brought from Grenewyche to the Tower of London, where after she was arreigned of high treason, and condempned. And at thesame tyme was likewyse apprehended, the lorde Rocheforde brother to thesayd Quene, and Henry Norrys, Marke Smeton, Wyllyam a Bruton and sir Fraunces Weston all of the kynges priuy chamber. All these were likewise committed to the Tower and after arreigned and condempned of high treason. And all the gentlemen were beheaded on the Skaffolde at the Tower hyll: But the Quene was with a sworde beheaded within the Tower. And these folowyng were the woordes that she spake the day of her death whiche was the xix day of May, 1536.

Good christen people, I am come hether to dye, for accordyng to the lawe and by the lawe I am iudged to dye, and therefore I wyll speak nothyng against it. I am come hether to accuse no man, nor to speake anythyng of that wherof I am accused and condempned to dye, but I pray God saue the king and send him long to reigne ouer you, for a gentler nor a more mercyfull prince was there neuer: and to me he was euer a good, a gentle, & soueraigne lorde. And if any persone will medle of my cause, I require them to iudge the best. And thus I take my leue of the worlde and of you all, and I hertely desyre you all to pray for me. O lorde haue mercy on me, to God I commende my soule. And then she kneled doune saying: To Christ I commende my soule, Iesu[154] receive my soule, diuers tymes, till that her head was stryken of with the sworde. And on the Assencion day folowyng, the kyng ware whyte for mournyng.

## Extract from a Letter from Mary of Hungary, Regent of the Netherlands, to her Brother, the Archduke Ferdinand, 23 May 1536, from the Archives at Brussels[155]

*Mary, Queen dowager of Hungary, the sister of Charles V, succeeded her aunt, and Anne's former employer, Margaret of Austria, as regent of the Netherlands. As the niece of Catherine of Aragon, she was no friend of Anne's as her letter demonstrates. The letter is of interest because it suggests that the swordsman who carried out Anne's execution was sent for from St Omer, rather than Calais, as previously stated. It also demonstrates that rumours of Anne's innocence began to circulate quickly. Chapuys also had doubts about Anne's guilt although, like Mary of Hungary, he believed that she deserved her death for other actions that she had carried out during her lifetime.*

*Finally, the letter is also of interest as an early demonstration of the fearsome reputation Henry VIII acquired as a husband: Mary of Hungary's niece, Christina of Denmark, would reportedly later echo her sentiments when she declined Henry's hand, stating that if she had two heads she would risk it ...[156]*

The English, I think, will not give us much trouble, especially now that we are quit of that damsel who was so good a Frenchwoman. You have no doubt heard that she has been beheaded, and in order that vengeance should fall on her from the subjects of his Majesty the Emperor, the King sent for the headsman from St Omer's to do the work. There was no one in England skilful enough.

The King has, I understand, already married another woman, who, they say, is a good Imperialist. I know not whether she will so continue. He had shown an inclination for her before the other's death; and as neither that other herself, nor any of the rest who were put to death, confessed their guilt, except one who was a musician, some people think he invented the charge to get rid of her. However it be, no great wrong can have been done to the woman herself. She is known to have been a worthless person. It has been her character for a long time, I suppose, if one may speak so lightly of such things, that when he is tired of his new wife he will find some occasion to quit himself of her also. Our sex will not be too well satisfied if these practices come into vogue; and, though I have no fancy to expose myself to danger, yet, being a woman, I will pray with the rest that God will have mercy on us.

# Notes

## Introduction

1. Recent biographies of Anne include Bernard 2010, Norton 2008, Ives 2005 and Denny 2004. Older biographies include Benger 1821, Friedman (originally 1884, reissued 2010), Sergeant 1923, Bruce 1972, Chapman 1974 and Erickson 1984. Round 1886, Wilkinson 2009 and Weir 2009 deal with particular aspects of Anne's life. Her life is also detailed in a number of group biographies of Henry's wives, including Fraser 2002, Starkey 2003 and Weir 1991.

2. Clifford 1887:80.

3. Lord Hunsdon's petition to Elizabeth I is from Round 1886:18.

4. Details of Margaret of Austria can be found in de Iongh 1954. Paget 1981 notes Anne's stay in Brussels.

5. Mary Boleyn was included in the list of gentlewomen appointed to attend Mary Tudor in France (L&P I:3348).

6. Anne's appearance is described in Wyatt 1825:182-183 and Sander 1877:25.

7. Anne's appearance in the Greenwich masque is noted in L&P III:155. The masque itself is described in Hall's Chronicle 1809:631.

8. Cavendish provides the information for Anne's relationship with Henry Percy (printed below and also in Cavendish 1825).

9. George Wyatt describes the rivalry between Henry VIII and Sir Thomas Wyatt (originally printed in Wyatt 1825 and printed in full below).

10. The Blackfriars trial is detailed in Cavendish and the *Life of Fisher* p. 65-66.

11. Herbert 1649:312-313 commented on the significance of Henry Percy carrying out Wolsey's arrest.

12. Anne's quarrels with the Duke of Norfolk are recorded in Chapuys to Charles V, 6 February 1530 (L&P IV:2781) and Augustine de Augustinis to the Duke of Norfolk, 3 June 1531 (L&P V:132).

13. Anne's relationship with the Duchess of Norfolk is detailed in Chapuys' despatches of 31 January 1531 (L&P V:31) and 14 May 1531 (L&P V).

14. Chapuys to Granville, 11 July 1532 (L&P V:514).

15. Chapuys to Charles V, 27 November 1530 (L&P IV:3035), Mai to Francis de los Covos, 22 January 1531 (L&P V:27), Chapuys to Charles V, 29 April 1531 (L&P V:101) and Muxetula to Charles V, 23 January 1531 (L&P V:28).

16. Du Bellay to Montmorency, 9 December 1528 (L&P IV:177).

17. Chapuys to Charles V, 29 July 1532 (L&P V:526).

18. Chapuys to Charles V, 1 October 1532 (L&P V:591).

19. Bernard 1993, Dowling 1984 and Foxe 1838:58 discuss Anne's religious beliefs.

20. The Praemunire Manoeuvres are discussed in Guy 1982.

21. Latymer 1990:50-61.

22. The dog's name is noted in letter 109 (John Husee to Lady Lisle, 7 January 1534) St Clare Byrne 1981 vol II:21.

23. Sir Francis Bryan to Lord Lisle, 20 January 1534 (number 114, St Clare Byrne 1981 vol II:30).

24. Thomas Broke to lady Lisle, 18 December 1534 (letter 299a St Clare Byrne 1981:331).

25. John Brown to Lady Lisle, 12 May 1534 (number 193, St Clare Byrne 1981, vol II:156).

26. John Husee to Lady Lisle, 13 January 1535 (number 307, St Clare Byrne 1981, vol II:380).

27. A number of historians have speculated on Anne's rapid fall. Bernard 1991, 1992 and 2010 considers that Henry had grounds for suspicion and that there was evidence of Anne's guilt. Ives 1992 and 2005 counters this view and considers that Cromwell actively worked to destroy her. Warnicke 1985 considers that a number of court factions grouped together behind Jane Seymour to oppose Anne. Warnicke 1989 controversially speculates that Anne gave birth to a deformed foetus which raised accusations of incest.

28. Both Smeaton's arrest and the interrogation of Norris are described in Constantyne 1831:64 (printed in full below).

29. Spelman 1977:71.

30. Lady Wingfield's deathbed statement is discussed in Warnicke 1989:120.

31. St Clare Byrne 1981:378.

32. Walker 2002:17.

33. Speculation over the fates of Wyatt and Page is contained in John Husee to Lady Lisle on 12 and 13 May 1536 (St Clare Byrne 1981).

34. Source books focussing on the break with Rome include Williams 1967 and Bray 1994.

# 1 George Wyatt's *Life of Queen Anne Boleigne*

1. George Wyatt's *Life of Queen Anne Boleigne* is taken from Wyatt 1825.

2. Details of George Wyatt's life and works can be found in Wyatt 1968 and Wyatt 1825.

3. i.e. George Wyatt obtained his information on Anne from two sources.

4. Mrs Anne Gainsford.

5. Wyatt is referring here to the dispensation granted to Henry VIII and Catherine of Aragon, allowing them to marry. He may have been unaware, or deliberately ignored, the relationship between Henry VIII and Mary Boleyn, which placed Anne and Henry within the first degree of consanguinity, the same as Henry and Catherine.

6. Wyatt claims that Anne had a second nail on one finger, the source of the rumours that she had a sixth finger. His description of Anne's appearance was intended to counter that written by Sander (see the extract from his work in the following chapter).

7. Wyatt suggests that Anne attracted a number of admirers.

8. Wyatt claims here that his grandfather wrote about Anne in his poetry. Poem 6 of his in the following chapter was linked to this section by Wyatt's earlier editor, Singer.

9. Henry VIII always claimed that he first became concerned over his marriage to Catherine when the French ambassador, the Bishop of Tarbes, voiced doubts over Princess Mary's legitimacy during negotiations for her marriage. This is unlikely. It was not uncommon for a widow to take the sibling of their deceased spouse as their next spouse. For example, Catherine of Aragon's eldest sister, Isabella, married Manuel I of Portugal. On her death, Manuel married her younger sister, Maria. On Maria's death, he married his first two wives' niece: Eleanor of Austria. The offspring of his marriage to Maria were always considered to be legitimate, in spite of the fact that their parents were within the first degree of consanguinity. The Emperor Charles V married their daughter, Isabella of Portugal.

10. A proposed French marriage for Henry.

11. Sander.

12. This refers to Sir Thomas Wyatt's two periods of imprisonment. The first was at the time of Anne's fall in May 1536.

13. 1533.

14. Tyndale's *Obedience of a Christian Man*.

15. The lady is Mrs Gainsford and her suitor Mr George Zouch. John Foxe further elaborates on the story.

16. 1534.

17. Shaxton and Latymer.

18. This is a considerable sum and likely to be a great over-exaggeration.

## 2 Early Life, *c.* 1501–1526

1. Taken from Sergeant 1923.

2. Taken from Sergeant 1923.

3. This perhaps refers to Catherine of Aragon and Anne's eventual anticipated return to England. Alternatively, it may be an error. Anne perhaps meant to refer to Margaret of Austria, who never achieved the rank of queen.

4. State Papers vol II p. 58.

5. State Papers vol II p. 49-50.

6. State Papers vol II p. 57.

7. The introduction in Hall 1904 gives details of the chronicler's life.

8. Taken from Hall 1809.

9. Richard Gibson's accounts for revels (L&P III:1557).

10. disvisered – i.e. unmasked.

11. Taken from Cavendish 1825.

12. Hunter 1827 and the preface to Singer's edition of Cavendish.

13. Details of George Cavendish's life can be found in the Introduction to

Lockyer's edition of his work.

14. Claude in fact died in 1524.

15. This implies that the couple were betrothed before witnesses. If the betrothal had been consummated, it would have been binding in the eyes of the church, rendering both Anne and Percy's subsequent marriages invalid.

16. Printed as an appendix to Cavendish 1825.

17. Wilkinson 2009b:70.

18. Printed in the *Oxford Magazine* Volume III, 1769:55-57. The author is anonymous.

19. Surrey's poem 'Description and Praise of his Love Geraldine' is printed in Surrey 1831:12. That Surrey was in love with Geraldine was often assumed by his earlier biographers, leading at least one editor of his work to add a reference to Geraldine to the titles of many of the Earl's poems. In fact, only one appears to refer to her at all (Introduction to Surrey 1831:xix-xxii). When the poem was written Geraldine would have been, at most thirteen years old.

20. Anne's relationship with Thomas Wyatt is discussed in a number of works, including Norton 2008 and Wilkinson 2009.

21. Bruce 1850:237.

22. Wyatt 1825:425. Wyatt's editor, Singer, made the link between poem six and Anne.

23. Wyatt 1858.

24. Wyatt 1858.

25. Wyatt 1858.

26. Wakeful.

27. 'chere' the expression of the countenance.

28. Originally: 'Her that did set our country in a rore'.

29. Wyatt 1858.

30. quenched.

31. Wyatt 1831.

32. Singer 1825.

33. Taken from Sander.

34. Details of Sander's life can be found in the introduction to his work by Lewis.

35. Quoted from Wilkinson 2009a:135.

36. He was the son of Elizabeth Howard's half sister, making him Anne's first cousin.

37. Here Sander appears to have confused Anne with her sister, who was indeed the mistress of Francis I.

## 3 The Love Letters of Henry VIII & Anne Boleyn

1. Warnicke 1990:35.

2. Slang for breasts.

3. Taken from Wood vol II:14-15.

4. Henry's letters are taken from Halliwell vol I.

5. Either there or nowhere.

6. Cardinal Campeggio.

7. Suffolk House, next to Whitehall.

8. Eleanor Carey, the sister of Anne's brother-in-law, William Carey.

9. Loneliness or misery.

10. Breasts.

11. Kiss.

12. The furnishing of Suffolk House.

13. Upon arrival in London Campeggio almost immediately took to his bed with gout.

14. Rumour.

## 4 Queen in Waiting, 1527–1532

1. Henry VIII to Wolsey (St Clare Byrne 1968:79).

2. Warnicke 1990:36-39.

3. Halliwell 1848 vol I.

4. Entirely, wholly.

5. *Harleian Miscellany* vol III p. 61.

6. Fiddes 1726. Strype vol I pt II p. 578 considers the letter to be addressed to Archbishop Cranmer, but this is unlikely due to Anne's marriage soon after Cranmer's appointment as Archbishop.

7. Wood vol II p. 45.

8. Wood vol II p. 48.

9. Taken from the appendix to Cavendish 1825.

10. Herbert 1649:312-313.

11. For this occasion only.

12. Before ('or' is used frequently for 'before' in the text).

13. Stephen Gardiner.

14. William Warham.

15. Thomas Boleyn.

16. Hunting season.

17. Wolsey was Bishop of Winchester in addition to being Archbishop of York.

18. Esher, Surrey.

19. Household.

20. Thomas Cromwell, who was a member of Wolsey's household. Cavendish implies that Cromwell was indeed a supporter of the religious reform movement, in spite of his claims of orthodoxy on his death (see Norton 2009b).

21. The noble lion, in his wrath, knows how to spare his victim: do likewise, whoever shall be the princes of this earth.

22. It is a glorious thing to do what ought to be done, not merely what is lawful.

23. Person who prays for another.

24. Anne Boleyn.

25. For the anger of the prince is death.

26. PRO SP 1/53 (also printed in Strickland vol IV p. 195).

27. Foxe to Gardiner, 11 May 1528 (L&P IV:187).

28. Taken from Halliwell 1848, vol I.

29. Anne Boleyn.

30. Journalistic account printed by Wynkyn de Worde printed in Pollard 1903.

31. The Field of the Cloth of Gold is discussed in Russell 1969. The same work also contains a transcription of the Bodleian MS Ashmole 1116 which details the event.

32. Henry Fitzroy, Henry VIII's illegitimate son by Bessie Blount.

33. Taken from CSP 4 pt 1 and CSP 4 pt2 (from 1 January 1531).

34. Details Chapuys' first meeting with Henry VIII.

35. A papal brief dating to the time of Henry and Catherine's betrothal, which confirmed the dispensation for the marriage, was held by Charles V. Henry had previously insisted that Catherine wrote to her nephew to obtain the original. She followed this letter with a secret verbal message, instructing Charles to keep the brief safe.

36. Wolsey.

37. Thomas Boleyn.

38. Mary of Hungary, Regent of the Netherlands (Charles V's sister).

39. i.e. that he found her a virgin at their marriage.

40. Henry and Catherine's daughter, Mary.

41. i.e. the 'White Queen', Mary Tudor, Queen Dowager of France.

42. This is probably a reference to Henry's relationship with Mary Boleyn, which placed him and Anne within the same degree of affinity (relatedness) as he was with Catherine (due to her marriage to his brother). The fact that Chapuys mentions an even greater affinity between Anne and Henry may also refer to the rumours of a relationship between Henry and Anne's mother, Elizabeth Howard.

43. Thomas More.

44. Anne Boleyn.

45. The French Ambassador.

46. Anne's aunt, the wife of the third Duke of Norfolk. She was estranged from her husband, who openly kept a mistress, Bess Holland.

47. Leicester, where Richard III's body was taken after the Battle of Bosworth Field.

48. He was sent for to advise the King on the correct interpretation of the Old Testament in relation to the legality of his marriage to Catherine.

49. John Fisher, Bishop of Rochester, was a devoted adherent of Catherine's. A sixteenth-century *Life* of the Bishop (printed in Bayne 1921) also describes this incident, as well as another apparent attempt on Fisher's life. Both were suggested to have been the work of Anne or her father.

50. York Place, later renamed Whitehall.

51. Gardiner.

52. Implied to be a threat due to the attempt to assassinate him the previous year which was blamed by Chapuys (and others) on Anne and her father.

53. Francis' mistress.

## 5 Queen Anne Boleyn, 1533–1536

1. Taken from Harspfield.

2. Hall's Chronicle p. 794

3. Dr Roland Lee. It is probable that he did indeed officiate at the secret marriage ceremony.

4. Taken from Ellis 1814.

5. i.e her hair loose down her back. A tradition generally followed by queens at their coronations.

6. Taken from Pollard 1903.

7. Anne's badge depicted a falcon.

8. Pollard 1903 from a manuscript in the royal collection.

9. Taken from Wriothesley 1875.

10. Hamilton's introduction to Wriothesley's Chronicle details the chronicler's life.

11. Anne's step-grandmother. The old duchess was later arrested for her role in the fall of another step-granddaughter, Catherine Howard, whom she had raised.

12. dais.

13. Bury St Edmunds.

14. burnt.

15. Latymer 1990 records Anne's patronage of the religious reform.

16. Taken from Furnivall 1869:408-409.

17. Taken from Strickland vol IV p. 233.

18. Taken from Wood vol II p. 186-188.

19. Taken from Wood vol II p. 188-189.

20. Taken from Wood vol II p. 190-191.

21. No Lincolnshire Abbey of this name – perhaps Vale-Royal in Cheshire?

22. Taken from Wood vol II p. 191-192.

23. Taken from Crawford 2002:192.

24. Ellis vol II first series p. 45.

25. Wolsey.

26. Taken from State Papers vol II pp. 302-3.

27. Ives 2005:209.

28. Levine 1982:121-122 convincingly demonstrates that Anne was not the queen who attempted to save Catesby. Norton 2009a:106-8 discusses the fate of Catesby Nunnery. The Prioress's letter is printed in Wood 1846:185-6.

29. i.e. Beadwoman – someone who prays for another.

30. Taken from Clifford.

31. Stevenson's preface to his edition of the *Life* provides details of Jane Dormer and Henry Clifford.

32. Norton 2009a details the courtship of Jane Seymour and William Dormer.

33. This wording strongly suggests that Clifford had read, and was influenced by, Nicholas Sander.

34. A transcript of the letter is contained in Chapuys to Charles V, 17 February 1536 (L&P X:117-118).

35. Taken from Wood vol II p. 193-197.

36. Taken from CSP 4 pt 2. From 17 January 1534 CSP 5 pt 1. From 9 January 1536 CSP 5 pt 2.

37. Catherine of Aragon. Chapuys continued to refer to her as queen, never applying the title to Anne.

38. George Boleyn.

39. A threat – Chapuys means that Anne wishes to poison Mary.

40. Since the husband of a ruling queen was expected to succeed to the throne with his wife, were Mary to marry a man with no following, it would be near impossible for her to win the crown in a disputed succession.

41. A suggestion that Catherine favoured an invasion of England by Charles.

42. Francis' second wife was Eleanor, the sister of Charles V and Catherine's niece.

43. Stepmother.

44. Maid of honour.

45. Elizabeth. Chapuys generally referred to her as the 'Little Bastard'.

46. Maria de Salinas, Lady Willoughby. Maria came to England from Spain in the train of Catherine of Aragon and was her dearest friend. Her only child, Catherine Willoughby, married the Duke of Suffolk after Mary Tudor, Queen Dowager of France's death.

47. Lady Shelton.

48. Anne's old suitor, Henry Percy.

49. Where Catherine was staying.

50. Mary of Hungary.

51. Actually stepmother.

## 6 A Memorial from George Constantyne to Thomas Lord Cromwell

1. Taken from Constantyne 1831.

2. Fox 2007:317-8 discusses the possibility that Constantyne's memorial is a forgery.

3. Weir 2009:339.

4. before.

5. Thomas Cromwell.

6. Christina of Denmark, dowager Duchess of Milan and Anne of Cleves. For details of Henry's attempts to find a fourth wife, see Norton 2009b.

7. Hans Holbein was sent by Henry to paint portraits of both Christina of Denmark and Anne of Cleves, among other candidates for his hand.

8. Christina of Denmark was the great niece of Catherine of Aragon. She was also the niece of Charles V and put forward as the Imperial candidate for Henry's bride.

9. Anne Boleyn.

10. Jane Seymour.

11. Henry Norris, one of the men that fell with Anne.

12. Sir William Kingston, lieutenant of the Tower.

13. Mark Smeaton. Due to his low birth he was commonly referred to by his Christian name.

14. Jousted.

15. Norris's confession is mentioned by no other source. If he did indeed confess it may have been in the hope of securing the pardon offered by Henry VIII.

16. Sir William Fitzwilliam, Treasurer of the Household. He was a conservative member of the court and, interestingly, also the half-brother of the Countess of Worcester, one of the women who helped to condemn Anne.

17. By convention, condemned prisoners were supposed to admit their guilt on the scaffold in order to be said to have had a good death. Constantyne suggests that, by not doing so, Brereton was either actually innocent, or that he died badly.

18. 'quit', i.e. found not guilty.

19. The statement that Norfolk wept as he gave judgment is interesting and says much about his relationship with Anne and George, his sister's children.

20. Carmarthen.

21. Before.

## 7 The Fall of Anne Boleyn, May 1536

1. Taken from CSP V pt 2.

2. Anne.

3. See the letter from Anne to Lady Shelton printed above.

4. The only occasion on which Chapuys recognised Anne as queen.

5. Anne.

6. i.e. the horns of cuckold – normally something that a man would find shameful.

7. A doctrine whereby the child of an invalid union could still be considered legitimate, providing that they were born at a time when both parents believed their marriage to be valid. This could not apply to Elizabeth since Henry knew of his relations with Mary Boleyn and Anne knew of her betrothal to Henry Percy.

8. Adequate – i.e. a reference to Henry VIII's alleged impotency.

9. Printed in Hume 1889.

10. Weir 2009:342.

11. Hume's introduction to the chronicle gives details of its authorship and reliability.

12. Friedmann 2010:275-6.

13. This story is taken and adapted by the chronicler from Boccacio.

14. The headsman is usually said to have come from Calais. The statement that he was from St Omer however agrees with the claim of Mary of Hungary, Regent of the Netherlands in a letter that she wrote in 1536 (printed below).

15. There is no other record that Anne said these words on the scaffold. It is unlikely that she would have dared be so provocative and, almost certainly, they are the product of the chronicler's imagination, or based on rumour.

16. Thomas Boleyn actually survived until 1539.

17. Taken from the appendix to Cavendish 1825.

18. Singer in his preface to his edition of Cavendish p. xix.

19. L&P X:357-8 (no. 869).

20. Coming towards me.

21. besprinkled.

22. punished.

23. Grave, sober.

24. prosperity.

25. places.

26. bowed.

27. Before.

28. disquieted.

29. ready.

30. bastard.

31. sour.

32. There is no help for it.

33. mate.

34. Bruce 1850, quoting a contemporary manuscript p. 239.

35. Taken from Wyatt 1858.

36. Taken from Wyatt 1997.

37. Taken from Wyatt 1997 (*circa regna tonat* – it thunders through the realms).

38. The deaths of the five men condemned with Anne.

39. Taken from Burnet vol I p. 320-1.

40. Printed in a slightly abridged form in Calendar of State Papers Foreign Series vol I no. 1303.

41. Charles V's brother, Ferdinand, King of the Romans (later Emperor).

42. The implication of this was that George Boleyn was the father of Anne's child.

43. Jane Seymour was, in fact, never crowned.

44. Henry never legitimised Mary or Elizabeth, although he did reinstate them in the succession.

45. Edward Seymour was appointed as Earl of Hertford by Henry VIII. He had to wait until the reign of his nephew to become Duke of Somerset.

46. Taken from the appendix to Cavendish 1825.

47. no.

48. laughing.

49. i.e. at the May Day jousts.

50. Worcester.

51. Stir.

52. without justice.

53. subject.

54. laughed.

55. Cousyns.

56. the queen's almoner.

57. dead men's shoes.

58. head were off.

59. Probably the name of one of her attendants – Madge Shelton her cousin and the King's former mistress?

60. unless.

61. Anne's aunt, Lady Boleyn, whom she disliked.

62. i.e. sleeps in the same room as her.

63. i.e. Kingston and his wife slept outside the door to Anne's chamber.

64. that.

65. that.

66. Madge Shelton.

67. Sir Nicholas Carew and Sir Francis Bryan.

68. Near.

69. Thomas Cromwell.

70. knew.

71. Mark Smeaton.

72. a noble.

73. an inferior.

74. a look.

75. almoner.

76. they.

77. laugh.

78. justice.

79. good deeds.

80. This sentence demonstrates that Anne cannot be considered a Protestant. She held the Catholic belief that salvation was by good works, not merely through faith.

81. Anne was unhappy with the women that Henry had selected to serve her in the Tower.

82. Almoner. This refers to the conversation between Anne and Norris, after which Anne bade Norris go to her almoner to swear that she was a good woman. As Kingston's letters show, Anne mentioned this herself while in the Tower.

83. note.

84. accepts.

85. that.

86. that.

87. what.

88. us.

89. that.

90. Antwerp. It appears that Anne hoped to be sent as a nun to a Continental monastery, something that would have allowed the King to marry again.

91. i.e. foreigners.

92. number.

93. hour (i.e. a set time for the execution to take place).

94. number.

95. i.e. that Anne would declare that she had carnally known no man other than the King.

96. Anne required Kingston to witness her swear on the sacrament that she was innocent. Given the piety of the age and the fact that perjury would have been believed to damn Anne's soul, this is strong evidence that she was indeed innocent.

97. no.

98. subtle, i.e. a quick death.

99. laughing.

100. almoner.

101. Harlean MSS. 2194 f.16 (transcribed in Furnivall 1869).

102. L&P X:361-363 (no. 876).

103. Henry Percy, Anne's old suitor.

104. Wood vol II p. 74-75.

105. Wood vol II p. 318-319.

106. Taken from Ellis 1825, first series vol II.

107. Fox 2007 is the only biography of Lady Rochford, which provides a very sympathetic portrayal. Her role in the fall of Anne Boleyn is also discussed in Weir 2009.

108. Morley's manuscript is in BL Add. MSS 12060. Details of his time with Margaret Beaufort can be found in Norton 2010.

109. poor.

110. poor.

111. poor.

112. Taken from the appendix to Cavendish 1825.

113. Morley.

114. The St Johns were a prominent gentry family. Margaret Beaufort had been the maternal half-sister of Lady Rochford's grandfather Sir John St John. Lady Rochford's mother was therefore a first cousin of Henry VII's.

115. Outrage.

116. Shent – i.e. injured, decayed or ruined.

117. Taken from Merriman 1902.

118. deferred.

119. devised.

120. done.

121. revealed.

122. heard.

123. duty.

124. Smeaton.

125. £200.

126. 300.

127. £100.

128. Sir Francis Bryan. He was nicknamed by the King 'The Vicar of Hell'.

129. Taken from Strickland 1844 vol IV p. 252-3.

130. Strype 1816 vol I:452.

131. Burnet vol IV:291.

132. Weir 2009:257.

133. Taken from Evans vol III 1810 p. 89-90.

134. Taken from the edition of the Chronicle printed in Nichols 1846.

135. a living man.

136. Taken from the edition of the Chronicle in Hamilton 1875.

137. Burnt.

138. L&P X p. 429 (1036). The original French version can be found in Ascoli 1927.

139. Ives 2005:60-61.

140. Mary Tudor, Henry VIII's sister.

141. Sir Anthony Browne or, perhaps, his half-brother, Sir William Fitzwilliam.

142. The Countess of Worcester.

143. Rochford's speech in de Carles is very similar to that recorded by the Portuguese gentleman (printed below).

144. Taken from *Excerpta Historica*.

145. *Excerpta Historica*.

146. Even if the writer was, indeed, an eyewitness to Anne's death, it would seem improbable that he would have been close enough to the scaffold to hear these words. They are mentioned in no other source and are likely to be fanciful.

147. Elizabeth was never acknowledged as the child of anyone other than Henry VIII (although Mary I apparently later claimed that she bore a resemblance to Mark Smeaton – see the extract from the *Life of Jane Dormer*). Mary was also never declared as legitimate by Henry VIII, nor named as heir to the throne (although she was later reinstated in the succession, along with Elizabeth).

148. Taken from Thomas 1861:116-117 (edited by Froude).

149. Weir 2009:337.

150. A gable hood rather than Anne's preferred French hood.

151. Taken from Townsend's edition of Foxe, vol V

152. A vast sum and clearly greatly exaggerated.

153. Taken from Hall 1809.

154. Jesus.

155. Taken from Thomas 1861:117.

156. Norton 2009b.

# Bibliography

## Primary Sources

Ales, A., 'Alexander Ales to the Queen, 1 September 1559' in Stevenson, J. (ed.), *Calendar of State Papers, Foreign Series, of the Reign of Elizabeth, vol I 1558-1559* (London, 1863).

Bayne, R. (ed.), *The Life of Fisher* (London, 1921).

Bray, G. (ed.), *Documents of the English Reformation* (Cambridge, 1994).

British Library Add. MSS. 12060: A Book of Miracles and Examples of Virtue for the Guidance of a Ruler, Dedicated to Queen Mary by Henry Parker Lord Morley.

Burnet, G. (ed.), *The History of the Reformation of the Church of England, vols I and IV*, Pocock, N., ed. (Oxford, 1865).

*Calendar of State Papers, Spanish vols IV-V*, De Gayangos (ed.) (London, 1882-1888).

Carles, L., de, 'Anne Boullant, Epistre contenant le process criminel faict a l'encontre de la royne Anne Boullant d'Angleterre', in Ascoli, G., *La Grande Bretagne devant l'opinion Francaise depuis la guerre de cent ans jusqu'a la fin du XVIe siecle* (Paris, 1927).

Cavendish, G., *The Life of Cardinal Wolsey*, Singer, S.W. (ed.) (Chiswick, 1825).

Cavendish, G., *Thomas Wolsey Late Cardinal His Life and Death*, Lockyer, R. (ed.) (London, 1962).

Clifford, H., *The Life of Jane Dormer, Duchess of Feria*, Estcourt, E. E. and Stevenson (ed.) (London, 1887).

Constantine, G., *Transcript of an Original Manuscript, Containing a Memorial from George Constantyne to Thomas Lord Cromwell*, Amyot, T. (ed.) (Archaeolgia 23, 1831).

Crawford, A., *Letters of the Queens of England* (Stroud, 2002).

Ellis, H. (ed.), *Copy of a Letter from Archbishop Cranmer to Mastyr Hawkyns, relating to Queens Catherine of Aragon and Anne Boleyn* (Archaeologia 18, 1814).

Ellis, H. (ed.), *Original Letters Illustrative of English History, vol II first series* (London, 1825).

Evans, R. H. (ed.), *Old Ballads, Historical and Narrative, with some of Modern Date, Collected from Rare Copies and Mss., vol III* (London, 1810).

*Excerpta Historica* (1831).

Foxe, J., *The Acts and Monuments,* Townsend, G., ed. (London, 1838).

Furnivall, Mr (ed.), *Ballad Society, First Report, January* (London, 1869).

Hall, E., *Hall's Chronicle* (London, 1809).

Hall, E., *Henry VIII, vol I,* Whibley, C. (ed.) (London, 1904).

Halliwell, J. O. (ed.), *Letters of the Kings of England, vol I* (London, 1848).

Harpsfield, N., *A Treatise on the Pretended Divorce Between Henry VIII and Catherine of Aragon,* Pocock, N. (ed.) (London, 1878).

Herbert, E., *The Life and Raigne of King Henry the Eighth* (London, 1649).

Hume, M. A. S. (ed.), *Chronicle of King Henry VIII* (London, 1889).

Latymer, W., *Chronickille of Anne Bulleyne,* Dowling, M. (ed.) (Camden Miscellany XX, Fourth Series, vol 39. 1990).

*Letters and Papers, Foreign and Domestic, of the Reign of Henry VIII, vols I, III, IV, V, X* Brewer, J. S., Brodie, R. H., Gairdner, J. (eds) (London, 1867-1920).

Merriman, R. B., *Life and Letters of Thomas Cromwell,* 2 vols (Oxford, 1902).

Nichols, J. G. (ed.), *The Chronicle of Calais* (London, 1846).

Oldys, W. (ed.), *The Harleian Miscellany, vol III* (London, 1809).

Pollard, A. F., (ed.), *Tudor Tracts* (Westminster, 1903).

Public Record Office SP 1/53 Letter of Anne Boleyn to Stephen Gardiner, 4 April 1529.

St Clare Byrne, M. (ed.), *The Letters of King Henry VIII* (London, 1968).

St Clare Byrne, M. (ed.), *The Lisle Letters,* 5 vols (Chicago, 1981).

Sander, N., *Rise and Growth of the Anglican Schism,* Lewis, D. (ed.) (London, 1877).

Spelman, J., *The Reports of Sir John Spelman,* Baker, J. H. (ed.) (London, 1977).

*State Papers Published Under the Authority of His Majesty's Commission, vol II (Henry VIII, Part III)* (1834).

Surrey, Henry Howard, Earl of, *The Poems of Henry Howard, Earl of Surrey* (London, 1831).

Thomas, W., *The Pilgrim: A Dialogue of the Life and Actions of King Henry the Eighth,* Froude, J. A. (ed.) (London, 1861).

Williams, N. (ed.), *English Historical Documents, vol V 1485-1558* (London, 1967).

Wood, M. A. E. (ed.), *Letters of Royal and Illustrious Ladies, vol II* (London, 1846).

Wriothesley, C., *A Chronicle of England,* 2 vols, Hamilton, W. D. (ed.) (London, 1875).

Wyatt, G., 'Extracts from the Life of the Virtuous Christian and Renowned Queen Anne Boleigne' in Singer, S. W. (ed.), *The Life of Cardinal Wolsey* (Chiswick, 1825).

Wyatt, G., *The Papers of George Wyatt Esquire of Boxley Abbey in the County of Kent,* Loades, D. M., ed. (London, 1968).

Wyatt, T., *The Poetical Works of Sir Thomas Wyatt* (London, 1831).
Wyatt, T., *The Poetical Works of Sir Thomas Wyatt*, Gilfillan, G. (ed.) (London, 1858).
Wyatt, T., *The Complete Poems*, Rebholz, R. A., ed. (London, 1997).

## Secondary Sources

Anon., *On the Past and Present Manners of the English Nation* (The Oxford Magazine, Vol. III, 1769:55-57).
Benger. E. O., *Memoirs of the Life of Anne Boleyn*, 2 vols (London, 1821).
Bernard, G. W., *The Fall of Anne Boleyn* (English Historical Review 106, 1991).
Bernard, G. W., *The Fall of Anne Boleyn: A Rejoinder* (English Historical Review 107, 1992).
Bernard, G. W., *Anne Boleyn's Religion* (The Historical Journal 36, 1993).
Bernard, G. W., *Anne Boleyn* (London, 2010).
Bruce, J., *Unpublished Anecdotes of Sir Thomas Wyatt the Poet, and of other Members of that Family* (The Gentleman's Magazine 34, New Series, 1850).
Bruce. M. L., *Anne Boleyn* (London, 1972).
Chapman, H. W., *Anne Boleyn* (London, 1974).
Denny, J., *Anne Boleyn* (London, 2004).
Dowling, M., *Anne Boleyn and Reform* (Journal of Ecclesiastical History 35, 1984).
Erickson, C., *Anne Boleyn* (London, 1984).
Fiddes, R., *The Life of Cardinal Wolsey* (London, 1726).
Fox, J., *Jane Boleyn, The Infamous Lady Rochford* (London, 2007).
Fraser, A., *The Six Wives of Henry VIII* (London, 2002).
Friedmann, P., *Anne Boleyn*, Wilkinson, J., ed. (Stroud, 2010).
Guy, J., *Henry VIII and the Praemunire Manoeuvres of 1530-1531* (English Historical Review 97, 1982).
Hunter, J., 'Who wrote Cavendish's Life of Wolsey? A Dissertation', in Cavendish, G., *The Life of Cardinal Wolsey, vol II* Singer, S.W., ed. (Chiswick, 1825).
Iongh, J., de, *Margaret of Austria* (London, 1954).
Ives, E. W., *The Fall of Anne Boleyn Reconsidered* (English Historical Review 107, 1992).
Ives, E. W., *The Life and Death of Anne Boleyn* (Oxford, 2005).
Levine, M., 'The Place of Women in Tudor Government', in Guth, D. J. and McKenna, J. W. (eds.), *Tudor Rule and Revolution* (Cambridge, 1982).
Norton, E., *Anne Boleyn, Henry VIII's Obsession* (Stroud, 2008).
Norton, E., *Jane Seymour, Henry VIII's True Love* (Stroud, 2009a)
Norton, E., *Anne of Cleves, Henry VIII's Discarded Bride* (Stroud, 2009b).
Norton, E., *Margaret Beaufort, Mother of the Tudor Dynasty* (Stroud, 2010).
Paget, H., *The Youth of Anne Boleyn* (Bulletin of the Institute of Historical Research 54, 1981).

Round, J. H., *The Early Life of Anne Boleyn* (London, 1886).

Russell, J. G., *The Field of the Cloth of Gold* (London, 1969).

Sergeant, P. W., *The Life of Anne Boleyn* (London, 1923).

Starkey, D., *Six Wives* (London, 2003).

Strickland, A., *The Lives of the Queens of England, vol IV* (London, 1844).

Strype, J., *Ecclesiastical Memorials: Relating Chiefly to the Reformation, Under the Reign of King Henry VIII, King Edward VI and Queen Mary the First, vol I* (London, 1816).

Strype, J., *Annals of the Reformation and Establishment of Religion, and Other Various Occurrences in the Church of England, During Queen Elizabeth's Happy Reign, vol I pt II* (Oxford, 1824).

Walker, G., *Rethinking the Fall of Anne Boleyn* (The Historical Journal 45, 2002).

Warnicke, R., *The Fall of Anne Boleyn: A Reassessment* (History 70, 1985).

Warnicke, R., *The Rise and Fall of Anne Boleyn* (Cambridge, 1989).

Warnicke, R., *Three Forged Letters of Anne Boleyn: Their Implications for Reformation Politics and Women's Studies* (Journal of the Rocky Mountain Medieval and Renaissance Associations 11, 1990).

Weir, A., *The Six Wives of Henry VIII* (London, 1991).

Weir, A., *The Lady in the Tower* (London, 2009).

Wilkinson, J., *Mary Boleyn* (Stroud, 2009a).

Wilkinson, J., *The Early Loves of Anne Boleyn* (Stroud, 2009b).

# Tudor History from Amberley Publishing

## THE TUDORS
Richard Rex

'The best introduction to England's most important dynasty'
**DAVID STARKEY**
'Gripping and told with enviable narrative skill... a delight'
**THES**
'Vivid, entertaining and carrying its learning lightly'
**EAMON DUFFY**
'A lively overview' **THE GUARDIAN**

£9.99    978-1-4456-0700-9    256 pages PB  143 illus., 66 col

## CATHERINE HOWARD
Lacey Baldwin Smith

'A brilliant, compelling account' **ALISON WEIR**
'A faultless book' **THE SPECTATOR**
'Lacey Baldwin Smith has so excellently caught the
atmosphere of the Tudor age' **THE OBSERVER**

£9.99    978-1-84868-521-5    256 pages PB  25 col illus

## MARGARET OF YORK
Christine Weightman

'A pioneering biography of the Tudor dynasty's most
dangerous enemy'
**PROFESSOR MICHAEL HICKS**
'Christine Weightman brings Margaret alive once more'
**THE YORKSHIRE POST**
'A fascinating account of a remarkable woman'
**THE BIRMINGHAM POST**

£10.99    978-1-4456-0819-8    256 pages PB  51 illus

## THE SIX WIVES OF HENRY VIII
David Loades

'Neither Starkey nor Weir has the assurance and command
of Loades' **SIMON HEFFER, LITERARY REVIEW**
'Incisive and profound. I warmly recommend this book'
**ALISON WEIR**

£9.99    978-1-4456-0049-9    256 pages PB  55 illus, 31 col

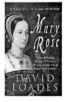   

## MARY ROSE
David Loades

£20.00  978-1-4456-0622-4
272 pages HB  17 col illus

## MARY BOLEYN
Josephine Wilkinson

£9.99  978-1-84868-525-3
208 pages PB  22 illus, 19 col

## JANE SEYMOUR
Elizabeth Norton

£9.99  978-1-84868-527-7
224 pages PB  53 illus, 26 col

## HENRY VIII
Richard Rex

£9.99  978-1-84868-098-2
192 pages PB  81 illus, 48 col

   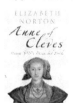

## THOMAS CROMWELL
Patrick Coby

£20.00  978-1-4456-0775-7
272 pages HB  30 illus (20 col)

## ANNE BOLEYN THE YOUNG QUEEN TO BE
Josephine Wilkinson

£9.99  978-1-4456-0395-7
208 pages PB  34 illus (19 col)

## ELIZABETH I
Richard Rex

£9.99  978-1-84868-423-2
192 pages PB  75 illus

## ANNE OF CLEVES
Elizabeth Norton

£9.99  978-1-4456-0183-0
224 pages HB  54 illus, 27 col

Available from all good bookshops or to order direct
Please call **01453-847-800** **www.amberleybooks.com**

# More Tudor History from Amberley Publishing

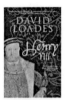

## HENRY VIII
David Loades

'David Loades Tudor biographies are both highly enjoyable and instructive, the perfect combination' *ANTONIA FRASER*

£12.99       978-1-4456-0704-7       512 pages HB  113 illus, 19 col

## ANNE BOLEYN
Elizabeth Norton

'Meticulously researched and a great read'
*THEANNEBOLEYNFILES.COM*

£9.99       978-1-84868-514-7       264 pages PB  47 illus, 26 col

## THE TUDORS VOL 1
G. J. Meyer

'His style is crisp and popular'
*PROFESSOR DAVID LOADES*

£12.99       978-1-4456-0143-4       384 pages PB  72 illus, 54 col

## THE TUDORS VOL 2
G. J. Meyer

'A sweeping history of the gloriously infamous Tudor era'
*KIRKUS REVIEW*

£12.99       978-1-4456-0144-1       352 pages PB  53 illus, 15 col

## ANNE BOLEYN
P. Friedmann

'A compelling and lively biography... meticulously researched and supremely readable classic of Tudor biography' *DR RICHARD REX*

'The first scholarly biography' *THE FINANCIAL TIMES*

£20.00       978-1-84868-827-8       352 pages HB  47 illus, 20 col

## MARY TUDOR
David Loades

£12.99       978-1-4456-0818-1       328 pages HB  59 illus, 10 col

## CATHERINE PARR
Elizabeth Norton

'Norton cuts an admirably clear path through tangled Tudor intrigues' *JENNY UGLOW*

'Wonderful... a joy to read'
*HERSTORIA*

£9.99       978-1-4456-0383-4       312 pages HB  49 illus, 39 col

## MARGARET BEAUFORT
Elizabeth Norton

£9.99       978-1-4456-0578-4       256 pages HB  70 illus, 40 col

IN BED WITH THE TUDORS
Amy Licence

£20.00   978-1-4456-0693-4

272 pages HB   30 illus, 20 col

THE BOLEYNS
David Loades

£10.99   978-1-4456-0958-4

312 pages HB   34 illus, 33 col

BESSIE BLOUNT
Elizabeth Norton

£25.00   978-1-84868-870-4

384 pages HB   77 illus, 75 col

ANNE BOLEYN
Norah Lofts

£18.99   978-1-4456-0619-4

208 pages HB   75 illus, 46 col

Available from all good bookshops or to order direct
Please call **01453-847-800 www.amberleybooks.com**